D0076979

Handbook of
Chinese
Popular Culture

Handbook of Chinese Popular Culture

EDITED BY

WU DINGBO

AND

PATRICK D. MURPHY

GREENWOOD PRESS

Westport, Connecticut
London

Library of Congress Cataloging-in-Publication Data

Handbook of Chinese popular culture / edited by Wu Dingbo and Patrick
   D. Murphy.
      p.   cm.
      Includes bibliographical references and index.
      ISBN 0–313–27808–3 (alk. paper)
      1. Popular culture—China—Handbooks, manuals, etc.   2. China—
   Social life and customs—Handbooks, manuals, etc.   I. Wu Dingbo.
   II. Murphy, Patrick D.
   HM101.H255   1994
   306'.0951—dc20   93–30979

British Library Cataloguing in Publication Data is available.

Library of Congress Catalog Card Number: 93–30979
ISBN: 0–313–27808–3

First published in 1994

Greenwood Press, 88 Post Road West, Westport, CT 06881
An imprint of Greenwood Publishing Group, Inc.

Printed in the United States of America

The paper used in this book complies with the
Permanent Paper Standard issued by the National
Information Standards Organization (Z39.48–1984).

10 9 8 7 6 5 4 3 2 1

Contents

Preface

PATRICK D. MURPHY

China, the most populous nation-state, has one of the oldest continuous civilizations on earth. Necessarily, then, its popular culture as much as its high culture, and probably more so, is extremely diverse and richly complex. It would be naive to believe that any single-volume study could possibly discuss such a popular culture in its entirety without being too heavy to lift. What a single reference volume can do is to provide a detailed and complete study of various aspects of that culture. This *Handbook of Chinese Popular Culture* provides the most comprehensive and up-to-date bibliographical and descriptive study of a wide range of popular culture subjects available in English. For the subjects treated in depth in its eighteen chapters, it provides a comprehensive survey of research materials as well as an overview of the major features and points of critical concern for each topic. The extensive selected bibliography at the end of the book also provides references for other subjects that could not be taken up in detail within this single volume.

The study of cultural tradition and popular culture reveals the complexity and fluidity of culture, as co-editor Wu Dingbo has elucidated in his introductory chapter. Such study requires careful and serious research to understand its character and development, and the relations of its various aspects. For decades, scholars around the world have done much work describing and interpreting Chinese popular culture. As the latest effort in that ongoing project, this book provides a balanced treatment of popular culture in many of its major manifestations as observed by a variety of scholars from China, the United States, and Canada. The chapters in this handbook, representing as they do a great diversity of views and backgrounds, have one thing in common: They all seek to explain what Chinese popular culture is. By analyzing the major features of various manifestations of that culture, they all contribute to our understanding of Chinese culture, Chinese people, and Chinese society.

One of the most difficult subjects to address in discussing popular culture is that of "lifestyles," since it has so many features and interrelated aspects. Nevertheless, Rebecca Weiner in "Lifestyles: Commercialization and Concepts of Choice" has managed to focus on the crucial characteristics of contemporary Chinese conceptions of lifestyle choices and concerns, while providing the reader with a wealth of bibliographical detail on every dimension of the subject, from economics and political struggles to sexuality and child care. E. N. Anderson turns our attention to an even more ubiquitous element of popular culture, "Food." Although this aspect of Chinese culture is perhaps the only one with which most Americans have some familiarity, Anderson demonstrates how much there is to know about the tremendous variety of Chinese food and the cultural implications of that diversity. Ione Kramer in "Tea Drinking and Its Culture" demonstrates the degree to which tea drinking is more a matter of cultural communication than of consumption. Particularly of interest to many will be her discussion of the revitalization of teahouses since the end of the Cultural Revolution.

Jordan Paper provides a new perspective on the conception of Chinese spirituality in "Religion," which focuses on the daily rituals and beliefs of the masses rather than on the formal philosophical and religious systems, such as Taoism, Confucianism, and Buddhism, that usually define this subject and exclude the bulk of actual popular religious practice. After having read his chapter, readers will more readily understand why we have placed Hsiao-Hung Lee's "Chinese Herbal Medicine" immediately after it. Cosmology and philosophy are crucial ingredients, alongside of herbs and attitudes, in the evolution and application of herbal medicine throughout China, as well in its adaptations by Westerners. Lee's study excels in providing information about both Chinese and English studies on this subject.

In some ways, it is difficult to determine whether Chinese traditional popular sports are part of the physical culture of sport as we understand it in the West or more a continuation of religion and medicine. Susan Brownell's chapter, "Sports," outlines the historical development of sport in China, including a discussion of the relationship of traditional sports and the introduction and popularization of Western sports, particularly those associated with the Olympics. J. A. English-Lueck's "*Taijiquan* and *Qigong*" provides a detailed examination of two of China's traditional sports, which remain widely popular and are practiced as components of maintaining psychic and physical health. Zhang Wei and Tan Xiujun, on the other hand, in their chapter on "*Wushu*" focus on the popular culmination of China's evolution of the martial arts.

The mass media are generally thought of as a contemporary phenomenon, and while Xu Xinyi's "The Chinese Mass Media" does emphasize the past half-century, it also details the long history of Chinese newspapers. Of special value is Xu's discussion of the ways in which government-controlled mass media are organized but nevertheless respond rapidly and extensively to audience opinions and preferences, particularly in the past decade or so. Wu Dingbo in "Film" provides a historical overview of the Chinese film industry, and analyzes specific major films in detail, emphasizing the past fifteen years. "Traditional Chinese Drama" is treated with the attention and care that only an insider such as Jiang Xingyun can provide. Known to most Westerners by only one of its variants, "Peking Opera," Chinese drama has a long history and complex conventions, as well as tremendous regional variations (nearly 400 styles), and Jiang's discussion of these features is admirable particularly for its wealth of specific examples. Cao Zhengwen in "Chinese Gallant Fiction" analyzes a particular form of highly popular prose virtually unknown in the United States, but certainly one that would appeal to many readers if it were available in translation. Wu Dingbo discusses "Chinese Science Fiction." Unlike gallant fiction, the unknown quantity for American readers is not its formal qualities—those of science fiction, introduced as Wu explains from Europe at the turn of the century—but the unique ways in which this international literary mode is rendered by its Chinese practitioners.

While Xu Xinyi educates the reader to the fact that newspapers are as old as printing in China, where the technology originated, John Lent in "Comic Art" demonstrates that cartoons are even older than the newspapers. From their earliest possible origins as suggested by archeological evidence to their latest political incarnations, comics, cartoons, and their various Chinese forms are discussed by Lent with a wealth of examples of the art and a plethora of biographical sketches of the artists. Qingxiang Wang contributes a chapter on another aspect of popular art: "Chinese Calligraphy." Not only does the artistic aspect of calligraphy have a long history in China, but also its current practice can be divided into several schools. Wang discusses these as well as differences among implements, brush strokes, and aesthetic philosophies.

In China, housing has never really been a lifestyle choice so much as it has been a result of lifestyle necessities, regional influences, and available materials. In "Popular Rural Architecture," Ronald Knapp introduces the reader to the major issues in understanding rural architecture as well as the diversity of reference materials in Chinese, English, and other languages available for study. John Marney displays a more personal style than our other authors in his study, "Transportation in the People's Republic of China." Combining solid research with recent personal observations, Marney provides interesting anecdotes supported by statistical details to overview a complicated, overworked, and absolutely essential feature of China's infrastructure.

We conclude with a selected bibliography that contains the majority of bibliographical entries from each of the chapters plus general and specific works in other subjects for which we were unable to provide detailed studies within this single volume.

Handbook of
Chinese
Popular Culture

Introduction: Cultural Tradition and Popular Culture

WU DINGBO

China's unswerving implementation of the open-door policy has been bringing about tremendous changes in all aspects of life. The open-door policy exposes the broad masses of the Chinese people to the outside world. When they compare the modernization in the West with the backward economy in China, they cannot but ponder the question: Why has China, which once led the world in science and technology, fallen far behind advanced world levels today? This question evokes a nationwide introspection of the Chinese cultural tradition. Chinese academic circles have shown great concern about and tremendous interest in the studies of Chinese culture and of the relations between Chinese culture and Western culture. The depth and scope of the present studies have surpassed those in the past.

One of the major controversies in such studies is over cultural tradition. Some people hold that the root cause of China's backwardness is its cultural tradition, a heavy burden that hinders progress and development. Equating modernization with the West and backwardness with China, they issue an antitraditionalist call. The antitraditionalists believe that the Chinese and the Westerners, being of the same species, share the same human nature. Therefore, what the Westerners are doing can be taken up immediately by the Chinese. Even though China lags far behind the West at present, it can catch up with the advanced level of the West if China pursues the policy of westernization.

It goes without saying that China can, sooner or later, catch up with the West economically, but the call for westernizing China is open to question. On the one hand, Western modernization is the outcome of Western efforts in inheriting, developing, and creating its cultural tradition. To equate modernization with westernization and backwardness with cultural tradition is not only to deny the evolutionary link between Western modernization and Western cultural tradition but also to put modernization and cultural tradition in opposition to each other. The two are not antagonistic to each other at all.

On the other hand, westernization implies that Western culture is the world's role model and urges mechanical imitation of everything Western. This is a naive view because it sees the difference between China and the West only in terms of economics and fails to see the true nature of cultural tradition. China is different from the West not merely in economical development, but also, and more fundamentally, in cultural tradition. As an independent body of cognition and practice, each nation has a unique national consciousness and national identity. With their different positions and experiences in the world, China and the West cannot establish the same cultural tradition. For instance, Westerners have been individualized thanks to their abstract philosophy of life whereas the Chinese have not been individualized due to their concrete philosophy of life; Westerners stress pluralism whereas the Chinese emphasize monism; Western culture is scientific, legalistic, and religious whereas Chinese culture is artistic and moralistic.

Obviously, the Chinese have set out on a course of cultural development apart and different from other nations and have built up a heritage that is still influencing their social and political behavior, their motivations and rationalizations, their moral and ethical compulsions and inhibitions. The time-honored Chinese culture has a history too long, strong, and stable to be replaced by any other culture. But this does not imply that China rejects all foreign influence. Modernization requires an open environment of creative vitality, and only by maintaining national tradition and assimilating all advanced cultures from other nations can China quicken the pace of its modernization. Therefore, it is detrimental to discard Chinese cultural tradition and advocate westernization in China.

The history of the development of human culture shows that enculturation, innovation, and acculturation are the three major processes in the progress of culture. Enculturation means the transmission of stable traditions from one generation to the next, innovation refers to the addition of new ideas to a given culture, and acculturation is the process whereby the people of one culture absorb fine traits from another culture. The development of a nation's culture results, on the one hand, from its own creative efforts to move from little to much, from shallow to deep, and, on the other hand, from the enrichment of the fine traits from alien cultures. A national culture can be strengthened and expanded through its clash, competition, exchange, and cooperation with foreign counterparts.

Evidently, cultural exchange is indispensable to the development of culture. If a nation should reject every possibility of innovation and acculturation and confine itself exclusively to the established ways of its tradition, its capability to change and grow could be lost. At the opposite extreme, if all traditional ideas should be discarded, the consequent loss of cultural stability would leave a nation bewildered and disorganized.

Moreover, judging from the development of contemporary culture in the world, the combination of the global consciousness of pluralized cultures and the national consciousness of indigenous cultures is the overwhelming trend as it guarantees the variety and splendor of human culture as a whole. Therefore, the culture of a nation like China, with a long history of cultural tradition, must develop with a global consciousness as well as the national consciousness. This reinforces the point that neither traditionalism nor antitraditionalism can promote the development of Chinese culture.

Chinese culture is largely homegrown. What is imported has usually been formulated in the Chinese style or tailored to suit Chinese tastes. One striking example is the acceptance and assimilation of Indian Buddhism in the period of the first century through the tenth century. Ever since Indian Buddhism was introduced into China, the Chinese not only have maintained the essence of Indian Buddhism, but also have transformed it into a native school of Chinese religion with a great following. This example demonstrates that the efficient acculturation of foreign cultures will not break up China's own cultural tradition but will enrich it instead. And the prerequisite for such efficient acculturation is a rich heritage of cultural tradition itself. Japan is a case in point. As Richard Gid Powers observes, ''The Japanese strategy for integrating the native and the imported aspects of their popular culture, while retaining the 'foreign' label on the imports, is remarkably precise and well developed'' (Powers, Kato, and Stronach ix). The Japanese are able to assimilate Western culture just because they are good at inheriting and developing their own cultural tradition. Much more modernized than mainland China, Singapore, South Korea, and Taiwan have all adhered to the Confucian cultural tradition conscientiously and persistently. This once again proves that modernization and cultural tradition are not antagonistic.

There is no denying that the Chinese cultural tradition contains negative elements that have exerted bad influence on the Chinese and have hindered the pace of China's progress and development. The Chinese cultural tradition, however, has lasted for thousands of years, but China lags behind the West only in recent centuries. Therefore, the cultural tradition is at most an indirect cause for China's backward situation at present. The direct causes are foreign imperialist invasions, corrupt government administrations, erroneous social systems, and detrimental party policies in the nineteenth and twentieth centuries. To overlook the direct causes and pursue the indirect cause is in fact an attempt to escape reality.

The call for westernizing China also reveals conceptual confusion about cultural tradition on the part of the antitraditionalists. Therefore, it is advisable, if not imperative, to make a distinction between ''traditional culture'' and ''cultural tradition.'' Culture is the long-term condensation of people's social lives and overall way of life with holism as its basic characteristic, and this condensation over generations acquires a national character. While traditional culture, which refers to the past culture in history, is a static condensation, cultural tradition, which refers to a living culture in reality, is a dynamic trend. Traditional culture may be studied as a historical phenomenon with affirmation or negation, but cultural tradition leaves only one choice for a nation: how to make it keep abreast of the times. The culture a nation maintains throughout history always exists in tradition, and for whatever changes national culture has undergone, it remains this nation's tradition.

For all nations, tradition is not a blood lineage, but a cultural phenomenon. It refers to ideas, systems, mores, and ethics that have passed down to the present from the past. Cultural tradition, once formed, is no longer monolithic. Instead, it becomes a unity of contradictions with multifarious aspects. The conservative force inherent in cultural tradition is an undeniable fact. For instance, the Chinese call their country *zhongguo,* meaning the "central nation." For a thousand years, they cherished the concept of China's being the central nation of a supposedly universal dominion, the most populous, the most affluent, the most powerful, and the most advanced in the world. They regarded other nations as barbarous, or at least not as cultured as themselves. The confidence in the superiority of their own culture produced the mental and psychological animus of the Chinese. This is revealed most strikingly in Emperor Qianlong's letter in 1793 to George III of Great Britain:

As to what you have requested in your message, namely to be allowed to send one of your nationals to reside in the Celestial Court to look after your country's trade, this does not conform to the Celestial Empire's system, and definitely cannot be done.... The Celestial Empire ruling all within the four seas . . . there is nothing we lack, as your principal envoy and others have personally seen. We have never set much store on strange and ingenious goods. Nor do we have any need of your country's manufactures.

The products of our Celestial Empire embrace all things. There is no need for imports from outside barbarous nations. But as the tea, porcelain, and silk, which the Celestial Empire produces, are necessities to the nations of the Western Ocean and your nation, we have already permitted, as a signal mark of favor, the establishment of *yanghang* ("Ocean Companies") at Macao so that all nations may participate in our beneficence and satisfy their wants. (Wu 398)

The ghost of Qianlong has haunted China for about two centuries, and the closed-door policy stems directly from such mental and psychological animus. For a thousand years China had turned a blind eye to what was going on outside. This narrow-minded conservatism slowed the pace of social progress in China. For this cruel reality, China has learned many bitter lessons in the past two hundred years.

Cultural tradition, however, represents both conservative and innovative forces. All cultures tend to strike a balance between these two forces. Therefore, it is a one-sided view to see only the conservative aspects of Chinese cultural tradition, and it is advisable to take a dialectic view and see cultural tradition as both a burden and an asset. China, with a recorded history of 4,000 years, is one of the world's most ancient civilized countries. According to archaeological data, primitive people lived on this land about one million years ago. Fossils of the ape-human were unearthed in Yuanmou, Yunnan Province (Yuanmou Man) and in Lantian, Shaanxi Province (Lantian Man). These were the earliest primitive people known in China so far. In 1929 a fossilized cranium belonging to Peking Man, who lived 690,000 years ago, was discovered. The site of a Neolithic village flourishing some 6,000 years ago was also unearthed in 1954 at Banpo in Shaanxi Province, revealing characteristics of the Yangshao Culture of matriarchy. During China's Neolithic period, which spanned the eighth to the second millennium B.C.E., finely executed styles of pottery appeared, foreshadowing the development of ceramics as a major Chinese art form. The appearance of bronze metallurgy in the second millennium B.C.E., during the Shang Dynasty, marked the end of the Neolithic period in China. And skilled craftsmen at that time produced ritual objects of clay, bronze, jade, and wood for the homes and tombs of rulers and nobles.

The immensely long history of continuous cultural development has left a rich legacy in many fields, and China's four greatest inventions—the compass, gunpowder, paper making, and movable-type printing—have had an enormous impact on world civilization. More significant than these four inventions is the cultural tradition that determines the behavioral contents of the Chinese people and serves as a cohesive force.

The Chinese stress conscientious moral disciplines and regard ethics and personality very highly. Chinese culture, although originating in remote antiquity and undergoing constant transformation, basically takes Confucianism as the core of its ideology, since Confucianism is the spiritual fruit of the productive labor and social practice of the Chinese over generations. Confucianism especially upholds humanism, justice, and virtue, and urges people to cultivate an independent personality and to abide by social ethics. With its dominating position in Chinese cultural tradition, Confucianism advocates rationalism, humanitarianism, and atheism, and helps to form a down-to-earth style of work on the part of the Chinese people. Confucianism stresses moral education instead of religion, advocates practical experience rather than supernatural forces, and upholds sovereign power instead of theocracy. As Confucianism stresses how to live life in the here-and-now and how the individual can relate meaningfully and harmoniously to other humans and to nature, it provides a basis for forming social ideology. Hence, the Chinese think more of this life than the next life. There are indigenous and foreign religions in China, but there has never been any religious fanaticism.

Cultural tradition is not monolithic but multidimensional. Every culture has a general tradition together with many specific traditions. In a sense, the general tradition is the condensation of these specific traditions, such as the philosophical tradition, literary tradition, religious tradition, and the tradition of popular culture. The process of modernization must start with the transformation of specific traditions. If not so, to materialize the modernization of a nation and its culture would be empty talk. This point may be illustrated by the unprecedented prosperity enjoyed in recent years by popular culture, one of the specific traditions in culture. On the one hand, popular culture appeals to the majority of the population because it caters to the tastes, ideas, habits, customs, interests, and psychology of the broad masses of the people who are the genuine carriers of cultural tradition. This would be impossible if popular culture did not take tradition as the basis and the point of departure for its development. On the other hand, popular culture acquires modern characteristics and reflects the fast development of a commodity economy and the rapid advancement of science and technology. The development and prosperity of popular culture relies on the progress of modernization and, in turn, manifests the progress of modernization. Therefore, in essence, the modernization of popular culture promotes the modernization of Chinese culture as a whole.

The development of a commodity economy and the enhancement of democratization are the necessary social conditions to develop popular culture. The development of the commodity economy calls for an end to the closed-door policy and promotes the opening. This expands human activities and international intercourse. Social democratization breaks up cultural confinement and ideological control so that people can enjoy great freedom in cultural activities, and a rich and colorful popular culture can evolve and reach the broad masses of the people. In our modern society, due to ever-increasing cultural exchanges between peoples and nations, cultural infiltration, absorption, and assimilation spread and become commonplace occurrences of acculturation. Consequently, modern culture of any nation or region can hardly maintain indigenous purity without absorbing any new traits from other cultures. And popular culture is especially active in absorbing alien traits to enrich itself. Therefore, popular culture is more often than not a medley of varied cultural traits.

The increasing demand for cultural commodities by the broad masses of the consumers of medium cultural refinement is the necessary cultural condition to develop popular culture. The prosperity of popular culture is determined by consumer demand, while demand and supply of cultural commodities are also determined by the cultural refinement of the consumers. The improvement of material conditions in life also stimulates the demand for the improvement of cultural conditions in life. When the consumers are aware of the need to enhance their cultural refinement so as to improve their cultural conditions in life, they welcome the market and production of popular culture.

While it is unrealistic to turn a blind eye to the negative aspects of popular culture, it is objective to observe that its positive aspects overwhelm its negative ones. A brief exposition of some social functions of popular culture can illuminate this point. All culture is created to satisfy human needs, and popular culture is especially so because it can be easily accepted by people of different occupations, different educational acquisitions, and different social strata. As popular culture meets the needs and demands of the cultural consumption of the majority of people, people can choose from popular culture what is suitable for their interest and appreciative ability. And this is what elite culture and folklore cannot provide. This is the satisfying function of popular culture.

Popular culture helps people observe and understand society. Like a mirror, popular culture reflects all aspects of society. Although the producer of popular culture might magnify or distort certain social phenomena for certain purposes, the spectators have the right to determine them according to their own understanding. In this way popular culture helps people realize social and individual values. This is the cognitive function of popular culture.

Directly related to the cognitive function is its reformative function. As popular culture helps people understand the world and makes people conscious of their value in society, it becomes an important tool for them to reform society and themselves. The problems in society and among the people are created by humans and can be solved only through human efforts.

Popular culture helps coordinate social activities and human relations. Society is a great system composed of people of various strata, various occupations, and various organizations, hence contradictions and conflicts are unavoidable. Popular culture is able to help establish appropriate contacts and coordinate the relations among people and between people and society. Only when a mutual understanding among different people is achieved can society have relative stability. This is the coordinative function of popular culture.

When some important events occur in society, people can learn about them immediately through mass media and decide what they should do about them. Many spontaneous and voluntary mass actions, such as donation, signature drive, and supportive rally, start as a feedback to the messages received from mass media. Popular culture sometimes plays a better role in mobilizing people than the order from the government administration high above. It is not merely because mass media are quick and widespread but also because they provide reliable information to be shared by the whole nation. This is the mobilizing function of popular culture.

As mass media often discuss the social issues with which people are most concerned, they provide opportunities for them to voice their opinions and to express their grievances. On the one hand, this helps people realize their individual value in society and enhance their self-consciousness. On the other hand, this serves as an "exhaust pipe" in society so that people can vent dissatisfaction and indignation. Otherwise, their dissatisfaction and indignation might sooner or later become so explosive as to affect social stability. This is the venting function of popular culture.

Popular culture is most sensitive to the change of the times and to the transformation of social structure, and it is most adaptable to such change and transformation. The plasticity of popular culture makes it commonplace for some aspects of popular culture to disappear and some other aspects to spring up. And such disappearance and appearance conforms to the fundamental interest and concern of the people as a whole. In this way popular culture strengthens the solidarity of the people of different social strata and enhances national identity. As a cohesive force, popular culture unites the people of the whole nation. This is the cohesive function of popular culture.

Evidently, popular culture is a complicated cultural system with contradictory characteristics and functions. Its advantages and disadvantages are closely entangled. This might be one of the reasons why many critics greet it with scorn. The intellectual establishment usually looks down upon popular culture. The major accusations from academia are that popular culture is a hotbed of poisonous weeds due to its commercial character and that it endangers the creation of an elite culture. Commercialism and creation, however, must not be absolutely contradictory. Without the consumer's demand there would be no market for production and creation. Therefore, consumption is the motive force of production. The creation and production of any form of culture have to consider the practical demand of society.

With its satisfying, cognitive, reformative, coordinative, mobilizing, venting, and cohesive functions in society, popular culture stimulates the development of the commodity economy, enhances national consciousness, and promotes cultural civilization. For all its positive social functions, however, popular culture is dualistic in nature. The dialectic view in regard to popular culture is to acknowledge its positive as well as negative aspects and see the close connection between the two. Popular culture is not a static phenomenon, but a dynamic trend, and it changes along with changes in social structure and social environment. It is unrealistic to deny the significant role popular culture plays in society; it is also unadvisable to overlook its potential for spiritual pollution.

WORKS CITED

Powers, Richard Gid, Hidetoshi Kato, and Bruce Stronach, eds. *Handbook of Japanese Popular Culture*. Westport, Conn.: Greenwood Press, 1989.
Wu Kuocheng. *The Chinese Heritage*. New York: Crown, 1982.

2

Lifestyles: Commercialization and Concepts of Choice

REBECCA HELEN WEINER

''Lifestyle'' has become a degraded term in the modern West, but not so in China. There *shenghuo fangshi* retains as yet a certain dignity by virtue of its promise of choice. After millennia rooted to family, home, work, and political relations handed down through generations with almost genetic force, after decades of extremist utopianism which denied the importance of individual lives, the phrase seems to promise that Chinese people at last are free to choose the directions (*fangshi*) in which to move their lives (*shenghuo*). Lifestyle, defined as a consciously chosen way of living, remains a newborn concept.

In ancient times, so popular wisdom holds, Chinese were born into lives fixed by fate, place, and economic necessity. According to this view, peasants tilled the same tenant plots as their ancestors; merchants handed the scales, bales, rigs, and ships of their trade from father to son; and royalty were born into riches and vices and palace intrigues as inevitable as the peasant's hoe and the merchant's strings of cash. To be sure, civil exams provided limited mobility for the brilliant and the wealthy, and marvellous inventions brought their creators riches and fame, and dynasties fell and new ones arose, and occasional individuals took shaping roles in these momentous events, transforming not only their own fate but the empire's. Still, most ancient lives are held to have been fixed by roots that led back through time, so that rulers good or bad were fated to be rulers while peasants' lifestyle choices were limited to eating rice soggy or dry.

The last century's transformations, so the mythology states, burst the old order and created a world in which Chinese became fully realized individuals in a brave new world of utopian socialism. But utopias carry their own exigencies, and the more China's continuing revolution overturned tradition, the more it created new requirements and restrictions in dress, food, actions, even thought. The concept of a consciously chosen lifestyle, impossible in the tradition-bound past, was equally impossible in a world where individual life was harnessed and sacrificed to the needs of the collective and the state.

After the ultimate disruption of the Cultural Revolution, however, politics lost command, and discussions of individual lifestyles have come to the fore. The post–Cultural Revolution world has left Chinese able and, indeed, forced to make choices of where and how to live, who to love, how to survive as a family, what job to take, and how to think about politics.

More than a century of war and revolution has ripped through China, stretching from the Opium Wars and the first broad-based contact with foreigners, to the Heavenly Kingdom (Taiping Tianguo) Rebellion in 1856, to the Xinhai of 1911, the May 4th of 1919, the civil war culminating in 1949, and the Cultural Revolution beginning in 1966. Revolution led to an explosion of ideas about choice, individuality, and personal needs—in short, about lifestyles. In the last half-century, discourse on such ideas permeated not only Chinese debate but also much foreign sinology. Entire literatures have examined Chinese choices in family and intimate life, housing and material life, working life, and political life.

To what extent this expansion of discussion represents actual increases in choice for average Chinese people remains to be seen. But certainly every field concerned with styles of life in China now breeds barrages of debate on tactics, possibilities, types of choices, and evaluations of effects. Compared with the land-bound peasant or fanatical cadre of yesteryear, the average Chinese today faces bewildering arrays of information, exhortation, advertisements, and enticements about lifestyle choices.

This massive discourse about lifestyle choice falls into several types: the official, the anti-official or underground, and the foreign. First, the Chinese government has striven to secure or to regain control over directions of lifestyle discourse, producing literature, magazines, films, images, lectures, and course books designed to channel debate to acceptable ranges of choice. These media constitute the official discourse. Second, an underground discourse has arisen in China concerning the making and exploiting of choices outside the realm of official discourse, be it how to swap houses to achieve choice in living space, or the politics of mass demonstrations as applied to choices of governance. Because this discourse is nonofficial, subject to censorship and silencing and fear, it exists in a largely oral or unpublished form, on telephone poles, in big character posters, in hand-copied volumes that pass from reader to reader, in private debates and quiet dinner conversations. This is the underground discourse. A third discourse on lifestyle choices in China comes from the foreign observer. Foreigners enjoy editorial freedoms unknown to writers in China. Standing outside the Chinese circle, however, the foreigner must make do with piecemeal observation, random oral histories, analysis of official sources, and selection of stray written items from the underground discourse.

Complicating this somewhat erratic collection process are two factors. First, many foreign sinologists lack the linguistic skills necessary to examine masses of original material on their own or to participate freely in the sort of informal conversation in which individual truths of the underground discourse in China most easily emerge. Thus handicapped, such sinologists must rely on assistants and interpreters, and are more than otherwise subject to control. Second, many foreigners bring to their China-watching biases and interpretations that inevitably shape their writings, be they anticommunist, pro-Marxist, or just fascinated by "Orientalia." The result is a sort of meta-discourse in which China becomes more sign and symbol than a country of living individuals, and which reveals perhaps more about the sinologists themselves than about China.

The truth, then, about lifestyle choices in China, if any exists, lies somewhere in the matrix of all discourses: the official, the underground, and the foreign. Only by examining various sources can readers come closest to knowledge of the individual realities of life and lifestyle in China, of degrees of freedom and choice, and of possibilities of change. The importance of all three sources informs the following historical outline and review of the field.

HISTORICAL OUTLINE

The century and a half of revolution which began with the Opium Wars was most essentially a revolution in ideas about individuality, the citizen's place in the nation, and personal power to shape destiny. Contact with foreigners followed the forced opening of the Treaty Ports, exposing many Chinese for the first time to non-Chinese, individualistic lifestyles. The coercive manner of that exposure bred much antiforeign sentiment, but ideas springing from that exposure gradually created a demand for change. The Heavenly Kingdom (Taiping Tianguo) movement, which began as antiforeign reaction and religious self-aggrandizement by the leaders, ended in a utopian proto-Marxist vision of control over capital, transformation of the old order, and women's and individual rights. Although the movement was brutally crushed, its legacy was a series of utopian-minded revolutionary acts and ideologies, from the Boxers to May 4th, workers' strikes to the Northern March, to the violent overthrow of patriarchy advocated by Qiu Jin. Central to many of these movements were quests to restructure material and political life through spiritual awakening, transformation of the family, and control by workers and peasants over their livelihoods. These quests became increasingly elided and confused with demands to restructure the compact between China's government and Chinese citizens.

It was perhaps this elision of personal, political, and spiritual goals that predisposed Chinese peasants and workers to support the utopian societal visions encompassed first by the Nationalist Party's (KMT's) Three Principles of the People, and later by the Marxist egalitarianism of the Chinese Communist Party (CCP). When the KMT was sullied by Chiang Kai-shek's flirtations with warlords and the Japanese, support swung overwhelmingly to the communists, with a force that not only vaulted the CCP to its 1949 victory, but also elevated Chairman Mao Zedong to the status of a god.

Mao's post-1949 continuing revolution, however, became an increasingly disastrous experiment with restructuring society's most fundamental norms. Art, literature, science, and trade were harnessed to this drive. Nationalization and collectivization movements, particularly in rural areas, strove to root out ancient concepts not only of privately held land and individual property but even of the virtue of family-based decisions on homemaking and marriage and the primacy of relations between parents and children. Antirightist movements sought to remold the New Socialist Person through confessions, struggle sessions, and self-examination, shaping a mind free from "old ways of thought." These movements culminated in the Cultural Revolution, ten years of anarchy the stated purpose of which was to transform the ideological foundations of culture itself, to free the individual from all tyrannies of birth, gender, place, or time, or even of native ability and talent.

In the search for a totally equal socialist society, Maoists nationalized land, houses, books, clothes, even pots and pans. Individual kitchens, gardens, chicken coops, and private enterprises of any kind were outlawed as bourgeois attempts to reestablish inequity, while citizens, especially in rural areas, ate from communal kitchens, read the same books, and wore the same clothes. Spouses, parents, and children were all encouraged to report on one another's ideological progress. In some "advanced" areas, children were taken from parents to be raised in communal nurseries. In the end, the very breadth and severity of the transformations required by Cultural Revolution goals dictated fanaticism on the part of the revolutionaries. The murders, forced suicides, imprisonments, beatings, struggle sessions, armed battles between Red Guard factions, and intrigues among central leaders all coexisted and were intimately intertwined with the dialogues of liberation, transformation, and remaking of society inherent in the Cultural Revolution, and perhaps in the entire utopian experiment from the start.

In the post–Cultural Revolution period, as individual Chinese tried to rebuild their lives, regather loved ones from prison and exile, and start anew in pursuit of careers and private dreams, as the Chinese government tried to return to the world community from isolation and economic and political stagnation, dialogue about choices in China entered a new phase. The new dialogue was infinitely more pragmatic and less utopian. The government promised stability, economic growth, and freedom from social experiment and political movements. Despite lapses into campaigns against crime and Western "spiritual pollution," the government has avoided large-scale mass movements since 1980.

Practical economics in China developed rapidly after the Cultural Revolution. Free markets and small private enterprises opened and, with them, choices of jobs, housing, and material goods unknown to Chinese of either the ancient or the less distant past. Workers and farmers began building houses, buying refrigerators, swapping jobs to be nearer loved ones, and generally making choices about their personal lives.

This relatively calm period of economic growth has undeniably increased choices in working, housing, and material life and has relaxed extremist experiments with choices in family and intimate life. The cost has inevitably, and perhaps not regrettably, been the abandonment of the experiment in liberation of spiritual and political life. Government has eased off the drive to remake a socialist man, calling instead for practical morality: Don't spit, kill rats, don't steal from your work unit, keep the family together as the base for a stable society. Meanwhile, the government has cracked down on dissident mass movements with fiercely consistent vigilance, both as a bulwark against backsliding into anarchy, and as a tool for aging party leaders to maintain their grips on power.

Indeed, in a very real sense, the reform and opening of China and the backing off from the goals of utopian spiritual transformation have meant a growth in commercial lifestyle choices, with a concomitant decrease in opportunities to experiment with spiritual or political life. Printing presses groan with the weight of new literature on housing, consumer goods, workplaces, courtship, marriage, and family. Political participation, however, once the foundation of Maoist mass-line politics, has been restricted, criminalized, and made an opposition phenomenon. The torrent of official literature exhorting, creating, and enforcing participation in mass movements has slowed to a trickle of documents explaining the proper role of the good citizen in the era of economic reform.

REVIEW OF THE FIELD

Four major categories of choices define lifestyle discourse in China. These concern family and intimate life, housing and material life, working life, and political life. Within each category, materials from both China and abroad discuss, define, and explicate the transformations in possibilities of the last hundred years.

Family and Intimate Life

Most modern writers view the traditional Chinese family as a relatively stable unit, largely patrilocal, patrilineal, and patriarchal. In the ideals of imperial-era social theorists, men controlled, women revered and obeyed, and children were filial. Although family structure did change over time, property restrictions, forms of inheritance, structures of marriage, and objects of sexuality all seem to have been tightly limited for most Chinese. Much literature explores the traditional Chinese family, from kinship structures and forms of ancestor worship to patterns of inheritance. Maurice Freedman's work is a good start, including *Family and Kinship in Chinese Society, Lineage Organization in Southeast China,* and *Lineage and Society in Fukien and Kwangtung.*

Relatively few surveys have emerged from China itself, but useful comparisons can be made with research done in Hong Kong and Taiwan. See, for instance, James L. Watson's *Emigration and the Chinese Lineage: The Mans in Hong Kong and London* and Patricia Buckley Ebrey and James L. Watson's

Kinship Organization in Late Imperial China, 1000–1940. Exhortative texts written by Chinese social theorists listing model women and ideal families also provide useful insights into social goals, if not realities. Lin Yueh-Hua's personal memoir *The Golden Wing* provides a useful individual insight, as does Alice Murong P. Lin's *Grandmother Had No Name* and Jonathan Spence's moving dramatization of traditional women's position, *The Death of Woman Wang*.

Of course, the traditional Chinese family, while stable by comparison with modern times, was never as static as the legend assumes, and much research into social history has revealed complex power relations in ancient Chinese family life. See Richard Guisso and Stanley Johannesen's *Women in China,* and Charles Meyer's *A History of Chinese Women: 4,000 Years of Power.*

The true explosion of discourse on the changing Chinese family, however, begins with the transformations in women's rights and kinship structures, ancestor worship, filiality, and attitudes toward nonprocreative sexuality, which began with the opening to the West. The official discourse on this period focuses on the positive effects of the liberation of women and the explosion of kinship structures in such stirring works as *Yingzi sashuang de Guangxi funu* (Heroic and Sacrificial Women of Guangxi Province), Hua Changming's *La Condition feminine et les Communistes Chinoises en action: Yan'an, 1935–46* (The Feminine Condition and the Chinese Communists in Action: Yan'an, 1935–46), and the English language *When They Were Young,* edited by the "Women of China." A semischolarly summary of this official history fills Chen Peng's *Zhongguo hunyin shi* (A History of Marriage in China). The underground discourse from this period is much harder to place, though it appears occasionally through the pages of oral histories taken down at the time, such as Ida Pruitt's *A Daughter of Han: The Autobiography of a Chinese Working Woman.*

Still more works have appeared from foreign observers, for whom perhaps the transformation of Chinese family structure resonated with the changes taking place in the West. Bobby Siu's *Fifty Years of Struggle: The Development of the Women's Movement in China, 1900–1949* is among the earliest of the genre, but throughout the 1970s and early 1980s dozens of Western publications covered these changes. Among the best are *Childhood in China,* edited by William Kessen; *Chinese Family and Kinship,* by Hugh D. R. Baker; *Chinese Kinship,* by Paul Chao; *The Family Revolution in Modern China,* by Marvin Leary, Jr.; *Patriarchy and Socialist Revolution in China,* by Judith Stacey; *Women in China,* by Katie Curtin; *Women in Chinese Society,* edited by Margery Wolfe and Roxanne Witke; and *Women of China: Imperialism and Women's Resistance, 1900–1949,* by Bobby Siu.

One particularly useful sort of study which emerged from this period followed individual villages or families through the many shifts of revolutions. Margery Wolfe's *The House of Lim* details the changing lives of one southern family. Isabel and David Crook's *Revolution in a Chinese Village: Ten Mile Inn* details the fortunes of their "Chinese home."

After the civil war and the CCP's victory, writers within and without China celebrated a new era of freedom for the Chinese family. Especially after the promulgation of the Marriage and Family Law and the Law on Equal Rights of Women, both in 1950, discussions implied that China had wholly overturned traditional ills. Chinese official volumes of this sort, such as *Zhongguo funu da fanshen* (The Great Transformation of Women in China) and *Lun funu jiefang* (On the Liberation of Women) were hardly surprising. Updates on this official view of the women's movement can be found in the journal *Funu zuzhi he yundong* (Women's Organizations and Movements). A bit more surprising were the many uncritical books that appeared from foreign authors about this period, such as *Women's Liberation in China* by Claudie Broyelle and Ruth Sidel's *Women and Child Care in China.*

As the Cultural Revolution progressed, official discourse on marriage and the family in China hardened. Very little was published during the "ten years of chaos," but immediately before and after the government produced much hard-line commentary on the "correct" socialist family, such as *Makesi, Engesi, Liening, Sidalin lun aiqing hunyin yu jiating* (Marx, Engels, Lenin, and Stalin on Love, Marriage and the Family) and *Pochu jiazu guannian* (Pushing out the Concepts of Ancestry). At this point, the break with both the underground discourse in China and the foreign discourse became clear. Within China nonofficial authors had little chance to publish books which baldly stated that Chinese liberation had failed to fully free women and the family. But fiction remained free of some controls. "Fiction" suggesting the limits still holding women, such as Ding Ling's stories, continued to appear.

At the same time, foreign writers began attacking the limits of marriage and family reform in China in such volumes as *Marriage en Chine* (Marriage in China) by Jean-Luc Domenach and Hua Changming; *La Chine: Une histoire de famille* (China: A History of the Family) by Claude Lemieux; *The Politics of Marriage in Contemporary China* by Elisabeth Croll; *Women, The Family, and Peasant Revolution in China* by Kay Ann Johnson; *Personal Voices: Chinese Women in the 1980s* by Emily Honig and Gail Hershatt; *Chinese Family Law and Social Change,* edited by David C. Buxbaum; *Chinese Women Since Mao,* by Elisabeth Croll; and *The Unfinished Liberation of Chinese Women: 1949–1980,* by Phyllis Andors.

With the fall of the Gang of Four and the rise of economic reform in China a new sort of publication joined the official discourse on marriage and family in China. Much was moralistic and prescriptive, though for practical rather than spiritual and political reasons. Grandparents' involvement in child care, for example, is urged in these materials both as a help for working mothers and as a familial role for the aged, while traditional Chinese sexual mores are urged as a bulwark against AIDS. Examples include *Jiating daode jiahua* (Moral Family Life), edited by Li Songnong; *Jiating wenti ershi jiang* (Twenty Answers to Familial Questions), by Xiu Dingben; *Hunyin jiating wenji* (Essays on Marriage and the Family) by the China Institute on Marriage and the Family; and *Hunyin jiating daode* (Morality in Marriage and Family). In some cases, these materials seem to warn of the power of the law as they urge parents to teach morality within the family, even in such recent books as Lao Feng's *Jiating yu shaonian fanzui* (Families and Juvenile Delinquency). More recently still, China has seen the rise of advice books dealing with such very prosaic matters as how to find a spouse and how to have a happy marriage, such as *Xinhun bidu* (Required Reading for Newlyweds), by Shi Tianyang, Ma Suwen, Li Yanshu, and Ying Xianyu; *Fuqi zhijian* (Between Husbands and Wives), by Li Saochen and Jiang Yuanming; and *Zenyang ban hunshi* (How to Get Married), by Can Shijie, You Zhonglun, and Tang Xiaoqing. Such titles reflect a changing society in which traditions of courtship and matchmaking have broken down, leaving a need for professional advice; at the same time, the Cultural Revolution–era belief that the individual family is unimportant has ended.

At the same time, such books reflect a certain commercialization of marriage and family life, the creation of love and courtship as provinces of advice givers and experts, whose wisdom and assistance have become marketable commodities. Thus China has seen the emergence of advice columnists on love, marriage, and family problems, such as Deng Weizhi, whose list of syndicated columns and books continues to grow, including *Jiating wenti zhongzhong* (Types of Family Problems), *Jiating de mingtian* (The Family Tomorrow), and, with Zhang Daiyu, *Zhongguo jiating de yanbian* (The Changing Chinese Family). Love as the province of experts emerges as well in the growing popularity of books on the psychology of marriage and family, such as Tang Tao's *Hunyin xinlixue* (The Psychology of Marriage).

Finally, starting around 1988, Chinese newspapers, magazines, and telephone pole message boards began hosting the ultimate commercialization of courtship: personal ads, in which the infinity of human characteristics is reduced to three lines or less and packaged to sell. To be sure, Chinese ads generally search for marital partners and are thoroughly tame by Western standards, but the fundamentally depersonalizing approach to relationships is the same.

One fascinating medium for viewing the transformation of official discourse on marriage and family over the last several decades is the popular magazines. Started mostly in the early 1960s, periodicals such as *Jiating* (The Family), *Hunyin yu jiating* (Marriage and Family), *Funu* (Women), and *Xiandai jiating* (Modern Family) began with drab layout and socialist-realist drawings of happy women on tractors as a way of propagandizing the masses about the new Chinese family. Over time, however, these magazines have all become glossier and thicker, begun accepting advertising, and given up publishing articles like "Chairman Mao's Thoughts on the Liberation of Women" and "Marx and Engels on the Meaning of Love under Socialism" for features like "Deng Weizhi's Love Advice," "The Twenty Best Refrigerators," "Quick and Easy Cantonese Recipes," and "The Call of Love," the title of the personals column in *Marriage and Family*.

Thus the official discourse on marriage and the family in China has followed a swift curve from early discussions of choice, to exhortations of extremist utopias, to commodification of choice. Foreign discourses in the same period have described tradition and discussed change, with mixed admiration and dismay. How foreign sinologists will react to the age of personal columns and Deng Weizhi remains to be seen. The underground discourse, always the most difficult to pinpoint, seems to have shifted focus as well, from Qiu Jin's mighty calls for women to arise, to the sadly familiar personal columns, which both genders use to arouse.

Two related issues have occupied much discussion on family and intimate life in China. One is population control and family planning as it relates to women's rights and family choices. Every aspect of China's family planning program has been thoroughly studied both within and without China, from statistical breakdowns, such as *Zhongguo chengshi jiating* (Chinese Urban Families) and the scholarly journal *Renkouxue* (Population Studies), to broad-based analyses, like *Jiating jihua* (Family Planning), by the Yinchuan Family Planning Committee. Foreign observers have also explored the effects of changing patterns of population growth. Such incisive papers as Ansley J. Coale, Shaomin Li, and Jing-Qing Han's *Distribution of Interbirth Intervals in Rural China, 1940s–1970s,* for example, offer powerful insight into the increased control rural Chinese women have gained over their reproductive lives through access to effective birth control. See also *Chinese Approaches to Family Planning,* a useful volume of translated documents, edited with an introduction by Robert Dunn.

Of course, the more repressive side of China's birth control policies has also been thoroughly detailed, from popularization by Steven Mosher in *Broken Earth: The Rural Chinese,* to more scholarly works, such as *China's One-Child Family Policy* by Elisabeth Croll, Delia Davin, and Penny Kane. Several of the most critical works come from Taiwan—see, for example, Ch'ou Pai-Yun's *Dalu nannu* (Men and Women on the Mainland). Some of the most interesting writing on China's birth control program in recent years, however, has been that specifically focusing on the ways government policy has affected family choices. Such issues as when families choose to have more than their allotted number of children, how they pay resulting fines, and what issues surround and inform such choices arise frequently. See, for instance, Ann-Ping Chin's oral history collection *Children of China: Voices from Recent Years* or the scholarly analysis *Marriage and Fertility in Tianjin, China: Fifty Years of Transition* by Burton Pasternak.

The other issue in family and intimate life emerging from recent writing is alternative sexual orientations. Despite a long history of homosexual culture in China, gay lifestyles were harshly oppressed after the CCP's victory in 1949. Maoists defined homosexuality as foreign "spiritual pollution" and criminalized it. In very recent times, however, more open choices of sexual orientation are reemerging from China and, with them, a small but growing literature on the subject. *Zhongguo tongxingai shilu* (A History of Homosexuality in China) by Xiao Mingxiong (pen name, Takeshi Koake) is more anecdotal than analytical.

Bret Hinsch's ground-breaking *Passions of the Cut Sleeve,* however, has opened
what promises to be a fruitful debate on intimate lifestyle choices.

Housing and Material Life

As the continuing revolution transformed choices in family relationships, so
it altered possibilities in housing and material life. Other chapters in this handbook treat the literature on actual housing and transportation. This section instead discusses the issue of material lifestyle choices.

Many of the movements of the last century focused on improving material
life, particularly for peasants. Land reform, protection against rapacious taxes,
and increasing general standards of living were central to the Taiping Tianguo
movement and were chief goals of the CCP in its drive toward liberation. Many
works, both Chinese and foreign, explore the extents and limits of these reforms.
Mark Selden's *The Yenan Way in Revolutionary China,* for example, offers
detailed insight into land reform, rent reduction, and the early cooperative movement. Works on specific areas, such as Jan Myrdal's *Report from a Chinese
Village* and William Hinton's classic *Fanshen,* explore structural reform in specific villages, with expert attention to how the CCP changed the choices available to various peasant groups. For a fascinating view of the end of utopianism
and the start of economic reform, read these books together with the follow-up
books the authors wrote on return trips to China: Myrdal's *Return to a Chinese
Village* and Hinton's *Shenfan.* The Chinese government throughout this period
published works extolling the glorious ways liberation created material improvement. These generally stressed growth for China as a whole, such as *Wo guo
ziran ziyuan* (Our Nation's Natural Resources), edited by Xiao Fengxi. Individual lifestyle improvement was not to be thought of during national development,
except for those classed as "deprived" in prerevolutionary times and granted
some of the nationalized spoils of those classed as "wealthy."

Even in the earliest stages of land reform and collectivization some dissenting
voices emerged. Wang Meng's early stories, for example, dissect the darker side
of "struggles" against the landlords, and by the late 1950s the response to
Mao's calls for a "Hundred Flowers" of dissent brought forth scores of articles
about the limits of reforms, many of whose authors later suffered dearly for
their honesty.

Reforms in housing and material life followed much the same pattern as
reforms in family life. Throughout the 1950s and 1960s, ever more extreme
forms of collectivization were first urged and then enforced, so that even as
official discourse in China praised freedom from tradition, real officials enforced
rigid new norms. Throughout the Cultural Revolution, official discourse in China
continued to glorify modernization, and countless books extolled the virtues of
socialist life. Shortly after the Cultural Revolution, the government produced
more muted but still highly optimistic studies, such as *Zhongguo jingji jinzhan*

(Chinese Economic Growth) and Chuan Weitian's *Zhongguo shaoshu minzu zibenzhuyi fazhan* (Developing Capitalism among China's Minorities).

Foreign discourse, predictably, moved ever farther away from official Chinese reality and explored not only the havoc wrought on individuals and families by economic collectivization, but also the strategies and tactics used by the Chinese people to achieve their material needs despite an illogical economic system. For an incisive analysis of the destructive economics of utopianism, see, for example, *Class and Social Stratification in Post-Revolutionary China,* edited by James L. Watson; *Class in China: Stratification in a Classless Society,* by Larry M. Wortel; and *La Chine apres l'utopie* (China after Utopia), by Jacques Gravereau.

With economic reform, China's official presses did an about-face and began to introduce and defend the new policies, sometimes in English publications written for foreigners. See, for example, *Smashing the Communal Plot: Formulation and Development of the Rural Responsibility System,* by Wang Guichen, or *Lun jingji xiaoguo* (On Economic Efficiency).

Foreigners, of course, also explored China's changed economic course, in such works as *China's Changed Road to Development,* edited by Neville Maxwell and Bruce McFarlane; *China and the Crisis of Marxism-Leninism,* by Franz Michael; *Asia Pacific Report: Focus—China in the Reform Era,* edited by Charles E. Morrison and Robert F. Dernberger; and *China's Unfinished Revolution,* by James M. Etheridge.

Meanwhile, as realism replaced idealism, new tactics for attaining scarce material goods emerged, and many recent works detail these strategies through oral history, anecdotes, and analysis. Topics such as black-market trading for residence permits (*hukou*); illegal sales of ration tickets and purchase coupons for rare items, such as televisions and refrigerators; house-swapping strategies (by which families strive for classification as hardship cases for housing allotment purposes); the entangled layers of connections necessary for purchasing bicycles, train tickets, and other scarcities; and the hows and whens of food hoarding emerge in detail in these works. See, for example, *Chinese Lives,* by Zhang Xinxin and Sang Ye, translated and edited by W.J.F. Jenner and Delia Davin; *The Family Rice Bowl: Food and the Domestic Economy in China,* by Elisabeth Croll; *Urban Life in Contemporary China,* by Martin King Whyte; *Living in China,* by Rebecca Weiner, Margaret Murphy, and Albert Li; and *Chinese Families in the Post-Mao Era,* edited by Deborah Davis and Steven Harrell.

Underground discourse on material life, as with family life, has appeared mostly in the form of fiction, notably in the "scar literature," fictionalizing Cultural Revolution horrors, which began appearing around 1980. Perry Link has edited two fine anthologies of translated short stories: *Roses and Thorns* and *Mandarin Ducks and Butterflies.* Much else remains untranslated; some of it is accessible only in hand-copied form. Some of the most interesting new "dissident literature" has appeared in the form of rock music and movies. Songs such as Cui Jian's "Xiang Yiba Dao" (Like a Knife) or movies such as Jiang

Wen's *Ben Ming Nian* (Black Rain) will be increasingly important windows into the underground discourse in years to come. Translating and presenting more such works in the West should help fill gaps in our understanding of underground discussions.

As both individuals and the government clamor for improved material life, advertising literature has developed in China, in forms not seen since 1949. Every newspaper, popular magazine, and city billboard in China teems with increasingly glossy and professional advertisements. Television "infotainment" ads, imitating those in the West, have become common; in some cities, the age of junk mail through direct mail marketing has begun. Studies of this burgeoning "literature" should provide important insight into choices in material lifestyles in China as well.

Interestingly, in very recent years, the official and underground discourses on material life have grown more similar to one another. With continued support for economic reform, particularly after Deng Xiaoping's journey to the south, official papers have begun exposing and vilifying corrupt local party cadres who have mismanaged, pilfered, or distributed public goods through favoritism. Such semi-internal government publications as *Duzhe Wenzhai* (Reader's Choice), a Beijing weekly publishing unclassified internal documents for Chinese readers, often seem indistinguishable in tone and content from, say, Liu Binyan's critical memoir, *A Higher Kind of Loyalty.* A fine collection of translations from *Reader's Choice* and other unclassified internal publications is *Economic Reform in the PRC: In Which China's Economists Make Known What Went Wrong, Why, and What Should Be Done about It,* translated and edited by George C. Wong. To some extent, even descriptions of the thousand petty strategies used by families to better themselves in China's current hybrid economy have reached the official press. Notably, the oral histories collected in Zhang Xin-xin and Sang Ye's *Chinese Lives* appeared first in China in serial form. Some were even translated into English and published by the Chinese government under the title *Chinese Stories.* Publication in English for a foreign audience of stories openly, if mutedly, critical of the government reveals the extent of current openness in this area.

Official and underground discourses still veer apart on larger issues, such as the overall value of a planned economy. The Chinese government seems willing to admit mistakes, corruption, and other difficulties in implementing economic plans nationwide, and to admit that economic plans need to be rationalized and that market forces must be taken into account. But to question the wisdom of a planned economy or the socialist way overall remains forbidden. It was after all Liu Binyan's questioning of the leadership role of the Communist Party, rather than his incisive criticism of economic flaws, that has forced him into exile.

Thus discourse about material lifestyle choices has changed from broad-based discussions of the nature of home and the values of the collective to focused attention on commercial choices in the market. Material life for the average Chinese is changing rapidly at present; choices and strategies for material lifestyles remain central to Chinese people's lives and a fruitful area for research.

Working Life

As China's economy developed, choices proliferated in jobs, conceptions of career, and ways of integrating working and nonworking life. A literature has developed that explores the variety of choices and strategies of Chinese people in their working lives.

Many early revolutions centered on freeing Chinese people from working roles they had been thrust into by tradition, whether as peasant, merchant, or laborer. Communist revolution, of course, transformed practices of child labor, tenant relationships, taxation, and enforced prostitution, and much literature both within and without China describes the many faces of early Communist labor reform. Within China triumphant tracts, such as *Lishi shi nulimen chuangzao de* (History Is Written by the Slaves), by the Youth Marxist-Leninist Studies Committee, coexisted with more general surveys, such as *Zhongguo minzhu shiqi de gongren yundong shilu* (A History of Workers' Movements in the Chinese Democratic Revolutions) by Tang Yuliang. Meantime, many foreign observers gathered information on how liberation affected workers. Good sources include Delia Davin's *Woman-Work: Women and the Party in Revolutionary China* and Stephen Andors's *Workers and Workplaces in Revolutionary China*. Many of the oral histories listed in the section on housing and material life also offer insights into ways CCP victory transformed the choices available to Chinese people in their working lives.

As with so many other aspects of life, normal work in China was cut off by the extremism of the late 1950s and the Cultural Revolution. Since the government began criticizing those years, an entire literature discussing the "ten years of destruction" has emerged from within China itself. Few sources criticize those years as poignantly as the once-banned *Shinian dongluan* (Ten Years of Chaos). Numerous other works, both Chinese and foreign, describe in horrifying detail the destruction both to individual lives and to China's economy wrought by a decade in which jobs were valued for political rather than economic virtues. Some of the most potent writings hail from Taiwan, such as *Zhongguo duidai gongren nongmin funu de zhencheng* (The Truth about How the Chinese Communists Treat Workers, Farmers, and Women), by the Chinese Researches Original Materials Committee. See also *Enemies of the People* by Anne F. Thurston and *A Year in Upper Felicity: Life in a Chinese Village during the Cultural Revolution* by Jack Chen.

Since 1980 employment opportunities have boomed. Reopening of free markets and of the responsibility system, however spottily applied, has allowed for the rebirth of whole categories of small-scale producers and minor salespeople bankrupted by the excesses of the 1960s and 1970s. Such topics as the responsibility system, free markets, developing entrepreneurship, the end of the job assignment system, unemployment, bankruptcy law, and guarantees for old-age pensions in the reformed economy fill many new government tomes. Such books rationalize and explain the economic reforms, assuring workers and farmers that they will not be abandoned in the new era. See, for example, *Guoying qiye laodong zhidu gaige dawen* (Answers to Questions on Reform of the State Enterprise Work System), edited by Xu Jianchuan, Tian Ming, and Yang Hao; *Laodong wenti jianghua* (Answers to Labor Questions) in the Central Peoples Broadcasting Station Lecture Series; and *Zhongguo laodong zhidu gaige* (Reforms in China's Work System), edited by Liu Jia-Lin and Mafeng Huadeng.

Other materials, written for reform-minded managers in state and cooperative enterprises, encourage modern management techniques. Almost quaint coming from the centralized leadership, such titles include *Banzu gongzuo yibai lie* (100 Ways to Improve Management Organization), edited by the Shanghai Municipal Union, which contains such remarkable chapters as "From Confronting Problems of Thought to Confronting Practical Problems." Useful sources also include semipopular magazines, such as *Gaige huhuan* (Voice of Reform) and *Jingji gaige* (Economic Reform).

China's official dialogue on working life has not abandoned discussions of the worker's paradise and the dictatorship of the proletariat, but materials produced now take a decidedly muted tone and refer to socialist self-organization more as a vague ideal than as an item on an immediate agenda. Many of the more recent books in China on the worker's movement, written clearly for a scholarly rather than a mass audience, are indistinguishable from similar books in the West. See, for example, *Bense, chuantong, shiming: Gongren jieji changshi duben* (Character, Tradition, and Historical Mission: A Working Class Reader) or the scholarly journal *Gongren zuzhi yu yundong* (Worker's Organizations and Movements). The government's lack of enthusiasm for publishing practical, mass-oriented books on labor organization is noteworthy.

Western literature on the new choices Chinese people face in working lifestyles remains sparse. A useful summary from a legal standpoint, although now somewhat dated, is Augusta Wagner's *Labor Legislation in China*. A good overall analysis can be found in *Communist Neo-Traditionalism: Work and Authority in Chinese Industry* by Andrew G. Walder. The oral history collection, *Lives: Chinese Working Women*, edited by Mary Sheridan and Janet W. Salaff, shows some of the strategies women have used to cope with reform. In the meantime, this remains a rich field for research.

Political Life

Most Chinese people, when asked about their political activities, still often respond that they are "uninterested in politics." This blanket mendacity covers a complex of choices Chinese people make about politics out of interest, necessity, and fear. In fact, it might be clearer to say that most Chinese people have participated too much in politics, having been forced all their lives to participate in movements, marches, and political study sessions and now fear the power of politics to corrupt ordinary life.

No aspect of Chinese lifestyles has inspired more writing, both Chinese and foreign, than political involvement. Beginning with mass involvement in the

Taiping Rebellion, and continuing through the peasant organizations that Mao observed in Hunan, to the "bandit" groups that formed in the War of Resistance against Japan, to Yanan-based CCP organizing of mass-based war, to the mass movements of Mao's continuing revolution, every aspect of political organization in the late Qing and Republican eras and in the People's Republic of China (PRC) has been dissected to the last minutiae. The list of works is far too extensive to attempt an exhaustive review of the literature on political participation here. This section merely attempts to note a few key works connected to the concept of choice in political participation.

Regarding Republican-era politics, China's government continues to release such victorious tomes as *Changzeng nu zhanshi* (Women Fighters of the Long March), by Zeng Zhi, and *Minzhu geming de minzhu yundong* (The Democratic Movement of the Democratic Revolution), by Qiu Qianshou, Yang Shubiao, and Wang Tianwen. Meanwhile, study of the history of the CCP is still considered an important enough subject to be an entire undergraduate major in many Chinese universities; it supports several scholarly magazines such as *Zhongguo gongchandang lishi yanjiu* (Researches into the History of the Chinese Communist Party) and *Sixiang yu zhengzhi gongzuo he yanjiu* (Thought, Political Work, and Research Magazine). At the same time, Taiwan authors continue to excoriate Communist "insurgents" during the Republican and Nationalist eras in such volumes as *Zhonggong jianyu sanshisan nian* (33 Years of Imprisonment by the Chinese Communists) by Chen Liaohsiang. Useful foreign perspectives on the period include, of course, those of the venerable Edgar Snow and the memoirs of Anna Louise Strong and Ilona Ralf Sues.

Post-1949 political action generally meant mass movements instigated top-down. Official literature from this era often presented models such as Lei Feng for the populace to follow, or gave glowing testimonies from those who had been happily reformed through labor. See, for example, *Qi ren zhi yu* (The Story of Seven Prisoners) by Sha Qianli or *Lao gai chun qiu* (A Spring and Autumn Annals of My Labor Reform) by Jia Wenqing.

Many foreign writers discuss the choices the Chinese faced about participation in mass politics throughout this period. Some of the best include *Political Culture and Group Conflict in Communist China,* by Alan P. L. Liu; *From Bandwagon to Balance-of-Power Politics,* by Avery Goldstein; *Citizens and Groups in Contemporary China,* edited by Victor C. Falkenheim; *The Dynamic of Factions and Consensus in Chinese Politics,* by Lucian W. Pye; *Groups and Politics in the People's Republic of China,* edited by David S. G. Goodman; *Chinese Democracy,* by Andrew J. Nathan; *The Mandarin and the Cadre: China's Political Cultures,* by Lucian W. Pye; *Political Participation in Rural China,* by John P. Burns; *Ten Mile Inn: Mass Movement in a Chinese Village,* by Isabel and David Crook; *Political Participation in Communist China,* by James R. Townsend; *Voices from the Whirlwind: An Oral History of the Cultural Revolution,* edited by Feng Jicai; and *Children of Mao: Personality Development and Political Action in the Red Guard Generation,* by Anita Chan.

Dissident political voices began to gain strength in China as the excesses of the Cultural Revolution became apparent. Despite lacking an organized permanent opposition, Chinese dissidents have published more often of late, frequently abroad, while students at home organized protests in 1979, 1984, 1987, 1988, and, most dramatically, 1989.

Official Chinese writings have tended either to ignore these movements, or to dismiss them as the work of ignorant youth being misled by counterrevolutionaries or foreign spies. Foreign writers, by contrast, have been fascinated with these evidences of the underground dialogue on political choice bubbling through to the surface. While many of the best dissident writers remain untranslated and uncollected in the West, such seminal voices as Liu Binyan, Fang Lizhi, and Cao Guanlong have appeared ever more frequently. While no opposition magazines can as yet be published in China, many dissident Chinese authors find publication venues in magazines produced in Taiwan, Hong Kong, or the United States, such as *Chaoliu* (Tide), *Jiushi niandai* (The Nineties), *Dalu yuekan* (Mainland China Monthly), and *Zhongguo zhi chun* (China Spring).

The outpouring of foreign writing on dissident political movements in China has been even greater. Amnesty International, Asiawatch, International Campaign for Tibet, Human Rights in China, and similar organizations regularly publish reports on human rights conditions in China, dissidents, political prisoners, and the state of political opposition. Meanwhile, foreigners have published various perspectives on dissident movements, from personal narratives like Alain Jacob's *Un Balcon à Pekin* (A Balcony in Beijing) to collections of documents and writings from the protest movements, such as *Beijing Street Voices*, by David S. E. Goodman, and *Documents on the Democratic Movement, 1978–1980*, edited by Claude Widor, to broad-based analyses of the goals and directions of the democracy movements, such as James D. Seymour's groundbreaking *The Fifth Modernization: China's Human Rights Movement, 1978–79*, or *Going against the Tide: On Dissent and Big Character Posters in China*, by Goran Leijonhufvud. Foreign fascination with dissident movements in China continues to grow, and indeed the 1989 student protests and the government crackdown following them have produced an explosion of materials; by my count so far, seventeen nonfiction analyses, twenty conference reports, five novels, six collections of personal narratives, four pictorial collections, seven anthologies of poetry, three statistical analyses of public opinion surveys, five collections of big character posters and other sources, one PBS documentary, and two television docudramas, with more on the way.

The Chinese government issued various works throughout the 1980s trying to recapture the lead in discourse on political choice. Many books codified for the first time the rights and responsibilities of Chinese citizenship, such as the handsomely printed *Gongmin shouce* (Citizen's Handbook), or *Zhongguo gongmin xuzhi* (What Every Chinese Citizen Needs to Know). Others take a more didactic tack, seemingly trying to revivify moribund popular idealism about mass political participation, such as *Zheng zuo yige guangrongde gongqing-*

tuanyuan (How to Become a Glorious Member of the Communist Youth League), or the sternly disciplinary *Woguo gongmin jiben quanli he ziren* (Basic Rights and Responsibilities of the Citizens of Our Nation), by Zhang Qingfu and Wang Deyang. At the same time, the government continues to require political study sessions, and to attempt to imbue those sessions with some of the lively faith of yesteryear, in semipopular magazines distributed to political educators, for example, *Zhengzhi jiaoyu* (Political Education), *Zhengzhixue yu falu* (Political Science and Law), and *Minzhu yu falu* (Democracy and Law).

Increasingly, however, it appears that China's leaders, moribund themselves in these pragmatic, antiutopian, black-cat/white-cat days, have abandoned hope of a truly popular mass movement supporting socialist leadership. Instead, official discourse speaks more of iron-fisted control.

While discourse on choices of political lifestyle in China is therefore the most repressed of the four categories we have examined, it remains perhaps the least commercialized as well, and therefore, in an odd way, it is the least defined, the most open in terms of debate on broad definitions. Liu Binyan advocates China's search for a true third way between Western capitalism and command socialism. Perhaps as the Chinese growing up in today's political atmosphere make their choices and arrange their political lifestyles, China will begin to find that way.

REFERENCE WORKS

Relatively few bibliographies exist regarding lifestyle choices in China, although a few detail specific areas that impact on lifestyle. Useful bibliographies on woman's rights, family, and intimate life include *The Women's Movement in China: A Selection of Readings, 1949–1973* (1974), edited by Elisabeth Croll; *Women in China: A Selected and Annotated Bibliography* (1984), by Karen T. Wei; *Women in China: Current Directions in Historical Scholarship* (1981), edited by Richard W. Guisso and Stanley Johannesen; and *Women in China: A Bibliography of Available English-Language Materials* (1984), edited by Lucie Chang, Charlotte Furth, and Hon-Ming Yip. Good bibliographies on political life include *Communist China: A Bibliographic Survey* (1971) and *Contemporary China: A Research Guide* (1967), Peter Berton and Eugene Wu. For bibliographies of economic developments in China as they affect choices about working and material life, see *The Chinese Economy Post-Mao: A Compendium of Papers* (1978), Joint Congressional Economic Committee, and the State Department Central Files on Chinese Internal Affairs. Some eighty reels of formerly classified microfilm on China's economic changes between 1949 and 1959 have been released to U.S. government document repository libraries, and they form an excellent source on the utopian-extremist years. For Chinese sources, see also *Zhongguo jingjishi tiyao* (A Bibliography of China's Economic History) (1988), by the Chinese Academy of Social Sciences.

Another important reference source for studies on lifestyle in China are the numerous topical dictionaries and compendia published in China. As topics emerge, become standardized and commercialized in China, increasing discourse on them requires codification, and a favorite form in China is the writing of dictionaries, compendia, and encyclopedias. For political participation, useful works include *Zhengzhixue cidian* (A Dictionary of Political Science) (1989), edited by Hu Fuming, with James Townsend, and *Zhengzhi lilun xuexie cidian* (A Student's Dictionary of Political Thought) (1987), edited by Zhang Nianzou. For family and intimate life, see *Hunyin yu jiating cidian* (1989) (A Dictionary of Marriage and Family). For economic reform and changes for workers, see *Laodong gongzi mingci jieshi* (A Directory of Labor and Salary Terms) (1983), by Li Fuye and Zhang Guoling.

RESEARCH COLLECTIONS

Research collections are rare on these topics. They are primarily useful in gaining access to varied documents from the underground discourse in China, such as hand-copied books and copies of big character posters. A number of useful sources exist for oral histories and other materials. On political life, the collections of the Center for International Studies at Columbia University in New York represent one of the most complete collections of materials on dissident writers, democracy movements, and the June 4th incident. Human Rights in China, Asiawatch, and the International Campaign for Tibet all maintain similar collections. On family life, the Yale University Manuscripts and Archives collection maintains a library of oral histories. On economic history, the Hoover Institute at Stanford University maintains an extremely broad collection of documents. Some early papers have been catalogued by Ming K. Chan in *Historiography of the Chinese Labor Movement, 1895–1945: A Bibliography of Chinese Source Materials at the Hoover Institute.*

BIBLIOGRAPHY

Books and Monographs

Andors, Phyllis. *The Unfinished Liberation of Chinese Women: 1949–1980.* Bloomington: Indiana University Press, 1983.

Andors, Stephen, ed. *Workers and Workplaces in Revolutionary China.* White Plains, N.Y.: M. E. Sharpe, 1977.

Baker, Hugh D. R. *Chinese Family and Kinship.* New York: Columbia University Press, 1979.

Bense, chuantong, shiming: Gongren jieji changshi duben (Character, Tradition, and Historical Mission: A Working Class Reader). Beijing: Workers' Publishing House, 1983.

Broyelle, Claudie. *Women's Liberation in China* (translated from *La Motie du ciel* and prefaced in English by Han Su-yin). New York: Hunter's Press, 1977.

Burns, John P. *Political Participation in Rural China.* Berkeley: University of California Press, 1988.

Buxbaum, David C., ed. *Chinese Family Law and Social Change*. Seattle: University of Washington Press, 1978.

Can Shijie, You Zhonglun, and Tang Xiaoqing. *Zenyang ban hunshi* (How to Get Married). Chengdu: Sichuan People's Publishing House, 1984.

Central People's Broadcasting Station Lecture Series. *Laodong wenti jianghua* (Answers to Labor Questions). Beijing: Guang Fan Publishing House, 1983.

————. *Zhengque chuli hunyin yu jiating wenti* (On the Correct Handling of Marital and Family Problems). Guilin: Guizhou People's Publishing House, 1979.

Chan, Anita. *Children of Mao: Personality Development and Political Action in the Red Guard Generation*. Seattle: University of Washington Press, 1985.

Chao, Paul. *Chinese Kinship*. London: Kegan, Paul, International, 1983.

Chen, Jack. *A Year in Upper Felicity: Life in a Chinese Village during the Cultural Revolution*. New York: Macmillan, 1973.

Chen Liaohsiang. *Zhonggong Jianyu Sanshisan Nian* (33 Years of Imprisonment by the Chinese Communists). Taipei: National Security Bureau, Political Work Section, 1982.

Chen Peng. *Zhongguo hunyin shi* (A History of Marriage in China). Beijing: Zhong Hua Publishing House, 1990.

Chin, Ann-Ping. *Children of China: Voices from Recent Years*. New York: Knopf, 1988.

China Institute of Marriage and the Family. *Hunyin jiating wenji* (Essays on Marriage and the Family). Tianjin: Legal Publishing House, 1984.

Chinese Researches Original Materials Committee. *Zhongguo duidai gongren nongmin funu de zhencheng* (The Truth about How the Chinese Communists Treat Workers, Farmers, and Women). Taipei: Li Min Cultural Affairs Company, 1984.

Ch'ou Pai-Yun. *Dalu nannu* (Men and Women on the Mainland). Taipei: Huan-Ning Press, 1968.

Chuan Weitian. *Zhongguo shaoshu minzu zibenzhuyi fazhan* (Developing Capitalism among China's Minorities). Kaifeng: Henan People's Publishing House, 1982.

Coale, Ansley J., Shaomin Li, and Jing-Qing Han. *Distribution of Interbirth Intervals in Rural China, 1940s–1970s*. Honolulu: East-West Center Press, Papers of the East-West Population Institute, no. 109, August 1988.

Croll, Elisabeth. *Chinese Women Since Mao*. London: Zed Books, 1983.

————. *The Family Rice Bowl: Food and the Domestic Economy in China*. (For the United Nations Research Institute for Social Development). London: Zed Press, 1983.

————. *The Politics of Marriage in Contemporary China*. New York: Cambridge University Press, 1981.

Croll, Elisabeth, Delia Davin, and Penny Kane, eds. *China's One-Child Family Policy*. New York: St. Martin's Press, 1985.

Crook, Isabel, and David Crook. *Revolution in a Chinese Village: Ten Mile Inn*. London: Routledge and Kegan Paul, 1959.

————. *Ten Mile Inn: Mass Movement in a Chinese Village*. New York: Pantheon, 1979.

Curtin, Katie. *Women in China*. New York: Pathfinder Press, 1975.

Davin, Delia. *Woman-Work: Women and the Party in Revolutionary China*. New York: Oxford University Press, 1979.

Davis, Deborah, and Steven Harrell, eds. *Chinese Families in the Post-Mao Era*. Berkeley: University of California Press, 1993.

Deng Weizhi. *Jiating de mingtian* (The Family Tomorrow). Guiyang: Guizhou People's Publishing House, 1986.

————. *Jiating wenti zhongzhong* (Types of Family Problems). Tianjin: Tianjin People's Publishing House, 1983.

Deng Weizhi, with Zhang Daiyu. *Zhongguo jiating de yanbian* (The Changing Chinese Family). Shanghai: Shanghai People's Publishing House, 1987.

Domenach, Jean-Luc, and Hua Changming. *Marriage en Chine* (Marriage in China). Paris: Presses de la Fondation Nationale des Sciences Politiques, 1987.

Dunn, Robert, trans. and ed. *Chinese Approaches to Family Planning.* White Plains, N.Y.: M. E. Sharpe, 1979.

Ebrey, Patricia Buckley, and James L. Watson. *Kinship Organization in Late Imperial China, 1000–1940.* Berkeley: University of California Press, 1986.

Etheridge, James M. *China's Unfinished Revolution.* San Francisco: China Books and Periodicals, 1990.

Falkenheim, Victor C., ed. *Citizens and Groups in Contemporary China.* Ann Arbor: Center for Chinese Studies, University of Michigan, Michigan Monographs in Chinese Studies no. 56, 1987.

Feng Jicai, ed. *Voices from the Whirlwind: An Oral History of the Cultural Revolution.* New York: Pantheon, 1991.

Freedman, Maurice. *Lineage and Society in Fukien and Kwangtung.* London: London School of Economics Monographs of Sociological Anthropology no. 33, University of London Athlone Press, 1971.

————. *Lineage Organization in Southeast China.* London: London School of Economics Monographs of Sociological Anthropology no. 18, University of London Athlone Press, 1966.

Freedman, Maurice, ed. *Family and Kinship in Chinese Society.* Palo Alto, Calif.: Stanford University Press, 1958.

Goldstein, Avery. *From Bandwagon to Balance-of-Power Politics.* Palo Alto, Calif.: Stanford University Press, 1991.

Gongmin shouce (Citizen's Handbook). Beijing: Huayi Publishing House, 1988.

Goodman, David S. E. *Beijing Street Voices.* Boston: Marian Boyars, 1981.

Goodman, David S. G., ed. *Groups and Politics in the People's Republic of China.* Armonk, N.Y.: M. E. Sharpe, 1984.

Gravereau, Jacques. *La Chine apres l'utopie* (China after Utopia). Paris: Berger-Levrault, 1983.

Guisso, Richard W., and Stanley Johannesen, eds. *Women in China: Current Directions in Historical Scholarship.* Youngstown, Ohio: Philo Press, 1981.

Hinsch, Bret. *Passions of the Cut Sleeve.* Berkeley: University of California Press, 1990.

Hinton, William. *Fanshen.* New York: Vintage, 1966.

————. *Shenfan.* New York: Random House, 1983.

Honig, Emily, and Gail Hershatt. *Personal Voices: Chinese Women in the 1980s.* Palo Alto, Calif.: Stanford University Press, 1988.

Hua Changming. *La Condition feminine et les Communistes Chinoises en action: Yan'an, 1935–46* (The Feminine Condition and the Chinese Communists in Action: Yan'an, 1935–46). Paris: Editions de l'Ecole des Hautes Etudes en Sciences Sociales, 1981.

Jacob, Alain. *Un Balcon à Pekin* (A Balcony in Beijing). Paris: Edition Grasset et Fasquelle, 1982.

Jia Wenqing. *Lao gai chun qiu* (A Spring and Autumn Annals of My Labor Reform). Beijing: Masses Publishing House, 1985.

Johnson, Kay Ann. *Women, the Family and Peasant Revolution in China.* Chicago: University of Chicago Press, 1983.

Kessen, William, ed. *Childhood in China.* New Haven, Conn.: Yale University Press, 1975.

Lao Feng. *Jiating yu shaonian fanzui* (Families and Juvenile Delinquency). Beijing: China People's Security University Press, 1987.

Leary, Marvin, Jr. *The Family Revolution in Modern China.* New York: Octagon Books, 1971.

Leijonhufvud, Goran. *Going against the Tide: On Dissent and Big Character Posters in China.* n.p.: Curson Press, Scandinavian Institute of Asian Studies Monograph Series no. 58, 1990.

Lemieux, Claude. *La Chine: Une histoire de famille* (China: A History of the Family). Montreal: Editions Saint Martins, 1984.

Li Saochen and Jiang Yuanming. *Fuqi zhijian* (Between Husbands and Wives). Jiangsu: Jiangsu People's Publishing House, 1983.

Li Songnong, ed. *Jiating daode jiahua* (Moral Family Life). Beijing: China Gong-guang Press, 1983.

Lianai, hunyin yu jiating (Courtship, Marriage, and Family). Beijing: China Youth Publishing House, "Lessons for Self-Improvement of Youth," 1980.

Lin, Alice Murong P. *Grandmother Had No Name.* San Francisco: China Books and Periodicals, 1988.

Lin Yueh-Hua. *The Golden Wing.* London: Kegan, Paul, Trachy, Trubner and Co., 1947.

Link, Perry, ed. *Mandarin Ducks and Butterflies.* Berkeley: University of California Press, 1981.

———. *Roses and Thorns.* Berkeley: University of California Press, 1984.

Liu, Alan P. L. *Political Culture and Group Conflict in Communist China.* San Francisco: Cho Books, 1971.

Liu Bin-Yan. *A Higher Kind of Loyalty.* New York: Pantheon, 1990.

Liu Hulin. *Hunyin jiating daode* (Morality in Marriage and Family). Beijing: Beijing Press, 1986.

Liu Jia-Lin and Mafeng Huadeng, eds. *Zhongguo laodong zhidu gaige* (Reforms in China's Work System). Jing'an: Economic Press, 1988.

Lun jingji xiaoguo (On Economic Efficiency). Beijing: Chinese Academy of Social Sciences Press, 1981.

Makesi, Engesi, Liening, Sidalin lun aiqing hunyin yu jiating (Marx, Engels, Lenin, and Stalin on Love, Marriage and the Family). Beijing: Red Flag Publishing, 1982.

Maxwell, Neville, and Bruce McFarlane, eds. *China's Changed Road to Development.* New York: Pergamon Press, 1984.

Meyer, Charles. *Histoire de la femme chinoise: 4000 ans de pouvoir* (A History of Chinese Women: 4,000 Years of Power). Paris: Editions Jean-Claude Lattier, 1986.

Michael, Franz. *China and the Crisis of Marxism-Leninism.* Boulder, Colo.: Westview Press, 1990.

Morrison, Charles E., and Robert F. Dernberger, eds. *Asia Pacific Report: Focus—China in the Reform Era.* Honolulu: East-West Center Press, 1989.

Mosher, Steven. *Broken Earth: The Rural Chinese.* New York: Free Press, 1983.

Myrdal, Jan. *Report from a Chinese Village.* New York: Vintage, 1965.

———. *Return to a Chinese Village.* New York: Pantheon, 1984.

Nathan, Andrew J. *Chinese Democracy.* New York: Knopf, 1985.

National Women's Democratic United Front, ed. *Lun Funu Jiefang* (On the Liberation of Women). Beijing: Xinhua Press, 1949.

Pasternak, Burton. *Marriage and Fertility in Tianjin, China: Fifty Years of Transition.* Honolulu: East-West Center Press, Papers of the East-West Population Institute, no. 99, July 1986.

Pruitt, Ida, ed. *A Daughter of Han: The Autobiography of a Chinese Working Woman.* Palo Alto, Calif.: Stanford University Press, 1967.

Pye, Lucian W. *The Dynamic of Factions and Consensus in Chinese Politics.* Project AIR FORCE Report, USAF, July 1980.

————. *The Mandarin and the Cadre: China's Political Cultures.* Ann Arbor: Center for Chinese Studies, University of Michigan, Michigan Monographs in Chinese Studies no. 59, 1988.

Qiu Qianshou, Yang Shubiao, and Wang Tianwen. *Minzhu geming de minzhu yundong* (The Democratic Movement of the Democratic Revolution). Changsha: Hunan People's Publishing House, 1986.

Selden, Mark. *The Yenan Way in Revolutionary China.* Cambridge, Mass.: Harvard University Press, 1971.

Seymour, James D. *The Fifth Modernization: China's Human Rights Movement, 1978–79.* New York: Human Rights Publishing Group, 1980.

Sha Qianli. *Qi ren zhi yu* (The Story of Seven Prisoners). Beijing: San Lian Publishing Company, 1984.

Shanghai Municipal Union, ed. *Banzu gongzuo yibai lie* (100 Ways to Improve Management Organization). Shanghai: Shanghai People's Publishing House, 1983.

Shao Qing-wen. *Pochu jiazu guannian* (Pushing Out the Concepts of Ancestry). Guangzhou: Guangdong People's Publishing House, 1975.

Sheridan, Mary, and Janet W. Salaff, eds. *Lives: Chinese Working Women.* Bloomington: Indiana University Press, 1984.

Shinian dongluan (Ten Years of Chaos). Beijing: Masses Publishing House, 1986.

Shi Tianyang, Ma Suwen, Li Yanshu, and Ying Xianyu. *Xinhun bidu* (Required Reading for Newlyweds). Nanjing: Nanjing People's Publishing House, 1985.

Sidel, Ruth. *Women and Child Care in China.* New York: Hill and Wang, 1972.

Siu, Bobby. *Fifty Years of Struggle: The Development of the Women's Movement in China, 1900–1949.* Hong Kong: Revomen Publications, 1975.

————. *Women of China: Imperialism and Women's Resistance, 1900–1949.* London: Zed Press, 1982.

Spence, Jonathan. *The Death of Woman Wang.* New York: Penguin, 1978.

Stacey, Judith. *Patriarchy and Socialist Revolution in China.* Berkeley: University of California Press, 1983.

Tang Tao. *Hunyin xinlixue* (The Psychology of Marriage). Shanghai: Shanghai People's Publishing House, 1986.

Tang Yuliang. *Zhongguo minzhu shiqi de gongren yundong shilu* (A History of Workers' Movements in the Chinese Democratic Revolutions). Beijing: Worker's Publishing House, 1985.

Thurston, Anne F. *Enemies of the People.* New York: Knopf, 1987.

Townsend, James R. *Political Participation in Communist China.* Berkeley: University of California Press, 1968.

Wagner, Augusta. *Labor Legislation in China.* New York: Garland Publishing, 1980.

Walder, Andrew G. *Communist Neo-Traditionalism: Work and Authority in Chinese Industry.* Berkeley: University of California Press, 1986.

Wang Guichen. *Smashing the Communal Plot: Formulation and Development of the Rural Responsibility System.* Beijing: New World Press, 1985.

Watson, James L. *Emigration and the Chinese Lineage: The Mans in Hong Kong and London.* Berkeley: University of California Press, 1975.

Watson, James L., ed. *Class and Social Stratification in Post-Revolutionary China.* Cambridge, England: Cambridge University Press, 1984.

Weiner, Rebecca, Margaret Murphy, and Albert Li. *Living in China.* San Francisco: China Books and Periodicals, 1991.

Whyte, Martin King. *Urban Life in Contemporary China.* Chicago: University of Chicago Press, 1984.

Widor, Claude, ed. *Documents on the Democratic Movement, 1978–1980.* Paris: Editions de L'Ecole des Hautes Etudes en Sciences Sociales, 1984.

Wolfe, Margery. *The House of Lim.* New York: Meredith Corp., 1960.

Wolfe, Margery, and Roxanne Witke, eds. *Women in Chinese Society.* Palo Alto, Calif.: Stanford University Press, 1975.

"Women of China," ed. *When They Were Young.* Beijing: China Spotlight Series, New World Press, 1983.

Wong, George C., trans. and ed. *Economic Reform in the PRC: In Which China's Economists Make Known What Went Wrong, Why, and What Should Be Done about It.* Boulder, Colo.: Westview Press, 1982.

Wortel, Larry M. *Class in China: Stratification in a Classless Society.* New York: Greenwood Press, 1987.

Xiao Fengxi, ed. *Wo guo ziran ziyuan* (Our Nation's Natural Resources). Baoding: Hebei People's Publishing House, 1957.

Xiao Mingxiong (pen name, Takeshi Koake). *Zhongguo tongxingai shilu* (A History of Homosexuality in China). Hong Kong: Fenhong Sanjian Press, 1984.

Xiu Dingben. *Jiating wenti ershi jiang* (Twenty Answers to Familial Questions). Xi'an: Shaanxi People's Publishing House, 1983.

Xu Jianchuan, Tian Ming, and Yang Hao, eds. *Guoying qiye laodong zhidu gaige dawen* (Answers to Questions on Reform of the State Enterprise Work System). Beijing: Worker's Publishing House, 1986.

Yinchuan Family Planning Committee. *Jiating jihua* (Family Planning). Yinchuan: Ningxia People's Publishing House, 1982.

Yingzi sashuang de Guangxi funu (Heroic and Sacrificial Women of Guangxi Province). Guangxi People's Publishing House, 1975.

Youth Marxist-Leninist Studies Committee. *Lishi shi nulimen chuangzao de* (History Is Written by the Slaves). Shenyang: Liaoning People's Publishing House, 1976.

Zeng Zhi. *Changzheng nu zhanshi* (Women Fighters of the Long March). Beijing: China Women's and Children's Publishing Company, 1987.

Zhang Qingfu and Wang Deyang. *Woguo gongmin jiben quanli he ziren* (Basic Rights and Responsibilities of the Citizens of Our Nation). Beijing: Masses Publishing Company, 1987.

Zhang Xin-xin and Sang Ye. *Chinese Lives.* Translated and edited by W.J.F. Jenner and Delia Davin. New York: Pantheon, 1987.

———. *Chinese Stories.* Beijing: Panda Books, 1989.

Zheng zuo yige guangrongde gongqingtuanyuan (How to Become a Glorious Member of the Communist Youth League). Shanghai: Shanghai Educational Press, 1984.

Zhongguo chengshi jiating (Chinese Urban Families). Jinan: Shandong People's Publishing House, 1985.

Zhongguo funu da fanshen (The Great Transformation of Women in China). Beijing:
    New Democracy Press, 1975.
Zhongguo gongmin xuzhi (What Every Chinese Citizen Needs to Know). Jiangsu: Jiangsu
    People's Publishing House, 1987.
Zhongguo jingji jinzhan (Chinese Economic Growth). Beijing: People's Publishing
    House, 1982.

Journals

Duzhe wenzhai (Reader's Choice). Beijing: Xinhua Press.
Funu (Women). Beijing: Xinhua Press.
Funu zuzhi he yundong (Women's Organizations and Movements). Beijing: Media Ma-
    terials Center, Chinese People's University.
Gaige huhuan (Voice of Reform). Shenyang: Liaoning Ministry of Economics.
Gongren zuzhi yu yundong (Worker's Organizations and Movements). Beijing: Chinese
    People's University Media Materials Center.
Hunyin yu jiating (Marriage and Family). Beijing.
Jiating (The Family). Beijing: Xinhua Press.
Jiating (Family). Guangzhou: Guangzhou People's Publishing House.
Jingji gaige (Economic Reform). Xi'an.
Minzhu yu falu (Democracy and Law). Shanghai.
Renkouxue (Population Studies). Beijing: Chinese People's University Media Materials
    Center.
Sixiang yu zhengzhi gonzuo he yanjiu (Thought, Political Work, and Research Magazine).
    Beijing.
Xiandai jiating (Modern Family). Shanghai: Yiwen Press.
Zhengzhi jiaoyu (Political Education). Beijing: Qinghua University Press.
Zhengzhixue yu falu (Political Science and Law). Shanghai.
Zhongguo gongchandang lishi yanjiu (Researches into the History of the Chinese Com-
    munist Party). Beijing: Qinghua University.

References

Berton, Peter, and Eugene Wu. *Contemporary China: A Research Guide.* Stanford, Calif.:
    Joint Committee on Contemporary China of the American Council of Learned
    Societies and the Social Science Research Council, Hoover Institute on War,
    Revolution, and Peace, 1967.
Chan, Ming K. *Historiography of the Chinese Labor Movement, 1895–1945: A Bibli-
    ography of Chinese Source Materials at the Hoover Institute.* Stanford, Calif.:
    Hoover Institute Press, 1981.
Chang, Lucie, Charlotte Furth, and Hon-Ming Yip, eds. *Women in China: A Bibliography
    of Available English-Language Materials.* Berkeley: University of California, In-
    stitute of East Asian Studies, 1984.
Chinese Academy of Social Sciences. *Zhongguo jingjishi tiyao* (A Bibliography of Chi-
    na's Economic History). Jinan: Social Sciences Press, 1988.
Communist China: A Bibliographic Survey. Washington, D.C.: U.S. Government Printing
    Office, 1971.

Croll, Elisabeth, ed. *The Women's Movement in China: A Selection of Readings, 1949–1973.* London: Anglo-Chinese Educational Institute, Modern China Series no. 6, 1974.

Guisso, Richard W., and Stanley Johannesen, eds. *Women in China: Current Directions in Historical Scholarship.* Youngstown, Ohio: Philo Press, 1981.

Hu Fuming, ed., with James Townsend. *Zhengzhixue cidian* (A Dictionary of Political Science). Hangzhou: Zhejiang Educational Publishing House, 1989.

Hunyin yu jiating cidian (A Dictionary of Marriage and Family). Beijing: International Broadcast Press, 1989.

Joint Congressional Economic Committee. *The Chinese Economy Post-Mao: A Compendium of Papers.* Washington, D.C.: U.S. Government Printing Office, 1978.

Li Fuye and Zhang Guoling. *Laodong gongzi mingci jieshi* (A Directory of Labor and Salary Terms). Nanjing: Nanjing People's Publishing House, 1983.

Wei, Karen T. *Women in China: A Selected and Annotated Bibliography.* Westport, Conn.: Greenwood Press, 1984.

Zhang Nianzou, ed. *Zhengzhi lilun xuexie cidian* (A Student's Dictionary of Political Thought). Beijing: Taijin Industrial Press, 1987.

3

Food

E. N. ANDERSON

"Popular" can have many meanings, and "popular culture" is hard to separate from the rest of culture, perhaps especially in regard to food. To the anthropologist, popular culture usually implies the aspects of culture that are shared widely by different groups within a large society, especially a modern "mass society." By this standard, China has had popular culture for a very long time, and serious study of China's premodern culture is well under way (the classic source is Johnson, Nathan, and Rawski 1985). Popular forms—songs, foods, stories, and the like—are typically created by professional specialists working for a mass audience. The contrast set includes the "elite" forms that are produced, often by skilled professionals, for public consumption by a ruling group and the "folk" forms that are produced, often by nonprofessionals, for local or informal consumption by a small (ideally face-to-face) community. Popular forms are often shunned (in public though often not in private) by the elite and the snobbish and may be out of reach of many of the folk; thus, a distinctive popular culture comes into existence. Naturally, these three categories blend into each other, and humans take a positive delight in mixing them. Thus, a hearty, coarse peasant dish will probably be discovered sooner or later by the elite, who elevate it to cult levels—usually "sophisticating" it in the process, by adding expensive ingredients or the like. This dish in turn is almost certain to propagate, via "status emulation," throughout society—thus becoming popular. It may even complete the cycle by going out of style except in one remote region of the country, thus returning to folk status. On the way, it has, of course, occupied intermediate positions. China has had few if any barriers to this process, especially in regard to food. I have heard a semiliterate folksinger chant a poem by Li Bo, an ancient folk song, and a recent popular song in rapid succession; similarly, a Chinese banquet may contain an ancient court dish, a local folk staple, and a modern Western-influenced creation. Moreover, food is usually prepared at home for the family, and thus is always more folk than popular in the strict sense, though a genuinely popular food culture has long existed in the inns, street stalls, and urban eateries of China. Recently, mass media have deeply influenced foodways, expanding the scope of popular food culture. However, in what follows, little attempt will be made to keep these categories pure. Widespread folk foodways will be discussed along with urban traditions that are popular in the stricter sense. Attempting to separate these would be pedantic, given the realities of Chinese society. This chapter, therefore, considers the ordinary foodways of China, especially urban China, without attempting to distinguish popular from folk in any rigid or narrow way.

This being said, there is still a large body of food that qualifies as focally popular by any definition. The small dumplings known as *jiaozi* are a good example. Few well-populated places in China are out of reach of a stand selling some form of this prototypic comfort food. Rich and poor, rural and urban, Han people and minorities eat crowded closely together in many a *jiaozi* house. At a more general level, the universal division of food into *fan* and *cai*—grain staple and dishes or vegetables to go with it—is a very ancient categorization that is clearly popular, cutting across all social distinctions. Both folk and mass media maintain it. Foods that do not consist of *fan* topped with *cai* may be simple *guo* (fruits and nuts) eaten out of hand, or the special and often complicated snack dishes known as *dianxin* (known in English as "dim sum," from the Cantonese pronunciation *tim sam*).

Chinese food has played a crucial part in popular life and culture since earliest times. Feasts, whether in dining halls, inns, or restaurants, have been the usual venue of important transactions and arrangements. They have also provided opportunities for entertainers, and much of China's popular music and dance developed partly as entertainments for feasts or for restaurant and inn settings. Such eating-place entertainment could range all the way from classical poems (chanted by dignitaries or by paid entertainers) to peasant dances. The lowest socioeconomic strata had access to the classical high culture through the former, and the highest strata kept up with the popular mood through the latter. The extreme eclecticism of restaurant, inn, singing-house, religious fair, and street entertainment guaranteed that all sectors of Chinese society had very wide access to each other's literary, musical, and choreographic productions.

Another food-related channel of communication from elite to popular and folk, and thence back to elite, was provided by the traditional doctors and pharmacists. In particular, the pharmacy—which dispensed tonic foodstuffs as well as drugs—was and is a neighborhood center of cultural activity. Some pharmacies have attached restaurants for serving tonic foods. Pharmacists had to be literate and at least somewhat educated, and often they were the most adept in literary forms of anyone in a small town or poorer urban neighborhood. They became advisers to local peasants and workers, helpers with writing and with complex medical and nutritional matters, and bearers or exemplars of a relatively sophisticated tradition for many a local family. Recent studies have brought out the relatively wide extent of literacy in premodern (as in modern) China (e.g., Rowe 1989, 23) and the great interpenetration of "great" and "little" traditions (see Johnson, Nathan, and Rawski 1985, *passim*). A look at China's popular world of food makes this latter phenomenon seem considerably more prominent than even Johnson, Nathan, and Rawski allow. Inns, markets, and drugstores served as great channels where individuals bearing many traditions could meet and stimulate each other.

HISTORICAL BACKGROUND

The full history of Chinese food culture is immensely complicated. The following is intended simply to convey a sense of this complexity, and especially of the outside influences that have always influenced Chinese food.

China has had a mass society for a very long time. Urbanization was well advanced by 1000 B.C.E., and a truly urban society, with its own distinctive popular cultural traditions, is reflected in the literature of the Warring States period (480–221 B.C.E.). At that time the typical food was boiled grain—most often some type of millet—topped with stew (*geng*). Special and ceremonial occasions required meat prepared in various ways, often elaborate, and large quantities of *jiu*—alcoholic liquor. (Often translated as "wine," *jiu* means any alcoholic liquid, from ale to medicinal tinctures.) The period saw the rise of specialized social categories such as bureaucrats and military leaders who were neither rulers nor peasants. Such new groups must have been part of a developing culture that was neither elite nor folk. The Han Dynasty (206 B.C.E.–220 C.E.) saw the continued rise of urban society, and what H. T. Huang calls "Chinese cuisine *in statu nascendi*" (Huang 1990). By late Han, the capital city may have held a million people and must have had its own mass society. Distilling may have been invented; at least, a primitive but unmistakable still, recently discovered, has been dated to this period on stylistic grounds (Ma 1990). If correctly dated, it is by far the oldest still in the world.

By the sixth century C.E., a full-blown popular food culture was in existence. The sixth century found China split north and south, each with its own empire and capital, until reunification occurred under the Sui Dynasty in 589. The north was a realm of wheat, millet, and sheep, while the south was a land of rice, fish, and paddy-grown vegetables. Central Asian cultures influenced the north, while the south was strongly influenced by Thai, Yao, and other local peoples. Northerners laughed at the southern taste for slimy water creatures, while southerners found the northern taste for yogurt and cheese to be barbaric. In the regional capitals and trading cities of the time, travelers saw merchants, bureaucrats, warriors, scholars, teachers, beggars, porters, monks, innkeepers, singers, and many more—to say nothing of foreign visitors from dozens of countries. The simple division into "great" and "little traditions" is evidently inadequate to deal with such a reality.

Shortly before the unification of the empire, a local official named Jia Sixie compiled an encyclopedia of agricultural and household lore, the *Qimin yaoshu* (Jia 1984; Sabban 1990b; Shih 1974). This was the culmination of a long line of extension manuals and practical handbooks designed to instruct an increasingly literate and book-oriented public on more efficient and sophisticated ways to produce and process food. The food-processing section alone runs to 222 pages in a modern edition (Jia 1984) and covers many forms of *jiu,* sauce, cakes, fish products, and the like, as well as a number of recipes that reflect the book's northern origin. At about the same time, in the southern realm, Tao Hongjing was compiling basic compendia of medicines (*bencao*) that include much food lore. While his books do not reflect a popular tradition in the narrow sense, they were produced by and for members of a wide stratum of society. True cookbooks—specialized compilations of recipes—may well have existed by then, as they certainly did in the Tang Dynasty (618–907). In the Song Dynasty (960–1279), there was something of a cookbook explosion, involving the production of many specialized works reflecting the foodways of many different segments of society. As is true of cookbooks throughout history, Song cookbooks tend to reflect the lifestyles of a comfortable middle class as well as those of the real elite in the imperial household. Production of agricultural books, *bencao,* and cookbooks has continued to the present, each generation adding new lore.

Before the Ming Dynasty (1368–1644), influences on China's popular cuisine came largely from the west, via the Silk Road through Central Asia. Wheat was probably the earliest arrival, long before urban civilization. In the Han Dynasty—the early days of empire—China acquired grape wine, improved flour, and oil milling machinery, and perhaps the wok. By Tang, Persians had introduced their characteristic raised bread covered with sesame seeds, which became an urban street food (Schafer 1963) and eventually evolved into today's *shaobing* (small sesame rolls). Turkic *mantu* became the ancestors—or at least the collateral relatives—of *mantou* (raised buns, originally filled) and *jiaozi.* The recipes in the *Qimin yaoshu* already show Turkic influence; this rose to a climax when the Mongols conquered China and established the Yuan Dynasty (1279–1368; see Sabban 1983b). The Ming Dynasty reacted against this Central Asianization. Moreover, during the Ming, New World food crops came to China (Ho 1955; Simoons 1990), many of them via Chinese merchants in the Philippines, who introduced, for example, the sweet potato and the chile pepper to their south coastal homelands in the seventeenth century. These foods were to have a revolutionary effect. Maize, sweet potatoes, peanuts, and chiles, in particular, removed ecological and nutritional constraints on rural growth and helped to unleash the population growth that continues today. Such minor crops as tomatoes and guavas had no such dramatic effect, but they did influence popular cuisine.

From the mid-nineteenth century until today, China, like the rest of the world, has been subjected to ever-increasing influences by the popular culture of the

West. Beer came with German imperialism, spreading from the German "sphere of influence" in Qingdao. In the twentieth century, perhaps the most widespread introductions have been carbonated soft drinks and monosodium glutamate. The latter was isolated from seaweed in Japan at the beginning of this century and popularized by the Aji-no-moto Company. It was virtually unknown and unused in China until some fifty years ago. Today it is universal, to the immense disgust of an older generation of Chinese epicures. Recent decades have seen the inevitable forward march of the Golden Arches and other franchise chains. In Hong Kong and Taipei one can obtain almost any type of food, Asian and Western; nor are Beijing and Shanghai far behind. Chinese food, however, holds its own, and it has spread throughout the world in its own right, profoundly influencing popular food culture in the United States, England, Germany, and elsewhere.

POPULAR FOODS

China's regional differences create problems for a definition of Chinese food. The Westerner automatically thinks of rice, but a third of China's people—living in the north and west—rarely saw rice until recent years and still depend largely on wheat, maize, and various millet species. Fortunately, local folk traditions are outside the scope of this chapter, and we can focus on the foods that define urban and mass traditions throughout the Chinese world.

Within the realm of *fan* and *cai*, the basic opposition of grain products and topping now usually takes the form of a milled grain product, boiled, topped with stir-fried or steamed vegetables with a bit of meat or fish added, and accompanied by thin soup. The grain is now usually rice, but wheat dumplings, maize cakes, buckwheat cakes, and boiled millet and sorghum are still locally abundant. Aware of the dangers of unboiled water, the Chinese consume most liquid in this latter form. Tea has only recently become part of truly popular culture; it was too expensive for anyone but the elite through most of its history in China. Produced primarily in the southeast and southwest, it is now widely available.

Next after ordinary boiled rice or its equivalent come the various flour foods, mostly made of wheat flour. Historically found primarily in the north and central parts of China, they have spread slowly and steadily southward, and recently they have become especially common as China moves to diversify supplies by bringing rice north and wheat south. A major use of wheat is in *mantou* (large breadlike loaves, usually steamed) and *bao* or *baozi* (smaller loaves or buns, filled with various stuffings). Still smaller relatives of these foods are the various dumplings, collectively *jiaozi*; these consist of thin sheets of dough wrapped around various stuffings. These are usually boiled in soup (such as the famous *hundun* or "wonton"; see Zee 1990). They are also fried or steamed. For instance, they may be fried without stirring, so that they stick to the pan, becoming "pot stickers" (*guotie*). Another wheat-flour food is the *youtiao* ("fried strip" of dough), a strip of leavened dough that is deep fried. It is equivalent to the crullers and *churros* of the Western world, but it is usually unsweetened.

Noodles occupy a special place in popular food culture. Very possibly invented in China (Sabban 1990a; cf. Ishige 1990) with uncertain degrees of Western influence (Anderson 1988), noodles of many kinds are important everywhere and the dominant staple in many areas. They provide half as many calories as rice in such nominally rice-dependent areas as the south central coast. Typically served as snacks, often in humble street stalls or informal cafes and inns, they are prototypic popular foods. The commonest noodles are *mian,* made of wheat, but rice and mung-bean-starch noodles are common, and noodles are even made of such things as maize, buckwheat, and sweet potatoes, in spite of the difficulty of getting such noodles to hold together in cooking. Durum wheat, used in the Western world for pasta, is virtually unknown; *mian* foods are made of ordinary wheat.

The soybean practically defines Chinese popular cuisine. Soy sauce and soybean pastes are the universal flavoring. Soybean curd (*doufu*) is the universal "poor man's meat," the cheap protein source of the ordinary people. Many types exist—soft or hard, flavored or natural, fermented or unfermented. (Recent increases in affluence, which have made meat more available, have led to a decline in bean curd use.) Soybean milk, *doufujiang,* has long been used as milk is used in other cultures. Even the skin (*doufupi,* "bean curd skin") that forms on boiling soybean milk is saved and used in many ways. Boiled or roasted soybeans make cheap snacks. Fermented bean pastes and bean curd products take the place of cheese, yogurt, and other fermented dairy products common in other cultures. A wealth of more specialized soy preparations has been developed, often for religiously motivated vegetarians. The latter, usually Buddhists, have developed a complex cuisine in which protein is derived from soybeans and wheat gluten. In parts of montane west China, broad beans and lima beans grow better than soybeans and partially replace them; broad bean curd and fermented pastes are important in Sichuan.

Elisabeth Rozin (1983:3–4) has defined Chinese food by its flavoring structure: soy sauce, rice wine, ginger (fresh root, slivered), garlic, and—locally— chile peppers and various fermented bean pastes. The popular tradition tends to dispense with the expensive alcoholic brews and to use more garlic and onions, often condemned by elites as too rank and offensive to use in large quantities. The characteristic flavors of unrefined sesame, maize, and peanut oils, heated to a very high temperature, also contribute to the unmistakable taste of Chinese popular cuisine. (As opposed to popular—urban or mass—traditions, home or folk traditions tend to use less strong flavorings and much less oil.)

Among ingredients of *cai,* the most widespread and truly popular are the Chinese cabbages (*Brassica* spp.; the taxonomy is confused). Other green vegetables are also exceedingly common, as are—in recent years—tomatoes and white potatoes. The popular taste is for vegetables, and such special products as young pea shoots and rare mushrooms traditionally command a much higher price than meat in the street markets. Among meats, the pig is the overwhelming favorite; the vast majority of the world's pigs are in China, and virtually every part of every pig is destined for human consumption. Chickens are popular but more expensive. Beef is traditionally avoided because cattle work so hard for humanity (there is an influence from India at work here), though this view is fading, especially where hamburgers have come. Fish and shellfish are exceedingly popular wherever found, and good, fresh seafood of the preferred species almost always commands the highest price of any food except for specialized medical products. Dairy foods are sedulously avoided—all the more surprising given the great popularity of these foods in medieval China (Sabban 1986; Simoons 1990,454–63). Today, milk and yogurt are available, but milk is in short supply and normally kept for children. This may be contrasted with the American popular preference for sugar, beef, dairy foods, and white flour products over fish and vegetables.

Fruits are enormously popular; among the most common are watermelon, citrus, peaches, Chinese pears, and apples. All are normally eaten plain, rarely candied—elaborate desserts are rare outside of elite cuisine. Nuts and seeds can be bought on almost any busy street corner, especially in winter, with melon seeds, peanuts, and roasted soybeans leading the lists. The popular enthusiasm for these has long been noted. Many nibble melon seeds to keep their mouths busy, as people in other cultures use chewing gum. Traditionally, sweets were far less common and popular than fruits and nuts, but today local stores offer a wide selection of candies and cookies, and these have transformed the eating habits of the young. This has led to a sharp rise in tooth decay. Popular food culture is moving rapidly in the direction of the rest of the world—toward fast-food items and factory-made sweets. Except in the most Westernized sectors of Hong Kong and Taiwan, however, traditional patterns still prevail.

Chinese food has always been a cooking of scarcity. The foods are those that yield the most nutrients per acre of land. Agriculture is "sustainable" and ecologically fine-tuned to a degree almost beyond belief (Anderson 1988; Bray 1984; Chao 1986; Ruddle and Zhong 1988). The cooking methods use the least fuel to produce the most effect, and they conserve nutrients effectively; for example, steaming vegetables or boiling them in soup, as opposed to boiling them and throwing away the water. Meat—expensive and hard to obtain—is chopped into small pieces and used with large quantities of vegetables. This is partly sheer economizing, but also the result of bitter lessons learned through thousands of years of famines (see the classic work of Mallory 1926, and the important review in Li 1982). With 25 percent of the world's population on 7 percent of the farmland, China must wring every possible nutrient from an oft-grudging environment. Nowhere does popular cuisine differ more from elite than in this regard; the elite kitchen uses wine and meat lavishly (as poets have complained for millennia), to say nothing of oil, expensive seafoods, and the like. Oil is perhaps the most revealing ingredient; elite dishes can be very rich, while folk dishes are usually oilless and almost never greasy. Popular cuisine falls between these extremes.

Popular evaluation of food is dominated by a deep concern for freshness and

for preserving the "pure" and "original/natural" flavor of the main ingredi-
ent(s). Spices are used to bring out this flavor, rather than to mask it or give a
wholly new taste. Steaming and stir-frying are considered especially appropriate
for this. The most favored texture is *cui*—crisp yet succulent, the texture of
fresh young vegetables very slightly cooked. The contrasting elite evaluative
universe, at least in so far as it can be seen in the records of court food and the
present practice of splendid restaurants, runs far more to complexity and to the
use of expensive ingredients for their own sake; it thus seems less concerned
with freshness and pure tastes. Traditional elite gourmets argued, however, for
the latter, and they denounced complex and expensive dishes as vulgar (see, for
example, the classic statements of the eighteenth-century gourmet Yuan Mei,
available in the excellent translation of Waley 1957).

China is divided into many regions, each with its special cuisine. The wheat-
eating north is fairly homogeneous, but often its south-central or southeastern
portion is separated off under some such name as "Shandong" cookery. The
rice region falls naturally into three divisions: east (the lower Yangtze Valley
and neighboring areas, characterized by much use of sugar, vinegar, oil, and
noodles); west (Hunan, Sichuan, and neighboring areas, characterized by heavy
use of chile peppers, brown pepper, and mountain products); and south (Guangdong and area, with heavy use of fermented soybeans, fresh seafood, lightly
cooked vegetables, and tropical fruits). Within these divisions, every province
and many particular parts of provinces have their own variants. Local pride is
marked, and most people will maintain that the food of their particular homeland
is the best. Minority ethnic and religious groups also have their own foodways,
which are only beginning to be well studied (Anderson 1988). Chinese Muslims,
of whom there are several million, must cope with the Islamic taboo on pork—
the most popular meat in China. The difficulty of doing this, and the social
tensions caused by it, are analyzed in great detail by Dru Gladney (1991, esp.
pp. 183–92) as part of a wider study of Chinese Muslims that gives details on
several regional food traditions. Tibet possesses a particularly distinctive tradition, autonomous and much influenced by India; it is the only minority area for
which a substantial food ethnography exists in English (Dorje 1985). As elsewhere in the world, food is routinely used as a self-conscious marker of ethnic
or religious identity. For example, members of Hong Kong's large Chaozhou
minority, however acculturated they may be to Cantonese ways, maintain large
restaurants where they gather to eat their traditional food in a quite explicit
reaffirmation of ethnicity. Urban Muslim life often centers around the restaurants
where "clean and pure" (*ching zhen*, i.e., *halal*) food is served (Gladney 1991).
Conversely, Han Chinese in Inner Mongolia maintain Han-style restaurants and
avoid Mongol foodways (W. Jankowiak, personal communication; see Jankowiak, *Sex, Death and Hierarchy in a Chinese City*).

Last, Chinese popular foodways are not unaffected by the worldwide spread
of familiar American items. Most widespread are beer and sodas, especially the
ever-present orange soda and cola drinks. Candy and small cookie or cracker

snacks are not far behind. Traditionally, fruit and local specialty products were obligatory gifts at formal house visits and minor ceremonial occasions. Today, large boxes of Western-style candy, crackers, and cookies are more popular. Sometimes, particularly beautiful boxes will be recycled—given to someone else—and thus a box of cookies may go through a succession of gift transactions until it is too stale to eat. This has enormously facilitated the spread of these food products in China. It is significant that during the anti-Western campaigns of the Gang of Four period, such large boxes of candies and cookies were among the few Western-style products that China continued to produce in large quantities.

Other Western products have lagged behind. Milk and milk products, promoted for many decades as health giving, are now universally available for children (though sometimes locally rationed), but the Chinese resistance to dairy products continues. Hamburgers have been even slower to win acceptance. There was effectively no consumption of such foods until the spread of MacDonald's in the last fifteen years. Today, most of the major fast-food franchise chains have branches in Hong Kong and Taiwan, and the mainland is following.

SETTINGS

In China, even more than in much of the rest of the world, most cooking and eating is done at home. Home cooking is somewhat outside the scope of this chapter, being more folk than popular, but some knowledge of Chinese home foodways is basic to further understanding. Chinese homes always have a kitchen area. Since it is typically small, cooks have learned to do a great deal in a limited space.

A typical day begins with breakfast, often boiled grain. In the south this will usually be rice congee with pickles or other flavorings added. Steamed rolls or noodles are common, especially in the north. *Youtiao* with hot soybean milk is another standard. The main meal of the day is often eaten around noon or early afternoon, though in today's work world it is often put off till evening. In the south it invariably consists of boiled rice with side dishes—typically including a stir-fried dish, a steamed dish, and a thin soup. In the north, noodles, thick pancakes, or steamed buns are the traditional starch staples. In the urban work world, lunch is rice with a topping or a large bowl of noodles with various meats and vegetables added. Supper is usually a light meal, often just the leftovers from lunch. Almost everyone who can do so will find an excuse to eat snacks between meals; thus, meals are often quite light. Any formal occasion is celebrated with a banquet that may start any time after noon—most often in early evening, today—and last for hours. Large quantities of rich meat dishes and rare, exotic ingredients are featured. Grain staples are not served or are kept to a minimum. The more important the occasion, the more valuable the food. A small family celebration involves a chicken; then progress is upward through other poultry and through increasingly large and rich cuts of pork. On especially important occasions, such as weddings and New Year feasts, rarities like sea cucumbers, birds' nests, and specially prepared meats occur.

The landscape of a Chinese city, town, or village is densely marked with eating places. They bulk even larger in the psychological landscape, the mental maps carried by the citizenry. In a Chinese town, any true citizen has views on where to get the best noodles, the best *jiaozi,* the best melons, and so on. No other culture, not even the French, is so focused on food. A conversation in China often turns quickly to themes of food, especially to the ever-burning question of which are the best restaurants, cafes, or street stalls for particular dishes. This goes beyond simple interest in food; like sports in some Western contexts, food provides the channel for any and all socializing, the topic that everyone shares and can intelligently discuss.

Food is produced by peasants and marketed through an elaborate network of markets. The classic description of the marketing network, by G. William Skinner (1964–65), has spawned a large literature of its own. Markets are arranged in a hierarchy, from the little roadside get-togethers where peasants meet to exchange fresh produce to the vast market areas of the great regional cities. At every level, markets not only sell raw materials and ingredients, but also provide some sort of cooked food. The green produce markets have their roving noodle sellers; the great regional cities have their streets lined with enormous and elaborate restaurants where wholesalers and retailers close million-dollar deals.

A hierarchy of settings dominates Chinese popular food culture. Lowest in prestige—but not necessarily lowest in quality—are the wandering vendors, who often carry or push small stoves and sell noodles, hot cakes, or other snacks. Above these are the street stalls—wooden stands, sometimes movable, that offer shelter and permit cooking of a small selection of dishes. These have an undeserved reputation for being unsanitary and inferior. They grade up into small sheds or cafes; many a cafe began as a street stall and gradually added more area of roof until chairs and tables could be accommodated. Larger cafes, often specializing in a particular type of dish, such as boiled noodles or rice with simple vegetable toppings, are perhaps the most important of all. They exist everywhere that people come together, and they can usually accommodate a large number of eaters (through a degree of crowding that visitors may find incredible). They are the quick lunch venue for the ordinary people of China. Specialized subvariants are the tea shops and teahouses. These are often open only for breakfast or breakfast and lunch. In south China and above all in Hong Kong, these have evolved into specialized tea shops that serve extremely elaborate arrays of snacks (*dianxin*). In these, "drinking tea" has evolved into a ritual that involves the consumption of large quantities of *dianxin* over an extended period of time. Many individuals spend the entire morning drinking tea. Community leaders and other locally important figures hold informal office hours at their habitual teahouses. Business ranging from simple deals to marriage arrangements is transacted. Poems and stories show this to be a very ancient pattern, going back at least as far as the literature does. Before tea became common, a glass of *jiu* was the equivalent social lubricant, as it still is in restaurant settings. This custom has spread to the West, where it has been enthusiastically adopted by many non-Chinese, who know *dianxin* as "dim sum," a corruption of *tim sam,* the Cantonese pronunciation of the word.

Cafes grade upward into restaurants—places that serve major meals, normally lunch and dinner, and have a wide selection of dishes. A typical restaurant has anywhere from one hundred to several hundred dishes on the menu and will make still others on special order. Often, in fact, the best dishes are not on the menu, thus being reserved for the cognoscenti. Restaurants range from simple neighborhood "mom and pop" operations to the huge, elaborate "wine palaces" (*jiu guan*) where patrons think nothing of spending thousands of dollars on a banquet. Governments have often attempted to eliminate such lavish displays, holding them wasteful, but in few places has this been successful. Banquets are too vital a part of social life, as they have been since the beginning of the historic record. Weddings, major business deals, alliances, personal triumphs, birthdays of senior members of one's family, and other such events must be socially validated with a banquet whose size and scope are determined by the importance of the event and the position of the host. Use of food to mark life-cycle events has been one of the most robust cultural survivals among emigrant Chinese (Newman, Ludman, and Lynn 1988). Such banquets must be held at restaurants; the Chinese home and its kitchen are not normally large enough. Naturally, this influences everyday life; ordinary entertaining and socializing tend to occur in restaurants rather than in homes. The necessity of closing deals over shared food (and alcohol) creates the aforementioned association of market zones and restaurants. Because of this, Chinese society is restaurant oriented to a unique degree. In Hong Kong and apparently some other places, well-to-do people spend a higher percentage of their income on food than do the lower socioeconomic levels—a reverse of the situation almost everywhere else in the world.

Among common types of specialty restaurants, perhaps the most popular are the seafood houses. Other common specialties include Mongolian barbecue and its relatives; vegetarian restaurants, and their ancestors the Buddhist monastery cafeterias; restaurants serving medicinal food; and restaurants specializing in one type of food, often also medicinal, such as mushrooms or snakes. All the major regions and minority groups of China have their special cuisines, with restaurants to cater to them. Since at least the fifth century C.E., such places have existed to serve the wants of travelers far from home. By Tang Dynasty times, we read of Persian restaurants—to say nothing of south Chinese restaurants and the like—in the imperial capital (see Schafer 1963, 1967). Today the larger cities have restaurants serving many regional cuisines, most frequently to travelers from the respective regions, but also to other visitors and to the curious and experiment-minded in general.

Finally, food and medicine are so entwined in China that traditional pharmacies sell many food products and sometimes have attached restaurants of the
medicinal variety.

HEALTH

Nutrition is outside the scope of this chapter, but it should be noted that
popular foodways have become fine-tuned through generations of famine, such
that a vast population can exist on a slender resource base. The diet of grain,
eked out with vegetables and small amounts of protein, is potentially deficient
in vitamins (especially A and C) and minerals (especially iron). The Chinese
have learned, through centuries of empirical observation and medical practice,
to make the best use of what they have, for example, by processing soybeans
to remove chemicals that inhibit nutrient uptake and by consuming such nutrient-
rich plants as Chinese wolfthorn when they are ill or physically stressed (Anderson 1990; Simoons 1990,470–515). No amount of care could prevent
environmental degradation and recurrent famine (Li 1982), but as early as 1406
a manual of famine foods was published under the patronage of Zhu Xiao of
the Ming royal family (Read 1946).

Popular Chinese culture makes no separation between foods and drugs. These
grade into each other. Many foods are eaten only for their medicinal value.
Others are tasty in themselves but owe their importance and high price to alleged
health benefits. Snakes, for instance, are eaten for warmth and vigor during
winter. Birds' nests—edible nests of swiftlets of the genus *Collocalia*—are believed to be easily digestible and have a tonic effect. Chrysanthemum tea is
drunk because of its cooling effect; it appears to reduce body temperature in
cases of fever, and certainly it makes summer sun seem more bearable. Literally
thousands of such medical foods are known (*Zhongyao da zidian* 1979; for brief
English language introductions, see Flaws and Wolfe 1983; Lu 1986).

The most important basic principle in much—but not all—of China is the
belief that the human body must maintain a balance of hot, cold, wet, and dry
qi (*ch'i*). Foods that seem hot or heating in some way (such as ginger, peppers,
and high-calorie foods) or that have been subjected to high heat (such as baked
foods) add heat and may overload the body. Foods that seem cooling (low-
calorie, watery/diuretic, or acidulous) may overload the cool side. Wet and dry
are much less salient but similarly must be kept in balance. For fever, gently
cooling foods are recommended. For chill and for such cold-seeming diseases
as anemia, gently heating foods are recommended. This parallels Western nutritional science in such things as using vegetables (cooling) recommended for
scurvy (a hot condition), or iron-rich meats (gently warming) for anemia. This
is only one of a large number of ways in which Chinese popular nutrition
paralleled or anticipated that of Western science.

Even more important to many people is the concept of *bu,* ''strengthening''
or ''supplementing.'' *Bu* foods supplement one's *qi* or the *qi* of some particular

physiological system. *Bu* foods are often recognized by their strange, striking, anomalous, or uncanny aspect, which shows unique *qi,* and this explains most of the Chinese foodways that seem strange to foreigners. Even the Chinese say that the Cantonese of the far south eat "anything with legs except the table and anything with wings except an airplane"; most of this wideflung consumption is due to the strength of the hot/cold and *bu* theories in the deep south. Warming and *bu* foods are an integral part of "doing the month," the period that a new mother spends recuperating from childbirth (Pillsbury 1978). Soups of chicken with ginger, wolfthorn berries, *jiu,* and vinegar, or of pork liver or pigs' feet, restore protein and minerals in women whose harsh lives have often left them sadly lacking in those nutrients.

Other foods may be *du,* which can mean either "poisonous" or "prone to potentiate poisons or pathologies in the body." *Du* foods of the latter type are held to make cancer worse, for example. More or less in contrast are foods that are *qing* ("pure") or that are believed to have a cleansing effect (see Gould-Martin 1978).

In modern China, there is a great range of belief in these traditional systems. Many dismiss them as sheer superstition, while others follow the systems with great care. The systems have spread into Japan and, recently, the Western world.

The effectiveness of Chinese dietary therapy is still under study, but already many valuable conclusions have emerged, and many vitamin-rich foods have been found. For example, the *guoji* plant (Chinese wolfthorn, *Lycium chinense*) has been used as a *bu* and tonic for centuries; we now know that it is one of the richest sources of vitamins and minerals in the plant world, and since it grows easily in many climatic settings it is a major resource for improving nutrition worldwide. Much more, no doubt, remains to be found.

However, a major problem has emerged: Many medicinal foods are derived from rare animals. Rhinoceri, bears, and pangolins have been locally exterminated and endangered worldwide because of their medicinal parts. Even once-abundant fauna such as edible-nest swiftlets, raccoon-dogs (*Nyctereutes procyonoides,* a *bu* food), and Chinese deer species have been reduced to dangerously low population levels. Farming or local management of wild stocks has been successful when tried, but in spite of this the problem is increasingly serious.

RITUALS

Chinese ceremonial practice has always been centered on rites in which foods and other consumption goods are offered to the entities to whom respect is being paid. These entities can be living humans (such as the emperor), gods, ghosts, or other supernaturals. The ceremonies are, of course, different for these different cases.

Secular rituals of eating, when they go beyond arbitrary (but elaborate) politeness codes, are designed to show respect to guests and to elders. An honored guest is seated by the host, and the host personally plies the guest with drinks and delicacies. Since speech tends to be formal to the point of emptiness on such occasions, these gestures often take the whole burden of expressing the real political and social dynamics of the situation. They are thus attended to with the utmost care. Honored elders are treated similarly, with even more respect, by their juniors. On the other hand, community and a kind of equality are maintained by eating from common dishes, the food being picked out with spoons or chopsticks. Usually, tables are round, and seating fairly open except for the most honored. There is often some degree of ordering of tables, according to nearness to the center of activities—where, of course, the most honored personages sit. The overriding principle is status inequality. Any sort of seniority in age or position is decisive, with men ranking above women within a seniority set. Whenever status can be downplayed, however, the emphasis is all on expressing the closest, most convivial sociability. Also, many if not most of the banquet and special-occasion foods are warming, strengthening, or nourishing, and are thus served as a mark of care and concern. Banquets are appropriate occasions for serving such *yang* foods, for reasons of health and of cosmological appropriateness. Warmth, strength, and energy are stressed at both microcosmic and macrocosmic levels: individual, social scene, and cosmos. (One could describe the social scene as a "mesocosm.")

In discussing rites for the supernaturals, we can speak (in English) of "sacrifice" and "religion." The typical minimal offering, such as a routine daily rite for a minor guardian spirit, involves incense and tea or wine. A slightly larger offering involves the addition of buns or cakes. Still larger offerings involve grain and vegetable foods and a chicken—the latter a vital part of most important sacred and secular rituals over thousands of years. The spirits eat the essence of these dishes; the humans usually consume the mere material substance, after the conclusion of the rite. Further increases in scale add, successively, more poultry, pork, and finally one or more whole pigs. (Muslim groups use sheep or dispense with the whole rite.) The exact foods used and the exact preparations (raw, boiled, roasted) differ with the ritual setting and the beings invoked. They also differ from place to place; adjoining villages may have very different rules for exactly how the ritual pig is prepared for the New Year. Some very local and distinctive usages have been described in detail; for three good and easily available recent case studies, see Emily Ahern (1973), Stuart Thompson (1988), and James L. Watson (1987). The government of the People's Republic formerly attacked all such ceremonies and celebrations as *mixin* ("superstition") and drove them underground to some extent, but they continue to flourish. In Taiwan, in spite of some similar problems, folk religion and its food offerings have grown and flourished over the years. There are several reasons for this, among which local and ethnic loyalty are prominent. The Durkheimian thesis that religion is the collective representation of the community (Durkheim 1961) is explicit in Chinese popular culture. Religious rituals are quite deliberately evoked to create and maintain social solidarity; the cited studies show how food is crucial in this.

Several religious minorities have their own foodways. In addition to the afore-mentioned Muslims, there are vegetarian Buddhist communities, who have per-fected imitation meats based on soy products and wheat gluten. Some small sects have their own food rules (see, for example, Jordan and Overmyer 1986,213–46).

The commonalities between secular and sacred rituals outweigh the differ-ences. Both involve status concession, offering of food as a sign of respect, and manipulation of food as the key communication channel for carrying social and political meanings. Etiquette can be manipulated in the service of requests, al-liance building, marking status changes, and any other important social expres-sion. However, the differences between humans and supernaturals force totally different structures on secular and religious events, and likewise the ghosts, gods, and other beings of the other world require different treatments. Some regional differences trace back to matters such as the elevation of a demon to a deity; one community may retain some demon-offering features which another, more respectful, has eliminated.

The centrality of food in rituals (sacred and secular) is an important part of the reason why China has never had a significant "puritan" reaction against the attention that popular culture lavishes on food quality. Critics have not been lacking, from the Taoists and Mohists of ancient times to many social reformers of today. However, the ideology of respect and sociability, concretely demon-strated through service of the best available foods, has prevailed.

Thus social norms, in the end, are a key shaping factor in Chinese popular food culture. Ecology can explain such things as the regional importance of rice or wheat; nutrition accounts for the importance of cabbages and Chinese wolf-thorn; health beliefs may be responsible for the use of chicken soup with ginger. China's long history of urban and mercantile culture guarantees a substantial set of foodways that are genuinely popular, as opposed to elite or folk. These fac-tors, however, are inadequate to explain the extreme importance of food in Chinese culture and the variety and richness of popular foodways. Such phe-nomena require an explanation rooted in social practice—especially the contin-ual pressure to express respect, care, and sociability through the material channels of highly valued foods. There is thus a continual pressure to serve dishes that are valued for their rarity, cost, local importance, or healthiness and medical value. Such dishes may take on secondary values by becoming canon-ical foods for royalty, or for the supernaturals, or for people of a given ethnic or regional background. As such matters are continually negotiated in everyday practice, Chinese popular foodways change. However, the paradigm of quality and variety, within a structure of grain staples garnished with meat and vegetable dishes, continues with no sign of pattern exhaustion.

REFERENCE WORKS

Literature on Chinese food is almost inconceivably vast. A bibliography of English language cookbooks alone runs to 724 items (Newman 1987), and the

Chinese language literature is comparable. There are also cookbooks in Japanese, Korean, and most European languages. Several Chinese language magazines are devoted to food. Also, the Chinese quickly seized on the concept of the "TV chef," and many cooking programs have flourished, especially in Taiwan. For convenience and brevity, only English language sources will be considered here, except for a few absolutely indispensable works. The Western literature is fairly comprehensively covered in *The Food of China* by E. N. Anderson (1988) and *Food in China* by Frederick Simoons (1990); the East Asian literature is surveyed in the Shinoda festschrift edited by Ishige Naomichi (1985; Osamu Shinoda and Ishige have been the leading Japanese historians of Chinese food).

If one looks solely at the scholarly literature, the picture is far narrower. Until very recently, little serious attention was paid to this critically important aspect of Chinese life. This was especially true in the Western world, where food traditionally has not been a serious topic of study. This has changed, thanks partly to the *Annales* school of historians and partly to the large number of scholars from East Asia who now work in the West.

Food in Chinese Culture (1977), edited by Kwang-chih Chang, was the first comprehensive historical work in English, and it is still standard. Its historical chapters, written by authorities on the periods in question, remain unexcelled. E. N. Anderson's *The Food of China* (1988) deals with the development of the food production system and with the correct scientific identification of ingredients. Frederick Simoons' recent book *Food in China* (1990) gives a geographer's comprehensive account of the foodstuffs of China and their geographic and agricultural history. It also reviews nutrition—an important question otherwise outside the scope of this chapter. Francesca Bray's "Agriculture" volume in the Needham *Science and Civilisation in China* series is absolutely indispensable for the student of food (Bray 1984). For contemporary China, Sylvan Wittwer, Yu Youtai, Sun Han, and Wang Lianzheng provide an important overview of production in *Feeding a Billion* (1987). Elisabeth Croll, in *The Family Rice Bowl* (1983), and Gong Dan, in *Food and Drink in China* (1986), do the same for consumption. A. Zee's *Swallowing Clouds* (1990) is a delightful introduction to foodways and food words, spiced with many folktales about the origins of the Chinese characters for various food terms. Thomas Gwinner, in *Essen und Trinken: Die klassische Kochbuchliteratur Chinas* (1988), provides an introduction to Chinese classical culinary literature, with translations (into German) of many of the cookbooks. The important collection of papers on famine edited by Lillian M. Li (1982) has been noted. Serious students of food will need to read widely in the literature on China's agriculture and agrarian economy, which is so vast as to be beyond hope of review here (see bibliographies in Anderson 1988; Bray 1984; Simoons 1990).

Particularly valuable sources in English on the technology used to make common foods include *China at Work,* by Rudolph Hommel (1937), *The Chinese,* by Cornelius Osgood (1975), and *T'ien-kung K'ai-wu,* by Sung Ying-hsing (1966).

Françoise Sabban has carved out a niche as the leading Western-world historian of Chinese food (Sabban 1983a, 1983b, 1986, 1988, 1990a, 1990b; Sabban-Serventi 1989). She provides extremely careful, thorough introductions to particular culinary works and to particular products and foodstuffs, based on comprehensive reading in the original languages. Donald Harper and a number of other younger scholars are carrying out research in this tradition.

In addition to the abovementioned works on food and medicine, attention should be called to Paul Unschuld's work on Chinese medicine, specifically his history of pharmaceutics (Unschuld 1986). This provides a basic reference on the classical Chinese medical works, which are usually also the major sources on the foods of their eras.

Turning to the Chinese language literature, there are several recent books on food history; a comprehensive one is *History of Chinese Food Culture and Food Industries* by Billy Wen-Chi Yang (1984). The really exciting development, though, has been the republication of the great classics of food and cooking, particularly the series *Zhongguo pengren guji cungkan* (Historic Records of Chinese Cooking), issued by the Chinese government over the last decade. These are annotated and often include a translation from classical to modern Chinese. They make infinitely easier the job of studying Chinese food history.

BIBLIOGRAPHY

Ahern, Emily. *The Cult of the Dead in a Chinese Village.* Stanford, Calif.: Stanford University Press, 1973.

Anderson, E. N. *The Food of China.* New Haven, Conn.: Yale University Press, 1988.

————. "Up against Famine: Chinese Diet in the Early Twentieth Century." *Crossroads* 1 (1990): 11–24.

Bray, Francesca. *Science and Civilisation in China.* Vol. 6, Part 2, *Agriculture.* Cambridge, England: Cambridge University Press, 1984.

Chang Kwang-chih, ed. *Food in Chinese Culture.* New Haven, Conn.: Yale University Press, 1977.

Chao, Kang. *Man and Land in Chinese History.* Stanford, Calif.: Stanford University Press, 1986.

Croll, Elisabeth. *The Family Rice Bowl.* London: United Nations Research Institute for Social Development and Zed Press, 1983.

Dorje, Rinching. *Food in Tibetan Life.* London: Prospect Books, 1985.

Durkheim, Emile. *The Elementary Forms of the Religious Life.* New York: Collier, 1961.

Flaws, Bob, and Honora Wolfe. *Prince Wen Hui's Cook: Chinese Dietary Therapy.* Brookline, Mass.: Paradigm Publications, 1983.

Gladney, Dru. *Chinese Muslims.* Cambridge, Mass.: Harvard University Press, 1991.

Gong Dan. *Food and Drink in China.* Beijing: New World Press, 1986.

Gould-Martin, Katherine. "Hot Cold Clean Poison Dirt: Chinese Folk Medical Categories." *Social Science and Medicine* 12 (1978): 39–46.

Gwinner, Thomas. *Essen und Trinken: Die klassische Kochbuchliteratur Chinas.* Heidelberger Schriften zur Ostasienkunde, Band 11. Heidelberg: Haag & Herchen, 1988.

Ho Ping-Ti. "The Introduction of American Food Plants into China." *American Anthropologist* 57 (1955): 191–201.

Hommel, Rudolph. *China at Work.* Cambridge, Mass.: Massachusetts Institute of Technology, 1937.

Huang, H. T. "Han Gastronomy—Chinese Cuisine *in statu nascendi.*" *Interdisciplinary Science Reviews* 15 (1990): 139–152.

Ishige, Naomichi. "Filamentous Noodles, *Miantiao:* Their Origin and Distribution." Paper presented at the Sixth International Congress on the History of Science in China, Session on the History of Food Science and Nutrition, Cambridge, England, 1990.

Ishige, Naomichi, ed. *Ronshu: Higashi ajia no shokuji bunka* (Collected Essays on East Asian Food Culture). Tokyo: Heibonsha, 1985.

Jankowiak, W. *Sex, Death and Hierarchy in a Chinese City.* New York: Columbia University Press, 1993.

Jia Sixie. *Qimin yaoshu (heshi bufen)* (Necessary Knowledge for the Ordinary People: Drinking and Eating Section). Beijing: Commercial Press, 1984.

Johnson, David, Andrew J. Nathan, and Evelyn S. Rawski. *Popular Culture in Late Imperial China.* Berkeley: University of California Press, 1985.

Jordan, David, and Daniel Overmyer. *The Flying Phoenix.* Princeton, N.J.: Princeton University Press, 1986.

Li, Lillian M. "Introduction: Food, Famine and the Chinese State." *Journal of Asian Studies* 41 (1982): 687–707.

Lu, Henry C. *Chinese System of Food Cures.* New York: Sterling, 1986.

Ma Chengyuan. "Archaeological and Experimental Investigations on a Han Bronze Still." Paper presented at the Sixth International Conference on the History of Science in China, Session on the History of Food Science and Nutrition, 1990.

Mallory, Walter. *China, Land of Famine.* New York: American Geographic Society, 1926.

Newman, Jacqueline. *Chinese Cookbooks: An Annotated English Language Compendium/Bibliography.* New York: Garland Publishing, 1987.

Newman, Jacqueline M., Elaine Kris Ludman, and Lois Lynn. "Chinese Food and Life-Cycle Events: A Survey in Several Countries." *Chinese American Forum* 4 (1988): 16–18.

Osgood, Cornelius. *The Chinese.* Tucson: University of Arizona Press, 1975.

Pillsbury, Barbara. " 'Doing the Month': Confinement and Convalescence of Chinese Women after Childbirth." *Social Science and Medicine* 12 (1978): 11–22.

Read, Bernard E. *Famine Foods Listed in the Chiu Huang Pen Ts'ao.* Shanghai: Henry Lester Institute of Medical Research, 1946. Reprint. Pasadena, Calif.: Oriental Book Store, 1977.

Rowe, William. *Hankow: Conflict and Community in a Chinese City, 1976–1985.* Stanford, Calif.: Stanford University Press, 1989.

Rozin, Elisabeth. *Ethnic Cuisine: The Flavor Principle Cookbook.* New York: Greene, 1983.

Ruddle, Kenneth, and Gongfu Zhong. *Integrated Agriculture-aquaculture in South China: The Dike-pond Systems of the Zhujiang Delta.* Cambridge, England: Cambridge University Press, 1988.

Sabban, Françoise. (1983a). "Cuisine à la cour de l'empereur de Chine: Les aspects culinaires du Yinshan Zhengyao de Hu Sihui." *Médiévales* 5 (1983): 32–56.

————. (1990a). "De la Main à la pâté." *L'Homme* 113 (1990): 102–37.

————. (1990b). "Food Provisioning: The Treatment of Foodstuffs and Other Culinary Aspects of the *Qimin Yaoshu*." Paper presented at the Sixth International Conference on the History of Science in China, Session on the History of Food Science and Nutrition, Cambridge, England, 1990.

————. "Un savoir-faire oublié: Le travail du lait en Chine ancienne." *Zinbun: Memoirs of the Research Institute for Humanistic Studies, Kyoto University* 21 (1986): 31–65.

————. "Sucre candi et confiseries de Quinsai: L'essor du sucre de canne dans la chine des Song (Xe–XIIIe siècle)." *Journal d'Agriculture Traditionelle et de Botanique Appliquée* 35 (1988): 195–214.

————. (1983b). "Le système des cuissons dans la tradition culinaire chinoise." *Annales: Economies, Sociétés, Civilisations* 1983:341–68.

Sabban-Serventi, Françoise. "Ravioli cristallins et tagliatelle rouges: Les pâtés chinoises entre XXie et XIVe siecle." *Médiévales* 16–17 (1989): 29–50.

Schafer, Edward. *The Golden Peaches of Samarkand.* Berkeley: University of California Press, 1963.

————. *The Vermilion Bird.* Berkeley: University of California Press, 1967.

Shih Sheng-han. *A Preliminary Survey of the Book Ch'i Min Yao Shu.* Beijing: Science Press, 1974.

Simoons, Frederick. *Food in China.* New York: CRC Press, 1990.

Skinner, G. William. "Marketing and Social Structure in Rural China." *Journal of Asian Studies* 24 (1964–65): 3–43, 195–228, 363–400.

Sung Ying-hsing. *T'ien-kung K'ai-wu.* Trans. E.-tu Zen Sun and Shiou-chuan Sun. University Park, Pa.: Pennsylvania State University, 1966.

Thompson, Stuart. "Death, Food and Fertility." In *Death Ritual in Late Imperial and Modern China,* edited by James L. Watson and Evelyn S. Rawski, 71–108. Stanford, Calif.: Stanford University Press, 1988.

Unschuld, Paul U. *Medicine in China: A History of Pharmaceutics.* Berkeley: University of California Press, 1986.

Waley, Arthur. *Yuan Mei: Eighteenth Century Chinese Poet.* New York: Grove Press, 1957.

Watson, James L. "From the Common Pot: Feasting with Equals in Chinese Society." *Anthropos* 82 (1987): 389–401.

Wittwer, Sylvan, Yu Youtai, Sun Han, and Wang Lianzheng. *Feeding a Billion.* East Lansing: Michigan State University Press, 1987.

Yang, Billy Wen-Chi. *History of Chinese Food Culture and Food Industries.* Beijing: Agricultural History Press, 1984. (In Chinese; bilingual title)

Zee, A. *Swallowing Clouds.* New York: Simon and Schuster, 1990.

Zhongyao da zidian. Beijing: Government of China, 1979.

4

Tea Drinking and Its Culture

IONE KRAMER

Tea is so much a part of Chinese culture that Chinese life without it is hard to imagine. Tea is quintessentially Chinese. Though there have been changes in styles for tea over the centuries, its place in Chinese life has remained essentially the same, even in the modern world.

The culture that has grown up around tea is the embodiment of politeness, and of a desire to share with others. A Chinese farmer has his tea every day if he can afford it, and the muddiest of the "old muddylegs" serves it to a guest with the politeness of a courtier.

This beverage is one of China's gifts to the world. The tea plant, a member of the camellia family (*Camellia sinensis*), is native to the China-India border area. A potion made from boiling its leaves may have been used medicinally by local mountain dwellers since time immemorial, but it was those on the Chinese side who from about 3,000 B.C.E. spread the use and later developed the processing for the beverage that became famous throughout the world.

Legend has it that Shen Nong, known in China as the God of Agriculture, was boiling water outdoors and some tea leaves fell into the pot, possibly a "tripod" of fired clay with three hollow legs that straddle the fire. He drank the brew and liked it. Thus tea was born. Shen Nong is credited with discovering many medicinal herbs. Another tale is that in testing these, when any proved to be poisonous, tea was his antidote.

HISTORICAL SURVEY

Tea began to be drunk as a beverage for enjoyment rather than purely medicine in the third century B.C.E. Tea drinking became an art in the Tang Dynasty (seventh to tenth centuries). One of China's golden ages, this was also a golden age for tea. The beverage was imbibed by rich and poor alike, north and south. In this period and in the subsequent Song Dynasty, tea was almost a fetish among the officials and literati. Tea-tasting contests were their great pastime, testing who could make the best cup and recognize rare varieties. Each in turn would prepare tea to be evaluated by a judge elected from among them, and discussion would follow on the quality of the leaf, water, and skill. Tales abound about acute tasters, especially the famous Lu Yu, called the Tea Sage.

The man of letters, Lu Yu, between 760 and 780, set down for all time the fine points of tea making in a work now called *The Classic of Tea*. Written at the request of the producers of the leaf for this now-popular beverage, his book was the first complete codification of information on its growing and processing. The original drawings show twenty-seven pieces of equipment needed, including brazier and fire tools, various containers, scoop, ladle, and bowls for drinking. He has a basket-ware carryall into which all the equipment could be fitted for an outdoor tea-and-poetry-writing excursion at a distant place. The two were often linked, and in ancient China (as in eighteenth-century England) many poems were written to the beverage.[1]

By the Song Dynasty (960–1297), tea had ceased to be a luxury and became a daily necessity even among the poorest as greater productivity improved the lives of the farming people. In *Mengliang Lu,* the famous description of the Southern Song capital Hangzhou, it is listed as one of the seven necessities of life, along with firewood, rice, oil, salt, soy sauce, and vinegar.[2] Another contemporary account describes night markets in the Northern Song capital Kaifeng running through the third watch (3:00–5:00 A.M.) with vendors bringing in their jars of tea all the while. Among the wealthy, tea drinking as an art rose to new heights. Many of the beautiful gardens that officials built for themselves, such as the famous ones at Suzhou, included a small rustic teahouse.

Hangzhou, the world's greatest city of its time, had numerous teahouses, but the beverage was only the catalyst for their real function, conviviality. Some were gathering places for off-duty officials or young men of wealthy families. Patrons played instruments, sang, or enjoyed professional performances, an important part of teahouse culture then as now. These teahouses featured flower arrangements according to season and displayed works of prominent painters on the walls. They also served soups and snacks.[3] Domestic servants, laborers, or artisans of different trades each had their favorite teahouses.

From about the fourth century, samples of the select first picking of the youngest, most tender leaves had been presented to the emperor, and soon these gifts, given as a sign of loyalty to him, turned into demands that were indeed a kind of tax. Among the common people, picking tribute tea in April was festival time. Thousands of young women would gather early in the morning on the mountains ringed with tea terraces. After the proper ceremonies, they plucked the tender green tips till noon, and the leaves were processed by men before nightfall.

For the processing, designated towns set up special wine shops and ''pleasure girl'' establishments for the occasion. Being forced during the busy plowing time to give labor at very low pay—much of which was lost in such pleasures—was a hardship on the peasants (Blofeld 1985, 10). The first picking is still a local festival today with traditional songs and dances. Many of these examples of ancient culture are continually being discovered by researchers and revitalized.

CONTEMPLATION AND CONVIVIALITY

Two tea traditions seem to have existed side by side. One is that of the quiet contemplation of the scholars and poets—through the art of tea escaping the cares of the world with a few select friends. The other might be termed the social role, the teahouses and teahouse entertainment that has run all through history.

The first is described by Lin Yutang, the famous popularizer of Chinese culture of the last generation, in *The Importance of Living*:

Tea is invented for quiet company as wine is invented for a noisy party. There is something in the nature of tea that leads us into a world of quiet contemplation of life. . . . Its enjoyment is appropriate in an atmosphere where all ostentation or suggestion of luxury is banished from one's eyes and one's thoughts.[4]

This association of tea with simplicity and purity may have its roots in the Taoist tradition, for Taoist monks, with their emphasis on health, contributed much to the spread of tea drinking.

It is interesting to note that Lin's own description and quotations from Song and Ming writers stress many things that are still practiced in China quite naturally without saying more about them, but which, formalized almost to the point of exaggeration, became vital parts of the Japanese tea ceremony. These include the total simplicity of decor; the complete removal from worldly matters; heightened sensitivity to fragrances, shadows, and muted sounds; and the enjoyment of handling the artistic tea things.

These two traditions, however, are not mutually exclusive, and in each there is much of the other. The quiet contemplation is done preferably with a sympathetic companion, and all of the above forms of appreciation can be practiced while enjoying a teahouse performance before a crowded company.

Setting the Stage: Kinds of Tea

Before we can visualize the Chinese at their tea drinking, a few words about the beverage in their cups are in order. Of the three main kinds of tea—green, black, and oolong—green is by far the Chinese drinkers' favorite, and they consume 90 percent of the national production.[5] Black tea, most familiar in the

West (known in Chinese as *hongcha,* red tea), undergoes a process called fermentation, which is really oxidation. The freshly picked leaves lie in piles for a few hours while the oxygen in the air creates chemical changes in them. Green tea is not fermented and quite soon the leaves go to be pan-fried and dried. Oolong, halfway between the two, is allowed to oxidize a shorter time and is called semifermented. Scented teas are a fourth main category. They may be made from any of the above dried with blossoms (such as jasmine) or treated with fruit juice (as with Lychee Black) to give them a distinctive flavor.

Oolong is the favorite in Fujian province on the southern coast, its birthplace and a main producer, and in Guangdong to the south. Popular in north China are scented teas, mostly green. The rest of the country prefers green teas of various kinds. China's minority nationalities have their own special preferences in brick tea, black or green.

Different authorities cite between 350 and 500 varieties of processed teas, reflecting various strains, topography (the best tea comes from high mountains says a Chinese adage), soil, climatic conditions, and methods of processing. Tea is grown, almost always in the mountains, in seventeen provinces from Hainan off the southern coast up as far north as Shandong and other Yellow River provinces. Zhejiang, Fujian, and Anhui provinces are the biggest producers.

Our tea tipplers may be savoring mellow-tasting yellow-green Lung Ching (Longjing), China's most famous green tea. The name means Dragon Well (the dragon is the king of the waters in Chinese mythology) and its home is the village of that name near beautiful West Lake and the city of Hangzhou, often called China's tea capital, in Zhejiang province southwest of Shanghai. Also favorites are the *mee* teas (meaning eyebrow, for the shape into which the leaves are hand-rolled). Among them are Chunmee and Showmee (Precious and Longevity Eyebrow). Lung Ching heads the list of the five best-known green teas, followed by Huangshan Mao Feng, Pi Lo Chun, Puto Fo Cha (made by the monks of Mt. Puto, an island off Shanghai), and Lu'an Guapian (leaves shaped like melon seeds through processing—and served to Henry Kissinger on one of his visits).

Oolongs are known for their distinctive aroma, and oolong drinkers, like brandy sippers, first raise the cup to the tip of the nose for a whiff, and then to the lips. Best known are Shui Hsien (Water Sprite, the same name as the narcissus flower) and Ti Kwan Yin (Tea of the Iron Bodhisattva) so named from a legend. (A devout man in Fujian province's Shaxian county, concerned that he could not afford to repair a rundown shrine with an iron statue of the Bodhisattva Guanyin, swept it regularly. She appeared to him and told him where to find the tea plants that enabled him and the village to prosper.) Both of these teas originated in Fujian, but now are also produced elsewhere.

An unusual oolong popular in China but until recently rarely seen outside is the dark, earthy-flavored Pu-erh made from the broad-leaved tea trees of Yunnan province. It is drunk as a beverage and often taken for relief of indigestion and diarrhea. Very few Chinese drink black tea regularly. The outstanding Chinese black on the world market is Keemun from Anhui province.

In a Chinese Home

Any time is teatime in a Chinese home, and the drink is always offered first thing after a guest enters. Serving tea is more than a matter of politeness, it is a symbol of togetherness, a sharing of something enjoyable. To not take at least a sip might be considered impolite. The custom was maintained even through the very hard years from 1959 to 1961, when families offered "white tea," that is, a cup of boiling hot water.

The hostess will freshen up the cup possibly from a second infusion. Some Chinese people used to consider refilling the pot and offering a third cup the signal that it was time to leave, but this custom does not hold among close friends, and many people pay no attention to it today. Blofeld recalls that it was a Qing dynasty custom for officials to signal the end of an interview by taking their second sip (Blofeld 1985, 28).

In Chaozhou, up the coast from Guangzhou (Canton) in Guangdong province, and in some other places, people sit around and converse over tea made in *gongfu* or "leisure" style (here meaning "brewed with great skill"; the name may also have come from the great amount of time needed for pickers to fill a basket with the finest small leaves). The tea set consists of a tiny pot and four handleless cups the size of walnut half-shells. The best are of Yixing stoneware.

The pot is filled half to three-fourths full of tea leaves, and then they are "rinsed" by pouring boiling water over them and immediately draining it off. The pot is then filled about four-fifths full of boiling water. After one minute the beverage is poured into the cups. Fine tea should be sipped and savored much like wine. The first cup is savored for its aroma before sipping. The second, after more water has been added to the pot, is the most flavorful, for by then the leaves are yielding full strength. By the third, there is no more aroma, but the flavor is still good. Oolong is particularly suited to this style.

Restaurant, Workplace, and Elsewhere

At home or in a restaurant, the teapot always appears on the table before any meal for the guests to refresh themselves while the cook is stirring and tossing the food, and again afterward to aid digestion. Tea is not served *with* food unless the guest asks for it. In Chinese style this is always green or oolong tea, and it is never drunk with milk or sugar.

Sometimes at the end of a seafood course, such as lobster or prawns that the diners have had to shell with their fingers, the waiter will bring a basin of hot tea and a few pieces of lemon. This is not for drinking but for washing hands before the next course. Jasmine or some other strong-flavored tea will likely be served to drink at the end of the meal, again to combat the fish odor.

Chinese teahouses, on the other hand, specializing in the beverage and serving lighter snack food, offer a wide selection of teas. Those in Cantonese style may have Pu-erh, Ti Kwan Yin, and Shui Hsien oolongs; Lung Ching and Show

Mee green; Jasmine scented; Chrysanthemum (made solely from tiny white chrysanthemum flowers); and Pu-erh with Chrysanthemum.

Public bathhouses are big sellers of tea, as after a hot bath people often lie down to cool off and relax with a cup of tea. The hot weather brings out numerous tea stalls. When small private businesses started up again after 1979 in China, these were the first to blossom along the busy streets.

Today, every office desk has its tea mug or glass and every office its table of big thermos bottles. Workmates rotate the task of filling them with hot water from a boiler elsewhere on the premises to serve the office all day. The first thing an office worker does in the morning is to make tea. Fresh hot water is added to the leaves of green tea and the brew is drunk at the desk throughout the day. There is no tea break as in England: In the Chinese work break, exercise or shopping is the thing. Everyone takes a tea mug along to meetings.

The farmer who toils in the fields of the hot south brings his tea in a hollowed-out bottle gourd. For easier carrying, he may weave a two-handled bamboo basket around it, or he may sling it over his shoulder on a string. In any other container, the tea would become hot from the sun in a few hours. But the gourd keeps the tea cool and preserves its natural flavor. Some people place their gourds in a spring for an even cooler drink.

Anyone who has traveled in China must wonder how many cups of tea he or she has been offered by the time the tour ended. Local favorites are served at every stop and during every "brief introduction" at every factory, museum, what-have-you visited, as well as before every meal. On all Chinese trains, clean covered mugs are supplied and hot water for tea is brought around by the conductors (formerly in beautiful, long-spouted, handmade brass kettles). You can buy a pack of green tea for a few *fen,* or use what you have brought along. Thermoses of hot water and packets of tea are provided in hotel rooms.

In ancient times, when a young woman was about to become engaged—the biggest step in her life—her fiancé's family would present her with a gift of tea, then one of the most precious and expensive things they could get. Her acceptance of it signaled the matchmaker to stop proposing candidates. Today, when a young woman becomes engaged she receives a present that is still called the "tea gift" (*chali*) but is not tea. This word has become the term for "engagement."

A related custom of "bride's tea" is followed in several variations in South China and among people of Chinese ancestry in southeast Asia, the United States, and elsewhere. On the day of the wedding, the bride offers a cup of tea to her mother-in-law. By accepting the tea, the elder woman signifies that she accepts the younger as her daughter-in-law.

The Teahouse: Center of Local Life

Not every village in rural China will have a teahouse, but every market or county town has one or more. The teahouse is believed to have begun in the

Tang dynasty when shops selling tea leaves began offering prepared tea. Passers-by dropped a few coins on the counter and helped themselves to a cup. Historically, the teahouse was a center of social life for the men, as women were supposed to stay at home, and in the rural areas this is mainly so still today. (For women, there was the line at the village well.)

Carters, and now truck drivers, and peddlers and farmers coming to town with their produce can have a cup, or a bite to eat, and rest up in the shade of a woven straw-mat awning. In a village, the teahouse may be only a low house of mud bricks with a shady yard filled with square tables of dark wood and stools or chairs fashioned of bamboo. These, however, are rapidly being upgraded to handsome red brick structures. There are many more teahouses in the rural areas now, as many as the traffic can bear, for they are one of the easier small private enterprises to start up under the new economic policy. In cities, a teahouse may be located above some other establishment, or may itself consist of several stories.

Most large city parks and scenic spots have teahouses, and serving is done out under the trees, weather permitting. Such spots are favorite haunts of elderly chess players, but on Sundays they are outnumbered by families, from grandmothers to babes, for this is just the spot for a rest while on a holiday outing.[6]

The teahouse is a place to exchange news and to meet and talk with friends. It was and is a popular hangout for elderly retirees, who park their pet caged birds on a nail and stay all day. Where there is no local club, the teahouse still has this function. "A rallying point for the scattered memories of the past, a recreational center in which to while away the time agreeably, an information center or gossiping shop," is the way a teahouse is described by reporter Yang Yi in the *China Daily*.[7]

For China's great novelist and playwright Lao She (1899–1966), the Beijing teahouse was a microcosm of urban life. He chose it for the setting of his 1957 play *Teahouse* because it was a place where people from all walks of life met.[8] Lao She shows the sadder side of teahouse life in grim times. The lives of altogether seventy characters, who pass through the Yutai Teahouse in Beijing for business or solace to their woes, reflect on the changes in the condition of the people in three periods: the late Qing Dynasty, the warlord decades, and the years just before the 1949 liberation.

Today's teahouses are quite different from Lao She's. They are places of conviviality and quiet bustle. Unsavory characters, should they crop up, are no longer prominent. As for gambling, which was also available in a corner of the old teahouses: Who is to say that there is none? But what may exist is among friends, not allowed to be organized, and kept within bounds. Each locality has its own viewpoint on such things.

A brighter side has always been the songs, storytelling, and opera in local style. The teahouse is the place for entertainment in towns that have no theater. How it also served as the poor man's theater even in a big city is vividly recalled by the well-known writer Deng Youmei:

The teahouses of old Beijing were not all places where members of high society passed the time, contrary to what some assume. Decades ago, the teahouses clustered around the Hademen, Gulou, and Qianmen city gates mainly catered to the poor.

They drew people from many walks of life, and not only because they offered good hot tea. Transport coolies came to swap job market tips. Dealers in small antiques showed up carrying their cloth packages. Editors occupied quiet corners with their contributors.

People gathered at teahouses in search of entertainment too. They included people who drove wagons, ran errands, performed skilled manual work or had just begun apprenticeships.

They could not afford to enter the big theatres or ballrooms, so they gathered in teahouses to give away ten *fen* for a full pot of tea and two *fen* for a moment of opera singing. For them, this kind of entertainment was affordable and worthy, and should never have been condemned as evidence of a decadent bourgeois lifestyle as it was termed during the cultural revolution (1966–76).[9]

While establishments merely serving tea survived, many places of this kind were closed down during the Cultural Revolution. Recently an old-style teahouse with drum singers and other folk artists opened in Beijing, appropriately called the Lao She Teahouse.

The city of Suzhou, south of the Yangtze, is famous for its ballads sung in heart-tugging tones to the accompaniment of a balloon guitar. In Guangzhou, capital of Guangdong province, it is bouncy Cantonese songs in the evening, or it is background for a *dim sum* brunch of little cakes of meat or sweets baked in a flaky pastry and served with the tea. Guangdong is a big tea producer, and its capital is the country's biggest consumer, racking up an annual 2.8 pounds per capita. An estimated 200,000 people there eat breakfast or brunch in the teahouses.

Sichuan province, possibly the birthplace of tea drinking, is famed for its many teahouses. Some say that the city of Chengdu has more than any other place in the country. Performances of arias from Sichuan opera are regular fare in many Sichuan teahouses, and some now offer opera videos. On this, opinion seems divided. Writer Yang Yi claims that they "distract the tea drinkers' attention and with it the enjoyment of free-flowing conversation" (Yang Yi 1991).

The custom in the rural areas with no auditorium has been to hold film showings outside on an open ground, often a threshing floor, to which everybody can come, bringing their own seats. When Chengdu officials found crowds dwindling, building on another older tradition, they set up "teahouse cinemas" or teahouses offering films. These places showed an average 600 films in 1990 for an audience of 100,000 and made a lot of money. Farming people can buy monthly or annual tickets and pay only half price when they come in in the middle of a film.[10]

In the past, the teahouse provided a place to clinch a business deal, and so it does today, too. Where it was perhaps the only "public building" around, it served as a site for mediation of landlord-tenant or other disputes. In some places, the phrase *shang chaguan* (to go to the teahouse) also means to take a dispute to be settled.

Today teahouse conversations may be among friends hatching ideas for further small businesses. Very recently a new figure, the business broker, has appeared, or perhaps one should say reappeared. In an economic situation where business is expanding faster than channels of information about raw materials and markets, brokers supply this information, and even commodities, meeting their clients in the teahouses.

In Sichuan's capital, Chongqing, everyone knows in exactly which teahouse to find brokers for each branch of business. Brokers and their clients make up 70 percent of one establishment's regular daytime customers, a local economic institute survey found. According to the Beijing magazine *Nexus,* they are easily identifiable by their almost de rigueur dark grey suits (worn unbuttoned) and black briefcases. While there have been some cases of fraud, under the present economic policy, the brokers are serving a purpose—and the teahouse is adapting to changing Chinese life.[11]

As for adaptation, the first teahouse in which patrons can *perform* Sichuan opera karaoke fashion opened in Chongqing in early 1991. In addition to seeing live performances and videotapes on eight color television sets, customers at the Bayu Teahouse can break into song for the house.

Taiwan Teahouses

So far we have been speaking of the traditional teahouse as it has existed in Chinese culture for generations. Although on the mainland there is now a family clientele, especially in park teahouses and on weekends, the traditional teahouse has remained chiefly a province of the male, and it is marked by elderly men, who come seeking companionship. Taiwan teahouses seem to have passed into a further stage of development since the 1970s with efforts to attract younger people of both sexes. Perhaps they might be called posttraditional, or the traditional revisited.

The first such attempt was the Chinese Kung Fu Tea House in Taipei in 1977. Some thirty others have opened since then. They are characterized by a quiet, restful atmosphere and tasteful decor "ranging from Japanese style, country flavor, and folkloric to teahouse-cum-art gallery, imitation study and straw-roofed cottage," as they are described by Cecilia Chang in an article in the *Free China Review.*[12]

"Tea in Taiwan used to be a dull affair with a foreign flavor," according to Fan Zongping, president of the Chinese Tea Culture Research Center in Taipei. This was the result of the various influences Taiwan suffered over the years—Japanese and then American, which brought coffeehouses. "A place that sold tea differed little from any other restaurant. Tea was drunk without flair, merely to quench thirst, and younger people preferred coffee or soda."[13]

Cecilia Chang (1983) lists four main types of the newer teahouses. The first is for a limited circle of tea connoisseurs who come "to drink, discuss, and criticize tea" and are knowledgeable about kinds, utensils, and accompanying pastries. The second (the majority of Taipei's teahouses) serves these persons, but is meant to attract a wider clientele by providing a cozy place for conversation and relaxation. The third has the characteristics of a coffee shop, which it once was, though is now converted to tea. The fourth kind consists of establishments with limited seating mainly in the business of selling teaware, or if art galleries, paintings or artifacts, and have limited concern for tea itself.

This "booming interest in tea drinking" represents "the desires of people living under contemporary urban pressures to slow down the bustle and hustle of their lives," Chang quotes the proprietor of the Lu Yu Tea Center as saying.

Serving Tea

In a teahouse, the brew is generally brought already prepared. At home, preparing good tea involves much more than just pouring hot water over some leaves. First there is the "spiritual" aspect. For Lin Yutang, "Without developing into a rigid system as in Japan, the preparation and drinking of tea is always a performance of loving pleasure, importance and distinction. In fact, the preparation is half the fun of the drinking" (1966, 227).

The procedure itself is an art, involving knowledge of the leaves, the water, and timing. For several cups, the tea will be briefly infused in a teapot (not steeped for a longer time, which "stews" the leaves and spoils the flavor), and the pot will almost always be ceramic. First the tea maker will warm the pot with hot water which is then poured off into the cups to warm them. This keeps the pot from chilling the water and prevents delicate china from cracking.

The leaves are placed at the bottom of the pot. Meanwhile the teakettle of water has just come to a boil. (On the temperature of water there are two schools of thought. Most Chinese tea makers feel that green tea should have water just before it reaches a boil. In no case should water be overboiled.) The tea maker will then pour in just a little liquid to soften the leaves. (Sometimes, particularly for Cantonese *gongfu* tea, the leaves in the pot are first "rinsed" with a potful of hot water which is immediately poured off.)

Depending on the style, the wait may be only a few seconds, or up to two minutes, and then with a flip of the wrist the tea maker pours on the rest of the water in three streams, raising the spout with a flourish after the final one. This is to keep the leaves rolling to bring out the full flavor. The first infusion will total three minutes, the second, five. Connoisseurs say that flavor is best on the second, but that the third, also five minutes, is still all right. High-quality teas need less of the leaf, and some claim that they can yield up to ten infusions.

When the time is up, the teamaker will arrange the cups with rims touching, and pour a little into each, and then a little more until all are filled. This is so that nobody gets tea that is too strong.

The tea maker will be careful to make only as many cups as are to be served at the moment. The beverage should not "stand on the leaves." If any of the infusion is left in the pot, it is poured off into another pot and kept warm. Thus the original pot and leaves are ready for the second infusion. The tea is always taken hot, not iced. The Chinese style does not use milk. Green tea is never taken with sugar, and black and oolong rarely.

This tea making, the pouring and the serving—proffering a cup of tea to the guest with both hands—while it has its rules and order, is still rather simple. The Chinese never had an elaborate ceremony like that of the Japanese, although the latter actually started in China. The Indian monk Bodhidharma (Dharuma) brought Zen Buddhism to China in 520. In his honor, from at least the Tang Dynasty on, Chinese monks used to sip a drink made from green powdered tea before a statue of him. In the Jingshan Temple northeast of Hangzhou, this seems to have developed into what records call a "tea meal" (*chayan*) with the public invited. Some say it was tea lovers getting together with monks as the hosts.

The rite, along with Zen Buddhism, was carried back home by a Japanese monk who visited the temple in 1291. While the custom later died out in China, in Japan it developed into an elaborate ritual. The temple building burned to the ground during fighting in the warlord years early in this century, but the site remains. The Chinese seem to regret that they now have no tea ceremony, although there are certain prescribed ways of serving. With the new interest in tea, research is being done on the temple and the origins of the ceremony.[14]

Tea Ceramics

The tea will most likely be sipped from small handleless porcelain cups, which came into style in the Ming Dynasty. The main tea styles in Chinese history, all green tea, are summarized in *All the Tea in China*.

Early days, fresh leaves boiled in water; third century on, leaves dried and powdered, then boiled; Tang, brick tea, made from leaves steamed, powdered, formed into cakes, and boiled to produce the beverage; Song, dry tea leaves ground to a powder and whipped in hot water with a fine bamboo whisk (this practice was taken to Japan in the eighth or ninth century and is still done in the tea ceremony there); Ming, loose tea much like ours today and prepared by infusion in hot water. Early in the Song dynasty the drink was enlivened by the addition of onions, pickle juice, ginger, and orange peel. Later it was drunk clear. (Chow and Kramer 1990, 9)

Tea's universal popularity had a marked effect on Chinese ceramics. When tea drinking became an art in the Tang Dynasty, it created a demand for teaware, thus stimulating the ceramics industry and then the creation of artistic designs— bowls of fine porcelain, which showed off the various teas and were pleasurable to handle, and, later, teapots and tea sets. In a true tea lover, says Lin Yutang,

"The pleasure of handling of the paraphernalia is such that it is enjoyed for its own sake" (1966, 228).

Bowls have been used for drinking since the beginning. For additives and whipped tea, they had to be quite large. Smaller handleless cups came in when the style changed in Ming. By then wide bowls were believed to dissipate the fragrance of the brew. Export pressures on the Chinese ceramics industry put handles on the cups, for the British had long had a handled posset cup. Now cups of both styles are used in China.

The teapot was also born in Ming. Previously, when tea was whipped in a bowl, teapots were not needed. When the style changed, the wine pot with a handle over the top was adapted for tea. The teapot often comes in a set with four cups on a small round tray of the same pattern.

For individual drinkers, a Qing Dynasty invention was the *zhong*, a bowl with saucer and a lid to keep the aroma from escaping. The tea is infused in the bowl. The saucer, balancing the bowl, is held in the left hand, while the right hand clamps on the lid, which is just slightly ajar. As one sips, the lid keeps back the leaves. The *zhong* is still used today.

A famous tea party in Chinese literature reveals the place of fine tea things in a wealthy home. This appears in *A Dream of Red Mansions,* the famous eighteenth-century novel of an aristocratic family. The Lady Dowager and young people visit a nunnery on the family's large estate. Even there the nun Miaoyu, who though described as leading an ascetic life, has the fine tea things that the family takes for granted. Among them are a carved lacquer tea tray in the shape of a crabapple blossom inlaid with a gold design, and on it a covered tea bowl of multicolor glaze from the Cheng Hua period (1465–1487). Later the nun serves tea in a pre-eleventh-century cup in the shape of a calabash. She herself usually drinks from a jade beaker.[15]

Teaware Today

An ordinary teahouse may serve in white porcelain cups with a transfer floral design around the edge. In a good restaurant or teahouse one popular porcelain may be *famille rose* in a curlicue design created with overglaze enamel before firing. This came into popularity in the Qing Dynasty, following technical advances in ceramics affording both overglaze and underglaze design application and many more colors.

Today teaware comes in all styles and glazes, including the renowned Ming blue and white and copies of famous teaware of ancient times such as the beautiful blue-green celadon of Tang and the Song "rabbit's hair" lines of white glaze on pure black. Lost techniques for making outstanding styles of the past are continually being rediscovered and applied to products for modern consumers.

With private tea drinkers, by far the most popular are Yixing pots, and every tea connoisseur treasures his. They are of a fine-grained stoneware made with a special kind of clay known as *zisha* (purple sand) for its reddish-brown color found near Yixing southwest of Shanghai in Jiangsu province. Buff or green can also be produced in firing. This ceramic town is the home of the first pots made especially for tea around 1500, crafted by a local monk after the wine pots made there. Yixing stoneware, being thicker than porcelain, is believed to keep tea warmer but also adjusts better to changes in temperature.

These pots were first used by monks in a nearby monastery and soon taken up by the officials and literati. Perhaps this espousal, according to K. S. Lo, who has made a study of Yixing ware, was a gesture to set themselves apart from the court, which used fine porcelain, and the vulgar rich, who displayed their wealth in gold and silver pots. With starkly simple lines that brought out the beauty of the material, or with a minimum of tasteful decoration, the pots made a statement about what their users regarded as the spirit of tea.[16]

Yixing pots were (and still are) created in many ingenious shapes, such as a bamboo trunk, a fruit known as Buddha's Hand (the fingered citron), and the lotus (a six-lobed pot). Some were decorated with verses in fine calligraphy. All were molded by hand. A scholar frequently would have a teapot made to order, with whatever artistic conceit he fancied. Many were tiny pots for individual use and the owner drank from the spout. In addition to their beauty, Yixing pots are prized by tea connoisseurs for their affinity for the beverage. A seasoned pot acquires a flavor of its own which contributes to the enjoyment.

For all-day drinking, the preferred vessel in China today is a tall mug about twice the size of an ordinary cup, with matching lid. While many of these are of very ordinary china, beautifully decorated cups are treasured and enjoyed throughout life. Covered mugs of reddish brown Yixing stoneware, inexpensive, practical, and artistic, are popular.

Drinking glasses, of very thin material so they do not crack even when hot water is poured in, have also been used in recent decades. One thing that can be said for them is that they show off the floating world created by certain kinds of green tea leaves as they unfold. With this criterion alone in mind, glasses might be recommended particularly for Gunpowder, Lung Ching, and several others.

Folklore and Fetishes

Tea connoisseurs can be most particular about certain aspects of their brew. These preferences are based on reason but sometimes can be carried to extremes. The young, tender leaves of the first picking in April are the most flavorful and are of the highest grade. But for some this was not enough, and they sought to get the leaves before they even burst from the bud. Thus White tea, a rare variety made entirely of unopened leaf buds, was born sometime before the twelfth century.

Water is very important, for the minerals in it affect the way the leaf components dissolve into the beverage, therefore its quality. Lu Yu said spring water was best, followed by river water, and then well water. Many traditional stories about Lu Yu and other tasters relate their acuity at recognizing not only the kind of tea, but the source of water used.

At the tea party in *A Dream of Red Mansions,* the first round was made with rain water saved from the previous year, and another from snow gathered from plum blossoms five years before and kept buried in the earth (Cao Xueqin 1980, IV: 9).

Every form of popular culture has its folklore, and tea is no exception. Tea became known to China first as a medicine, and only later as a beverage, so naturally a rich store of folk beliefs on cures is associated with it. An old proverb runs: "Drinking a daily cup of tea, Will surely starve the apothec'ry." Though now tea is drunk by social and dietary custom, everybody of Chinese tradition knows in his bones that tea drinking helps keep you well.

Probably the most important way in which tea has helped health in China through the ages is the use of boiling water to make it, so that now today, even for drinking without tea, hot water (*kai shui,* meaning that it has been boiled) is the custom, and very few Chinese will drink cold water. Tea is held to have a cheering effect and contribute to longevity.

Lung Ching in particular is believed to be cooling and is widely drunk in hot weather. In both popular belief and Chinese traditional medical practice, tea, particularly green tea and especially certain kinds, is held to aid digestion, particularly of fats. Green teas are taken for diarrhea, and Liuxi tea for constipation. Guangdong people will travel a long way each spring to get a fresh supply of this tea. In the cosmology of Chinese medicine, certain kinds are said to combat dampness in the body.

Chinese folk beliefs did not explain how teas could do these things, but all of the above have been proved true to some extent in initial tests by modern medical research in China, Japan, the United States, and some other countries.[17] In recent years, there has been a popular belief that tea drinking helps prevent cancer. Initial modern scientific tests indeed suggest at least two ways in which tea might have this effect: through inhibiting cell mutation and by detoxifying cancer-causing substances.

Tea among the Nationalities

We have thus far been speaking of tea customs among the Han people, China's majority. But China embraces altogether fifty-five other nationalities, and these minorities, some of them sizable, have a host of colorful tea customs. Introduced to the herding peoples on China's frontiers, tea seems to have been an instant hit as an aid to digestion and (we know today) a source of vitamin C, for these were herding peoples with a diet composed largely of meat and milk and few if any vegetables. This must have happened at least as early as 476 C.E., the year Chinese records note its use in barter trade with Turkic peoples in the north. In fact the Chinese government used tea as a way of "controlling" the nomads by withholding it from trade if they became too warlike.

Tea leaves pressed into a brick shape became the style for most of the herding peoples, for easier transport to remote areas and easier carrying while moving with the herds. Mongolians grind up a piece of green brick tea and drop the leaves into either boiling water or cold water which is then brought to a boil. After the tea has cooked a few minutes at low heat, milk and salt are added and sometimes pan-roasted millet. In Xinjiang and Qinghai, milk is cooked with the tea.

Although the early inhabitants of the Tibetan plateau may have boiled tea leaves in water for medicine, tea as a beverage is believed to have been introduced to the Tibetans in 641, when the Tang Dynasty Chinese princess Wen Cheng went there as the bride of its king Songstan Gambo. Now in Tibet, after a piece of ground tea brick (black) has boiled a few minutes, the leaves are strained off and the liquid poured into a tall tea churn where it is thoroughly mixed with salt and the ever-present Tibetan yak butter. The beverage is then transferred to a kettle where it is kept warm, ready to drink at any time. Often a handful of ground *tsamba* (highland barley) is added for a filling meal.

Demonstrations of nationality styles of making and serving tea can be seen at the National Tea Museum which opened in the city of Hangzhou in 1991. One alcove is furnished in the style of a well-to-do Tibetan home with the teapot atop a central brazier and walls lined with elaborately carved low green-and-gilt cupboards. Others include a room in a stilt house of the Dais (related to the Thais of Thailand) and a Mongolian tent of thick felt. In these rooms costumed guides demonstrate tea making and explain customs of serving.

TEA DRINKING IN MODERN CHINA

Is tea being threatened by the tide of other beverages being introduced to China from abroad?

One of the first joint ventures under the new economic policy was, Coca-Cola's "imperialist" reputation notwithstanding, a bottling plant in Beijing that supplies Coke to all of East Asia. In addition, there are several sweeter, syrupier Chinese products that call themselves colas, the best known of which is Xinfu (Happiness). Shopkeepers display both prominently, for that is where the profit is, and tea is, after all, old hat. After the reforms began, television viewers of foreign films and language programs, like English on Sunday, were bombarded with a Hongkong commercial for Maxwell House, extolling the lip-smacking goodness of instant coffee.

There is tremendous receptivity among the young Chinese to take up almost anything that they hear is popular abroad—a thirst to be *mo dun* (modern). This is not unusual in youth anywhere, but in China it is compounded by a long-standing feeling of inferiority stemming from China's historical backwardness in terms of the modern world. Carbonated drinks are also a status symbol for the newly affluent who have made their pile in free market street sales (and partly perhaps as compensation for their doing such work and being unable to fulfil an older and somewhat unrealistic Chinese dream of getting a higher education).

So while the postindustrial United States, enlightened about the dangers of too much caffeine and sugar, turns away from coffee and soft drinks and toward tea, among urban Chinese youth, who have had insufficient benefit of such education, the trend is the other way. Thus praise for the "convenience" of colas and instant coffee, and words like these from the *China Daily:* "It is common for many families to greet their guests with Coca-Cola and other drinks in summer and coffee in winter," and even, "Some younger people feel ashamed to offer tea to their guests."[18]

But for real drinking, such beverages will never endanger the time-honored custom of tea, even among this small urban group. Tea mugs still sit all day on office desks. One reason is the cost. A can or bottle of Coca-Cola costs three yuan in a restaurant, Xinfu Chinese cola about two, many times the price of a glass of tea. And for the working and farming millions throughout the vast countryside who little heed nor can afford such folderol, tea has been one of the staples of life for centuries, and it is not likely to suffer. Sales keep rising, partly because the population does, but also because a general rise in income has brought greater consumption.

"Traditional-style teahouses still stand firm despite mushrooming numbers of modern coffee bars in cities," was the conclusion of Chang Weimin in another *China Daily* article. "Tea is still the most favored drink in China despite the influx of soft drinks and foreign beverages."[19]

THE TEA CULTURE MOVEMENT

Recent years have seen a new development, the tea culture movement. Tea culture can roughly be defined as the social and cultural life associated with tea drinking, and that can cover a vast territory. The movement is much more than mere publicity to stimulate the sale of tea or provide a focus for tourist visits to tea areas, two roles which it indeed has. At its heart—I observed at a 1990 tea culture meeting in Hangzhou—are some of the most charming, scholarly, almost courtly, men and women of the older generation. For them drinking tea is the grace of living, extreme humanity, politeness, and consideration, certainly in social relations involving tea, hopefully in other relations too.

Tea culture is one of the things that reasserted itself after the ravages of the Cultural Revolution turned everybody against each other (and perhaps also in answer to recent emphasis on money—now recognized as overemphasis—that came with economic reform)—an attempt at a renaissance of virtues which have always been held to be the essence and best of Chineseness.

In this context it is also a medium of bonding with Hongkong and Taiwan. Tea culture is already serving as a vehicle for contact with other Asian tea-drinking countries, whose tea cultures share aspects of China's. A start is being made on this, too, with lands of the West.

On the mainland itself, numerous tea culture festivals and exhibitions on tea art, ceramics, and related subjects have been held, and such activity is not confined to the tea-producing areas. One of the best books on the subject, *Cha yu wenhua* (Tea and Culture), edited by Kong Xianlo, was published not in a southerly tea province but in Liaoning on the northern coast. These events draw big crowds and certainly help people realize that the beverage they drink every day, and more particularly the culture associated with it, is a national treasure worthy of study and research. Tea culture societies have been formed in many cities. Tea drinking as Chinese popular culture is as lively as ever.

REFERENCE WORKS

Chinese tea drinking as popular culture seems to be a virtually untouched field of research, and even tea drinking itself has only recently become a matter of research interest. There are, however, a few basic works on tea in relation to contemporary China.

Chen Chuan's *Cha ye tongshi* (History of Tea) (1974) offers complete coverage of the subject. I was unable to buy it in China in 1990 and could find a copy only in the National Library in Beijing, and nowhere outside China.

In English for Chinese tea, its growing, customs, and health benefits as well as its passage to the West and tea customs there, the newest is *All the Tea in China* (1990), by Kit Chow and Ione Kramer. The authors hope that it will remain the definitive authority on Chinese tea for some time to come. The last chapter describes fifty famous Chinese teas in terms of growing, relation to health, legends, and other colorful material.

William Ukers's encyclopedic two-volume 1935 work, *All about Tea,* is the basic reference on all aspects of tea, with considerable material about production. Unfortunately it is sadly out of date for terminology, and much else has changed. The references to Chinese things are quite unreliable. Its overview of tea in Chinese literature, however, might suggest things that the researcher could check on and follow up. This book and a shorter one by Ukers, *The Romance of Tea* (1936), are also useful on tea in Western art and literature.

John Blofeld's *The Chinese Art of Tea* (1985) is a chatty, highly personalized, Taoist-oriented account of history and lore, rare and legendary teas. Included are his translations of Tang and Song tea poems and excerpts from the tea book by Song dynasty Emperor Hui Zong, the Ming *Cha shu* by Xu Cishu, and a chapter on his travels through the teahouses and tea gardens of China.

The most exhaustive study I have found in English on modern Chinese tea production, recent development, problems, and prospects is ''The Complex Case of the Chinese Tea Industry'' by Dan M. Etherington and Keith Forster (1989). This work does not deal with the cultural aspects. It uses figures from Chinese and international sources. An earlier and perhaps more accessible version of the same material appeared in the *Tea and Coffee Trade Journal* (1988). Etherington and Forster provide newer information, and that related to foreign investment, in "Reading between the Leaves," in *The China Business Review* (1991). Their theme is that the industry is falling behind.

For paintings and photos, as well as some historical and cultural information, there are two large-size books, *5,000 Years of Tea, a Pictorial Companion* (1983) by Derek Maitland and *China, Homeland of Tea* (1989) edited by Wang Yuefen with text in Chinese and English. The latter has nuggets of information and lists tucked away among the photos, including a short bibliography giving the names in English of a few books on tea in Chinese, a list in both languages of the most important writings that mention tea over the last 3,000 years, a list of addresses of tea research institutes, and descriptions of odd kinds of tea and customs that have not been treated in basically mainstream accounts. This lavish and expensively produced book was published for special visitors during the celebration of the fortieth anniversary of the founding of the people's government. It may now be sold in tea shops in Hongkong. In the United States, some tea importers may have a copy, or possibly the Sunry Corporation office in Paramus, New Jersey (Suite 125, Paramus Plaza 2, 120 Route 17 North, Paramus, N.J. 07652; phone: 201/967-7320). In China, it can be seen at the office of the China National Tea Import and Export Corporation, 82 Donganmen Dajie, Beijing 100747; phone: (1) 512-4673.

Current production figures and feature articles in English frequently appear in the *China Daily* published in Beijing and the *Tea and Coffee Journal,* a trade journal published in New York City. Annuals with figures and summary information can be found in *Ukers' International Tea and Coffee Buyers Guide.*

Papers from the "Tea, Quality, and Human Health, International Scholarly Symposium" (Hangzhou, November 1987) and *A Collection of Research Papers at the First China Tea-Culture Festival* (Hangzhou, October 1990) are now available in English as well as Chinese. The first deals with tea chiefly from the health angle. The other will have considerable material on international exchange, but also certainly more research on tea in China. They may also be available in Japanese. The best place to inquire is the Tea Research Institute, Hangzhou, Zhejiang province, China; phone: 61824, cable: 4423. Papers were also presented at the International Tea Festival '91 (Hangzhou, April 1991) and the Second International Tea Culture Symposium (Tao Hua Yuan, Hunan province, March 1992) and presumably will also be available in these languages.

Two new and useful books in Chinese with essays on historical-cultural topics are *Zhongguo cha shi jielun* (Some Conclusions on Chinese Tea History) (1988), edited by Zhuang Wansu—Kexue Chubanshe, Dong Beichenggen Jie 16, Beijing, China. It has a four-page list of the important tea classics and other historical references chronologically by dynasty, but no page numbers for its references. And there is the more recent *Cha yu wenhua* (Tea and Culture) (1990), edited by Kong Xianlo—Chunfeng Wenhua Chubanshe, Nanjing Jie 6 Duan 1 Li 2 Hao, Shenyang, China.

Yixing teaware has recently been the subject of several fine books updating Yixing expert K. S. Lo's *The Stonewares of Yixing from the Ming Period to the Present Day* (1987). Big and beautiful, *The Art of the Yixing Potter. The K. S. Lo Collection, Flagstaff House Museum of Tea Ware* (1990) was produced by the Hongkong Urban Council for the collection's 1990–1991 North American tour. It has a concise history; notes on important designers, engravers, and producers; sections on outstanding examples from the Shanghai Museum; photos with insets of seals, glazes, and calligraphy; an index-chart of signature seals; and an appendix showing the potter's hands at three techniques (luting, beating, and pinching).

An earlier council book, *Innovations in Contemporary Yixing Pottery* (1988), includes an article by K. S. Lo on the influence of patronage on Yixing pots. Both books are bilingual (English and Chinese).

What may prove the ultimate for now is *Yixing zisha taoci* (Yixing Purple Clay Pottery) (1993) edited by Gu Jingzhou. Illustrations in the silkbound volume include 180 of the most representative and valuable pieces from China's famous museums and private collections.

All three may be hard to get, though perhaps they can be found in museums and libraries. Pots can be purchased in some museums and other shops. The World Treasure Trading Company, P.O. Box 50213, Long Beach, CA 90815-61213, a mail-order firm, has a very wide selection (catalog free on request).

RESEARCH COLLECTIONS

The United States has several collections with good material on the tea trade with China, but they contain little about tea in China itself. These are the China Trade Museum in Milton, Massachusetts, and the Peabody Museum in Salem, Massachusetts.

The Brandsten Collection in the Bancroft Library of the University of California, Berkeley, is the only specialized tea collection I have used. It contains a miscellany of material in English on tea in relation to the West, the tea trade particularly with the U.S. West Coast, some on tea history East and West, and processing in China and Japan. It has an extensive collection of illustrations related to tea.

In China, sociological research on popular culture is a relatively untouched thing. Some material on tea itself, however, may be available. The Tea Research Institute (TRI, Chinese Academy of Sciences, Hangzhou, China) has vast resources in Chinese and some in English about tea chemistry, processing, and history, and since the advent of the tea culture movement, perhaps more material on customs. It has a great number of tea utensils collected over the years. The Tea Culture Society, which can be reached through the institute, currently serves as a center for Chinese research on tea culture.

The China Tea Museum in Hangzhou has an excellent display of visual material and, though a new institution and still getting set up for research, may prove helpful.

For tea artifacts, significant Yixing collections can be found in the Asian Art Museum, San Francisco; the Nelson-Atkins Museum of Fine Arts, Kansas City, Missouri; the Art Institute of Chicago; the Seattle Art Museum; and the Smithsonian's Freer Gallery. As far as is known, there is no museum in the United States devoted specifically to Yixing pottery. The Flagstaff House Museum in Hongkong displays the Yixing collection of K.S. Lo. A good display can be found in the ceramics museum in the town of Yixing in China's Jiangsu province, and of course there are many examples in the Palace Museum in Beijing.

NOTES

1. Lin Yutang lists as the best-known ancient tea writings (translations of names of works, where no commonly known ones exist, are my own): Tang Dynasty: Lu Yu, *Cha jing* (The Classic of Tea); Song: Cai Xiang, *Cha lu* (Tea Record); Ming: Tian Yiheng, *Chuchuan xiaopin* (Essay on Boiling Spring Water), Tu Long, *Cha chien* (Zhuang Wanfang gives the title of Tu's work as *Cha shuo* (Speaking of Tea) (as Lin does not give characters, it is not clear if this is the same work), and Xu Cishu, *Cha shu* (Random Notes on Tea), which contains a delightful poem on the twenty-four good times for drinking tea (translated in Blofeld 1985, 41–42 and Lin Yutang (1966), "On Tea and Friendship").

To these I would add Song Hui Zong, *Da guan cha lun* (Treatise on Tea) by the Song Dynasty emperor who reigned from 1100 to 1125, and the famous poem by the Tang Dynasty tea lover Lu Tong, "Thanks to Imperial Censor Meng for His Gift of Freshly Picked Tea." The complete poem appears in translation in Blofeld 1985, 11–13, and a portion appears in the introduction to Chow and Kramer, *All the Tea in China* (1990).

2. Wu Tzumu, *Mengliang lu* (literally "The Dream of Happiness," but actually meaning a "millet dream"—of splendors in the midst of deprivation in the Southern Song capital while the north was held by the Mongols), quoted extensively in Etienne Balazs, *Chinese Civilization and Bureaucracy* (1964, 93). The passage is translated into English from a translation into French by Balazs, who titles it "Account of the Remembered Splendors of the Former Capital."

3. See John Blofeld, *The Chinese Art of Tea* (1985, 52–56), for a detailed description of such tea rooms in ancient China, and Balazs quoting Wu Tzumu (1964, 93–94). The date is 1274, the year of Marco Polo's arrival in China.

4. Lin Yutang, "On Tea and Friendship" in *The Importance of Living* (1966, 223–31).

5. While in this book Chinese words appear in the pinyin romanization now used in China, in this section names of teas are those under which they are marketed internationally.

6. See Blofeld (1985). His reminiscences of the more enjoyable side of teahouses in preliberation China are delightful, but his complaints that all such teahouses vanished after the 1949 liberation are not to be taken too seriously. Teahouses with entertainment had a hard time during the Cultural Revolution, but I was served in many others in parks and scenic spots.

7. Yang Yi, "Chengdu Teahouse—A Superb Place to Relax" (1991, 4).
8. Lao She, introduction to *Teahouse* (1978).
9. Deng Youmei, "High Time for Teahouses" (1989, 6).
10. Li Jiangtian, "Rural Films" (1991).
11. Mao Hao, "Teahouse Business Brokers" (1988, 26–27).
12. Cecilia Chang, "Teatime in Taiwan" (1983, 57–63).
13. Conversation with the author.
14. Conversations with members of the China Tea Culture Association in Hangzhou.
15. Cao Xueqin, *A Dream of Red Mansions* (1980), vol. II, ch. 41, pp. 7–10).
16. K. S. Lo, *The Stonewares of Yixing from the Ming Period to the Present Day* (1987, 35–36).
17. Scientific papers on initial research on tea and health were brought together for the first time in 1987 at a conference "Tea, Quality and Human Health, International Scholarly Symposium" sponsored by the Tea Research Institute of the Chinese Academy of Agricultural Sciences. Facts from the conference and other sources were brought together in English for the first time in Chow and Kramer, chapter 9, "Tea and Your Health," (1990, 91–112). March 4–5, 1991, saw the first Western meeting on this topic in New York City, an international symposium entitled "Physiological and Pharmacological Effects of *Camellia Sinensis*—Implications for Cardiovascular Disease, Cancer and Public Health." Its findings were reported in a forty-inch article in the *New York Times* of March 14. For information on those papers that have been published and an expected report of the proceedings, contact Dr. John H. Weisburger, Director Emeritus, American Health Foundation, Dana Road, Valhalla, New York, 10596, (914) 592–2600.
18. Li Xing, "The History and Culture of Tea in China Is on Exhibit" (1989, 5).
19. Chang Weimin, "Increased Sales Just China's Cup of Tea" (1990, 1).

BIBLIOGRAPHY

Atterbury, Paul, ed. *The History of Porcelain.* New York: Wm. Morrow, 1983.
Balazs, Etienne. *Chinese Civilization and Bureaucracy.* Translated by H. M. Wright. New Haven, Conn.: Yale University Press, 1964.
Blofeld, John. *The Chinese Art of Tea.* Boston: Shambhala, 1985.
Cao Xueqin. *A Dream of Red Mansions.* Translated by John Howard Gibbon. Beijing: Foreign Languages Press, 1980.
Chang, Cecilia. "Teatime in Taiwan." *Free China Review* (July 1983): 57–63.
Chang Weimin. "Increased Sales Just China's Cup of Tea." *China Daily,* February 7, 1990, 1.
Chen Chuan. *Chaye tongshi* (History of Tea). Beijing: Agriculture Press, 1974.
Chow, Kit, and Ione Kramer. *All the Tea in China.* San Francisco: China Books, 1990.
Deng Youmei. "High Time for Teahouses." *China Daily,* February 7, 1989, 6.
Etherington, Dan M., and Keith Forster. "The Complex Case of the Chinese Tea Industry." Palo Alto, Calif.: Food Research Institute Studies, Food Research Institute of Stanford University, vol. 21, no. 3, 1989.
Gu Jingzhou, ed. *Yixing zisha taoci* (Yixing Purple Clay Pottery). Hongkong: Joint Publishers, 1993.
Hongkong Urban Council. *The Art of the Yixing Potter. The K. S. Lo Collection, Flagstaff House Museum of Tea Ware.* Hongkong: 1990. (Bilingual English/Chinese.)

————. *Innovations in Contemporary Yixing Pottery.* Hong Kong: 1988. (Bilingual English/Chinese.)

Kong Xianlo, ed. *Cha yu wenhua* (Tea and Culture). Shenyang: Chunfeng Culture Press, 1990.

Kramer, Ione. "Serving Tea Traditionally." *China Today* 40 (March 1991): 44–45.

————. "Tea Culture, a New-Old Tradition." *China Today* 40 (March 1991): 46–47.

————. "Tea Gets Its Own Museum." *China Today* 40 (March 1991): 48–49.

Lao She. *Teahouse.* Translated by Yang Xianyi and Gladys Yang. Beijing: Foreign Languages Press, 1978.

Li Jiangtian, "Rural Films." *Economic Daily* (Jingji Ribao), June 9, 1991. Excerpted in *China Daily.*

Li Xing. "The History and Culture of Tea in China Is on Exhibit." *China Daily,* September 13, 1989, 5.

Lin Yutang. "On Tea and Friendship." In *The Importance of Living.* 1937. New York: John Day, 1966.

Lo, K. S. *The Stonewares of Yixing from the Ming Period to the Present Day.* Hongkong: Sotheby's and Hongkong University Press, 1987.

Lu Yu. *The Classic of Tea.* Translated with an introduction by Francis Ross Carpenter. Boston: Little, Brown, 1974.

Maitland, Derek. *5000 Years of Tea, a Pictorial Companion.* Hong Kong: CFW Publications, Ltd., 1983.

Mao Hao. "Teahouse Business Brokers." *Nexus* (Spring 1988): 26–27.

Medley, Margaret. *The Chinese Potter, A Practical History of Chinese Ceramics.* Oxford, England: Phaidon, 1976.

Tea Research Institute of the Chinese Academy of Agricultural Sciences. *Cha—pinzhi—renlei jiankang guoji xueshu taolun hui, taolun wenzhang gaoyao* (Tea, Quality and Human Health, International Scholarly Symposium, papers presented, November 4–9, 1987). Hangzhou, 1988.

Ukers, William. *All about Tea.* Whitestone, N.Y.: Tea and Coffee Trade Journal Co., 1935.

————. *The Romance of Tea.* New York: Alfred A. Knopf, 1936.

Wang Yuefen, chief ed. *China—Homeland of Tea.* Beijing: China National Native Produce and Animal By-Products Import and Export Corp., and Hongkong: Educational and Cultural Press, 1989.

Yang Yi. "Chengdu Teahouse—A Superb Place to Relax." *China Daily,* June 17, 1991, 4.

Zhuang Wanfang, Tang Qingzhong, Tang Li-xing, Chen Wen Huai, and Wang Jiabin. *Zhongguo mingcha* (Famous Chinese Teas). Hangzhou: Zhejiang People's Publishing House, 1979.

Zhuang Wansu, ed. *Zhongguo cha shi jielun* (Some Conclusions on Chinese Tea History). Beijing: Science Press, 1988.

5

Religion

JORDAN PAPER

The term "religion" exists only in Western languages; in other languages, terms have to be created to serve as its equivalent. Often, this creates a confused understanding. This is particularly the case with regard to China. Five hundred years ago, Matteo Ricci, an Italian Jesuit, the first Catholic missionary to successfully reside in China, understood the Chinese term "Three Teachings" (*sanjiao*)[1] to mean "Three Religions," although the Chinese at the time considered him to be in error. It has since been normative in the West to assume that there are three religions in China: Confucianism, Taoism, and Buddhism.

At the beginning of this century, the Chinese borrowed the Japanese word for religion, itself taken from an obscure Chinese Buddhist text, and understood the term *zongjiao* to indicate primarily foreign phenomena. Currently, given the Chinese predilection for the number five, it is said that there are five religions in China, the above three plus Islam and Christianity. If one were to ask the average Chinese about Chinese religion, the answer is usually quite simple: The Chinese do not have one. In other words, religion is understood to be a phenomenon pertinent to foreign cultures.

The reason for this confusion is that the concept of three or five religions excludes most of Chinese religious practices and understanding, which are officially considered superstition. The terms, three religions or five religions, refer to institutions outside normative religion. Buddhism is, of course, of Indian origin. Institutional Taoism developed after Buddhism became established in China and in part was modeled on it. Confucianism, that is the establishment of Confucian temples in cities, developed as a response to the success of the first two. Chinese religion per se is considerably older than any of these traditions.

HISTORICAL SURVEY

Chinese culture is humanity's oldest continuing civilization and can be traced back at least four thousand years. Throughout these four millennia can be found a pattern of religious rituals and understanding that is at the center of both elite and popular practices, a pattern that is determinative of Chinese society and culture.

In essence, these rituals consist of the offering of a meal and other necessities to the spirit realm, particularly those most important to humans, the departed members of the family. This meal is then eaten by the living members of the family. Similar offerings are also made to nature and cosmic spirits.

In the early development of Chinese civilization, from ca. 2000 to 800 B.C.E., we are only aware of the lives of a hereditary aristocracy. They were organized in patrilineal clans hierarchically arranged, the clan chieftain of the superior clan being the king. The leading male of each clan and his wife made offerings to his deceased parents, grandparents, and the clan founders; the sacrifice was simultaneously a clan feast. The cast bronze sacrificial vessels, made with a highly advanced technology, were the most important material items of the culture. The clan sacrifice of the king was, in effect, the primary state ritual, establishing and maintaining both cosmic and social order. The place of sacrifice, the clan temple of the king, was the center of state authority; its destruction symbolized its end and the beginning of a new regime. Some of these sacrificial vessels became emblematic of kingship itself.

With the creation of the Chinese empire two thousand years ago, the various traditions of the different cultures hitherto found in the area of greater China slowly coalesced into the religion that continued into the early twentieth century on the state level and still continues on the popular level. This religion has been the determinative feature of Chinese culture and its lack marks the limits of cultural expansion.

On the state level, the primary function of the emperor was that of the chief priest; it was his ritual function that justified his political role. Given that the imperial clan was obviously the most important clan, the departed clan founders and previous emperors were the most important of the human spirits, and only the most direct descendant, the emperor with his spouse, could sacrifice to them. Also, only the emperor had the prerogative of sacrificing to Heaven and Earth, the primary cosmic spirits. One of the titles of the emperor, the Son of Heaven, specifically indicates this ritual role. Hence, the emperor was responsible for the well-being in every respect of the empire.

At the same time, approximately two thousand years ago, we find ordinary people had family names, whereas previously only the aristocracy had them. Having a family name meant adopting the clan concept of family, a family that existed at the macro-level, the clan, and micro-level, the nuclear or three-generation family. The family name included the rituals of sacrificial offerings and an understanding of family that includes the deceased members as powerful spirits and the unborn as a religious obligation, an obligation to continue the patrilineal family. What the rituals of ordinary people were previous to the adoption of this concept of family we do not know, except that it undoubtedly included sacrifices to the soil for farming families, sacrifices to patron deities of trades and crafts for urbanites, and sacrifices to local deities for everyone, as these practices continued.

Buddhism entered China also at this time, but it did not spread among Chinese to any extent until the collapse of the first Chinese empire. In the centuries of resulting disorder, Buddhism became of major importance. Simultaneously, Taoist churches developed. Institutionally, these were modeled to a degree on Buddhist monasteries and temples, but ideologically they were based on previous uninstitutionalized religious developments and a number of subsidiary religious practices of the court. When China was reunified fourteen hundred years ago, the traditional practices slowly regained ascendance. Since that time, both Buddhism and Taoism have remained as alternative and adjunct practices to normative Chinese religion.

Chinese religion, a religion some have called "familism," is a religion which has at its center the family itself, with a focus on the dead. Another scholar has called Chinese religion a "cult of the dead," but it is the family per se, which includes the dead, that is of central importance. The emperor was also called the "Father and Mother of the People"; the Chinese empire was in theory a centralization of families into a single grand family with the emperor as the family patriarch.

Chinese religion, as with most religions aside from Christianity and Islam, is not imbued with a particular ideology or concept of truth but with a set of ritual practices, most of which focus on the deceased members of the family. The various calendrical rituals center on family meals which begin with the offering of a complete banquet, both food and wine, to the departed members of the family. After these spirits are satisfied, the living members of the family sit down to consume the meal.

One ceremony held in the spring, Qingming, takes place at the grave site. The grave is cleaned and offerings are made, to be later consumed by the family. All other offerings are made in the home and in clan temples.

The most important yearly ritual is the Spring Festival, referred to in the West as Chinese New Year. Based on the lunar calendar, it takes place toward the end of winter and marks the new year. Rituals take place over half a month, beginning with a family sacrifice and ending with the colorful Lantern Festival. A number of other festivals take place throughout the year.

Every traditional Chinese home is a temple, a shrine to the family's dead. In the center of the main room will be an altar with the name tablets of the immediate deceased with candles, or red lightbulbs in modern times, wine cups, an incense burner, and vases for flowers. In front of the altar will be a table on which the food at times of sacrifice is placed before it is removed to the dining table for consumption by the family.

Many families also bring the food to be offered to clan temples prior to its being offered in the family home. Here there are far more name tablets, listing the important deceased members of the family for many generations.

Of the various rituals that denote the changes in a person's life, the most important are funerary rituals. Because the deceased are understood to be influential on the fortunes of a family, how they are treated is of utmost importance. There are elaborate rituals surrounding the care of the corpse, its burial, and subsequent rituals at various times following the death. All of these rituals involve food offerings as well as the burning of representative items made of paper to be used in the afterlife: (spirit) money, gold and silver ingots, television sets, automobiles, houses, clothing, and so on.

These offerings are indicative of the Chinese understanding of life which is very much this worldly, in contrast, as examples, to Therevada Buddhism and Christianity. The world of the dead is understood as another version of this life, connected by the interaction of the living and dead members of the family.

Often also involved in the funeral are Taoist priests who perform particular rituals and, at fixed periods after the death, Buddhist monks or nuns who chant sutras. Money may also be offered to Buddhist monasteries for the periodic chanting of memorial masses.

The deceased are not the only spirits in Chinese religion, but they are the most ubiquitous and central. All of nature is imbued with spirituality, and particular bodies of water, mountains, and even trees have become considered especially efficacious. Sacrifices to these were carried out at imperial shrines in the capital, performed on pilgrimages to special mountains and bodies of water by emperors and still by ordinary people, made at small shrines by sacred trees, and so on.

Of particular importance with regard to nature spirits is the earth itself. Mentioned above was the imperial sacrifice to Heaven and Earth, so important that it was treason for anyone else to make the offering. But the earth is understood in many modes. In southeastern China, at every grave is a shrine to the Lord of the Soil, the keeper of the very earth in which the body is laid. At the Qingming festival, offerings are also made to this deity. Farming families have shrines in the fields to Grandmother and Grandfather Soil as well as on the family altar for fertility of the fields. And it is not uncommon to hear references to Mama Soil.

Also important until recently were a plethora of deities with specific functions, such as city-protecting deities, fertility deities, martial deities, examination success deities, and occupational deities. Offerings were made to these deities in city, guild, and other types of temples. The most important general deity is Guanyin.

Although Guanyin is nominally a male Buddhist bodhisattva of Indian origin, approximately eight hundred years ago there was a gender shift, and the bodhisattva became a female deity not limited to Buddhism. Her image is omnipresent and will be found on or above family altars among those who have no specific links to Buddhism. She has multiple functions including fertility with regard to human progeny and as protector of the deceased. She is linked to the story of a young unmarried woman who after death became a deity, following the pattern of the majority of Chinese deities.

Throughout China, one will find numerous local deities, some of whom achieve regional and even national recognition, for example, Mazu, the most important deity in southeastern China, who is a sea goddess. Aside from heroes and other famous historic persons, most deities are people who died under circumstances that do not lead to their being cared for by the living. Accordingly, they become wandering, potentially malevolent ghosts, who possess the living and need to be exorcised. Some, who on possessing the living are benevolent and benefit the community, have temples built for them. If their benefits become major, their fame will become widespread and their temples will increase in size and number.

Because of the patrilineal nature of the Chinese family and religion, unmarried females have no family status. Once married, they become part of their husband's family and after death will be sacrificed to by their children. But an unmarried female, unless there is a spirit marriage (a marriage of a dead female to a living male), becomes a wandering ghost. This probably is part of the reason that the majority of popular deities are female.

The phenomenon of trance possession also illustrates a major feature of Chinese religion: It is experiential. Chinese religion is not a matter of faith. People directly experience the spirits and deities; they meet them face to face.

On the family level, the spirits to whom sacrifice is made are those of recent memory—one's parents or grandparents. In earlier times, during the aristocratic clan sacrifices, a grandson or granddaughter-in-law of the deceased was chosen to be possessed by the recipient of the sacrifice so he or she could be present and eat and drink the offerings. On the natural level, spirits are the very earth in which we lay the dead and plant our crops, or especially old trees and particularly tall mountains. On the local temple level, mediums in trance are possessed by the temple spirits during festivals and, on request, by the spirits of the deceased if a family has problems, so that the deities and spirits can heal or deal with the family's problems.

It is at the local temple, whether village or urban neighborhood, that families can interact. Since the primary aspect of Chinese religion is religion of the family, until recently, without the local temple, community would be impossible. Local temples usually are the locus of several deities meaningful to the community and function as community centers. This is where community meetings can be held, where dramatic performances can take place—nominally for the spirits, but everyone attends and enjoys them—where old people can meet each other to play chess, where people can get together to play musical instruments, and where many other activities take place. It is also where people will come whenever the need is felt to make offerings to the deities. Women might stop after shopping and offer the food they bought at the local market before taking it home. And on sacrifice days, the uncooked food will often be brought to the local temple to be offered to the deities before it is cooked and offered in the home to the family spirits.

It is at the temple too that one can ask questions of the deities concerning important decisions to be made, of the cause and cure for illnesses, and other problems. One can ask the deities through possessed mediums or, more commonly, through various divination practices. The most ubiquitous are a pair of kidney-shaped blocks of wood and a container of numbered bamboo slips. The former are thrown for a yes-no response, based on how the blocks fall. In the case of the latter mode, the container is shaken until a single slip is ejected. The number on the slip is then matched to an almanac or prepared statements available on a side wall of the temple.

At the local temples, as in the home, there are no clergy. Caretakers will be appointed, often retired persons; otherwise, families will take turns in caring for the building. In larger temples, a small shop will be on the premises for purchasing incense, spirit money, and other items used in worship. But these are available from neighborhood stores in any case. Mediums, who have other occupations, will be present only if requested or during a festival of one of the temple's deities.

Family rituals, such as marriages and funerals, do not take place at the temples but in the home, or in urban areas with generally smaller homes, in restaurants, or in long tents erected in the street in front of the home. In North American cities with a significant Chinese population, one will find large restaurants with, along two different walls, often in neon lights, a "dragon" and a "phoenix" for weddings and the sign for longevity for sixtieth-birthday celebrations. This function of urban restaurants can be traced back many centuries. In Chinese religion, it is the marriage feast itself that socially signifies the union of the marital pair, and such feasts are a mainstay of urban restaurants.

Other than local temples, Buddhist monasteries, Taoist temples and shrines, and pilgrimage sites are utilized by people on various occasions. People who do so are not necessarily Buddhists or Taoists. Until the twentieth century, only those who became Taoist priests or Taoist and Buddhist monks and nuns, or who took special vows as laypersons, would be so considered. Chinese religion encompassed all the different possibilities in a single totality; only those who became monks or nuns and thereby renounced family limited the many possibilities of religious life and experience.

The present century has seen change and continuity in the practice of Chinese religion similar to the changes that have taken place in Chinese culture. Chinese civilization, long ahead of others in technology and similar developments, due in part to an increasingly rigid control of the educated by the government, was in a state of decay at the time the West was expanding its technology in the service of imperialistic ambitions. By the mid-nineteenth century, the Chinese government itself had become ineffectual in the face of Western economic and territorial expansion. Finally in the early twentieth century, the Chinese empire collapsed into regional strife and loss of major territories to the West and later Japan.

Chinese intellectuals began to seek a Western education and look toward Western models for solutions to Chinese problems, and Western education in China was largely controlled by Christian missionaries. Traditionally, the educated, who composed an aristocracy based on a civil service examination system, looked down on the culture of the common people. A Western orientation, along with chaotic conditions that saw the breakup of many families, led the educated away from traditional religion toward a twentieth-century Western agnosticism. In the mid-twentieth century, the Chinese Communist Party succeeded in reunifying China and creating a relatively stable socioeconomic situation, but their ideology included a Soviet-influenced official atheism. A small remnant of the opposing side of the civil war, the Nationalist Party, fled to Taiwan, then recently liberated from a half century of Japanese control. There, after the Chinese entered the Korean War to stop an assumed invasion of China by the United Nations forces, the Nationalist Party received major financial and military support from the United States. In effect, two patterns of religious development have evolved, one in China itself, the "Mainland," and one in Taiwan, Hong Kong, and Singapore.

In China, the government distinguishes between religious institutions, which are under tight government control, and theoretically have a constitutional right to religious freedom, and superstition, which is outside the law and subject to official suppression. During the Cultural Revolution, from the late 1960s to the late 1970s, all Chinese traditions suffered heavily, including every aspect of religion. Temples and shrines, indeed all old structures, throughout China underwent massive destruction. Since that time, there has been a slow resurgence in state support for religious institutions, particularly those that are useful in foreign intercourse. Supported religions include centralized Buddhist, Taoist, and Christian churches, as well as Islam. All reconstructed temples and pilgrimage sites which are not explicitly Buddhist are termed Taoist, including many that had no such designation in the past.

Mainstream Chinese religion as described above, however, is considered superstition rather than religion and is frowned upon by the government. Such practices continued to take place in secret, especially in rural areas and among families that had maintained themselves in urban areas. Popular religious practices were suppressed not only because of the biases of the educated, reinforced by Western and Marxist viewpoints, but also because a religion based on and reinforcing a strong concept of family was inimical to the concept of a communist society, in which the focus should be on the people as a whole.

With the recent changes in socioeconomic policies and values, a slow revitalization of traditional religious practices is taking place, although it is still officially deemed superstition. This chapter was written just after my return from

China where many examples of traditional religion were in evidence, particularly with regard to burials, in comparison to the recent past. The situation in China, however, is far different from that in Taiwan, Hong Kong, and Singapore.

In Hong Kong, the far southern variation of Chinese religion continues unabated. In Taiwan, although there was superficial influence from the Japanese occupation, Fujien (southeastern coastal) culture continued. When the Nationalist Party government moved to Taiwan, martial law was imposed and all institutions were rigidly controlled. Although Chiang Kai-shek was nominally a Methodist Christian and Taiwan became completely open to Christian missionaries, traditional family and clan religious practices continued unchanged.

With the tremendous growth in economic prosperity, there has been a flourishing of traditional religion, as well as the building of new and the refurbishing of older local temples in the traditional Fujien exuberant style. The recent lifting of martial law has seen a rapid increase in many new religions, all variations of normative Chinese religion, which do not replace but are in addition to the traditional family-oriented practices. As well, certain traditional practices are being institutionalized. For example, there is now an association of spirit possession trance mediums with several thousand members, and they have recently begun a training school.

Modernization, including the development of science and technology on a par with Western countries, has not led to the diminution of Chinese religion, but rather the opposite. This is because, as David K. Jordan (1972,177) has pointed out, Chinese religion is flexible and not linked to any particular ideology. Family and religion are coterminous in Chinese culture; as long as one survives, so will the other.

Chinese Buddhism has also flourished in the twentieth century. In the early part of the century, Buddhists used the model of the YMCA and created modern, responsive institutions. The mistaken Western assumption that Chinese were Buddhists affected Western-influenced Chinese. The breakup of families with the constant warfare of the first half of the century and particularly the loss of family by those who fled to Taiwan or Hong Kong made Buddhism attractive for some, as Buddhism per se denied the importance of family. In overseas Chinese communities in Christian countries, the similarity of Buddhist and Christian institutions made Buddhism a viable alternative to Christianity. All of these factors have led to an increased visibility of Chinese Buddhism, and it has attained an importance not seen for the last thousand years. To give but one example, in the last year or so, it has become popular to wear the smaller Buddhist rosary as a bracelet. Shops selling them have appeared in every town, and spirit possession mediums, who are not Buddhists, wear them as sign of their calling.

Taoism too is beginning to flourish. Continuing cosmic renewal rituals carried out in the imperial court two thousand years in the past, Taoist priests are hired by communities in the present improved economic situation to perform these elaborate ceremonies. In China, all continuing government-approved, popular religious practices have been put in the control of a centralized national Taoist establishment that, as with the Buddhist church, is under the control of the government.

In summary, popular Chinese religion is the oldest continuing religious tradition of which we are aware. It is not in conflict with modernity and tends to flourish with improved economic circumstances.

REFERENCE WORKS

There are many good introductions to Chinese culture and history that would serve as a background to the understanding of popular Chinese religion. One that is both comprehensive and highly readable and, as well, focuses on those aspects central to understanding Chinese ideology is Wolfgang Bauer's *China and the Search for Happiness* (1976). An analysis and description of Chinese religion as a unitary construct over the last four millennia will be found in Jordan Paper's "The Ritual Core of Chinese Religion" (1987).

The earliest Chinese religion is known through two sources: archaeology and a collection of odes, the *Shi*, recorded over two and a half millennia in the past. Two collections of articles concerning very early Chinese religion, the first by an archaeologist and the second by an historian of early Chinese culture are available: K. C. Chang's *Art, Myth, and Ritual: The Path to Authority in Early China* (1983) and Sarah Allan's *The Shape of the Turtle: Myth, Art and Cosmos in Early China* (1991). There are a number of translations of the collection of odes, which include what seem to be ritual songs and myths of dynastic clan origins. The easiest to read remains Arthur Waley's *The Book of Songs* (first published in 1937); the most accurate, Bernhard Karlgren's *The Book of Odes* (1950).

More explicit references to the practice of elite Chinese religion in its early developed phase are found in the three books of ritual, edited about two thousand years ago, that formed part of the canon of the civil service examination system, called the Classics. Available translations of each are by John Steel, *The I-Li or Book of Etiquette and Ceremonial* (first published in 1917); James Legge, *The Li Ki* [Liji] (1885); and Edouard Biot, *Le Tchou-Li ou Rites des Tchou* (first published in 1851). An analysis of these developments will be found in Lester Bilsky's *The State Religion of Ancient China* (1975), and an analytical description of early Chinese festivals has been made by Derk Bodde in *Festivals in Classical China, New Year and Other Annual Observances during the Han Dynasty, 206 B.C.–A.D. 220* (1975). An interesting collection of early accounts of Chinese religious practitioners will be found in Kenneth DeWoskin's *Doctors, Diviners and Magicians of Ancient China: Biographies of Fang-shih* (1983). Popular early religious practices are covered in Michael Loewe's *Ways to Paradise: The Chinese Quest for Immortality* (1979).

Early concepts of cosmology and cosmogony are analyzed in a comparative framework in Norman Girardot's *Myth and Meaning in Early Taoism: The*

Theme of Chaos (hun-tun) (1983). General introductions to the development of Taoism will be found in Holmes Welch's *The Parting of the Way: Lao Tzu and the Taoist Movement* (1958) and Max Kaltenmark's *Lao Tzu and Taoism* (1969). An anthology of related scholarly studies will be found in Holmes Welch and Anna Seidel's, *Facets of Taoism: Essays in Chinese Religion* (1979). Seidel's *La divinisation de Lau Tseu dans le Taoisme des Han* (1969) describes a major development in the formation of institutionalized Taoism.

The introduction of Buddhism into China is analyzed by E. Zürcher in *The Buddhist Conquest of China: The Spread and Adaptation of Buddhism in Early Medieval China* (1959). Chinese Buddhist history is well covered in Kenneth Ch'en's *Buddhism in China, An Historical Survey* (1964). A major aspect of later Buddhism, especially as it impinged on popular traditions, is treated in Daniel Overmeyer's *Folk Buddhist Religion, Dissenting Sects in Late Traditional China* (1976).

Discussion of some later developments in elite Chinese religion will be found in Howard Wechsler's *Offerings of Jade and Silk: Ritual and Symbol in the Legitimation of the T'ang Dynasty* (1985). An interesting study of popular religion in a slightly later period is Valerie Hansen's *Changing Gods in Medieval China, 1127–1276* (1990). The rituals of the ordinary elite in the medieval period is the subject of Patricia Ebrey's *Chu Hsi's Family Rituals* (1991). Shen Fu's unusual autobiography, *Six Records of a Floating Life* (1983), provides an understanding of the integration of religion in a middle-class eighteenth-century person's life. An anthology of studies that bridges the premodern and modern periods with regard to both elite and popular religion is *Death Ritual in Late Imperial and Modern China* (1988), edited by James Watson and Evelyn Rawski.

Modern Popular Religion

The best introduction that focuses on Chinese religion as it is lived is found in Lawrence Thompson's *Chinese Religion: An Introduction* (1989); hence, it is also the recommended introduction to Chinese popular religion. Thompson is also the author of the most important bibliographic reference work in the field, *Chinese Religion in Western Languages: A Comprehensive and Classified Bibliography of Publications in English, French and German through 1980* (1985). An excellent introduction to Chinese religious practices is found in Michael Saso's *Blue Dragon White Tiger: Taoist Rites of Passage* (1990). The subtitle is unfortunate and inaccurate as Saso, a Taoist priest, follows a contemporary trend to label all indigenous religious practices as Taoist. Finally, David Jordan's superb *Gods, Ghosts and Ancestors: Folk Religion in a Taiwanese Village* (1972), although focusing on the practices of southeastern China, contextualizes and explains the interrelationships of popular Chinese religious understanding in general.

The earliest and still the best major source for the details of Chinese religion is J.J.M. de Groot's comprehensive *The Religious System of China* (originally published 1892–1910). De Groot pioneered participant-observation techniques. Similar but incorporating a Christian missionary perspective is Henri Doré's *Researches into Chinese Superstitions* (originally published 1914–1938).

Numerous useful reference works are available. Most important is E.T.C. Werner's *A Dictionary of Chinese Mythology* (1961). Werner is also the author of the more compact *Myths and Legends of China* (1922). Valentine R. Burkhardt's *Chinese Creeds and Customs* (1952–1958) and C.A.S. Williams's *Outlines of Chinese Symbolism and Art Motives* (1932) are also useful specialized encyclopedic dictionaries. Clarence Burton Day's *Chinese Peasant Cults: Being a Study of Chinese Paper Gods* (1969) not only introduces a major aspect of popular religious imagery but also depicts the deities. Wolfram Eberhard's slim *Chinese Festivals* (1972) is a good compendium of the subject. Dun Lichen's *Yenjing suishi ji* (Annual Customs and Festivals in Beijing) (1936), which provides more complete descriptions of all the festivals of one region, also presents a more complete picture of the Chinese ceremonial year as lived. Finally, *T'ung Shu, The Ancient Chinese Almanac* (1986), edited by Martin Palmer, introduces the most popular Chinese book relevant to religion.

There have been a number of sociological studies of Chinese religion, the first major one of which is C. K. Yang's *Religion in Chinese Society* (1961). A good collection of these studies will be found in *Religion and Ritual in Chinese Society* (1974), edited by Arthur Wolf.

One of the best anthropological studies is Emily Ahern's *The Cult of the Dead in a Chinese Village* (1973). Also recommended in this regard is Philip Chesley Baity's *Religion in a Chinese Town* (1975). David Crockett Graham's *Folk Religion in Southwest China* (1961) covers an entire region rather than just a single town. A highly complex but intriguing comparative and historical analysis of particular regional practices is Wolfram Eberhard's *The Local Cultures of South and East China* (1968).

A major analysis of an important set of Chinese sects, those surrounding the creation of texts created by possessed spirit mediums, combining the work of an anthropologist and a historian of religions, is David Jordan and Daniel Overmeyer's *The Flying Phoenix: Aspects of Chinese Sectarianism in Taiwan* (1986). The importance of spirit possession in Chinese religion can also be seen in Alan Elliot's *Chinese Spirit Medium Cults in Singapore* (1955). Jack Potter discusses the phenomenon in Hong Kong in his "Cantonese Shamanism" (1974), and Julian Pas discusses related practices in Taiwan in "Journey to Hell: A New Report of Shamanistic Travel to the Courts of Hell" (1989). His "Temple Oracles in a Chinese City" (1984) discusses a common and important function of Chinese temples.

There are several descriptions of Chinese pilgrimage sites. Dwight Baker's *T'ai Shan* (1925) is of interest because it describes the most important sacred mountain in China, one that has been a sacrificial site for emperors, both mythic and historical, as well as ordinary people from as far back as we can trace

Chinese history up to the present. Baker's description of Mount Tai is also important because it was written prior to much of the destruction of sacred sites that has taken place this century.

Contemporary Taoist practices are covered in two books by Michael Saso: *The Teachings of the Taoist Master Chuang* (1978) and *Taoism and the Rite of Cosmic Renewal* (1972). Early twentieth-century monastic Buddhist practices are covered in Holmes Welch's *The Practice of Chinese Buddhism, 1900–1950* (1967). Sidney Shapiro has compiled a number of studies about Chinese Judaism written by Chinese scholars in his *Jews of Old China* (1984). Christianity in China into the early twentieth century is comprehensively presented by Kenneth Scott Latourette in *A History of Christian Missions in China* (originally published 1929). Contemporary Christianity in China is discussed by G. Thompson Brown, *Christianity in the People's Republic of China* (1986); although, written from a Christian position, it may overly state the growth of Christianity in China. The indigenous Chinese response to Christianity can be found in Jordan Paper's "The Normative East Asian Understanding of Christian Scriptures" (1989).

Of studies of Chinese deities, Glen Dudbridge's *The Legend of Miao-shan* (1978) presents the major popular myth of Guanyin's origin. Steven Harrell's "Men, Women and Ghosts in Taiwanese Folk Religion" (1986) discusses gender aspects of Chinese deities, which also is the subject of Jordan Paper's "The Persistence of Female Spirits in Patriarchal China" (1990).

Until quite recently, the study of Chinese popular religion was primarily a provenance of anthropologists and sociologists in the West; few historians of religions considered it an appropriate subject for study. Catherine Bell in a review article, "Religion and Chinese Culture: Toward an Assessment of 'Popular Religion' " (1989), discusses some of the recent studies being made by religionists. Hubert Seiwert's *Volksreligion und nationale Tradition in Taiwan: Studien zur regionalen Religionsgeschichte einer chinesischen Provinz* (Popular Religion and National Traditions in Taiwan: Studies on the Regional Religious History of a Chinese Province) (1985) is a good example of one of the more recent studies. And it is not until quite recently that Chinese studies of popular religion of the Chinese people have begun to appear. Two good examples are Zong Li and Liu Chun's *Zhongguo minjian zhushen* (Chinese Folk Deities) (1986) and Zhen Zhiming's *Zhongguo shanshu yu congjiao* (Chinese 'Good Books' and Religion) (1988).

As interest in the study of Chinese popular religion among scholars is again growing; although it barely reaches the output of early twentieth-century studies, more insightful, comparative studies can be expected. Julian Pas's "The Human Gods of China, New Perspectives on the Chinese Pantheon" (1991) exemplifies this expected development.

The contemporary resurgence of religion in China has been the subject of a fair number of articles, many included in the anthology, *The Turning of the Tide: Chinese Religion Today* (1989), edited by Julian Pas. The most recent developments in Taiwan and China are sketched in Jordan Paper's "Notes on

Recent Developments Regarding Religion in Taiwan'' (1990) and "Further Notes on Religion in China—1992'' (1992).

NOTE

1. Chinese words in the text are romanized in Pinyin currently used in China. Most of the books cited, however, use the earlier Wade-Giles system, still in use in Taiwan, except titles in French or German, whose languages have their own respective systems. Romanization in article and book titles will not be changed.

BIBLIOGRAPHY

Ahern, Emily. *The Cult of the Dead in a Chinese Village.* Stanford, Calif.: Stanford University Press, 1973.

Allan, Sarah. *The Shape of the Turtle: Myth, Art and Cosmos in Early China.* Albany: State University of New York Press, 1991.

Baity, Philip Chesley. *Religion in a Chinese Town.* Taipei: Orient Cultural Service, 1975.

Baker, Dwight Condo. *T'ai Shan.* Shanghai: Commercial Press, 1925.

Bauer, Wolfgang. *China and the Search for Happiness.* Translated by Michael Shaw. New York: Seabury Press, 1976.

Bell, Catherine. "Religion and Chinese Culture: Toward an Assessment of 'Popular Religion.' " *History of Religions* 29 (1989): 35–57.

Bilsky, Lester James. *The State Religion of Ancient China.* 2 vols. Taipei: Orient Cultural Service, 1975.

Biot, Edouard, trans. *Le Tchou-Li ou Rites des Tchou.* 2 vols. 1851. Reprint. Taipei: Ch'eng-wen Publishing, 1969.

Bodde, Derk. *Festivals in Classical China, New Year and Other Annual Observances during the Han Dynasty, 206 B.C.–A.D. 220.* Princeton, N.J.: Princeton University Press, 1975.

Brown, G. Thompson. *Christianity in the People's Republic of China.* Rev. ed. Atlanta: John Knox Press, 1986.

Burkhardt, Valentine R. *Chinese Creeds and Customs.* 3 vols. Hong Kong: South China Morning Post, 1952–1958.

Chang, K. C. *Art, Myth, and Ritual: The Path to Authority in Early China.* Cambridge, Mass.: Harvard University Press, 1983.

Ch'en, Kenneth K. S. *Buddhism in China, An Historical Survey.* Princeton, N.J.: Princeton University Press, 1964.

Day, Clarence Burton. *Chinese Peasant Cults: Being a Study of Chinese Paper Gods.* 2d ed. Taipei: Ch'eng-wen Publishing, 1969.

DeWoskin, Kenneth J., trans. *Doctors, Diviners and Magicians of Ancient China: Biographies of Fang-shih.* New York: Columbia University Press, 1983.

Doré, Henri. *Researches into Chinese Superstitions.* Translated by M. Kennedy et al. 13 vols. 1914–1938. Reprint. Taipei: Ch'eng-wen Publishing, 1966–1967.

Dudbridge, Glen. *The Legend of Miao-shan.* London: Ithaca Press, 1978.

Dun Lichen. *Yenjing suishi ji* (Annual Customs and Festivals in Beijing). Translated by Derk Bodde. Hong Kong: Henri Vetch, 1936.

Eberhard, Wolfram. *Chinese Festivals.* Taipei: Orient Cultural Service, 1972.

————. *The Local Cultures of South and East China.* Translated by Alide Eberhard. Leiden, Netherlands: E. J. Brill, 1968.

Ebrey, Patricia Buckley. *Chu Hsi's Family Rituals.* Princeton, N.J.: Princeton University Press, 1991.

Elliot, Alan J. A. *Chinese Spirit Medium Cults in Singapore.* London: Royal Anthropological Institute, 1955.

Girardot, Norman. *Myth and Meaning in Early Taoism: The Theme of Chaos (hun-tun).* Berkeley: University of California Press, 1983.

Graham, David Crockett. *Folk Religion in Southwest China.* Washington, D.C.: Smithsonian Press, 1961.

Groot, J.J.M. de. *The Religious System of China.* 6 vols. 1892–1910. Reprint. Taipei: Ch'eng-wen Publishing, 1972.

Hansen, Valerie. *Changing Gods in Medieval China, 1127–1276.* Princeton, N.J.: Princeton University Press, 1990.

Harrell, Steven. "Men, Women and Ghosts in Taiwanese Folk Religion." In *Gender and Religion: On the Complexity of Symbols,* edited by Caroline Walker Bynum, Steven Harrell, and Paula Richman, 97–116. Boston: Beacon Press, 1986.

Jordan, David K. *Gods, Ghosts and Ancestors: Folk Religion in a Taiwanese Village.* Berkeley: University of California Press, 1972.

Jordan, David K., and Daniel L. Overmeyer. *The Flying Phoenix: Aspects of Chinese Sectarianism in Taiwan.* Princeton, N.J.: Princeton University Press, 1986.

Kaltenmark, Max. *Lao Tzu and Taoism.* Translated by Roger Greaves. Stanford, Calif.: Stanford University Press, 1969.

Karlgren, Bernhard, trans. *The Book of Odes.* Stockholm: The Museum of Far Eastern Antiquities, 1950.

Latourette, Kenneth Scott. *A History of Christian Missions in China.* 1929. Reprint. Taipei: Ch'eng-wen Publishing, 1966.

Legge, James, trans. "The Li Ki." In *The Sacred Books of the East,* edited by F. Max Müller. Vols. 27 and 28. Oxford, England: The Clarendon Press, 1885.

Loewe, Michael. *Ways to Paradise: The Chinese Quest for Immortality.* London: George Allen and Unwin, 1979.

Overmeyer, Daniel L. *Folk Buddhist Religion, Dissenting Sects in Late Traditional China.* Cambridge, Mass.: Harvard University Press, 1976.

Palmer, Martin, ed. *T'ung Shu, The Ancient Chinese Almanac.* Boston: Shambhala, 1986.

Paper, Jordan. "Further Notes Regarding Religion in China—1992." *Journal of Chinese Religion* 20 (1992): 215–220.

————. "The Normative East Asian Understanding of Christian Scriptures." *Studies in Religion* 18 (1989): 451–65.

————. "Notes on Recent Developments Regarding Religion in Taiwan." *Journal of Chinese Religion* 18 (1990): 163–65.

————. "The Persistence of Female Spirits in Patriarchal China." *Journal of Feminist Studies in Religion* 6 (1990): 25–40.

————. "The Ritual Core of Chinese Religion." *Religious Studies and Theology* 7, 2–3 (1987): 19–35.

Pas, Julian. "The Human Gods of China: New Perspectives on the Chinese Pantheon." In *From Benares to Beijing: Essays on Buddhism and Chinese Religion in Honour of Prof. Jan Yün-hua,* edited by Koichi Shinohara and Gregory Schopen. Oakville, Ont.: Mosaic, 1991.

————. "Journey to Hell: A New Report of Shamanistic Travel to the Courts of Hell." *Journal of Chinese Religion* 17 (1989): 43–60.

————. "Temple Oracles in a Chinese City." *Journal of the Hong Kong Branch of the Royal Asiatic Society* 24 (1984): 1–45.

Pas, Julian, ed. *The Turning of the Tide: Chinese Religion Today.* Hong Kong: Royal Asiatic Society, Hong Kong Branch, 1989.

Potter, Jack M. "Cantonese Shamanism." In *Religion and Ritual in Chinese Society,* edited by Arthur P. Wolf, 207–31. Stanford, Calif.: Stanford University Press, 1974.

Saso, Michael. *Blue Dragon White Tiger: Taoist Rites of Passage.* Washington, D.C.: The Taoist Center, 1990. (Distributed by the University of Hawaii Press.)

————. *Taoism and the Rite of Cosmic Renewal.* N.p.: Washington State University Press, 1972.

————. *The Teachings of the Taoist Master Chuang.* New Haven, Conn.: Yale University Press, 1978.

Seidel, Anna K. *La divinisation de Lau Tseu dans le Taoisme des Han.* Paris: Ecole Française d'Extrême-Orient, 1969.

Seiwert, Hubert. *Volksreligion und nationale Tradition in Taiwan: Studies zur regionalen Religionsgeschichte einer chinesischen Provinz.* Stuttgart, Germany: Franz Steiner Verlag, 1985.

Shapiro, Sidney, ed. and trans. *Jews of Old China.* New York: Hippocrene Books, 1984.

Shen Fu. *Six Records of a Floating Life.* Translated by Leonard Pratt and Chiang Su-hui. Harmondsworth, England: Penguin Books, 1983.

Steel, John, trans. *The I-Li or Book of Etiquette and Ceremonial.* 2 vols. Taipei: Ch'eng-wen Publishing, 1966.

Thompson, Lawrence. *Chinese Religion: An Introduction.* 4th ed. Belmont, Calif.: Wadsworth Publishing, 1989.

————. *Chinese Religion in Western Languages: A Comprehensive and Classified Bibliography of Publications in English, French and German through 1980.* Tucson: University of Arizona Press, 1985.

Waley, Arthur, trans. *The Book of Songs.* New York: Grove Press, 1960.

Watson, James L., and Evelyn S. Rawski, eds. *Death Ritual in Late Imperial and Modern China.* Berkeley: University of California Press, 1988.

Wechsler, Howard J. *Offerings of Jade and Silk: Ritual and Symbol in the Legitimation of the T'ang Dynasty.* New Haven, Conn.: Yale University Press, 1985.

Welch, Holmes. *The Parting of the Way: Lao Tzu and the Taoist Movement.* London: Methuen, 1958.

————. *The Practice of Chinese Buddhism, 1900–1950.* Cambridge, Mass.: Harvard University Press, 1967.

Welch, Holmes, and Anna Seidel. *Facets of Taoism: Essays in Chinese Religion.* New Haven, Conn.: Yale University Press, 1979.

Werner, E.T.C. *A Dictionary of Chinese Mythology.* New York: Julian Press, 1961.

————. *Myths and Legends of China.* New York: Brentano's, 1922.

Williams, C.A.S. *Outlines of Chinese Symbolism and Art Motives.* 2d ed. Shanghai: Kelley and Walsh, 1932.

Wolf, Arthur P., ed. *Religion and Ritual in Chinese Society.* Stanford, Calif.: Stanford University Press, 1974.

Yang, C. K. *Religion in Chinese Society.* Berkeley: University of California Press, 1961.

Zhen Zhiming. *Zhongguo shanshu yu congjiao* (Chinese 'Good Books' and Religion). Taipei: Hsüeh Sheng Shu Chü, 1988.

Zong Li and Liu Chun. *Zhongguo minjian zhushen* (Chinese Folk Deities). Shijiazhuang, China: Hebei renming chubanshe, 1986.

Zürcher, E. *The Buddhist Conquest of China: The Spread and Adaptation of Buddhism in Early Medieval China.* 2 vols. Leiden, Netherlands: E. J. Brill, 1959.

6

Chinese Herbal Medicine

HSIAO-HUNG LEE

To look at medical services in China today as part of its cultural tradition, one would expect to see the dominance of herbal medicine. Surprisingly, the commonest medical practice in contemporary China is *xi yi* (Western medicine). Statistics show that out of 65,911 hospitals (1980), only a few more than 800 were designated to Chinese medicine. As for medical doctors, Western medical doctors[1] apparently outnumber their traditional Chinese counterparts (out of 1,244,000 doctors, only 300,000 were traditional Chinese medical doctors in 1980).[2] The lopsided figures reveal a sign of China's giant move toward modern systems of medical and health care.

Despite the prevalence of Western medicine in modern China, herbal medicine is unquestionably the "national medicine" with its deep roots both in the country and urban areas. Such household names as *gan mao chong ji* (herbal soup for the treatment of cold and influenza) and *yin huang pian* (herbal pills for the treatment of fever, carbuncles, and inflammation) not only sell well in China, but also find some remarkable ready markets elsewhere in East Asian countries.

The survival of Chinese herbal remedies in spite of the challenge of Western medicine demonstrates their proven medicinal properties rather than their being "old wives' tales." In one case, for example, statistics indicate that a prescription with a history of more than 400 years for the treatment of hemorrhoids has been 96 percent effective on 40,000 patients in the Beijing area (Reid 1987, 10).

Chinese herbal medicine is, on the one hand, a natural healing art. On the other hand, there is always something unknown behind it, its mysterious curing power and ancient tradition. The availability of herbs as medicine has long been recorded as peasant wisdom, the combination of simplicity and complexity, facts and fiction, superstition and folk culture. The Chinese character *yi* (medicine), which is composed of both medicine (*yi*) and sorcery (*wu*), best describes that combination. The development of Chinese herbal medicine, however, has always been connected to the changes of society and the evolution of civilization.

At the dawn of Chinese history, health care was dominated by shamans (*wu*) who used incantation, along with ashes as well as some herbs for the treatment of diseases. No matter how much they knew about the herbs they used, they simply called them ''divine herbs.'' The growing recognition of the application of herbs in treatment of diseases came along with the development of agriculture. While tilling in the field, people began to notice the multiple functions of the ''weeds'' they were ready to eradicate. These weeds were good not only for fertilizer, but also for health care. Ironically, the process of weeding made possible the increasing knowledge of the special functions of herbs.

The legendary figure whose name has been the symbol of both agriculture and medicine is Shen Nong, the ''Divine Husbandman.'' He has been identified as the founder of Chinese herbal medicine. According to some ancient accounts, Shen Nong tasted hundreds of herbs after being inflicted with seventy poisons one day. Shen Nong's story, though a legend, testifies to the fact that the understanding of the medical functions of herbs has been acquired gradually through daily life struggles against diseases. No matter whether people believe stories about Shen Nong, his herbal observations were recorded in *Shen Nong ben cao* or *The Classic of the Materia Medica of the Divine Husbandman,* which includes 364 entries. Each entry is designated to a day of the year.

Nevertheless, the origin of *Shen Nong ben cao* has not been determined. Many sources point out that the book was compiled by anonymous authors in the time period of the first to the second century C.E. (Bensky et al. 1986, 4; Hyatt 1978, 19). During the Southern and Northern Dynasties (420–589 C.E.), the famous Taoist, Tao Hong-Jing (452–536 C.E.), added to *Shen Nong ben cao* 365 herbal entries. Under the Tang Dynasty (618–907 C.E.), *Ben cao* was expanded to 844 entries with twenty-five volumes of illustrations under different classifications. *Shen Nong ben cao* was again revised during the Song Dynasty (960–1279 C.E.). As a result, a brand new herbal classic came into being with 1,746 entries. Doubtless, *Shen Nong ben cao* laid a cornerstone for the establishment of Chinese herbal medicine.

There are many other contributions to that establishment. Huang Di, one of the legendary founding fathers of Chinese history and civilization, is credited with the Yin-Yang and the Five Elements theory as the bases of Chinese herbal medicine. *Huang ti nei ching su wen* (*The Yellow Emperor's Classic of Internal Medicine*) has long been considered the first, most important Chinese medicinal classic. This book summarizes the medical achievements during or before the Spring and Autumn, and Warring States periods (770–221 C.E.). Based on the theory of yin and yang and Five Elements, it explains the relationship between humans and nature and the interrelationship between the inner organs of the human body.

It establishes a complete theoretical system in medicine under which principles of diagnosis, prevention, treatment, and physiology can be developed.

Throughout the history of Chinese civilization, the yin-yang theory has dominated not only philosophy, history, and literature, but also medicine and health care. To explain yin-yang in simple terms, one can find the concept embodied in all natural phenomena. As two primordial cosmic forces, yin and yang are opposing yet complementary to each other. They represent forces of alternating growth and decay. Yin is defined as female, negative, passive, weak, dark, destructive, and characteristic of water; yang as male, positive, active, strong, bright, constructive, and symbolic of fire.

The association of the yin-yang principle to the condition of the human body sets the tone for both the practice and theory of Chinese herbal medicine. Since the practice of Chinese herbal medicine mainly deals with the balance and harmony of yin and yang in the body, the application of herbal drugs for medical treatment aims at the restoration of that balance and the ability of the body to cure itself. Yin and yang control different portions of the body. Yin governs blood and the body's interior. Yang rules *qi* (body atmosphere or vital energy in the body) and the body's exterior. Herbal medicine is used to combat diseases caused by excessive yang or yin in the body. The following are some examples of Chinese herbal medicine in pill form for the treatment of various diseases caused by the imbalance of yin and yang.

The first group comprises medications for clearing inner body heat and excessive yang, including infections, sore throat, and wounds: *jiang ya ping pian* (tablets to decrease blood pressure) clears liver heat, settles excessive liver yang, reduces internal wind, and decreases high blood pressure. *Shuang liao hou feng san* (double ingredient powder for sore throat disease) treats oral infections or disorders; for example, tonsillitis, mouth ulcer, canker sore, toothache, scarlet fever, and other throat disorders caused by heat.

The second group is composed of herbal medicines to dispel cold and to warm the interior: *wu shi cha* (noontime tea) is used to treat wind-cold syndrome such as the flu or common cold.

Apart from the medicines for heat and cold, one unique characteristic of Chinese herbal medicine is the nourishment of yin and yang: *bu zhong yi qi wan* (pills to nourish *qi*) strengthens *qi* and causes *yang qi* to ascend. It is used to treat deficient *qi* in the spleen and stomach with the symptoms of fatigue, shortness of breath, headache, and general feeling of coldness. *Xi yang shen* (American ginseng) nourishes the yin. It is applied to deficient yin, a febrile illness with the symptoms of thirst, weakness, and irritability.

The Five Elements theory presents the traditional Chinese descriptions of the interactivity of the body's organs according to the symbolic representations of natural forces. The sequences of these forces are based on the generative-destructive cycles, wood, fire, earth, metal, and water. Wood produces fire; fire nourishes earth (a popular practice in Chinese agriculture is to burn weeds and stalks for fertility); earth provides ground for mining that makes metal possible; metal can be fused and liquified by heat; water accelerates the growth of wood. The destructive cycle negates the positive cycle of generation. Water extinguishes fire; fire destroys metal by melting it; metal changes the shape of wood by chopping it; wood subjugates earth by penetrating it; earth soaks up water.

Each element represents certain parts of the human body. Wood stands for the liver; fire relates to the heart; earth symbolizes the spleen; metal represents the lungs; and water is associated with the kidneys. The diagnostic functions of the five elements helps to trace the sources of diseases to the imbalance of natural forces in the human body and the deficiencies of the vital organ interrelationship. For example, a specific Chinese herb, *bai zhu* (rhizome), is used when a deficiency in the spleen (earth) and an excess in dampness (water) occur. This particular rhizome strengthens the spleen and dries dampness. Doubtless, Chinese herbal medicine attempts to reflect and to explain the interactivities and relationships among the vital organs of the human body.

As subdivisions of yin and yang, the Five Elements symbolize the five basic elements that encompass not only all the phenomena of nature, but also all bodily functions of a human being. The organs of human bodies, like the Five Elements, are mutually inhibitive and interrelated. With the application of yin-yang and Five Elements theory in Chinese herbal medicine, people are able to see inner-body imbalance as the cause of diseases in dialectical ways. More and more people believe in the existence of both ''pure and evil atmosphere'' in the human body (neither a religious nor a social meaning is attached to pure and evil atmosphere, which simply points to a balance or imbalance in the body). The battles between these two forces never end.

The view of the complementary opposites of yin and yang and the Five Elements dominated the early development of Chinese herbal medicine. Zhang Zhong-Jing (c. 150–219 C.E.) combined his own medical experience and herbal knowledge with philosophical concepts exemplified in yin-yang theory. His time-honored classic, *Shanghan lun* (Treatise on Febrile and Miscellaneous Diseases), summarizes the applications of yin-yang and Five Elements theory in medicine. His major contribution includes the classification of diseases into six types: three yin and three yang. Zhang Zhong-Jing's treatise, which provides detailed prescriptions and manuals, is considered a valuable guidebook for traditional Chinese physicians.

Around the same period of time, Hua Tuo (c. 136–208 C.E.) became the first doctor in Chinese medical history to use herbal ''narcotic soups'' as anaesthesia to operate on patients' stomachs without causing any pain. According to Hua Tuo, the herbal narcotic soups have the function of numbing the patient and helping sufficient recovery with no side effects.

Perhaps the best-known herbal medicine doctor and scholar in China was Li Shi-Zhen, who compiled the classic herbal encyclopedia, *Ben cao gang mu, Grand Materia Medica,* or *Chinese Medicinal Herbs.* Li Shi-Zhen was born in a doctor's family. His father, Li Yan-Wen, was known for his medical skills around his hometown. Since the medical profession at that time had a very low social status, Li Shi-Zhen's father wanted him to study for imperial exams so that he could have a better career than a medical doctor. However, Li Shi-Zhen was too sick to endure the hardship of the exam preparation. Instead, Li fell in love with the studies of herbal medicine. He started a huge project of compiling a complete *Ben cao,* the herbal medica. It took Li Shi-Zhen twenty-seven years to finish the book, which is composed of fifty-two volumes with 1,892 entries of medicinal herbs. During that period, Li Shi-Zhen traveled from south to north to collect sample herbs. He climbed mountains, walked more than 10,000 miles, and visited hundreds of local farmers to get first-hand information about the applications of various medicinal herbs.

Unfortunately, *Ben cao gang mu* was not published during Li's lifetime because he could not afford to print this massive project. In 1596, three years after his death, the book was published owing to help from his friends. *Ben cao gang mu,* which has become a valuable guide as well as a great contribution to the studies of Chinese herbal medicine, summarizes the experience and development in Chinese herbal medicine up to the sixteenth century. Around 1765, Chao Xue Ming, another scholar of Chinese herbal medicine, wrote a book entitled *Supplement to Materia Medica,* adding 716 entries of herbs to Li's book. At that time, the number of herbs for medical purposes had reached 2,608 entries.

The first half of the twentieth century witnessed the decline of traditional Chinese herbal medicine due to social upheavals and Western influences. As a cultural issue, Chinese herbal medicine was under attack by both government personnel and medical doctors for its lack of a scientific basis. The movement toward a scientific and modern China led to a partial rejection of Chinese herbal medicine as ''national medicine'' (see Croizier 1968, 105–31). Economic necessity and political realism, however, urged the preservation of herbal medicine to provide medical services to the rural areas of China, which could not afford to purchase most needed modern pharmaceuticals and hospital equipment. Herbal medicine was not only a part of the Chinese philosophy that reflects the syncretic and symbolic approaches to health and diseases, but also an alternative to Western medicine. Its dialectical theory, tongue and pulse diagnoses, and emphasis on *qi* address the balance of yin and yang in the body, the tonification of the weakened organs, and the strength of the body's resistance to outside attack by germs. In addition, Chinese herbal medicine provides a more affordable and economic health care system to Chinese farmers and workers than Western medicine.

Recently in China, efforts have been made to rehabilitate traditional Chinese herbal medicine by encouraging Western medical doctors to study herbal medicine and by facilitating modern technology to improve the practice of traditional Chinese medicine. The government's new policy of synthesizing Chinese and Western medicine has paved the way for the new era of Chinese medicine. Even in the modern urban hospitals, Chinese medicine departments have become indispensable parts of the medical service and practice. As an important component of China's cultural heritage, traditional herbal medicine will further flourish in the future.

In general, Chinese herbal medicine is an interesting but complicated subject. Any attempt to understand fully the subject should take into account the complexity of Chinese philosophy and cosmology, and their relationship with herbal medicine. In order to examine thoroughly the theory and the practice of Chinese herbal medicine, one has to grasp the essence of Taoism, yin-yang, and the Five Elements theory, as well as the culture that has prevailed for a thousand years.

REFERENCE WORKS

Historical Survey

Since Chinese herbal medicine embodies the classical thought of Taoism, yin-yang theory, and other ancient Chinese philosophy and cosmology, historical surveys and scholarly treatments of Chinese philosophy and cosmology will shed light on the study of Chinese herbal medicine. The most extensive and thorough study of the history of Chinese philosophy is the two-volume *A History of Chinese Philosophy* (1952) by the late Fung Yu-Lan, a world-renowned scholar on Chinese philosophy. Professor Fung's expertise in Chinese philosophy and his exhaustive research have resulted in his clear explanations of yin-yang theory and its applications in Chinese society.

A similar study, *The Chinese Mind: Essentials of Chinese Philosophy and Culture* (1967), edited by Charles A. Moore, although not as thorough and extensive as Fung's book, nonetheless includes valuable information on the concept of the Five Elements. Another book on the classical Chinese philosophers is *The Philosophers of China* (1962) by Clarence Burton Day, a fine study, particularly on ancient Chinese philosophers' contributions to Chinese culture, tradition, civilization, and social development.

Cosmology is an invaluable source of traditional Chinese medical theories because, according to many medical classics, the human body is a microcosm of the natural world. The principal study of Chinese cosmology, John B. Henderson's *The Development and Decline of Chinese Cosmology* (1984), probes the connections between medicine and correlative cosmology. The author examines the relationship between the cycle of the seasons and the occurrence of diseases. Another aspect of traditional Chinese medicine reflects the Taoist way of life and its effects on health. Yet, there is no comprehensive study done on that subject in English. A list of studies and translations of *Tao te ching* by Lao Zi (Tzu), the frequently quoted masterpiece of Taoism, however, offers a key to the Taoist view of the road to healthy body and soul. Victor H. Mair's new translation of *Tao Te Ching: The Classic Book of Integrity and the Way* (1990) is a very faithful and readable one. Thomas Cleary's translation of Chang Po-tuan's *Understanding Reality: A Taoist Alchemical Classic* (1987) is also an excellent translation. *Taoism: The Road to Immortality* (1985) by John Blofeld compares the spirit of Tao with the healthy way of life. The author also explains the fundamental concept of Taoism and its relationship with cosmology, meditation, and the sciences.

Alongside the growth of Chinese herbal medicine, as a part of the Chinese medical system, has been its gradual emergence as an academic discipline. The major recognition of Chinese herbal medicine's place in science and civilization began with Joseph Needham's unprecedented study, *Science and Civilisation in China*, fourteen volumes to date (1954–). Needham reveals the development of Chinese herbal medicine as an important facet of Chinese civilization and science. In Volume 2, *History of Scientific Thought* (1969), Needham explores the relations among health patterns, sexual techniques, and the methods of nourishing life by means of yin and yang. More discussion on herbal medicine can be found in Volume 5, parts 3 (1976) and 4 (1980). In the lengthy chapter, "Alchemy and Chemistry" (parts 3 and 4), Needham surveys the theories and practices of such great physicians and pharmaceutical botanists as Tao Hong-Jing (Tao Hung-Ching) and Li Shi-Zhen. Needham also delves into the relations between alchemy and medicine. Particular sections are given over to the healing property of herbs, herb cultivation, drug production, and the Chinese belief in herbs of immortality. Needham's work of ecumenical scholarship is well indexed. Each volume contains detailed bibliographies.

Other important studies of Chinese medicine as a significant part of the history of Chinese science and civilization include *The Genius of China: 3,000 Years of Science, Discovery, and Invention* (1986), by Robert Temple, and *Heritage of China: Contemporary Perspectives on Chinese Civilization* (1990), edited by Paul S. Ropp. In the chapter "Medicine and Health," Temple traces the historical developments and inventions in the field of medicine and health care. Chronologically, Temple lists such impressive records as the theory of the circulation of the blood,[3] the theory of circadian rhythms in the human body, the science of endocrinology, the treatment of deficiency diseases, and the use of the thyroid hormone. The chapter "Science and Medicine in Chinese History," by Nathan Sivin in *Heritage of China*, provides a further discussion of the interrelations among astrology, medicine, and alchemy.

The primary sources for research and study of Chinese herbal medicine are the Chinese medical classics, most of which are not available in English. Among the more valuable classics in English are *Huang Ti Nei Ching Su Wen, The Yellow Emperor's Classic of Internal Medicine*, translated by Ilza Veith (1972); Li Shi-Zhen's *Chinese Medicinal Herbs*, translated by F. Porter Smith and G. A. Stuart (new edition, 1973); and *Nan-Ching* (The Classic of Difficult Issues), translated by Paul Unschuld (1986).

Despite its legendary myth and symbolic ramifications, Chinese herbal medicine, the world's oldest, safest, most comprehensive medical system, has not been thoroughly explored in the West. Study has been hampered by the lack of appropriate translations of Chinese medical classics, unavailable herbal sources in the West, and poor information exchange between China and the West concerning the development of herbal medicine. Chinese herbal medicine is inarguably the most important part of traditional Chinese medicine. K. C. Wong and Lien-Teh Wu's old but still useful *History of Chinese Herbal Medicine* (1936) offers a comprehensive historical survey of the subject. The authors discuss the much acclaimed medical works of each historical period, their features, and their contributions to Chinese medical literature. The second part focuses on the development of Western medicine in China, the establishment of modern hospitals, the training of medical doctors and nurses, and general analyses of public health in China from 1600 up to 1932.

Another old introductory book on the history of traditional Chinese medicine is *Chinese Medicine* (1934) by William R. Morse. Not as detailed as the *History of Chinese Herbal Medicine,* Morse's book, nevertheless, touches on the major aspects of traditional Chinese medicine: Chinese concepts of human anatomy, herbal treatments, and their interrelationship. The author also discusses individual works on medicine and philosophy in different periods of time that have shaped traditional Chinese medical theories.

Another substantial study on the history of traditional Chinese medicine is *Medicine in China: A History of Ideas* (1985) by Paul U. Unschuld. In this book, Unschuld looks beyond Chinese classical medicine to socioeconomic and political factors that have effected changes in medicine. Excellent as a scholarly survey of traditional Chinese pharmaceutical literature from the third century B.C.E. through the present is Unschuld's *Medicine in China: A History of Pharmaceutics* (1985). As a serious scholar on the history of Chinese medicine, Unschuld introduces classical works on Chinese medicine in *Introductory Readings in Classical Chinese Medicine* (1988). The book contains sixty readings that cover the time period from 90 B.C.E. to 1891 C.E. Other books about the history of Chinese medicine include *Roots of Chinese Culture and Medicine* (1990) by Wei Tsuei and *Forgotten Traditions in Ancient Chinese Medicine* (1989) by Hsu Ta-chun.

Chinese Herbal Medicine

Until recently, there were few scholarly works on Chinese herbal medicine. Even now, the bulk of influential studies on that subject are in Chinese and are very difficult to translate. Nevertheless, books available in English on Chinese herbal medicine have successfully brought the issue of Chinese herbal medicine to the attention of the Western world. Designed as an introduction to Chinese pharmacopeia, Richard Hyatt's *Healing with Chinese Herbs* (1978) opens with two chapters on the historical development of Chinese herbal medicine. Most interestingly, the author examines the application of yin-yang theory to traditional herbal treatments of diseases, and further differentiations of Yin and Yang are described in the book in connection with the principles of diagnosis and pathology.

A useful introduction to the art of practicing Chinese herbal medicine is found in Daniel P. Reid's highly illustrated *Chinese Herbal Medicine* (1987), which includes a list of 200 major herbs. Reid expounds the Taoist theory of cosmic law and structure, humanity's place within that structure, and physical health as an integral part of the law of Chinese medical theory. The book presents insightful analyses of *qi* (vital energy) and the applications of it to Chinese herbal medicine. A large portion of both Hyatt's and Reid's books is the herbal companion. The best part of Reid's book is the color illustration of the herbs with their Latin, Chinese, and English names, followed by detailed descriptions of the herbal parts used and their natural distribution, affinity, effects, dosage, and indications.

Another valuable guide to the use of Chinese herbs, spices, and other foods with medical functions is *Chinese Herbal Medicine* (1984) by Albert Y. Leung. Detailed information is given for each herb: nutritious elements, medical functions, physical characteristics, effects on the human body, and its availability in the United States. The book's unique contribution to the study of Chinese herbal medicine is a clear distinction between the traditional and modern uses of a particular herb or a healthy food.

Delineating Chinese herbal medicine as an art of healing characterizes Stephan Palos's *The Chinese Art of Healing* (1971). The book is divided into two parts: The first states the basic principles of traditional Chinese medicine as an art of healing; the second deals with individual methods of medical treatment, such as acupuncture, moxibustion, respiratory therapy, remedial massage, physiotherapy, and herbal medicaments. Other books that provide a general survey of Chinese herbal medicine are *Herbal Emissaries: Bringing Chinese Herbs to the West* (1992), by Steven Foster and Yve Chongxi; *The Herbs of Life: Health and Healing Using Western and Chinese Techniques* (1992), by Leslie Tierra; *Secrets of the Chinese Herbalists* (1987) by Richard M. Lucas; *Chinese Herbology Made Easy* (1986), by Maoshing Ni; *Survey of Traditional Chinese Medicine* (1986), by Claude Larre, Jean Schatz, and Elisabeth Rochat de la Valle; and *Chinese Tonic Herbs* (1987), by Ron Teeguarden.

Dr. John H. Shen's *Chinese Medicine* (1980) offers a professional herbalist's perspective of the topic. Born in 1914 in Shanghai, Shen is a native Chinese who has practiced traditional Chinese medicine for more than fifty years in mainland China, Taiwan, Hong Kong, Malaysia, Indonesia, Thailand, Japan, Korea, and the United States. Although this book gives the author's insights on the creative and control cycle of the Five Elements, forms of energy, the causes of sickness, and the conditions of illness, it is more geared to professionals than to a general audience. Henry C. Lu's *Legendary Chinese Healing Herbs* (1991) is another book written by a practitioner and teacher of traditional Chinese medicine on the topic of the Chinese materia medica. Lu discusses Chinese herbal remedies and therapeutic uses of herbs that have also appeared in many Chinese legends.

In addition to the general surveys and herbal companions, Margaret A. Naeser's *Outline Guide to Chinese Herbal Patent Medicines in Pill Form* (1990) is the first book to introduce patent medicine, a form of traditional Chinese medicine, to the Western world. Patent medicines are mostly made out of medicinal herbs and animal parts. Therefore, Naeser's book marks an emphasis on contemporary pharmaceutical products from traditional herbal sources. Each of the more than 175 patent medicines has a sample picture to show the general front design and the trade mark. The patent medicines are classified into different categories according to their medical functions, such as "Treat Exogenous Conditions," "Expel Summer Heat," "Clear Heart," and "Warm the Interior." There is also a list of stores in the United States where Chinese patent medicines can be purchased.

More specialized topics on Chinese herbal medicine can be found in *Immunology and Chinese Herbal Medicine* (1986), by Pi-Kwang Tsung and Hong-yen Hsu; *Zang Fu: The Organ Systems of Traditional Chinese Medicine* (1985), by Jeremy Ross; *How to Stay Healthy a Lifetime without Medicines* (1979), by Betty Yu-Lin Ho; *Chinese Herbs: Their Botany, Chemistry and Pharmacodynamics* (1991), by John Keys; *Signs of Health: Traditional Chinese Medicine for Modern Living* (1991), edited by Ramona A. Moody and Lee C. Overholser; *Second Spring: A Guide to Healthy Menopause through Traditional Chinese Medicine* (1990), by Honora L. Wolfe; *AIDS and Its Treatment: According to Traditional Chinese Medicine* (1991), by Bing-shan Huang; *Allergies and Chinese Herbal Medicine* (1987) and *Arthritis and Chinese Herbal Medicine* (1987), by Pi-Kwang Tsung and Hong-yen Hsu; and *Regeneration of Health: Nourishing Body Systems with Chinese Herbal Formulas* (1991) and *Regeneration of Health: Nourishing Body Systems with Chinese Food Herb Formulas* (1989), by John Finnegan.

The following group is composed of medical doctors whose books reflect their experiences during visits to China and their thoughts on Chinese health care in which herbal medicine plays an important role. David Eisenberg's *Encounters with Qi: Exploring Chinese Medicine* (1985) is one of the very few texts written by an American that touches knowledgeably on the essence of traditional Chinese medicine and the important basis for the practice of herbal medicine. As the first exchange medical student from the United States to study traditional Chinese medicine from 1977 through 1985, Eisenberg had the privilege of having the finest teachers, a custom-tailored curriculum, and one-on-one tutorials offered by one of the best traditional Chinese medical colleges in China, the Beijing Institute of Traditional Chinese Medicine. In this well-written and very readable book, Eisenberg has recorded the essence of his classes, the conversations between him and his professors on such topics as *Qi* (vital energy), the theory of yin and yang and the Five Elements, diagnoses of tongues and pulses, and the functions of acupuncture. As part of his studies of traditional Chinese medicine, Eisenberg was assigned to work in the acupuncture, massage, and herbal medicine clinics to practice as a traditional Chinese medical doctor. With his previous training at Harvard Medical School, the author is able to compare the Western and traditional Chinese medical systems and to synthesize what he has learned about traditional Chinese medicine.

K. K. Jain is another medical doctor who has offered observations and analyses of the traditional Chinese medical system through first-hand experience. *The Amazing Story of Health Care in New China* (1973) incorporates his own observations during his visit to China and information he collected from other physicians who had visited China after 1971. Jain is particularly interested in the joint efforts between Western medicine and traditional Chinese medicine. A specific chapter is devoted to discussion of herbs and modern drugs. The author offers very brief information about the testing of herbs in modern hospitals, especially in surgical conditions. He has also conducted surveys on research in herbs and on the pharmaceutical industry in China.

The rising tide of new studies on political influences on the Chinese health care system has brought to readers such pioneer works as Ralph C. Croizier's *Traditional Medicine in Modern China* (1968), Marilynn M. Rosenthal's *Health Care in the People's Republic of China* (1987), and *Health Care and Traditional Medicine in China, 1800–1982* (1983) by S. M. Miller and J. A. Jewell. Although these books deal with the Chinese health care system in general, they, to some degree, all discuss the relationship among social changes, political influence, and the development of traditional Chinese herbal medicine. Croizier examines the events and issues in the history of traditional Chinese medicine in great detail and depth. He discusses the interrelationship between medicine and the cultural background in contemporary China. A variety and a great amount of documents have been searched to reveal and to reflect both Chinese Communist Party and Nationalist Party policies on traditional medicine. By tracing the debate on traditional medicine in modern China, Croizier's book illuminates some important issues aroused by the medical controversy: the drive for modernization and the concern for cultural continuity.

Rosenthal's impressive study of the Chinese medical system, *Health Care in the People's Republic of China,* gives extensive attention to the relations between modernization and the fate of traditional medicine in China. Rosenthal moves away from a simplistic concern with the Chinese health care system to the political driving forces behind Mao's attempt to preserve traditional Chinese medicine and to bring it to the modern world. The author's analyses of the Chinese medical system and facilities present a clear picture of how herbal medicine is used in rural areas in China.

Part 3 of *Health Care and Traditional Medicine in China, 1800–1982,* ''Traditional Medicine,'' examines the theoretical basis of traditional Chinese medicine, acupuncture and moxibustion, Chinese materia medica, and the integration and separation of traditional Chinese medicine and modern Western medicine. The authors have explored topics of early Western contacts, the Chinese medical system under the attack of a new generation of intellectuals, government regulations concerning the practice of traditional Chinese medicine, and its remaining problems under communist leadership.

Materia Medica

Very few reference works on Chinese herbal medicine are available to the English reader since research on that subject is not fully developed. Information about Chinese herbal medicine can be found in broader-based works on the history of Chinese medicine, Chinese science and technology, Chinese philosophy and cosmology, and the Chinese health care system. The starting place for any serious exploration of the subject is materia medica. The single most important materia medica in Chinese with an English translation is Li Shi-Zhen's *Ben cao gang mu* (*Chinese Medicinal Herbs* or Grand Materia Medica, reprinted in 1973). Other useful historical materia medica in Chinese are Tao Hong-jing, *Ben cao jing ji zhu* (Collection of Commentaries on the Classic of the Materia Medica, 500); authors unknown, *Shen Nong ben cao jing* (Divine Husbandman's Classic of the Materia Medica, later Han Dynasty); Xu Yan-Chun, *Ben cao fa hui* (Elaboration of the Materia Medica, Ming Dynasty); Wang Ang, *Ben cao bei yao* (Essentials of the Materia Medica, Qing Dynasty, 1751); Kou Zong-Shi, *Ben cao yan yi* (Extension of the Materia Medica, Song Dynasty, 1116); Lu He, *Shi wu ben cao* (Food as Materia Medica, Ming Dynasty); Chen Jia-Mo, *Ben cao meng quan* (Hidden Aspects of the Materia Medica, Ming Dynasty, c. 1560); Wu Rui, *Ri yong ben cao* (Household Materia Medica, Yuan Dynasty, c. 1350); Su Song, *Tu jing ben cao* (Illustrated Classic of the Materia Medica, Song Dynasty, 1061); Zhang Lu, *Ben jing feng yuan* (Journey to the Origin of the Classic of Materia Medica, Qing Dynasty, c. 1670); Tang Shen-Wei, *Zheng lei ben cao* (Materia Medica Arranged According to Pattern, Southern Song Dynasty, 1082); Wang Hao-Gu, *Tang ye ben cao* (Materia Medica for Decoction, Yuan Dynasty, 1306); Li Xun, *Hai yao ben cao* (Materia Medica of Herbs from Seas, Tang Dynasty); Zhen Quan, *Yao xing ben cao* (Materia Medica of Medicinal Properties, Tang Dynasty, c. 600); Zhao Xue-Min, *Ben cao gang mu shi yi* (Omissions from the Grand Materia Medica, Qing Dynasty, 1765); Li Zhong-Li, *Ben cao yuan shi* (Origins of the Materia Medica, Ming Dynasty); author and date unknown, *Ben cao zheng* (Rectification of the Materia Medica); author and date unknown, *Ben cao zai xin* (Renewed Materia Medica); Zhu Zhen-Heng (also known as Zhu Dan-Xi), *Ben cao yan yi bu yi* (Supplement to the Extension of the Materia Medica, Yuan Dynasty, c. 1347); Wu Yi-Luo, *Ben cao cong xin* (Thoroughly Revised Materia Medica, Qing Dynasty, 1751).

Although most of the materia medica listed above are not available in English, one recent and relatively comprehensive English version of Chinese materia medica, *Chinese Herbal Medicine: Materia Medica* (1986), compiled and translated by Dan Bensky, Andrew Gamble, Lilian L. Bensky, and Ted Kaptchuk, is a great addition to the Western scholarship on Chinese herbal medicine. The sources of this book are from Chinese materia medica, dictionaries and handbooks of Chinese herbal medicine, and leading textbooks used in traditional Chinese medical colleges. This materia medica is categorized by herbal functions. Each entry contains pharmaceutical, botanical, Mandarin, Japanese, Korean, and English names, as well as their literal English translations; properties; texts in which the herbal description first appeared; functions and clinical use; major combinations; cautions; dosage; major known ingredients; and pharmacological and clinical research. Libraries with a research collection of Chinese medicine should obtain this book.

An excellent translation of Yanchi Liu's *The Essential Book of Traditional Chinese Medicine*, translated by Fang Tingyu and Chen Laidi (1988), provides a good example of collaboration between American and Chinese scholars to introduce more scholarly books on the modern practice of traditional Chinese medicine to the West. The first volume introduces the theoretical bases of traditional Chinese medicine; the second volume contains a detailed, well-arranged materia medica. Other materia medica available in English include Bernard E. Read's *Chinese Materia Medica*, vol. 1, *Dragon and Snake Drugs* (1934), vol. 2, *Fish Drugs* (1939), vol. 3, *Insect Drugs* (1941), *Chinese Materia Medica: Turtle and Shellfish Drugs* (1937), *Avian Drugs* (1932), *A Compendium of Minerals and Stones* (1936), and *Chinese Materia Medica: Animal Drugs* (1931). See also, G. A. Stuart, *Chinese Materia Medica: Vegetable Kingdom* (1911); Hong-yen Hsu, Yuh-pan Chen, and Shuenn-jyi Shen, *Oriental Materia Medica* (1986); and *Chinese Tonic Herbs* (1992), published by Gordon Press Publishers.

The title, *A Barefoot Doctor's Manual,* is somewhat misleading, since "barefoot doctors" are paramedical practitioners who have only partially gone through strenuous medical training but are given permission by the government to practice medicine in the rural areas because of the great demand for a large number of medical professionals in the country.[4] The volume, *A Barefoot Doctor's Manual* (1977), however, is more suitable for Western doctors without Chinese herbal medicine background than the title suggests. A guidebook by nature, this manual contains chapters of traditional Chinese understanding of the human body and Chinese medical plants, which can be useful for Western practitioners of Chinese herbal medicine. Altogether, 522 medicinal herbs are depicted with their Chinese and scientific names and synonyms, properties and action, conditions, and preparations. Extensive descriptions of folk treatments, such as acupuncture, skin scraping, blood letting, and Chinese massage, make this manual a good reference guide for anyone who is interested in traditional Chinese medicine.

Readers seeking information about traditional Chinese herbal medicine have several fine dictionaries and handbooks to consult. Wee Yeow Chin and Hsuan Keng's *An Illustrated Dictionary of Chinese Medicinal Herbs* (1992) has rich illustrations and concise definitions for commonly used Chinese medicinal herbs that are not familiar to Western readers. Less significant to scholars of Chinese herbal medicine, Nigel A. Wiseman's *Glossary of Chinese Medical Terms,* Vol. 1, *Points and Terms* (1989), however, is helpful for understanding the terms and medical jargon that readers will encounter in reading translated versions of original documents and materials on Chinese herbal medicine. The growing demand for a concise but accurate translation of Chinese herbal terminology can find a satisfactory answer in *Dictionary of Traditional Chinese Medicine* (1984), published by China Books and Periodicals in San Francisco. A welcome addition to Chinese medicine dictionaries, F. Liu and Yan Mau Liu's *Chinese Medical*

Terminology (Chinese and English, 1980) and *English-Chinese Medical Terminology* (English and Chinese, 1980) represent early efforts to provide readers access to Chinese medical terminology from Chinese to English and from English to Chinese. Another comprehensive medical dictionary is *English-Chinese Medical Dictionary* (1980), published by French and European Publications, New York City.

Although there is no specific bibliography designated for traditional Chinese herbal medicine, Theodora Andrews's *A Bibliography on Herbs, Herbal Medicine, "Natural" Foods, and Unconventional Medical Treatment* (1982) has several entries on Chinese medicinal herbs, the Chinese way in medicine, and Chinese herbs: their botany, chemistry, and pharmacodynamics. The most valuable medical index for Chinese herbal practitioners and scholars is *Index Medicus* available through online search or on CD ROM, which provides citations and abstracts of a wide range of topics on Chinese herbal medicine and its applications from professional journals throughout the world.

RESEARCH COLLECTIONS

Traditional Chinese herbal medicine is found in great profusion in research collections in China. Almost all traditional Chinese medical colleges and institutions have good research collections in their libraries. Beijing College of Traditional Chinese Medicine and Shanghai College of Traditional Chinese Medicine should be considered as good places for research collections of Chinese herbal medicine. The Academy of Traditional Chinese Medicine will help any scholar or researcher locate rare books or original documents concerning the theory and practice of herbal medicine in China.

In the United States, the most complete collection for medical research is in the National Library of Medicine, 8600 Rockville Pike, Bethesda, Maryland, 20209. Gest Oriental Library at Princeton University has a fine collection of traditional Chinese medicine. The collection emphasis is on pre-twentieth century works on traditional medicine in all areas. Contemporary works on acupuncture and materia medica are also collected. The University of California, San Francisco, has collections of Chinese medicine that consist of titles in Chinese, Japanese, and other languages from the twelfth century on. Another American center for traditional Chinese medicine is the Francis A. Countway Library of Medicine, 10 Shattuck Street, Boston, Massachusetts, 02115. Combining resources of the Harvard Medical School and the Boston Medical Library, Francis A. Countway Library is able to provide strong research collections. Other university libraries that have limited collections of traditional Chinese herbal medicine include Yale University, Medical Historical Library, 333 Cedar Street, New Haven, Connecticut, 06510; Johns Hopkins University, Institute of the History of Medicine, 1900 E. Monument Street, Baltimore, Maryland, 21205; Columbia University, Butler Library, 535 W. 114 Street, New York, New York 10027; and the University of Michigan, Asia Library, Ann Arbor, Michigan 48109.

NOTES

1. In China, Western medical doctors are those medical doctors who have been trained by and have worked under medical systems other than the traditional Chinese medical system.

2. Statistics come from the following books: *China ABC,* Beijing: New World Press, 1985, pp. 149–51; *China: An Introduction,* Beijing: Foreign Languages Press, 1984, pp. 61–65. See also Marilynn M. Rosenthal, *Health Care in the People's Republic of China: Moving Toward Modernization* (1987, 193–95).

3. Temple points out that the idea of the circulation of the blood ''occurred in China about two thousand years before it found acceptance in the West'' (1986, 123–24).

4. The term ''barefoot doctor'' originates from the popular practice in the rural areas in China, especially in the southern part, where paramedical professionals work in the field barefooted to help farm as well as to provide first aid and other medical treatments.

BIBLIOGRAPHY

A Barefoot Doctor's Manual (Contemporary Chinese Paramedical Manual). Philadelphia: Running Press, 1977.

Academy of Traditional Chinese Medicine, Peking Staff. *An Outline of Chinese Acupuncture.* Monterey Park, Calif.: Chan's Corporation, n.d.

Andrews, Theodora. *A Bibliography on Herbs, Herbal Medicine, "Natural" Foods, and Unconventional Medical Treatment.* Littleton, Colo.: Libraries Unlimited, 1982.

Austin, Robert, and Koichiro Ueda. *Bamboo.* New York: Walker/Weatherhill, 1970.

Bailey, Liberty Hyde. *Manual of Cultivated Plants.* New York: Macmillan, 1949.

––––––. *The Standard Cyclopedia of Horticulture.* 3 vols. New York: Macmillan, 1942.

Beijing Institute of Traditional Chinese Medicine Staff. *Fundamentals of Chinese Medicine.* Translated by Nigel Wiseman and Andrew W. Ellis; edited by Paul Zmiewski. Brookline, Mass.: Paradigm Publications, 1987.

Bensky, Dan, and Randall Barolet. *Chinese Herbal Medicine: Formulas and Strategies* (translation from Chinese). Seattle: Eastland Press, 1990.

Bensky, Dan, Andrew Gamble, Lilian L. Bensky, and Ted Kaptchuk, comp. and trans. *Chinese Herbal Medicine: Materia Medica.* Seattle: Eastland Press, 1986.

Berk, William, ed. *Chinese Healing Arts: Internal Kung Fu.* Translated by John Dudgeon. Burbank, Calif.: Unique Publications, 1979. Reprint. 1986.

Blofeld, John. *Taoism: The Road to Immortality.* Boston: Shambhala, 1985.

Bowers, John Z., J. William Hess, and Nathan Sivin, eds. *Science and Medicine in Twentieth-Century China.* Ann Arbor: University of Michigan, Center for Chinese Studies, 1989.

Braun, R. *List of Medicines Exported from Hangkow and Other Yangtze Ports.* Shanghai: Inspector General of Customs, 1909.

Buchman, D. D. *Herbal Medicine.* New York: Outlet Book Company, 1988.

Buchman, Dian D. *Herbal Medicine: The Natural Way to Get Well and Stay Well.* New York: McKay, David, Company, 1979.

Chang, Chun-yuan. *Creativity and Taoism.* New York: Harper and Row, 1970.

Chang, H. M., and P. P. But, eds. *Pharmacology and Applications of Chinese Materia Medica.* Vol. 1. River Edge, N.J.: World Scientific Publishing Company, 1988.

Chang, Jolan. *The Tao of Love and Sex*. London: Granada, 1979.

Chang, Po-tuan. *Understanding Reality: A Taoist Alchemical Classic*. Translated by Thomas Cleary. Honolulu: University of Hawaii Press, 1987.

Chen, C. R. *Zhong chao yao bai ke quan shu* (Encyclopedia of Chinese Drugs). 2 vols. Hong Kong: Shanghai Publishing Co., 1962.

Cheung, S. C., and N. H. Li, eds. *Xiang Gang de Zhong yi chao yao* (Chinese Medicinal Herbs of Hong Kong). Vol. 1. Hong Kong: Commercial Press, 1978. (In Chinese and English)

Chinese Herbs Made Easy. Provo, Utah: Woodland Health Books, n.d.

Chinese Pharmacopeia. Vol. 1. Beijing: People's Medical Publishing House, 1977. (In Chinese)

Chinese Tonic Herbs. New York: Gordon Press Publishers, 1992.

Claus, Edward P. *Phamacognosy*. 4th ed. Philadelphia: Lea and Fibiger, 1961.

Croizier, Ralph C. *Traditional Medicine in Modern China*. Cambridge, Mass.: Harvard University Press, 1968.

Current Topics in Chinese Science, Section G: Medical Science. Vol. 2. New York: Gordon and Breach Science Publishers, 1984.

Current Topics in Chinese Science, Section G: Medical Science. Vol. 3. New York: Gordon and Breach Science Publishers, 1984.

Dale, Ralph A. *The Complete Guide to Acupuncture: The Five-Volume Reference Library*. North Miami Beach, Fla.: Dialectic Publications, 1990.

Day, Clarence Burton. *The Philosophers of China*. New York: Philosophical Library, 1962.

Dictionary of Traditional Chinese Medicine. San Francisco: China Books and Periodicals, 1984.

Eisenberg, David, and Thomas Lee Wright. *Encounters with Qi: Exploring Chinese Medicine*. New York: W. W. Norton, 1985.

Ellis, Andrew W. *Fundamentals of Chinese Acupuncture*. Edited by Richard Feit. Rev. ed. Brookline, Mass.: Paradigm Publications, 1991.

English-Chinese Medical Dictionary. New York: French and European Publications, 1980.

Faiservis, Walter A., Jr. *The Origins of Oriental Culture*. New York: New American Library, 1959.

Femald, M. L. *Gray's Manual of Botany*. New York: American Book Company, 1950.

Finnegan, John. *Regeneration of Health: Nourishing Body Systems with Chinese Food Herb Formulas*. 3d ed. Mill Valley, Calif.: Elysian Arts, 1989.

————. *Regeneration of Health: Nourishing Body Systems with Chinese Herbal Formulas*. 5th ed. Mill Valley, Calif.: Elysian Arts, 1991.

J. E. Fogarty International Center for Advanced Study in the Health Sciences. *A Barefoot Doctor's Manual*. Washington, D.C.: National Institutes of Health, 1974. (U.S. Department of Health, Education, and Welfare Publication no. NIH 75-695; translation of Chinese text)

Foster, Steven, and Yve Chongxi. *Herbal Emissaries: Bringing Chinese Herbs to the West*. Rochester, Vt.: Inner Traditions International, 1992.

Fulder, Stephen. *Tao of Medicine*. Rochester, Vt.: Inner Traditions International, 1991.

Fung Yu-Lan. *A History of Chinese Philosophy*. 2 vols. Princeton, N.J.: Princeton University Press, 1952.

Gosselin, R. E., et al. *Clinical Toxicology of Commercial Products: Acute Poisoning*. 4th ed. Baltimore, Md.: Williams and Wilkins, 1976.

Grieve, Maude. *A Modern Herbal.* 2 vols. New York: Dover, 1971.

Griffin, LaDean. *The Return to Herbal Medicine.* Salt Lake City, Utah: Hawkes Publishing, 1979.

Gumbel, Dietrich. *Principles of Holistic Skin Therapy with Herbal Essences.* Translated by Ritva Abao. Portland, Oreg.: Medicina Biologica, 1986.

Hallowell, Michael. *Herbal Healing: A Practical Introduction to Medicinal Herbs.* Garden City Park, N.Y.: Avery Publishing Group, 1989.

Hammer, Leon. *Dragon Rises, Red Bird Flies: Psychology and Chinese Medicine.* Barrytown, N.Y.: Station Hill Press, 1980.

Henderson, John B. *The Development and Decline of Chinese Cosmology.* New York: Columbia University Press, 1984.

Herbal Pharmacology in the People's Republic of China: A Trip Report of the American Herbal Pharmacology Delegation. Washington, D.C.: National Academy of Sciences, 1975.

Ho, Betty Yu-Lin. *How to Stay Healthy a Lifetime without Medicines.* New York: Juvenescent Research Corporation, 1979.

————. *Immediate Hints to Health Problems.* Edited by Betty Elkan. New York: Juvenescent Research Corporation, 1991.

Holmes, Peter. *The Energetics of Western Herbs: Integrating Western & Oriental Herbal Medicine Traditions.* Vol. I. Boulder, Colo.: Artemis Press, 1989.

Hsu, Hong-yen, Yuh-pan Chen, and Shuenn-jyi Shen. *Oriental Materia Medica.* Long Beach, Calif.: Orient Heal Arts, 1986.

Hsu Ta-chun. *Forgotten Traditions in Ancient Chinese Medicine.* Brookline, Mass.: Paradigm Publications, 1989.

Huang, Bing-shan. *AIDS and Its Treatment: According to Traditional Chinese Medicine.* Translated by Di Fu and Bob Flaws. Boulder, Colo.: Blue Poppy Enterprises Press, 1991.

Huang ti nei ching su wen—The Yellow Emperor's Classic of Internal Medicine. New ed. Translated by Ilza Veith. Berkeley: University of California Press, 1972.

Huard, Pierre, and Ming Wong. *Chinese Medicine.* New York: McGraw-Hill, 1968.

Hume, Edward H. *Chinese Way in Medicine.* 1940. Reprint. Westport, Conn.: Hyperion Press, 1975.

Hyatt, Richard. *Healing with Chinese Herbs.* New York: Schocken Books, 1978.

Jain, K. K. *The Amazing Story of Health Care in New China.* Emmaus, Pa.: Rodale Press, 1973.

Johnson, Obed S. *A Study of Chinese Alchemy.* 1928. Reprint. Salem, N.H.: Ayer Company Publishers, 1974.

Kan, Lai-bing. *Parasitic Infections of Man & Animals: A Bibliography of Articles in Chinese Medical Periodicals, 1949–1964.* Ann Arbor, Mich.: Books on Demand, 1966. Reprint. 1991.

Kaptchuk, Ted J. *The Web That Has No Weaver: Understanding Chinese Medicine.* Chicago: Congdon and Weed, 1985.

Keys, John. *Chinese Herbs: Their Botany, Chemistry and Pharmacodynamics.* Boston: Charles E. Tuttle, 1991.

Kleinman, Arthur, Peter Kunstadter, E. Russell Alexander, and James L. Gale, eds. *Medicine in Chinese Cultures: Comparative Studies of Health Care in Chinese and Other Societies.* Washington, D.C., National Institutes of Health, 1974.

Koo, A., H. W. Yeung, and W. W. Tso, eds. *Advances in Chinese Medicinal Materials Research: Proceedings of the International Symposium.* River Edge, N.J.: World Scientific Publishing Company, 1985.

Lampton, David M. *The Politics of Medicine in China: The Policy Process, 1949–1977.* Boulder, Colo.: Westview Press, 1977.

Lao Tzu. *Tao Te Ching: The Classic Book of Integrity and the Way.* Translated by Victor H. Mair. New York: Bantam Books, 1990.

Larre, Claude, Jean Schatz, and Elisabeth Rochat de la Valle. *Survey of Traditional Chinese Medicine.* Columbia, Md.: Traditional Acupuncture Institute, 1986.

Leung, Albert Y. *Chinese Herbal Medicine.* New York: Universe Books, 1984.

———. *Encyclopedia of Common Natural Ingredients Used in Food, Drugs and Cosmetics.* New York: Wiley-Interscience, 1980.

Li Shi-Zhen. *Ben cao gang mu. (Chinese Medicinal Herbs).* Translated by F. Porter Smith and G. A. Stuart. New ed. San Francisco: Georgetown Press, 1973.

Liang, Jian-Hui. *A Handbook of Traditional Chinese Dermatology.* Edited by Bob Flaws; translated by Zhang Ting-Liang. Boulder, Colo.: Blue Poppy Enterprises Press, 1987.

Liu, F., and Yan Mau Liu. *Chinese Medical Terminology.* Hong Kong: Commercial Press, 1980.

———. *English-Chinese Medical Terminology* New York: French and European Publications, 1980. (In English and Chinese)

Liu, Yanchi. *The Essential Book of Traditional Chinese Medicine.* Translated by Fang Tingyu and Chen Laidi. New York: Columbia University Press, 1988.

Lu, Henry C. *Legendary Chinese Healing Herbs.* New York: Sterling Publishing Company, 1991.

Lu, K. S. *Encyclopedia of Chinese Drugs and Their Chemical Constituents.* Hong Kong: Shanghai Press, 1955. (In Chinese)

Lu, S. *Chinese Drugs in the West.* Hong Kong: Deli Book Co., 1978.

Lucas, Anelissa. *Chinese Medical Modernization: Comparative Policy Continuities, 1930's–1980's.* Westport, Conn.: Greenwood Press, 1982.

Lucas, Richard M. *Secrets of the Chinese Herbalists.* Rev. ed. New York: Prentice Hall, 1987.

Lust, John B. *The Herb Book.* Simi Valley, Calif.: Benedict Lust, 1974.

Mann, Felix. *Acupuncture: The Chinese Art of Healing.* 3d ed. London: William Heinemann Medical Books, 1978.

Maoshing Ni. *Chinese Herbology Made Easy.* Santa Monica, Calif.: Shrine of the Eternal Breath of Tao, 1986.

March, Kathryn G., and Andrew L. March. *The Wild Plant Companion: A Fresh Understanding of Herbal Food and Medicine.* Lakewood, Colo.: Meridian Hill Publications, 1986.

Miller, S. M., and J. A. Jewell. *Health Care and Traditional Medicine in China, 1800–1982.* London: Routledge and Kegan Paul, 1983.

Moody, Ramona A., and Lee C. Overholser, eds. *Signs of Health: Traditional Chinese Medicine for Modern Living.* San Diego, Calif.: Empire Publishing, 1991.

Moore, Charles A. *The Chinese Mind: Essentials of Chinese Philosophy and Culture.* Honolulu: University of Hawaii Press, 1967.

Morse, William R. *Chinese Medicine.* New York: Paul B. Hoeber, 1934.

Naeser, Margaret A. *Outline Guide to Chinese Herbal Patent Medicines in Pill Form.* 2d ed. Boston: Boston Chinese Medicine, 1990.

Nan-Ching: The Classic of Difficult Issues. Translated by Paul U. Unschuld. Berkeley: University of California Press, 1986.

Needham, Joseph, et al. *Science and Civilisation in China.* 14 vols. to date. Cambridge, England: Cambridge University Press, 1954– .

Palos, Stephan. *The Chinese Art of Healing.* New York: Herder and Herder, 1971.

Porkert, Manfred, and Christian Ullmann. *Chinese Medicine.* New York: Henry Holt and Company, 1990.

Read, Bernard E. *Chinese Materia Medica: Animal Drugs.* Hong Kong: Commercial Press, 1931. Reprint. Pasadena, Calif.: Oriental Book Store, 1982.

———. *Chinese Materia Medica: Insect Drugs, Dragon and Snake Drugs, Fish Drugs.* Hong Kong: Commercial Press, 1934. Reprint. Chinese Materia Medica no. 2. Pasadena, Calif.: Oriental Book Store, 1984.

———. *Chinese Materia Medica: Turtle and Shellfish Drugs, Avian Drugs, a Compendium of Minerals and Stones.* Hong Kong: Commercial Press, 1932. Reprint. Chinese Material Medica no. 3. Pasadena, Calif.: Oriental Book Store, 1982.

———. *Chinese Medicinal Plants from the Pen T'sao Kang Mu.* Pasadena, Calif.: Oriental Book Store, 1977.

———. *Famine Foods List in the Chiu Huang Pen Ts'ao.* Pasadena, Calif.: Oriental Book Store, 1977.

Reid, Daniel P. *Chinese Herbal Medicine.* Boston: Shambhala, 1987.

Risse, Guenter B., ed. *Modern China and Traditional Chinese Medicine.* Springfield, Ill.: Charles C. Thomas Publisher, 1973.

Ropp, Paul S., ed. *Heritage of China: Contemporary Perspectives on Chinese Civilization.* Berkeley: University of California Press, 1990.

Rosenthal, Marilynn M. *Health Care in the People's Republic of China: Moving Toward Modernization.* Boulder, Colo.: Westview Press, 1987.

Ross, Jeremy. *Zang Fu: The Organ Systems of Traditional Chinese Medicine.* 2d ed. New York: Churchill Livingstone, 1985.

Said, Hakim Mohammed. *Medicine in China.* Karachi, Pakistan: Hamdard Foundation, 1981.

Shen, John H. *Chinese Medicine.* New York: Educational Solutions Incorporated, 1980.

Shen Nong ben cao (The Shennong Herbal). Taipei: Five Continent, 1977.

Sidel, Victor W., and Ruth Sidel. *The Health of China.* Boston: Beacon Press, 1982.

———. *Serve the People: Observations on Medicine in the People's Republic of China.* Boston: Beacon Press, 1973.

Sivin, Nathan. *Traditional Medicine in Contemporary China.* Science, Medicine, and Technology in East Asia Series no. 2. Translated from Chinese. Ann Arbor: University of Michigan, Center for Chinese Studies, 1987.

Stuart, G. A. *Chinese Materia Medica: Vegetable Kingdom.* Shanghai: American Presbyterian Press, 1911. Reprint. Taipei: Southern Materials Press, 1976.

Teeguarden, Ron. *Chinese Tonic Herbs.* Briarcliff Manor, N.Y.: Japan Publications (U.S.A.), 1987.

Temple, Robert. *The Genius of China: 3,000 Years of Science, Discovery, and Contemporary Perspectives on Chinese Civilization.* New York: Simon and Schuster, 1986.

Tierra, Leslie. *The Herbs of Life: Health and Healing Using Western and Chinese Techniques.* Freedom, Calif.: Crossing Press, 1992.

Tsuei, Wei. *Roots of Chinese Culture and Medicine.* Academy of Chinese Culture and Health Sciences Series no. 1. Oakland, Calif.: Chinese Culture Books Company, 1990.

Tsung, Pi-Kwang, and Hong-yen Hsu. *Allergies and Chinese Herbal Medicine.* Educational Series on Chinese Medicine no. 3. Long Beach, Calif.: Oriental Healing Arts Institute, 1987.

———. *Arthritis and Chinese Herbal Medicine.* Long Beach, Calif.: Oriental Healing Arts Institute, 1987.

———. *Immunology and Chinese Herbal Medicine.* Educational Series on Chinese Medicine no. 1. Long Beach, Calif.: Oriental Healing Arts Institute, 1986.

Unschuld, Paul U. *Medical Ethics in Imperial China: A Study in Historical Anthropology.* Berkeley: University of California Press, 1979.

———. *Medicine in China: A History of Ideas.* Berkeley: University of California Press, 1985.

———. *Medicine in China: A History of Pharmaceutics.* Berkeley: University of California Press, 1985.

Unschuld, Paul U., ed. *Approaches to Traditional Chinese Medical Literature: Proceedings of an International Symposium on Translation Methodologies and Terminologies.* Norwell, Mass.: Kluwer Academic Publishers, 1989.

———. *Introductory Readings in Classical Chinese Medicine.* Norwell, Mass.: Kluwer Academic Publishers, 1988.

Wee Yeow Chin and Hsuan Keng. *An Illustrated Dictionary of Chinese Medicinal Herbs.* Sebastopol, Calif.: C R C S Publications, 1992.

Willmott, Jonathan C. *Western Astrology and Chinese Medicine.* Rochester, Vt.: Inner Traditions International Limited, 1985.

Wiseman, Nigel A. *Glossary of Chinese Medical Terms,* Vol. 1, *Points and Terms.* Edited by Robert L. Felt. Brookline, Mass.: Paradigm Publications, 1989.

Wiseman, Nigel A., and Ken Boss. *Complete Chinese Materia Medica.* Brookline, Mass.: Paradigm Publications, 1991.

Wolfe, Honora L. *Second Spring: A Guide to Healthy Menopause through Traditional Chinese Medicine.* Edited by Bob Flaws. Boulder, Colo.: Blue Poppy Enterprises Press, 1990.

Wong, K. C., and Lien-Teh Wu. *History of Chinese Herbal Medicine.* 2 vols. Shanghai: National Quarantine Service, 1936. Reprint. New York: Gordon Press Publishers, 1976.

Wu, Shan M. *The Mending of the Sky and Other Chinese Myths.* Translated by Xiao M. Li. Durham, N.H.: Oyster River Press, 1989.

Yang, Jwing-Ming. *The Root of Chinese Chi Kung.* Jamaica Plain, Mass.: Yang's Martial Arts Association, 1989.

Zhang Zhong-Jing. *Shanghan lun* (Treatise on Febrile and Miscellaneous Diseases). Shanghai: Commercial Press, 1983.

Zhong chao yao he chao yao shi pu (Chinese Herbs and Herbal Recipes). Hong Kong: Commercial Press, 1970.

7

Sports

SUSAN E. BROWNELL

Most of the sports to which we commonly refer in modern usage, such as soccer, basketball, volleyball, boxing, and track and field, took their present form in England and the United States during the nineteenth century, and are therefore closely connected with a specific culture—Anglo-Saxon. The cultural distinctiveness of this connotation of ''sport'' is reflected in the fact that, around the world, whenever Anglo-Saxon sports were adopted, the word ''sport'' was simultaneously adopted to describe them. Mandarin Chinese is a notable exception. The official Chinese phrase is *tiyu* (physical culture). *Tiyu* is an overarching term that refers to three categories: competitive sports (*jingji tiyu* or *tiyu yundong*), physical education in the schools (*xuexiao tiyu* or simply *tiyu*), and recreation and physical fitness for the masses (*qunzhong tiyu*). The meaning of *jingji tiyu* is much more restricted than that of ''sports'' in English, so there is a genuine translation problem in dealing with sports-related concepts. Because of the specific cultural background of the word ''sport,'' it is often questionable whether it should be used to refer to traditional (pre–twentieth century) Chinese physical culture. The following definition will allow me to delineate a field of inquiry.

Sport consists of a variety of activities that range outward from an ideal type. The ideal type of sport is found in ballgames like soccer and basketball, or in individual contests like boxing and track (Lüschen and Sage 1981, 5). The focus of this chapter is on the competitive sports found in the modern Olympic Games and the traditional Chinese sports that more or less resemble them. These activities grade into other types of activities; most notably, the line between traditional martial arts (*wushu*) and hand-to-hand combat sports (wrestling, boxing, *leitai*) is not at all clear.

A cultural analysis of sport should describe sport practices as one facet of the overall cultural configuration, taking the symbolic functions of sport as most important. There is a root metaphor inherent in sporting practice; it derives from the fact that, on a behavioral level, sport is distinguished from other human activities by two distinctive features: it is competitive, and it is based primarily on the physical ability of the participants (Lüschen and Sage 1981, 5–6). The outcome is determined by superiority in physical skill, tactics, or strategy. This interaction of biological and cultural factors imitates, on a more concentrated scale, the interaction between biology and culture that occurs in everyday human social life, giving sport its metaphoric appeal. Sport especially embodies two things: competition and the establishment of some sort of physical superiority. These two concepts form the root metaphor of sport. The metaphor, in turn, allows sport to generate meanings about different fields of human behavior. The main task of a cultural analysis of sport should be to ascertain what a given sport signifies in a given social context, and to reveal the relationship between these meanings and the power structures dramatized, legitimated, or contested by them.

TRADITIONAL CHINESE SPORTS

China possesses the rich sporting heritage that one would expect in a complex and ethnically diverse civilization. Although the Chinese have perhaps the most comprehensive and accurate historical records of any people, there are remarkably few references to sports as a result of bias on the part of the Confucian scholars who were writing the histories. For over 2,000 years, Chinese society has been grounded in a profound respect for education as a means of social mobility. The dichotomy between learning and physical prowess was and is expressed in the opposition of the words *wen* (civility, literacy) and *wu* (martiality). Sports were and are associated with the second half of the equation.

In feudal Zhou times (ca. 1100–256 B.C.E.), a warrior aristocracy occupied the highest social position, but the balance of power shifted over time toward the scholar-official class. This was largely the result of the imperial examination system, commonly said to date to 165 B.C.E. when examinations were first required for men recommended for government service. The scholar-officials finally gained ascendance in state politics during the Song Dynasty (960–1279) (Levenson 1964, 36–37). At that time, esteem of education became the key configuration in Chinese culture that it remains today. The relative importance of the two spheres of *wen* and *wu* is reflected in the saying, "Esteem literacy and despise martiality" (*zhong wen qing wu*), which Chinese people still assert to be a central feature of Chinese culture that accounts for a lack of attention to physical education.

The lack of scholarly literature on Chinese sports in the West may be due to a similar bias. Until recently, Western scholars who specialized in Chinese history tended to be more interested in elite than popular culture. They concentrated on religion, philosophy, literature, the arts, and imperial politics. When they began to turn their attention to popular culture, they merely shifted their focus to popular religion, to popular literature and the arts, and to popular rebellions.[1]

In recent years, however, a number of overviews have appeared as chapters in books, beginning to fill the void in the history of Chinese sports.[2] Unfortunately, these all-too-brief essays tend to repeat the same information. Reflecting the Communist Party's promotion of sports, two key English language sources, *Sports and Games in Ancient China* and *Sports in Ancient China,* have been published in the People's Republic of China (PRC). Articles on traditional Chinese sports also frequently appear in the English language magazines *China Sports, Beijing Review,* and *China Today* (formerly *China Reconstructs*), as well as the newspaper *China Daily.* These sources are published in English for a non-Chinese audience, and there is an agenda behind their production. China rejoined the Olympic Games in 1984 and since that time has been eager to play an active role in international sports. Histories of ancient Chinese sports demonstrate that China has a sporting tradition every bit as illustrious as the ancient Greek tradition upon which the Olympic Games are based. Thus, scholarship on ancient sports can be viewed as one strategy in China's effort to establish itself as a world power with a proud cultural heritage of its own to contribute to the Western-dominated global culture.

The traditional Chinese state was an amazing accomplishment, given the limitations of premodern technology. Historically, cultural beliefs gave the ideals of social order, harmony, and obedience to the state a powerful emotional appeal. Religion, ritual, and symbol were in a high degree of harmony with the political and social structures at every level of society, from the imperial court to the rural village. This high level of cultural integration was in large part responsible for the stability of traditional states, even when they were headed by ethnic minorities that conquered the Han majority. China's traditional sports were also in harmony with the overall sociocultural system. They embodied the prevailing cultural notions about the positioning of human bodies in space and time and their relationship with the cosmos.

This integrated sociocultural system was disrupted by Western imperialism in the nineteenth century and never recovered. Contact with the West led to a series of rebellions and revolutions, the complete reshaping of the traditional political and economic systems, and the intrusion of Western beliefs into Chinese culture. Modern sports were inculcated by the missionaries, promoted by the Nationalists (1912–1949), imposed by the Japanese (during their occupation of the northeast in 1931–1945), and systematized by the Communists (est. 1949). Modern sports are characterized by their reliance on technology and on highly rules-regulated and standardized practices, and they embody the notions of space and time that accompanied capitalist industrialization.[3] As a cultural form, they are not completely in harmony with traditional Chinese culture. Sports are just one example of the disjunctures in Chinese culture today.

In premodern sports around the world, three general fields of behavior tend to be symbolically represented: sexual competition, economic production, and military preparation. Each type, as it existed in imperial China, will be considered briefly.

Sexual competition is often symbolized through ritualized competitions for mates. Although such competitions have become less common in the industrialized West, they are common in many societies (Sansone 1988, 33–34). A number of popular games that occur during seasonal festivals among China's minorities are forms of courtship ritual. These games are often viewed askance by representatives of the state, who fear they may incite social disorder. An example is "Girls Chase" among the Kazakhs, a form of tag on horseback in which boys "say naughty things" to the girls and try to prevent them from crossing a line. If a girl does cross the line, turn around, and overtake the boy, then she is allowed to whip him and he must remain silent. This game is said to often end in marriage (*Sports in Ancient China* 1986, 89–90).

Contests involving sexual symbolism are unusual in that they often involve both sexes. However, when males and females engage in the same sport, it may signify different things. In China during the Song Dynasty, women appeared in prestigious wrestling contests (*Sports and Games* 1986, 131). Sometimes they fought in the nude; this indecency was the cause for a petition written to the emperor by a scholar-official (Van Gulik 1961, 229). One might suspect that the sport's entertainment value lay in its prurient appeal rather than in the military ideals associated with men's wrestling. During the Song, kick ball also became popular among the female populace, even though the practice of foot binding spread simultaneously. Again, it seems unlikely that this was seen as a form of military training as it was for the imperial troops who practiced it.[4]

The connection between sports and the economic infrastructure is considered most important in traditional Marxist theory. The Marxist view is that sports arose primarily from productive labor. The best example in English of the Eastern Bloc Marxist view of sports is Bero Rigauer's *Sport and Work* (1981); in a Chinese work, Cao Xiangjun discusses a revised view in *Tiyu gailun* (A General Theory of Physical Culture), which acknowledges the military connection but still places primacy on production (Cao 1985, 45). The Marxist view notwithstanding, sports with economic meanings are hard to find. Two notable Chinese examples are bullfighting and bull grappling; however, these are rather distant from the ideal type of sport because in the former case the contest was between two animals, and in the latter case it is unclear that one victor was declared.

Historical bullfighting and grappling are described in four short articles based mostly on archaeological evidence.[5] Reliefs from the Han Dynasty (206 B.C.E.– 221 C.E.) depict contests between two bulls and between men and bulls. The former type of contest was common in southern China and is still practiced in Southeast Asia. It is part of a ceremony for welcoming the spring, and the victor is sacrificed to guarantee the fertility of the fields.

Contests between men and animals, on the other hand, are no longer known. Han Dynasty sources suggest that famous animal fighters and visiting "barbarians" wrestled the animals to demonstrate their bravery. They fought the bulls barehanded, perhaps even attempting acrobatic feats over the animals' backs. As analyzed by Mark Edward Lewis, these contests represented men's subjugation of natural forces and played an important role in the symbolic construction of imperial power (1990, 150–63).

Dragon boat racing is another type of contest that was associated with the agricultural calendar. There is a fascinating English translation of a 300-year-old Ming Dynasty description by Yang Ssu-ch'ang (1943); this translation is also the basis for a more detailed but highly speculative analysis of the festival by Goran Aijmer (1964). According to these accounts, the Dragon Boat Festival was much more elaborate in southern than in northern China and was associated with rice cultivation. In the Ming, it was called *jingdu,* or "fight and cross," because fighting played as important a role as paddling in the contest. It neither resembled modern boat races nor even dragon boat races in today's China. Each boat was associated with a "boat region" which provided most of the crew of up to eighty members. The spectators, who watched the ceremony in tall buildings and along the riverbanks, were highly partisan. A spectator who crossed into another boat region's viewing area would be beaten. The boat crews attacked and grappled with each other, sang rhyming songs insulting the other boats, and fought with bamboo canes and stones the size of goose eggs stored in the bottom of the boat. Men were wounded, drowned, and killed. It is not clear whether one victor was declared. By the time of Yang's description, local Ming authorities had (unsuccessfully) forbidden the races due to the level of violence.

This Ming Dynasty description of dragon boat racing illustrates that traditional "sports" do not always fit our modern conception. Often, they are not zero-sum contests; no single victor is established.

Above all, the dragon boat race seems to have been a symbolic expression of hostility between local lineages. Sulamith Heins Potter and Jack M. Potter (1990) note that dragon boat races were revived in rural China in the 1980s as lineages regained socioeconomic importance. They give a brief but vivid description of a race held in a Cantonese district in 1985 (1990, 258–61). A colorful video by Zhuang Kongshao (1992) also shows a dragon boat race that resulted in intervillage antagonism.

Bullfighting and dragon boat racing were two contests that were associated with agricultural production; however, such sports are few. Even though some sports may have accompanied harvest festivals—as is true in parts of rural China today—the technology of the harvest does not seem to have penetrated the practice of the sports themselves. In China today, contests with sexual and agricultural meanings are limited almost entirely to ethnic minorities. With the increasing focus on the Western model of sport, it is possible that these sports will lose their traditional form (as has the dragon boat race) or die out entirely.

Bullfighting also has military associations; it and hand-to-hand combat sports trace their roots to the same myth. This myth involves a trio of Chinese gods: the Divine Husbandman (*Shen Nong*); Chi You, a horned beast; and the Yellow

Emperor. Bullfighting is sometimes interpreted as a ceremony held in honor of the Divine Husbandman.

The myth is significant for the history of Chinese martial arts because Chinese historians commonly name it as the origin of hand-to-hand combat sports. In the "Chi You Play," a ritual reenactment of the battle between the Yellow Emperor and Chi You, the combatants put horns on their heads and charged at each other like goats. Lewis provides an excellent discussion of the Chi You myth and its use as a charter for the reformulation of state power in the Zhou Dynasty (Lewis 1990, 165–212). In the Western Zhou Dynasty (ca. 1100–770 B.C.E.), warriors were required to practice *jiaodi* (literally, "horn resistance"), a military drill in which they wore horns and butted each other (*Sports and Games* 1986, 109). It was also called *jiaoli* (horn strength), a word which today means "wrestling." The basic form spawned many different varieties of combat sports, which became increasingly popular. *Jiaodi* is said to have evolved into the Chinese martial arts (*wushu*—popularly called kungfu in English), wrestling (*jiaoli* or *shuaijiao*), platform fighting (*leitai*), and sumo wrestling (*xiangpu*). In the Qin and Han, *jiaodi* matches were featured at local festivals and were accompanied by all sorts of competitions and magic acts, and the word gained a broader definition referring to all sorts of ritual performances. The modern word *jiao* has the meanings of "horn" and "theatrical role," among others.[6]

Among Chinese physical activities, *leitai* was perhaps most similar to the Greek sporting tradition. Like the king of Greek sports, pankration, it was a combination of wrestling and boxing that allowed all sorts of holds and blows and attracted large numbers of spectators. *Leitai* was most commonly fought on an open-air platform in a "king-of-the-mountain" style of contest, where the man who occupied the platform took on challengers until he was defeated, at which point the challenger occupied the platform. Pictures of such contests usually show a group of athletes lined up on the side, waiting their turn. When no more challenges were made, the occupier was declared the victor. One source suggests that contestants may have been "seeded" (*Tiyu cidian* 1984, 321). That there were some rules in Chinese combat sports is indicated by the presence of a judge in many depictions of *leitai* and wrestling, but none of the available sources describe the rules. *Leitai* competitions were popular at court and among the populace. In the Western Han, the Emperor Wu entertained foreign guests with a *jiaodi* performance which attracted spectators from afar (*Tiyu* 1984, 130). The Tang, Song, and Qing imperial courts maintained groups of professional wrestlers to entertain the emperor and perform at important banquets (*Tiyu* 1984, 132). In the Tang Dynasty (618–906 C.E.), matches were held at the foot of a hill so spectators could sit on the slopes. Whole towns would turn out to watch these matches (*Sports and Games* 1986, 109). The classic novel *Outlaws of the Marsh* (or *The Water Margin*) describes a match in which thousands of spectators showed up, including high-ranking officials; even the roofs were dotted with watchers. The prizes came from different parts of the country, "suggesting that the contest was actually a national championship" (*Sports and Games* 1986,

110). There were special platforms in the imperial palaces as well. In the Qing court (a dynasty headed by ethnic Manchu), the wrestlers formed a regiment of the royal guard. The court established a wrestling camp, and those who passed the examination received a state salary and held permanent jobs (Chang 1978, 24–25). In contrast to their Han subordinates, the Manchu were quite fond of wrestling and *leitai*. As a reaction, the Han elite considered these sports examples of the vulgar tastes of the "Qing barbarians" (Van Gulik 1961, 18).

While wrestling and *leitai* are associated with the beast Chi You, the invention of kick ball, a form of soccer, is attributed to his nemesis, the Yellow Emperor. Kick ball is another very ancient Chinese game. The most comprehensive discussion of the game is found in Lewis's *Sanctioned Violence in Early China,* which also gives an excellent analysis of the symbolism of the game and its role in the changing nature of state power. Kick-ball stadiums were a feature of many ancient palaces, and a book on the sport was written as early as the Western Han (206 B.C.E.–9 C.E. (*Sports and Games* 1986, 78). Although many of the surviving early portrayals show women, it was also considered to have military functions. The Yellow Emperor is said to have introduced it as a type of military training (Lewis 1990, 147). One manuscript states that, after his victory over Chi You, the Yellow Emperor stuffed the monster's stomach and made it into a ball; another report is that the ball represented Chi You's head (Lewis 1990, 148). In the *Book of Han,* the game was said to be a simulacrum of the regulation of the state: The square walls and the round ball represented the Chinese belief that the heavens were round and the earth square. Two teams of six represented the six yin and six yang months that made up the year. The movement of the ball from one side of the stadium to the other mimicked the yin and yang cycles of the heavenly bodies. Thus, the kick-ball game was an allegory of the annual cycle of Heaven and Earth. It was a simulacrum of the well-regulated state because the virtuous ruler was supposed to regulate the state according to the heavenly cycles (Lewis 1990, 149–50). In other words, the game was played according to the same cosmic principles that were supposed to underlie good government.

According to Lewis's interesting cultural analysis, the *jiaodi* wrestling matches associated with the Yellow Emperor's victory over Chi You demonstrated that "the emperor's power extended to and was rooted in the natural world" (1990, 162). The game of kick ball, also identified with the Yellow Emperor's victory over savagery, was one indication of a shift in the elite interpretation of the role of violence in the state. As Lewis concludes, "[T]he actual performance of violence that had been central to the Zhou nobility became the sphere of the commoner masses who filled the ranks of the armies, while authority inhered in those who organized the violence and gave it pattern" (1990, 161). Thus, this cycle of Chinese myths reveals a relationship between sport, violence, and the consolidation of state power.

Kick ball clearly embodied traditional notions of humankind's place in the cosmos. It was played by a primarily agricultural people for whom time was measured by the cyclical movement of heavenly bodies and productivity was a natural occurrence of the cycle of sowing and reaping. This contrasts with modern sports, which are played by a primarily industrial people for whom time is measured by the clock, and productivity is the result of the greatest output in the shortest amount of time. Perhaps it is not surprising that this game, which had symbolized the orderly state for 2,500 years, declined and then disappeared in the social unrest of the late Qing Dynasty.

Along with kick ball, polo was a popular game at court, reaching its zenith in the Tang (618–906 C.E.). Carl Diem's masterwork on Asian equestrian games, *Asiatische Reiterspiele,* is one of the major sources on Chinese polo. Unfortunately, there is no English translation. There is, however, a brief, beautifully illustrated essay on polo by Virginia L. Bower in the *Asian Art* issue on ''Games.''

There is also an interesting article by James T.C. Liu on ''Polo and Cultural Change,'' which is a social history of the sport. According to Liu, during the Tang, polo was played by two teams of sixteen players on horses or donkeys. Dressed in elegant, embroidered jackets, and accompanied by a military band, they hit a leather or wood ball with a curved stick (Liu 1985, 206–7). The game was criticized by the scholar-officials because it was dangerous and hurt the ''vitality'' of the horses and players. Their concern was not unjustified; in the late Tang, polo games were reportedly the pretext for killing an emperor and several generals.

Polo had fallen into disfavor by the Song, and Liu associates this with the nature of the Song scholar-officials, a nonhereditary class of highly educated men (1985, 217). By the Southern Song (1127–1279), according to Liu, ''the overwhelming majority of scholar-officials paid no attention either to ball games or players'' (1985, 223). Players came from the army rather than from court circles. Liu concludes that the decline of polo was a result of the transition away from the Tang frontier spirit toward the genteel, refined, and elegant pursuits of the Song (1985, 224). He notes:

The non-aristocratic scholar-official class, refined, urbane, and genteel, cared little for the vigorous sports they viewed as inappropriate, pointless, harmful, and even risky. Under their influence, court circles gave up such games as polo. In fact, this negative attitude permeated the culture and persisted until the early twentieth century when modern sports were newly introduced from the West and Japan, as if China had never had them or their equivalents at all. (Liu 1985, 204)

Bull grappling, dragon boat racing, *leitai,* kick ball, and polo are the traditional sports on which the most information is available, so I have dealt with them in some detail. Many other sports were also practiced, including the lifting of heavy bronze tripods, archery, high jump, long jump, running, swimming, speed skating, figure skating, and kick ball played on the ice. Unfortunately, aside from a few paragraphs on each in *Sports and Games in Ancient China* and *Sports in Ancient China,* there is almost no information on these sports in English. In addition, acrobatics and juggling were highly developed; and, of course, I have only briefly touched upon the martial arts tradition, which is covered elsewhere in this volume, and which is somewhat better documented in English.

By the end of imperial times, most of the sports discussed above had declined or disappeared. Only the martial arts (*wushu*) flourished—not surprising in the civil unrest that ended the Qing Dynasty. A comparison of the rise of the martial arts in late Qing China with the development of modern sports in England is found in Susan E. Brownell's "Sports in Britain and China, 1850–1920: An Explanatory Overview." Nationalistic fervor increased with the fall of the Qing, and ten years after the establishment of the republic (1912), a "martial arts revival period" occurred in which *wushu* was linked to the welfare of the nation. In the early years of the republic, there was widespread agreement that sports served the good of the state, but there was a great deal of conflict over whether the traditional martial arts or Western sports did it best. *Wushu* was reshaped to fit the Western model with the establishment of the newly named "national art" (*guoshu*) as a competitive sport in 1928. In the 1930s, a conflict arose between those who supported *guoshu* as a means of strengthening China on the one hand and those who supported Western sports on the other. The conflict contained all the elements of the clash of cultures that has confronted the Chinese for the last century. Traditionalists argued, "If we want to quickly train our skills, *guoshu* is the path to start upon. . . . Only with a strong body, a strong race, a strong nation will our national spirit develop and expand, and only then will there be hope for world peace" (Xie 1988, 6). Reformers countered heatedly, "In cultivating the skills of running, jumping, scrambling, and climbing, indigenous physical culture is completely ineffective" (Xie 1988, 7).

The Chinese solution to the clash between indigenous and foreign physical culture was to recommend the combination of the strengths of both types of physical culture. This has been considered the proper program for Chinese culture as a whole. However, this combination has not yet been achieved in sports. On the one hand, *wushu* has been "sportized,"[7] and competitions are now held based on a ten-point judging scale, as in gymnastics. Although it attracts a wide audience, it is not widely practiced. The more popular types of *wushu* are practiced nearly in their original form; *taiji* and *qigong* (meditational breathing exercises) together probably comprise the most popular forms of exercise. They have absorbed little Western influence, while the imported Western sports have absorbed few of the elements of traditional sports. If sport is representative, then the difficulty of melding East and West in other areas of culture will be very great indeed.

INTRODUCTION OF MODERN SPORTS IN CHINA

The history of sports in the Republican (1912–1949) and Communist periods is more comprehensively documented than the history of traditional Chinese sports. The most complete discussion of the introduction of Western sports into China is found in Jonathan Kolatch's *Sports, Politics, and Ideology in China*. A brief but good overview is also found in Gu Shiquan, "Introduction to Ancient and Modern Chinese Physical Culture." Each book has major shortcomings (Kolatch was unable to actually visit the PRC; Knuttgen et al. is translated from articles written by Chinese scholars, which necessarily reflect the Communist Party viewpoint[8]); however, these two books are the major English language sources on modern sports in China.

Modern sports were first introduced into China in association with the concept of physical education. The first physical education program was instituted in 1875 at the Nanking Military Academy. Programs in other military schools followed. These programs, which centered on military drills rather than on sports, were generally directed by German or Japanese instructors (Kolatch 1972, 4). After the demise of the imperial examination system in the early 1900s, the new government schools included military drills. In 1922 they were dropped and Western sports were substituted; they have been the main content of physical education classes ever since. This marked a switch from the imitation of the Japanese and German school systems to the imitation of the American system (Gu 1990, 16).

In 1890 the first modern sports event, a track and field meet, was held at St. John's University in Shanghai. Between 1900 and 1927, the YMCA and YWCA were the dominant influences on sports in China (Kolatch 1972, 29). In 1910 the first national athletic meet was held. The main contribution of the YMCA was to organize the first national athletic meets and the Far Eastern championship games, which directed considerable public attention to sports (Kolatch 1972, 13, 26). The championship games were a series of ten international meets held between 1913 and 1934 in which China, Japan, and the Philippines participated. They were the first international team competitions in the Far East (Kolatch 1972, 52).

The YMCA influence waned with the formation of the Nanking government in 1928 and the increasing involvement of that government in sports. The Republican leaders recognized the importance of national sports games as a means of promoting national unity; the fifth and six national athletic meets were held on October 10, the anniversary of the founding of the republic (Kolatch 1972, 42–43). China became an active member of the International Olympic Committee (IOC) in 1931 and sent one athlete to the 1932 Olympic Games held in Los Angeles.

During the Republican period, sports became a pastime and sometime source of income for a handful of people attached to schools headed by Westerners or modeled after the Western system. Coaching jobs were only part-time and were combined with the teaching of other subjects. A story that illustrates the low esteem in which sports were held is that of the famous sports leader Ma Yuehan (John Ma). A professor at Qinghua (Tsinghua) University, he was once demoted for coaching the soccer team. It was only after the team won the North China championship that his position was restored (Shih 1963, 14).

Sports were also promoted as a means of military training in the Communist revolutionary bases. They provided an escape for the soldiers, boosted their morale, and helped maintain their physical fitness. Of particular renown is the Combat Basketball Team (*zhandou lanqiudui*) in the Yan'an revolutionary base. The team was founded by He Long, who later became the first director of the State Sports Commission.

ESTABLISHMENT OF THE COMMUNIST SPORTS SYSTEM

The Republican period was a time in which some of the basic infrastructures of the Chinese sports system were laid. However, sports were much more important to the Communist state. The definitive Chinese history of sport in the People's Republic is *Dangdai zhongguo tiyu* (Contemporary Chinese Sports), by Rong Gaotang et al. Though unavailable in English, its contents are summarized in a review by Brownell in the *International Journal of the History of Sport*.

In 1955 the People's Republic of China established the system of sports schools based on the Soviet model that is still in place today. The most thorough and up-to-date description of the sports commission system can be found in Knuttgen et al., *Sport in China* (1990); Kolatch (1972) gives a thorough description of the system up to 1972. A number of sources give briefer and less current descriptions.[9] All of these sources tend to present a picture of a static, highly structured system of institutions; in reality, the sports system adapts itself to local conditions and is not nearly as systematic as these descriptions imply.

The sports commission system consists of a hierarchical structure of sports training centers under the ultimate direction of the State Sports Commission, which is equal in status to a government ministry (equivalent organizations include the Education Commission and the Ministry of Culture). At the base of the pyramid are the local (county, township, and city) sports commissions; above them are the provincial and municipal sports commissions (there are thirty provinces and three municipalities, or federally administered cities—Beijing, Shanghai, and Tianjin); at the top is the State Sports Commission. The sports commissions at each level control the training centers under their jurisdictions. The local commissions preside over the county, township, and city sports schools; the provincial commissions preside over the provincial training center, usually located in the provincial capital; at the same level as the provincial commissions, the Beijing, Shanghai, and Tianjin City Sports Commissions preside over the training centers in those municipalities; and the State Sports Commission presides over the national team training center (*Beijing tiyuguan*) located near the Temple of Heaven in the southwest of the nation's capital. The State Sports Commission also presides over national-team training centers for individual sports located in other parts of the country. In addition, it sets policies for the national-level institutes of physical education located in Beijing, Chengdu, Xi'an, Shenyang, Wuhan, and Shanghai. These are college-level educational institutes. This pyramidal system is designed to recruit promising athletes at the grass-roots level and move the superior ones level by level up through the system until they arrive at the pinnacle: the national team.

At the grass-roots level, training centers may be of several types. One of the most widespread is the "spare-time sports school" (*yeyu tixiao*), where students train before or after their regular school hours. Spare-time sports training is often offered by a regular "sports school" (*jingji tixiao*). This is a training center where students live, train, and attend classes. After they reach a certain age, they may stop taking classes; until recently, many athletes completed only nine years of schooling. These sports schools, in turn, are often attached to a provincial or municipal training center or an institute of physical education. There are also "traditional sports middle schools" (*chuantong tiyu xiangmu zhongxue*). These are regular middle schools which have traditionally been strong in one or two sports events. I have described here only the bare bones of a system which is actually extremely complex. There are all sorts of variations.

According to articles written by He Zhenliang (1987) and Kang Bing (1988), there were reportedly, in 1986, 3,411 sports schools and traditional sports middle schools, with a total of more than 270,000 students. Among these, 300 schools were "high-level" schools which train most of the top junior athletes, and they had a total of around 30,000 students. That these schools are the key to China's sports success is shown by the fact that, in 1984, 85 percent of the athletes chosen for international competition had trained in them.

After the establishment of the sports school system in 1955, China's sports made rapid improvement, many events reaching world-class level. From 1955 on, female athletes enjoyed essentially equal opportunities with the men (a situation still not found in the West), and a woman even broke the world high jump record in 1957. Like the other world records in swimming and track and field, it was not internationally recognized because the PRC had not officially been accepted into the IOC. Conflict over the "Two China" question eventually led to China's withdrawal from the 1956 Olympic Games and a complete break with the international sports community in 1958. Chinese participation in the Olympic Games as one aspect of international relations has been described by a number of authors.[10] In fact, the political history of Chinese sport is more thoroughly covered in English than any other aspect. This chapter, by contrast, attempts to fill in some of the social and cultural history of sports in China.

The Communist Party has actively promoted physical fitness activities, the most notable example being the daily radio broadcast exercises that have involved hundreds of people at a time. The party's promotion of sports had two causes. First, during the revolution, leaders had found the general health of the Chinese people so poor that many recruits were unfit for military service. During the occupation, the Japanese had insulted the Chinese by calling them the "sick men of East Asia." This label achieved legendary proportions, as the Chinese imagined it was commonly known around the globe; they will often say that the goal of their efforts in sports is to erase it. A second reason for the party's promotion of sports was that national sports games proved to be an effective means of creating a new Chinese nationalism.

Under the Communists, sports careers began to gain in prestige. Before 1958, many top athletes were college students—a remnant of the Western-inspired model. After that, sports schools became increasingly important. In the patriotic atmosphere that followed the founding of the PRC, "winning glory for the nation" was a strong motivation for becoming an athlete. However, the pre-Communist attitude that athletes have "four developed limbs and an underdeveloped brain" (*sizhi fada, tounao jiandan*) still existed—indeed, this saying is still popular today.

Kolatch's book (1972) and John M. Hoberman's two articles (1984, 1987) are the best sources on Maoist sport ideology. Chairman Mao was a strong believer in physical education. His reported swim across the Yangtze River in 1956 was a national propaganda event. In 1952 Mao penned the slogan still more often quoted than any other: "Develop physical culture, strengthen the people's physiques" (*fazhan tiyu, zengqiang renmin tizhi*). Chinese scholars consider such guiding slogans, like the national games, to be important markers along the path of the cultural history of sports.

Each of the main eras in Chinese political history was symbolically marked by a national games. The official title of this multisport festival is the National Games of the People's Republic of China (*Zhonghua Renmin Gongheguo yun-donghui*). They imitate the Olympic Games and are supposed to be held once every four years, but the schedule has been repeatedly disrupted by social and economic turmoil. These games illustrate party-orchestrated symbolism and media dissemination at its height. The choreography of the opening ceremonies, in particular, derives from the current economic, political, and cultural fabric of Chinese life. The heart of the opening ceremonies is always the mass calisthenics display performed to music and presented in several acts. The symbolism of the opening ceremonies is discussed in Susan E. Brownell's "The Olympic Movement on Its Way into Chinese Culture" (1990, 68–133), and is summarized in *Sports and Public Health* (1983, 7–8).

The first national games were held in 1959, ten years after the establishment of the PRC. They were intended to consolidate the gains made since liberation and to motivate the people to continue to work for the future. In 1959 the central theme of the mass calisthenics display was "The Entire Nation Simultaneously Celebrates."

Despite the optimism, China was actually on the verge of disaster due to the Great Leap Forward and the floods and droughts that unfortunately came shortly after. Along with the establishment of the sports school system, the State Sports Commission had established a system of food subsidies based on the level of the athlete. In the late 1950s, many parents encouraged their children to join sports schools so that they would receive the food subsidy. Parents considered that the added nutrition would help the child study better, balancing out their concern that sports would detract from studies. (In 1988, the food subsidy was still one of the main reasons that parents agreed to let children participate in sports schools.)

SPORTS IN THE CULTURAL REVOLUTION

The second national games could not be held until six years later, and even then they were greatly scaled down. At that time, China was on the brink of the Cultural Revolution, and this was clearly reflected in the theme for the opening ceremonies of the 1965 games: "A Song of Praise for the Revolution." One of the acts had the inspiring title of "Tightly Grip the Gun in Your Hand."

With the start of the Cultural Revolution in 1966, sports entered a dark phase. Sports schools were closed down from 1966 to 1971, and outstanding sports figures were targets of attack for their "medals-and-trophyism." In 1968 the rustication campaign began, in which a million urban youths were sent each year to rural areas to live and work. China was in chaos, but the restoration of sports teams in 1971 provided a haven for not a few youths who otherwise would have been sent down to the countryside.

In the late 1970s, the guiding slogan of Chinese sports was "Friendship first, competition second" (*youyi diyi, bisai dier*). This ideology was consistent with the anti-individualist rhetoric of the Cultural Revolution, and was also opposed to the perceived imperialism of Western-controlled international sports. The slogan accompanied China's "Ping-pong Diplomacy," the most notable accomplishment of which was the restoration of Sino–U.S. relations in 1972 after two Sino–U.S. table-tennis exchanges. China's use of sports in international diplomacy is discussed in David B. Kanin's "Ideology and Diplomacy: The Dimensions of Chinese Political Sport."[11]

The Cultural Revolution lasted ten years, and the games were suspended until its very end. The theme for the third national sports games, in 1975, was still very revolutionary: "Ode to the Red Flag."

SPORTS IN THE ERA OF ECONOMIC REFORM

The revolution ended after the death of Chairman Mao in 1976 and the overthrow of his wife and her allies, the Gang of Four, in 1978. The new regime, headed by Deng Xiaoping, celebrated its victory a little over a year later with the largest games held to that date. The theme of the 1979 games reflected the idea of starting over, with a realization of the hard work ahead: "The New Long March." Chinese society began to return to a more normal state, and the era of reform began.

Many people mark the victory of the women's volleyball team in the 1981 World Cup as the beginning of the revival of Chinese patriotism after the devastation of the Cultural Revolution. It was possibly the most significant event in the realm of public culture in the time period after the death of Mao and before the Tian An Men protests of 1989. It aroused more optimism than the event that was officially supposed to have done so: the Party Congress in 1978 during which the Cultural Revolution was declared at an end and the era of reform begun.

This was China's first world championship in a major sport. The victory had special patriotic significance since China had defeated Japan for the victory. The championship became a symbolic victory over China's longtime Asian rival. When the live broadcast came to an end, people across the nation spontaneously flooded the streets, setting off firecrackers and weeping openly. Approximately 30,000 letters were sent to the women on the team, many of them written in blood (a customary way of expressing deep sentiment).

Yuan Weimin, the male coach who led the team to its first three world championships, began a meteoric rise to power that culminated in his selection to the Central Committee of the Chinese Communist Party in 1987. He was also one of the most popular public figures in China.

The women eventually won five consecutive world titles and were often held up as examples of what women can achieve under the socialist ideology of equality. When they slipped to bronze in the 1988 Seoul Olympics, a newspaper headline explained, ''They Are Human, They Aren't Divine.''

By the fifth national games in 1983, the political changes in China had gone full cycle. Once again China was recovering from ruin, and the party was attempting to inspire optimism for the future, and so the symbolism of springtime, which had been utilized for the first games in 1959, appeared again. The theme for the opening ceremonies was ''A Beautiful Healthy Spring.''

China's reentry into the national politicoeconomic arena was symbolically marked by its reacceptance into the IOC. In 1984, China participated in the Los Angeles Olympic Games. When China won the very first gold medal awarded in the games, it finally, as they say, ''broke the big duck egg''—referring to the erasure of its ''zero'' record in Olympic Games. The new international orientation of China's leaders was also embodied in a new guiding slogan for sports: ''Break out of Asia, advance on the world'' (chongchu Yazhou, zou xiang shijie). As China became the dominant nation in the Asian Games, and finally held its first Asian Games in 1990, this goal was close to realization.[12]

In the 1987 national games, modernization appeared for the first time as the major theme, reflecting China's latest concerns. The mass calisthenics display was appropriately entitled ''Great Aspirations.'' These games were significant because many new policies were implemented specifically for the occasion. Media coverage repeatedly depicted the games as an illustration of the success of the economic policies whose correctness had been reasserted at the Party Congress, which had convened less than a month before the games started. These reforms in the sports system are discussed in greater detail in Susan E. Brownell's ''The Changing Relationship between Sport and the State in the People's Republic of China.'' A general discussion of sport during the socialist transformation in the Soviet Bloc, with reference to China, is found in James Riordan's Sport, Politics and Communism. During the heights of the policy of openness, a journalist named Zhao Yu published a scathing critique of the Chinese sports system that attracted national attention (Zhao Yu 1988). He received international notice when he was jailed after the Tian An Men protests of 1989.

The Chinese sports system was encouraged to become self-supporting through better management of existing facilities, corporate sponsorship and advertising, lottery tickets, and other means. These practices would supplement the state physical culture budget. The national industrial systems were also encouraged to support teams in order to provide competition for the state sports system, which had a virtual monopoly on the organization of sports teams.

The economic improvements of the 1980s also made possible a grass-roots movement in sports outside of the state-sponsored system. The best example is the sport of bodybuilding (see Brownell, "Olympic," 1990). Unlike other sports, which were imposed from the top down by the State Sports Commission, bodybuilding began as a grass-roots movement and continued to grow despite resistance from the official state apparatus. State leaders opposed bodybuilding for two reasons: first, they disapproved of the baring of the body, especially by women; second, because bodybuilding was not an Olympic sport, no gold medals could be gained. The growth of bodybuilding illustrates the changing nature of Chinese cultural attitudes toward the body, and the roles of economic decentralization and global culture in that change. Bodybuilding athletes for the most part rely on private and corporate sponsorship for financial support. Teams are funded by corporations, national industries, work units, wealthy peasants, and private entrepreneurs.

The early history of bodybuilding in China was almost entirely one of Western influence. In the 1930s, a few missionary school students began to practice and promote it. In 1953 bodybuilding was denounced as "bourgeois" and banned; it was not officially sanctioned again until 1983, when the first formal competitions were held. In 1985 China joined the International Bodybuilding Association. In the national competition of that same year, the women gave an exhibition wearing one-piece bathing suits. Competitions for women were held in 1986, and bikinis were approved for the first time. The question of whether or not China's women bodybuilders should be allowed to wear bikinis was the subject of a heated debate at the highest state levels. It was only because of the support of the State Sports Commission that the women were permitted. The first event attracted remarkable nationwide attention, but when it proceeded without incident, women's bodybuilding slowly became just one more global cultural import.

POSITION OF ATHLETES IN CHINESE SOCIETY

State policies on wages, bonuses, and subsidies for sportspeople up to the early 1980s are set out in an invaluable resource book available only in Chinese, *Tiyu yundong wenjian xuanbian 1949–1981* (Selected Sport and Physical Culture Documents 1949–1981), published by Guojia tiwei zhengce yanjiushi

(State Sports Commission Policy Research Division). In recent years, several articles in *Sports Illustrated* and the *New York Times Magazine* have portrayed the human side of Chinese sports, though not without a bit of sensationalism with regard to the poverty of conditions and the treatment of young athletes (see Gary Smith, 1984, and Trip Gabriel, 1988). In fact, in the late 1980s, the living standards of professional athletes began to improve along with the national economy as a whole. It is true that they still lagged far behind those of the average American. Athletes typically lived from four to six to a room in dormitories with one communal toilet room to a floor and a washroom with cold running water. They had access to communal shower halls as often as six times a week, unlike an average college student who might go once or twice. Athletes' wages, too, were unremarkable. National team athletes might receive a total of about 90 yuan per month, which included a 70 yuan basic wage and 20 yuan in subsidies for shoes, showers, housing, and other things (at the 1988 exchange rate of $1 = 3.7 yuan, 90 yuan converts to $24). An athlete's position on the wage scale depended on performance and age. Performance levels are divided into grades according to the standards set for each sport event. At the top of the scale is the "international master sportsperson" (*guoji jianjiang*); ranging downward are the "master sportsperson" (*jianjiang*), "first grade," "second grade," "third grade," and the "junior athlete." Each jump in grade is accompanied by certain benefits: a one-time bonus, an increase in wages and food subsidies, and/or the addition of points to the National College Entrance Exam score. In 1987 performance bonuses reached substantial amounts by Chinese standards: as much as 10,000 yuan ($2,700) for a gold medal at China's national games or the Olympic Games. Even at that time, however, if you asked an athlete if it was a good occupation to have, he or she would most likely respond, "It's average, except we eat a little better." The food subsidy of up to 20 yuan per day was enough to guarantee dairy products at every meal and two kinds of meat for both lunch and dinner. This was beyond the range of the average family or student budget.

In their 1988 study of occupational prestige among Beijing residents, Lin Nan and Xie Wen concluded that athletes ranked eighteenth out of fifty occupations (1988, 805). They generally ranked below "mental workers" (university and secondary schoolteachers; high-, middle-, and low-ranking officials; accountants; secretaries; and others) and above "physical workers" (mechanics, machinists, and typists were fairly close categories). They also ranked above elementary schoolteachers and actors. Thus, athletes currently have a relatively high social status in Chinese society.

A closer examination of the success of the volleyball team and other women athletes shows that the sports school system gives women opportunities in sports that are not so accessible in other arenas. Female children of working-class or peasant families are especially likely to pursue sports as an avenue of social mobility; coaches often attribute their success to the fact that their hard lives made them better able to "eat bitterness and endure hard labor" (*chi ku nai lao*). As among black athletes in the United States, the few who succeeded spurred a multitude of others to try their luck at sports.

Nevertheless, an enduring aspect of Chinese culture began to present obstacles to the further development of Chinese sports. This conflict is also described in more detail in Brownell, "Changing Relationship" (1991). Education has become increasingly important since the National College Entrance Exam was reinstituted in 1976. A college education has become essential for entering a desirable occupation, because modernization requires scientific and technical skills. The College Entrance Exam is a gruelling, three-day examination that requires a huge amount of memorization. Since fewer than 10 percent of middle-school graduates are accepted into college, the competition is intense. School-children who participate in sports fall behind when they go away for competitions. Athletes at sports boarding schools may spend only half a day in class, and the academic demands are not very rigorous. Many athletes stop schooling altogether. With such a poor educational background, it is impossible for them to score well on the College Entrance Exam, and thus they have sacrificed their education for sports.

In the 1980s, parents were increasingly reluctant to allow their children to join sports teams, and sports schools were having trouble finding enough students. By 1988 the top-level teams had trouble replacing their aging stars, and many sportspeople were concerned that China's hard-won status in the international arena would begin to backslide.

Because of their lack of education, athletes were also unable to get desirable job assignments after retirement. The local Labor Bureau was responsible for finding them jobs. The majority were retained in the sports system as assistant coaches, cadres, office workers, and so on. Coaching a high-level team was considered the best job, but only a limited number of these positions were available. Many of the athletes who received jobs outside the sports system were assigned to factories. Most of these job opportunities were not especially appealing, and many parents, especially well-educated ones, were not happy with the long-term prospects for their athletically gifted children.

The state is now forging a closer link between the sports system and the educational system. In 1982 a national collegiate games was established to promote college sports. Along with the general sports boom, this quadrennial event gained in scale and importance. Since the founding of the PRC, outstanding accomplishments in sports have been rewarded with the addition of points to the entrance exam score; however, in preparation for the second national collegiate games, held in 1986, some colleges began recruiting athletes who scored hundreds of points below the minimum. In some cases, they reportedly had not taken the test at all.

The State Sports Commission saw lowered admission standards as a way to solve the post-retirement problems of professional athletes, but the Education Commission resisted. Finally, in the winter of 1987, the Education Commission gave outright permission to fifty-five colleges nationwide to create "high-level sports teams'' by recruiting former professional athletes. Because of China's cultural history and social structure, the American model of high-level college sports may be more appropriate than the old Soviet model of specialist athletes.

SUMMARY: SPORT AND SOCIAL CHANGE IN CHINA

There is very little continuity between the sports of premodern and modern China. Modern sports were introduced through contact with Japan and the West. They were promoted from the top down in the process of nation building by the Nationalist and Communist states. The Communist Party's promotion of sports is a strategy for promoting China's image in the international arena and for promoting the party's image in the domestic arena.

Modern sports are not firmly grounded in the Chinese beliefs about human physiology and morality. The traditional forms of physical culture were in greater harmony with an overall view of the cosmos and the proper relationships among the cosmos, the person, and the body. The symbolism of traditional sports was firmly located within a worldview whose significant elements included the agricultural seasons, local and ethnic identities, shared myths and customs, and the ritual trappings of imperial power. These elements have now lost much of their importance in daily life. The symbolic appeal of modern sports is chiefly based on the fact that they represent ''modernity'' and participation in global culture, notions that arouse patriotic and nationalistic fervor. However, this appeal is only superficial. In their everyday lives, people are still much more likely to practice *qigong, taiji,* or other traditional activities. In rural southern China, the dragon boat races have become bigger and more heated in recent years.

An exception to the top-down model of Western sports is the grass-roots popularity of bodybuilding, which may indicate that some of the traditional concepts of the body are changing. In the case of bodybuilding, these changes are due on the one hand to the desire of the Chinese people to participate in transnational trends; on the other hand, to their increasing ability to do so under economic decentralization and growing prosperity. This picture is overly simplified, however, because it is also true that sport as a cultural form helps people at the local level adjust to the changing socioeconomic structures in which they find themselves enmeshed. Hence, the adoption of new sport forms is not just a result of the changing worlds in which Chinese live; it also enables the changes that are taking place in those worlds.

NOTES

1. Perhaps the best source on these aspects of Chinese popular culture is found in David Johnson, Andrew J. Nathan, and Evelyn S. Rawski, eds., *Popular Culture in Late Imperial China* (Berkeley: University of California Press, 1985).

2. See Gu Shiquan (1990, 3–24), Gene Rizak (1989, 101–20), Kohsuke Sasajima (1973, 35–44), and Jonathan Kolatch (1972). The most thorough Chinese history appears

to be *Zhongguo gudai tiyu* (Ancient Chinese Physical Culture) (1983), edited by Xu Yongchang.

3. On the debate over what is "modern" about modern sports, see *From Ritual to Record* (1979) by Allen Guttmann and *Ritual and Record* (1990) edited by John Marshall Carter and Arnd Krüger.

4. These gendered differences of meaning were suggested to me by the discussions of ancient Spartan women who engaged in physical training. The Spartans most likely considered it training for motherhood or a means of inspiring young men to marry, rather than training for war. See Anton Powell 243–45 and Licht 95.

5. See Edward A. Armstrong, "Chinese Bull Ritual and Its Affinities" (1945), Carl W. Bishop, "The Ritual Bullfight" (1925), Richard Rudolph, "Bull Grappling in Early Chinese Reliefs" (1960), and Edward H. Schafer, "Hunting Parks and Animal Enclosures in Ancient China" (1968).

6. Western sources often transcribe the character as *jue* when referring to *jiaodi* and theatrical performances, but I have found that in colloquial speech, the Chinese say *jiao;* the New World Press also transcribes it in this way.

7. On the notion of "sportization," see Norbert Elias, *Quest for Excitement: Sport and Leisure in the Civilizing Process,* edited by Norbert Elias and Eric Dunning (Oxford: Basil Blackwell, 1986), pp. 22, 129–31.

8. For a review of *Sport in China,* see Susan E. Brownell, in *Journal of Sport Management* 5.2 (1991): 193–94.

9. See Rizak, Clumpner, Pendleton, Riordan, and Amos.

10. Chinese participation in the Olympic Games as one aspect of international relations is described in Richard Espy, *The Politics of the Olympic Games* (1979), David B. Kanin, "Ideology and Diplomacy: The Dimensions of Chinese Political Sport" (1978), and Kolatch, *Sports, Politics, and Ideology* (1978). A chart listing the world and Asian sports organizations of which China is a member, and years of withdrawal and resumption of membership, is listed in *Sports and Public Health* (1983), 112–17.

11. See also Kolatch, *Sports, Politics and Ideology;* and *Sports and Public Health* (1983).

12. The Beijing Asian Games are discussed in an English language booklet distributed to foreigners at the games: *XI Asian Games, Beijing, 1990,* edited by Beijing Review. The Asian Games and the Games of the New Emerging Forces (which include Asian, African, and Latin American countries) are discussed in Kolatch, *Sports, Politics and Ideology* and in Swanpo Sie, "Sports and Politics: The Case of the Asian Games and the Ganefo" (1978).

BIBLIOGRAPHY

Aijmer, Goran. *The Dragon Boat Festival on the Hupeh-Hunan Plain, Central China: A Study in the Ceremonialism of the Transplantation of Rice.* Stockholm: Stockholm Statens Etnografiska Museum (The Ethnographical Museum of Sweden, Stockholm) Monograph Series Publication no. 9, 1964.

Amos, Daniel Miles. "Marginality and the Hero's Art: Martial Artists in Hong Kong and Guangzhou." Ph.D. diss., University of California at Los Angeles, 1983.

Armstrong, Edward A. "Chinese Bull Ritual and Its Affinities." *Folk-lore* 56 (1945): 200–207.

Beijing Review, ed. *XI Asian Games, Beijing, 1990.* Beijing: New Star Publishers, 1990.

Bishop, Carl W. "The Ritual Bullfight." *China Journal of Science and Arts* 3 (1925): 630–37.

Bower, Virginia L. "Polo in Tang China: Sport and Art." *Asian Art* 4,1 (Winter 1991): 25.

Brownell, Susan E. "The Changing Relationship between Sport and the State in the People's Republic of China." In *Sport . . . the Third Millennium,* 295–302. Proceedings of the International Symposium, May 21–25, 1990. Quebec City, Canada: Les Presses de l'Université Laval, 1991.

————. "The Olympic Movement on Its Way into Chinese Culture." Ph.D. diss., University of California, Santa Barbara, 1990.

————. Review of *Dangdai zhongguo tiyu* (Contemporary Chinese Sports), by Rong Gaotang et al. *International Journal of the History of Sport* 6, 1 (May 1989): 140–41.

————. Review of *Sport in China,* by Howard Knuttgen, Ma Qiwei, and Wu Zhongyuan, eds. *Journal of Sport Management* 5,2 (1991):193–94.

————. "Sports in Britain and China, 1850–1920: An Explanatory Overview." *International Journal of the History of Sport* 8,2 (1991): 114–20.

Cao Xiangjun. *Tiyu gailun* (A General Theory of Physical Culture). Beijing: Beijing Institute of Physical Education Press, 1985.

Carter, John M., and Arnd Krüger, eds. *Ritual and Record: Sports Records and Quantification in Pre-Modern Societies.* Westport, Conn.: Greenwood Press, 1990.

Chang Ying-jen. *The Rise of Martial Arts in China and America.* Ph.D. diss., New School for Social Research, 1978.

"China's Fear of the Bikini." *Time,* December 15, 1986, 48.

Clumpner, Roy, and Brian B. Pendleton. "The People's Republic of China." In *Sport under Communism: The U.S.S.R., Czechoslavakia, the G.D.R., China, Cuba,* edited by James Riordan, 103–39. Montreal, Quebec: McGill-Queen's University Press, 1978.

Diem, Carl. *Asiatische Reiterspiele: Ein Beitrag zur Kulturgeschichte der Völker.* Berlin: Deutscher Archiv-Verlag, 1941.

Elias, Norbert, and Eric Dunning, eds. *Quest For Excitement: Sport and Leisure in the Civilizing Process.* Oxford: Basil Blackwell, 1986.

Espy, Richard. *The Politics of the Olympic Games.* Berkeley: University of California Press, 1979.

Gabriel, Trip. "China Strains for Olympic Glory." *New York Times Magazine,* April 24, 1988, 30–40, 112.

Giles, Herbert A. "Football and Polo in China." *Nineteenth Century and After* 59 (1906): 508–13.

Gu Shiquan. "Introduction to Ancient and Modern Chinese Physical Culture." In *Sport in China,* edited by Howard G. Knuttgen, Ma Qiwei, and Wu Zhongyuan. Champaign, Ill.: Human Kinetics Books, 1990.

Guojia tiwei zhengce yanjiushi (State Sports Commission Policy Research Division). *Tiyu yundong wenjian xuanbian 1949–1981* (Selected Sport and Physical Culture Documents 1949–1981). Beijing: Renmin tiyu chubanshe, 1982.

Guttmann, Allen. *From Ritual to Record: The Nature of Modern Sports.* Boulder, Colo.: Colorado University Press, 1979.

He Zhenliang. "Sport for Our Children." *China Sports* October (1987): 25–29.

Hoberman, John M. "Purism and the Flight from the Superman: The Rise and Fall of Maoist Sport." In *Sport and Political Ideology,* Austin: University of Texas Press, 1984. 219–31.

———. "Sport and Social Change: The Transformation of Maoist Sport." *Sociology of Sport Journal* 4 (1987): 156–79.

Kang Bing. "Schools for Champions." *China Daily,* February 3, 1988.

Kanin, David B. "Ideology and Diplomacy: The Dimensions of Chinese Political Sport." In *Sport and International Relations,* edited by Benjamin Lowe, David B. Kanin, and Andrew Strenk, 263–78. Champaign, Ill.: Stipes Publishing, 1978.

Knuttgen, Howard G., Ma Qiwei, and Wu Zhongyuan, eds. *Sport in China.* Champaign, Ill.: Human Kinetics Books, 1990.

Kolatch, Jonathan. *Sports, Politics, and Ideology in China.* Middle Village, N.Y.: Jonathan David Publishers, 1972.

Kong Xiang'an, Niu Xinghua, and Qiu Bo. "A Summary of Sport Sociology Research in the PRC." Translated by Susan E. Brownell. *International Review for the Sociology of Sport* 25,2 (1990): 93–108.

Levenson, Joseph R. *Confucian China and Its Modern Fate: Vol. 2, The Problem of Monarchical Decay.* Berkeley: University of California Press, 1964.

Lewis, Mark Edward. *Sanctioned Violence in Early China.* Albany: State University of New York Press, 1990.

Lin Nan and Xie Wen. "Occupational Prestige in Urban China." *American Journal of Sociology* 93, 4 (1988): 793–832.

Liu, James J. Y. *The Chinese Knight-Errant.* Chicago: University of Chicago Press, 1967.

Liu, James T. C. "Polo and Cultural Change: From T'ang to Sung China." *Harvard Journal of Asiatic Studies* 45, 1 (1985): 203–24.

Lüschen, Gunter R.F., and George H. Sage, eds. *Handbook of Social Science of Sport.* Champaign, Ill.: Stipes, 1981.

McIntyre, Thomas D. "Sport in the German Democratic Republic and the People's Republic of China: A Sociopolitical Analysis." *Journal of Physical Education, Recreation and Dance* (January 1985): 108–11.

People's Sports Editorial Group. *Minzu tiyu jijin* (Outstanding examples of minority physical culture). Beijing: Renmin tiyu chubanshe, 1985.

Potter, Sulamith Heins, and Jack M. Potter. *China's Peasants: The Anthropology of a Revolution.* Cambridge, England: Cambridge University Press, 1990.

Rigauer, Bero. *Sport and Work.* Translated by Allen Guttmann. New York: Columbia University Press, 1981.

Riordan, James. *Sport, Politics and Communism.* Manchester, England: Manchester University Press, 1991.

Rizak, Gene. "Sport in the People's Republic of China." In *Sport in Asia and Africa: A Comparative Handbook,* edited by Eric A. Wagner, 101–20. Westport, Conn.: Greenwood Press, 1989.

Rong Gaotang et al. *Dangdai zhongguo tiyu* (Contemporary Chinese Sports). Beijing: Chinese Academy of Social Sciences Press, 1984.

Rudolph, Richard. "Bull Grappling in Early Chinese Reliefs." *Archeology* 13 (Winter 1960): 241–45.

Sansone, David. *Greek Athletics and the Genesis of Sport.* Berkeley: University of California Press, 1988.

Sasajima, Kohsuke. "Early Chinese Physical Education and Sport." In *A History of Sport and Physical Education,* edited by Earle F. Ziegler, 35–44, Champaign, Ill.: Stipes Publishing, 1973.

Schafer, Edward H. "Hunting Parks and Animal Enclosures in Ancient China." *Journal of the Economic and Social History of the Orient* 11 (1968): 318–43.

Seban, Martha. "Political Ideology and Sport in the People's Republic of China and the Soviet Union." In *Sport in the Sociopolitical Process,* edited by Marie Hart, 306–16. Dubuque, Iowa: Wm. C. Brown, 1972.

Shih Chi-wen. *Sports Go Forward in China.* Peking: Foreign Languages Press, 1963.

Sie, Swanpo. "Sports and Politics: The Case of the Asian Games and the Ganefo." In *Sport and International Relations,* edited by Benjamin Lowe, David B. Kanin, and Andrew Strenk, 279–96. Champaign, Ill.: Stipes Publishing, 1978.

Smith, Gary. "The Great Leap Upward." *Sports Illustrated* 18 (July 1984): 522–33.

Sports and Games in Ancient China. Beijing: New World Press, 1986.

Sports and Public Health. Beijing: Foreign Language Press, 1983.

Sports in Ancient China. Hong Kong: Tai Dao, 1986.

"Sports in China: The Birth of an Athletic Power." *Sports Illustrated,* 15 August 1988, 8.

Tiyu cidian bianji weiyuanhui (Physical Culture Dictionary Editorial Committee). *Tiyu cidian* (Physical Culture Dictionary). Shanghai: Shanghai Dictionary Publishing House, 1984.

Van Gulik, R. H. *Sexual Life in Ancient China: A Preliminary Survey of Chinese Sex and Society From ca. 1500* B.C. *till 1644* A.D. Leiden, Netherlands: E.J. Brill, 1961.

Xie Lingzheng. *Shixi Zhongguo jindai tiyushi shang de "tu yang zhi zheng"* (A Preliminary Analysis of the Conflict between Indigenous and Foreign Physical Culture in Modern Chinese History). Master's thesis. Beijing Institute of Physical Education, 1988.

Xu Yongchang, ed. *Zhongguo gudai tiyu* (Ancient Chinese Physical Culture). Beijing: Beijing Normal University Press, 1983.

Yang Ssu-ch'ang. "The Dragon Boat Races in Wu-ling, Hunan." Translated by Chao Wei-pang. *Folklore Studies* 2 (1943): 1–18.

Zhao Yu. "Qiangguo meng" (Superpower Dream). *Dangdai* (Contemporary Times), February 1988, 163–98.

Zhuang Kongshao, producer and director. *The Dragon-Boat Festival* (videocassette). Seattle: University of Washington Press, 1992.

8

Taijiquan and Qigong

J. A. ENGLISH-LUECK

The mind is the commander, and the body is subservient to it.[1]

A powerful image is associated with China, portraying a disciplined mind, mastering and merging with the body as it slowly plays the forms of *taijiquan* (t'ai-chi-ch'uan)[2] or concentrates vitality through the breath control techniques of *qigong* (chi kung). This association not only conjures an internal Chinese image of authentic Han identity, it is internationally recognized and, to a certain extent, globally enacted. The dual perspective, internal and external, is one that runs through the English language literature on both *taijiquan* and *qigong*. The English language sources on these subjects come from varied perspectives.

Few come directly from the People's Republic of China. Useful and available Chinese sources on *taiji* include *Yang Style Taijiquan*, edited by Yu Shenquan; *T'ai Chi Ch'uan: The Basic Exercises*, by Wang Peikun and Shing Yen-Ling; *Wu Style Tradition: A Detailed Course for Health and Self-defence and Teachings of Three Famous Masters in Beijing*, by Wang Paisheng and Zeng Weiqi; and *Simplified ''Taijiquan,''* compiled by the China Sports Editorial Board. These books are primarily written as instruction manuals, but they also contain asides on history, application, and popular use. Chinese sources on *qigong* combine the approach of the instruction manual with glowing essays on medical effectiveness. Examples of these texts include *The Wonders of Qigong: A Chinese Exercise for Fitness, Health and Longevity*, edited by China Sports Magazine; *Traditional Chinese Fitness Exercises*, compiled by China Sports and New World Press; and Zhang Mingwu and Sun Xingyuan's *Chinese Qigong Therapy*.

These sources are augmented by foreigners' observations, often tinged with romanticism, about *taiji* or *qigong* in Chinese popular culture. Particularly fertile and detailed sources exist expressing the sympathetic foreign practitioner's viewpoint regarding *qigong*. Especially noteworthy are David Eisenberg and Thomas Lee Wright's *Encounters with Qi: Exploring Chinese Medicine*, Masaru Takahashi and Stephen Brown's *Qigong for Health: Chinese Traditional Exercises for Cure and Prevention*, and Philip Lansky and Wu Shen's ''Qigong: Its Hidden Agenda.''

The instructional materials prepared by the overseas Chinese *taijiquan* practitioners yield a richer source of information, reflecting the martial arts tradition of the Yang, Wu, and Chen schools. Historic masters set up schools and taught students throughout China and, in time, experts in Taiwan acquired overseas Chinese students who contributed significantly to *taiji* literature. Such sources are interesting for students of overseas Chinese culture and often yield historic tidbits on the development of the schools or offer English translations of classic commentaries written in China. A standard reference set would include the series by Zheng Manqian (listed in bibliography under Cheng Man-Ch'ing): *T'ai Chi Ch'uan: A Simplified Method of Calisthenics for Health and Self-defense, Cheng Tzu's Thirteen Treatises on Tai Chi Ch'uan, Cheng Man-Ch'ing's Advanced T'ai-chi Form Instructions*, as well as the volume coedited with Robert Smith, *T'ai-chi: The ''Supreme Ultimate'' Exercise for Health, Sport, and Self-defense*. Douglas Wile's *T'ai-chi Touchstones: Yang Family Secret Transmissions* is also on Zheng's style of *taijiquan*. Other useful references by Taiwanese or overseas Chinese practitioners include Tsung Hwa Jou's *The Tao of Tai-chi Chuan: Way to Rejuvenation*, Douglas Lee's *Tai Chi Chuan: The Philosophy of Yin and Yang and Its Application*, T. T. Liang's *T'ai Chi Ch'uan for Health and Self-defense: Philosophy and Practice*, Da Liu's *The Tao of Health and Longevity*, and Wenshan Huang's *Fundamentals of T'ai Chi Ch'uan*. Huang's work is probably the most erudite of these resources, and it also includes information on *qigong*. Overseas Chinese commentaries on the classical practice of Taoist breathing and *qigong* include Jane Huang and Michael Wurmbrand's *The Primordial Breath* and Chee Soo's *The Chinese Art of K'ai Men*. Both books are more interested in philosophy and historic practice than in contemporary culture.

Finally, foreign—European, American, or Japanese—adherents of both *taiji* and *qigong* write guides and commentaries on the traditions. Much of that international literature is so highly cast in New Age language that it reveals more about European or American popular culture and values than it does about *Chinese* popular culture. The greater portion of this foreign literature is omitted here. Manuals that include interesting historic and philosophical items include *The T'ai Chi Workbook*, by the British martial artist, Paul Crompton; *T'ai-Chi Ch'uan: Body and Mind in Harmony, the Integration of Meaning and Method*, by the dancer *taiji* advocate, Sophia Delza; and *Tai Chi Ch'uan: The Technique of Power*, written as an inspirational guide by Tem Horwitz, Susan Kimmelman, and H. H. Lui. Robert C. Sohn's *Tao and T'ai Chi Kung* is heavily influenced by Western concepts of Taoism.

There are also peripheral studies, by both Chinese and foreign scholars, on traditional Chinese medicine (TCM) that may briefly touch on the assumptions and practices of *taiji* and *qigong* as they relate to classic or folk medical practices. Highly erudite theoretical considerations include Manfred Porkert's "The Intellectual and Social Impulses behind the Evolution of Traditional Chinese Medicine," and Porkert and Christian Ullman's *Chinese Medicine.* Ilza Veith's translation of *The Yellow Emperor's Classic of Internal Medicine* gives useful access to the chief work of traditional Chinese medicine.

Much of the literature in medical anthropology and medical sociology has focused on three areas: the epistemology of Western/Chinese synthesis of medical beliefs, the social context of practitioner training and professionalization, and the description of traditional folk beliefs. Empirical research on urban popular health practices needs to be further developed. Finally, there is a lacuna of etic works analyzing *taiji* or *qigong* as *cultural phenomena,* either as symbols of Chinese ethos or as social movements.

Before addressing bibliographic concerns per se, it would be useful to discuss the development and current practices of *taiji* and *qigong* in China. Some discussion of international diffusion will be necessary so that the diverse sources of information can be put in their proper context. Indeed, it is a source of pride for China that the ethos attached to *taiji* and *qigong* is part of the international scene in both sports and health. For the world to recognize a special Chinese affinity to health, longevity, and spiritual mastery reinforces those concepts in the motherland.

HISTORICAL SURVEY

The Development of *Taijiquan*

In the late twentieth century, *taiji* has come to be known as a specific form of *wushu,* or martial arts, with implications for health. The importance of health as the primary venue of discourse, however, has been a relatively recent innovation. For much of its history, *taijiquan* was clearly a martial art. *Taiji* reflects a multitude of applications including boxing, sword, and javelin. The "boxing" element is most well known as a set of solitary postures and movements using circular, gentle, and even motions. The key is physical and mental coordination, balancing the external and internal. Visions materialize of synchronized elders "playing *taiji*" in a park. More advanced skill is required for *tuishou,* or push hands. Two *taiji* adepts pair off. One partner pushes; the other turns his waist to ward off the blow and neutralize it, and then presses back. The internal focus is on sensing the opponent's motion, effortlessly redirecting it, and cycling into pushing toward the opponent's waiting redirection. This emphasis on the internal has placed *taiji* in the "soft" or "internal" forms of *wushu.* In international martial arts, it is not as nonaggressive and reactive as the Japanese aikido, whose roots stem from *taiji,* but neither is it a technique that relies on force or aggression to overwhelm, such as the Chinese Shaolin traditions or the Korean tae kwon do. In a martial exchange, the principles of *taiji* would translate into reacting to the opponent's motions and seizing each opportunity to turn that motion into an awkward movement that can be aggressively exploited. *Taiji* in competitive action is not slow, nor necessarily gentle. The pinnacle of martial prowess, however, is not necessarily the goal sought by modern advocates of *taiji*, who may concentrate on the solitary forms that reinforce the principles of the discipline to enhance health and promote longevity. The latter illuminates the popularity of *taiji* in contemporary China, especially among the elderly.

The current forms of *taiji* are the culmination of a long series of innovations and traditions, particularly in the last two centuries. The history of *taiji* can be divided into three phases: masters from antiquity, the development of major schools, and the codification and international expansion of contemporary forms.

In the distant past, the historic roots of *taiji* are obscured by mythic narrative. Zhang Sanfeng (Chang San-feng), a Yuan dynasty Taoist priest, reputedly created a primal *taiji* form in the Wudang mountains nearly 800 years ago. His inspiration was a dream in which he was taught boxing by Emperor Xuan Wu. Regardless of the mythic quality of this tale, the key point is that a new approach to *wushu* was created, the *nei jia,* the internal form. This style was clearly different from the *wai jia,* the external forms of the active and aggressive Buddhist Shaolin style.

On a more historical note, during the late Ming or early Qing Dynasty, the Chen family tradition developed in Chenjiagou, Wenxian County, Henan province, nearly 300 years ago. It probably evolved from a folk variation of the *nei jia* martial arts tradition that used eight key postures. The key figure in this tradition was Chen Wangting, reputedly a garrison commander in Wenxian County. He cultivated a new style of ''subduing the vigorous by the soft'' that used thirteen forms, the essential core of *taijiquan.* This nucleus of postures and movements is also called *Changquan,* translated as ''long boxing,'' poetically referring to the flow of the Changjiang, or Yangtze, river. In the late eighteenth-century, Wang Zongyue (Wang Tsung-yueh) gentrified the folk forms of the Chen family tradition by adding the classical concepts of yin and yang, and named the boxing style *taijiquan.* Henan province, the home of the Chen family, continued to be the haven of this new *wushu.*

In the nineteenth and twentieth centuries, the second phase of *taijiquan* development ensued as the five major schools of *taiji* were systematized. A serious student of the art will identify with one of these five major traditions. *Taiji* adepts should know their teachers' ''lineages,'' extending back several generations. This is especially critical in the competitive arena but may also be significant to the burgeoning health-related aficionados. The five key schools are the Chen (*lao jia*—old frame), Yang (*da jia*—big frame), Wu (*zhong jia*—middle frame), a different Wu (*xiao jia*—small frame, also called Hao style), and Sun (*huobu jia*—lively pace frame). Details of the different styles of the Chen, Yang, and Wu/Hao schools are well defined in Jou's *The Tao of Tai-chi Chuan.*

The still extant Chen family style uses gentle and vigorous motions and is filled with jumps, leaps, and explosions of strength—all worked out in circular paths. Meanwhile other traditions have continued to emerge. The Wu tradition uses more moderate postures—lithe and more dance-like. The name is derived from a royal guard captain of the Manchu nationality, Wu Quanyu (Wu Chuan Yu, 1834–1902), who in turn taught his son, Wu Jianquan (Wu Chien-chuan, 1870–1942), who popularized the Wu form. Wang Paisheng (b. 1919) in Beijing continues this tradition, having simplified (in 1953) the eighty-one posture form to thirty-seven. The dance-like motions of this style have contributed to its international popularity. *T'ai-Chi Ch'uan: Body and Mind in Harmony, the Integration of Meaning and Method* is devoted to this style. It was written by Sophia Delza, a popular international figure who has emphasized the dance side of *taiji*. She has been pivotal in the transition of Chinese *taiji* into the international artistic set.

The second Wu school, or Hao style, was established by Wu Yuxiang (Wu Yu-Hsing, 1812–1880), a fellow villager and student of Yang Luchan, the founder of the Yang school. This style was popularized by Hao Weizhen (Hao Wei-jin, 1849–1920). The series of forms, which are simple and quick, use short range movements, especially the opening and closing of one's arms. The Sun school was developed by Sun Lutang (1861–1932), who incorporated elements from other internal forms of *wushu* such as nimble movements and a quick tempo. This "lively pace" form is closely related to the second Wu, or Hao, school.

The Yang school is by far the most popular in China and elsewhere. In 1852 Yang Luchan (1799–1872) acquired *taijiquan* from the Chen family, who had dominated it in circumstances shrouded in mystery and legend. Yang reportedly returned with this knowledge to his home, Yongnian County, in Hebei. Over the next few generations, the standardized Yang form evolved. Yang Luchan (also known as Yang Fukui) then taught his sons, Yang Banhou (Yang Panhou, 1837–1892) and Yang Jianhou (Yang Chien-hou, 1839–1917). Yang Jianhou taught his two sons, Yang Shaohou (1862–1930) and Yang Chengfu (1883–1936). Yang Banhou and Yang Shaohou were reputed to be "bellicose" and developed a more vigorous, martial style. In contrast, Yang Chengfu (1883–1936), Yang Luchan's grandson, expanded the style and promoted the concept of strength concealed in gentle movements. Yang Chengfu was the one who systematized the unique features of the Yang school—extended and natural postures, slow and even motions, and light, steady, curving movements. Yang Chengfu taught *taiji* in Nanjing, Shanghai, Hangzhou, and Guangzhou and spread it to southern and eastern China. This began the third, modern phase of the dissemination of *taiji*. Yang Chengfu's heyday coincided with the aftermath of the May 4th movement, in which intellectuals reappraised various aspects of tradition and the discussion was directed to "self-strengthening." Young intellectuals embraced martial arts. Yang Chengfu himself wrote about the need to strengthen the Chinese people against Japanese imperialism and Western models of modernization (Wile 1983, 153).

The lineage of Yang Chengfu's students defines the key *taijiquan* masters of the early twentieth-century: Zheng Manqin (Cheng Man-Ch'ing, a leading international master in Taiwan), Chen Weiming, Wu Huichuan, and Fu Zhongwen, to name a few. Yang Chengfu's own sons, Yang Zhenji (Yang Chen-chi), Yang Zhenduo (Yang Chen-to), Yang Zhenming, and Yang Zhenguo (Yang Chen-kuo), also developed reputations into the middle and later twentieth century as repositories of the Yang tradition. Yang Zhenduo (Yang Chen-to) in Taiyuan, Shanxi, is sometimes regarded as the heir to the orthodox Yang school.

The forms became increasingly relaxed in the twentieth century. The most popular Yang forms eliminated foot stomping and explosive strength moves. Both in post-liberation China and internationally, the Yang tradition increasingly has focused on health and has become accessible to men and women, old and young. The key to accessibility was the 1956 simplification of *taijiquan*. This set was derived from the Yang school, using twenty-four forms flowing from easiest to the most difficult. This act was the single greatest stimulus to popularization. In 1959, again based on Yang forms, a comprehensive set of eighty-eight forms (referred to as the national forms) became the basis of competition in the Chinese physical culture community.

The creation of the five schools, and the many resulting subschools, set the stage for the massive popularity of *taijiquan* in the late twentieth century. The growth of health consciousness in the New China was concurrent with the changes in *taiji* form. The publication and dissemination of classic works in both traditional Chinese medicine and *wushu* have allowed for an unprecedented synthesis of different traditions and a revitalization of health-related traditions.

The Development of *Qigong*

There is a huge void in the English language literature regarding the direct description and discussion of the health-related beliefs of the urban popular culture. Indirectly, *taiji* occupies that niche. Another element of the popular, health-related belief is *qigong*. This term reflects a whole range of practices, derived from Taoist breath control exercises, that are intimately tied into the epistemology of classic traditional Chinese medicine. Yet the writings on *qigong* in the modern Chinese press reflect such diverse material as psychic phenomena, cancer therapies, and the unique mystique of the Han people.

Qigong is a collection of methods designed to enhance *qi,* the essential energy of the universe. *Qi* is not an undifferentiated substance, but reflects the varying conditions of life. In particular, distinctions are drawn between the life force at conception, in the fetal stage, and after birth. Breathing and eating are links between the internal body and external nature. Mastery of the different *qi* forms is the key to *qigong. Gong,* the act of attaining mastery in a method, as in *gongfu* (kungfu), provides the second character in *qigong.*

The system is reputed to be 5,000 years old, although this probably refers to some of the techniques rather than to *qigong* as an organized system. For brief histories of *qigong,* consult Li Meibin's "Qigong: Its Origin and Development"

(1985, 11–12), Lili Cui's "Fitness and Health through Qigong" (1989, 16–20), Gu Shiquan's "Introduction to Ancient and Modern Chinese Physical Culture" (1990, 10–13), and Wu Yan's "Qigong—Chinese Keep-fit Exercises" (1991, 59–60). Traditionally, ritual dances were used to combat arthritis, muscle ailments, and skin diseases. During the Spring and Autumn Period (770 B.C.E.– 475 B.C.E.), the founder of Taoism, Lao Zi, is said to have elaborated on the relationships among *qigong,* morality, behavior, and self-cultivation, lifting the context of the dances from health to philosophy. In health care, the elaboration continued. Nearly 2,400 years ago, the *Huangdi nei jing* (The Yellow Emperor's Classic of Internal Medicine), translated by Veith, united *qigong* theory and treatment by recommending mental disciplines and breath control for kidney disease.

One of the most exciting pieces of evidence for the antiquity of *qigong* was the discovery of a site dating to the second century B.C.E. in the archaeological excavations at Mawangdui near Changsha, Hunan province (Gu 1990, 11). This Western Han Dynasty site contained a silk scroll picturing forty *qigong* postures. During the Eastern Han Dynasty (25–220 C.E.), a renowned fabled physician, Hua Tuo, formalized the five animal exercises (tiger, deer, bear, ape, bird): the *wuqinxi.* These became a core set for *qigong* postures. A Sui Dynasty medical tome discussed 260 *qigong* methods. Later, an eighteenth-century collection of ancient and modern books cited *qigong* as one of the four methods of traditional Chinese medicine (Cui 1989, 16).

Since 1949 significant efforts have been made to coordinate *qigong* endeavors in medical use, teaching, and popularization. In 1986 the State Education Commission included *qigong* as a sports department subject in teacher training colleges and other tertiary institutes. Another emphasis has been on scientific research. There are at least ten national and many local *qigong* scientific research associations. Official support is substantial. The China Qigong Scientific Research Association is one of forty-six branches of the China Scientific and Technological Association. The bulk of the material reflects medical case studies or surveys of patients that cite and describe improvements attributed to *qigong.*

Out of the six schools, the thirty methods, and the more than four hundred varieties of *qigong,* the theme emerges that the techniques should raise resistance to illness. The mind can be regulated through relaxation and concentration of mental and physical powers, with a maximum of ease and self-control. Ultimately, an individual should develop a strong constitution. This notion is an essential one in the naturalistic medical belief systems, the Great Tradition of traditional Chinese medicine, India's Ayurvedic medicine, and Europe's Hippocratic tradition. In such systems, the body is the ultimate defense against illness. Strengthening its systems by balancing energetic forces and elements is integral. In traditional Chinese medicine, self and nature are intertwined, so therapies must strive for coordination with nature. Maintaining a balance of yin and yang while permitting *qi* to circulate is the prime focus of the entire medical system, but especially *qigong.* In both the folk and the Great Tradition, enhanced *qi* protects against the six "evil" pathogenic factors—wind, fire, heat, wetness, dryness, cold, and fluctuating emotions.

The contemporary focus of *qigong* has gone beyond the realm of medicine into physical culture to increase general fitness and augment a psychological and physical edge in competition. *Qigong* is used in martial arts to enhance self-control and endurance. This direction is highlighted by the close kinship of *taiji* and *qigong*.

The multiplicity of perspectives can be illustrated by examining the three overlapping approaches to *qigong:* as a reflection of medical science, as a manifestation of traditional mystical Chinese power, or as an example of psychic phenomena. As mentioned before, the medical science framework dominates the literature coming out of China on *qigong*. Interestingly, American practitioners of naturalistic medicine (holistic health) rely on this Chinese literature and write in much the same style—overwhelmingly anecdotal—with each case representing a unique demonstration of power.[3] Hence stories such as the successful use of *waiqi* anesthesia in Shanghai's No. 8 People's Hospital would represent an illustration of validity (Bian 1985, 104). Even though aggregate data, based on many cases, is presented in the Western style of science language and statistics, controlled experimentation is conspicuously absent. This empirical style has led to international skepticism in the very realm of science and medical discourse. Their acceptance is complicated by the alternative forms of discussing *qigong*, particularly as a mystical power. This fashion of discussion itself may take two, often overlapping, forms. One mode is to see *qigong* as a religious manifestation of Taoism. This blends well with the classical tradition so strongly favored by overseas Chinese and sinological enthusiasts. Yet this is also the tone of everyday discussion. From 1988, for eighteen months, I lived in Chengdu, in the heart of Sichuan, near the Taoist Quingcheng Mountain. Both residents and other Chinese perceive Chengdu as a more traditional community, one deeply connected to ancestral wisdom, such as *qigong* and TCM. The power of traditional mysticism was given at least a nodding acceptance even in the university setting.

The second, less traditional, approach to the mysterious *qigong* is to view it as a "psychic" phenomenon, related to reputedly exceptional human functions (EHFs) such as the ability to channel electricity to illuminate lightbulbs. Paul Dong's *The Four Major Mysteries of Mainland China* and Dong and Aristide Esser's *Chi Gong: The Ancient Way to Health* provide examples of this tone, along with popular magazine articles. Again, drawing an analogy to alternative medical traditions in the United States and Europe, this parallels the distinctions made between the laying on of hands, a religious healing steeped in ancient Christian tradition, and psychic healing that reflects a worldview tied to ideas that are part of the nineteenth- and twentieth-century European esoteric tradition. In China, both the religious master and psychic specialist may be linked to the use of *waiqi qigong* (using outside *qi* forces to heal a client), which is a defining feature of masters of *qigong*.

As a system, *qigong*'s basic categories are more flexible than those in *taiji*.

There are divisions based on both form and function. Based on form, the essential division of *qigong* is into *Jinggong* and *Donggong*. The former is passive; it focuses on training breath postures, standing, sitting, or lying down. This category would include *Daoyin* styles, the oldest form of *qigong,* which unite breathing from the *dantian* (a focus below the navel) and sensing the sticky energy of *qi.* In one exercise, a person might concentrate on sensing the *qi* between one's hands while standing, knees slightly bent, with hands thirty centimeters apart. *Donggong* is more active, ranging from the nonstrenuous *Yijinjing* exercises to forms of *wushu,* especially *taiji.*

The divisions of *qigong* based on function are even more important for understanding the cultural context of the discipline. There are six basic schools of *qigong* whose missions encompass Confucian, Taoist, Buddhist, martial, and medical concerns. The final school is the collection of folk traditions associated with *qigong.* The Confucian school primarily reflects the works of Meng Zi (Mencius) on cultivating peace of mind (Liu 1986, 30–32). For a discussion of the differing approaches of Taoist and Confucian thought, refer to Liu's *The Tao of Health and Longevity* (1978). The Taoists balance the contemplation of nature with the practice of *qigong.* This school appears strongly in the international discourse that is concerned with Taoist classics. The Buddhist approach emphasizes the power of the mind over the body. Shaolin *si wushu* heralds the next school of *qigong,* the martial style. Other important forms include the Taoist internal martial art *bagua* (eight diagrams) and *taiji.* These indirectly promote health, but the key goals are to protect and strengthen oneself against moral assaults.

Of course, the overwhelming focus of *qigong* is medical, both in China and internationally. The goals are to treat disease, promote health, and prolong life. *Qigong* is cited in reference to a long list of diseases including stomach ulcers, nervous system disorders, cardiovascular problems, hypertension, pulmonary tuberculosis, chronic bronchitis (*gongmao*), hepatitis, nephritis, and impotence. One of the latest popular health practices is to use *qigong* in dieting, an urban pursuit that lacks much foundation in the classical literature of Chinese medicine, but looms large in the late twentieth century. The most striking discussions of *qigong* are on cancer. Examples of this can be found in Cui's "Fitness and Health through Qigong," Zhang and Sun's *Chinese Qigong Therapy,* Hou Ruili's "Cancer Victims Think Recovery," Takahashi and Brown's *Qigong for Health* (1986, 14), and Hong Xia's "Qigong Helps Life, Love." The Recovery Society of the China Anticancer Association founded in Beijing in 1990 is a case in point. It has several thousand members in twenty-seven cities in China (Hou 1991, 31). The basic thrust is the desire to "conquer" cancer and to aid the recovery process by doing *qigong* three to four hours each day. Joined with "communication therapy," a patient support group gives advice, provides lectures, and maintains an avenue of hope. Consider the following story. The artist Guo Lin developed cancer in 1949. She developed a new form of *qigong* and refined it until she died of a cerebral hemorrhage, not cancer, in 1984 at the age of seventy-five. Her technique and life continue to inspire cancer patients, and she is virtually a folk hero. The story of an individual healed or led to hope is a common motif.

The other form of discussion is less anecdotal, harnessing the language and forms of science writing to demonstrate physiological evidence to back up *qigong* theory. Both the research work on possible mechanisms and survival rates reflect the medicalization of *qigong*. The use of *qigong* by the patient is perceived as another in an arsenal of therapies. This reflects a deeper cultural issue, implying the need to redesign the epistemology of Chinese medical presentation—away from its naturalistic form to one more suitable to an urban audience—both internally and internationally. In such a presentation, the evidence is marshaled to demonstrate that *qigong* lessens the side effects of chemotherapy and radioactive treatments. Other physiological explanations for *qigong* include inducing a neurological state of relaxation, reducing energy consumption, and generating gastric juices and bile. Although Western medical practitioners may chide that literature for its lack of control subjects or unspecified sampling strategies, it represents a departure in the way in which the essentially spiritual discipline is approached.

On another level, however, the interests medical *qigong* expresses can be reduced to concern with longevity, a theme certainly in keeping with traditional Chinese medicine. This moral is brought to the forefront when examining *taijiquan*. Huang, one of the most academic of the authors on *taijiquan*, quotes the motto that the practice of *quan* (boxing) without studying *gong* (breathing system) would certainly end in failure when it comes to old age (1973, 9). It is the *qigong* of *taiji* that is essential in promoting longevity. Both *qigong* and *taiji* are considered suitable exercise for the elderly, especially women. Along with old people's disco, it is seen as a way of getting both necessary exercise and inner spiritual strengthening (Lu 1991, 19). In addition, the underlying theme of the special quality of *qigong* to transform physics and improve world health belies the tone of scientific objectivity (Cui 1989, 20).

Zajia (folk *qigong*) is the final form of *qigong*. The most telling aspect of this category in contemporary China may be the use of *waiqi*, external *qigong*. In this form, energy is released by a practitioner and emitted to patients. The patient is then healed by the projection of *qi*. Unlike the naturalistic forms of the Great Medical Traditions, this bears a closer resemblance to personalistic medicine, in which powerful individuals manipulate spirits or spiritual forces to effect healing. The references to the *qigong* masters who perform *waiqi* have this modern shamanic tone. Yet, this too has been medicalized by citing experiments of *waiqi* on cancer patients, as well as studies in which rat immunity is enhanced, and seeds mature earlier with more resistance to the cold (Cui 1989, 19).

CURRENT SCENE

Taiji is part of the international sports scene. As such it is useful both as a diplomatic tool and as a statement of Chinese identity (Blanchard and Cheska

1985, 270–74). *Taiji* can "enhance cultural interflow between peoples of the People's Republic of China and different countries of the world" (Wang and Zeng 1983, foreword). It is certainly a statement of Chinese identity in overseas Chinese communities. Taiwanese Zheng Manqian has been a key figure in teaching, revising, and simplifying the popular Yang style, and he has had a profound impact throughout Asia, Europe, and the United States. In the last decade, there has been an international renewal of the physical culture scene as an influx of teachers from the People's Republic of China have brought the National and Yang simplified forms, as well as other schools, to the rest of the world. In China, *taiji* has emerged on the physical culture scene as a martial arts sport. It was represented in the 1990 Eleventh Asian Games in Beijing as a formal competitive event. In popular sport, *taiji* ranges from a competitive to a casual exercise system, and grades into *taiji qigong* as a health-promoting regime. The focus is particularly on individually performed postures broadly appealing to women, the elderly, or the ill. Within China, *taiji* is geographically widely spread. In the competitive sphere, *taiji* is housed in physical culture departments in universities and, as such, is concentrated in Beijing, Shanghai, and provincial capital cities. Popular use extends far beyond the strict milieu of competitive sports. As a basic fitness system, *taiji* is ubiquitous. A Chinese article on the heavily physical sports of bodybuilding and Western aerobics refers to *taiji* as a *Chinese* way of exercising (Lu 1991, 19). *Qigong* is said to have 600,000 adherents in Jiangsu province alone.[4] In an article defining traditional Chinese sports, Wang Zeshan emphasizes the distinctiveness of the Chinese attitude in physical culture. Chinese sports, including *taiji* and *qigong,* uniquely blend mimicking nature, implementing philosophical values, and seeking health improvement (1990, 90).

Zheng Manqian and Robert Smith discuss the critical concept of effortlessness as a key to the *taiji* and *qigong* philosophy (1986, 2). Both disciplines subdue the self and are humbling. In reference to classical *taiji,* this discussion is heavily invested with the languages of Taoism and Confucianism. Other values are also expressed regarding *taiji.* "Self-strengthening" was a phrase used in the early part of this century to refer to the need to build Chinese moral character to withstand the onslaught of the outside. It is reflected in the literature by the key figures Yang Chengfu and Zheng Manqian, and it remains a part of the discourse in Taiwan. Again, the critical concept is that *taiji* is part of the Chinese national character, defining Chinese, that is, Han identity, hence its importance for overseas Chinese. In the People's Republic, this self-strengthening may still play a part, but it is expressed in terms of reducing the negative, early twentieth-century image of China as the "sick man of Asia," emphasizing the shift to healthy, improved conditions. Contemporary *taiji* and *qigong* are themselves considered improved forms, stemming from more scientific theories of anatomy, sports physiology, and biomechanics.

Currently, there are a proliferating number of *qigong* centers. Some may be specific to *qigong,* such as the well-known Beidaihe Qigong Therapy Institute, developed by Dr. Liu Guizhen, or they may be part of a college of traditional medicine, such as the Qigong Research Unit affiliated with the Shanghai Institute of Traditional Chinese Medicine. Others may conduct research and *qigong* practice housed in "Westernized" hospitals that seek to synthesize traditional Chinese medicine with the rationalist tradition of the West. Huaxi, West China Medical University in Chengdu, is an example of the latter. The organizations are primarily regional, but some are international, such as the World Academic Society of Medical Qigong organized in 1989.[5] At the other end of the spectrum, there has been an expanding number of practitioners of medical *qigong*. Regulation of that sector has proven tricky, and swindling has become an issue. In 1989 regulations were issued to "reestablish order in medical qigong." Practitioners must acquire a doctor's qualification and have conducted clinical work on at least thirty cases in designated hospitals to obtain a license. This authorization would be required for both practice and teaching.[6] The necessity for this regulation stems from the impossibility of externally validating the practitioners of *waiqi*, who use *qi* on clients. While *waiqi* is also subject to experimentation, the key concept is that a master has *internally* powerful *qi* that can reach out and effect a change in an ill person.

Coupled with this application of soft *qigong* is the concept of hard *qigong*, breaking steel rods by hand or foot, or injuring someone with a finger (Dong 1984, 145–53; Dong and Esser 1990, xxiii). The extraordinary powers may reflect traditional motifs of *wushu,* or may be styled EHF, such as mysteriously being able to read with the ears or see through objects (Dong 1984, 154–56). Three of the most interesting foreign writings on this "mystic aspect" of *qigong* in China are Eisenberg and Wright's *Encounters with Qi,* Dong's *The Four Major Mysteries of Mainland China,* and Dong and Esser's *Chi Gong.* Eisenberg, a Western medical student, studied TCM in the early 1980s. He later joined a team of medical scholars at Harvard to examine various aspects of TCM, including *qigong.* He is sympathetic, but his insights translate well to a rationalist Western intellectual audience. Paul Dong is an overseas Chinese journalist who traveled in China in the late 1970s through the 1980s. He has written for the *People's Daily* and Shanghai's *Nature Magazine.* Dong's books reflect the tone of many English language writings on *qigong*—awed and filled with the excitement of the esoteric.

Chinese ethos is a theme that spans a range of activities—competitive *wushu,* exercise and physical culture, health-promoting *taiji,* medical *qigong,* Taoist mastery, and psychic mystery. The theme is the essential *Chinese* flavor of *taiji* and *qigong.* The international attention paid to these disciplines only highlights that they are not Western. In social science and in cultural studies, much could be done to help comprehend the proliferation of a uniquely Chinese worldview as it revitalizes and renews Han life. To date, this has yet to be done.

REFERENCE WORKS

Two references come to the foreground on the subject of *taiji.* The first is Randy Nelson and Katherine C. Whitaker's *The Martial Arts: An Annotated*

Bibliography (1988). It includes resources on general aspects of *taiji*, history, biographies and profiles, philosophy, and instruction (335–52). An additional source is Nelson's *Martial Arts Reader: An Anthology of Historical and Philosophical Writings* (1989). It has a short section on *taijiquan* (338–39). No corresponding bibliography exists for *qigong*. Standard references, however, such as Tsuen-Hsuin Tsien and James K. M. Cheng's *China: An Annotated Bibliography of Bibliographies* (1978), yield a few resources, mostly in Chinese, under the headings of Taoism and traditional medicine.

Most of the works on both *taiji* and *qigong* have relatively sparse referencing. Paul Crompton's *The T'ai Chi Workbook* (1986), Sophia Delza's *T'ai-chi Ch'uan: Body and Mind in Harmony, the Integration of Meaning and Method* (1961), Tem Horwitz, Susan Kimmelman and H. H. Lui's *Tai chi Ch'uan: The Technique of Power* (1976), and Huang Wen-shan's *Fundamentals of T'ai Chi Ch'uan* (1973) do have bibliographies. Paul Dong and Aristide Esser have footnoted references in *Chi Gong: The Ancient Way to Health* (1990), as do David Eisenberg and Thomas Lee Wright in *Encounters with Qi: Exploring Chinese Medicine* (1985). Jane Huang and Michael Wurmbrand provide a bibliography on Taoism and *qigong* in *The Primordial Breath* (1987), volume 1.

Journals

In addition to the English language Chinese paper, *The China Daily*, which often contains tidbits on *taiji*, but especially on *qigong*, there is the ever useful monthly publication of the China Welfare Institute, *China Today* (formerly *China Reconstructs*). Both deal with aspects of *taiji* and *qigong* that reflect a somewhat conservative view of Chinese popular culture. Both sources are highly accessible.

There are also two English language specialty magazines that present a consistent flow of articles, primarily on *taiji*, but also on *qigong*. One is *Black Belt*, a specialty journal of the martial arts. The other is *T'ai Chi Magazine*, published through Wayfarer Publications, an American press based in Los Angeles. It includes articles from and about contemporary China and focuses on both *taiji* and *qigong*. Wayfarer Publications also specializes in books and videotapes about *taiji* and *qigong*. Along with China Books in San Francisco, it provides an avenue of cultural brokerage for the international market on Chinese culture.

RESEARCH COLLECTIONS

While English language resources do not have collections on either *taiji* or *qigong* per se, there are nonetheless collections with material on martial arts and traditional Chinese medicine. The Amateur Athletic Foundation of Los Angeles has a large research collection on international sports, including an on-line and compact disk database: sportdatabase. They carry *Black Belt* magazine and are on the OCLC interlibrary loan network. Among the best resources for the Chinese medical connection are the University of California, San Francisco Medical Library Oriental Collection, and Princeton University's Gest Oriental Library's Asian Collection. Overseas collections on Chinese medicine include the Brion Research Institute of Taiwan in Taipei (affiliated with the Oriental Healing Arts Institute of Palo Alto, California) and the Academy of Traditional Chinese Medicine's medical library in Beijing. Of course, more general research collections, in which a person might find relevant material in both English and Chinese, include:

- The Institute of Chinese Studies in Pasadena, California
- The Chinese Collection of Ohio State University in Columbus (with a functioning *taiji* program)
- The Center for Chinese Studies Library at the University of California, Berkeley
- The East Asian Library in the University of Kansas, Lawrence
- The Asia Library at the University of Michigan, Ann Arbor
- The East Asian Collection of Yale University, New Haven, Connecticut
- The Asian Collection of St. John's University, Jamaica, New York (focusing on Taoism).

NOTES

1. This saying was used by Yang Chengfu, one of the key figures in the Yang school of *taijiquan* (Yang and Chen 1988, 15).
2. Also commonly romanized in the Wade-Giles fashion as *t'ai chi ch'uan* and *chi kung*. Since much of the English language literature either comes through a Taiwanese connection or refers to "classical" English translations of Taoist literature, such romanizations may be more common than Pinyin. To adjust for this, Wade-Giles spellings will be given in parentheses following the Pinyin renderings.
3. For a discussion of American holistic health discourse, see J. A. English-Lueck, *Health in the New Age: A Study of California Holistic Practices* (Albuquerque: University of New Mexico Press, 1990), 73–75.
4. As claimed by the staff article, "Qigong Art Praised by Followers in Jiangsu." *China Daily,* July 7, 1989.
5. See Zhu Baoxia, "New Group to Promote Qigong," *China Daily,* November 18, 1989.
6. See Zhu Baoxia, "New Rules Will Affect Medical Qigong Practices," *China Daily,* November 20, 1989; Staff, "New Regulation," *China Daily,* November 29, 1989.

BIBLIOGRAPHY

Anderson, E. N., and Marja L. Anderson. "Folk Dietetics in Two Chinese Communities, and Its Implications for the Study of Chinese Medicine." In *Medicine in Chinese Cultures: Comparative Studies of Health Care in Chinese and Other Societies,* edited by Arthur Kleinman, 143–75. Washington, D.C.: U.S. Government Printing Office, 1975.

Bian Ji. "A Newfound Therapy." In *The Wonders of Qigong: A Chinese Exercise for Fitness, Health and Longevity.* Edited by *China Sports Magazine,* 104–6. Los Angeles: Wayfarer Press, 1985.

Blanchard, Kendall, and Alyce Taylor Cheska. *The Anthropology of Sport.* South Hadley, Mass.: Bergin and Garvey Publishers, 1985.

Cheng Man-Ch'ing. *Cheng Man-Ch'ing's Advanced T'ai-chi Form Instructions.* Translated and edited by Douglas Wile. Brooklyn, N.Y.: Sweet Ch'i Press, 1985.

———. *Cheng Tzu's Thirteen Treatises on Tai Chi Ch'uan.* Translated by Benjamin Pang Jeng Lo and Martin Inn. Berkeley, Calif.: North Atlantic Books, 1985.

———. *T'ai Chi Ch'uan: A Simplified Method of Calisthenics for Health and Self-defense.* Translated by Beauson Tseng. Berkeley, Calif.: North Atlantic Books, 1981.

Cheng Man-Ch'ing and Robert Smith. *T'ai-chi: The "Supreme Ultimate" Exercise for Health, Sport, and Self-defense.* Rutland, Vt.: Charles E. Tuttle, 1986.

China Sports and New World Press. *Traditional Chinese Fitness Exercises.* China Spotlight Series. Beijing: New World Press, 1984.

China Sports Editorial Board. *Simplified "Taijiquan."* Revised. China Sports Series. Beijing: Foreign Languages Press, 1983.

China Sports Magazine. The Wonders of Qigong: A Chinese Exercise for Fitness, Health and Longevity. Los Angeles: Wayfarer Publications, 1985.

Crompton, Paul. *The T'ai Chi Workbook.* Boston: Shambhala Publications, 1986.

Cui, Lili. "Fitness and Health through Qigong." *Beijing Review,* April 24–30, 1989, 16–20.

Delza, Sophia. *T'ai-Chi Ch'uan: Body and Mind in Harmony, the Integration of Meaning and Method.* 1961. Rev. Albany: State University of New York Press, 1985.

Dong, Paul. *The Four Major Mysteries of Mainland China.* Englewood Cliffs, N.J.: Prentice-Hall, 1984.

Dong, Paul, and Aristide Esser. *Chi Gong: The Ancient Way to Health.* New York: Paragon Press, 1990.

Dunn, Fred. "Medical Care in the Chinese Communities of Peninsular Malaysia." In *Medicine in Chinese Cultures: Comparative Studies of Health Care in Chinese and Other Societies,* edited by Arthur Kleinman, 297–326. Washington, D.C.: U.S. Government Printing Office, 1975.

Eisenberg, David, and Thomas Lee Wright. *Encounters with Qi: Exploring Chinese Medicine.* New York: Norton, 1985.

"Eyewitness: Heal It!" *Asiaweek* 21, 10 (1988): 42–47.

Gu Liuxin. "The Evolution of the Yang School of Taijiquan." In *Yang Style Taijiquan,* edited by Yu Shenquan, 4–9. Beijing: Morning Glory Press, 1988.

Gu Shiquan. "Introduction to Ancient and Modern Chinese Physical Culture." In *Sport in China,* edited by Howard Knuttgen, Ma Qiwei, and Wu Zhongyuan, 3–25. Champaign, Ill.: Human Kinetics Books, 1990.

Hong Xia. "Qigong Helps Life, Love." *China Daily,* July 13, 1989, n.p.

Horwitz, Tem, Susan Kimmelman, and H. H. Lui. *Tai Chi Ch'uan: The Technique of Power.* Chicago: Chicago Review Press, 1976.

Hou Ruili. "Cancer Victims Think Recovery." *China Today* (October 1991): 31–32.

Huang, Jane, and Michael Wurmbrand. *The Primordial Breath.* Translated by Jane Huang. Torrance, Calif.: Original Books, 1987.

Huang Wen-shan. *Fundamentals of T'ai Chi Ch'uan*. 1973. 5th rev. ed. Seattle, Wash.: South Sky Book Company, 1984.

Jou, Tsung Hwa. *The Tao of Tai-chi Chuan: Way to Rejuvenation*. Edited by Shoshana Shapiro. 1981. 3d rev. ed. Rutland, Vt.: Charles E. Tuttle, 1983.

Knuttgen, Howard, Ma Qiwei, and Wu Zhongyuan, eds. *Sport in China*. Champaign, Ill.: Human Kinetics Books, 1990.

Lansky, Philip, and Wu Shen. "Qigong: Its Hidden Agenda." *East West* (December 1989): 46–75.

Lee, Douglas. *Tai Chi Chuan: The Philosophy of Yin and Yang and Its Application*. Burbank, Calif.: Ohara Publications, 1976.

Li Gaozhong. "Wuqin Qigong." In *The Wonders of Qigong: A Chinese Exercise for Fitness, Health and Longevity*, edited by China Sports Magazine, 41–42, Los Angeles: Wayfarer Press, 1985.

Li Meibin. "Qigong: Its Origin and Development." In *The Wonders of Qigong: A Chinese Exercise for Fitness, Health and Longevity*, edited by China Sports Magazine, 11–12. Los Angeles: Wayfarer Publications, 1985.

Liang, T. T. "My Experience." *Martial Arts Reader: An Anthology of Historical and Philosophical Writings*. Edited by Randy Nelson. Woodstock, N.Y.: Overlook Press, 1989.

———. *T'ai Chi Ch'uan for Health and Self-defense: Philosophy and Practice*. Edited by Paul Gallagher. 1974. Rev. New York: Vintage Books, 1977.

Liu, Da. *T'ai Chi Ch'uan and Meditation*. New York: Schocken, 1986.

———. *The Tao of Health and Longevity*. New York: Schocken, 1978.

Lo, Benjamin Peng Jeng, ed. *The Essence of T'ai Chi Ch'uan: The Literary Tradition*. Richmond, Calif.: North Atlantic Books, 1979.

Lu Hui. "For the Sake of a Body Beautiful." *China Today* (October 1991): 20–23.

Lu Yin. "Women Find a Full Life after Retirement." *China Today* (March 1991): 17–19.

Nelson, Randy, ed. *Martial Arts Reader: An Anthology of Historical and Philosophical Writings*. Woodstock, N.Y.: Overlook Press, 1989.

Nelson, Randy, and Katherine C. Whitaker. *The Martial Arts: An Annotated Bibliography*. New York: Garland, 1988.

Porkert, Manfred. "The Intellectual and Social Impulses behind the Evolution of Traditional Chinese Medicine." In *Asian Medical Systems: A Comparative Study*, edited by Charles Leslie, 63–76. Berkeley: University of California Press, 1977.

Porkert, Manfred, and Christian Ullman. *Chinese Medicine*. Translated by Mark Howson. New York: William Morrow, 1988.

Sohn, Robert C. *Tao and T'ai Chi Kung*. Rochester, Vt.: Destiny Books, 1989.

Soo, Chee. *The Chinese Art of K'ai Men*. New York: Gordon and Cremonesi Publishers, 1977.

Staff. "New Regulation." *China Daily*, November 29, 1989, n.p.

———. "Qigong Art Praised by Followers in Jiangsu." *China Daily*, July 7, 1989, n.p.

Takahashi, Masaru, and Stephen Brown. *Qigong for Health: Chinese Traditional Exercises for Cure and Prevention*. New York: Japan Publications, 1986.

Tsien, Tsuen-Hsuin, and James K. M. Cheng. *China: An Annotated Bibliography of Bibliographies*. Boston: G. K. Hall, 1978.

Veith, Ilza, trans. *The Yellow Emperor's Classic of Internal Medicine* (Huang di nei jing). New ed. Berkeley: University of California Press, 1972.

Wang, Paisheng, and Zeng Weiqi. *Wu Style Tradition: A Detailed Course for Health and Self-defence and Teachings of Three Famous Masters in Beijing.* Beijing: Zhaohua Publishing House, 1983.

Wang Peikun and Shing Yen-Ling. *T'ai Chi Ch'uan: The Basic Exercises.* Translated by Sue-Shion Mei. Vol. 1, Chinese Martial Arts Series. Tokyo: Minato Research and Publishing, 1990.

Wang Zeshan. "Traditional and Popular Sports." In *Sport in China,* edited by Howard Knuttgen, Ma Qiwei, and Wu Zhongyuan, 89–105. Champaign, Ill.: Human Kinetics Books, 1990.

Weng, Chi-Hsiu Daniel. *Ch'ang Style T'ai-Chi-Ch'uan.* Taipei: n.p., 1987. Available through Dr. Daniel Weng, P.O. Box 1221, Cupertino, Calif., 95015.

Wile, Douglas. *T'ai-chi Touchstones: Yang Family Secret Transmissions.* Translated by Douglas Wile. Brooklyn, N.Y.: Sweet Ch'i Press, 1983.

Wu Xiaoming. "Role for Qigong in the Western Way." *China Daily,* October 10, 1988, n.p.

Wu Yan. "Qigong—Chinese Keep-fit Exercises." *China Today* (November 1991): 59–60.

Xu Jie. "Dieters Praise Qigong." *China Daily,* July 18, 1989, n.p.

Yang Chengfu, and Zhang Hongkui. "Talks on the Practice of Taijiquan." In *Yang Style Taijiquan,* edited by Yu Shenquan, 10–13. Beijing: Morning Glory Press, 1988.

Yang Chengfu, and Chen Weiming. "The Ten Essentials of Taijiquan." *Yang Style Taijiquan,* edited by Yu Shenquan, 13–15. Beijing: Morning Glory Press, 1988.

Yang Zhenduo. "Foreword." In *Yang Style Taijiquan,* edited by Yu Shenquan, 1–3. Beijing: Morning Glory Press, 1988.

Yu Shenquan, ed. *Yang Style Taijiquan.* Beijing: Morning Glory Press, 1988.

Zhang Mingwu and Sun Xingyuan. *Chinese Qigong Therapy.* Translated by Yang Entang. Jinan: Shangdong Science and Technology Press, 1985.

Zhu Baoxia. "New Group to Promote Qigong." *China Daily,* November 18, 1989, n.p.

———. "New Rules Will Affect Medical Qigong Practice." *China Daily,* November 20, 1989, n.p.

9

Wushu

ZHANG WEI AND TAN XIUJUN

As a priceless cultural heritage developed and enriched in the long process of social practice of the Chinese people, *wushu,* which literally means "martial arts," enjoys great popularity among the broad masses of the people. It consists of two general forms, namely, exercising sport and fighting sport. Based on simulated fighting with bare hands and with weapons, the Chinese *wushu* combines the techniques of attack and defense, such as kicking, throwing, holding, striking, falling, chopping, and stabbing. With its tremendous appeal to people of all ages, sexes, and races, *wushu* has now been studied and practiced by people in China and abroad, and it is becoming an important part of international sports.

Since ancient times, the great interest of the Chinese people in *wushu* and their high appreciation of the great *wushu* masters for their marvelous skills have exerted a significant impact on the makings of Chinese character and Chinese traditional culture and art. In a sense, *wushu* is not only a kind of sport, but also a unique kind of physical culture. Throughout Chinese history, *wushu* has always been regarded as more than a kind of sport. Before the appearance of firearms, *wushu,* with its fighting capacity of high military significance, embodied tactical ideas and the collective wisdom of many strategists in ancient China. Furthermore, *wushu* was looked upon as an important part of self-cultivation by prominent intellectuals of various historical periods from Confucius (551–479 B.C.E.) to modern scholars. They took writing and *wushu* as two required courses to cultivate individual morality, to rule the state, and to bring peace to the world.

In the history of Greek civilization, the ancient nude athletics, though its

This chapter was translated by Wu Dingbo.

influence is still felt today, only lasted for three or four hundred years. *Wushu,* however, claims a history as long as China's civilization, and it is still developing vigorously. Being a unique kind of physical culture integrating philosophy and science, *wushu* has exerted a much deeper impact on the Chinese people's psychology and character and on various aspects of Chinese culture. *Shuobo* and *jiandao* in the Han Dynasty (206 B.C.E.–220 C.E.) were in a sense primitive forms of modern *quanshu* (barehand exercises) and *jianshu* (swordplay). Devised by the famous doctor Hua Tuo (?–208), *wuqinxi* (five-animal play) was probably the earliest set of exercises for fitness building. This set of exercises imitates the movements of the tiger, deer, bear, ape, and bird. In the Tang Dynasty (618–907), dance and acrobatics flourished. The Xiho Sword Dance, designed and performed by Madame Gong Sun and Sister Li, was a superb combination of swordplay and dance, and the momentous music titled ''Qinwan buzhenqu'' (Ode to King Li Shimin Who Breaks the Enemy's Battle Formation) was also produced under the impact of *wushu.* In the Song Dynasty (960–1279), *baixi,* literally meaning ''a hundred games,'' was very popular in the army. It was also known as a variety show since it was in essence a combination of performance arts originated from combat skills. It is evident that *wushu* as a special kind of physical culture promoted the performing arts in the Tang and Song dynasties.

One of the reasons for traditional Chinese drama being viewed as one of the world's three major theatrical systems is its rich array of varied and dazzling acrobatic fighting on stage based on *wushu.* Judging from stage performances worldwide, one can hardly discover any other nation that is able to present the battle scene on the stage as vividly as China. No matter whether it is on earth or in heaven, on the mountain or in the sea, combat scenes on whatever scale can be put on the stage symbolically and momentously through the splendid and colorful theatrical performance of dance and acrobatic fighting based on *wushu.*

Chinese *wushu* provides a technical basis for the fighting skills in traditional Chinese drama. This is an all-inclusive influence of multichannel and multilayer cultural atmosphere. The acrobatic fighting found in Beijing drama (customarily called Peking opera) is a typical example of the artistic application of Chinese *wushu.* It is by no means accidental that Beijing drama formed and developed in the Daoguang reign (1821–1851) of the Qing Dynasty when three modern forms of *wushu* developed in Beijing, namely, *taijiquan* (shadow boxing), *baguazhang* (eight-diagram palm), and *xingyiquan* (pictographic boxing). The famous performing artists of Beijing drama—Tan Xinpei (1847–1917), Yang Xiaolou (1877–1937), Gai Jiaotian (1888–1970), Mei Lanfang (1894–1961), Cheng Yanqiu (1904–1958), and others—have all integrated these three forms of *wushu* with their respective performing artistry. The unique skills and artistry of kicking, striking, leaping, and somersaulting with or without arms on the stage are all developed from *wushu,* including *taijiquan, baguazhang,* and *liuhequan* (six-direction boxing—*liuhe* refers to six directions, namely, east, west, south, north, upward, and downward).

Biaoju, establishments that provided escorts and bodyguards for private security, especially for merchant caravans, developed rapidly during the Ming (1368–1644) and Qing (1644–1911) dynasties. As the bosses and managers of these establishments were mostly well versed in *wushu,* their adventurous experiences in business were so appealing to people that they stimulated the development of military plays and gallant fiction. On the stage of traditional Chinese drama appeared many military plays about gallant escorts and woodland heroes. *Sanchakou* (At the Crossroads), *Yandangshan* (The Yandang Mountain), *Ehulin* (The Vicious Tiger Woods), *Luomahu* (The Fallen Horse Lake), *Lianhuantao* (Interlocking Stratagems), and *Shisanmei* (The Thirteenth Sister) are just a few of the military plays in the repertoire of Beijing drama. With their distinctive features, these military plays aroused strong interest in *wushu* on the part of the spectators, and at the same time promoted the popularization of *wushu.*

With the appearance of firearms and the development of telecommunications and railroads, *biaoju* as private security services declined, and these gallant escorts and bodyguards had to retire from public life or change their trade. Some became street performers of *wushu* in the temple fair, and some joined drama troupes to be coaches of *wushu.* Those who were good enough to perform could reclaim dear memories of their good old days as errant gallants on the stage.

After the founding of the People's Republic, the Chinese dancers, in order to explore national characteristics of dance drama, devoted themselves to the study of *wushu.* Celebrated dance drama routines, such as *The Small-Sword Society* and *The Leifeng Pagoda,* have all assimilated a great variety of *wushu* footwork and movements. Some famous dancers study *wushu* with great concentration and benefit from it all their lives. The combination of swordplay sequences has become one of the basic teaching materials for classic dance in the dance colleges.

Wushu in China has a history as long as Chinese culture. As far back as remote antiquity, people fought with beasts and fought with other people. Once the weapons fell from their hands, they had to fight with their bare hands and feet, striking, kicking, dodging, wrestling, jumping, and sometimes even engaging in barehanded fight against weapons. With the accumulation of experiences through practice, the movements for both attack and defense gradually became sets of routines. The conscious application of these routines evolved the primitive forms of the Chinese boxing system—*wushu.* Each form of *wushu* includes starting position, final movements, and a certain number of routines in between. All movements go on one after another in regulated sequence. The Chinese *wushu* lays special emphasis on the work of the hands, eyes, torso, and feet, and each of these has its own set of rules.

SCHOOLS OF *WUSHU*

The conscious practice of *wushu* for thousands of years has evolved various forms and schools which indicate the technical advancement of the Chinese martial arts system. They include *shaolinquan, neijiaquan, taijiquan, xingyi-*

quan, baguazhang, changquan, liuhequan, tantui, jingchaquan, huaquan, pa- ochui, yanqingquan, meihuaquan, mianquan, qinna, zuijuiquan, houquan, yingquan, shequan, tanglangquan, nanquan, and others.

Shaolinquan

Originated in the sixth century, *shaolinquan* is one of the oldest and most famous forms of Chinese *wushu*. It got its name from the Shaolin Monastery in the Songshan mountains in Dengfeng county, Henan province. *Shaolinquan* has a great variety of routines with interesting names. Vigorous and simple in move- ments, *shaolinquan* is performed with flexible and changeable postures. It serves practical purposes for best attack and defense. Being a unique form in Chinese *wushu, shaolinquan,* known as "the kernel of Chinese *gongfu*" (kung fu), en- joys high esteem at home and abroad. It is often said that "all *gongfu* originates from *shaolin,*" or that "the *shaolin gongfu* is the greatest under heaven."

Several words in Chinese indicate the major features of *shaolinquan:* dynamic as billows, static as mountains, rising as an ape, falling as a magpie, standing on one leg as a golden pheasant, rising straight as a pine tree, turning as a wheel, curving as a bow, quick as a whirlwind, slow as a gliding eagle, light as a leaf, heavy as iron, waiting as a lying cat, advancing as a leaping tiger. The whole set of routines moves on one line and in a space just "big enough for a lying bull" as the saying goes. On the brick floor of the One Thousand Buddha Hall in the Shaolin Monastery are forty-eight hollows, each about fifty centimeters in diameter, with a space of two meters in between each pair of them. It is said that these hollows were shaped by the Shaolin monks' stamping feet during exercises.

Shaolinquan in the Songshan mountains emphasizes fighting skills and pro- ceeds from the needs of actual combat. Each and every movement serves the purpose of either attack or defense. There are defensive tactics in attack and offensive tactics in defense. In essence, it strives for victory through quick, accurate, and fierce attacks. In actual combat, *shaolinquan* not only pays atten- tion to the changing maneuvers of advance, retreat, feint, and attack, but also tries to blend force with grace and hardness with softness, as the saying puts it: "Acting like a maiden in defense but a tiger in attack."

All postures are tactical, such as "making a feint to the east and attacking in the west," "pointing to the upper part but striking the lower part," "making an attack in appearance but retreating in essence," "retreating in form but ad- vancing in fact," "attacking continuously with closely concentrated tactics," "knocking down your opponent by taking advantage of his own striking force," "avoiding a direct confrontation with a fierce opponent and subduing him with wits and stratagems," and "looking fierce in appearance and remaining inwardly calm." The characteristics of the varied tactics of *shaolinquan* are also described in the following Chinese martial art expressions: agile as a cat, energetic as a tiger, moving as a dragon, striking as a lightning bolt, and loud as a thunder.

Taijiquan

While there is no conclusive evidence as to who created *shaolinquan,* it appears that *taijiquan* was first devised by Chen Wangting in Chenjiagou, Wenxian county, Henan province. Chen Wangting was a garrison commander in the late Ming Dynasty. After the fall of the Ming Dynasty, he returned home, did farm work and devised *taijiquan,* a new form of the Chinese boxing system, in his later years. Different from other forms of *wushu,* his movements of *taijiquan* are initiated from a half squatting position, with the legs as a base and the waist as the axis. Through long years of dissemination among the people, *taijiquan* has gradually evolved into many different styles. Among them the following five are most outstanding: Chen, Yang, Wu, another Wu, and Sun.

Chen Style. The Chen style has the longest history. Compared with other styles of *taijiquan,* the Chen style is most energetic with jumps, leaps, and explosions of strength. It contains vigorous as well as gentle movements which follow a circular path. As it blends force with grace, force and grace supplement each other. One motion of any part affects all other parts of the body. With the concentrated mind in command, body movement and breathing are in perfect coordination, and thus the internal energy circulates to the extremities or "four tips" (fingertips and toe tips of hands and feet) as the jargon has it. The inward force is so solid and flexible that it can "topple a weight of 1,000 catties by exerting a force of only four ounces," as the popular saying goes. The Chen style is also known by the name of *laojia taiji* (old-frame *taiji*).

Yang Style. The Yang style was originated by Yang Luchan (1799–1872) of Hebei province. In his childhood, Yang Luchan learned *taijiquan* from Chen Changxing, an excellent follower of Chen Wangting. Later, Yang brought *taijiquan* with him to Beijing and taught Chinese boxing there for years. For his superb command of martial arts, he was called the "peerless Yang." After his death, his grandson Yang Chengfu (1883–1936) systematized the Yang style and thus put an end to the exclusive domination of the Chen style in the field. The main features of the Yang style are extended and natural postures, slow and uncluttered motions, light and steady movements, and curved and flowing lines of performance. As is required, while making a stride, it must be as quietly as a cat walks and, while putting forth strength, the exertion must be so mild that it looks like reeling off raw silk from a cocoon. There are two key rules governing the practice: relaxing and sinking. The complete relaxation of all muscles, viscera, vessels, and nerves opens all the passages for the circulation of internal energy in the whole body. Sinking means the concentration of consciousness on the *dantian* (a spot 1.97 inches below the umbilicus). The Yang style is also called by the name of *dajia taiji* (big-frame *taiji*).

Wu Style. The Wu style was established by Wu Quanyu (1834–1902), and his son Wu Jianquan (1870–1942) made great contributions to systematizing this style of *taijiquan.* The Wu style is also known by the name of *zhongjia taiji* (medium-frame *taiji*) for its moderate postures and curved motions. Without explosions of strength, its movements are spry and light, soft and natural, but well balanced and steady, one after another in uninterrupted, rhythmic harmony.

Another Wu Style. This Wu style was developed by Wu Yuxiang (1812–1880). Assimilating the essence of both the Chen style and the Yang style, Wu Yuxiang devised a new style of his own. Because Hao Weizhen (1849–1920), one of Wu Yuxiang's followers, contributed much to popularizing this style, it is also known as the Hao style *taijiquan.* This style stresses both the coordination of opening and closing movements and the concentration of consciousness. The mind which commands the body directs the circulation of the internal energy, and the internal energy directs the movements. While exercising, one always keeps his trunk straight and moves with ease and lightness in solid steps. As the Wu style is a well-knit series of routines with simple, quick, and short-range movements, it is also known by the name of *xiaojia taiji* (small-frame *taiji*).

Sun Style. The Sun style was founded by Sun Lutang (1861–1932), an expert in *xingyiquan* (pictographic boxing) and *baguazhang* (eight-diagram palm). In the early years of the Republic, he learned the Wu style *taijiquan* from Hao Weizhen. Having achieved mastery through a comprehensive study of the three forms of Chinese boxing, Sun devised a *taiji* style of his own with dexterous and nimble movements performed at a quick pace and with lively footwork. The change of the movement directions is followed by opening and closing movements. Therefore, it is also known as "opening-closing-lively pace *taiji*" or simply *huojia taiji* (lively pace *taiji*).

Although each of these five styles has distinctive features of its own, the basic requirements in exercises are similar: well-balanced and steady movements, natural and fluid motion, deep and even breathing, combination of vigor and gentleness, concentration of consciousness, and coordination of body movements so that the hands, eyes, torso, and limbs perform as a whole unity.

Baguazhang

Baguazhang (eight-diagram palm), originally called *zhuanzhang* (turning palm), is a form of Chinese boxing which turns round in circles while assimilating the fighting skills of attack and defense with *daoyingong* (breathing exercises with movements made to imitate animals). *Baguazhang* calls for a wide range of variations in the movements of the hands, legs, feet, and body, and it involves constant changes in directions. It attaches great importance to changing tactics according to changing conditions and strives to attack one's opponent in different ways and at different points.

Changquan

Changquan (long-range boxing) is said to have been developed by the first Emperor Taizu of the Song Dynasty before he came to the throne. Therefore, it is also named after him as *taizuquan.* The complete set of *taizuquan* has very long routines with about thirty-two postures. After the founding of the People's Republic of China in 1949, the concept of *changquan* changed. All forms of Chinese boxing that have the following features belong to this category: extended and natural postures, agile and dexterous movements, quick and energetic explosions of strength, and rhythmic actions, such as scurrying, jumping, leaping, dodging, turning, prancing, stretching, somersaulting, shifting, rising, and falling. Thus *changquan* includes *chaquan, huaquan, hongquan, paochui,* and even *shaolin. Changquan* contains long-range movements with high demands on the flexibility of joints and the elasticity of ligaments. As it helps develop speed and agility, it is especially good for teenagers.

Nanquan

Nanquan (southern-style boxing) originated in the south of China. This form of Chinese boxing has a great variety of styles and schools in China. Among them five styles are most prominent: Hong, Liu, Cai, Li, and Mo. Although each of the five has characteristic features of its own, they share the following essentials. So far as the hand is concerned, *nanquan* has more movements of upper limbs with vigorous explosions of strength. So far as the body is concerned, *nanquan* requires flexible and changeable movements of leaning backward and bending forward, engulfing and blowing, leaning and prancing, dodging and turning. So far as footwork is concerned, *nanquan* requires steady and balanced footwork with each landing as if firmly rooted on the ground. *Nanquan* stresses energetic explosions of strength with strong arms and firm footing, confronting the tough with toughness, going ahead steadily, and striking sure and powerful blows. As all the exercises are full of power and grandeur, people describe them in these words: "One shout changes the color of the wind and clouds, and one strike splits the mountains."

Houquan

Houquan (monkey boxing) has enjoyed a long history in China. It evolved from the dance in imitation of a monkey's movements more than 2,000 years ago. A silk painting of the earlier Han Dynasty, unearthed from the No. 3 Han Tomb at Mawangdui, east of Changsha, Hunan province, contains a picture with the inscription of "A Bathing Monkey Calls." In fact, this picture shows an ancient style of *houquan* practiced 2,100 years ago. Another example recorded in the Chinese classics treats Tan Changqing, an official of the Han Dynasty, who once gave a performance of the Monkey Dance at a feast. His dance was based on the actions of the macaque, a short-tailed monkey.

Houquan became one of the major forms of *wushu* with thirty-six routines in the Ming Dynasty. Although *houquan* is basically an imitation of the monkey's movements, it assimilates the combat skills of attack and defense, such as kicking, striking, locking, pressing, grasping, throwing, holding, jumping, dodging, turning, hooking, stretching, and somersaulting. While exercising, one must remember the five basic requirements known as "the five canons" of monkey boxing: physical resemblance, spiritual likeness, concentrated tactics, light steps, and a nimble body. The major features of *houquan* can also be summarized in the following twenty-two expressions: firmness, litheness, lightness, agility, persistence, shrewdness, elusiveness, wariness, vigor, restraining, grasping, throwing, plucking, chopping, tricking, holding, pressing with palm, pushing, entwining kick, thrust kick, snap kick, and springy kick. *Houquan* has a good effect on body metabolism, and constant practice increases the body's resistance to disease.

Zuiquan

Zuiquan or *zuijuiquan* (drunkard's boxing) is a pictographic form of Chinese boxing in imitation of a drunkard's movements. Although it has a great variety of schools, the major features are similar. In the drunken state of wriggling and stumbling, one displays his unique skill of attack and defense, such as tricking, puckering, shoving, smashing, kicking, springing, hooking, hanging, brushing, grazing, brushing, squeezing, jostling, dodging, stretching, pouncing, rolling, somersaulting, and entwining. The traditional routines stress the movements of falling, pouncing, rolling, and somersaulting. All the drunken postures are composed of boxing motions of dodging, turning, prancing, and shifting. The drunken stance is only the deceptive form; the fighting ability is the essence, and the two are blended as an organic whole.

WEAPONS IN *WUSHU*

Apart from barehanded exercises in *wushu,* there are many more forms of armed exercises. Although "eighteen kinds of weapons" is a set phrase commonly used in China to refer to the arms used by ancients, more than eighteen kinds of weapons are used in *wushu.* Here are a few examples commonly seen in armed exercises:

1. Short weapons: axe, hammer, sword, and broadsword
2. Long weapons: spear, cudgel, pike, long-hilt broadsword, gisarme, flying fork, halberd
3. Flexible weapons: nine-section whip, three-section cudgel, two-section short cudgel, two-section long cudgel, meteoric hammer, rope dart
4. Double weapons: double broadswords, double swords, double two-headed spears, double hooks, double daggers, Emei daggers
5. Shield.

Among these weapons, the broadsword, sword, spear, and cudgel are the most popular. Almost all forms of Chinese *wushu* have developed their own routines with weapons. With barehanded exercises and armed exercises, *wushu* embodies the superb Chinese *gongfu* (kung fu).

PHYSICAL BENEFITS OF *WUSHU*

Wushu is a unique form of national sport in China. From *wuqinxi* (five-animal play) and *taijiquan* to modern therapeutic exercises and functional training, all ancient and modern exercises have drawn nourishment from this inexhaustible legacy. As *wushu* can strengthen bones, muscles, and nerves; improve health; cure diseases; temper willpower; teach the art of self-defense, and mold temperament, it has been widely practiced among the Chinese people, not only as a kind of physical exercise but also as a means of fitness building and kinesitherapy.

Medical assessments show that the therapeutic effects of *taijiquan* are very satisfactory in regard to such chronic diseases as neurasthenia, pulmonary tuberculosis, hypertension, cerebral thrombosis, coronary heart diseases, and arthritis. The reason for all physical exercise therapy is to keep each part of the body in constant motion. *Taijiquan* is just one of such exercises. Different from other sports, *taijiquan* not only stimulates the movements of bones, muscles, and joints, but also assimilates the breathing exercises of *qigong*. As a result, while keeping the body in constant motion, it ensures an adequate supply of oxygen to the tissues of the various organs and facilitates substance metabolism. All this increases the body's resistance to disease and prolongs life.

Furthermore, the constant motion of all the muscles stimulates the blood circulation. Therefore, regular practice of *taijiquan* increases the blood supply to the coronary arteries, strengthens heart contractions, and improves hemodynamic processes. Thus, it wards off diseases caused by clogged blood circulation. *Taijiquan* requires a high degree of concentration with the mind free from any distractions. This enhances the regulatory functions of the central nervous system. As the eyes, hands, waist, and feet perform in rhythmic harmony uninterruptedly, they force the mind to coordinate various organs in the human body and thus overcome morbid psychology and other distractions. Different from other sports and pure *qigong*, *taijiquan* combines physical training and breathing exercises. Therefore, it enhances both external and internal strength and energy. Externally, *taijiquan* strengthens the bones and muscles with visible active movements of the body; internally, it adjusts one's respiration and guards one's mind against distractions. In this way it achieves high efficacy in fitness building and in preventing and curing diseases. Regular *taijiquan* practitioners can enjoy its salubrious effects all their lives. Since the founding of the People' Republic of China, *taijiquan* has undergone unprecedented development. It not only has become a popular form of health-building sport, but it also now forms an important part of the kinesitherapy often prescribed in hospitals and sanatoriums all over the country. Apart from *taijiquan, baguazhang* is also used to treat Ménière's syndrome.

Wushu as a fruitful therapy in traditional Chinese medicine has many advantages. First, *wushu* is effective for treating many internal, surgical, gynecological, and ophthalmological diseases; second, the processes are simple. If one practices it conscientiously, wholly absorbedly, and persistently, satisfactory results can be obtained. Third, it does not need special equipments or drugs. While exercising, one feels relaxed, comfortable without any suffering. With all these advantages, *wushu* has been in vogue among people of all ages, sexes, and races. It has been so well received by the broad masses of the Chinese people that one can always see crowds of people practicing various forms of *wushu* in urban and rural areas, in parks and schools, and even on the sidewalks of the streets. In the schools of all levels, *wushu* has been a regular course in the curriculum in China.

WUSHU AS AN INTERNATIONAL SPORT

The significance of *wushu* is self-evident, and such far-reaching significance urges the Chinese *wushu* circles to consider two issues concerning *wushu*'s orientation. The first issue is how to make Chinese *wushu* head for the international arena; in other words, how to make *wushu* an internationally recognized and accepted sport. Since the establishment of the Preparatory Committee of the International *Wushu* Federation (IWF) in 1985, *wushu* has developed rapidly worldwide. Asian *wushu* has a very good foundation. Immediately after its establishment in 1986, the Asian Wushu Federation successfully sponsored the first session of Asian Wushu championships in China, and the second session in Hong Kong the next year. During the 24th Olympics in Seoul, South Korea, in 1988, the Plenary Session of the Asian Council passed a resolution accepting *wushu* as one of the official events at the 11th Asian Sports Championships, thus opening a new page in the history of international *wushu.*

In 1985 China held her first invitational tournament of *wushu* in Xian, with no more than one hundred participants from fourteen countries. Six years later, China successfully held the First World *Wushu* Championships in Beijing in October 1991, with about 600 participants from forty-one countries and regions representing every member of the IWF founded in 1990.

At the First World *Wushu* Championships in Beijing, there were eight official events: *changquan, nanquan, taijiquan,* broadswordplay, spearplay, swordplay, cudgelplay, and triathlon. All used optional routines in competition. There were also nine demonstration events of men's free sparring. Although the China team did not send all its eminent masters of *wushu* to join the competition, it won first place with twelve gold medals and two silver medals in the official events. The Japanese team won two gold medals, five silver medals, and four bronze medals; the Hong Kong team, one gold medal, five silver medals, and four bronze medals; the Philippines, one gold medal and one silver medal; the United States and Chinese Taipei, one silver medal and one bronze medal, each; Aomen (Macao), one silver medal; Malaysia, four bronze medals. Singapore, South Korea, the Soviet Union, France, and Nepal won the fourth to sixth places in the events. In the men's free-sparring events, China won four gold medals, the Soviet Union, two; Spain, Brazil, and Chinese Taipei, one, each.

A *wushu* symposium was also held during this world championship in Beijing, October 12–16, 1991. Apart from the theses presented by the Chinese academics, three papers were presented by foreign specialists. "Internationalizing the Value of Chinese *Wushu*," by Antonio Florase of Mexico, and "Developing a Method of Teaching *Wushu* for Youngsters in the West," by Marc Theeboom of Belgium both explored the issue of how to make Chinese *wushu* more international in scope.

Another issue concerning *wushu*'s orientation is how to broaden prospects for *wushu*. Whenever *wushu* is mentioned, people think of a wide variety of routines of Chinese boxing or the complex fighting skills shown in a combat between two opponents. People judge and appreciate *wushu* according to its technical skills of each movement and each posture, or according to its function of fitness building and self-defense. This is only a narrow view in regard to *wushu*. *Wushu* has been developing in China for thousands of years. In the long process of its development, it has assimilated the rich heritage of Chinese culture. Consequently, it embodies philosophy, aesthetics, and medical science. Much needs to be done to explore these aspects of *wushu*.

Today, while practicing *wushu*, many people study *taiji* and *bagua* and even try to trace the philosophical origin of *taijiquan* in the *Yijing* (Book of Changes), an ancient classic written about 3,000 years ago. Some *wushu* practitioners also explore the theory of yin and yang and the theory of *jinruo* (the main and collateral channels) in Chinese medicine, and apply these theories in treating diseases. From this comes *wushu* therapy. It is commonplace for *wushu* coaches in China and abroad to work as physicians concurrently. They are good at bone adjustment and zone therapy (massage).

Wushu also exerts tremendous influence on Chinese literature and art. In ancient China there were military dance, military music, military drama, and gallant fiction. They formed a unique genre of literature and art, all drawing nourishment from *wushu*. In our modern society, there are kung fu movies and teleplays with various themes. The close relationship between *wushu* and literature and art urges one to think of a new field to be opened up: *wushu* economics. Along with the development and popularization of *wushu* in China and elsewhere, a promising market has appeared for commercial goods related to *wushu*, such as *wushu* apparatus, *wushu* jackets, *wushu* books, *wushu* movies and television shows, *wushu* souvenirs, and so on. All these goods need to be produced in one way or another to satisfy customers' demands. It is believed that *wushu* economics has great potential and will open new prospects gradually in China and abroad.

REFERENCE WORKS

As a vast, inexhaustible heritage of Chinese sports, *wushu* deserves serious academic attention. However, in China only a few books are devoted to the study of the history of *wushu*, and only two books are currently available for this purpose. With high academic value, *A Brief History of the Chinese Wushu* (1984) by Matsuda Takachi of Japan and *Zhongguo wushu shi* (A History of the Chinese *Wushu*) (1985) by Xi Yuntai both offer historical accounts.

After *wushu* was introduced to Japan, especially in the Ming Dynasty, the Japanese developed a high regard for it. Matsuda Takachi has not only learned various forms of *wushu*, but also has collected about 500 books and journals related to *wushu*. After several years of painstaking efforts, he produced *A Brief History of the Chinese Wushu*. This book was later translated into Chinese and published in 1984 in China. His contribution to the study of the Chinese *wushu* embarrassed the Chinese *wushu* circles. Therefore, Professor Xi Yuntai of the Chengdu Physical Culture Institute published *A History of the Chinese Wushu* in 1985. This is the first comprehensive academic book on the history of *wushu* written by a Chinese.

Similar to national histories or literary histories, *wushu* history also follows a chronological sequence, one year after another, one dynasty after another. However, different from national histories or literary histories, the history of *wushu* must deal with multifarious forms and schools which have their respective histories of development. Drawn from the rich but scattered historical materials of Chinese *wushu*, Matsuda used two different disciplines to unfold the sport's history. One follows a chronological order, and the other follows the development of the various forms and schools. As a result, his well-knit book presents in a clear, logical way the development of *wushu* as a whole and the development of the major forms and schools in particular.

In *A History of the Chinese Wushu*, Xi also adopts the two disciplines. However, since Xi was born in China and is himself a good master of *wushu*, he not only could easily get access to the fragmentary statements about the origin and development of *wushu* in a tremendous number of historical books of all ages, but also could intuitively comprehend the classic sources about the varied forms and schools of *wushu* produced in all dynasties. As a result, Xi Yuntai's book is more comprehensive, more coherent, more substantial, and more characteristic of textual research and historical study than Matsuda's clearly expounding the long process of Chinese *wushu*'s appearance, variation, and development. So far as the chronological sequence is concerned, Xi's book proceeds from the Spring and Autumn period (770–476 B.C.E.), Qin Dynasty (221–207 B.C.E.), Han Dynasty (206 B.C.E.–220 C.E.), Sui Dynasty (581–618), Tang Dynasty (618–907), Five Dynasties (907–960), Song Dynasty (960–1279), Yuan Dynasty (1271–1368), Ming Dynasty (1368–1644), Qing Dynasty (1644–1911), the Republic (1912–1949), to the People's Republic (1949–). So far as the forms and schools are concerned, Xi's book proceeds from *shaolin, neijia, taiji, xingyi* . . . forty-six forms altogether, plus twenty-seven kinds of weapons. Although Xi's book shares the same disciplines in exposition, it is more accurate and comprehensive than its Japanese counterpart.

Applying the scientific method and historical conception of *wushu*, both books discard the dross and select the essential from the historical source materials about *wushu*. For instance, *A Brief History of the Chinese Wushu* takes Tang Hao's "Shaolin Wudang kao" (Historical Accounts of Shaolin School and Wudang School) for a guide. Tang's article was later included in *Shenzhou wuyi* (Chinese Martial Arts, 1986). Tang Hao is an outstanding textual researcher. Although he does not quote much from Tang Hao, Xi Yuntai, in fact, follows Tang Hao's historical conception of *wushu* in his own exposition.

Wushu is a national sport of the Chinese people with a history of several thousands of years. Yet for a long time it remained abstract in historical conception without much penetrating and convincing textual research. Therefore, the publication of these two academic studies on *wushu* has great significance. They trace *wushu*'s origin and development through the constant change and variation, confirm and publicize *wushu* and its functions in practical and realistic approaches, and provide necessary guidance and solid ground for further study.

However, there are also some weak points in the two books. First, they fail to provide a clear-cut exposition of *wushu*'s definition, scope, and evolution. *Wushu* has been practiced for thousands of years, but its complex nature leads to conceptual confusion among its practitioners. Hence, controversies over its definition continue in academic circles, and it remains an important task for academics to clarify the concept of *wushu*.

Second, the two books fail to elucidate systematically and penetratingly the relations of *wushu* with politics, economics, the military, and literature and art in all historical periods. All nations in the world have combat and struggle, and so fighting skills are part of their cultures. Then, why have they not created *wushu* as China has? From ancient times onward, China had been the most war-ridden nation in the world. As it required superb fighting skills to win victory, *wushu* emerged and developed accordingly. This should have been a major issue in dealing with the history of *wushu*. *A Brief History of the Chinese Wushu* does not touch on this issue at all. *A History of the Chinese Wushu* mentions the Spring and Autumn and Warring States Period, and touches on the improvement of *wushu* along with the change from the Stone Age and Bronze Age to the Iron Age. It deals with the issue, however, rather vaguely and narrowly on the whole.

The two books also overlook the close relations between *wushu* and literature and art. In fact, their relations are complementary. *Wushu* enriches literature and art, and literature and art in turn popularize *wushu* among the people. Most classic dances are military dances; the regional styles of traditional Chinese drama are full of military plays about Xiang Yu the Conqueror (232–202 B.C.E.), Monkey King, and Guan Yu the General. As almost half of their repertoire are military plays, combat skills are required learning for actors and actresses. Many classic literary works take combat as their major theme, such as *Dongzhou lieguo zhi* (The Romance of the Big Powers in the Eastern Zhou Dynasty), *Shuo Tang quanshu* (The Complete Romance of the Tang Dynasty), *Sanguo yanyi* (The Romance of the Three Kingdoms), *Shuihu zhuan* (Outlaws of the Marsh);

let alone the gallant fiction of the new schools which evolved later, such as *Sanxia wuyi* (Three Heroes and Five Gallants), *Shigong an* (The Cases of the Lord Shi), *Penggong an* (The Cases of the Lord Peng), *Shushan jianxia zhuan* (Swordsmen in Sichuan Mountains), and *Qijian xia Tianshan* (Seven Swordsmen to Tianshan Mountains). More recently, *wushu* has been adapted to the screen and exerts an influence worldwide. All movies and teleplays depicting the chivalry and prowess of ancient swordsmen and Chinese boxers display the fascinating splendor of the mysterious romance of *wushu*.

All these aspects, and more, demonstrate the scope and depth of Chinese *wushu*, which are much broader and deeper than what Matsuda Takachi and Xi Yuntai have offered us in their books. Therefore, it is expected that more academic works will reach the broad reading public in the near future.

BIBLIOGRAPHY

Li Cheng, ed. *Wushu daquan* (Compendium of Wushu). Beijing: Beijing Physical Culture Institute Press, 1990.

Matsuda Takachi. *Zhongguo wushu shilue* (A Brief History of the Chinese Wushu). Translated by Lu Yan and Yan Hai. Chengdu: Sichuan Science and Technology Press, 1984.

Tang Hao. *Shenzhou wuyi* (Chinese Martial Arts). Changchun: Jilin Culture and History Press, 1986.

Xi Yuntai. *Zhongguo wushu shi* (A History of the Chinese *Wushu*). Beijing: People's Physical Culture Press, 1985.

Xu Cai, ed. *Wushu kexue tanmi* (Exploring Science in *Wushu*). Beijing: People's Physical Culture Press, 1990.

10

The Chinese Mass Media

XU XINYI

HISTORICAL SURVEY

Mass media develop with printing and telecommunication technologies. China, the homeland of papermaking and printing, possessed its version of newspapers several hundred years before any other country. Those early newspapers, however, did not constitute the origin of mass media in the modern sense, since they served exclusively for the royal court to transmit imperial edicts and memorials. Modern newspapers and journals came to China with Western religious missions and imperialist advances in the early nineteenth century. About 100 years later, radio was introduced into the country in the same manner by foreigners. Television made its debut to the Chinese media in 1958, twenty-two years after the first television broadcasting in the world. Initiated by the Chinese themselves, it has become the most rapidly growing form of mass media in China.

Newspapers

The most ancient Chinese newspaper was *Dibao* (Court Gazette) which could be traced back as early as the Han Dynasty (206 B.C.E.–220 C.E). *Dibao*, compiled by imperial scholars, was distributed within the feudal court as an official medium. The early *Dibaos* were handwritten on nonpaper materials. Beginning in the Tang Dynasty (618–907), paper was used. Censorship appeared in the Song Dynasty (960–1279) when unofficial newspapers, called *Xiaobao*, became popular among the civil society. Printing was put into application in the Southern Song Dynasty (1127–1279). It was not widely used, however, until the mid-sixteenth century when the official *Jingbao* and folk newspapers formed a recognizable enterprise.

The Western version of newspapers and periodicals began with the publication by foreigners of the first Portuguese newspaper, *A Abelha da Chine* (Mifeng Huabao), in 1822, and the first Chinese journal, *East Western Monthly Magazine* (Dongxiyangkao Meiyue Tongjizhuan), in 1833, within the country. After the Opium War, foreign newspaper publishers gradually extended their publishing base and readership from the coastal areas to the eastern, central, and northern parts of the country. For about fifty years, until the end of the nineteenth century, they published about 170 Chinese and foreign language newspapers and periodicals, 95 percent of the total throughout the period. Among them, the main Chinese language newspapers and journals were *Xiaer guanzhen* (Chinese Serial), 1853–1856, Hong Kong; *Huazi ribao,* the Chinese edition of *China Mail* (Dechen Xibao), established in 1864, becoming independent in 1919, published until 1941, one of the earliest newspapers with the longest history; *Zhongwai xinwen qirilu* (Chinese and Foreign Weekly News), 1865– , Guangzhou; *Jiaohui xinwen* (The Church News), 1868, established in Shanghai, renamed in 1874 as *Wanguo gongbao* (The Globe Magazine and a Review of the Times), published until 1904; *Shenbao,* established in 1872, transferred to Chinese ownership in 1912, becoming the largest daily in Shanghai; and *Zhongguo shibao* (China Times), 1886– , Tianjin. Foreign language newspapers and periodicals were dominated by English, followed by Japanese, Russian, French, Portuguese, and German for 100 years after the Opium War. The well-known included *Daily Press* (Zici xibao), *China Mail, South China Morning Post* (Nanhua zaobao), *North China Daily News* (Zilin xibao), the *Shanghai Mercury* (Wenhuibao), and the *Peking Tientsin Times* (Jingjin Taiwusi shibao). Chinese-owned modern newspapers came late amidst foreign dominance and imperial conservatism. The earliest, which appeared in Hong Kong, Guangzhou, Shanghai, and Hankou, include *Zhaowen xinbao,* 1873, Hankou; *Xinhuan ribao,* 1874, Hong Kong; *Huibao,* 1874, Shanghai; and *Guangbao,* 1886, Guangzhou. Significant growth occurred when reform movement leaders began to use the media to rally people and to spread new thoughts. After the China-Japan War, hundreds of newspapers and magazines were published in the country and abroad. In Shanghai, among thirty-two newspapers and forty-six periodicals, *Zhongwai jiwen, Qiangxuebao, Shiwubao,* and *Subao* were directly edited by the well-known reformers Liang Qichao and Kang Youwei. In Tianjin, Yan Fu established *Guowenbao.* In Changsha, *Xiangbao* was a forum for Tan Citong to make claims for changes.

Like reform advocates, revolutionaries led by Sun Yat-sen also turned to newspapers and periodicals for mass mobilization. Before the 1911 revolution, sixty-eight newspapers and more than fifty magazines were published for their agenda, including *Subao,* 1897, Shanghai; *Zhongguo ribao,* 1899, Hong Kong; *Guominbao,* 1901, Tokyo; *Dagongbao,* 1902, Tianjin; *Jinzhong ribao,* 1904, Shanghai; and *Shenzhou ribao, Minhuabao, Minyubao,* and *Minlibao,* from 1907. After the emperor was ousted, with freedom of speech, writing, and publishing declared by the temporary constitution, about 500 newspapers appeared across the country. News agencies were also flourishing. The first Chinese news agency, Zhongxing News Agency (Zhongxing Tongxunshe), was established in 1904. In 1912 several more agencies were founded. By 1918 there were about twenty operating in Shanghai, Beijing, Guangzhou, Wuhan, and Changsha.

The nationalists did not hold power for very long. China was soon driven into imperial restoration under Yuan Shikai and the division of separatist warlord regimes after his death. Newspaper publishing, following the political change, experienced ups and downs. In 1919 a group of young intellectuals published *Xinqingnian* (New Youth), *Xinsichao* (New Thoughts), *Fendou* (Struggles), and other newspapers to agitate for science and democracy against warlord regimes and imperialism, all of which led to the historically influential May 4th movement. In 1926 the Northern Expedition was declared in Guangzhou. After a series of field battles and political maneuvers, the nationalist government claimed a unified country under its rule in 1929. The news media were then able to take on a stable development. From 1931 to 1936, news services totaled 4,040, among which there were 1,763 newspapers, 759 news agencies, and 1,518 magazines or journals. The Kuomintang (KMT) government's newspaper was the *Zhongyang ribao* (Central Daily).

In 1937 Japan staged its full-scale invasion. The nationalist government transferred from Nanjing to Chongqing. The main newspapers followed and became concentrated in the new capital. In 1939 more than three months of Japanese bombardment led to the closing of almost all capital newspapers. Only a collective edition was compiled in air-raid shelters. Nevertheless, throughout the entire anti-Japanese war, the news media did grow. By 1946 officially registered newspapers went up to 1,781, news agencies to 729, magazines to 1,763, and the total news services to 4,273. In the communist controlled area, there were another several hundred newspapers and periodicals.

In 1949 the KMT nationalist government was driven to Taiwan. After consolidation, in 1964, Taiwan had 31 newspapers, 747 magazines, and 43 news agencies. The *Central Daily* remains the KMT government's newspaper.

On the mainland, the Chinese Communist Party (CCP) established main national and city newspapers as soon as it liberated cities and took over national power from the KMT. *Xinshimen ribao* (Xinshimen Daily) was published as its first large-city newspaper. Afterward, *Xinhua ribao* (Xinhua Daily) in Nanjing, *Jiefang ribao* (Liberation Daily) in Shanghai, *Changjiang ribao* (Yangtze Daily) in Wuhan, *Qunzhong ribao* (Mass Daily) in Xian, *Tianjin Daily* in Tianjin, and *Dazhong ribao* (The Public Daily) in Jinan acclaimed their establishment one after another. *Xinminbao* (Xinmin News) and *Wenhuibao* (Wenhui News) were reinstated in Shanghai. In 1949 *Guangming ribao* (Guangming Daily) and *Gongren ribao* (Workers' Daily) were published. *Renmin ribao* (People's Daily) in North China was proclaimed the CCP's official newspaper. By 1950 there were 281 newspapers, among which 116 were run by the state, 58 by people's organizations, 55 by private publishers, 33 by the army, and 19 by others.

By 1957 all 1,325 newspapers published on the mainland were under state operation. From 1958 to 1959, during The Great Leap Forward, the number of newspapers increased to 1,776. Then came three years of economic hardship, which caused the number to plunge to 308 in 1962. The following period of economic improvement brought some increase; by 1965, there were 413 newspapers with a total circulation of 27.8 million copies.

During the period of the Cultural Revolution, newspaper titles in the country were cut down to as low as 42 from 1968 to 1970. By 1976, 236 were back in production, but still the figure was lower than it had been in 1950. Deng Xiaoping's economic reforms brought about a newspaper boom. From 1980 to 1985, one new newspaper appeared every one-and-a-half days. As a result, by 1985, there were 2,191 newspapers across the country. Among them, 227 were daily newspapers, 10.36 percent of the total. The total circulation was 207.22 million copies, about one copy per five citizens in the country.

Radio

Radio was first used for internal communications in 1905. In 1922 an American businessman, P. Osborne, created a radio company in Shanghai and started China's first broadcasting. A Chinese-owned broadcasting station appeared four years later in Harbin. In 1928 the nationalist government began its radio service; by 1929, there were two official and three private radio stations.

In the 1930s, private radio stations flourished in major cities. Official stations also extended to most of the provinces. Radio broadcasting was becoming a crucial tool and a salient target for political actions. In 1936 Zhang Xieliang and Yang Hucheng took control of the Xian Diantai (Xian Radio Station) after they abducted Jiang Jieshi, and made the Xian event immediately well known to the country. The Japanese invaders targeted various radio stations and inflicted significant damage to the nationalist government's broadcasting system. In 1941 they bombed the KMT's central and international broadcasting building in Chongqing and nearly aborted the broadcasting service. In destroying the Chinese broadcasting system, the Japanese lost no time in building up their own radio stations. By 1944 they operated nineteen radio stations in occupied areas.

The victory of the anti-Japanese war in 1945 brought about a short period of rapid development. The nationalist government took over the radio stations in the main cities and expanded them to a larger broadcasting capacity. Private broadcasting services also swelled to a considerable number. In Shanghai, there were as many as 108 private radio stations in 1946; In 1947, 41 broadcasting stations were under the government's direct control. In 1948 the official Shanghai Diantai (Shanghai Radio Station) successfully carried out a live broadcast of the 7th National Games. In 1949 the KMT government landed on Taiwan and continued some broadcasting services in their original call signs. In 1950 there were ten broadcasting stations on the island. Development afterward picked up moderately. By 1981 the number of radio stations reached 134, with a total transmitting volume of 460 kilowatts.

The CCP founded its first station in 1940 in Yanan. By 1949 the number of radio services under its control had risen to forty, with 1,800 announcers and staff members. In 1950 the State Council defined radio broadcasting as functioning for news delivery, policy transmission, social education, and cultural entertainment. The following basic policies were laid out: expanding the Zhongyang Renmin Guangbo Diantai [Central People's Broadcasting Station (CPBS)], establishing a radio reception network across the country, developing minority language broadcasting, and strengthening broadcasting to Taiwan and overseas.

Rapid growth occurred from 1957 to 1966. In 1958 the CPBS main building was put into use. Not long after, a self-designed and manufactured 500-kilowatt medium-wave transmitter started operating. In 1959 the Beijing Guangbo Xueyuan (Beijing Broadcasting College) was established. By the end of 1960, the number of staff and workers in the country's broadcasting services rose to 44,080. Foreign broadcasting was enhanced. By 1966 the number of foreign languages used in programs had increased to thirty-three, doubling the 1956 figure. The broadcasting time was also lengthened, about 4.16 times that in 1957.

The Cultural Revolution featured a rough and slipshod development of radio services. Numerous loudspeakers were installed in offices, on farms, and under families' roofs. From 1966 to 1976, wired stations swelled to 2,503. Loudspeakers roared to more than 100 million, and the total transmitting watts were nearly doubled.

Since 1976 it has been a stable development period. Previously established stations have been consolidated, some new stations opened, equipment updated, and transmitting techniques greatly improved. But more saliently, programs have been depoliticized and diversified. More and more people have turned to radio for news, information, and entertainment, and the reception rate continues to increase.

Television

China's first television broadcasting occurred on May 1, 1958, when Beijing Dianshitai (Beijing Television Station) was inaugurated. A trial broadcast, it lasted less than one hour. Formal operation started on September 2, 1958. One month later, Shanghai Dianshitai (Shanghai Television Station) came into being, taking up its trial broadcasting. At the year's end, the first National Television Conference was called to formulate a national strategy for television development. Provincial or municipal television stations were founded subsequently in Tianjin, Helongjiang, Guangdong, Shaanxi, Liaoning, Jiangsu, Shandong, Hubei, Sichuan, Yunnan, and other provinces. By 1960 there were twenty-three stations in operation across the country. Around that time, Taiwan launched its effort for television development; in 1962, its first television station was established.

Economic difficulties in the early 1960s caused a setback to television development on the mainland. Most of the stations were closed. Only several stations in Beijing, Tianjin, Shanghai, Guangzhou, Shenyang, Harbin, Changchun, and Xian were retained. Not long after came the Cultural Revolution. During its peak, even the remaining stations were forced to stop broadcasting. Fortunately, the interruption did not last as long as the Cultural Revolution itself. From 1968 provincial stations began to be restored or established. In 1969 a collective effort was called for color broadcasting. By 1971 all provincial governments except Tibet and Beijing owned their own stations. Some of them began to experiment with color broadcasting. In 1972 Chairman Mao's meeting with President Richard Nixon was filmed in a color documentary. Beijing television station programs began to be transmitted to the world through a ground satellite station set up in Beijing. One year later, color programs were broadcast.

Reform after Mao ushered in a fast growing era for television in the Chinese media. In 1978 the former Beijing Television Station changed its name to the Zhongguo Zhongyang Dianshitai [Chinese Central Television (CCTV)]. A Xinwen Lianbo (News Hookup Broadcast) program was introduced. In 1980 the CCTV was connected through international communication satellites with Viz News of Britain and United Press Independent Television News of the United States, enabling the Chinese people to view world news one day after occurrence. Other programs, such as television films, sports, live reporting, and commentaries, were also extended and updated. In 1985 the CCTV broadcast 148 hours, 26 minutes a week; 21 hours, 12 minutes a day; its programs were received by 69.65 million television sets across the country.

MASS MEDIA TODAY

Today, newspapers, radio, and television have all taken root in terms of scale, market, and audiences. The newspapers, with their long historical legacy and detailed news and information service, remain the largest enterprise. Radio is simple, mobile, and quick. Television presents concrete situations to viewers. Its attraction in news and information services is so irresistible that every Chinese household strives to have a television set under its roof. In recent years, in tune with economic development, television has become the fastest growing medium in the country.

Newspapers

Newspaper editors, reporters, administrative staff, and business personnel constitute a major employee army in the cultural enterprise. They total 100,000 working for 1,618 publicly published and 4,014 internally circulated newspapers across the nation.

The publicly published newspapers are registered with and granted a publishing number by the government. They are distributed either through the postal service or through their own delivery networks. The circulation can be as wide as across the entire population or as small as a corporation, a segment of production, or a profession. The national total ran as high as 151.48 million copies in 1989.

The internally circulated newspapers are not necessarily confined to a working unit or a local community. They can be nationally distributed among a particular group of elites at a particular layer. For instance, the CCP compiles many internal reference newspapers or news reports that are delivered across the country to the party cadres and act as an important vehicle to run the party and governmental bureaucracy. The well-known *Cankao xiaoxi* (Reference News), which carries first-hand news from international media, was originally an internal newspaper within the CCP bureaucracy. It now turns out to be one of the most popular newspapers accessible to the public.

The distinction between internal and public newspapers lies essentially in how the government defines readership and rations news in terms of CCP ranks and connections. It therefore signifies how the entire newspaper industry is organized around the CCP in the country. The mechanism is that the CCP edits its official newspapers and uses them to set the example for all other specialized or non-party newspapers. From the Central Committee's *People's Daily,* down to provincial, municipal, prefecture, and county committees' dailies under various names, there are about 426 CCP official newspapers with a stable circulation of 28 million copies.

Around the CCP's official newspapers are newspapers for various areas and specialties. There are urban-life-oriented morning or evening papers, people's political consultative papers, and many different papers for workers, peasants, youth, juniors, women, old people, overseas Chinese affairs, economic affairs, legal practices, education, sports, science and technology, culture and arts, population, health and medicine, environmental protection, social life, radio and television, book publishing, lines of business, enterprise, university, and military. Among them, economic, scientific, and business papers rank highest in the quantities of both titles and circulations. In the middle are youth, workers, education, legal practices, health, and evening papers. In 1989 there were 39 workers' papers, 24 peasants' papers, 78 scientific and technological papers, 14 overseas Chinese affair papers, 51 industrial papers, 135 commercial and business papers, and 43 evening papers. The circulation for commercial and business papers totaled 4.16 million copies in 1988. In 1989 evening papers were sold at 10 million copies a day.

The main language used in newspapers in Chinese. In 1989, 95.2 percent of newspapers were published in Chinese. In addition, there appear scores of newspapers using minority languages including Mongolian, Tibetan, Korean, Uygur, and Kazak. In 1989 there were seventy-six such papers in thirteen minority languages across eleven provinces or autonomous regions. There are also a few foreign language newspapers and periodicals published for international circulations. The most well known are *China Today* (previously *China Reconstructs*), *People's China, Beijing Review,* and *China Daily.* The English language edition of *China Daily* was inaugurated in 1981. Printed and distributed daily in Beijing,

Hong Kong, and New York, it has become an important source for foreigners to know about China's political, economic, cultural, and social situations.

An interesting note to Chinese newspapers is the anti-CCP papers and magazines that are circulated underground. Originating from big posters on democratic walls, they first appeared in 1978. In 1979 and 1980, two big surges were recorded in titles and circulations. In Beijing, the highest went up to more than twenty titles and thousands of copies. In other large cities, such as Tianjin, Shanghai, Guangzhou, and Wuhan, they were also printed and distributed on a considerable scale. They mainly exposed CCP corruption and propagandized democracy. As such, they have played a great role in instigating people to conduct street protests and mass movements.

Radio

The national radio network is well developed. Central and local, wired and wireless broadcasting services have been organized to cover a majority of the country's population and to reach most of the regions in the world. By the end of 1988, the national total of wireless radio stations was 461. They provided 4,968 hours of broadcasting a day, covering 70.6 percent of the population. Wired stations numbered 2,521. They were connected to 82.06 million loudspeakers, with service hours reaching 14,746 a day. The reaction from the audience is measured by the number of letters from listeners. In 1988 there were 261.97 million radio receivers in the country. Letters to wireless stations ran at nearly 5 million from domestic listeners and 0.17 million from abroad. Wired stations received about 0.55 million letters from their audiences.

The Central People's Broadcasting Station takes the lead in the country's radio services. It has exchange programs with the broadcasting stations of about 100 countries and regions. In its repertoire, there are two programs broadcast in standard Chinese to all parts of the country; one FM program to the Beijing region; one program beamed to ethnic minority areas in Mongolian, Tibetan, Uygur, Kazak, and Korean; and two programs beamed to Taiwan in standard Chinese and in the southern Fujian and Kejia dialects. Each program consists of news, education, art, and service sections. The best-known and highest-received programs are "Xinwen Baozhi Zhaiyao" (News and Paper Extracts) in the morning and "Gedi Renmin Guangbo Diantai Lianbo" (All People's Radio Stations Hookup Broadcasting) in the evening. In 1989 the latter received 1.08 million letters from listeners.

Local broadcasting stations are ranked from provincial through municipal or prefecture down to county levels. In addition to transmitting the CPBS and upper-level stations' programs, they broadcast local news, programs, and entertainment for local audiences under the corresponding government jurisdiction. Municipal stations serve mainly urban and suburban residents. Most of the prefecture or county stations turn to peasant listeners. In minority or dialect regions, broadcasting is conducted in the corresponding ethnic languages and local dia-

lects. By the end of 1988, there were 34 provincial, 179 municipal and prefecture, and 246 county broadcasting stations. They had 562 programs, broadcasting 4,722 hours a day. Besides standard Chinese, about thirty-three dialects
and ethnic languages were used in broadcasting.

Wired broadcasting is an important component. In terms of scale and function,
it is a unique characteristic of the Chinese mass media. Wired networks are built
up as large as covering a region or as small as circulating in a unit. Programs
are transmitted directly to loudspeakers in offices or households. In cities, networks are centered on municipal or district broadcasting stations, spreading to
various factories, companies, work units, streets, and residential compounds.
Large enterprises, farms, or ranches install their own networks. Transportation
stations, passenger trains, or ships also have their own broadcasting systems. In
rural areas, a county station functions as the center, township stations as relay
stops; the entire network is thereby connected to thousands of villages and
households, sending various news, warnings, and agricultural knowledge to
peasants, even in remote mountains.

A unique aspect is the broadcasting to Taiwan. Originally, it was designed to
spread Communist ideology, to expose the KMT, and to bolster the CCP's effort
to liberate Taiwan for unification. As early as the 1950s, the CPBS, Fujian, and
Jiangsu stations began to beam their special programs to Taiwan. *Haixia zhisheng guangbo diantai* (Radio Voice of the Strait Station) devoted its entire broadcasting to the island. In recent years, with the liberation intention and
confrontation atmosphere receding, news, services, arts, entertainment, and other
special programs have begun to take the lead in programming. Broadcasting to
Taiwan has become a positive means to promote understanding and cohesion
among the Chinese across the strait.

Broadcasting overseas is also a considerable activity, contributing to the
CCP's effort to build its international image. The main station in charge of this
is the Zhongguo Guoji Guangbo Diantai (Chinese International Broadcasting
Station) whose call sign in foreign languages is Radio Beijing. Its programs,
which are aired in thirty-eight foreign languages, reach most of the regions in
Asia, Africa, North America, Latin America, Europe, and Oceania. To serve
overseas Chinese in particular, programs are also announced in standard Chinese
and four local dialects including Cantonese, Xiamen, Hakka, and Chiuchow.
Total daily broadcasting time averages more than 140 hours, ranking number
three in all countries' overseas radio services in the world. Radio Beijing has
thirty-two domestic and seventeen foreign correspondent stations. It receives
from fifteen to twenty thousand letters from foreign listeners a year.

Television

China's television broadcasting system is organized in the same way as the
radio system. Chinese Central Television takes the lead in programming and
broadcasting. Local television stations are set up from the provincial, municipal

level down to the county level. They transmit the central station's programs and supply the best local programs back to it. But most of the time, they broadcast local news, practical information, entertainment, and other programs that fit local interests or situations. In 1989 there were 469 local stations, reaching 77.9 percent of the country's population.

Television programs are generally diverse and abundant. The program with the highest rate of reception is the CCTV's "News Hookup Broadcast," which provides a thirty-minute survey of daily domestic and international news and attracts several hundred million viewers in the evening prime time. News broadcasting plays an important part overall. Apart from "News Hookup Broadcast," CCTV has opened subsequently since 1984 "Wujian Xinwen" (Noon News), "Wanjian Xinwen" (Evening News), "Zaojian Xinwen" (Early Morning News), "Yingyu Xinwen" (News in English), and "Tiyu Xinwen" (Sport News). Local stations, in addition to transmitting CCTV's news, also develop their own daily news programs. Shanghai, Guangdong, and other advanced coastal city stations are even able to provide up to four or five different news services a day. The three Autonomous Regions' stations translate the CCTV's news into corresponding ethnic languages. Local news, in those languages, is also broadcast regularly.

Column programs, commentaries, and documentaries have developed very quickly, forming a tradition. The CCTV's well-known columns and commentaries are "Guancha yu sikao" (Observation and Contemplation), "Dianshi luntan" (TV Forum), "Shehui liaowang" (Social Outlook), "Xinwen toushi" (News Perspective), "Jizhe xinguancha" (Correspondent's New Observation), "Jinri shijie" (World Today), "Guoji liaowang" (International Outlook), and "Shijie zongheng" (World in Length and Breadth). Influential news documentaries include "Shenpan Lin Biao, Jiang Qing Fangeming Jitan Tebie Jiemu" (Special News on the Trial of Lin Biao, Jiang Qin Reactionary Clique); "Rang lishi gaosu weilai" (History Foretells the Future), a documentary of sixty years of the People's Liberation Army; "Hongqi Chashang Qiaozhiwangdao" (Red Flag on the King George Island), a news compilation of the Long March Expedition to the South Pole; "Hongshui Hepan Nucanshen" (The Goddess of Wealth on the Beach of Hongshui); and "Heshang" (Elegy).

Continuous reports, series reports, and spot coverage have grown strong, becoming a fashion. Continuous reports follow a particular event, presenting a full picture of the event's occurrence, process, and outcomes. The Daxinan Mountain forest fire report lasted more than one month, turning out more than 100 pieces of news on the air. Series reports revolve around a subject or a problem, giving a multiple-aspect report about its nature and development. The most influential televised in recent years include "Gaige zai nishenbian" (Reform with You), "Kan jinzhao" (See Today), and "Tanzhi yihuijian" (A Snap of Fingers), which broadcast on CCTV for two months, consisted of 180 pieces of news in 500 minutes. In spot coverage, correspondents on the scene interview people, film happenings, and report directly to viewers. It is different from the nonparticipatory live coverage of political conferences. It is also different from regular news reports, which are usually rehearsed and edited by producers.

Television films have a big share of broadcasting time. CCTV and many local stations have the capacity to produce films and translate foreign films into Chinese. In 1989 CCTV received 1,973 television films from local television stations and film studios and aired 1,189, totaling 59,450 minutes. It also broadcast 197 domestic movies and 275 foreign television films in Chinese.

Another big time taker on television is educational programming. China was the first country in the world to have a "television university." Currently, most of its education programs have been institutionalized as university courses, being broadcast in low-reception time or even through special channels. In 1988 there were forty-three radio and television universities in the country. They had 453,700 students and 9,659 formal and 12,474 affiliated faculty members.

With various program needs growing, television techniques have been greatly enhanced. Electronic news gathering and editing are widely applied. Trunk microwave lines are laid out from Beijing to most of the provincial capitals. In many provinces, they further branch out to lower governmental seats. Ground reception stations continue to be set up, connecting satellites, microwave lines, and television stations into a nationwide communication network. By 1988 there were 8,233 ground stations across the country. Wired television systems are also being rapidly developed. In 1988 it was estimated that 8,000 networks operated to serve 5 million households.

MESSAGES, AUDIENCES, AND MACHINERY

At the center in the newspaper, radio, and television media is what is being passed on to the masses, and how the masses react. Also important is how the media's physical systems are run and supported by technological advances and human resource development.

Programs

The Chinese mass media are run by the CCP. The party nature of the media is emphasized all the time and stressed after every noticeable adjustment, transition, or event. In the aftermath of the 1989 Tiananmen Square event, the CCP secretary-general elaborated the point unequivocally and unambiguously to a high-ranking press research class. He said that the press's party nature requires all newspapers and radio and television stations to align with the CCP Central Committee, in a clear-cut stand against bourgeois liberalization. Concretely, newspapers and radio and television broadcasting take the CCP's political views and policies to the masses through every possible means and in every possible form.

The CCP's hope to spread its views and policies in various forms, in a sense, helps the media develop full diversity. Also, the CCP presents itself as representing the masses. Needs and demands from the grass-roots level are generally heard and integrated into program development. Program titles in the entire media repertoire reflect a variety of interests, focuses, and concerns. Even at the provincial level, main newspapers and radio and television stations can have sections, columns, or programs as diverse as covering all basic subjects of human knowledge and social activities. For example, Jiangsu Renmin Guangbo Diantai (Jiangsu People's Radio) has several dozens of columns, including private entrepreneurs talking about their experiences, love, marriage and family ethics, listeners' letters, rural youth, policy questions and answers, casual talks at villages, youth forums, courses on economic responsibility, dialogues on contemporary history, heroes and the nation, youth cultural museums, Jiangsu history, biographical surveys of Jiangsu novelists, informal talks on philosophy, informal discussion on markets, energy saving, and so on.

Among diverse media columns and programs, the favored are those that introduce objective situations about the outside world and raise real questions as to social problems. For example, "Guoji rexian" (International Hotline) in *Zhongguo qingnianbao* (China Youth Daily), the CCTV's "Waiguo yizhipian" (Translated Foreign Films), "Jinri shijie" (World Today), and "Guoji tiyu" (International Sport) bring current world events and foreign social life to the eyes of readers and viewers. "Gongkai diaocha" (Public Investigation) in *Nantong ribao* (Nantong Daily), "Zai qiangweihua xia" (Under the Rose) in *Xinmin waibao* (Xinmin Evening News), "Qianjia wanhu" (Hundreds of Families and Thousands of Households) in Harbin People's Radio, and the CCTV's "Guancha yu sikao" (Observation and Contemplation) expose social problems and raise questions as to the rationality of many social practices. They have all become popular among their audiences.

News Supply

News and information carried by newspapers, radio, and television are monopolized by Xinhua She (Xinhua News Agency), the country's only official news supplier. Through Xinhua, the CCP is able to make certain that the news and information transmitted serve its own interests.

Xinhua News Agency was originated from the Hongse Zhonghua She (Red China Agency) in the CCP's guerrilla war and has grown into a giant network since the CCP came into power. Xinhua now has more than 6,000 staff members, working in the Beijing head office, forty domestic offices, and ninety-six overseas branches. At home, it supplies from forty to fifty thousand words a day to all levels of newspapers, radio, and television stations through four different communication lines. Internationally, it has news and photo exchanges with media organs of more than sixty countries. Each day, it delivers about 150 items of news and information in English, French, Russian, Spanish, Arabic, and Chinese to most of the regions in the world. It also receives and duplicates from 1.3 to 1.5 million words through forty-three lines from thirty-four foreign news agencies or broadcasting stations. Xinhua ranks as one of the six largest news agencies in the world.

Technological Support

In the early years, without much access to Western markets, China resorted to self-reliance and hard work for technological progress in newspaper, radio, and television. In 1970 China launched its first satellite into orbit. In 1973 it started color television broadcasting. By the end of the 1970s, Chinese factories were competent to produce film and video cameras, most sound equipment, lighting equipment, and some tape recorders. The bulk of the studio equipment in the country is Chinese produced.

In the 1980s, opening up to the outside world brought about many fresh impetuses to the media's technological supporting systems. Western advanced equipment was imported. Foreign technologies were learned to improve domestic capacity for invention and innovation. China now has sizable television, radio, and printing research facilities and production capacities. From 1979 to 1986, China produced 52.36 million black and white and 10.94 million color television sets. In 1988 China launched two communication satellites. The Ministry of Radio, Film, and Television (Guangbo Dianying Dianshi Bu) developed twenty-one new technologies and had a total of 24.98 million yuan of industrial output in radio and television broadcasting, recording, editing, and transmitting equipment.

Main research organizations include the Academy of Designing (Sheji Yuan) and the Institute of Broadcasting Science (Guangbo Kexue Yanjiusuo) under the Ministry of Radio, Film, and Television; the Institute of Broadcasting Technology (Guangbo Jishu Yanjiusuo) in Beijing Broadcasting College; institutes of journalism (Xinwen Yanjiusuo) in the Chinese Academy of Social Sciences (Zhongguo Shehui Kexue Yuan) and in Xinhua News Agency; institutes or departments of broadcasting science (Guangbo Kexue Xi) or journalism (Xinwen Xi) in several provincial bureaus of radio and television, universities, or academies.

Human Resources

The old generation of media staff members was mostly converted from other disciplines. In recent years, advanced and professional education for journalists, editors, announcers, and studio technicians has been established across the country. It has now become the main source for qualified media staff members. Advanced educational institutions include the Chinese College of Journalism (Zhongguo Xinwen Xueyuan), Beijing Broadcasting College, and schools or departments of journalism or broadcasting in Fudan, Wuhan, and Lanzhou, People's Universities (Renmin Daxue), and several dozens of other universities. At the middle level, most of the provinces and some cities have their polytechnic schools for radio and television broadcasting.

Audiences

The Chinese media obtain their feedback from the audience mainly through letters and surveys. Receiving, compiling, and responding to letters has been a tradition for a long time. Surveying was introduced only recently. Hundreds of surveys have been conducted concerning the audience's makeup, interest distribution, reading, listening or viewing habits, and wishes or suggestions.

Audience Makeup. Hunan ribao conducted a survey in 1989 and found its readership's occupational, educational, and age makeups respectively as follows: 32.5 percent officials, 25.9 percent professionals, 11.7 percent workers, 5.5 percent peasants, 14.7 percent students, 1.9 percent military members, 7.8 percent others; 31.9 percent undergraduate and above, 49 percent polytechnic and senior high school, 19.1 percent below junior high school; 52 percent under the age of thirty-five, 33.9 percent between thirty-six and fifty-five, 14.1 percent over fifty-six. Henan Renmin Guangbo Diantai (Henan People's Radio Station) did a sample survey, which showed its listenership split up by gender and residency as 60 percent male and 40 percent female, and 60 percent rural and 40 percent urban and township. Radio Beijing found in a 1988 sample survey its Italian listeners' makeup: mainly male, young and middle-aged, white-collar employees followed by professionals, and geographically concentrated in northern and middle Italy. In 1985 the CCTV survey showed its viewership consisting of 86 percent city or township and 14 percent rural residents. By 1988, however, another survey found that the television coverage rate in economically advanced rural areas was up to 98.5 percent of the general population. In moderate areas, it was 54 percent. The proportion of rural viewers in various television stations' viewerships has been dramatically increased in the past years and has begun to take its due share.

Interest Distribution. A general pattern displayed by various surveys is that television has the highest reception among newspaper, radio, and television. The urban audience has higher contact with newspapers and television, but their frequency of contact with radio is lower than that of the rural audience.

Common audience interests found in regard to programs are domestic and international news, social problem reports and critiques, and knowledge or information services. The CPBS's 1988 national survey indicated their highly received programs as follows: news and newspaper extracts, all people's stations news hookup, international news and current affairs, concise news, sports, broadcasting to rural regions, legal field, scientific knowledge, hygiene and health, around the country, radio opera, long story series broadcasting, folk art, eight-thirty this evening, selected songs, weather and ocean forecasts, economic information, and program forecasts. Zhongguo Shehui Diaocha Yanjiusuo (the Chinese Social Survey Institute) interviewed both rural and urban television viewers and obtained information about their watching interests. Among urban viewers, 77.8 percent said they watched television mostly for news and current affairs; 68.8 percent, for pleasure and entertainment; 29 percent, for knowledge; 8.4 percent, for policy awareness; 6.9 percent, for amateur interests; 4.2 percent, for business information; and 2 percent, for secondary training. Among rural viewers, the main interests are pleasure or entertainment (66 percent), news and current affairs (49 percent), knowledge (38.5 percent), and policy awareness (18.5 percent). The survey allowed respondents to check more than one reason for watching.

Advertisements have appeared in the media for some time, but generally they have been resisted by the audience and restricted by the CCP. In the open city of Xiamen, the municipal television station surveyed its viewers in 1988 and found that, although 82.7 percent of its viewership watches advertisements, only 13.7 percent do so voluntarily. Among the voluntary viewers, 39.5 percent are private entrepreneurs or individual laborers; only 15 percent are officials, professionals, and teachers.

Reading, Listening, and Viewing Behavior. Listening to the radio in the early morning, reading newspapers at noon, and watching television in the evening is a general pattern and has become a standard saying in the Chinese media.

Newspaper reading behavior is shaped by both availability and work schedule. Because private subscription is rare, it is common for officials, professionals, and students to read newspapers in offices or libraries where various newspapers are available. The CCP's main newspapers are often collectively read in work units' political study. In recent years, short evening papers and radio or television program guides have begun to enter urban households.

Both television and radio have prime reception time and are therefore able to arrange programs according to the reception situation. For radio, the highest reception time is generally from 7:00–9:00 P.M., followed by 6:30–8:00 A.M. and 11:30 A.M.–1:30 P.M. Golden time for television is basically from 5:00–9:00 P.M. Prime time can be adjusted slightly by seasons and program arrangements. For example, Beijing Television Station, by scheduling its "Dongwu shijie" (Animal World) at 6:00 P.M., "Xiaoshuo lianbo" (Storytelling Series) at 6:25 P.M., and "Beijing xinwen" (Beijing News) at 6:45 P.M., locates its own golden time from 6:00 to 7:00 P.M., right before the CCTV's overwhelming "News Hookup Broadcast."

Wishes and Suggestions. The masses in the Chinese media are generally active. Various wishes and suggestions are expressed through different channels such as letters, telephone calls, meetings with media staff members, and surveys.

From surveys conducted in recent years, common concerns can be generalized as follows: (1) People want to see differences in news programs and distinctive features such as factual reports or reflective analyses of social problems, which might indicate a tiredness with the CCP's one-voice propaganda; (2) people hope to hear more critical reports on the negative side; the CCP stresses positive reports on good things and often intentionally covers up bad happenings—this hope reflects the people's awareness of the gap between what they see in the media and what they encounter in reality; (3) people are eager to obtain practical knowledge and hope that the media will act as basic reference sources; (4) people are desperate for objective reports and analyses on current affairs and hot issues. Although skeptical of the media, people believe more is better than less.

All the major media forms, including newspapers, radio, and television, in response, display considerable willingness and flexibility to make changes. However, on the substantial matters concerning the CCP's ingrained beliefs and practices, compromise and progress are not easy to make.

REFERENCE WORKS

Publications on China's mass media in English are scarce. In Chinese, they have grown moderately in the past ten years.

General

One of the most comprehensive references is *Zhongguo xinwen nianjian* (The Chinese Press Almanac). It was first published in 1982 and its tenth volume was published in 1991. Main sections include development surveys; specialized theses; reform experiences; reader, listener, and viewer investigations; important news and commentaries; important events in the press; awarded press work; press organizations; press books and publications; and who's who in the press. The most important is the development survey under which both a historical review and a calendar year's survey on newspapers, radio, television, and other main press sectors are provided. Also helpful are press organizations that offer a concise description of almost all the publicly registered and internally circulated newspapers, radio and television stations, education and research institutions, professional associations, journals and periodicals, and other related organizations across the country and in Taiwan, Hong Kong, and Macao. The almanac is coedited by Xinwen Yanjiusuo (the Press Institute) in the Chinese Academy of Social Sciences and the Association of the China's Press Societies (Zhongguo Xinwen Xuehui Lianhehui) and is published in Chinese by the Chinese Social Science Press (Zhongguo Shehui Kexue Chubanshe).

Another comparable reference is *Zhongguo guangbo dianshi nianjian* (China's Radio and Television Yearbook). Beginning in 1986, it has published six volumes for each year until 1991. The first volume included a comprehensive history on national radio and television development, particularly on the CPBS, the CCTV, and Radio International. The later volumes focus on corresponding years. Main sections include national conferences, legal documents, general situations, theses, special selections, experiences, selected programs, award activities, investigations and reactions, professional associations, theoretical and professional meetings, organizations, biographies, major events, books and journals, statistics, new technologies, foreign exchanges, radio and television production units, and Taiwan, Hong Kong, and Macao's radio and television. The important sections are general situations, selected programs, and organizations that provide a general picture of China's radio and television. The yearbook, edited by a special board, is published in Chinese by Beijing Guangbo Xueyuan Chubanshe (Beijing Broadcasting College Press).

For noted figures and their interactions with important media organizations and historical events, *Xinwenjie renwu* (Who's Who in the Press) is a systematic source. Edited by the Press Institute in the Chinese Academy of Social Sciences, it includes correspondents, editors, announcers, writers, columnists, publishers, and leaders for news agencies, newspapers, radio, and television stations and provides a biographical review of their lives and an analysis of their thoughts, working styles, and contributions to the press enterprise. The book series has run more than ten volumes.

Introductory English materials are found in several encyclopedias. *The Cambridge Encyclopedia of China* has two short descriptions about radio and television in its 1991 edition. *Encyclopedia of New China,* published in 1987 by Beijing Foreign Language Press (Beijing Waiguo Yuyan Chubanshe), contributes a small section to cultural undertakings in which a concise introduction to newspapers, radio, television, and publishing is located. Monograph studies are rare. James W. Markham's *Voices of the Red Giants,* published in 1967 by Iowa State University Press, contributes half of its contents to China's traditional and Communist media. On the Communist media, it covers all the aspects including the media's function, structure, control, performance, and effects. The most valuable is its analytical comparison between China and the Soviet Union in the concluding chapter. John Howkins's *Mass Communication in China,* published by Longman in 1982, is based upon the author's interviews in Beijing with government officials and media professionals in the late 1970s. Its sections on publishing, film, and radio and television broadcasting are very informative. Won Ho Chang's *Mass Media in China: The History and the Future,* published by Iowa State University Press in 1989, provides a survey of the area with a projection into the future. Several theses in mass communication and journalism completed in recent years are also a worthy reference source. For example, Lin Sun's ''Television Development in China toward the 21st Century'' (1987) includes a historical review of important events and an analysis of their impact on future policy formation in Chinese television development.

Newspapers

Publications are plentiful, but most of them are in article form, scattered among several dozen press journals. Books are relatively fewer.

The ancient Chinese newspaper is studied in a monograph published in 1983 by the Renmin Ribao Chubanshe (People's Daily Press). Entitled *Zhongguo gudai baozhi tanyuan* (An Exploration into China's Ancient Newspapers) by

Huang Zhuomin, it traces the origins of Chinese newspapers to the Han Dynasty and details historical developments in newspaper printing, distribution, titles, contents, and sponsorship from the Tang Dynasty to the Qing Dynasty.

For modern newspapers, several valuable sources have become available. One is Zhongguo jindai baokan shiliao congshu (A Book Series of China's Modern Newspaper History). The series, published by Xinhua Chubanshe (Xinhua Press), is designed to collect all the articles concerning the origin, changes, and publishing activities of China's modern newspapers. Its first volume, *Zhongguo jindai baokan fazhan gaikuang* (A General Survey of China's Modern Newspaper Development) by Yang Guanghui et al., includes articles written from 1840 to 1919 by famous newspaper editors or publishers. Valuable information can be found about the period's newspaper publishing in main cities, among main groups, and the general relationship with revolution. The second is Fang Hanqi's *Zhongguo jindai baokanshi* (A History of China's Modern Newspapers) published in 1981. In two volumes, the book provides an analytic description of the Chinese newspaper from its historical origin to the early nationalist period when warlords and nationalists vied for power. The third is Lin Dehai's *Zhongguo xinwen shumu daquan 1903–1987* (An Annotated Bibliography of Chinese Press Publications 1903–1987). Published in 1989, it is the first ever to survey more than 1,900 publicly and internally published monographs, textbooks, thesis collections, research material compilations, and references in the eighty-five years since 1903. For newspapers under the nationalist government, the Department of Police in the nationalist government published *Quanguo baoshe tongxunshe yilan* (A Nationwide List of Newspapers and News Agencies) in 1947. Lai Kuang-lin's *Qishinian zhongguo baoyeshi* (Seventy Years of China's Newspapers), published by the KMT's Central Daily Press in 1981, provides a historical survey of newspaper publishing from the KMT perspective.

Historical study on newspaper publishing in the CCP's era is just under way. *Quanguo baokan neirong huibian* (A Nationwide Compilation of Newspaper Contents) provides the original title in the Chinese calligraphy and a concise description of all the newspapers and magazines in the country. Compiled by the Beijing Municipal Bureau of Postal Service (Beijingshi Youzhengju), it has been published annually since 1985. Huanlong Xu's *Zhongguo xiandai xinwenshi jianbian* (A Concise History of the Chinese Press) contains a section reviewing newspaper publishing since 1949. *Xinwenxue yanjiu shinian 1978–1988* (The Ten Years of Press Study 1978–1988), edited by the Press Institute in the Chinese Academy of Social Sciences and published in 1989, gives clues to current theoretical controversies and important references about the CCP's newspaper enterprise.

Case studies on particular kinds of newspapers are becoming more available. He Huang and Zhihua Zhang's *Zhongguo renmin jiefangjun baokanshi* (A History of the Chinese People's Liberation Army's Newspapers) was published in 1986. Yunjia Xu's *Hangzhou baokanshi gaishu* (A General Survey of Hangzhou's Newspapers) appeared in 1989. Xinhua Press published Jigen Fang and Wenying

Hu's *Haiwai huawen baokan de lishi yu xianzhuang* (Historical and Current Situations of the Overseas Chinese Newspapers) in 1989. Monographs on several newspapers have also been published internally or publicly. For instance, the *Wenhui Daily* published publicly in 1986 *Wenhuibao dashiji* (A Record of Big Events of Wenhuibao), and the *Harbin Daily* compiled *Harbin Ribao sishinian* (Forty Years of the *Harbin Daily*) for internal circulation in 1989.

Dictionaries for newspaper reading and writing are very useful, especially for those who are not familiar with CCP newspaper styles. The earliest, published in 1950 by the *Yangtze Daily,* was entitled *Dubao shouce* (A Handbook for Newspaper Reading). Another handbook under the same name was compiled by the *Yunnan Daily* (Yunnan Ribao) thirty years later in 1981. It swelled to two volumes. The *Guangming Daily's Dubao cidian* (Newspaper Dictionary) in 1985 has similar features as the aforementioned handbooks. It gives a short explanation of all the frequently appearing terms in newspapers. *Zhongguo baokan xinciyu* (New Words in the Chinese Newspapers), published in 1987 by Zhengjie Li et al., focuses on those words newly formed in CCP newspaper writings. It is intentionally designed for foreigners and overseas Chinese. *Current Chinese Communist Newspaper Terms and Sayings,* prepared in 1971 by the Center for Chinese Studies at the University of California at Berkeley, is outdated but still usable for English readers. Xinhua Press published *Zhongguo baokan tougao zhinan* (A Manuscript Submission Guide for the Chinese Newspapers), by Wenhai Yu et al., in 1988. It is one of a very few books devoted solely to amateur newspaper contributors.

For underground newspapers, two sources can be cited for reference. One is the Institute of Current China Studies' (Dangdai Zhongguo Yanjiusuo) *Zhongguo dalu dixia wenxue mulu* (Catalog of Chinese Underground Literature) edited by T.C. Chang et al., published in 1981 in Taipei. The other is Liu Sheng-chi's 1985 *Zhongguo dalu dixia kanwu yanjiu 1978–1982* (A Study of Underground Periodicals in Mainland China 1978–1982). Both include main titles, articles, editorials, and related analyses.

To aid readers or researchers to access newspaper articles, main newspapers compile content indexes. The most well known are *Renmin Ribao suoyin* (People's Daily Indexes) and *Guangming Ribao suoyin* (Guangming Daily Indexes). Both subject indexes have been published for dozens of years. For the entire country, indexes to current newspapers and periodicals are compiled by the Shanghai Library, *Quanguo baokan suoyin* (A Nationwide Index to Newspapers and Periodicals), from 1979, and the Center for Book and Newspaper Materials, *Quanguo baokan suoyin* (An Index to the Country's Newspapers and Periodicals), from 1980, in People's University. Shanghai Library's indexes, which cover hundreds of newspapers and thousands of periodicals, are published monthly in two editions for philosophy and social sciences and for natural sciences. For example, its February 1991 issue for philosophy and social sciences includes 10,577 items from 145 newspapers and 2,273 periodicals. It is indexed by both subject and author. People's University's indexes are devised to cover a calendar year. They appear in several volumes with each volume dealing with one or several subjects. Shanghai Library also compiled in 1979 a title index to modern newspapers and periodicals from 1857 to 1918. Its six volumes include all the article titles in more than 11,000 issues of 495 newspapers and periodicals. Indexes are generally broken down by subjects.

Radio and Television

The most comprehensive reference is *Zhongguo guangbo dianshi shiliao xianbian* (Selected Collection of Chinese Radio and Television History). Compiled by a special editorial board under the same name and published by Beijing Broadcasting College in series, it has covered the following topics in several volumes: major events for Chinese radio and television, China's radio stations, China's broadcasting programs, China's wired radio, China's television stations, and China's radio and television technology.

General historical reviews are available in both books and articles. For the nationalist years, Shih-kuang Wen's *Zhongguo guangbo dianshi fazhanshi* (A Development History of China's Radio and Television), published in 1983, traces radio to its origins in the 1920s and talks about the possibility of the development of television in the late 1940s. Its post-1949 part is mainly devoted to Taiwan. The CCP's perspective on radio broadcasting under the KMT is reflected in two books about the KMT's central broadcasting station. One is Xueqi Wang's *Disi Zhanxian: Guomindang Zhongyang Guangbo Diantai Duoshi* (The Fourth Front: The KMT Central Broadcasting Station), published in 1988; the other is *Guomindang Zhongyang Guangbo Diantai Gaikuang 1928–1949* (General Situations about the KMT Central Broadcasting Station 1928–1949), edited by the Jiangsu Institute of Radio and Television News in 1988 for restricted circulation.

Radio broadcasting under the CCP is traced back to the early 1940s by *Zhongguo renmin guangbo huiyilu* (A Reminiscence of the Chinese People's Radio) from the editorial board of the Chinese Broadcasting Press in 1983. *Jiefangqu guangbo ziliao xianbian 1940–1949* (A Compilation of Historical Materials on Broadcasting in the Liberated Areas 1940–1949), published by the editorial board of the Chinese Radio and Television Press in 1985 for internal circulation, is a collection of historical materials especially dedicated to the CCP's broadcasting before 1949. A general survey of both KMT and CCP broadcasting is provided by Yuming Zhao's *Zhongguo xiandai guangbo jianshi* (A Concise History of China's Modern Radio Broadcasting), published in 1987.

Case studies on main stations are also available. The CPBS has a group to study its own history. In 1987 the Chinese Radio and Television Press published that group's monograph, entitled *Zhongyang Renmin Guangbo Diantai Jianshi* (A Concise History of the Central People's Broadcasting Station). The CCTV compiled its own history and published it in 1988 through the same press, under the title of *Zhongguo Zhongyang Dianshitai Sanshinian* (Thirty

Years of China's Central Television Station). The Chinese International Radio Station has also documented its development historically; *Zhongguo zhisheng youyi zhiqiao* (Voice of China and Bridge of Friendship) was published in 1987.

Current situations and policy orientations are found in a variety of publications. At the general level, Moye Zuo's *Dangdai zhongguo de guangbo dianshi* (Contemporary Radio and Television in China) was published in 1987 by the Chinese Social Science Press. Fudan University Press (Fudan Daxue Chubanshe) published Tianchuan Shi's *Guangbo dianshi gailun* (An Introduction to Radio and Television) in 1987. The Bureau of Propaganda in the Ministry of Radio, Film, and Television compiled in 1987 *Xinshiqi yu xinwen guangbo* (New Era and News Broadcasting) and *Guangbo jiemu gaige chutan* (Broadcasting Program Reform Exploration). Another two were turned out by the Bureau of Policy Research in the Ministry of Radio, Film, and Television in 1988: *Guangbo dianshi gongzuo wenjian xianbian 1978–1980* (A Selection of Radio and Television Documents 1978–1980) and *Guangbo dianshi fagui guizhang huibian* (A Compilation of Rules and Regulations for Radio, Film, and Television).

Other important references include compilations of audience letters and surveys, winning programs and news, and award-winning radio operas and television films. For instance, *Beijing duzhe tingzhong guanzhong diaocha* (Beijing Survey on Readers, Listeners, and Viewers) was published in 1985 by the Workers' Press (Gongren Chubanshe). Brantly Womack edited the English version in 1986 under the title of *Media and the Chinese Public: A Survey of the Beijing Media Audience. Diwujie quanguo youxiu guangbo jiemu gaoxian* (A Selection of the Fifth Nationwide Winning Programs) was published in 1987 by the editorial board of the Chinese Radio and Television Press.

RESEARCH COLLECTIONS

To save time when accessing research materials and researchers in the Chinese media, consult first with the professional associations. These associations, established for media practitioners in specific fields nationwide or locally, are able to provide information on a wide range of research-related issues. The main associations are as follows: Zhonghua Quanguo Xinwen Gongzuozhe Xuehui (All-China News Workers' Federation), 50 Xijiaominxiang, Beijing 100031, phone 656149; Association of China's Press Societies, 2 Jintaixilu, Zhaoyangmenwai, Beijing 100020, phone 5025694; Zhongguo Guangbo Dianshi Xuehui (Association of China's Radio and Television), 2 Fuxinmenwaidajie, Beijing 100866; nationwide associations for different disciplines or fields, for example, societies for China's scientific newspapers, youth papers, and press history, located mostly in Beijing; and local associations for press workers, press study, or radio and television broadcasting, established in the main cities and all the provinces. Addresses and telephones can be found in municipal telephone books, *The Chinese Press Almanac,* and *The Chinese Radio and Television Yearbook.*

The information provided by associations might be crucial to visit important figures, newspapers, radio or television stations, and news agencies. Main national media units have their own research team and research collection. They are valuable sources for studying the history and current situations for the unit and even for the entire country. The following are important addresses to visit: *People's Daily:* 2 Jintaixilu, Zhaoyangmenwai, Beijing 100733, phone 5092121; *Guangming Daily:* 106 Yonganlu, Beijing 100050, phone 338561; the Central People's Broadcasting Station: 2 Fuxinmenwaidajie, Beijing 100866, phone 8012435; the Chinese International Broadcasting Station: the same address as the CPBS, phone 8013189; the Central Chinese Television Station, 11 Fuxinlu, Beijing 100859, phone 8011144; Xinhua News Agency: 12 Nanjie, Baiwanzhuang, Beijing 100037, phone 8315012; provincial radio and television stations; and the CCP's provincial newspapers, located in the provincial capitals.

Written, aural, and visual data can be obtained in most of the above places. For written materials at the general level, Beijing Library (Beijing Tushuguan), the Chinese Academy of Social Sciences, and the main universities with a department of journalism or radio and television broadcasting are also important sources. The academy and universities, in most cases, have both general libraries and subject collections.

Special collections have appeared in recent years, mainly for radio, film, and television. The Chinese Archives of Photography (Zhongguo Zhaopian Danganguan) in Xinhua News Agency stores up all the news photos collected and delivered through the country's only official news agency. The CCTV's Material Center (Ziliao Zhongxin) is a national authority in television data collection. Based upon its collection of films, television records, radio tapes, books, and periodicals, it conducts national studies on television theories, organizes research activities and exchanges both domestically and internationally, publishes books and periodicals, offers consultation services, and monitors international television development. There are also several provincial aural and video libraries. Beijing Aural and Video Library (Beijing Yinxiang Ziliaoguan) is under the auspices of the Beijing Municipal Bureau of Radio and Television (Beijingshi Guangbo Dianshi Ju). Its collection runs from domestic to international products. The service is conducted mainly for the municipal government and professionals in the Beijing region. Jiangxi Aural and Video Library (Jiangxi Yinxiang Ziliaoguan) was opened in 1988 on the basis of the provincial Bureau of Radio and Television's (Jiangxisheng Guangbo Dianshi Ting) formal aural and video collection. Its materials come primarily from local radio and television stations within the province. Guizhou Aural and Video Library (Guizhou Yinxiang Ziliaoguan) and similar libraries or collections in other provinces or main cities are similar to Beijing and Jiangxi in contents, functions, and services.

BIBLIOGRAPHY

Books and Monographs

Beijing Municipal Bureau of News Publications. *Xinwen chuban zhengce guizhang xian-bian* (A Selective Compilation of Rules and Regulations for News Publications). Beijing: The Beijing Municipal Bureau of News Publications, 1989.

Beijing Municipal Bureau of Postal Service. *Quanguo baokan neirong huibian* (A Nationwide Compilation of Newspaper Contents). Beijing: Beijing Municipal Bureau of Postal Service, 1985– .

Bureau of Policy Research in the Ministry of Radio, Film, and Television. *Guangbo dianshi gongzuo wenjian xianbian 1978–1980* (A Selection of Radio and Television Documents 1978–1980). Beijing: Chinese Radio and Television Press, 1988.

———. *Guangbo dianshi fagui guizhang huibian* (A Compilation of Rules and Regulations for Radio, Film, and Television). Beijing: Chinese Radio and Television Press, 1988.

Bureau of Propaganda in the Ministry of Radio, Film, and Television. *Guangbo jiemu gaige chutan* (Broadcasting Program Reform Exploration). Beijing: Chinese Radio and Television Press, 1987.

———. *Xinshiqi yu xinwen guangbo* (New Era and News Broadcasting). Beijing: Chinese Radio and Television Press, 1987.

CCTV's Group for History. *Zhongguo Zhongyang Dianshitai Sanshinian* (Thirty Years of China's Central Television Station). Beijing: Chinese Radio and Television Press, 1988.

CCTV's Group for Mass Correspondence. *Zhongyang dianshitai guanzhong laixin xian-bian* (A Selective Compilation of the CCTV's Letters from Viewers). Beijing: Chinese Radio and Television Press, 1989.

Center for Book and Newspaper Materials. *Quanguo baokan suoyin* (An Index to the Country's Newspapers and Periodicals). Beijing: People's University Press, 1980– .

Center for Chinese Studies. *Current Chinese Communist Newspaper Terms and Sayings.* Berkeley: University of California, 1971.

Chang, T. C., et al., eds. *Zhongguo dalu dixia wenxue mulu* (Catalog of Chinese Underground Literature). Taipei: Institute of Current China Studies, 1981.

Chang, Won Ho. *Mass Media in China: The History and the Future.* Ames: Iowa State University Press, 1989.

Chinese International Radio Station. *Zhongguo zhisheng youyi zhiqiao* (Voice of China and Bridge of Friendship). Beijing: Chinese International Broadcasting Press, 1987.

Chu, Godwin C., ed. *Popular Media in China.* Honolulu: East West Center, 1978.

Chu, Godwin C., and Francis L. K. Hsu, eds. *China's New Social Fabric.* Melbourne, Australia: Kegan Paul International, 1983.

CPBS's Group for History. *Zhongyang renmin Guangbo Diantai Jianshi* (A Concise History of the Central People's Broadcasting Station). Beijing: Chinese Radio and Television Press, 1987.

Department of Police. *Quanguo Baoshe Tongxunshe Yilan* (A Nationwide List of Newspapers and News Agencies). Nanjing: Department of Police, 1947.

Editorial board. *Beijing duzhe tingzhong guanzhong diaocha* (Beijing Survey on Readers, Listeners, and Viewers). Beijing: Workers' Press, 1985.

Editorial board. *Dangdai zhongguo guangbo dianshi* (Contemporary Radio and Television in China). Vols. 1–2. Beijing: Chinese Social Sciences Press, 1987.

Editorial board. *Diwujie quanguo youxiu guangbo jiemu gaoxian* (A Selection of the Fifth Nationwide Winning Programs). Beijing: Chinese Radio and Television Press, 1987.

Editorial board. *Encyclopedia of New China.* Beijing: Beijing Foreign Language Press, 1987.

Editorial board. *Jiefangqu guangbo ziliao xianbian 1940–1949* (A Compilation of Historical Materials on Broadcasting on the Liberated Areas 1940–1949). Beijing: Chinese Radio and Television Press, 1985.

Editorial board. *Zhongguo guangbo dianshi nianjian* (China's Radio and Television Yearbook). Beijing: Beijing Broadcasting College Press, 1986– .

———. *Zhongguo guangbo dianshi shiliao xianbian* (Selected Collection of Chinese Radio and Television History). Vols. 1–5. Beijing: Beijing Broadcasting College Press, 1987–1988.

Editorial board. *Zhongguo nujizhe* (China's Female Correspondents). Vols. 1–2. Beijing: Xinhua Press, 1989.

Editorial board. *Zhongguo renmin Guangbo huiyilu* (A Reminiscence of the Chinese People's Radio). Beijing: Chinese Broadcasting Press, 1983.

Editorial board. *Zhongguo xiandai baokanshi congshu* (A Book Series of China's Modern Newspaper History). Beijing: Xinhua Press, 1983– .

Fang Hanqi. *Zhongguo jindai baokanshi* (A History of China's Modern Newspapers). Taiyuan: Shanxi People's Publishing House, 1981.

Fang Jigen and Wenying Hu. *Haiwai huawen baokan de lishi yu xianzhuang* (Historical and Current Situations of the Overseas Chinese Newspapers). Beijing: Xinhua Press, 1989.

Harbin Daily, comp. *Harbin Ribao sishinian* (Forty Years of the *Harbin Daily*). Harbin: Daily's Internal Reference, 1989.

Hook, Brian, ed. *The Cambridge Encyclopedia of China.* New York: Cambridge University Press, 1991.

Howkins, John. *Mass Communication in China.* New York: Longman, 1982.

Huang, He, and Zhihua Zhang. *Zhongguo renmin jiefangjun baokanshi* (A History of the Chinese People's Liberation Army's Newspapers). Beijing: PLA Press, 1986.

Huang Zhuomin. *Zhongguo gudai baozhi tanyuan* (An Exploration into China's Ancient Newspapers). Beijing: People's Daily Press, 1983.

Jiangsu Institute of Radio and Television News, ed. *Guomindang Zhongyang Guangbo Diantai Gaikuang 1928–1949* (General Situations about the KMT Central Broadcasting Station 1928–1949). Nanjing: Jiangsu Institute of Radio and Television News. 1988.

Lai Kuang-lin. *Qishinian Zhongguo baoyeshi* (Seventy Years of China's Newspapers). Taipei: Central Daily Press, 1981.

Li Zhengjie et al. *Zhongguo baokan xinciyu* (New Words in the Chinese Newspapers). Beijing: Chinese Language Learning Press, 1987.

Lin Dehai. *Zhongguo xinwen shumu daquan 1903–1987* (An Annotated Bibliography of Chinese Press Publications 1903–1987). Beijing: Xinhua Press, 1989.

Liu, Alan P. L. *Communications and National Integration in Communist China.* Berkeley: University of California Press, 1971.

Liu Sheng-chi. *Zhongguo dalu dixia kanwu yanjiu 1978–1982* (A Study of Underground Periodicals in Mainland China 1978–1982). Taipei: Commercial Publishing House, 1985.

Lu Yunfan. *Zhongguo shida mingjizhe* (China's Contemporary Top Ten Correspondents). Hefei: Anhui People's Press, 1985.

Markham, James W. *Voices of the Red Giants.* Ames: Iowa State University Press, 1967.

Material Group. *Guangming Ribao suoyin* (An Index to the *Guangming Daily*). Beijing: Guangming Daily Press, 1968– .

———. *Renmin Ribao suoyin* (An Index to the *People's Daily*). Beijing: People's Daily Press, 1950– .

Press Institute in the Chinese Academy of Social Sciences. *Xinwenxue yanjiu shinian 1978–1988* (Ten Years of Press Study 1978–1988). Beijing: People's Publishing House, 1989.

Press Institute in the Chinese Academy of Social Sciences, ed. *Xinwenjie renwu* (Who's Who in the Press). Vol. 1– . Beijing: Xinhua Press, 1983– .

Press Institute in the Chinese Academy of Social Sciences and the Association of the Chinese Press Societies, eds. *Zhongguo xinwen nianjian* (The Chinese Press Almanac). Beijing: Chinese Social Science Press, 1982– .

Radio and Television Group, ed. *Quanguo guangbo xinwen youxiu zuopin xianping* (A Selective Commentary of All-China's Excellent Broadcasting Works). Beijing: People's University Press, 1989.

Shanghai Library. *Quanguo baokan suoyin* (A Nationwide Index to Newspapers and Periodicals). Shanghai: Shanghai Library, 1979– .

———. *Zhongguo jindai qikan pianmu huilu 1857–1918* (A Compilation of China's Modern Newspapers and Periodicals 1857–1918). Shanghai: Shanghai People's Publishing House, 1979.

Shi Tianchuan. *Guangbo dianshi gailun* (An Introduction to Radio and Television). Shanghai: Fudan University Press, 1987.

Sun, Lin. "Television Development in China toward the 21st Century." Master's thesis, University of Hawaii, 1987.

Wang, Ting. *A Compilation of Press Articles on Peking's News Policy during the Cultural Revolution.* Hong Kong: Chinese University of Hong Kong, 1973.

Wang Xueqi. *Disi Zhanxian: Guomindang Zhongyang Guangbo Diantai Duoshi* (The Fourth Front: The KMT Central Broadcasting Station). Beijing: Chinese Culture and History Press, 1988.

Wat, Kit-Bing Teresa. "Similarity and Diversity in the News: A Study of Three National Media and Five Regional Broadcasting Stations in China." Master's thesis, University of Hawaii, 1980.

Wen Shih-kuang. *Zhongguo guangbo dianshi fazhanshi* (A Development History of China's Radio and Television). Taipei: Three People's Principles Publishing House, 1983.

Wenhui Daily. Wenhuibao dashiji (A Record of Big Events of Wenhuibao). Shanghai: Wenhui Press, 1986.

Womack, Brantly, ed. *Media and the Chinese Public: A Survey of the Beijing Media Audience.* Armonk, N.Y.: M. E. Sharpe, 1986.

Xiao Ho and Yu Yan. *Dubao cidian* (Newspaper Dictionary). Beijing: Guangming Daily Press, 1985.

Xu Huanlong. *Zhongguo xiandai xinwenshi jianbian* (A Concise History of the Chinese Press). Zhengzhou: Henan People's Publishing House, 1989.

Xu Yunjia. *Hangzhou baokanshi gaishu* (A General Survey of Hangzhou's Newspapers). Hangzhou: Zhejiang University Press, 1989.

Yang Guanghui et al. *Zhongguo jindai baokan fazhan gaikuang* (A General Survey of China's Modern Newspaper Development). Beijing: Xinhua Press, 1986.

Yangtze Daily. Dubao shouce (A Handbook for Newspaper Reading). Wuhan: Yangtze Daily Press, 1950.

Yu Wenhai, et al. *Zhongguo baokan tougao zhinan* (A Manuscript Submission Guide for the Chinese Newspapers). Beijing: Xinhua Press, 1988.

Yunnan Daily. Dubao shouce (A Handbook for Newspaper Reading). Kunming: Yunnan Daily Press, 1981.

Zeng Xubai. *Zhongguo xinwenshi* (A History of the Chinese Press). Vols. 1–2. Taipei: University of Politics Press, 1966.

Zhao Xin, ed. *Zhongguo xinwenxue daxi—Dianshipian 1976–1982* (China's New Literature—Television 1976–1982). Beijing: China's Literature Association Press, 1990.

Zhao Yuming. *Zhongguo xiandai guangbo jianshi* (A Concise History of China's Modern Radio Broadcasting). Beijing: Chinese Radio and Television Press, 1987.

Zhuang Chunyu. *Zhongguo dianshi gaishu* (An Introduction to Chinese Television). Beijing: Chinese Radio and Television Press, 1985.

Zuo Moye. *Dangdai Zhongguo de guangbo dianshi* (Contemporary Radio and Television in China). Beijing: Chinese Social Science Press, 1987.

Periodicals

Beijing Guangbo Xueyuan Xuebao (Journal of Beijing Broadcasting College). Beijing: Beijing Broadcasting College, 1979– .

Dazhong dianshi (Mass TV). Hangzhou: Zhejiang Provincial Bureau of Radio and Television, 1979– .

Dianshi yuekan (TV Monthly). Wuhan: Hubei Provincial Bureau of Radio and Television, 1982– .

Dianshiju yishu (TV Film Arts). Shanghai: Shanghai Television Station, 1985– .

Duiwai xianchuan cankao (Overseas Propaganda Reference). Internal. Beijing: Xinhua News Agency.

Guangbo dianshi jishu (Radio and Television Technology). Beijing: Ministry of Radio, Film, and Television, 1974– .

Guangbo dianshi yewu (Radio and TV Enterprise). Hangzhou: Zhejiang Provincial Bureau of Radio and Television, 1979– .

Guangbo dianshi zhanxian (Radio and Television Front). Beijing: Ministry of Radio, Film, and Television, 1982– .

Shanghai dianshi (Shanghai Television). Shanghai: Shanghai Television Station, 1982– .

Shitingjie (Listening and Viewing). Jiangsu Provincial Bureau of Radio and Television, 1986– .

Xinwen aihaozhe (News Amateur). Zhengzhou: Henan Daily, 1986– .

Xinwen caibian (News Collecting and Editing). Taiyuan: Shanxi News Workers' Association, 1959–61, 1982– .

Xinwen chuanbo (News Propagation). Harbin: Helongjiang News Workers' Association, 1985– .

Xinwen guangbo dianshi yanjiu (Radio and Television News Study). Beijing: Press Institute in Beijing Broadcasting College, 1981– .

Xinwen jizhe (News Reporters). Shanghai: Shanghai Press Institute, 1982– .

Xinwen luntan (News Forum). Huhehaote: Mongolia Press Institute, 1986– .

Xinwen qianshao (News Front). Wuhan: Hubei Daily, 1988– .

Xinwen sanmei (News Conscience). Beijing: Workers' Daily, 1984– .

Xinwen shijie (News World). Hefei: Anhui News Workers' Association, 1989– .

Xinwen tongxin (News Communication). Nanjing: Jiangsu Press Institute, 1984– .

Xinwen xiezuo (News and Writing). Beijing: Beijing Daily, 1984– .

Xinwen yanjiu (News Study). Beijing: Press Institute in the Chinese Academy of Social Sciences, 1985– .

Xinwen yanjiu ziliao (News Study Materials). Beijing: Press Institute in the Chinese Academy of Social Sciences, 1979– .

Xinwen zhanxian (News Battlefront). Beijing: People's Daily, 1957–1966, 1978– .

Xinwen zhishi (News Knowledge). Xian: Shaanxi Daily, 1984– .

Xinwenchao (News Tide). Nanning: Guangxi News Workers' Association, 1988– .

Zhongguo guangbo dianshi (China's Radio and Television). Beijing: Ministry of Radio, Film, and Television, 1982– .

Zhongguo jizhe (China's Correspondents). Beijing: Xinhua News Agency, 1987– .

11

Film

WU DINGBO

Shortly after the world's first public showing of motion pictures was held in Paris on December 28, 1895, and America's first public showing was held in New York City on April 23, 1896, Chinese audiences saw a Western film for the first time at the Youyicun Teahouse in Shanghai's Xu Garden on August 11, 1896. This was an immediate success as the audiences were amazed and delighted to see real people and things reproduced on screen. Thus film as a new commercial entertainment based on modern technology was gradually introduced to China. James Ricalton of America was probably one of the earliest to see the lucrative market in China. In 1897 he began to import movies to China and show them at teahouses. More and more foreign film entrepreneurs followed suit, and they soon dominated the film markets in big cities such as Beijing and Shanghai. Early imports came mainly from France, but beginning in the 1920s, Hollywood movies dominated the Chinese markets for almost thirty years. Foreign films, though aiming at enormous commercial value, not only entertained Chinese audiences but also exerted a positive influence on the Chinese film industry.

The first attempt to produce a Chinese film was made by Ren Jingfeng, a businessman from Shenyang. He opened the Fengtai Photo Studio in Beijing in 1892 and then set up a theater showing Western films. As there was a shortage of Western films in the market, he gradually lost audiences. Then the idea occurred to him to make a Chinese film. He bought a French camera and fourteen reels of film from a German merchant and began his experiment. In the fall of 1905, in the courtyard of the Fengtai Photo Studio, the first Chinese film, *Dingjun shan* (Dingjun Mountain), was produced with Ren Jingfeng as producer, Liu Zhonglun as cameraman, and Tan Xinpei, the prominent actor of Beijing drama (Peking opera), as the main actor. It took three days to finish the three-reel project. Based on an episode from the classic novel *Sanguo yanyi* (Romance of the Three Kingdoms) by Luo Guanzhong (c. 1330–1400), *Dingjun Mountain* is a classic item in the repertoire of Beijing drama. Obviously, China's first film is in fact a record of an old drama performed not on stage but in a photo studio. The nature of the dramatic original helped define the early cinema audience that in turn influenced the films made to attract it.

Theatrical traditions were so strong that the cinema spent its early years working with dramatic conventions, and even acting styles were transferred from stage onto screen. The transition from the traditional form of old drama to the new art of cinema is significant because, on the one hand, Chinese audiences could feel on familiar ground with mellow falsetto or violent swordplay, and on the other hand, old drama films could establish themselves as a unique type in Chinese cinema. For decades, Chinese filmmakers have continuously made use of traditional materials from theater repertory and historical tales. Later, many more famous actors of Beijing drama put their art on camera in the Fengtai Photo Studio, such as Yu Jusheng, Zhu Wenying, Xu Deyi, Yu Zhenting, and Mei Lanfang.

It was not until 1913, however, that the first Chinese feature film, *Nanfu nanqi* (The Suffering Couple), was produced by the Asia Film Company in Shanghai. The foreign businessman who owned the company invited Zhang Shichuan as the advisor in filmmaking. Zhang accepted the invitation out of his curiosity about the new gadget, though he knew little about it. Therefore, he in turn invited his literary friend Zheng Zhenqiu to work with him. As Zheng believed that film must help reform society and educate the broad masses, he readily accepted the invitation and wrote the script and directed it with Zhang Shichuan. Since there were no actresses at that time, all the female parts were played by men. *The Suffering Couple* was first shown in Shanghai's Xinxin Theater in September 1913. Although this was only a four-reel short film, it had great social significance because it exposed and condemned China's feudal marriage system through the tragedy of the young couple.

With the success of this film, Zhang went to make more and more short films, although most of them were trivial nonsense that pandered to cheap laughter, and Zheng Zhenqiu was mainly engaged in the new drama movement and only returned to film ten years later. This is how China's two film pioneers made their debut. Their collaboration resumed in 1922 when they sponsored the Mingxing (Bright Star) Film Company. Zheng Zhenqiu not only wrote screenplays but also directed them and played some parts in them. He died in 1935 at the age of forty-eight; he is highly acclaimed as a great artist in Chinese cinema with over eighty titles from his pen. Zhang Shichuan learned his trade through practice. In a strict sense, he was not an accomplished director, but he made great contributions to the Chinese film industry as a capable production manager. Through his efforts, the company set up China's first film school to train young film artists. Many young people thus became engaged in the field.

As an attempt to create a domestic product sufficient in quantity to counterbalance the influx of Western films, the Shanghai Commercial Press set up its motion picture department in 1918. For a decade, this department produced various kinds of films on Chinese scenic spots, political affairs, and educational issues to promote progressive ideas and enhance consciousness. Moreover, as this department was well funded and fully equipped with its own production and distribution system, it helped two other film studios to produce two of China's three earliest full-length features: *Yan Ruisheng* and *Hongfeng kulou* (Female Skeleton), ten reels and twelve reels, respectively. The Shanghai Film Company produced the third one, the six-reel feature titled *Haishi* (Sea Vow) in 1922.

The achievements made by the Motion Picture Department of the Commercial Press and the production and exhibition of China's early full-length feature films marked the beginning of Chinese film production on certain scales. As the film industry was quick to see the potential in this new era of mass communication, more and more film studios emerged. According to the statistics, there were 175 film companies all over China around 1925—there were 141 in Shanghai alone—but most of these companies closed down without a single film. In the late 1920s, dozens of companies in China produced more than a hundred films annually, most of them dealing with sentimental romances and martial arts adventures. Among these companies, the Mingxing, the Tianyi, and the Lianhua made the greatest contributions to the development of the national cinema.

During the 1920s, the Mingxing Company produced two box-office hits which not only saved the company from financial reverses but also inspired talented young artists to work in the field. *Guer jiu zu ji* (Orphan Saves His Grandpa, 1923) concerns social morals; Zheng Zhenqiu served as scriptwriter, Zhang Shichuan as director, Zhang Weitao as cameraman, and Zheng Xiaoqiu (Zheng Zhenqiu's son) played the main role. The film deals with Yang Shouchang's family. Yang is very rich, but one day his son falls from a horse and dies leaving behind a pregnant wife, Yu Huiru. Daopei, Yang's nephew, becomes eager to inherit Yang's wealth, but he is afraid that Yu Huiru might give birth to a son. Therefore, he accuses Yu of immorality in front of Yang Shouchang. Yang is taken in, and he drives Yu out. Yu returns to her father's house and later gives birth to her son Yu Pu. Later Yu Pu studies in a free school set up by Yang Shouchang. When Daopei becomes impatient waiting for Yang's death, he plans to kill Yang. However, Yu Pu comes to rescue his grandpa just in time. The Yang family celebrates their reunion happily.

With its educational and artistic values, *Orphan Saves His Grandpa* was an immediate success which ushered in a period of prosperity in early Chinese filmmaking. In 1928, the company turned out China's first kung fu movie, *Huoshao Hongliansi* (The Burning of the Red Lotus Temple). Although it took three years for the company to finish the eighteen-part serial, the enormous profit gained from the film was encouraging. The success of kung fu films lies in the fact that they are geared to the popular taste for thrilling entertainment.

So far as Chinese cinema is concerned, the 1930s were of special significance in at least three aspects. First, talkies reached Chinese audiences for the first time in 1931. The early films were all silent. Shortly after Will Hays of America became the first person in the world to talk on screen in 1926 and *The Jazz Singer* became the first feature with sound shown in New York in 1927, China turned out its first feature-length film with sound, *Genu Hongmoudan* (Red Peony, the Singing Girl). This was coproduced by the Mingxing Company and Pathe Gramophone Records in 1930, with Hong Shen as scriptwriter, Zhang Shichuan as director, and Hu Die (Butterfly Hu) playing the main role.

The film tells the story of Red Peony, a beautiful girl with a sweet voice. She is married to a villain, who spends money without restraint, and she is so depressed that her voice gradually loses its charm. Since she cannot make enough money to support the family, her husband mistreats her. He kills a man accidentally and goes to jail. Red Peony still visits him in prison and even manages to set him free. This film shows the poisonous influence of feudal ethics on benighted Chinese women who have been oppressed all their lives but still have no urge to change their tragic lot. It was first shown on March 15, 1931, in Shanghai. Although Mingxing lost money on this film, their efforts were commendable as it ushered in a new era of filmmaking in China.

It was certainly a great honor for Hu Die to play the main role in China's first talkie, but *Red Peony, the Singing Girl* is by no means her best performance. *Jiemei hua* (Twin Sisters) is generally regarded as her representative work. *Twin Sisters* was produced by Mingxing in 1933 with Zheng Zhenqiu as scriptwriter and director. It tells about the drastically different experiences of the twin sisters, one married to a poor carpenter and the other to a warlord as his seventh wife. Because the twin sisters were separated from each other in childhood, they do not know each other when the elder sister secures a job as a wet nurse to her younger sister's son. The younger sister treats the wet nurse arrogantly until she realizes their relationship. By making a striking contrast between the extravagant life of the warlord's family and the poverty-stricken life of the poor working people, the film exposes inequality and injustice in society and advocates reformist ideas. Because the film touched the heartstrings of the audiences, it was shown for sixty days running.

Hu Die played the two roles of the twin sisters with entirely different dispositions. She entered Mingxing in 1928 and after that acted in dozens of titles and played about eighty roles. Her great attainments in performance won her the honor of the film queen in the 1930s. She was also the first Chinese film actress to attend the First International Film Festival held in Moscow in 1935 and then visited France and England. She died in Canada in 1988, but her artistic contribution to Chinese cinema is everlasting.

More and more talkies emerged, such as *Taoli jie* (Disaster after School, 1934) with scenario by Yuan Muzhi and directed by Ying Yunwei. This film vividly depicts the harsh life of the intellectuals in China. In the film, Yuan Muzhi also played the main role as the schoolteacher who tastes the bitterness of life but still passes on democratic and nationalistic ideas to his students and encourages them to realize their social responsibility. The talkies became popular in China during the mid-1930s.

The 1930s were significant also because Chinese cinema entered its golden age with high annual production, high artistic level, and numerous young creative artists emerging in the field. When China was torn by civil strife and foreign aggression during the 1930s, the progressively minded young artists were eager to use film as a tool to raise political consciousness to reform society and save the nation. Therefore, they produced many successful silent films and sound films with high artistic and educational values.

Outstanding silent films during this period include Shen Xiling's *Shanghai ershisi xiaoshi* (Twenty-four Hours in Shanghai, 1934), Sun Yu's *Gudu chunmeng* (Spring Dream in the Old Capital, 1930) and *Xiao wanyi* (Toys, 1933), Cai Chusheng's *Sange modeng nuxing* (Three Modern Girls, 1933), Wu Yonggang's *Shennu* (Goddess, 1934), and Xia Yan's *Chuncan* (Spring Silkworms, 1933). Among them, *Goddess* has exerted a far-reaching influence in Chinese cinema for its realistic style. Produced by the Lianhua Film Company, *Goddess* is about the miserable life of a woman struggling for survival in Old China. Raped by a villain, she tries several times to escape from his control but in vain. Later, she becomes a prostitute in order to support the family and pay for her son's education. When the school authorities learn that she is a prostitute, they expel her son from school. Not totally discouraged, she believes that she can use her savings to send her son to study in a remote place. When she discovers that all her savings have been stolen by the villain, she is so enraged that she throws a vase at him, killing him accidentally. Consequently, she is sentenced to twelve years in prison. Full of deep sympathy for downtrodden women, this film reflects their misery with great artistic power. Its success shows the progress made in technique and direction as well as in acting.

Ruan Lingyu in the title role reached the acme of perfection in her vivid portrayal of an oppressed woman in an evil society. Her superb performance was highly appreciated not only by the Chinese audience in the 1930s but also by foreign cinematic experts half a century later. As a great film star of original talents, Ruan Lingyu played the main roles in twenty-nine films, most of them depicting injured and humiliated women in Old China. Whatever roles she took, she always revealed the heartrending persecution of women by evil forces from various perspectives. Her ingenious integration of naturalness with artistry is best illustrated in such classic titles as *Spring Dream in the Old Capital, Goddess, Three Modern Girls, Toys,* and *Xin nuxing* (The New Women, 1935). It is a pity that her personal life was deplorable. Ruined by two villains one after another and humiliated by ill-willed gossip from newspapers and journals, she committed suicide on Women's Day, March 8, 1935, at the age of twenty-five. Thus Chinese cinema suffered a great loss.

During the early 1930s, when Japan escalated its aggression in northeastern China, the Chinese people became more and more involved in antifeudal, anti-Japanese activities. Under such circumstances, headed by Xia Yan, a member of the Chinese Communist Party, many talented young writers and artists initiated the left-wing movement in literature and art, including cinema. Under their influence, many filmmakers gave up romance and kung fu projects and turned to serious films with antifeudal and anti-Japanese themes.

For instance, among the more than seventy films produced in 1933 in China, over forty advocated democratic and nationalistic ideas. Mingxing alone turned out twenty-five features that year with twenty-two left-wing products. The Lianhua Company and the Yihua Company also produced a dozen progressive films, such as Tian Han's *Minzu cunwang* (Survival of the Nation), Yang Hansheng's *Zhongguohai de nuchao* (The Angry Tide of the East China Sea), and Xia Yan's *Kuangliu* (The Wild Torrent). Influenced by the left-wing film production, even the Tianyi Company, which specialized in kung fu films, began to present movies with progressive ideas.

Outstanding sound films in the period from 1933 to 1937 include Xia Yan's *Zhifen shichang* (Face Powder Market, 1933), Cai Chusheng's *Yuguang qu* (Song of the Fishermen, 1934), Yuan Muzhi's *Malu tianshi* (Street Angel, 1934), Shen Xiling's *Shizi jietou* (Crossroads, 1937), and Ma Xu Weibang's *Yeban gesheng* (Song at Midnight, 1937). *Face Powder Market,* directed by Zhang Shichuan, portrays the miserable life of Chinese women. The film advocated that women could achieve real emancipation only by joining the national salvation movement.

Song of the Fishermen depicts the harsh life of Chinese fishermen. It begins with a fishermen's song while three children are playing on the shore. Two of them are the poor twins Xiaomao and Xiaohou, and the third one, Wenying, is the son of a rich shipowner. Eighteen years later, Wenying finishes his studies abroad and meets the penniless twins by chance in Shanghai. Wenying gives them some money, but the policemen take for granted that the twins have stolen the money and put them in jail. After their release, the twins return home to be fishermen. Xiaohou falls seriously ill and dies in his sister's arms while listening to her singing the fishermen's song. Written and directed by Cai Chusheng, a highly accomplished artist in camera techniques, composition, and editing, *Song of the Fishermen* created a box-office hit of eighty-four days nonstop. Moreover, it won an honorary prize at the First International Film Festival in Moscow and was thus the first Chinese film to receive an international cinematic prize.

Written and directed by Yuan Muzhi, *Street Angel* is a tragicomedy about the love story of a poor trumpeter and a slave girl. Zhao Dan, Zhou Xuan, and Wei Heling, three great stars in Chinese cinema, played the principal roles. This film is considered to be a good example of Chinese neorealism. *Crossroads* depicts the sufferings and affections of unemployed young people who finally join the anti-Japanese war. Written and directed by Shen Xiling, the film was another box-office hit. Its success is mainly attributed to Shen's skillful direction and narrative style and to Bai Yang's excellent presentation of the main role in the film. Although only sixteen, she had already made a name for herself. Bai Yang became a professional actress, and her innumerable accomplishments make her one of the most popular film stars in China.

Song at Midnight, written and directed by Ma Xu Weibang, shows the love between a young intellectual and a landlord's daughter. Their relationship is ruined by a villain who pours nitric acid on the young man's face. The young man hides himself away from the sight of his girlfriend. At the end, he takes revenge on the villain and dies with him. This film is often regarded as China's first horror film since the hair-raising scenes appear one after another: an old broken-down cart in a gloomy street, a ghastly shadow moving in the dark attic of an empty theater, and a thin hand with long fingernails stretching through a cobwebbed gate. The director was an expert in creating an atmosphere of horror with cinematic artistry.

The 1930s were also significant because, along with the Chinese cinema reaching its maturity, young talented artists emerged in the field in large numbers and soon became its mainstay. Among the directors were Zheng Zhenqiu, Zhang Shichuan, Hong Shen, Cheng Bugao, Pu Wancang, Cai Chusheng, Sun Yu, Ying Yunwei, Xu Xingzhi, Situ Huimin, Fei Mu, Shen Xiling, Zhu Shilin, and Ma Xu Weibang. Among the scriptwriters were Shen Xiling, Sun Yu, Cai Chusheng, Pu Wancang, Wu Yonggang, Xia Yan, Tian Han, Yang Hansheng, Yuan Muzhi, Sun Shiyi, Fei Mu, Shen Huangmei, Ke Ling, Xu Changlin, Cheng Jihua, Li Shaobai, Luo Yijun, and Liu Niantong. Among the actors were Zheng Xiaoqiu, Jin Yan, Zheng Junli, Liu Qiong, Zhao Dan, Wei Heling, Jin Shan, Wang Xianzhai, and among the actresses were Ruan Lingyu, Hu Die, Li Lili, Zhou Xuan, Bai Yang, Lin Chuchu, Hu Ping, and Ai Xia. Even film scores appealed tremendously to the audiences, young people in particular. Nie Er and Xian Xinghai both composed music and songs for many movies. With lyrics by Tian Han and music by Nie Er, "Song at Midnight" and "Hot Blood" from the film *Song at Midnight* have been immensely popular for decades. "March of the Volunteers," a song Nie Er composed for the film *Fengyun ernu* (Children of the Storm, 1935) later became the national anthem of the People's Republic in 1949. It is through all their concerted efforts that Chinese cinema achieved its national character.

During World War II, the Chinese film industry was greatly hampered by the Japanese invasion. In northeastern China, the Japanese aggressors controlled the film industry and produced more than 200 "enlightening films," more than 120 entertainment films, and more than 300 documentaries from 1937 to 1945. Although about 240 features were made in Shanghai from 1938 to 1941, most of them were ancient history costume dramas roughly produced. When the Japanese seized all the concessions in Shanghai in December 1941, they also took control of filmmaking there. In Shanghai, from 1942 to 1945, more than 130 features were produced under the Japanese occupation. All these films were intended to prettify the Japanese presence in China and to nullify the Chinese people's national spirit. However, in cities like Wuhan and Chongqing, the

China Film Studio, the Central Film Studio, and the Northwest Film Company did produce some documentary films and more than a dozen features eulogizing the Chinese people's heroic struggle against the Japanese; for example, Shi Dongshan's *Baowei women de tudi* (Defend Our Land, 1938) and Yang Han-sheng's *Babei zhuanshi* (Eight Hundred Soldiers, 1938).

After World War II, there were state-funded film studios, such as the China Film Company, in Shanghai, Beijing, and Nanjing, as well as privately owned independent studios, such as the Kunlun Company and the Wenhua Company in Shanghai. The national productions faced serious challenges from imported American films. From 1945 to 1949, 1,896 films were imported in Shanghai alone, but Chinese filmmakers were not utterly discouraged in the face of such a serious situation. From 1946 to 1949, they produced more than 240 films in the areas under Kuomintang (Nationalist Party) rule, of which more than 40 were written and directed by progressive artists. Successful films during this period include *Baqian lilu yun he yue* (Eight Thousand *li* of Clouds and Moon, 1947), *Yijiang chunshui xiang dongliu* (The Spring River Flows East, 1947), and *Yanyangtian* (Bright Day, 1949).

Eight Thousand li of Clouds and Moon was the first feature that the Lianhua Film Studio produced under rather poor material conditions after the war. Shi Dongshan wrote and directed the film, and Bai Yang and Tao Jin played the principal roles. The story tells of the adventures of two artists who work in a wartime theater group. Through their encounters and experiences, the film shows, on the one hand, the patriotic enthusiasm of the artists, and, on the other hand, the corrupt officials who escape the battle front when the anti-Japanese war breaks out and return to usurp power and properties after the war. It is said that this film was based on Shi Dongshan's personal experience in a wartime theater group.

After the production of *Eight Thousand li of Clouds and Moon,* the Lianhua coproduced *The Spring River Flows East* with the Kunlun Company, with Cai Chusheng and Zheng Junli as scriptwriters and directors, and Bai Yang, Tao Jin, and Shui Xinwen playing the principal roles. Through the separation and reunion of a family during and after the anti-Japanese war, the film realistically portrays the tragic experiences of the Chinese people. It was such an appealing tearjerker that it was shown for more than three months running, with more than 710,000 tickets sold.

Bright Day was Cao Yu's first attempt in filmmaking. He wrote and directed it for the Wenhua Film Company. Shi Hui played the main role as a lawyer who is ever ready to uphold justice in defiance of personal danger. Finally he succeeds in exposing the villain as a traitor who once served the Japanese aggressors. The villain is sent to prison, and the lawyer continues to defend people against injustice. Cao Yu is one of the greatest playwrights in China, so *Bright Day* cannot but reveal some of his writing characteristics: ingenious conception, concise structure, dramatic plot, distinct characterization, lively dialogue, and light humor.

The Adventures of Sanmao, the Waif (1949) was adapted from the comic strip series by the great cartoonist Zhang Leping who started this cartoon figure in 1935. Yang Hansheng transformed the materials into a polished screenplay with cutting satire. The film was directed by Zhao Ming and Yan Gong. Wang Longji played the role of Sanmao. With bitter humor, this film exposes the evils of the corrupt society through the misfortunes of a homeless boy who struggles for mere survival, and at the same time, the film praises a pure and innocent child with stubborn character. The Kunlun Film Company began this juvenile in October 1948, but it was not finished until August 1949 when Shanghai was taken over by the People's Liberation Army. In order to welcome the new government, the film added a new ending in which Sanmao cheers the People's Liberation Army.

The film industry also developed in Communist areas before the founding of the People's Republic in 1949, but under very poor material conditions. Following Zhou Enlai's instructions, the Yanan Film Workshop was set up in the fall of 1938, with one of the cameras donated by the famous filmmaker Joris Ivens from Holland. Then, in 1939, the workshop set up a projection team. This workshop produced a few documentary films, but it dissolved when all of its forty members went to northeastern China to take control of the film institutions there from the Japanese after their surrender. The Yanan Film Studio was set up in 1946, but it produced only a few newsreels and an unfinished feature, Chen Boer's *Bianqu yingxiong* (Heroes in Communist Areas). In October 1946, the Northeast Film Studio was also set up under the leadership of the Communist Party. The footage produced in Communist areas in these days was not for commercial profits, but to carry the propaganda of Communist ideas. Although it mainly produced documentary films, the studio also turned out animations such as Chen Boer's *Huangdi de meng* (Emperor's Dream, 1947) and a four-reel feature, Lin Qi's *Liuxia ta da laojiang* (Leave Him Behind to Fight Chiang Kai-shek, 1948).

Since the founding of the People's Republic in 1949, Chinese filmmakers have been working in Hong Kong, Taiwan, and on the mainland under different governments. Hong Kong's filmmaking has its own traditions. From the very beginning in the 1920s, the filmmakers in Hong Kong showed their awareness of social responsibility. They held that film was a tool for social reform and that it should entertain as well as educate people. After the anti-Japanese war, the Hong Kong film industry developed rapidly and produced about 200 films annually, and it reached its golden age in the 1950s and 1960s with about 3,500 titles on various subjects. Among the best were *Chun* (Spring) (1958), and *Lan yu hei* (Blue and Black) (1966).

The film industry in Hong Kong declined in the late 1960s, and it restored its prestige in the early 1980s with the emergence of young, creative filmmakers who initiated a new wave in the field. They have made outstanding achievements in kung fu films and neorealistic films. Fang Yuping's *Fu zi qing* (Father and Son) (1981) and Yan Hao's *Shishui liunian* (Time Flows) (1984) appeal tremendously to audiences even on the mainland. These New Wave films are greatly influenced by the Western cinematic aesthetics. At present, there are hundreds of film studios in Hong Kong. The largest among them are the Yindu, the Shaoshi, the Xinyicheng, the Jiasu, the Jinlie, and the Debao. As they are all independent studios, the competition is extremely great. But such competition also nurtures great numbers of artists. Among the famous directors are Zhang Che, Hou Xiaoxian, Li Hanxiang, Hu Jinquan, and Liu Jiachang. There are many film stars in Hong Kong who have received cinematic prizes at home and abroad, such as Zhou Renfa, Liu Dehua, Wan Ziliang, Cheng Long, Li Xiaolong, Zhong Chuhong, Zheng Yuling, Li Zhi, Zhang Manyu. Hong Kong has been issuing annual film prizes since 1982.

In 1949, after Chiang Kai-shek's government moved to Taiwan, it still controlled three state-owned studios: the China film Studio, the Central Film Studio, and the Taiwan Film Studio. They produced films in Beijing dialogue whereas some independent film studios produced films in Taiwanese dialogue. The government made "wholesome realism" the basic policy in filmmaking in Taiwan, and some studios turned out films like *Yangya renjia* (The Duck-raising Family) (1963), which received an award at the Asia Film Festival. It was not until in the early 1980s that the Taiwan film industry made a big leap forward with the emergence of a new generation of filmmakers who had studied abroad and returned to Taiwan. They were engaged in the New Wave movement after their Hong Kong counterpart. Among the representative works of the New Wave were *Guangyin de gushi* (The Story of Time) (1982), codirected by Tao Dechen, Yang Dechang, Ke Yizheng, and Zhang Yi; *Xiaobi de gushi* (The Story of Young Bi) (1983), codirected by Hou Xiaoxian, Chen Kunhou, and others; and *Haitan de yitian* (One Day on a Beach) (1983), directed by Yang Dechang. Among the directors, Hou Xiaoxian is said to have made the greatest contributions to the New Wave movement in Taiwan.

Meanwhile, Li Hang took the lead in producing local color films in Taiwan. In the 1960s and 1980s, he launched two upsurges in making films of native flavor and themes. Another phenomenon in Taiwan's filmmaking is the adaptations of Qiong Yao's sentimental fiction, which formed a craze for years among the audiences, high school students in particular. The films adapted from Qiong Yao's stories also overwhelmed the audiences on the mainland. The prominent film stars in Taiwan include Ke Junqiong, Sun Yue, Qin Han, Qin Xianglin, Zhang Aijia, Lin Fengjiao, Yang Huishan, Hu Weizhong, Wang Zuxian, and Lin Qingxia. Taiwan has been issuing the Golden Horse Prize annually since 1962, commending the achievements in cinematic art gained by Taiwan's best film artists.

In the People's Republic, the Central Film Bureau became the leading body to take care of all production, distribution, and exhibition of films on the mainland after 1949. As the film industry was funded by the new government, it naturally followed the strict guiding principles set by the government. Hence the films were to advocate class struggle; portray workers, peasants, and soldiers;

and eulogize the state and the Communist Party. From 1949 to 1951, the Northeast Film Studio, the Shanghai Film Studio, and the Beijing Film Studio produced 35 features, 280 documentaries, and 6 animations. With few exceptions, they all glorified the party and the government. In the next ten years, more studios were set up one after another, including the Bayi (PLA), the Zhujiang, the Xian, the Emei, the Xinjiang, the Central Documentary Film Studio, the Shanghai Scientific and Educational Film Studio, and the Agricultural Film Studio.

Outstanding films produced from 1949 to 1965 include *Bai maonu* (The White-Haired Girl, 1950), *Wo zhe yibeizi* (My Whole Life, 1950), *Weile Heping* (For Peace, 1956), *Zhufu* (The New Year's Sacrifice, 1956), *Lin Zexu* (1959), *Liu Sanjie* (1960), *Honghu zhiweidui* (Red Guards in the Honghu River, 1961), *Nongnu* (The Serf, 1963), *Tianshan de honghua* (The Red Flower on Tianshan Mountain, 1964), and *Nianqing yidai* (The Younger Generation, 1965). To commend their great contributions to the cinematic art, the Ministry of Culture issued official photos of twenty-two film stars to all cinemas in China in the early 1960s: Bai Yang, Zhao Dan, Zhang Ruifang, Sun Daolin, Shangguan Yunzhu, Wang Danfeng, Qin Yi, Wei Heling, Cui Wei, Xie Tian, Chen Qiang, Yu Lan, Zhang Ping, Yu Yang, Xie Fang, Wang Xingang, Tian Hua, Wang Xiaotang, Pang Xueqin, Zhang Yuan, Li Yalin, and Jin Di.

Hampered by natural disasters and political struggles, one after another, the film industry developed tortuously, and the crashing blow came when the Cultural Revolution broke out. From the beginning of the Cultural Revolution to 1973, except for several "models" under the auspices of Jiang Qing, Mao Zedong's wife, no feature films were produced for seven years on mainland China. What is even worse, the films produced since 1949—603 features, more than 100 animations, and several thousand documentaries—were under malicious examination. Most of them were condemned as "poisonous weeds." Most of the cinematic artists were persecuted, and many died as a result.

After the downfall of the Gang of Four, the film industry tried hard to catch up in its development and began a new phase in its history. From 1978 to 1988, it produced more than 1,100 features, and the film studios expanded to twenty-two. Of these, sixteen were designated to produce features; namely, the Beijing, the Changchun, the Shanghai, the Bayi (PLA), the Zhujiang, the Emei, the Xian, the Xiaoxiang, the Guangxi, the Tianshan, the Inner Mongol, the Fujian, the Shenzhen, the Yunnan, the Children, and the Youth. In addition, there are the Shanghai Animation Studio, the Shanghai Dubbing Studio, and the scientific and educational film studios in Beijing, Shanghai, and Liaoning. Considering the market, the annual output for features has been set at around 120 on the mainland since 1982.

Since then, filmmakers have been encouraged to open new grounds in subject matter and in experimental styles. They have not only resumed their realistic tradition but also have explored sophisticated techniques and styles in both content and form. Generally speaking, in the early 1980s, retrospective films, though highly critical of the party's policies, appealed to audiences tremendously. Among the box-office hits were *Tianyun shan chuanqi* (The Legend of Tianyun Mountain, 1980), *Bei aiqing yiwang de jiaoluo* (A Corner Forgotten by Love, 1981), and *Rendao zhongnian* (At Middle Age, 1982).

The Legend of Tianyun Mountain was directed by Xie Jin of Shanghai. The film was adapted from Lu Yanzhou's short novel, dealing with Luo Chun, a young intellectual, who was wrongly persecuted in the 1957 antirightist movement and suffered from it for more than twenty years. This film took first place in five categories—including best feature, best director, and best screenplay at the First Golden Rooster Prizes held in 1981.

A Corner Forgotten by Love was directed by Li Yalin and Zhang Ji of Emei. The film was adapted from Zhang Xian's short story dealing with a poverty-stricken peasant family in a destitute and forgotten corner of a remote county. It focuses on Huangmei's love for the young cadre Xu Rongshu, who believes that collectivization leads to poverty in the countryside. As Huangmei's father was branded a rightist because of just such a view in 1958, Huangmei's mother is afraid that the same misfortune might befall the family again, and she marries her daughter off in a hurry for only 500 yuan to pay the family debt. This film was criticized for its exposure of rural misery in the People's Republic, but it was acclaimed as one of the best in 1981 and won two awards at the Second Golden Rooster Prizes in 1982.

At Middle Age was directed by Wang Qimin and Sun Yu of Changchun. The film was adapted from Chen Rong's novella, which reveals the burden of life on a middle-aged woman doctor: low salary, poor living conditions, heavy household chores, oppressive workload, and a problematic party policy about intellectuals. Even though the story was attacked by hostile critics for its challenge of the party's policy about intellectuals, the film was a box-office hit and received high acclaim from many professionals. It won the best feature at the Sixth Hundred Flowers Prizes, and Pan Hong who played the woman doctor won the best actress at the Third Golden Rooster Prizes in 1983.

The success achieved by the retrospective films lies in the daring efforts of filmmakers who have evaded the mainstream of official ideology and have voiced the dissenting views of ordinary people. More significant, these films have called for a reexamination of the Party's policy, not just during the Cultural Revolution, but from the early days of the Communist reign, such as collectivization in 1956 and the antirightist movement in 1957.

In the late 1980s, the call for political reform and opening up became nationwide. The filmmakers tried their best to fight for full freedom of creative expression and produced many experimental films. The passion for experiment is eternal, but young directors recently graduated from the Beijing Film Academy seemed to have a much stronger passion for it in filmmaking. Because they had all experienced the social turmoil and had lived at the bottom of society before they grew up and because they all had received systematic higher education, they detested the backward aspects in the People's Republic and had a vehemently strong urge for reform. Because they felt disgusted about commercial and fake-serious fare, they explored new ground for new aesthetic values. They were well prepared for such efforts, and the films they produced demonstrated their sophistication and subtleties in form and content.

Their films reexamined China's traditional values with a critical eye. Although they were rather subjective in speculation, they were filled with profound philosophical ideas. Their themes were very serious; their cinematic techniques were symbolic and impressionistic; and stereophonic sound, special optical effects, and color processes were used. The significance of their films can be best illustrated by the following examples.

Huang tudi (Yellow Earth, 1984), directed by Chen Kaige, is a lyrical film that tells a story about a young army artist who goes to a remote village on the Loess Plateau. The scenes of the bleak plateau implied the heavy traditional burdens the natives had to bear from generation to generation. The cinematography demonstrated a successful blend of feature and documentary film shooting techniques. Zhang Yimou received the best cameraman award at the Fifth Golden Rooster Prizes in 1985.

Hong gaoliang (Red Sorghum, 1987) looked through the eyes of a child at the bitter experiences of a peasant wine distillery in Shandong province in the 1930s and 1940s before and during the Japanese occupation. The director, Zhang Yimou, made special efforts to control the lighting while shooting this gloomy picture of rural life. His adroitness at presenting rural life won the film the Golden Bear Prize at the 38th West Berlin International Film Festival in 1988.

Wanzhong (Evening Bell, 1988), directed by Wu Ziniu, tells about the dramatic encounter of five Chinese soldiers with thirty-two Japanese soldiers immediately after Japan's surrender in 1945. The Japanese soldiers are guarding an arsenal in a cave without any idea that the war has ended. In order to intensify the inner conflicts of both the Chinese and Japanese soldiers, the film applied a delicate treatment of sound.

The Chinese film industry also made tremendous achievements in 1992. It not only produced 150 features but also won international awards for 10 features, 4 animations, and 4 scientific and educational films. Most noteworthy is the success of the director Zhang Yimou and the actress Gong Li in the film titled *Qiuju da guansi* (Qiuju Goes to Court). The film shows the radical changes made in rural areas by portraying a young village woman who fights for dignity, understanding, and equal rights in modern China. The film won the Golden Lion Prize at the 49th Venice International Film Festival, and Gong Li was honored as the best actress.

It was said that 1992 was Gong Li's year since she received the most publicity in her field at home and abroad. In fact, she became famous abroad first, but the repercussions were soon felt at home. The filmmakers in Taiwan and Hong Kong appreciated her performance so much that they had already signed many contracts with her. Ever since the production and exhibition of *Red Sorghum*, Gong Li's collaborations with Zhang Yimou have all been rewarded with cinematic awards of various kinds.

Significant also in 1992 was the first session of Golden Rooster and Hundred

Flowers Film Festival held in Guilin, Guangxi province, in November. The China Film Association honored Xia Yan and Yang Hansheng with lifelong achievements awards. *Da Juezhan* (Decisive Campaigns) won the best feature for both prizes, and Wang Tiecheng, who played the main role in this film, also won the best actor for both prizes. Song Xiaoying won the best actress award of the Golden Rooster while Zhao Lirong won the best actress award of the Hundred Flowers.

On the mainland, there are three major film prizes. The Best Film Prizes, issued by the Ministry of Culture, was first held in 1956, second held in 1979, and then held annually. This prize embodies the official standards of evaluation. The Hundred Flowers Prizes, sponsored by the magazine *Dazhong dianying* (Popular Cinema), was first held in 1962, second held in 1963, and then cancelled. It was not until 1980 that it was resumed as an annual prize. The prize decision is made according to the ballots from the readers of the magazine. Therefore, it reflects the grass-roots view of the ordinary audience. The Golden Rooster Prizes, sponsored by the China Film Association, began in 1981. Winners are chosen through appraisals of a twenty-two-member panel of leading film artists and critics. Hence it is often called the Chinese Oscar.

It is estimated that at present more than 20,000 professional scriptwriters, more than 500 professional directors, and more than 600 professional actors and actresses are working in the Chinese film industry. Among the directors are Shui Hua, Xie Tieli, Xie Tian, Ling Zifeng, Xie Jin, Chen Huiai, and Zhao Huanzhang (third-generation directors, who have been working in the field since 1949); Wu Yigong, Wu Tianming, Zhang Aixin, Zheng Dongtian, Ding Yinnan, Luo Xiaoya, and Huang Jianzhong (fourth-generation directors, who graduated from the film academy in the 1960s); Chen Kaige, Zhang Yimou, Wu Ziniu, Huang Jianxin, Tian Zhuangzhuang, and Liu Miaomiao (fifth-generation directors, who graduated from the academy in the 1980s). Among the prominent stars are Liu Xiaoqing, Xiang Mei, Chen Peisi, Song Jia, Pan Hong, Ge Cunzhuang, Ge You, Jiang Wen, Xiao Xiong, and Gong Li.

In 1978 the China Film Cooperation Company was established to take charge of the cooperation between the Chinese filmmaking and its counterparts abroad. So far it has made arrangements with a dozen countries and regions, and more than thirty films have been finished and twenty-five are in process. The cooperation generally follows three approaches: investment and production by both parties; investment by foreigners but production by the Chinese; and, on a reciprocal basis, each party sends its own team to make its own film on a foreign land and the production expenses there are paid by the host party. At present, more and more foreign filmmakers seek cooperation with their Chinese counterparts.

China has made significant progress in its film industry; however, the tremendous achievements made in the field cannot overwhelm the whirlwind of the market economy. Challenged by television, imported films and video tapes, and other entertainment outlets, the film studios and the cinemas have lost audiences in great numbers. The film market is in the doldrums. In order to halt the slide of cinema attendance, the filmmakers are taking drastic measures to reform. For decades, the government monopolized all the production, distribution, and exhibition and hence formed an overstaffed film industry of 500,000 people who received their regular pay from the state. This raised the costs of production, distribution, and exhibition. To change the situation, independent producers are encouraged now to find money, organize the team, and make money by themselves without government interference. After 1993, the film studios have the right to sell their copies directly to local companies or overseas markets, which removes the official obstacles between production and distribution. The state will still fund the production of films about important revolutionary and historical events since films of this kind might not make a profit. Last but not least, the appeal of the films lies in the high quality in themes and styles. The numbers of audiences increase along with the appearance of more and more good films. This calls for talented artists and their hard work. The government and society must provide favorable conditions for the artists to make contributions in the field.

REFERENCE WORKS

The most basic problem confronting English speaking people interested in studying Chinese films is the lack of sufficient reference materials. To date, apart from articles occasionally carried in journals, only a few books in English are devoted to the field, namely, *Perspectives on Chinese Cinema* (1991), edited by Chris Berry; *Chinese Cinema: Culture and Politics Since 1949* (1988), by Paul Clark; *Chinese Film: The State of the Art in the People's Republic of China* (1987), edited by George Stephen Semsel; *Dianying: An Account of Films and the Film Audience in China* (1972), by Jay Leyda; and *Film: Chinese Film and Film Audience* (1972), by Chen Li. Of these five, the edited volumes by Berry and Semsel provide the most wide-ranging and critically diverse overviews (Paul Clark's essay in the Berry volume, originally presented in 1985, provides an example of the kind of analysis appearing in his 1988 monograph). Chen Li's book is necessarily dated, given the advances in Chinese cinema over the past twenty years. In Berry's *Perspectives,* Leo Ou-Fan Lee provides a historical overview of Chinese film, while Catherine Yi-Yu Cho Woo studies the intertextuality of film and painting. Berry and Clark focus on gender and politics, respectively; Esther C. M. Yau makes cross-cultural comparisons with Western cinema. Over half of the chapters focus on the new Chinese cinema and its fifth-generation filmmakers. Particularly pertinent for further research, *Perspectives* contains a list of major directors and a chronology of Chinese films. Semsel's edited volume is a very helpful reference book for Westerners interested in the film industry exclusively in the People's Republic. The book mainly consists of five parts: Semsel offers a brief survey of the filmmaking in China; Pat Wilson deals with the establishment of the Northeast Film Studio in the period from

1946 to 1949; Xia Hong introduces the research work on film theory in the new period; Ma Ning recommends the new generation of film artists; and Semsel recalls his interviews with Xie Jin, Zhang Aixin, Chen Kaige, Tian Zhuang-zhuang, Zhang Yimou, and others. In the book, Semsel sees the great impact of the economic reform on filmmaking since 1978 in China.

There are many authoritative works on film in China for all researchers conversant with the Chinese language. The following works are recommended as the first choices for specialists as well as novices who intend to explore the field.

Dangdai zhongguo dianying (Contemporary Chinese Film, 1989), edited by Chen Huangmei, is the most comprehensive survey of the film industry in China from 1949 to 1985. Contributed to by sixteen critics and specialists in the field, the two volumes provide authoritative data and information on various aspects of the film industry, such as the production of feature films in each historical period; the production of animations, documentaries, and scientific and educational films; film education and film theory; distribution and exhibition; and international relations. The eight appendices to the book list the major events in filmmaking, the major film studios in China, all the titles of films produced since 1949, and all awards won at home and abroad. The coverage ends in 1985, although it was published in 1989.

Zhongguo dianying fazhan shi (The History of the Development of Chinese Film, 1963), edited by Cheng Jihua, focuses on film production before October 1949 in China. From the very first showing of the motion picture in Shanghai to the last film made before the Communists took over the mainland, the three contributors present valuable data and information in great detail. The book also deals with filmmaking in Communist areas before the founding of the People's Republic.

Zhongguo dianying nianjian (China Film Yearbook) has been edited by the China Film Association and published by the China Film Press annually. The yearbook is no doubt a good source for research studies. It has reached readers regularly since 1982. A dozen film journals are published monthly in many big cities in China. They not only offer up-to-date coverage of the cinematic activities in the field but also carry criticisms of the works recently shown. These include *Dazhong dianying* (Popular Cinema), *Dangdai dianying* (Contemporary Cinema), *Dianying yishu* (Cinematic Art) in Beijing, *Shangying huabao* (Shanghai Film Pictorial) in Shanghai, *Xibu dianying* (Western Cinema) in Xian, and *Dianying shijie* (Cinema World) in Changchun. Among them, *Popular Cinema* is the most prestigious film journal with a monthly readership of several hundred thousand.

BIBLIOGRAPHY

Chen Huangmei, ed. *Dangdai zhongguo dianying* (Contemporary Chinese Film). Beijing: China Social Science Press, 1989.

Chen, Li. *Film: Chinese Film and Film Audience.* London: Massachusetts Institute of Technology Press, 1972.

Cheng Jihua, ed. *Zhongguo dianying fazhan shi* (The History of the Development of Chinese Film). 1963. Reprint. Beijing: China Film Press, 1980.

China Film Association, ed. *Zhongguo dianying jia liezhuan* (Biographies of the Chinese Film Artists). Beijing: China Film Press, 1991.

———. *Zhongguo dianying jinjijiang wenji* (A Collection of the Golden Rooster Prize Essays). Beijing: China Film Press, 1983.

———. *Zhongguo dianying nianjian: 1989* (China Film Yearbook: 1989). Beijing: China Film Press, 1991.

Clark, Paul. *Chinese Cinema: Culture and Politics Since 1949.* Cambridge, England: Cambridge University Press, 1988.

Fonoroff, Paul. "Perhaps the Beginning of a Vital Film Culture." *Far Eastern Economics Review,* May 3, 1989, 37–53.

Leyda, Jay. *Dianying: An Account of Films and the Film Audience in China.* Cambridge, Mass.: Massachusetts Institute of Technology Press, 1972.

Mei Duo. *Mei Duo dianying pinglun ji* (Mei Duo's Critical Essays on Films). Chengdu: Sichuan Literature and Art Press, 1985.

Pearson, Margaret. "Film in China: The Domestic System and Foreign Imports." In *U.S. Department of State Cultural Background Series, U.S. Embassy.* Beijing, January 21, 1982.

Pickowicz, Paul. "Popular Cinema and Political Thought in Post-Mao China: Reflections on Official Pronouncements, Film, and the Film Audience." In *Unofficial China, Popular Culture and Thought in the People's Republic,* edited by Perry Link, Richard Madsen, and Paul C. Pickowicz. Boulder, Colo.: Westview Press, 1989, 37–53.

Semsel, George Stephen, ed. *Chinese Film: The State of the Art in the People's Republic of China.* New York: Praeger, 1987.

Yang Sheng et al., eds. *Zhongguo dianying yanyuan beiren zhuan* (Biographies of a Hundred Chinese Film Stars). Wuhan: Changjiang Literature and Art Press, 1984.

Yang Wenming and Xie Xizhang, eds. *Zhongguo dianying mingxing lu* (Chinese Film Stars). Beijing: Xuewan Press, 1990.

12

Traditional Chinese Drama

JIANG XINGYU

TRADITIONAL DRAMA IS NOT OPERA

Before the appearance of modern drama in China, introduced from the West directly or via Japan, there had been indigenous kinds of traditional Chinese drama. In order to distinguish the two from each other, modern drama in imitation of the manner of Ibsen, Shaw, and other moderns is called *huaju* (spoken drama), and traditional Chinese drama with special stress on singing is called *xiqu* (traditional drama). *Xiqu* is a general term for all the various styles of *difangxi* (regional drama) in China.

Song Yuan xiqu kao (A History of Traditional Drama under the Song and Yuan Dynasties), written in 1915 by the famous modern scholar Wang Guowei (1877–1927) lays the foundation for scientific and systematic studies of the history of Chinese drama. Since then academics in China and in other countries have basically accepted the term *xiqu* and its concept.

Traditional Chinese drama is an integrated art, more integrated than Western drama. It is the result of a longtime assimilation, absorption, and integration of various genres in literature and art, such as music, dance, ballad medleys, comic sketches, acrobatics, and poetry. Opinions vary on how to determine the beginning of Chinese drama. In *Tang xi rong* (Drama under the Tang Dynasty), written in 1958, Ren Erbei alleges that Chinese drama began in the Tang Dynasty (618–907), but he has not presented sufficient grounds for his assumption. In the Song Dynasty (960–1279), Meng Yuanlao's *Dongjing menghua lu* (Reminiscences of the Eastern Capital, 1147) and Zhou Mi's *Wulin jiushi* (Tales of the Old Capital, 1279) both recorded the theatrical activities in Kaifeng, capital of the Northern Song Dynasty (960–1127), and in Hangzhou, capital of the

This chapter was translated by Wu Dingbo.

Southern Song Dynasty (1127–1279). So far as the dramatic forms are concerned, some were song and dance performances with a little plot; some were forms similar to modern cross talks in the north or one-man shows in the south. Only one script has been handed down, namely, *Zhang Xie zhuangyuan* (Number One Scholar Zhang Xie) of *nanxi* (southern drama), popular in Fujian Province.

The Yuan Dynasty (1206–1368) was the golden age of traditional drama. *Zaju* (variety drama), set to northern music in the northern dialect, and *nanxi,* set to southern music in the southern dialect, flourished at the same time. However, academic circles hold controversial views about whether the Yuan drama was a natural growth of Chinese culture and art or if it came through the exotic influence of foreign culture and art. The second view also makes sense because, on the one hand, the Yuan rulers were Mongols who had conquered Mid-Asia and part of Europe before they entered Xanadu (Beijing), and on the other hand, Quanzhou and Ningpo already had good transport facilities at that time and the dramatic forms of Mid-Asia and Europe could be introduced to China by land and sea.

Drama under the Ming and Qing dynasties (1368–1644, 1644–1911) developed vigorously. The playwrights in the Yuan Dynasty mainly portrayed the intellectuals who were among the lower classes of society. Zhu Yuanzhang, the first emperor of the Ming Dynasty, attempted to use drama as a supplementary tool for his feudal rule. Therefore, he highly appreciated *Pipa ji* (The Story of a Lute), which advocates filial piety. Later, his son Zhu Quan and grandson Zhu Youdun both became playwrights. With the social economy reaching high prosperity during the Wanli Reign of the Ming Dynasty (1573–1620), *kunqiang,* melodies originating in Kunshan, Jiangsu province, was the major dramatic form appreciated by aristocrats as well as common folks. Widespread performances were seen in imperial palaces, teahouses, and restaurants.

The ruling classes of the Qing Dynasty were originally Manchus from the Liaodong Peninsula. They did not stop assimilating the Han culture even after they established themselves as the rulers of the land. They favored *kunqiang,* but it declined because it was too elegant to be popular. At the end of the Qianlong Reign (1736–1796) and the beginning of the Jiaqing Reign (1796–1821), *huiju* (Anhui drama) troupes toured the capital. Anhui drama is mainly set to the music of *gaobozi* and *chuiqiang.* Having interlaced with *hanju* (Hubei drama) and *bangziqiang* (Clapper drama, performed to the accompaniment of wooden clappers from Shanxi and Shaanxi), it gradually developed into a new style of drama—*jingju* (Beijing drama, or Peking opera as people used to call it).

Beijing drama is different in form and content from the southern drama and variety drama of the Song and Yuan dynasties, and from *kunqiang* of the Ming Dynasty. But it has reserved part of the repertoire from *kunqiang* and Anhui drama. For instance, Mei Lanfang, the great master of Beijing drama, once staged *Youyuan jingmeng* (A Startling Dream of Wandering through the Garden) and *Si fan* (Longing for the Secular World), which are *kunqiang* items.

With poor transport facilities in China, the ethnic cultures and regional cultures did not have much contact with the outside world until the 1940s. As a result, there are more than 300 styles of regional drama. Most northerners are unable to make a distinction between *huju* (Shanghai drama) and *xiju* (Wuxi drama), and most southerners cannot tell *qinqiang* (Shaanxi drama) from *jinju* (Shanxi drama). The same is true with minority nationalities. It can be well imagined that the Western audience has even greater difficulty in distinguishing the various styles of traditional Chinese drama.

Beijing drama is the most popular and widespread of all styles of Chinese drama, and it tours abroad most frequently. In Western literature and art, drama, opera, and ballet coexist, but each has a unique style. When drama without song and dance was introduced into China, it was called *huaju* (spoken drama). There seems no exact synonym in the West to translate the Chinese term of *xiqu* (traditional drama). Therefore, many scholars translate *xiqu* into opera.

Although this translation has been used for decades, it needs to be revised. *Xiqu* is traditional Chinese drama, and it is not opera at all. In *Sanchakou* (At the Crossroads), Ren Tanghui and Liu Lihua fight at close quarters in the dark. In the play little singing or recitation occurs, but much difficult footwork and many somersaults take place. *Yandang shan* (The Yandang Mountain), adapted in 1953, is a play of collective fighting. There are no utterances during the entire play. Could it be called opera? *Si jinshi* (The Four Successful Candidates) tells of Song Shijie who, outraged by an injustice done to Yang Suzhen, lodges a complaint on her behalf with the local authorities. In the play there are only two arias, and the rest is dialogue, to be exact, tit for tat argument. Could it be called opera? As to Mei Lanfang's famous plays *Bawang biji* (The Conqueror Bids Farewell to Lady Yu) and *Guifei zuijiu* (The Drunken Beauty), both of them have as much dancing and singing. They might be viewed at best as song-and-dance dramas, but not as operas. Furthermore, China stages Chinese operas, such as *Jiangjie* (Sister Jiang) and *Baimaonu* (The White-Haired Girl), as well as Western operas, such as *La dame aux Camelias* and *Turandot*. If we should call traditional Chinese drama opera, we would confuse the two genres.

ACROBATICS AND FACIAL PAINTING

I have stated earlier that traditional Chinese drama is an integrated art of music, dance, ballad medleys, comic sketches, acrobatics, and poetry. Therefore, many breathtaking acrobatic feats are still seen in current performances. The old styles of traditional drama, such as *kunju, chuanju* (Sichuan drama), *qinqiang,* and Beijing drama, place special stress on acrobatic skills and often use them as major standards to evaluate the artistic achievements of performers.

The acrobatic feat most often seen on the stage is called *dachushou* (brutal attack). *Wudan* (warrior maiden) often performs this feat. In general, she has to fight against more than four opponents who throw spears or other similar weapons at her from various directions and heights. She uses her hands, feet, and the weapons in her hand simultaneously to throw, kick, and push back these spears and other similar weapons to the hands of her opponents. This skill demands that the performer be quick of eye and deft of hand. She must study diligently and practice very hard from her childhood. It would be too late to learn this skill as an adult. There are thrilling performances of *dachushou* in the traditional works of *Sishui cheng* (The City of Sishui) and *Dao xianchao* (Stealing the Celestial Herb). There is also a scene of *dachushou* in the adapted play of *Huo fenghuang* (A Fiery Phoenix). Qi Shufang, who now lives in the United States and was once an actress in the Shanghai Troupe of Beijing Drama, acted these three plays and became famous for her consummate *dachushou.*

Special acrobatic feats are mostly performed by the *chou* (clown). Sichuan drama presented *Zeng tipao* (Presenting a Robe as a Gift) in 1953. The famous clown Liu Chenji played the role of Xu Jia. In 1956 the famous *kunju* clown Wang Chuansong played the role of the thief and murderer Lou Ashu (literally Liu the Rat) in the play *Shiwu guan* (Fifteen Strings of Cash). All his footwork and eye movement are in imitation of a rat.

Acrobatic feats are not merely performed by a warrior maiden or clown. In the traditional drama, even the most important role, *laosheng* (old man), performs it. Also in the 1950s I saw Yan Fengchun in the role of a *jinju* (Shanxi drama) *laosheng*. In *Sha yi* (Murder at the Post), he wore a black gauze cap as did all the feudal officials. To show the restlessness of the character, Yan Fengchun displayed his consummate skill of stirring the two wings on his black gauze cap in various directions, sometimes mildly and sometimes violently.

Wusheng (male warrior) possesses great acrobatic skills as he is most often engaged in combat on the stage. This is also the case with *jing* (painted face). The *jing* actor is able to blow fire from his mouth while taking the role of Zhong Kui in *Jiamei* (Marrying off His Sister).

Like acrobatics, facial painting is characteristic of these time-honored styles of traditional drama. Many new styles of regional drama, however, like Shanghai drama, Shaoxing drama, and Huangmei drama have never used facial painting.

In these old styles, like *kunju*, Beijing drama, *qinqiang*, Sichuan drama, and Henan drama, only the roles of *jing* and *chou* paint their faces. As *jing* has his whole face painted, he is also called *dahualian,* ''fully painted face.'' And *chou* has only a part of his face painted (around his nose), so he is also called *xiao-hualian,* ''slightly painted face.''

Jing is usually a bold and forthright character or a rash and ridiculous one. For instance, Liu Bei, Guan Yu, and Zhang Fei are three sworn brothers in the period of the Three Kingdoms (220–65 B.C.E.). The role of Liu Bei is usually performed by a *laosheng* without facial painting. Zhang Fei's facial painting usually takes the butterfly pattern which matches the straw hat he wears. The role of Guan Yu is also performed by a *laosheng*. Because his face is painted all red basically without any design, he is also called a red *jing* or red *sheng*.

The facial painting of *jing* character has various functions. Some indicate unique temperaments, and some indicate unusual capacities. Furthermore, each style of traditional drama has its own conventions in facial painting. More complicated is the fact that the same role played by different actors might have different designs of facial painting. For instance, the famous *jing* actors Jin Shaoshan, Hao Shoucheng, and Yuan Shihai all played the part of Cao Cao of the Three Kingdoms, but they all used different designs of facial painting for this very same character.

Although each style of traditional drama has its own conventions in facial painting, the differences are not very striking. For instance, Bao Zheng, an upright official of the Song Dynasty, is called Bao Gong (Lord Bao) in all styles of traditional drama. He is deified to such an extent as to be able to handle cases at the Prefecture of Kaifeng in daytime and in nether regions at night. Even Yan Wang (King of Hell) is afraid of him. With such a capacity, Lord Bao's face is painted all black with a crescent moon or *taiji* design on his forehead. Black indicates his impartiality and incorruptibility, and the crescent moon or *taiji* design indicates his ability to go to hell to redress mishandled cases and even to resurrect those who have been wrongly killed.

Facial painting is done by the actor himself in front of a mirror. No full-time assistant does the job for any actor. But an exception is made when acrobatics and facial painting are simultaneously required in the play to produce "face change." This is mostly seen in Sichuan drama. When an actor is to show the change a character undergoes or the different moods a character has, he needs to change facial paintings twice or more in a very short period. It is impossible to paint the face on the spot. Therefore, the actor prepares several facial paintings on paper or plastic film beforehand. While on the stage he skillfully tears off the old one and sticks on the new one.

EMPERORS AND KINGS, GENERALS AND MINISTERS, SCHOLARS AND BEAUTIFUL LADIES

The story aspect is of the first importance in traditional drama. Almost all plays tell complicated and intriguing stories about people. Therefore, the drama in the Ming Dynasty was termed *chuanqi* (romance), and these are very romantic, indeed.

The repertoire of traditional drama is mostly based on historical materials. *Weishui he* (The Weishui River) of Beijing drama deals with Jiang Shang who, not until the age of eighty, meets the Zhou Dynasty emperor Wen Wang and becomes his military counselor. This historical legend comes from 3,000 years ago.

The decline of the Zhou Dynasty ushered in the period of the Spring and Autumn and Warring States (770–221 B.C.E.). With armies of their own, dukes and princes were engaged in wars for several hundred years. In this historical period occurred many events that can move one to song and tears, and from it emerged many brave warriors, resourceful counselors, gallants, beautiful ladies, and loyal servants. They form a thematic reservoir for dramatic adaptation.

The variety play *Zhaoshi guer* (The Orphan of the Zhao Family), written by

Ji Junxiang of the Yuan Dynasty, is a great tragedy. It tells of Tu Anjia, wicked minister of the Jin Dynasty, who tries to exterminate Zhao Dun's entire family. Cheng Ying, one of Zhao's friends, saves Zhao's family name by substituting his own son for a child of the Zhao family. Cheng's son is murdered, and Cheng brings up Zhao's orphan as his own son. Later this young man takes revenge on the enemy of his family. This play was later adapted in the Ming Dynasty. *Kunju* often performs some highlights from the play. This play is also included in the repertoire of *qinqiang* and Beijing drama now, sometimes titled *Zhaoshi guer* and sometimes *Sougu jiugu* (Searching for the Orphan and Rescuing him).

There are many plays that deal with Wu Zixu, a native of the land of Chu. After his father was wrongly killed, he defected from the land of Chu to that of Wu. With his wisdom and talents, he helped the king of Wu to administer the state in perfect order. Hence the state of Wu became increasingly strong and prosperous. Then he commanded troops southward and conquered the state of Yue. Gou Jian, king of Yue, presented Xi Shi the Beauty to the king of Wu. The king of Wu indulged himself in sex and neglected administration. Wu Zixu tried to dissuade him from his indulgence but in vain. He died of worry and indignation. With deep remorse, Gou Jian of Yue cleared up the mess and was restored to power. He finally destroyed the state of Wu. The plays that depict these historical events include *Er Xu ji* (The Story of Shen Baoxu and Wu Zixu) of the Ming Dynasty drama, *Wen Zhaoguan* (The Pass of Zhaoguan in Peace), and *Wu Zhaoguan* (The Pass of Zhaoguan in Battle) of Beijing drama.

Around the 1950s, all styles of traditional drama staged the play *Jiangxiang he* (The Prime Minister Makes Peace with the General). Its theme is "unity is strength." The play tells about General Lian Po of the state of Zhao who claims credit for himself and is very arrogant toward Lin Xiangru, the prime minister. Lin, taking the interest of the state into account, endures humiliation from Lian Po. Having learned of the discord between Lin and Lian of the state of Zhao, the king of Qin is ready to invade the state of Zhao. But Lian Po is finally impressed by Lin's forbearance and feels ashamed of himself. He goes to Lin and apologizes to him for his arrogance. When the king of Qin learns of this, he dares not attack the state of Zhao. This story is based on a recorded historical fact in the period of the Warring States.

So far as the subject matter of traditional drama is concerned, the period of the Three Kingdoms is as important as the period of the Spring and Autumn and the Warring States. After the decline of the Southern Han Dynasty (25–220), Liu Bei of the state of Shu (221–263), Sun Quan of the state of Wu (222–280), and Cao Cao of the state of Wei (220–265) became the real rulers of their respective regions. Because their relations were subtle and complicated, many plays are based on the anecdotes about the three kingdoms: variety drama in the Yuan Dynasty; the romances in the Ming Dynasty; and Beijing drama, Sichuan drama, Anhui drama, and *kunju* in the present time.

All the plays based on the historical events of the three kingdoms share one distinct feature: The playwrights, with few exceptions, stand on the side of Liu

Bei and portray Cao Cao and Sun Quan as negative characters representing reactionary forces. The plays *Sanqing Zhuge Liang* (Paying Three Visits to Zhuge Liang), *Jie dongfeng* (Borrowing the East Wind), *Kongcheng ji* (The Ruse of the Empty City), and *Baidi cheng* (The City of Baidi) all show how Zhuge Liang is able to command with perfect ease and foretell with miraculous accuracy. At the same time, his opponents Zhou Yu and Sima Yi are both portrayed in a sense as rather foolish and narrow-minded. This creates some distance between the plays and the objective facts in history. The plays of *Gucheng hui* (Meeting in an Ancient City), *Huarong dao* (The Huarong Passage), *Dandao hui* (Meeting Lu Su Single-handedly), and *Shuiyan qijun* (Drowning Seven Troops) all praise Guan Yu for being invincible. The image of Guan Yu in these plays is much exaggerated and deified, although it is recorded in *Sangguo zhi: Guan Yu zhuan* (Annals of the Three Kingdoms: Biography of Guan Yu) that Guan Yu is "known far and wide in China for his military prowess." Likewise, as recorded in history, Cao Cao was not only an outstanding statesman and strategist but also achieved high literary attainments. But envy and suspicion are his fatal weaknesses. The plays of *Zhuofang Cao* (Capturing and Releasing Cao Cao), *Gefa daishou* (Cutting Hair as of Head), *Zhan Wancheng* (Attacking the City of Wancheng), and *Dagu ma Cao* (Beating the Drum While Cursing Cao Cao) are on the whole based on historical materials, though with a bit of exaggeration. *Cao Cao yu Yang Xiu* (Cao Cao and Yang Xiu), staged by the Shanghai Troupe of Beijing Drama during its visit to the Soviet Union in 1990, also stressed Cao Cao's envy and suspicion.

In addition, some historical events and historical figures of the Tang, Song, and Ming dynasties have been adapted into plays. The most handy examples are those eulogizing national heroes and upright officials, such as *Mu Guiying guashuai* (Mrs. Mu Guiying Takes Command) and *Shiwu guan* (Fifteen Strings of Cash).

The aforementioned plays all deal with emperors, kings, generals, and ministers. In proportion to them in the repertoire of traditional drama are those dealing with scholars and beautiful ladies. However, the plays about literary men and beautiful ladies are mostly not based on historical materials. There are a few exceptions, of course. For instance, the story about Sima Xiangru and Zhuo Wenjun really occurred in the Western Han Dynasty (206 B.C.E.–25 C.E.) In her bitter solitude, the widow Zhuo Wenjun met Sima Xiangru. She was daring enough to elope with him to Chengdu. Later, Zhuo opened a wineshop to make a living. There are many plays written about this story in the Yuan, Ming, and Qing dynasties, such as *Danglu yan* (Beauty Opens a Wineshop). The tragic love between the Southern Song poet Lu You and his cousin Tang Huixian has also drawn great interest from playwrights. *Chaitou feng* (The Phoenix Hairpins), staged by the Shanghai Troupe of *Kunju,* is one of the great influential works of this theme.

Without being engaged in social activities, women in ancient China had little contact with the outside world. Only the female entertainers of low social status cherished some deep friendship with literary men, and some such friendships even developed into marital union. However, due to feudal ethics or due to some abrupt changes in political situations, their love was seldom long lasting. Their relations often ended in separation in life or in parting at death. Themes arising from such a tragic ending offer many attractions to traditional drama. Tang Xianzhu (1550–1617) of the Ming Dynasty wrote *Zichai ji* (The Story of Purple Hairpins) about the love story between the Tang Dynasty poet Li He and Huo Xiaoyu. Kong Shangren (1648–1718), of the Qing Dynasty, wrote *Taohua shan* (The Peach Blossom Fan) about Li Xiangjun's love for the literary man Hou Fangyu of the Ming Dynasty.

Many plays about literary men and beautiful ladies, however, bear no specific reference to history. Most characters are invented. The following story line is typical. The literary man is from a poor family. He is long engaged to a girl from a rich family. The girl appreciates his talents, but her parents insist on her marrying another man. The girl refuses. With the help of her maid, the girl meets her lover and offers him financial support. When he finally wins the highest honors at the imperial examinations and becomes *zhuangyuan* (Number One Scholar), the girl's parents immediately change their minds and hold a wedding ceremony for the young lovers. *Zhenzhu ta* (The Pearl Pagoda) is a typical example of this theme. In traditional drama, making a literary man *zhuangyuan*, Number One Scholar, has been a stereotypic formula to solve all conflicts in the play. This stereotype, characteristic of traditional drama, is called "happy endings." People who favor this formula argue that this is what the audience expects whereas those who disfavor this formula argue that this goes counter to the reality of life.

All formulas of performance in traditional drama are extracted and refined from the realities of ancient life. That is why it is somewhat difficult for traditional drama to present modern themes. This is especially true with the time-honored styles of traditional drama, which have rather fixed conventions. They have more difficulties in presenting modern life on the stage than other styles of regional drama.

As a result of painstaking efforts in creation, revision, and polishing on the part of the theatrical workers, there are, of course, some successful plays which combine traditional forms with modern content. The following are a few examples: *Xianglin sao* (Xianglin's Wife), adapted from Lu Xun's short story "Zhufu" (New Year's Sacrifice) by Shaoxing drama; *Zhaoyang gou* (The Zhaoyang Village), about life in the countryside staged by Henan drama; *Hongdeng ji* (The Red Lantern), *Shajia bang* (The Shajia Creek), and *Zhiqu weihushan* (Taking Tiger Mountain by Strategy), presented by Beijing drama. They have all attained rather high artistic levels. During the Cultural Revolution, Jiang Qing and her clique claimed credit for all these achievements and called them "model revolutionary theatrical productions." After fifteen years, people can view these modern plays dispassionately now. The occasional presentations of these plays still win some audiences.

PERFORMANCE IS NOT IMITATION OF LIFE

Traditional Chinese drama reflects life, but its approaches are not as direct and straightforward as those of modern drama. Its final objective is not representation of the prototype of life. The life it reflects has been selected and refined according to definitive conventions. Besides, it reflects life in a much broader sense than modern drama does. As the plays are presented on a bare stage with minimum props, the actors must portray characters through stylized gestures and movements fit to the specific role categories of these characters. Moreover, the actors must make believe the time, space, and the nonexistent props on the bare stage with their body language, gleams of their eyes, and other artistic means. The actors of the Western-styled drama are not obliged to do this. But this is one of the important criteria to evaluate the artistic accomplishment of an actor in traditional Chinese drama.

When the curtain rises, the audience does not know whether the bare stage represents an imperial palace, the prime minister's mansion, a young lady's boudoir, a monk's temple, a mountain fastness of greenwood heroes, or a teahouse that welcomes customers from all corners of the land.

A torch, an oil lamp, or an electric lamp is used to light the stage. From the beginning to the end of any performance in traditional drama, the light never changes. Its brightness, angle, or color will not change in accordance with the development of the plot. *Sancha kou* (At the Crossroads) and *Wu Song dadian* (Wu Song Fights the Innkeeper) are both set in the night, but the stage is fully bright all the time. In *Wu Song Fights the Innkeeper,* shortly before the curtain falls, the innkeeper holds out a lit candle which indicates the time of the happenings. But the brightness on the stage never changes, with or without a candle.

Xu Ce paocheng (Xu Ce Runs across the Imperial City) is set in an imperial city. There are many movements of climbing steps up and down, right and left. The actor almost has no time to stop running. But on the stage there are no walls, no steps. The actor's singing and dancing make spectators feel as if they could see the wall of the imperial city on the stage. Such an effect demonstrates the artistic accomplishment on the part of the actor. In the play *Zhui Han Xin* (Chasing Han Xin), the character Xiao He takes a longer and harder journey. It is nothing but the actor's singing and changing footwork that indicate how the character is crossing deep waters and climbing high mountains. *Qiujiang* (The Autumn River) tells of Chen Miaochang, who takes an old boatman's boat in an attempt to catch up with her sweetheart Pan Bizheng. On the stage there is neither river nor boat, only the oar in the old man's hand. When the actor makes the pantomime of paddling or poling the boat, his body must shake and move synchronously. This is also true in representing some minute details in life. In *Shi yuzhuo* (Picking up a Jade Bracelet), Sun Yujiao sits at the door doing needlework, and she also feeds a handful of chickens and scatters them from time to time. When she makes the pantomime of feeding or scattering chickens, the audience seems to visualize that there were many biddable chickens on the stage.

The horse is an especially important animal in traditional Chinese drama, but it is a riding whip instead of a horse that indicates a horse on the stage. If a character holds a riding whip in his hand, that means he is on horseback. The way he waves his whip in dance shows whether the horse is tamed or not, is galloping, or is engaged in a battle.

Two plays merit special attention. *Tiao huache* (Overturning Chariots with a Spear) tells about Gao Chong of the Song Dynasty who fights the troops of the state of Jin. When he and his horse are strong and vigorous, he wins the battles continuously. Later he feels sorry for his spent horse, but he keeps on overturning chariots with his spear. However, more and more chariots rush toward him. He gets weary and is finally run down by them. He dies in the field of battle. It is rather difficult to show the development of the plot in performance. Only a vigorous performer can put on such an amazing show. *Zhaojun chusai* (Wang Zhaojun Goes Beyond the Frontier) deals with Wang Zhaojun who leaves on imperial orders for a barbarous state to be married to the king of Xiongnu, an ancient tribe in China. There are altogether three characters in the play: Wang Zhaojun, her bodyguard Wang Long, and her groom. From the beginning to the end, the groom continuously displays all kinds of acrobatic feats to show that the horse is getting more and more stubborn and out of control beyond the frontier.

Many styles of Chinese drama in the north can present *Wang Xiao ganjiao* (Wang Xiao Rides a Donkey), a short play about everyday life in the countryside. There is no donkey on the stage, but Wang Xiao's humorous words and acting create a make-believe donkey for the audience. Moreover, the audience can visualize in the mind's eye the donkey Wang Xiao rides: rather foxy and mischievous, though thin and small.

The conventions of singing and recitative can also manifest the fact that traditional Chinese drama does not imitate the realities of everyday life. In traditional drama, when a major character or even a minor one first appears on the stage, he or she must introduce himself or herself to the audience in a monologue because he or she is the only person on the stage. *Liyuanxi* (a classic style of Fujian drama) has *Chen San Wuniang* (Chen San and His Sister-in-Law Wuniang) in its repertoire. As soon as Chen appears on the stage, he speaks to himself: "I am called Chen Boqing. Having been coming along with my elder brother who is to take his office in the southern Guangdong, I arrive here in Caozhou." At that time Wuniang has not yet appeared on the stage, so Chen San introduces himself directly to the audience. In *Shuang tuimo* (The Lovers Turn the Mill Together) of Wuxi drama, Su Xiaoe comes onto the stage and sings: "After the night watchman beats the first watch on his drum, Su Xiaoe, that's me, comes out of the house. My husband died two years ago and I have lived alone for more than three years." At that time, He Yidu, her long-term hired hand, is not on the stage. Obviously, she introduces herself directly to the audience. This conventional technique is called *zibao jiameng* (self-introduction).

Conventionally, characters at their first appearances on the stage sing or recite two sentences or a poem to tell the audience about their mode or circumstances then and there. Generally speaking, an army general would recite these words: "Testing horses by a willow camp in Spring, discussing military maneuvers in a tiger tent at night." By saying so, the general not only introduces his own capacity but also plays up the atmosphere of military life. When a scout appears on the stage, he usually recites these words: "I have taken a thousand-li journey and my horse has passed ten thousand hills." This indicates either the elapsing of a long period of time or the trials of a long journey. According to the number of sentences or different content, these prologues are termed either *dingchangshi* (a scene-setting verse) or *yinzhi* (an introduction).

When the play is about to end, there is *xiachangshi* (a leaving-stage verse). Sometimes each of the characters recites one line to express his or her sad or happy emotion for his or her fate; sometimes just one person sings four or more lines to summarize the ethical values of the whole story, either admonishing people to be kindhearted, or cherish a deep love for prominent personages in the past. This formula is mostly replaced by an offstage chorus now.

In traditional drama, there are also some conventional patterns for common dialogues. For instance, when he reports some urgent matter to his master or general, a servant or scout always says, "A disaster is imminent." Then the master or general always asks, "What's up?" After hearing a complete report, the master or general always orders, "Go and see again." There are numerous examples to show such conventional patterns.

One of the criteria of evaluating and appreciating the artistic accomplishment of an actor is to see how proficient he is in practicing all kinds of theatrical conventions in speech and action and what artistic levels he has achieved. This has its own weakness because it leads an actor to follow convention for convention's sake. It is rather difficult to improve the stylized conventions, and it is even more difficult to create new formulas of speech and action in accordance with the realities of modern life and to be accepted by the audience.

MEN FOR FEMALE ROLES AND WOMEN FOR MALE ROLES

In the budding period of Chinese drama, men dominated the whole field. The recorded performances before the Song Dynasty were almost all done by men. In the last years of the Yuan Dynasty, Xia Tingzhi wrote *Qinglou ji* (Records of the Green Chamber, 1366) which is the first biographical work about actors and actresses of Chinese drama, mostly actresses. And it is the actresses who played almost all the leading roles. Famous as she was, Zhu Lianxiu kept close contacts with officials and literary men like Hu Zhiyu, Lu Zhi, and Guan Hanqing. She was a versatile actress who could play both male parts, such as the role of an emperor, and female parts like *huadan* (young woman). Obviously, hers was not the only case, at that time, of a performer to play both male and female roles.

Originally called Guo Fangqin, Shun Shixiu was another outstanding actress like Zhu Lianxiu. She was able to play both male and female parts. She also had a close association with such officials and literary men as Yu Ji and Wang Yuanding. When she was ill and wanted to eat horse intestines, Wang Yuanding killed his own steed and cooked its intestines for her. Later, this story became one of the key episodes in *Xiuru ji* (The Embroidered Jacket), a romance written in the Ming Dynasty, which deeply impressed the audience of the day.

In the Ming Dynasty, the plays shown in the imperial palaces were performed by eunuchs. Ah Chou and some other eunuchs are mentioned in the historical records for their performances. The practice of actors for male roles and actresses for female roles was still prevalent among the common folks. Ma Jin of Nanjing, an outstanding actor of the late Ming Dynasty, played the role of *jing*— a painted face. In order to observe the manners of a notoriously wicked official, he worked as a servant in the official's mansion for three years. As a result, he became a great success when he played the part of the wicked prime minister Yan Song in *Mingfeng ji* (The Story of Mingfeng). Ma Jin's experiences were on everyone's lips at that time. Another touching story is that of Shang Xiaoling, a famous actress in Hangzhou. When she played the part of Du Liniang in Tang Xianzhu's classic *The Peony Pavilion,* she identified herself with the character so much that she is said to have died of sorrow on the stage.

Wang Zijia of the Kangxi Reign (1662–1723) and Wei Changsheng (1744–1802) of the Qianlong Reign (1736–1795) were actors of high attainment. They were both good at acting the role of *huadan,* deep in romantic affairs. Later, they were both condemned for bawdiness by feudal officials who asserted that their performances would encourage sexual misdemeanors. Wang Zijia was executed by the magistrate in Suzhou. The representative plays in Wei Changsheng's repertoire are *Gunlou* (Rolling Downstairs) and *Beiwa rufu* (Carrying the Kid to the Mansion). His plays, however, were often banned, and he himself was often expelled from Beijing.

From the middle period of the Qing Dynasty to the revolution of 1911, traditional drama was the domain of male performers. It was especially true with *kunju* and Beijing drama, although there were actresses in the regional styles of drama in the small towns and the countryside who played the male as well as female roles.

In the 1920s and 1930s, under the influence of new ideas from the West, traditional drama as a genre of literature and art began to draw greater attention, and its artists began to enjoy higher social status. Some specialists and professors who studied Western literature and drama gradually engaged themselves in adapting, directing, and teaching traditional drama, thus adding new life to Chinese drama.

For nearly half a century, the representatives of the traditional drama circles have been the four *dan*s in Beijing drama: Mei Lanfang (1894–1961), Cheng Yanqiu (1904–1958), Xun Huisheng (1900–1968), and Shang Xiaoyun (1900–1976). These extremely skilled male actors specialized in playing female roles. Each had his unique styles of performance. Mei Lanfang is celebrated for his clear, resonant falsetto and elegant, poised stage image. His plays *The Conqueror Bids Farewell to Lady Yu* and *The Drunken Beauty* are both combinations of classical dances and songs, highly acclaimed at home and abroad. He was well received in his first performance in the United States in 1930, and the University of California awarded him an honorary doctorate. Mei paid several visits to other countries and exchanged views with many masters of art, such as Charles Chaplin, Konstantin Stanislavski, and Bertolt Brecht. Most performers in the role of *dan* in our time are his students or his students' students. Cheng Yanqiu was an expert in tragedy, for example, in *Huangshan lei* (The Bleak Mountain Tragedy) and *Yingtai kanghun* (Zhu Yingtai Defying an Arranged Marriage). These dramas convey thematic messages against unjust wars or parents' arranged marriages. In *kunju* Han Shichang and Zhang Chuanfang, who played female roles, were well-known actors representing the northern school and southern school, respectively. Mei Lanfang often took them along with him during his visits to other countries so that he could consult with them about artistic problems and take their views for reference.

In Sichuan drama, Zhou Mulian (1900–1961) and Yang Youhe (1913–1989) were extremely influential actors who played female roles. They were highly acclaimed for their roles as Jiao Guiying in *Qingtan* (Testing His Love) and the White Snake in *Baishe zhuan* (The Romance of the White Snake). Fu Quanxiang of Shaoxing drama and Liang Guyin of *kunju* are both actresses. While they were rehearsing *Testing His Love*, they found it difficult to comprehend the feminine emotion of Jiao Guiying, and they consulted with these two male performers of the female role.

Among the actresses of male roles, Meng Xiaodong was most outstanding. With intense contemplation, she mastered Yu Shuyan's style much better than any of the male performers.

Generally speaking, Shaoxing drama troupes are composed entirely of women. The only exception is the No. 3 Shanghai Shaoxing Troupe, which consists of both actors and actresses. Women play the male parts in all other troupes of Shaoxing drama in Shanghai, Zhejiang, Jiangsu, Fujian, and Anhui provinces. Yin Guifang, over seventy now, was once the head of the Fanghua Troupe of Shaoxing Drama. She is well known for her role of *xiaosheng* (young man), talented in letters, and unconventional in lifestyle. Most performers of Shaoxing drama today who play the role of *xiaosheng* belong to the Yin school called after her surname. Xu Yulan is another influential actress who also plays the role of *xiaosheng* in Shaoxing drama. Xu has formed her own school with her peculiar style in singing and acting, but a bit later than Yin Guifang. *Shamo wangzi* (The Prince of the Desert) and *Honglou meng* (A Dream of the Red Mansions) are their representative productions.

Pei Yanling is an outstanding actress who plays such male roles as the ghostbuster Zhong Kui in the *Zhong Kui* in the Bangzi drama of Hebei. Having studied diligently and practiced hard for years, she is capable of many highly difficult acrobatic skills with amazingly agile movements of her back and legs.

In the past fifty years or so, Yu Zhenfei, who played the role of *xiaosheng* in *kunju*, is most accomplished among the actors who play male roles. With his high literary attainments, he played the part of bookish and naive scholars without conforming to conventional patterns. Hou Yongkui, who played the part of red *jing* (painted face) in *kunju*, successfully created the image of an ancient hero in his unique portrayal of the bold and unrestrained general Guan Yu. Hua Chuanhao, who played the part of *chou* (clown) in *kunju*, was good at all kinds of humorous body movements. Ma Shizeng, who played the part of *laosheng* (old man) in Guangdong drama, acted many kinds of old men in the plays. He was especially successful in the role of Guan Hanqing in the play *Guan Hanqing*.

Zhao Yanxia, a famous actress of Beijing drama, plays female roles. She adopts an unconventional style of singing to enunciate each word distinctly, and hence she wins a large audience. Du Jinfang, Yan Huizhu, and Shen Xiaomei are all talented actresses who have studied under Mei Lanfang. Yan Huizhu also played some parts in *kunju* and in motion pictures. She committed suicide during the Cultural Revolution. Hong Xiannu of Guangdong drama and Yao Xuanqiu of Chaoju drama are actresses who play the role of *huadan*. Both of them enjoy a large audience in Hong Kong, Taiwan, and Southeastern Asian countries.

Yan Fengyin of Huangmei drama is worth special comment. Among the many actresses of traditional drama, she had the greatest artistic charm. Huangmei drama was originally a local style of drama in Anqing county, Anhui province. It had never put on any shows in big cities like Shanghai or Beijing. Yan Fengyin flexibly and ingeniously applied her past acting experiences as an actress in Beijing drama and Wuxi drama after she became an actress in Huangmei drama. With her sweet voice and charming appearance in costume and makeup, she instantly appealed to the audiences. Her productions of *Da zhucao* (Gathering Greenfeed for Pigs) and *Tianxian pei* (Marrying an Angel) once enjoyed such popularity in the theater that they became models for emulation even in the dance circles and music circles. Huangmei drama was soon shown in other countries. Now it exerts as much influence abroad as Shaoxing drama and Henan drama.

Whether men play male parts and women play female parts or men play female parts and women play male parts, traditional Chinese drama, due to its unique conventions, has no unyielding restriction on the sex and age of its performers.

SINGING AND RECITATIVE

Singing is one of the major elements in traditional Chinese drama, even though some plays have no aria or only a few arias from the beginning to the end.

It might seem incredible to Western audiences that singing in traditional Chinese drama has strict regulations in regard to its rhythms, melodies, and volumes. As a performer is required to follow all these phonetic rules for singing and recitative, he or she can make few innovations. There are even more restrictions on writing music. The composer is usually obliged to make certain alterations of the original basic melodies according to the singing conditions of a performer. The composer sometimes has to put down the score after hearing the performer's rehearsal and then collate and polish it afterward.

According to different styles of traditional drama, the music for voices can be divided into three groups. The classic styles of traditional drama such as *kunju* and *liyuanxi* use *qupai*, the system of the tunes to which verses for singing are composed. For instance, in the act of "A Startling Dream" in Tang Xianzhu's *The Peony Pavilion*, all the verses are set to twelve tunes, namely, *raochiyou*, *bubujiao*, *zhuifugui zaoluopao*, *haojiejie*, *gewei*, *shanpoyang*, *shantaohong*, *baolaocui*, *shantaohong*, *miandaxu*, and *weisheng*. The sequence of these tunes is set as illustrated above. There are very strict regulations about how to repeat the same tune in a play and under what conditions.

If the original tunes might not be fit for certain scenes of a new plot, it is a common practice to put together the first half of one old tune and the second half of another to form a new tune. For instance, the tune "Huamei shang haitang" is made up with the tune "Huameixu" and the last three lines of the tune "Yueshanghaitang." Some tunes allow the addition of words, even one or two lines. Some old tunes allow simplification. The tunes resulting from addition or simplification might sound like new tunes, indeed.

The sequence of the tunes in traditional drama generally starts with a prologue and ends with an epilogue. Although the tunes of traditional drama are different from the movements of the symphony, and the former are not so well-organized as the latter, they share similar musical theories governing the alternation of high or low, rising or falling, strong or weak tones.

Regulations also govern the number of words in a verse set to a tune. The additional words in a regular verse are called *chenzi*. The music scores of the Ming Dynasty, such as *Taihe zhengyin pu* (Taihe Northern Drama Music) and *Jiugong zhengshi* (Jiugong Southern Drama Music), pointed out the tonal patterns and rhyme systems. During the Qianlong Reign of the Qing Dynasty, Ye Tang of Suzhou produced *Nashu yingqu pu* (A Collection of Drama Music). His musical notation is called *gongche*, a traditional Chinese musical scale system. The Shanghai Literature and Art Press recently published *Zhengfei qupu* (Yu Zhengfei Drama Music), a comprehensive collection of *kunju* music based on the tunes Yu Zhengfei sang or heard. This book has numbered musical notation.

Beijing drama, *qinqiang*, Hunan drama, and some other styles of traditional drama use *bangqiang*. According to this system, one type of music can be divided into tunes of various measures. For instance, Beijing drama mainly uses two types of music: *xipi* and *erhuang*. The music of *xipi* is fit for conveying the impassioned, lively, happy, unrestrained, and elegant moods. It can be divided into tunes of leading measure, slow measure, original measure, fast measure, and loose measure. The music of *erhuang* is fit for deep, bleak, sad, and sentimental moods. It can also be divided into tunes of leading measure, slow measure, original measure, fast measure, and loose measure.

There is no rigid rule governing the choice and sequence of the tunes in one play. Arias may not be all set to *erhuang* or *xipi,* and the tunes of original measure may not be preceded by that of slow measure and followed by that of fast measure. Necessity determines choice. For instance, when Mei Lanfang played the role of the courtesan Su San in *Qijia* (Transferring Su San under Escort), he first sang to the tune of the loose measure of *erhuang,* next to the tune of the slow measure of *erhuang,* and then to the tune of *xipiliushui.*

Popular ballads and ditties are adopted without restrictions by these styles of traditional drama developed from the popular folk entertainment consisting of flower-drum, flower-lantern, picking-tea song and dance, and other artistic forms of singing and recitative. Popular ballads and ditties are more flexible than *bangqiang.* They leave more room for performers to give free rein to their artistic pursuit and make theatrical innovations. The audience is ready to accept the occasional use of new melodies if they coordinate well with other melodies.

There are only a few musicians in the orchestra of traditional drama; hence, the drum serves as a baton. On the whole, the instruments include *huqin* (a two-stringed fiddle), *pipa* (a lute), *sanxian* (a three-stringed banjo with a round soundbox), *yueqin* (a four-stringed banjo with a round soundbox), *xiaoluo* (a small gong), *jiuyinluo* (a nine-tone gong), and others. *Kunju* stresses the use of *dizi* (a flute). There is a tendency for using a bigger orchestra with foreign musical instruments in the traditional drama. Many Western musical instruments have been used in performances, such as the violin, viola, electric piano, and others. Take Beijing drama for instance. In the play *Zhiqu Weihushan* (Taking Tiger Mountain by Strategy), when Yang Ziyong climbs up the mountain and fights a tiger on his way, the French horn is used to accompany his action.

Speech in traditional drama is called *bai.* The performer is required to enunciate each word correctly, distinctly, and loudly enough to reach all corners of the theater. There was a saying popular in the drama troupes in the past: ''Thousand *jin* of speech but four *liang* of singing'' (one *jin* = 16 *liang* = 0.5 kg). This saying greatly emphasizes the importance and difficulty of speech in performance.

The speech requirements vary in accordance with the content of a play. Some plays demand modulation in tones and some demand eloquence in argument. For instance, in *The Four Successful Candidates,* Song Shiji argues at the tribunal. No other actor can play the part so eloquently as Zhou Xinfang did in accordance with the plot as well as with the capacity and temperament of the character Song Shiji. Their voices all sound rather weak in comparison. If Song Shiji should fail to overwhelm his opponent in argument, the later development of the story would be logically unconvincing. Similar to the term of *bai* is *nian,* which means recitation in our modern sense. When he was in Zhongqing during the anti-Japanese war, Hong Shen (1894–1955), professor and dramatist, wrote *Xi de nianci yu shi de langsong* (Recitations of Drama and Poetry). This is the only academic work dealing with this subject.

The Chinese language is extremely complicated. What kind of language should be used for arias and speech in traditional drama? Whether staged in Xanadu (Beijing) in the north or in Hangzhou in the south, the variety plays of the Yuan Dynasty used one common language. Zhou Deqing of the Yuan Dynasty produced *Zhongyuan yinyun* (Phonology of the Central Plains), which classified the pronunciation of the Chinese words into nineteen groups based on everyday usage of the words in the north. This set the rule for the pronunciation of the Yuan Dynasty variety drama.

The styles of traditional drama, such as *kunju*, which sing to the southern tunes cannot apply Zhou Deqing's *Phonology of the Central Plains.* They follow the rule set in the books on phonology by Jiang Xiao, Shen Jing, and others.

Different from the Yuan Dynasty variety drama or *kunju*, Beijing drama applies another phonology called "Shisan zhe" (thirteen rhymes). The language Beijing drama uses is, on the whole, Beijing dialect or *putonghua* (common speech) based on the popular pronunciation in the north.

Flower-drum, flower-lantern, picking-tea song and dance, and other regional styles of drama all use their respective regional dialects. As a result of having been performed in big cities for a long time, however, they have been transformed unconsciously, and their local accents are gradually getting weaker and weaker.

Traditional drama is faced with a rather grim crisis at present. The decade of the 1950s was a booming period, but it is gone forever. The present situation is so bleak that it cannot even be compared with the flourishing theatrical activities after the Cultural Revolution and before 1980. The major issue is the loss of the audience in great numbers. Old and young people have changed their aesthetic standards along with the radical changes of the times. There are no regular performances of traditional drama even in many big cities. People in the theatrical circles sometimes attribute the decrease of the audience to the rapid development of movie, television, and radio broadcasting services. There is some sense in their argument. Nowadays people are all very busy and have little free time. Listening to the radio or watching a movie or a show on television does not require them to go to the theater. There is, however, another aspect worth noticing. Movies, television shows, and radio broadcasting have, in fact, won and trained a great number of audiences for traditional drama. For instance, Huangmei drama was, at first, popular only in some regions of Anhui province, and later it toured in Shanghai and Beijing. Only when the play *Tianxian pei* (Marrying an Angel) was adapted for the screen and released nationwide did people all over the country become familiar with this style of drama. Some of the audiences even became its fans. People in other countries also came to know Huangmei drama through this medium. So far as financial benefits are concerned, the production of a movie or television show gains much more profit than theatrical performances. Therefore, screen adaptation is beneficial to both drama troupes and their members because they can earn extra money.

The production of traditional drama in movie, television, and radio broadcasting, however, cannot be realized without the stage performance that is still its lifeblood. If there had been no audience for the stage performance of Beijing drama or Shaoxing drama, no one would have adapted their repertoire or music.

What of its future? No one can tell exactly. But as a unique part of the nation's cultural heritage, traditional drama will never disappear. By keeping with the changing mood of the times, following new aesthetic interests on the part of audiences, and absorbing nourishment through cultural exchange with all countries at all times, traditional drama will present its new image on the stage.

REFERENCE WORKS

About thirty academic works on traditional Chinese drama were produced annually from 1979 to 1989. Most of them were published officially, but their quality varies. In the fifty years from the publication of Wang Guowei's *A History of Traditional Drama under the Song and Yuan Dynasties* (1915) to 1966, no more than 200 academic works on traditional drama reached the reading public, yet they are of higher quality than the works produced in the recent decade.

Wang Guowei's book was published in 1915, and has been reprinted again and again. This book lays the foundation for the studies of the history of traditional Chinese drama. Wang believed that traditional drama did not become mature until the Song Dynasty. His is a sound argument which can stand close scrutiny. Due to lack of reference materials, his book makes very simple statements about the performing art. Therefore, it is at its best a literary history of traditional drama. This work was included in the 1957 edition of *Wang Guowei xiqu lunwen ji* (Wang Guowei's Treatises on Traditional Drama) published by China Drama Press. The Writers Press turned out Ren Erbei's *Tang xi rong* (Drama under the Tang Dynasty) in 1958. It was supplemented and republished by the Shanghai Ancient Books Press later. With painstaking efforts, the author not only presents a wealth of data but also makes an extensive exploration and textual research of the budding styles of drama before the Song Dynasty. The author is a bit subjective when he states that the entertainment of song and dance with little plot, such as *Tayaoniang,* can be classified as traditional drama. He also argues without sufficient grounds that traditional drama formed and developed without the influence of exotic cultures.

Mei Lanfang's *Wutai shenghuo sishi nian* (My Forty Years of Stage Life) is based on Mei Lanfang's reminiscences of his forty years' engagement in the performance of Beijing drama. He recounted his life orally and Xu Jichuan put it down in writing. The Shanghai Pingming Press published the first volume in 1952 and the second volume in 1954. The People's Literature Press reprinted the two in 1957. Later China Drama Press reprinted it again. The first volume not only reveals the ins and the outs of the Fu Liancheng Drama School, which is most influential in the development of Beijing drama, but also records in great detail the productions of *Yu Tangchun, Jinshan si* (The Jinshan Temple), *Duanqiao* (At the Broken Bridge), *Hongni guan* (At the Pass of Hongni), *Fanjiang guan* (At the Pass of Fanjiang), *Fenhe wan* (The Fenhe River Bend), *Muke zhai* (The Muke Mountain Redoubt), *Yuzhoufeng* (A Woman Feigning Madness), and *Youyuan jingmeng* (A Startling Dream of Wandering through the Garden). The second volume deals mainly with Mei Lanfang's theatrical experiences from 1913 to 1917, stressing Mei's creative efforts in reversing the tradition in the aspects of singing, acting, and recitation. This volume provides a great number of valuable photos. In *My Forty Years of Stage Life,* Mei Lanfang treated himself rather objectively without prettifying himself politically or artistically.

Before 1949, no outstanding artist of traditional drama received a high education. Without much education, most of them had some difficulty in creative writing. Since the publication of *My Forty Years of Stage Life,* many artists of traditional drama have been working with their collaborators to produce reminiscences of this kind. Few of their publications, however, can be compared with *My Forty Years of Stage Life* in quality.

Compiled by the joint efforts of the Beijing Art Research Institute and the Shanghai Art Research Institute, and published by China Drama Press in 1990, *Zhongguo jingju shi* (A History of China's Beijing Drama) is the first comprehensive history book of Beijing drama. It provides a detailed exposition of the gradual formation of this new style of drama through interaction with and assimilation of various styles of drama, such as Anhui drama, Hubei drama, and *qinqiang*. Divided into many chapters and sections, this book not only makes systematic analyses of the development of the art of Beijing drama in each period but also provides biographical notes of all outstanding actors and actresses. These two aspects complement each other in such a way as to avoid omissions of important points.

Jiang Xingyu's *Xixiang ji kaozheng* (Textual Studies on *The West Chamber*) was published by Shanghai Ancient Book Press in 1988. So far there have been about a dozen works on *The West Chamber,* but they are alike except for slight differences. They discuss in general the evolution from *Huizhen ji* (The Biography of Yingying) to *The West Chamber* and make general expositions on its theme and artistry. Jiang's book and his previous publication *Mingkanben Xixiang ji yanjiu* (On the Editions of *The West Chamber* in the Ming Dynasty, 1982) are twin scholarly works. The 1988 book explores the history of various versions of the *West Chamber* in the Ming and Qing dynasties and corrects some of the mistakes made by Wang Jisi and Dai Bufan. Before anyone else, Jiang makes the first exploration about the relations between the *West Chamber* and Chinese painting, calligraphy, and novels such as *Jinpinmei* (1610). He also illustrates several examples to show the influence of the *West Chamber* on Tang Xianzhu's four classic plays, known as *Linchuan simeng* (Four Romances from

Linchuan), in the aspects of phraseology and style. Another special feature of Jiang's work is its commentaries on the illustrators of the various versions of the *West Chamber,* such as Chou Shizhou, Tang Bohu, Qian Shubao, and others, including their artistic attainments, their unique styles, and the depth of their understanding of the play.

The 1987 International Symposium on Traditional Chinese drama, held in Beijing, was attended by more than 100 specialists and professors from China, the United States, Japan, Britain, France, the Soviet Union, Czechoslovakia, and other countries. The theses presented at the symposium were published under the title of *Zhongguo xiqu yishu guoji xueshu taolunhui wenji* (Papers from the 1987 International Symposium on Traditional Chinese Drama) by the Culture and Art Press in 1988. So far as the history of the traditional drama is concerned, the theses touch upon the Yuan Dynasty theaters which have been preserved now, the temple frescoes adapted from traditional drama, the role classification of ancient drama, and other subjects. "Traditional Chinese Music-Drama and China's Ruling classes (1736–1911)" by Collin Mackerras of Australia concerns the impact of China's ruling classes on the development of traditional Chinese drama. He argues that the ruling classes in feudal times made a positive contribution to the development of traditional Chinese drama. More papers in this collection deal with drama's literary aspects and performing artistry. Generally speaking, all the papers can be divided into four groups: (1) comparative studies of Chinese and foreign dramas in structure, acting, form, acrobatics, and other aspects; (2) reports about the ongoing major projects in China, such as the compilation of *A History of China's Beijing Drama* and *Xiqu zhi* (Records of Regional Drama) in some provinces and cities; (3) accounts about understanding and carrying out government policies concerning traditional drama; and (4) the current status of foreign academic interest in traditional Chinese drama in other countries, including research, translation, introduction, adaptation, performance, and so on. Although this collection makes great contributions to the exchange of information, it has not yet reached the broad reading public.

BIBLIOGRAPHY

Allen, B. S. *Chinese Theater Handbook.* Tianjin: Oriental Press, n.d.

Beijing Art Research Institute and Shanghai Art Research Institute, comp. *Zhongguo jingju shi* (A History of China's Beijing Drama). Beijing: China Drama Press, 1990.

Giles, Herbert A. *A History of Chinese Literature.* New York: D. Appleton and Company, 1915.

Hong Shen. *Xi de nianci yu shi de langsong* (Recitations of Drama and Poetry). Beijing: China Drama Press, 1962.

Jiang Xingyu. *Mingkanben Xixiang ji yanjiu* (On the Editions of *The West Chamber* in the Ming Dynasty). Beijing: China Drama Press, 1982.

———. *Xixiang ji kaozheng* (Textual Studies on *The West Chamber*). Shanghai: Ancient Books Press, 1988.

Johnston, R. F. *The Chinese Drama*. Hong Kong: Kelly and Walsh, 1921.

Mei Lanfang. *Wutai shenghuo sishi nian* (My Forty Years of Stage Life). 2 vols. Shanghai: Pingming Press, 1952 and 1954.

Ren Erbei. *Tang xi rong* (Drama under the Tang Dynasty). Beijing: Writers Press, 1958. Reprint. Shanghai: Shanghai Ancient Books Press, 1984.

Scott, A. C. *An Introduction to the Chinese Theatre*. New York: Theatre Arts Books, 1960.

Snow, Lois Wheeter. *China on Stage: An American Actress in the People's Republic*. New York: Random House, 1972.

Stanton, William. *The Chinese Drama*. Hong Kong: Kelly and Walsh, 1899.

Wang Guowei. *Song Yuan xiqu kao* (A History of Traditional Drama under the Song and Yuan Dynasties). Shanghai: Commercial Press, 1915.

———. *Wang Guowei xiqu lunwen ji* (Wang Guowei's Treatises on Traditional Drama). 1957. Reprint. Beijing: China Drama Press, 1986.

Yu Zengfei. *Zengfei qupu* (Yu Zengfei Drama Music). Shanghai: Shanghai Literature and Art Press, 1983.

Zhongguo xiqu yishu guoji xueshu taolunhui wenji (Papers from the 1987 International Symposium on Traditional Chinese Drama). Beijing: Culture and Art Press, 1988.

Zucker, A. E. *The Chinese Theater*. London: Jarrolds, 1925.

13

Chinese Gallant Fiction

CAO ZHENGWEN

Gallant culture is a unique and important part of traditional Chinese culture. And gallant fiction, which evolved from gallant culture, has a long history in China. It enjoys broader readership and exerts greater influence than any other literary genre in Chinese literature. In order to comprehend Chinese popular culture, it is imperative to acquaint oneself with Chinese gallant culture and fiction.

GALLANTS IN THE HISTORIC RECORDS OF THE QIN DYNASTY

Before gallant fiction came into being as a literary genre, there had been early images of gallants in Chinese history. As distinct personalities, they were active in classic literature in the Pre-Qin period, Western Han, and Eastern Han dynasties (before 221 B.C.E. to 220 C.E.). *Zuo zhuan* (Zuo's Commentaries on the Spring and Autumn Annals), *Zhanguo ce* (Strategies of the Warring States), *Shiji* (The Historical Records), and *Wuyue chunqiu* (Annals of the States of Wu and Yue) all carry anecdotes about the earliest Chinese gallants. Even classics like *Zhuangzi* (The Prose of Master Zhuang and His Disciples), *Liji* (The Records of Rites), *Hanfeizi* (The Prose of Master Han Fei), and *Mozi* (The Sayings of Master Mo) make different commentaries on the concept of gallantry and righteousness.

The word *xia* (gallant) first appeared in "Wang Du" from *The Prose of Master Han Fei*. Han Fei, a legalist in the last years of the Warring States (c. 280–233 B.C.E.), asserted that "Confucius confuses laws with literature while gallants violate prohibitions with martial arts" (Han, 670). He defined a gallant

This chapter was translated by Wu Dingbo.

as one who "carries a sword, gathers around him a group of disciples, sets up rules, and tries to be famous" (Han, 680). According to Han Fei, ancient gallants shared the following features: disregarding laws and discipline, gathering a mob of rascals, indulging in martial arts and fame, and specializing in assassination. The great historian Sima Qian (c.145 B.C.E–?) of the Western Han, however, held a different view. He stated, "Gallant-errants of the present time, though they do not always act for justice, are true in word and resolute in deed. They keep their promises and are willing to sacrifice themselves to save others" (Sima, 896). Sima Qian also pointed out other features of the gallants: robbing the rich to help the poor, finding it a pleasure to help others, keeping promises unswervingly, demanding no payment of gratitude, being duty bound to friends, cherishing their good reputation, being ready to lay down their lives for righteousness, and facing death unflinchingly. Sima Qian's *The Historical Records* is China's first great history book that portrays gallants and righteous heroes, such as Cao Mo, Zhuan Zhu, Yu Rang, Nie Zheng, Jing Ke, Tian Guang, Gao Jianli, Guo Hu, Zhu Jia, and others.

Ancient Chinese gallants can be divided into five groups: gallant errants, gallant assassins, gallant heroes, gallant outlaws, and gallant officials. Some were hangers-on of aristocrats like Jing Ke, some were hermits like Lu Zhonglian, some were common people like Guo Hu, some were artists and craftsmen like Gao Jianli, some were butchers like Zhu Hai, some were generals like Ji Bu, and some were aristocrats like the four princes of the Warring States: Tian Wen, Wei Wuji, Zhao Shen, and Huang Xi.

From the Pre-Qin period to the Eastern Han Dynasty, gallants had been continuously recorded in various historical documents, which could serve as a prelude to the emergence of gallant fiction because Chinese fiction appeared later than poetry and prose. Gallant culture, however, gradually moved from historical gallantry to literary gallantry with the appearance of the first Chinese gallant fiction at the end of the Eastern Han Dynasty.

FICTION IN HAN, WEI, AND SIX DYNASTIES: THE BUDDING PERIOD OF GALLANT FICTION

What is gallant fiction? It is a combination of martial arts, gallantry, and fiction. Each of the three is indispensable to gallant fiction. Ban Gu of the Eastern Han (25–220) was the first writer who began to pay attention to the genre of fiction. In *Hanshu—Yiwenzi* (The Han Dynasty History—Biographies of Artists and Writers), Ban Gu collected fifteen titles of fiction. At that time, fiction generally referred to *zashi* (miscellaneous writings); in other words, literary sketches. In the last years of the Eastern Han, an anonymous author wrote "Yandanzi" (Prince Dan of the State of Yan) based on historical facts. "Prince Dan of the State of Yan" can be regarded as the first gallant fiction in China.

This story tells of Prince Dan of the state of Yan in the period of the Warring States who sends Jing Ke as an assassin to kill the first emperor of the Qin

Dynasty. Jing Ke fails in his attempt, but he faces death unflinchingly and dies for righteousness. His high-spiritedness commands admiration. This story is thematically progressive as it exposes the ruthlessness of Chinese feudal rulers and condemns the injustice of big nations swallowing small nations. Artistically, there are twists and turns in the intriguing plot, careful depictions of setting, and subtle psychological descriptions that reveal the personalities of the characters.

After the appearance of "Prince Dan of the State of Yan," numerous titles emerged in the Jin, Wei, and Six Dynasties (220–589). *Sou shenji* (Records of Spirits) by Gan Bao of the Jin Dynasty exemplifies the development of gallant fiction in China. "Li Ji zhanshe" (Li Ji Kills the Snake) and "Sanwang mo" (The Tomb of Three Kings) are two stories from Gan Bao's collection. They are both gallant stories with a strong moral sense.

"Li Ji Kills the Snake" is set in the east region of Zhejiang province where a snake monster appears. The local people are so superstitious that they consecrate maidens to the snake to avoid disasters. Before long, nine girls have been swallowed up by the snake. Li Ji, a gallant girl, ventures into the snake's lair. With her courageousness and sharp-wittedness, she kills the snake. This beautiful and daring girl is the first female image of a gallant in Chinese history. "The Tomb of Three Kings" tells of the king of Chu who executes innocent Gan Jiang. Chibi, Gan Jiang's son, defies tyranny and makes up his mind to take revenge. With the help of mountain gallants, he finally avenges his father and has his wishes fulfilled. This story manifests the distinctive features of gallant fiction thematically and artistically. The gallant fiction in the Jin, Wei, and Six Dynasties also told stories about cutting huge snakes, killing flood dragons, and piercing fierce tigers. They reflected the spirit of gallantry through wondrous fantasy.

In its budding period, gallant fiction had already distinguished itself as a unique form of fiction. Its authors, however, had not yet entered into the conscious state of genre creation. As a result, they failed to display the strength of humanism and gallantry from multiple dimensions. It is the appearance of the Tang Dynasty romance that marks the gradual movement of Chinese gallantry toward maturity.

TANG DYNASTY ROMANCE: THE DEVELOPING PERIOD OF GALLANT FICTION

Chinese gallant fiction entered its developing period in the Tang Dynasty (618–907). The emergence of the Tang Dynasty prose romances provided a broad arena for Chinese fictitious gallants, and the unprecedented prosperity of the Tang Dynasty promoted the development of literature and art and ushered in the flourishing phase of gallant fiction.

The Tang Dynasty gallant fiction can be divided into four groups. The first group deals with gallants who dedicate themselves to helping the poor and the weak and are always ready to take up the cudgel for victims. Pei Xing's "Kun-lun nu" (The Slave Girl from Kunlun Mountain), Du Guangting's "Qiuranke zhuan" (The Man with the Curly Beard), and Bi Diao's "Wushang zhuan" (The Story of Wushang) are some examples in this group. The second group deals with gallants who are adept in mysterious swordsmanship and martial arts. Duan Chengshi's "Lanling laoren" (The Old Man of Lanling) and "Sengxia" (The Monk Gallant), Huangfu Mei's "Chezhong nuzi" (The Woman in Cariole) and "Jiaxing shengji" (Feats with a Whip in Jiaxing County) are good examples of the group. The third group portrays gallants with clear senses of gratitude and resentment who requite kindness and take revenge. Pei Xing's "Nie Yin-niang" and Yuan Jiao's "Hongxian" are good examples. The fourth group reveals social upheavals as in the stories "Mashizhong xiaonu" (Magistrate Ma's Young Slave), "Weimingdi" (The Emperor Mingdi of the State of Wei), and "Li Lang."

Before the Tang Dynasty, gallant fiction stressed only chivalry, but the Tang romances combined martial arts and gallantry closely. Amazing swordsmanship and thrilling martial arts lend more bold and unconstrained features to gallant fiction. Another breakthrough the Tang romances made is manifested in the depiction of chivalry by extolling love in gallant fiction, and the result is more meticulous and splendid narration. This plays an important role in the development of Chinese gallant fiction as it exerts great impact on gallant fiction in the Qing Dynasty and in the Republic, and even on the contemporary new-school gallant fiction. Nevertheless, the Tang romances are all short stories. This form is not adequate for gallant fiction as a unique literary genre to show great momentum. For all this, the Tang romance forms a connecting link between the preceding and the following productions of gallant fiction in history.

GALLANTS IN THE LATE QING DYNASTY: THE MATURING PERIOD OF GALLANT FICTION

The Song, Yuan, and Ming dynasties (960–1279, 1206–1368, and 1368–1644) were the transitional periods of Chinese gallant fiction. The short gallant stories written in classical Chinese in the Song Dynasty inherited the style of the Tang romance. *Taipin guangji* (Taipin Miscellany), compiled by Li Fang, Xu Xuan, and others, includes twenty-five titles about gallants. In the Song and Yuan dynasties, the historical romances in *huabeng* (the promptbooks for storytellers) touched upon gallants. Feng Menglong (1574–1645) of the Ming Dynasty produced *Jingshi tongyan* (Stories to Warn People), *Yushi mingyan* (Stories to Enlighten People), and *Xingshi hengyan* (Stories to Awaken People). Some stories in each of these three books are about gallants. Feng is the first author who wrote stories in the vernacular. Shi Naian's *Shuihu zhuan* (Outlaws of the Marsh, 1610), another magnum opus about gallants, helped lay the foundation for gallant fiction to reach its maturity.

From the last years of the Ming Dynasty to the late Qing Dynasty (1636–

1911), Chinese gallant fiction drew attention in the literary circles and developed into three schools: (1) gallant fiction about legal cases, such as *Sanxia wuyi* (Three Heroes and Five Gallants, 1879), *Shigong an* (The Cases of Lord Shi, 1903), and *Penggong an* (The Cases of Lord Peng, 1891); (2) gallant fiction about chivalry and romance, such as *Ernu yingxiong zhuan* (The Gallant Maid, 1878) and *Hongbi yuan* (The Romance between Gallants Lu and Hua, 1831); and (3) gallant fiction about skilled swordsmen, such as *Qijian shisanxia* (Seven Swordsmen and Thirteen Gallants, 1894).

The confluence of gallant fiction and case fiction actually indicated that righteous gallants and upright officials joined forces in feudal society. The authors of the stories of this kind held that both righteous gallants and upright officials embodied justice in feudal society. Their joining forces could defend the broad masses of the people, strike blows at corrupt officials, and reform society. Objectively, this reflected the wishes of the people at that time. *Three Heroes and Five Gallants* is one of the best among those works. This novel is based on the scripts of the promptbooks of the storytellers. Shi Yukun, a storyteller in Tianjin well known for his exquisite narration of gallant fiction, revised, polished, and finally turned these scripts into a novel. It became an immediate success after its publication in 1879.

Three Heroes and Five Gallants consists mainly of two parts. The first half deals with the southern hero Zhan Zhao who serves under the upright prefect Bao Zheng and fights against the wicked high official Pang Taishi. It also tells of five gallants who are impressed by Prefect Bao and accept posts under him. The second half of the novel deals with these five gallants who help another upright official, Yan Chasan, to wipe out Prince Xiangyang and his clique. The theme of the novel is praise of loyalty and condemnation of treachery, eulogizing righteousness and punishing the wicked. So far as the investigation of cases is concerned, this novel highlights Prefect Bao's sharp-sightedness in seeing through the real criminals and punishing them for benefit of the people. So far as the depiction of gallantry is concerned, the novel extols the chivalrous conduct of Zhan Zhao, Ouyang Chun, Bai Yutang, Lu Fang, Jiang Ping, Ai Hu, and some other heroes who rescue the victims and wipe out the wicked. The greatest achievement this novel makes is its consistent stress on the creation of character while unfolding the story. It portrays characters' distinct dispositions and inner worlds in a consummate style of classic Chinese fiction. For instance, Bai Yutang is a proud, adventurous, and ruthlessly radical gallant who indulges in self-admiration and craves success. The lifelike portrayal of this character indicates that the author is already good at handling the dual features of fictitious images. Other characters in this novel also show supplementary personality characteristics. Being a masterpiece of classic Chinese fiction, this novel is vivid in description, and clear and well-knit in organization. It has widespread clues and closely linked suspense episodes. There are sequels to *Three Heroes and Five Gallants,* such as *Xiaowuyi* (The Five Younger Gallants). These novels have greatly inspired the later development of gallant fiction. Strictly speaking, *Three*

Heroes and Five Gallants is the first actually complete and mature gallant novel in China.

The Gallant Maid by Wen Kang of the Qing Dynasty is a representative work of gallant fiction about chivalry and romance. This novel was produced in the Daoguang Reign (1821–1851). Wen Kang came from an aristocratic family and served as a local official for some time, but in his old age he lived alone with pen and ink for company and wrote this novel to amuse himself. *The Gallant Maid* tells of the upright official An Xuehai who is incriminated. His son An Ji goes to the trouble of traveling a long long distance in an attempt to rescue him. When he is in danger on his way, the gallant maid He Yufeng, who calls herself Thirteenth Sister, saves his life. She tries to be An Ji's matchmaker, too. Finally, An Xuehai is rescued, An Ji becomes a high official, and He Yufeng is married to him. This novel depicts chivalry and tenderness, and combines heroic bravery with romantic love. The development of the story is full of twists and turns. For instance, when Thirteenth Sister He Yufeng ventures to the temple to rescue the victim in the dark of night, she fights with fierce and tough monks. All this is described in mysterious and thrilling detail, successfully highlighting the courage and resourcefulness of the gallant maid. So far as language is concerned, the author writes in colloquial Beijing dialect with easy fluency and high liveliness. Besides, his diction is so exquisite and dialogue so dynamic that his novel is well worth its ranking among the best.

Seven Swordsmen and Thirteen Gallants by Tang Yunzhou of the Qing Dynasty consists of 180 chapters. It was published around 1894 in the Guangxu Reign (1875–1909). This story inherits and develops the wondrous swordsmanship of the Tang romance and merges heavenly and secular worlds into one. It tells of Xu Minggao, Yi Zhimei, and other gallants who kill tyrants for the people and suppress the strong to help the weak. Under the leadership of upright officials, they put down the rebellion headed by the prince of Ning. The gallants in this novel are able to summon wind and rain and spread beans to turn into soldiers, and thus they bring real-life martial arts to fairy land. This fantastic type of gallant fiction is unique in its style, though with many irrational aspects. It serves as a precursor for the swordsman fantasy that emerged in the period of the Republic (1912–1949). *Seven Swordsmen and Thirteen Gallants,* however, is not as well written as *Three Heroes and Five Gallants* or *The Gallant Maid.* Its narration is often interrupted by the author's commentaries, which ruin the structural compactness of the novel.

The production of gallant fiction in the Qing Dynasty indicated that Chinese gallant fiction had in fact become a literary genre. There were over fifty novels of various sorts with gallants as protagonists. These novels were good and bad intermingled. Generally speaking, however, they made three breakthroughs. First, they truly manifested the concept of gallant fiction, integrating martial arts, gallantry, and fiction into a unified whole. Second, they formed various schools and styles of gallant fiction. Third, this genre moved from short story to novel, from classic language to the vernacular. Obviously, the production of gallant fiction in the Qing Dynasty showed that gallant fiction had entered a new phase in the literary arena and had been accepted as a literary genre enjoying the greatest readership in China.

GALLANTS AMONG THE PEOPLE: THE SURGING PERIOD OF GALLANT FICTION

It is in the period of the Republic (1912–1949) that Chinese gallant fiction set off such a new upsurge in production that the genre became known to all, including women and children. From the early 1920s to the late 1940s, gallant fiction reached its unprecedentedly flourishing stage. According to the reminiscences of the newspaper editors at that time, six or seven out of every ten novels were gallant fiction. If one looks over the newspapers of the 1930s and 1940s, almost all of them carried columns for serialization of gallant fiction. When the renowned novelist Zhang Henshui (1895–1967) wrote *Tixiao yinyuan* (A Sad and Happy Marriage) in the 1930s, he catered to the reader's taste and created chivalrous gallants Guan Shoufeng and Guan Xiugu. In this way, he added gallantry to romance.

Evidently, the appearance of gallant fiction in great numbers in the period of the Republic was, on the one hand, related to the economic growth of the Republic and the rising interest in martial arts as a popular sport, and, on the other hand, related to novelists' awareness of the entertaining nature of fiction in the time of prosperity of commodity economy in China. Literary works that try to enjoy great popularity must give consideration to both the influence of traditional Chinese culture and the demand of townspeople's consciousness, and this was further evidenced by the expanding contingent of the writers of gallant fiction in the first half of this century.

The authors of gallant fiction in ancient China were mostly literary men in dire straits or artists among the common people. But in the period of the Republic those who were well known in the fields of newspapers and journals almost all had produced some gallant fiction. Among them were the famous translator Lin Qinnan; the outstanding editors Zhang Henshui, Fan Yanqiao, Zhen Yimei, and Yao Mingai; the masters of martial arts Jiang Xiahun and Zheng Zhengyin; and novelists Gu Mingdao and Gong Baiyu. Those who became eminent in literary circles by writing gallant fiction were Pinjiangbuxiaosheng [Xiang Kairan], Huanzhulouzhu [Li Shouming], Zhu Zhengmu, Wang Dulu, and others. Through their concerted efforts, gallant fiction among the people formed various schools and different styles. By combining the old literature and art with the new, gallant fiction advanced to its mature stage in structure, language, and characterization.

So far as subject matter is concerned, gallant fiction among the people can be divided into three groups. The story of the first group is based on historical facts and tradition. The major characters in the story are real, but the author has made artistic elaboration by mixing facts with unofficial history and anecdotes.

Against the true historical background, all the protagonists are not identical with their historical counterparts in such works as Wen Gongzhi's *Bixue danxing daxia ji* (The Story of a Loyal Gallant Hero, 1930), and Pinjiangbuxiaosheng's *Jindai xiayi yingxiong zhuan* (The Stories of Modern Chivalrous Heroes, 1923–24).

The story of the second group deals with factional strife among the gallants. Characters and episodes are all fictitious, but the story is set in human society and the swordsmanship has nothing to do with supernatural powers. The author has followed such a realistic approach in writing that his story was believable. Gong Baiyu's *Shier jingqian biao* (The Twelve Goldcoin Darts, 1938–48), Zheng Zhengyin's *Yingzhuawang* (Eagle-Talon King, 1941), and Gu Mingdao's *Huangjiang nuxia* (The Gallant Maid of Desolate River, 1929) are examples of this group.

The third group tends to be fantastic. Its representative author is Huanzhulouzhu. In his *Shushan jianxia zhuan* (Swordsmen in Sichuan Mountains, 1923–32), characters are able to mount the clouds and ride the mist, to blow white light from their mouths, and strike their enemies from the other side of a hill. Their swords can fly by themselves to kill their enemies. In this way, the author has combined God-demon fiction with gallant fiction. Because the author had a rich imagination and wrote climax following climax, his fiction had a unique charm.

Gallant fiction produced in the period of the Republic can be divided into two schools: the southern school and the northern one. The former is represented by Pinjiangbuxiaosheng, Gu Mingdao, Yao Mingai, Zhao Tiaokuang, Wen Gongzhi, Wang Jingxing, Jiang Dieru, He Yifeng, Lu Shier, and Zhang Genong; and the latter by Wang Dulu, Gong Baiyu, Zhu Zhengmu, Zhao Huanting, Zheng Zhengyin, and Huanzhulouzhu. Although the northern school could not compete with the southern school in the number of the writers and in the quantity of production, it on the whole created novels of higher quality than the southern school. The author who produced more titles of gallant fiction than any other writer is Zheng Zhengyin with eighty-six novels to his name. The author who produced more words in gallant fiction than any other writer is Huanzhulouzhu with thirty-seven novels to his name; his *Swordsmen in Sichuan Mountains* alone consists of fifty-five volumes of 3.5 million words. Among those who produced over fifteen titles are Gong Baiyu, Lu Shier, He Yifeng, Gu Mingdao, Zhang Genong, Wang Dulu, and Wang Jingxing. Since gallant fiction stressed plot and organized episodes with suspense, it appealed to the reading public tremendously when it was serialized in newspapers. Therefore, many writers ventured into the field. When some tried to pass off the sham as the genuine, some cheap imitations appeared in the market.

In the period of the Republic there were over 100 authors of gallant fiction. Among them, only ten formed their own unique styles: Pinjiangbuxiaosheng, Zhao Huanting, Yao Mingai, Gu Mingdao, Wen Gongzhi, Wang Dulu, Zhu

Zhengmu, Zheng Zhengyin, Gong Baiyu, and Huanzhulouzhu. They were called the ten masters of the gallant fiction in the Republic.

Pinjiangbuxiaosheng (1890–1957, real name Xiang Kairan) was born in Pinjiang county, Hunan province; graduated from Chuyi Engineering college in Changsha; and studied both science and martial arts in Japan. After his return from Japan, he set up the Hunan Chinese Martial Arts Club and sponsored a national competition of martial arts in Changsha. His first publication was *Quanjing jiangyi* (The Manual of Pugilism, 1930). Afterward he used Pinjiangbuxiaosheng as a pseudonym to publish gallant fiction, and he became famous in the field. *Jianghu qixia zhuan* (The Story of an Extraordinary Gallant Errant, 1923) and *The Stories of Modern Chivalrous Heroes* (1923–24) are his representative works. His fiction appeals very much to the reader for its terse language, ingenious structure, and lively narration.

Zhao Huanting (1877–1951) shared the same popularity with Pinjiangbuxiaosheng; people used to say "Xiang in the South and Zhao in the North." There is little biographical information about him. It seems that he had a good command of classic literature and knew many historical anecdotes. He wrote both classical and vernacular Chinese excellently. The novel that made him famous is *Qixia jingzhong zhuan* (Loyalty of an Extraordinary Gallant, 1923–27). In literary creation, he was especially careful about conception, and his depiction of local customs was exquisite.

Yao Mingai (1894–1938) was an eminent newspaper editor. Born in Changshu, Jiangsu province, he was a dwarf with a facile imagination. He once joined the Southern Society, a progressive literary organization founded in 1909 in Suzhou. He became well known after publishing gallant fiction about secret societies and underground gangs. In *Jianghu haoxia zhuan* (The Story of a Gallant Errant, 1930) and *Sihai Qunlong ji* (Heroes of the Four Seas, 1929), he revealed the inside story of secret societies in humorous language with well-knit plots. Although his stories propagandize patriotism, they lack thrilling combat scenes.

Gu Mingdao (1897–1944), born in Suzhou, Jiangsu province, was a novelist of manners in the early years of the Republic. His popularity can be compared favorably with Zhang Henshui and Zhou Shoujuan (1897–1968). Even his gallant fiction is very sentimental as represented by *The Gallant Maid of Deserted River*. This novel, which runs six volumes of 1.2 million words, was quite a hit at that time. It gets rid of the storytelling approach of folk literature. Instead, it applies new literary and artistic devices in the portrayal of characters and the narration of events. Its weakness lies in excessive elaboration and a poor denouement.

Wen Gongzhi (1898–?) was once a member of Tongmenghui (China Alliance Society founded in 1905; antecedent of the Kuomintang), and he took part in the struggle against Yuan Shikai and for a constitution. He was chief editor of the newspaper *Pacific Afternooner* for some time. The trilogy *Bixue danxing daxia zhuan* (The Story of a Loyal Gallant Hero, 1930–33) is his representative work. Influenced by *Shuihu zhuan* (Outlaws of the Marsh, 1610), Wen Gongzhi maintained close links between fiction and history and unfolded his story with the confrontation of loyalty and treachery. His story, however, is not very complicated in plot, and his narration is rather straightforward.

Wang Dulu (1909–1977) was often called a "sentimental gallant" because he followed the plaintive and sentimental style of *The Gallant Maid*. His best known work is *He ti sanbuqu* (The Trilogy of Crane and Iron). *Hejing Kunlun* (The Crane Startles the Kunlun Mountain), *Baojian jingcha* (The Sword and the Hairpins), *Jianqi zhuguang* (The Sword and the Pearl), *Wohu canglong* (The Sleeping Tiger and the Hidden Dragon), and *Tieqi yinping* (The Horseman and His Lover) are a series of novels connected with one another, yet each is also independent by itself. All were published in the 1940s. Wang Dulu was good at minute description of characters and events and at psychological studies of men and women in love. His novels are very realistic and readable.

Zhu Zhengmu was born in Shaoxing, Zhejiang province, but he made a living by writing stories in Beijing and Tianjin. He produced several gallant novels such as *Qisha bei* (The Seven-Kill Tombstone), *Ruojian furen* (Mrs. Ruojian), and *Longxiao huning* (The Roar of Tiger and Dragon). Splendid in style and crafty in conception, they depict numerous kinds of weapons and unfathomable martial arts. They also advocate feudal morals in regard to the relations between men and women.

When he was young, Zheng Zhengyin (1900–1960) learned martial arts and was good at the nine-ring broadsword. He was known as a gallant novelist of super pugilism. Full of tough masculine characters, his representative work *Eagle-Talon King* demonstrates his simple yet vigorous style of writing, but his narration is sluggish and his structure is loose.

Gong Baiyu (1898–1966, real name Gong Zhuxin) was born in Hebei province. He wrote about new-styled literature and art but became famous overnight with the publication of his gallant novel *Twelve Goldcoin Darts*. His production of gallant novels showed his talent in the field. He paid great attention to setting and characterization, and his diction and dialogue are also exquisite, but he did not display much imagination, and hence his plot was too simple.

Huanzhulouzhu (1902–1961, real name Li Shoumin) was born to an official family in Changshou county, Sichuan province. In his teens, he traveled north and south, three times over the Ermei Mountains and four times over the Qingcheng Mountains. Later, he used Sichuan mountains and rivers as the setting for his marvelous gallant novels, such as *Swordsmen in Sichuan Mountains* and *Qingcheng shijiu xia* (Nineteen Gallants on the Qingcheng Mountains, 1935–49). His fiction is characteristic of tremendous momentum, surprising twists, magnificent scenes, and graceful language. There is undulating development in his narration, but its structure, with many diversions and without an overall consideration, is not closely knit. For all this, his fiction appeals very much to the reader. He was the first author who tried to apply the philosophy of Confucianism, Buddhism, and Taoism to gallant fiction and thus paved the way for the emergence of new-school gallant fiction.

These ten masters of gallant fiction in the Republic made their respective achievements and played important roles in promoting the genre. Generally speaking, however, gallant fiction produced in the Republic had not yet gotten rid of the narrative method used in the promptbooks by storytellers. Hence its narration was often one-dimensional; its transitions used cliches, such as ''The flower blooms on the two branches and let's talk about them one by one''; and the depiction of character psychology was not penetrating in detail. Gallant fiction in the Republic played an important role in the transition from the Qing Dynasty gallant fiction to the new-school gallant fiction.

NEW-SCHOOL GALLANTS: THE CONSUMMATE PERIOD OF GALLANT FICTION

Chinese gallant fiction has experienced three climaxes. The first occurred during the late Qing Dynasty, the second happened during the Republic, and the third took place in Hong Kong and Taiwan in the 1950s–1970s. After the founding of the People's Republic of China, the guiding principles of literature and art on the mainland took a negative attitude toward some old forms of literature and art (including gallant fiction) and even banned them. It was not until the 1980s that the situation changed. In the early 1950s gallant fiction was also looked down upon in Hong Kong and Taiwan because the old-school gallant fiction was written and published excessively and in low quality, and readers were dissatisfied with it.

In Hong Kong, in 1954, Wu Gongyi, propagator of the Taiji School, and Cheng Kefu, propagator of the White Crane School, had a bitter wrangling over their different factional views on martial arts and agreed on a contest in fighting skills in Aomen (Macao). In order to win over a greater readership, Hong Kong's *Xin Wanbao* (New Evening Paper) took advantage of the event and began to serialize *Longhu dou jinghua* (Contesting of Dragons and Tigers in Capital) written by its own staff member Zheng Wentong under the pseudonym of Liang Yusheng, in 1954.

Once he ventured into this field of gallant fiction, there seemed no way for him to stop halfway. As a result, he has produced thirty-five gallant novels so far. He has been extremely popular among readers because he pours new wine into the old bottle by applying new writing techniques to describe setting, to portray character, and to play up scenic atmosphere. He is good at classic poetry, and his style is so elegant that even his narration of heated combat is rich in poetic flavor.

Then Jin Yong produced *Shujian enchou lu* (A Scholarly Gallant's Revenge) in 1955. Jin Yong's gallant fiction is wide in scope and penetrating in knowledge. Succinct language, ingenious conception, and lifelike characterization are his major achievements in writing. In a word, he has overcome the stereotype of the old-school gallant fiction.

The successes of Liang Yusheng and Jin Yong spurred a craze for gallant fiction in Hong Kong and Taiwan. Following in their steps were Wo Longsheng, Zhuge Qingyun, Shangguan Ding, Sima Ling, Liu Chanyang, Wulinjiaozi, Banxialouzhu, Dong Fangyu, Ni Kuang, Gu Long, Xiao Yi, Weng Reian, Yu Donglou, Ding Qing, and others. They formed an impressive contingent of gallant fiction writers. The gallant fiction authors came forth in vast numbers, but most prominent among them are Jin Yong and Gu Long, followed by Liang Yusheng, Xiao Yi, and Weng Reian.

Jin Yong (1924– , real name Zha Liangyong) born in Haining, Zhejiang province, studied international law and then entered the journalistic circles. In the early 1950s he worked as an editor for the Hong Kong newspaper *Dagong Bao* (Dagong Daily), as a movie reviewer. He became famous by writing gallant fiction, and later he became an outstanding journalist after running *Ming Bao* (Mingbao Daily) by himself.

Jin Yong has produced fourteen novels and the short story "Yuenu jian" (Yue Maiden's Sword). If Liang Yusheng can be regarded as the founder of the new-school gallant fiction, Jin Yong can be considered its leader. Jin Yong's gallant fiction is grotesque in plot, ingenious in conception, and proficient in language. His depiction of character psychology and temperament reaches unprecedentedly high artistic consummation. His representative works include *Ruding ji* (On Ruding Mountain, 1969), *Xiaoao jianghu* (The Peerless Gallant Errant, 1967), *Tianlong Babu* (Eight Books of the Heavenly Dragon, 1965), and *Yitian tulong ji* (The Sword and the Knife, 1964). The most impressive characters he has created are Ling Huchong, Qiao Feng, Yang Guo, Hu Fei, Zhang Chuishan, Wei Xiaobao, Huang Rong, and Ren Yingying.

Although his gallant fiction is "adult fairy tale," Jin Yong is so erudite that he enriches gallant fiction with the essence of Buddhism, Confucianism, and Taoism. Moreover, he applies the modern devices and techniques of Western literature to his depiction of characters and events. As a result, his novels not only appeal to many readers, who are unable to tear themselves away from them, but also leave a great deal for the readers to ponder. So, beginning with Jin Yong's creative efforts, Chinese gallant fiction has really reached high literary and artistic standards and has become a qualified literary genre most unique and most representative in the history of Chinese literature.

Gu Long (1936–1985, real name Xiong Yaohua) spent his childhood in Hong Kong and settled down with his parents in Taiwan at the age of thirteen. He once studied at Danjiang College, a famous school in Taiwan. He first tried poetry and prose and then ventured into gallant fiction. Of his seventy-one novels, *Lu Xiaofeng* (1972), *Xiadao Chu Liuxiang* (Gallant Outlaw Chu Liuxiang, 1970), *Duoqing jianke wuqing jian* (The Affectionate Gallant and the Affectionless Sword, 1969), and *Juedai shuangjiao* (Two Peerless Heroes, 1967) are most representative. The reading public is very familiar with the gallants he has portrayed, including Li Xunhuan, Chu Liuxiang, Lu Xiaofeng, and Jiang Yuer.

Gu Long's gallant fiction strives for something new, for change, and for artistic breakthroughs. Its structure is exquisite, grotesque, and compact, and its style is terse, trenchant, yet free and easy. The author changes his sentence structure frequently and demonstrates expertise in phrases with profound philosophical implications. He organizes thrilling stories of gallantry in his graceful style and combines gallant fiction with detective fiction. Drawn by one suspense after another throughout the story, the reader follows the flexible and incredible arrangement of events and probes the mysteries of the mazes of the plot.

Liang Yusheng (1926–) was born in Mengshan, Guangxi province, and graduated from Lingnan University, where he majored in economics. He loved classic literature and history and played the game of go in his spare time. He worked as an editor for the newspapers *Dagong Bao* and *Xin Wanbao,* one after another, where he was an expert in chess reviews and short essays about literature and history. Since the publication of *Contesting of Dragons and Tigers in Capital* in 1954, he has been writing gallant fiction for over thirty years and has produced five books. Among his representative works are *Pingzong xiaying* (Tracks of a Gallant, 1958), *Qijian xia Tianshan* (Seven Swordsmen to Tianshan Mountains, 1956), *Kuangxia tianjiao monu* (The Wild Gallant Maid, 1970), *Nudi qiying zhuan* (The Story of a Gallant Empress, 1961), *Yunhai yugong yuan* (The Jade Bow Romance, 1963), *Baifa monu zhuan* (The Story of the White-Haired Gallant Maid, 1958), *Huanjian qiqing lu* (The Return of a Sword, 1963). Liang Yusheng's gallant fiction has strong political color because it uses historical background and national conflict for its plot. His language inherits the national style of classic Chinese literature with poetry and songs interweaved in the plot. Sometimes the author describes geographical beauty in great detail, and sometimes he elaborates the romantic encounters of men and women. The characters under his pen are all dazzlingly brilliant, such as Zhang Danfeng, Yun Rei, Lu Siniang, Feng Ying, Feng Ling, Geng Zhao, and Meng Hua.

Xiao Yi (1936– , real name Xiao Jingren) was born in Hezhe, Shandong province. He went to Taiwan with his parents in the 1940s, and then moved to Los Angeles, California, in the 1970s. He has produced over fifty titles of gallant fiction. Of his representative works are *Gan shijiumei* (The Nineteenth Sister of the Gan Family, 1986), *Wuyou gongzhu* (The Carefree Princess, 1987), *Yinma Liuhuahe* (Watering a Horse at Liuhua River, 1988), and *Maming fengxiaoxiao* (Horse Neighing and Wind Soughing, 1989). Xiao Yi's gallant fiction as a whole stresses the depiction of chivalrous feats and tender feelings; even the description of heated combat is rich in poetic flavor. Xiao Yi pays much attention to the rhythms of his language. The beginning of his fiction is full of great momentum, but its denouement is comparatively weak. His novels appeal very much to overseas readers. Xiao Yi also writes film scripts and newspaper columns.

Weng Reian (1954–), who was born in Malaysia, belongs to the younger generation of the new-school gallant fiction. He was originally a Malaysian Chinese. In his teens he went to study in Taiwan. He began to write poetry in his early years, started the poetry magazine *Oasis* at the age of thirteen, and even founded the Sirius Poetry Society. Weng also writes prose and science fiction. He is acclaimed mainly, however, for his gallant fiction, and he may be the best author in the field since the death of Gu Long. Only thirty-nine years old, Weng has already produced 247 titles. His well-known gallant novels include *Sida minbu* (The Four Famous Detectives, 1988), *Baiyi Fang Zhenmei* (The Commoner Fang Zhenmei, 1983), *Daxia Xiao Qiushui* (The Great Hero Xiao Qiushui, 1980), and *Shenxiang Li Buyi* (The Fortune Teller Li Buyi, 1982). Weng's style is similar to that of Gu Long, good at short phrases and psychological depiction. He solves difficult cases by inference but beyond readers' expectations. His best story is "Shachu" (An Incredible Case, 1988), which is one of the four volumes in *The Four Famous Detectives*. Weng also writes book reviews about gallant fiction and represents the gallant fiction writers who are expert in practicing martial arts.

There are over 100 gallant fiction authors in Hongkong and Taiwan, but the good and the bad are intermingled. With Jin Yong, Gu Long, Liang Yusheng, Xiao Yi, and Weng Reian taking the lead, however, gallant fiction has experienced one upsurge after another. In the early 1980s, they also stimulated great mass fervor for the genre in mainland China. Jin Yong's *Shediao yingxiong zhuan* (The Hero with Two Falcons, 1958) alone has 800,000 copies in print. The major gallant fiction authors in Hong Kong and Taiwan are now all very popular in mainland China.

Liang Yusheng and Jin Yong have already stopped writing gallant fiction. Gu Long is dead. Xiao Yi and Weng Reian are turning out some good stories occasionally. But the new generation of gallant fiction authors is emerging. Gallant fiction as a popular literary genre will never be stagnant.

GALLANT FICTION IN MAINLAND CHINA

In the mid-1980s, more and more gallant novels from Hong Kong and Taiwan were being reprinted by publishing houses in mainland China. This drew the attention of mainland Chinese writers. In only five years, they have produced about 100 titles. Though their works have not reached the high standards of their counterparts in Hong Kong and Taiwan, the tremendous craze for gallant fiction has compelled the literary circles here to reconsider the genre.

The mainland authors of gallant fiction can be divided into two groups. The first group consists mainly of storytelling artists. Jin Shengbo's *Bai Yutang* is adapted from the story of *Three Heroes and Five Gallants,* but the author has made revisions and highlighted the heroic image of one gallant, Bai Yutang. With her unique skill of storytelling, Shan Tianfang has adapted *Baimei daxia* (The White-Eyebrowed Gallant), *Fengcheng zhixia* (The Gallant Errant), and *Daming fengliu pu* (Great Heroes of the Ming Dynasty). The second group is made up of the mainstream writers who have ventured into the popular genre of gallant fiction. The woman writer Liu Xi produced *Dadao Yanzi Li San chuanqi* (The Story of the Great Outlaw Yanzi Li San, 1984), Feng Yunan wrote *Jinmeng daxia Huo Yuanjia* (Huo Yuanjia the Hero of Tianjin, 1984) and

Zhongtong yu daxia (The President and the Gallant, 1988), Feng Jichai turned out *Shenbian* (The Extraordinary Whip, 1984), Cao Zhengwen published *Sanduo furongjian* (Three Attempts for the Lotus Sword, 1990) and *Longfeng shuangxia* (The Dragon-Phoenix Twin Swords, 1985), Li Rongde created *Bajian wu tianfeng* (Brandishing the Sword, 1990), Song Wugang wrote *Kunlun qianli xing* (A Thousand *li* Trip to Kunlun Mountain, 1988), and Cao Bula produced three gallant novels. Although these authors are all members of the Chinese Writers' Association, they do not look down upon popular literature. They have made new efforts to promote gallant fiction. In addition, some writers of popular literature, such as Nie Yunlan, Can Mo, and Ouyang Xuezhong, have turned out gallant fiction.

The recent upsurge of gallant fiction in mainland China not only evidences the writers' attention to readers' demands but also the thorough application of "Let a hundred flowers blossom"—the guiding principle for literature and art in the People's Republic of China. Gallant fiction has been accepted as one of the flowers in the garden of Chinese literature and art.

COMPARISON BETWEEN GALLANT FICTION AND KNIGHT FICTION

Gallant fiction is a unique genre in Chinese literature, but the spirit of gallantry is universal. The European knight literature of the Middle Ages is similar to the stories about Chinese gallants. Thematically, Western knights and Chinese gallants share some common features. They are all dedicated to the cause of justice, they rob the rich only to help the poor, and they are ready to help the weak and fight against the evil forces in a dark society. They have much in common spiritually; however, Western knights are also different from Chinese gallants. First, knights come from aristocratic families and believe in religion; Chinese gallants are mostly errant vagabonds and commoners of low social status. Chinese gallants in early literature do not believe in religion until the emergence of the new-school gallant fiction. Only then do they believe in Buddhism and Taoism. For all this, Chinese gallants generally act according to their personal judgment of right and wrong and strive for unique personalities. This feature, in addition to their low social status, deprives Chinese gallants of the exquisite manners of aristocracy.

The most striking difference between Western knights and Chinese gallants lies in their different attitudes toward love. In Western knight literature, knights and fair ladies are usually the protagonists. An ideal knight is also an ideal lover. He defies all dangers for love. Most gallants in Chinese gallant fiction, however, cherish little love with women but stress the vows of brotherhood and are loyal to their friends. This is especially true with the works of Gu Long, an author of the new-school gallant fiction. In his novels, the protagonists Chu Liuxiang, Li Xunhuan, and Lu Xiaofeng, although they do have some romantic attachments with women, are not lady-killers. On certain occasions, they also show the traditional concept that "friends are brothers whereas women are clothes." In *The Affectionate Gallant and the Affectionless Sword,* romantic errant Li Xunhuan gives up his wife-to-be for the sake of friendship; in *Wulin waishi* (The Story of the Capital, 1968), the protagonist Shen Lang is a man of honor in his encounter with women; in *Tiexue daqi* (The Iron Blood, 1969), the protagonist Tie Zhongtang shows more sympathy than affection for women. The most striking example is seen in *The Affectionate Gallant and the Affectionless Sword.* The first-class killer, A Fei, slips in his martial arts skill whenever he associates with women. As soon as he leaves women, he makes rapid progress in martial arts skill. This indicates the corrosive influence of women to the practice of martial arts. Obviously, this author's attitude toward women is influenced by traditional Chinese culture. Gu Long's novels not only exemplify the striking difference of Chinese gallant fiction from the Western knight literature, but also evidence the enormous impact of national psychology on literary creation.

Also, the depiction of combat skills in Western knight literature is extremely simple. In China, however, along with the development of gallant fiction, the depiction of combat scenes is such a dazzling display of martial arts that the eye cannot take it all in. To a certain extent, Chinese gallant fiction truly demonstrates the genre formula of "martial arts + gallantry + fiction." Being a literary genre with the most distinct features of Chinese literature, gallant fiction is an important research topic for foreign literary circles all over the world. It is also an important aspect of Chinese culture worth studying by foreign literary circles the world over.

REFERENCE WORKS

The earliest book review on gallant fiction appeared in the early years of the Republic. Before the upsurge of gallant fiction in the Republic, some fans had devoted themselves to the compilation of short stories about gallantry. Lu Shie compiled *Jingu yixia qiguan* (The Amazing Stories of Gallants Ancient and Modern); Xu Muxi, *Qingdai sanbainian qixia zhuan* (The Gallant Stories in the Qing Dynasty); Chen Langxian, *Lidai jianxia daguan* (A Collection of Swordsmen of the Past Dynasties); and Zhang Genong, *Xiandai wuxue daquan* (A Collection of Modern Martial Arts). Jiang Xiahun not only compiled *Nuzi wuxia daguan* (A Collection of Gallant Maids), *Feixian jianxia haiwen* (Astounding Anecdotes of Flying Swordsmen), and other books, but also published the first short theoretical comment on gallant fiction, "Du wuxia xiaoshuo zhi renshengguan" (The Outlook on Life in Reading Gallant Fiction).

Xu Guozhen made the first serious study of the genre, and his *Huanzhulouzhu lun* (On Huanzhulouzhu) is the first academic work in the field. In the mid-1960s, Chinese American James J. Liu published *The Chinese Knight-Errant* (1967), and in the 1970s there appeared several theoretical studies on gallant fiction in Hong Kong. Ni Kuang initiated the study of Jin Yong's fiction. He wrote *Wokan Jin Yong xiaoshuo* (My Reading of Jin Yong's Fiction, 1987),

Erkan Jin Yong xiaoshuo (My Second Reading of Jin Yong's Fiction, 1987), and *Sankan Jin Yong xiaoshuo* (My Third Reading of Jin Yong's Fiction, 1987). Later, the Yuanjin (Long-range) Press of Taiwan turned out a series of works on Jin Yong under the general title *Jinxue yanjiu congshu* (Books on Jin Yong's Fiction). Among its over twenty volumes is *Zhuzi baijia kan Jin Yong* (Hundred Schools' Views on Jin Yong, 1986), contributed to by San Mao and others. Luo Longzhi, Zeng Zhaoxu, Yang Xingan, Dong Qianli, Lin Yiliang, Lin Yanni, Shu Guozhi, Su Zhaoji, Chen Peiran, Liu Tianci, and Wu Aiyi have all written comments on Jin Yong's fiction. Among them, Ni Kuang and Wu Aiyi have the greatest appeal. Their academic works are good references for the study of Jin Yong's fiction.

During the mid-1980s, some newspapers and magazines in mainland China also began to pay attention to gallant fiction, and even some college journals carried articles on gallant fiction. Among these articles are Hou Jian's "Wuxia xiaoshuo lun" (On Gallant Fiction, 1978), Liu Yongqian's "Lun xiayi xiaoshuo" (On Gallant Fiction, 1985), He Xin's "Xia yu wuxia wenxue yuanpai yanjiu" (Studies on the Origin of Chivalry and Gallant Fiction, 1988), Feng Yunan's "Luelun jinnian wuxia xiaoshuo zhai Zhongguo zhi shengxing" (A Brief Comment on the Recent Popularity of Gallant Fiction, 1988), Luo Liqun's "Tanjian shuoxia" (About Swords and Gallants, 1988), and Cao Zhengwen's "Jin Yong Gu Long bijiao shuo" (Comparing Jin Yong with Gu Long, 1990). These articles not only deal with gallant fiction from the Tang to the Qing dynasties, but also touch upon the new-school gallant fiction. In the last years of the 1980s, magazines and newspapers like *Dushu* (Reading Books), *Wenshizhishi* (Knowledge of Literature and History), *Wenhui bao* (Wenhui Daily), and *Xinmin wanbao* (Xinmin Evening Paper) have carried introductions and commentaries on the new-school gallant fiction.

The publishers in mainland China produced academic works on gallant fiction in the late 1980s and early 1990s. Wang Hailin turned out *Zhongguo wuxia xiaoshuo shilue* (A Brief History of Chinese Gallant Fiction) in 1988, and Luo Liqun published *Zhongguo wuxia xiaoshuo shi* (A History of Chinese Gallant Fiction) in 1990. Both of these academic works systematically introduce and comment on the genre; Luo Liqun's book is especially comprehensive with substantial detail. Academic studies on individual authors also appeared in 1990; for example, Cao Zhengwen's *Wuxia shijie de guaicai—Gu Long xiaoshuo yishu tan* (A Rare Genius in the World of Gallant Fiction—Gu Long's Artistry) and Chen Mo's *Jin Yong xiaoshuo shangxi* (Appreciating Jin Yong's Fiction). Cao Zhengwen also wrote *Jin Yong bixia de yibailingba jiang* (One Hundred and Eight Heroes in Jin Yong's Novels) in 1991. These systematic studies of gallant fiction have stimulated the publication of related dictionaries, such as *Zhongguo wuxia xiaoshuo cidian* (A Dictionary of Chinese Gallant Fiction) edited by Hu Wenbin, Wang Hailin, and Luo Liqun, in 1992, and *Zhongguo xiandai wuxia xiaoshuo jianshang cidian* (A Dictionary of Modern Chinese Gallant Fiction Appreciation) edited by Hu Wenbin in 1992. The Lijiang Press of Guangxi province is going to publish *Wuxia wenhua cidian* (A Dictionary of Gallant Culture), and at least five presses in mainland China plan to turn out a series of academic studies on gallant fiction.

There is also a tremendous interest in the studies of gallant fiction in Taiwan. Ye Hongsheng, an outstanding specialist in gallant fiction, wrote prefaces to *The Swordsmen in Sichuan Mountains, The Gallant Maid of Desolate River,* and *Eagle-Talon King;* published a series of comments on Wang Dulu, Zhu Zhengmu, and Gong Baiyu; and is compiling *Jindai Zhongguo wuxia xiaoshuo mingzhu daxi* (The Collection of the Masterpieces of Modern Chinese Gallant Fiction) and *Zhongguo wuxia xiaoshuo fazhan shi* (A History of the Development of Chinese Gallant Fiction), which will be a brilliant survey of Chinese gallant fiction, especially of the new-school gallant fiction.

Beyond doubt, the theoretical studies of Chinese gallant culture and of the thematic and artistic values of gallant fiction not only have contributed to the development of Chinese gallant fiction but also have showed the reading public how to read and appreciate gallant fiction. The craze for gallant fiction and for the studies of the genre will certainly broaden the field of gallant fiction and will at the same time provide valuable academic reference for Western scholars to enable them to study traditional Chinese gallant fiction.

BIBLIOGRAPHY

Cao Zhengwen. *Jin Yong bixia de yibailingba jiang* (One Hundred and Eight Heroes in Jin Yong's Novels). Hangzhou: Zhejiang Literature and Art Press, 1991.
———. *Wuxia shijie de guaicai—Gu Long xiaoshuo tan* (A Rare Genius in the World of Gallant Fiction—Gu Long's Artistry). Shanghai: Xuelin Press, 1990.
———. *Zhongguo xia wenhua shi* (A History of Chinese Gallant Culture), Shanghai: Shanghai Literature and Art Press, 1993.
Chen Mo. *Jin Yong xiaoshuo shangxi* (Appreciating Jin Yong's Fiction). Nanchang: Baihuazhou Literature and Art Press, 1990.
Gu Long [Xiong Yaohua]. *Duoqing jianke wuqing jian* (The Affectionate Gallant and the Affectionless Sword). Taiwan: Wansheng Press, 1969.
———. *Juedai shuangjiao* (Two Peerless Heroes). Taiwan: Wansheng Press, 1967.
———. *Lu Xiaofeng.* Taiwan: Wansheng Press, 1972.
———. *Xiadao Chu Liuxiang* (Gallant Outlaw Chu Liuxiang). Taiwan: Wansheng Press, 1970.
Han Fei. *Hanfeizi* (The Prose of Master Han Fei, annotated). Nanjing: Jiangsu People's Press, 1982.
Hu Wenbin, ed. *Zhongguo xiandai wuxia xiaoshuo jianshang cidian* (A Dictionary of Modern Chinese Gallant Fiction Appreciation). Shijiazhuang: Huashan Literature and Art Press, 1992.
Hu Wenbin, Wang Hailin, and Luo Liqun, eds. *Zhongguo wuxia xiaoshuo cidian* (A Dictionary of Chinese Gallant Fiction). Shijiazhuang: Huashan Literature and Art Press, 1992.
Jin Yong [Zha Liangyong]. *Ruding ji* (On Ruding Mountain). Hong Kong: Minghe Press, 1969.

————. *Shujian enchou lu* (A Scholarly Gallant's Revenge). Hong Kong: Minghe Press, 1955.

————. *Tianlong Babu* (Eight Books of the Heavenly Dragon). Hong Kong: Minghe Press, 1965.

————. *Xiaoao jianghu* (The Peerless Gallant Errant). Hong Kong: Minghe Press, 1967.

————. *Yitian tulong ji* (The Sword and the Knife). Hong Kong: Minghe Press, 1964.

Liang Yusheng [Zheng Wentong]. *Longhu dou jinghua* (Contesting of Dragons and Tigers in Capital). Hong Kong: Tiandi Press, 1954.

Liu, James J. *The Chinese Knight-Errant.* Routledge and Kegan Paul, 1967.

Luo Liqun. *Zhongguo wuxia xiaoshuo shi* (A History of Chinese Gallant Fiction). Shenyang: Liaoning People's Press, 1990.

Ni Kuang. *Erkan Jin Yong xiaoshuo* (My Second Reading of Jin Yong's Fiction). Taiwan: Yuanliu Press, 1987.

————. *Sankan Jin Yong xiaoshuo* (My Third Reading of Jin Yong's Fiction). Taiwan: Yuanliu Press, 1987.

————. *Wokan Jin Yong xiaoshuo* (My Reading of Jin Yong's Fiction). Taiwan: Yuanliu Press, 1987.

Ning Zongyi and Lin Guohui, eds. *Zhongguo wuxia xiaoshuo jianshang cidian* (A Dictionary of Chinese Gallant Fiction Appreciation). Beijing: International Culture Press, 1992.

San Mao, et al. *Zhuzi baijia kan Jin Yong* (Hundred Schools' Views on Jin Yong). Taiwan: Yuanjin Press, 1988.

Sima Qian. *Shiji* (The Historical Records, annotated). Changsha: Yuelu Press, 1988.

Wang Hailin. *Zhongguo wuxia xiaoshuo shilue* (A Brief History of Chinese Gallant Fiction). Taiyuan: Beiyue Literature and Art Press, 1988.

Weng Reian. *Baiyi Fang Zhenmei* (The Commoner Fang Zhenmei). Hong Kong: Dunhuang Press, 1983.

————. *Daxia Xiao Qiushui* (The Great Hero Xiao Qiushui). Hong Kong: Dunhuang Press, 1980.

————. *Jianghu xianhua* (An Errant's Chitchat). Taiwan: Wansheng Press, 1988.

————. *Shenxiang Li Buyi* (The Fortune Teller Li Buyi). Hong Kong: Dunhuang Press, 1982.

————. *Sida minbu* (The Four Famous Detectives). 4 vols. Hong Kong: Dunhuang Press, 1988.

————. *Xi Xueshanfeihu yu Yuanyangdao* (*The Flying Fox in Snow Mountain* and *The Twin Swords*). Taiwan: Yuanjin Press, 1987.

14

Chinese Science Fiction

WU DINGBO

The era of science nurtures scientific literature and art which, in turn, reflect the era of science.[1] Science fiction as a modern genre that emerged after the industrial revolution has developed along with the development of science. With the impact of science felt by people everywhere all the time, rapid changes in all aspects of society stimulate people's interest in exploring the nature of such changes and in anticipating possible changes in the future. Such interest is undoubtedly universal. The best expression of such interest is found in the popular genre of science fiction, the literature of change. Therefore, science fiction is a universal language for all those who have interest in science and in the changes brought about by science.

Science fiction, however, is also a cultural phenomenon which has to develop in accordance with the specific conditions in a given nation. There is no universal path to follow in its national development. Moreover, the development of science fiction in a given nation is unavoidably restricted by its unique characteristics of race, social history, and cultural conditions.

Chinese science fiction has developed in its own way. On the one hand, China is a nation rich in imagination, and the Chinese are eager to reach advanced world levels in all aspects. This lays the foundation for developing the genre of science fiction. On the other hand, China is also a nation with a history of more than 2,000 years of feudalism, and China's closed-door policy had been practiced much longer. For thousands of years, the ruling classes tried to make people believe that China was the central nation of a supposedly universal dominion. This belief had served as a practical guideline for China's conduct toward her neighboring nations, and this belief had also formed the mental and psychological animus of the Chinese people who considered their central nation the most populous, the most affluent, the most powerful, and the most advanced in culture. The long-term condensation of the feudal ideas, ethics, and the way of life has formed the introversive character and conservative tendency of the Chinese. In their collective unconsciousness, the Chinese tend to maintain the status quo and resist anything alien. This has hindered the development of China's national culture and economy.

The open-door policy, practiced since 1979, has opened the eyes of the Chinese people to the outside world. The mental and psychological animus condensed in thousands of years, however, cannot be changed overnight. It still exerts its influence on all aspects of life in China consciously and unconsciously. Therefore, science fiction, with its origin in the West, has developed in a tortuous way in China, experiencing a rise and fall in recent years. As change, however, represents the dynamic force for progress, science fiction as the literature of change has great potential in China.

China has a long tradition of the fantastic, which prepares the way for and leads up to modern Chinese science fiction, which in turn respects and challenges that tradition. The pedigree of Chinese science fiction can be traced back to the earliest Chinese literature, such as the *Shan hai jing* (The Book of Mountains and Seas, 500 B.C.E.), "Tian wen" (Questioning Heaven) in *Chu ci* (The Songs of the South) by Qu Yuan (347–278 B.C.E.), "Hou Yi sheri" (Hou Yi Shooting the Suns) and "Chang E benyue" (Chang E Goes to the Moon) in *Huai nan Zi* (Works of Master Liu An) by Liu An (197–122 B.C.E.), and others. As mountains and seas are fertile grounds for myths and legends, *The Book of Mountains and Seas* is full of tales about mythological encounters, unusual experiences, and extraordinary adventures. "Questioning Heaven" is a collection of cosmological queries asking heaven 172 questions on the creation of the world, the nature of light and darkness, the locations of Heaven's nine divisions, and the motions of the sun and the moon. "Hou Yi Shooting the Suns" tells of a time when ten suns appear in the sky scorching the crops so that the people can hardly survive. To save the people from starvation, a hero named Hou Yi comes forward and shoots down nine of the suns, leaving only one in the sky, the same one we see now. "Chang E Goes to the Moon" tells of Hou Yi's wife who flies to the moon after she drinks an elixir of immortality that she has stolen from her husband. This tale is very probably the world's earliest fantasy about space travel.

Robotics is one of the conventional themes of science fiction. The earliest robot story, as a matter of fact, appeared in China in the fourth century. In Zhang Zhan's "Tangwen" in *Lie zi* (The Book of Lie Zi, circa 307–313), there is a story about Yanshi's robot. Yanshi is a clever craftsman who produces a robot capable of singing and dancing. While entertaining the Zhou emperor, however, the robot constantly stares at the queen. This so enrages the emperor that he issues an order to kill Yanshi. Before his execution, Yanshi requests permission to open the robot's chest. When the emperor sees with his own eyes that all of the organs inside the entertainer's body are made of artificial materials, he is greatly relieved. With his jealous anger turning to appreciative joy, he praises Yanshi for his craftsmanship. Robot stories can also be found in other historical records. From the seventh century, in Zhang Zhou's *Chao ye qian zai* (The Complete Records of the Court and the Commoners), there are two robot stories. Shen Kuo (1031–1095) also told a story about a robot rat killer in his *Meng xi bi tan* (Sketches and Notes by Dream Creek).

Some classic novels also display the fantastic tradition of Chinese literature precursive of modern science fiction. *Xi you ji* (Journey to the West), written late in the sixteenth century by Wu Chengen (1500–1582); *Feng shen yanyi* (The Canonization of the Gods), written at the end of the seventeenth century by an unknown writer; *Liao chai zhi yi* (Strange Stories from a Chinese Studio, 1679), by Pu Songling (1640–1715); and *Jinghua yuan* (Flowers in the Mirror, 1828) by Li Ruzhen (1763–1830) are all fine examples. The Chinese tradition of wondrous stories includes tales of extraordinary events, fairy-tale romances, supernatural interventions in secular human affairs, heroic explorers on holy missions, unusual experiences during journeys, and close encounters with aliens of various kinds. Such stories all depict people's pursuit of fantastic possibilities in alternate worlds. The subject matter of those stories has been constantly borrowed and extended by modern science fiction writers.

The above-mentioned myths, legends, fantastic voyages, and utopias, however, can be regarded only as prototypical predecessors of science fiction because this genre is a distinctly modern form of literature. The industrial revolution in England ushered in the rapid development of science and technology, which in turn brought about tremendous changes in Western life. Human knowledge of the world and the universe greatly increased, and human exploration of fantastic possibilities was intriguingly stimulated. Science fiction emerged as the times required, and it emerged first of all in the West.

At that same historic period of industrialism, China was forced to yield to the powerful military machines of the Western countries in a series of disastrous wars. The nation was fast disintegrating. People, especially young intellectuals, became worried about China's future. They hated foreign aggression, but when they compared China's backwardness with Western power and wealth, they could not but admire its accomplishments in science and technology. They came to see the importance of science and technology for a nation's civilization and development, became aware of the inexorable laws of nature, and realized the need to cope with them both.

In order to stimulate people's interest in science and technology, some enlightened intellectuals discovered science fiction and began introducing this new literature to the Chinese reading public. Lu Xun (1881–1936) is one of them. He highly praised science fiction in his preface to his 1903 translation of Jules Verne's novel *From the Earth to the Moon:*

More often than not ordinary people feel bored at the tedious statements of science. Readers will doze over such works before they can finish reading. It is simply inevitable because these readers are pressed to go over them. Only by resorting to fictional pres-

entation and dressing them up in literary clothing can works of science avoid their te-
diousness while retaining rational analyses and profound theories. . . . So far as the
Chinese fiction is concerned, if we talk about love story, historical story, social story,
and fantasy, they are too numerous to enumerate. Nonetheless, only science fiction is as
rare as unicorn horns, which shows in a way the intellectual poverty of our time. In order
to fill in the gap in the translation circles and encourage the Chinese people to make
concerted efforts, it is imperative to start with science fiction. (Lu 1973, 9)

Thus, translations of Western science fiction began to reach Chinese audiences
one after another beginning at the turn of the century. Chinese readers first came
into contact with science fiction not through original creation but through Chinese translations of Western stories. The dissemination of Western science fiction in China played a very important role in the emergence and development
of its Chinese counterpart. Among the earliest of translations is that of Jules
Verne's *Around the World in Eighty Days.* It was interpreted orally by Yi Ru
and put down in writing by Xiu Yu, published by Shiwen Press in 1900. In
these early years, Jules Verne was by far the most heavily translated of international science fiction authors.

Foreign science fiction stories, in spite of their tongue-twisting names and
unfamiliar terms, were devoured avidly by wild-eyed young Chinese intellectuals, and they also opened the eyes of Chinese writers and stimulated them to
venture into this new field of literature. Ever since then, nourishment from
abroad has periodically sustained the development of Chinese science fiction.

It is estimated that modern Chinese science fiction really began in 1904 with
the serialization of *Yueqiu zhimindi xiaoshuo* (Tales of Moon Colonization) in
Xiuxiang xiaoshuo (Portrait Fiction). A novel of approximately 130,000 words
in Chinese, it was written by Huangjiang Diaosou (Aged-Angler of Desolate
Lake), whose real name remains unknown. The story describes the settlement
of a group of earthlings on the moon.

Another important work in the early period of Chinese science fiction is Xu
Nianci's "Xin falu xiansheng tan" (New Tales of Mr. Absurdity), published
under the pseudonym of Donghai Juewo. It was included in *Xin falu* (New
Absurdity), published by Fiction Forest Press in 1905. The short story tells about
Mr. Absurdity whose body and soul are separated by a typhoon. While his body
sinks down toward the center of the earth, his soul travels to Mercury and Venus.
On Mercury his soul watches the transplantation of brains as a method of rejuvenation, and on Venus it discovers that rudimentary plants and animals appear at the same time, thus refuting biologists' assertions that rudimentary plants
historically preceded rudimentary animals. At the earth's core, his body encounters a nearly immortal man and watches, through his invention of a "lens,"
wonderful scenes. Then accidentally, his soul falls from outer space to merge
with his body in the Mediterranean Sea. He has the good luck of being rescued
by a warship heading east so that he is able to return to Shanghai safe and
sound. Once there he founds a university with an enrollment of 100,000 students

and teaches just one course: ''Brain Electricity''—sitting still as a way to produce electricity. In his six-day sessions, students learn how to generate and transmit electricity and how to use, memorize, analyze, and synthesize symbolic codes. As a result, brain electricity becomes widely applied in everyday life and proves amazingly effective and economical.

During the 1910s, translation was in vogue. Some magazines and publishers published stories without differentiating original creations from translations. And even though some stories were published as being science fiction translations, they might actually have been written by Chinese authors and sold as translations to enhance their market value. This confusion causes great trouble for critics attempting to determine the real identity of some works, which could be original Chinese creations, adaptations of foreign works, or straight translations. Many such works require further scrutiny before the decade's history of science fiction production and publication can be accurately told. It is in the following decades that original Chinese works can be more readily identified.

Lao She (1899–1966) is one of the major figures in contemporary Chinese literature. Although he himself expressed his regret for the publication of *Maocheng ji* (Cat Country; also translated as The City of Cats), this work of about 110,000 words remains one of the most significant of Chinese science fiction novels. It was first serialized in the magazine *Xiandai* (Modern) from 1932 to 1933, and then published as one of the modern serials by the Modern Book Company in 1933. A second edition appeared in 1947. *Cat Country* is a dystopian story about catlike Martians. An earthling from China travels to outer space in a plane, and when the plane crashes on Mars he is the only survivor. There are about twenty countries on Mars, but he lands in the country of the natives with catlike heads. These natives are greedy, and they cheat and even murder each other for money and for the ''reverie'' drug, although everything is done in ''poetic ways.'' The scholars there behave like beasts and regard women as playthings. The rich men's main interest is to have more concubines. Young people try to mimic foreigners because they think everything foreign is good, and the emperor controls the entire nation while the people enjoy no rights at all. Revolutionaries only pay lip service to revolution, and although the people hate foreign invasions, no one is bold enough to resist even the ''dwarf'' aggressors. When another foreign invasion occurs, the cat people fight among themselves instead, aiding in the complete genocide of their people. After the country has been destroyed, the earthling boards a French exploration plane and returns to his ''great, glorious, and free China.'' The happenings in the cat country on Mars bear a strong resemblance to those in Old China: avarice, opium smoking, government corruption, incompetent education, moral degeneration, and foreign invasions. It is a biting satire of Old China.

Xu Dishan (1893–1941) is another major figure in mainstream literature who has also written science fiction. His story ''Tieyu de sai'' (Ironfish Gills) was first published in 1941 and is included in the *Selected Works of Xu Dishan*. It tells of a Mr. Huang who, although terribly impoverished, invents a kind of submarine equipped with iron gills. People aboard the ship can use these gills to work underwater for days. Huang thinks that his invention will play a great role in the anti-Japanese war, but the government shows no interest in it. When the aggressors are approaching his homeland, Huang has to flee. He puts his invention in a wooden box and brings it aboard a ship. It so happens that the box falls overboard and sinks to the seabed. Huang sighs bitterly: It seems that ironfish gills should not have been invented so early! This story illustrates the inventor's misfortunes in Old China.

Lao She and Xu Dishan wrote their science fiction without knowing that their stories were part of this new genre. Gu Junzheng (1902–1980), on the other hand, self-consciously wrote science fiction and even acknowledged his debt to H. G. Wells. By 1937 he had written six science fiction short stories and published them in *Quwei kexue* (Science Delight), a magazine he launched in Shanghai. Among the six, "Heping de meng" (Dream of Peace), "Lundun qiyi" (The Strange Epidemic in London), and "Zai Beiji dixia" (Under the North Pole), were later collected in a booklet entitled *Heping de meng,* published by Cultural Life Press in Shanghai in 1940.

"Dream of Peace" tells of the American special agent Sean Marlin who, at the risk of his own life, returns to the United States to find that all of his countrymen are appealing to their government for reconciliation and against war with the Far Eastern State. He is greatly puzzled by this. Back home, he turns on his radio and discovers that hypnotic electric waves are being projected from a secret radio station by Li Guer of the Far Eastern State. He realizes that this is how the pro-Far Eastern State ideas are being instilled in the minds of lethargic Americans. Marlin pilots his private plane over the Tennessee mountains and discovers the secret radio station. After a fierce struggle, he kills three bodyguards, catches Li Guer red-handed, and forces him to instill anti–Far Eastern State ideas in the minds of Americans continuously for fourteen hours. When Marlin finally hears the radio announcer's clarion call to all Americans to unite and fight the Far Eastern State, he falls into a sound sleep on his couch. "The Strange Epidemic in London" details the dirty chemical warfare scheme of the German spy Stegil. He sprays a special catalyst he has developed into the London air and creates a strange epidemic that causes thousands of deaths. American chemist Ingram discovers the secret of this catalyst and slips into his enemy's lair; there he destroys the catalyst generator and puts an end to this strange disease. The third story, "Under the North Pole," tells of the anthropologist Kean's exploration of the Arctic. Kean discovers an enormous factory, under the ice, run by Cameron, a scientist who is studying magnetism. Cameron has not only developed a kind of iron alloy that has permanent magnetism, but also has discovered that the geomagnetic pole is caused by a huge magnetic iron deposit under the North Pole. In order to make a tremendous fortune from his invention, he tries to bury the original deposit deep beneath the earth's crust and replace it with his alloy, so that magnets everywhere will need to be made of this same alloy. He is so excited by his own evil scheme that, while exploding the deposit, he missteps and falls into an abyss. Compasses all over the world fail to work properly for three hours due to the explosion, but they soon return to normal because the iron alloy begins functioning as a new geomagnetic pole for both the alloy and genuine iron.

Gu Junzheng's stories display three distinguishing features: An ingenious combination of literary imagination and scientific conception enhances their aesthetic appeal; the exposition of future discoveries and inventions, based on the latest achievements of science and technology, inspires readers' determination and confidence in harnessing nature; and the scientific knowledge and ideas presented in these stories stimulate readers' interests in science and technology. Gu Junzheng pays much attention to the scientific basis for his imagination. He devotes considerable space in his stories to explaining scientific principles and formulas. Whereas Lu Xun advocated the translation of science fiction to popularize science, Gu Junzheng is the first Chinese author to advocate the popularization of science through science fiction. In his preface to *Dream of Peace,* he explicitly states:

In the United States, science fiction almost enjoys the same popularity as detective story. Whether in books, on screen, or on the radio, H. G. Wells's story about the future war disturbs the whole city, and people run pell-mell to seek refuge in the countryside. That is enough to show the great impact science fiction can exert on people; no less than that of mainstream literature. Then, can and shall we make use of this genre to carry a few more scientific ideas so as to popularize people's education in science? I think it is possible and worth trying. These three stories as collected in this booklet are the result of my attempt. (1940, 2)

Chinese history in that period, however, was chaotic, with the collapse of the Qing empire followed by the warlord era, the war of resistance against Japan, and the civil wars. Few people showed much concern for the development of science and technology, much less science fiction. Works of science fiction were scarce during the first half of the twentieth century in China.

The People's Republic of China was founded in 1949. The new government, facing many new problems in building the country, was determined to learn from the Soviet Big Brother and apply the Soviets' "advanced experience" in all fields. From this came the all-pervasive influence of the Soviet Union throughout China. Zhu Yulian's article, "A Chart of Sino-Soviet Economical and Cultural Cooperations" in *Renmin Ribao* (People's Daily) of April 19, 1957, revealed the extent of this influence: From 1949 to 1956, over 12,000 Russian books were translated into Chinese, with 191 million volumes printed (5). Among these books were Soviet science fiction. The numerous translations of Soviet science fiction seemed, purposely or not, to set out the guiding principles for science fiction writing in China. The result was that Chinese science fiction authors followed their Soviet counterparts in form, techniques, spirit, and ideology.

Probably also influenced by the Soviet science fiction circle's preference for Jules Verne's short-range extrapolations, based on the knowledge and technology already achieved, over H. G. Wells's hypothetical scientific romance, the Chinese Youth Press systematically published selections of Jules Verne's works throughout the 1950s and into the 1960s. The meticulous translation and systematic publication of Jules Verne's science fiction helped Chinese readers to understand his themes and style more comprehensively and thoroughly, with the result that he remains the most familiar and popular science fiction writer to the Chinese reader. And so, once again, in the 1950s and early 1960s foreign science fiction stories and theories had a profound impact on Chinese science fiction writing.

During this period, almost all Chinese science fiction stories were written for juvenile readers. Therefore, the authors saw their publications only in children's magazines, and then they were directly published by juvenile presses, mainly the Juvenile Press in Shanghai and the Chinese Juvenile Press in Beijing. Those science fiction writers who had been accepted as members of the Chinese writers's Association all belonged to the subgroup of children's literature.

Zheng Wenguang (1929–) wrote his first science fiction story in 1954, "Cong Diqiu dao Huoxing" (From Earth to Mars), which was first carried in *Zhongguo shaonian bao* (Chinese Juvenile Daily), in Beijing. It depicts a girl called Zhen Zhen who slips into a rocket ship together with her younger brother and her classmate Wei Xinzhen. They pilot the rocket ship away from Earth toward Mars and come across a meteor stream halfway there. Another rocket ship appears at this crucial moment. Inside it are Zhen Zhen's father and two other older scientists. They have come to rescue the children and bring them back to Earth.

Yu Zhi (1919– , real name, Ye Zhishan) authored "Shizong de gege" (The Missing Elder Brother) in 1957. First serialized in *Zhongxuesheng* (High School Student), in Beijing, it won a second place trophy in China's Second Juvenile Literary and Artistic Creation Awards. The story tells of a mischievous elder brother who gets into a cold storage for fun, only to be locked inside and frozen. More than ten years later, refrigeration workers repairing the bin find this frozen boy. Scientists successfully bring him back to life, producing the science fiction comedy of the younger brother being older than the elder brother (American readers may recall a short-lived television series in which a similar reversal occurred between a father and son).

Xiao Jianheng (1931–) also published an interesting story entitled "Buke de qiyu" (Pup Buke's Adventures), which is a story about a puppy named Buke. After it gets run over by a car, some scientists transplant its head onto another dog's body, resulting in a series of miracles. This story also won a second place trophy in China's Second Juvenile Literary and Artistic Creation Awards.

Other authors who experimented in this genre during this period include Chi Shuchang, Cui Xingjian, Guo Yishi, Ji Hong, Lu Ke, Su Pingfan, Tong Enzheng, Wang Guozhong, Xu Qingshan, Yan Yuanwen, Yang Zijiang, Zhang Ran, and

Zhao Shizhou. Nearly twenty authors produced approximately sixty works between 1950 and 1965. Due to Soviet influence, science fiction was regarded as
a subcategory of popular science. Therefore, all the stories of this period fall
into one of two modes: (1) intriguing accidents plus scientific explanation or (2)
an interesting visit to the future or another planet. They are short, simple, and
written in children's language; they are crude and incidental in nature while
meager in plot and characterization; and they contain too much reasoning
squeezed into action-oriented linear narratives. These stories are not comparable
in literary and artistic quality with the stories of the 1980s. They received scanty
attention in Chinese literary circles and existed merely as a weak subgenre in
juvenile literature.

The next ten years or so witnessed the unprecedented catastrophe of the Great
Cultural Revolution in China (1966–1976). This notorious "revolution" swept
away almost everything creative and meaningful. Arbitrary leadership at the top
level suspended most magazines and sent writers and editors to the factories and
the countryside to learn from the workers and poor peasants. Little in the way
of fiction or poetry was produced, except that which conformed to the immediate
political purposes of each successive campaign. Not a trace of science fiction
could be found in the whole of China.

The Gang of Four collapsed in the fall of 1976. The late Premier Zhou Enlai's
speech of June 19, 1961, which called for moderate policies for literary and
artistic creation, was released in its entirety on February 4, 1979. The Fourth
National Congress of Writers and Artists, held in Beijing from October 30 to
November 16, 1979, promised writers and artists a new era of creative freedom.
A flood of responses followed. New magazines were launched, writers experimented with new genres and techniques, and a group of new authors gained the
limelight. The Chinese science fiction scene was also permeated with a remarkable resurgence of creative vitality. Stories superior both artistically and thematically to the earlier ones appeared one after another.

"Shanhudao shang de siguang" by Tong Enzheng (1935–) (Death Ray on
a Coral Island) was the first science fiction story published in the prestigious
mainstream magazine *Renmin wenxue* (People's Literature) in August 1978. It
depicts Hu Mingli (later known as Dr. Matai), a Chinese laser specialist who,
deceived by a foreign consortium, engages in laser gun research work on a
desolate coral island. The consortium tries to use his invention for military
purposes. Realizing the actual state of affairs, Hu Mingli fights back and dies a
martyr's death. Before he dies, however, he entrusts his invention to the young
scientist Cheng Tianhong, who then brings it back to China. The success of the
story lies in its clear-cut portrayal of characters and the intriguing plot. It won
China's best short story award of 1978. This was a great honor, because, in all
the years that this nationwide literary award has been offered, this is the only
science fiction story ever to receive it. This story was later adapted to film,
theater, Shanghai local drama, and radio. The appearance of this story not only
indicated the improvement of characterization and plot in Chinese science fiction

writing but also a break from the bondage of its juvenile literature classification. It heralded the booming period of science fiction creation that lasted from 1979 through 1982. According to incomplete statistics compiled by Wei Yahua in a talk given in April 1985, 1978 saw the production of about 32 works, 1979 about 80, 1980 about 120, 1981 about 270, and 1982 about 340.

Magazines provide the playground for thought experiments which create a sense of wonder. In addition to all the popular science journals that carried science fiction, other magazines were also active in publishing science fiction during that period. Some influential newspapers with circulations over one million also serialized science fiction stories, such as *Gongren ribao* (Worker's Daily) and *Beijing wanbao* (Beijing Evening Paper) in Beijing; *Wenhui bao* (Encounters) and *Xinmin wanbao* (Xinmin Evening Paper) in Shanghai; and *Yangcheng wanbao* (Goat City Evening Paper) in Guangzhou. Moreover, a dozen presses published large numbers of science fiction books during this period.

With magazines and publishers as their powerful mainstay, more and more people made their contributions to the development of Chinese science fiction. Nearly 150 science fiction authors were active in China in the late 1970s and early 1980s. Among them were some old-time writers and some novices, such as Zheng Wenguang, Xiao Jianheng, Tong Enzheng, Liu Xinshi (1931–), Wang Xiaoda (1939–), Ye Yonglie (1940–), Song Yichang (1942–), Wei Yahua (1945–), Ji Wei (1954–), and Jin Tao (1940–).

Because most of China's science fiction authors are engaged in scientific research or in the popularization of science, they are not, for the most part, professional writers. They write in their spare time. In China, science fiction writing is institutionally affiliated with the popularization of science, with the result that science fiction activities have all been attached to the China Popular Science Creative Writing Association instead of the Chinese Writers' Association. When the China Popular Science Creative Writing Association was established in 1979, nearly all of the science fiction authors joined this organization. Up to the present time there has been no national science fiction organization per se in China.

Although not a few of the works produced in this period from 1978 to 1982 still fell into the category of juvenile literature, some did make conspicuous breakthroughs in form, content, and techniques, not merely breaking the bonds of juvenile literature but also the bonds of short fiction. There appeared novels, novellas, plays, and film scripts. Among the many works produced in this booming period, the following three examples are the most influential and representative ones.

Zheng Wenguang's novel *Feixiang Renmazuo* (Forward Sagittarius) depicts the sudden takeoff of China's spaceship "The East" as a result of enemy sabotage. The ship was originally destined for Mars. With its fuel exhausted, however, it heads straight toward Sagittarius, far, far away, and comes across a black hole on the way there. Against tremendous odds, the three young people on this ship succeed in harnessing the black hole's energy and in linking their ship with "The Advance," another spaceship sent by China to rescue its sistership and crew. "The East" returns to Earth safe and sound. This novel pays great attention not only to characterization but also to the presentation of accurate information.

Meng Weizai (1933–) is a famous contemporary mainstream writer. *Fangwen shizong zhe* (Call on the Missing People) is his only work of science fiction. It is a utopian novel, but it mirrors the reality of Chinese society by way of science fiction. The historical setting of the story is the "Tianan Men Incident"—the spontaneous rally of April 5, 1976, that honored the memory of the late premier Zhou Enlai. The Gang of Four suppressed the mourning masses. *Call on the Missing People* tells of nine people who are missing after the Tianan Men incident. It so happens that they board an alien flying saucer and reach a far-off planet named Songlu. They find that Songlu is an Edenic land for the planet's natives, who enjoy happiness all their lives. The nine Chinese happily join the natives in singing and dancing to extol the wealth and prosperity of Songlu. As a utopian story, it is just wish fulfillment on the author's part, but it sincerely expresses many Chinese people's strong yearning for a peaceful and happy life without political upheavals and disastrous social chaos.

Wei Yahua's "Wenrou zhixiang de meng" (Conjugal Happiness in the Arms of Morpheus) is a story of great impact. It tells of a scientist who marries a robot. The robot wife is so docile, gentle, and beautiful that the young scientist becomes intoxicated with love. He is so indulged in the conjugal happiness of his married life that he neglects his work and even unintentionally burns up all the research data of an important project. The complete subservience of the robot wife to all of the whims of her husband eventually leads him to disaster. He is handed over to a special court for investigation and determination of his responsibility in the case. The scientist finally awakens from his rosy dream and realizes how hateful subservience and excessive love are. He makes up his mind to divorce his robot wife. The sequel to this story was later carried in *Yanhe* (Yanhe River, nos. 3–4, 1982), a magazine in Jilin province.

More science fiction stories appeared in the prestigious mainstream magazine *People's Literature.* Ye Yonglie's "Fushi" (Corrosion) deals with scientists' attitudes toward fame and financial gain when a great scientific discovery is made. Xiao Jianheng's "Shaluomu jiaoshou de miwu" (Professor Solomon's Delusion) shows that human beings are beyond simulation by robots.

Science fiction during this period also found expression in other media such as film, television, radio broadcasting, and comic books. In film, for instance, the movie version of Tong Enzheng's "Death Ray on a Coral Island" was filmed in 1980, and Ji Hongxu's *Qianying* (Hidden Shadow) was released in 1982. On television, Zhou Yongnian, Zhang Fengjiang, and Jia Wanchao's *Zuihou yige aizheng sizhe* (The Last Man Who Dies of Cancer) and Wu Boze's *Yinxing ren* (The Invisible Man) were shown in 1980, while Ye Yonglie's *Xiongmao jihua* (The Panda Project) was shown in 1983. Ye Yonglie's *An dou*

(Veiled Strife) was broadcast daily over the radio as a serial by the Central People's Broadcasting Station in 1981, while his *Mimi zhongdui* (The Secret Column) was broadcast by Hunan and Sichuan People's Broadcasting Stations in 1981. In comic books, Ye Yonglie's detective science fiction series consisting of 8 million copies of twelve booklets, under the general title of *Scientific Sherlock Holmes,* was published by Popular Science Press in 1982, and Jin Tao's juvenile science fiction series, consisting of ten booklets under the general title of *Adventures of Foolish Ma, Junior,* was published by Ocean Press in 1983.

Chinese science fiction differs in some aspects from its counterparts abroad, due to different social systems, cultural traditions, and attitudes toward science, technology, and the future. Chinese science fiction seldom tackles the subjects of space colonization, galactic empires, alternative histories, cataclysms, apocalyptic visions, telepathy, cybernetics, religion, sex, and taboos. On the whole, Chinese science fiction is optimistic. People always get the upper hand over nature, science, evil, or whatever enemy or obstacle they may face. The hero is supposed to succeed, emerging triumphant and unscathed from difficulties. Visions of the future are always bright and promising, although a spectrum of possibilities for that bright future is projected. In China, where most science fiction writers are engaged in scientific work and most of the protagonists in their stories are scientists or scientists-to-be, science fiction is, in a sense, a kind of literature that presents scientists' collective aspirations in the form of an explorative excursion into an alternate reality. The conflicts in the stories always reveal the most prominent characteristic of the Chinese scientists: their patriotism. This key virtue is their indispensable guarantee in overcoming all kinds of difficulties and emerging victorious.

As critics in China emphasize that imagination in science fiction has to be based on experienced science, the fantasy elements in the stories are bound by known scientific facts or extrapolations from them. Therefore, writers usually look ahead a few decades, and the readers seem to expect that the imaginary in the story will come true in their lifetimes. As a result, Chinese science fiction stories mostly depict the near, foreseeable future. In China, science fiction's main function is utilitarian rather than aesthetic. It aims to create interesting stories in a simple and effective prose and to teach moral lessons, often in the form of an admonition, expressed in definite terms at the end of the story. In his afterword to *Forward Sagittarius,* Zheng Wenguang writes:

We eulogize science. We eulogize the glorious future which a highly developed science will give to human life. We eulogize all the fine things working people create with the help of science and we eulogize millions of people who heroically strive for the materialization of the four modernizations. (1979, 282)

Science fiction entered the classroom for the first time in China in 1979 when Dr. Philip Smith, from the University of Pittsburgh, offered the first science fiction course in the English Department of the Shanghai Foreign Languages

Institute, now named the Shanghai International Studies University. With his help, Wu Dingbo began to offer science fiction as a one-term (about twenty weeks) optional course for the third- and fourth-year students in 1980. The course relied on independent readings, class discussions, lectures, and video presentations. The textbooks were based on Robert Silverberg's *Science Fiction Hall of Fame*. The objective of the course was to provide an introduction to the history, writers and their works, and themes of British and American science fiction. Wu Yan of the Beijing Teachers University also offered science fiction as an optional course in 1990 with emphasis on the theoretical studies of the genre. In 1989 Guo Jianzhong of Hangzhou University sponsored the Science Fiction Research Center with over 1,500 texts, mainly from Japan and the United States.

The rapid growth of Chinese science fiction has drawn the attention of both scientific and literary circles. Different schools of thought and different viewpoints appear, giving rise to enthusiastic theoretical debates inside and outside science fiction circles, a normal and healthy phenomenon in the process of developing a creative genre and one that demonstrates the health and vitality of science fiction in China. Currently, there are six major controversies about science fiction.

The first controversy concerns which category science fiction falls into. Some say that science fiction falls into the category of literature because the author conveys ideas by means of images. Science fiction is obliged to create typical characters in a typical environment so as to best demonstrate the theme. Besides, science fiction is a literary genre that takes scientific exploration as its subject matter, imaginative extrapolation as its approach, and fiction as its form. Others maintain that science fiction is part of popularizing science. The eclectic view holds that it stands entirely independent from both popular science and literature.

The second controversy is what the mission of science fiction is. Some hold that the mission of science fiction is to expound a scientific outlook of life. It explores what may be, not what will be; and it portrays a world different in some way from the everyday world we know. Just as other artistic and literary works do, science fiction expresses the author's ideas, philosophy, realistic attitude, and truth-seeking spirit. It has no obligation to introduce any specific scientific knowledge, though it may stimulate thought on the part of the readers and arouse their interest in science and technology. Others assume that science fiction must undertake the task of popularizing scientific knowledge. If science fiction does not do so, then its soul must have become a disembodied one.

The third controversy involves the definition of science fiction. *Ci hai* (Encyclopedia of Chinese Words, 1979) provides this definition in the entry of "Kexue huanxiang xiaoshuo" (Science Fiction): "Fantasized fiction about humankind's efforts to work miracles by applying new discoveries, new achievements, and plausible predictions in science." Many people, however, question the validity of this authoritative statement. Views vary so greatly that it is hard to pick up any single one as representative.

Fourth is the scientific feature of fantasy in science fiction. Some hold that scientific fantasy is based on certain scientific knowledge and that it can offer a plausible explanation for its fantastic aspects. If writers can make things sound plausible through the artistic use of pseudoscience, then there can be no denying their literary effects. But others hold that scientific fantasy means imagination that sticks strictly to experienced science. Otherwise it conducts propaganda for pseudoscience and fails to usher readers into the hall of science.

Fifth, is detective science fiction all right? Some think it is a new type of writing that deserves encouragement, since it appeals to many readers. Others view it as a harmful trend.

Finally, what is the orientation of science fiction creation in China? Some believe that Chinese science fiction is still immature. Most of the authors are newcomers and beginners lack experience. Therefore it is imperative to encourage the policy of "Let a Hundred Flowers Blossom," which would allow science fiction writers to tackle different subjects and try different techniques and styles. Others believe that the current tendency of science fiction writing is unhealthy. They argue that the formulas of "fantasy + love" and "fantasy + thriller," in particular, should be discarded.

Although these issues remain controversial and unresolved, the debates over them have drawn more public attention to this new genre of Chinese writing. They encourage the people who are concerned about science fiction to make serious studies of the genre and the writers to produce high-quality works.

Science fiction treats change, particularly human-made change. Yet the greatest irony lies in the fact that, when certain changes really take place, science fiction is hushed and becomes dead silent. The most prominent of these is a change in the political climate. Just as Chinese writers were busy writing and publishing science fiction with great enthusiasm, the political drive against "spiritual pollution" began, and it swept the whole of China in 1983. Ideas and practices that were publicly criticized in mass media were bourgeois individualism; writing as self-expression; modernism; works without theme, character, or plot; abstract humanism; "socialist alienation"; the profit motive; sexual promiscuity; and various other "noxious" influences. Unexpectedly, science fiction became a scapegoat, and its golden period ended overnight. Science fiction publication was virtually stopped; some books that had already been half-printed were snatched from the presses. Chinese science fiction creations of the previous five years came under severe criticism.

Chinese science fiction has suffered involuntarily from the change of political climate, and it remains at a very low ebb, with annual production lingering around forty titles from 1984 to the present. Science fiction is, however, still alive, and *SF World* has played an indispensable role in its survival. This magazine, established in 1979 and holding its ground in 1983, has been turning out twelve issues annually, with a circulation of 10,000 or more during these years. It not only publishes science fiction stories and commentaries but also does its best to unite around it all those in China interested in science fiction. In 1985 it launched the first nationwide contest for the best science fiction short stories, and in 1986 it issued the first Milky Way awards to eleven winners.

This magazine has done its job quite well, and its editor in chief, Yang Xiao, has worked efficiently for years. In 1987, at the invitation of Japan's Chinese Science Fiction Research Association (JCSFRA), Ms. Yang led a delegation of four editors of *SF World* to visit Japan. After their arrival in Tokyo, they called on Dan Fukami, the head of JCSFRA, and other eminent Japanese science fiction writers, and they exchanged their views on science fiction creation and publication. Accompanied by Osamu Iwagami and Mrs. Takumi Shibano, the editors visited three Japanese publishing companies with long-running science fiction lines.

In order to support the Chengdu bid for hosting the 1991 World Science Fiction Annual Meeting, Ms. Yang led the Chinese delegation to the World Science Fiction meetings in 1989 and 1990, in San Marino and The Hague. Her courage and will overwhelmed most of the World Science Fiction members. The 1991 World Science Fiction Annual Meeting turned out to be such a great success, with the distinct theme of "Science Fiction, Peace, and Friendship," that it won all attendees' high appreciation. In his "Chengdu—A Personal View," carried in the *World SF Newsletter,* Brian Aldiss comments, "Since the foundation in the cold mid-seventies, WSF has achieved nothing better than the meeting in Chengdu this May" (1991, 2). The Chengdu meeting lasted for five days, from May 20 to May 24, with 150 participants from all parts of China and forty-five science fiction professionals from other countries in Asia, Europe, and America. At the meeting, *SF World* won the Best Magazine Award together with the Czechoslovak *Spaceship*. Apart from the routine proceedings of the WSF meeting, the Chengdu meeting also held an academic exchange meeting, the third Milky Way (Forest Cup) awarding ceremony, and a trip to the Wolong Wild Animal Reserve to meet Panda An An.

Science fiction has again drawn public attention in recent years. It is rather unusual for several articles on the same subject to appear in China's most authoritative party newspaper, *Renmin Ribao* (People's Daily), in 1987 and 1988. Tan Kai's "Why Has Cinderella Withdrawn from the Stage?" and Jiang Yunsheng's "Spread SF Wings" are most representative of such articles. All of these articles tend to analyze the causes of the low ebb of Chinese science fiction production. Writers sometimes complain about the readers for their skin-deep knowledge of science and technology and their lack of imagination, whereas readers blame the writers for their limited understanding of science and their poor writing skills.

The critics have a view different from either of these complaints. According to them, the major reason for the low production of science fiction in China is the erroneous guiding principle found in Chinese science fiction writing: Science fiction stories must deal with and popularize known scientific facts. For over forty years, this restrictive principle has limited imaginative flexibility and has hindered the development of Chinese science fiction. To compensate for it, writers, critics, and readers are being encouraged to spare no effort in stressing the view that science fiction is a literature about change and that imagination is more important than science. The second reason is the rare appearance of high-quality stories in China. The critics believe that once high-quality stories reach the reading public, the situation will improve accordingly. As Chinese science fiction has not yet reached its maturity, the advisable step to be taken at present is to translate and introduce the best foreign science fiction works, as people in Japan have done. The third reason is the interference of various cadres who do not know the nature of science fiction but too heavily influence its production. Given that Chinese science fiction is studied and respected abroad but not so much at home, critics have urgently called on the cadres in the circles of both literature and popular science to be aware of this abnormal situation and to show sincere concern for the development of Chinese science fiction. Critics also suggest that more Chinese participation in international activities be encouraged.

Science fiction has also developed in Hong Kong and Taiwan in a similar pace as on the mainland. Although the term ''science fiction literature'' was first used by Lu Yingzhong in 1980, the Asian Press in Hong Kong published in 1956 Zhao Zifan's *Feidie zhengkong* (The Flying Saucer Conquers the Sky), *Taikong lixian ji* (Adventures in Space), and *Yueliang shang kan Diqiu* (Watching Earth from the Moon), which probably marks the beginning of Chinese science fiction creation outside the mainland. In coordination with the 1957 International Geophysics Year, Zhao introduced the solar system by means of science fiction. The three books all deal with the space exploration of a scientist and his grandson. Zhao's stories mainly play the role of popularizing known scientific information. Ni Kuang, who often writes under the pseudonym of Wei Shili, is the most productive science fiction writer in Hong Kong. Since 1965 he has turned out about twenty-five volumes of stories, mostly sword and sorcery. As his stories are more fantasy than scientific speculation, some critics doubt if his works belong to the genre. Li Weicai has also produced some well-received science fiction stories. Sponsored by Li Weicai, Du Jian, and others in Hong Kong, *Kexue yu kehuan congkan* (Science and Science Fiction), a quarterly, started in January 1990 but closed down in 1991, after publishing only four issues.

In Taiwan, Zhang Xiaofeng published ''Pan Duna'' in *Zhongguo shibao* (China Times); Huang Hai [Huang Binghuang] turned out ''Hangxiang wuya de lucheng'' (A Boundless Voyage) in 1968; and Zhang Xiguo published ''Chaoren liezhuan'' (The Biography of a Superman) in *Chun wenxue* (Mainstream Literature) in March 1969. These three represent the major trend in science fiction writing in Taiwan. Dealing with the theme of science creating human lives, Zhang's story demonstrates the author's concern about human nature. As a mainstream writer, Zhang's cross-line attempt is worth commending. Divorcing himself from the writing style of realism, Huang Hai follows the tradition of the fantastic. He is best known for his high literary quality and scientific speculation. Among his best-known works are *Tianwei yixiang ren* (A Stranger from Outer Space), *Yinghe mihang ji* (Drifting Off Course in the Galaxy), *Liulang xingkong* (Wandering in Starry Skies), *Xinshiji zhelu* (Voyage to a New Era), and *10101* (The Year of 10101). His persistent venture into the field of science fiction, especially into the science fiction short story, has won him the honor of being considered the best science fiction writer in Taiwan today.

Zhang Xiguo, a computer specialist who teaches at the University of Pittsburgh in the United States, has shown much concern about the development of science fiction in Taiwan. He has written, translated, commented on, and edited a great number of science fiction works for more than two decades. He is the mainstay of Taiwan's science fiction circles. Among his representative works are *Yiyumao* (A Feather), *Longcheng hujiang* (Heroes in the Dragon City), *Yequ* (Nocturne), *Wuyudie* (A Five-Jade Plate), and *Xingyun zuqu* (Nebula Suite).

Lu Yingzhong is a devoted editor of science fiction publication. In 1977 he sponsored the first science fiction magazine in Taiwan: *Yuzhou kexue* (Cosmic Science), which lasted for only one year. Together with Huang Hai and Zhang Zijian, Lu edited and published *Zhongguo dandai kehuan xianji* (Selections of Contemporary Chinese Science Fiction), in 1981. At present he is the chief editor of *Huanxiang* (Mirage), the only science fiction magazine in Taiwan. For decades Lu has been a zealous propagator of the genre in Taiwan. Among other noted science fiction writers in Taiwan are Huang Fan, Ye Yandu, and Ye Lihua, who are celebrated for *Shangdi men* (Gods), *Haitian longzhan* (Dragon Wars in Ocean and Sky), and *Shikong youxi* (The Game of Space and Time), respectively.

To accompany the production of science fiction stories in recent years, criticism and guidebooks have quickly developed. Lu Yingzhong of Taiwan produced *Kehuan wenxue* (Science Fiction Literature) in 1980, which is a theoretical exposition of science fiction as a literary genre. The author is the first person in Taiwan to use the term ''science fiction literature.'' By introducing and analyzing the best authors and their best works in Taiwan and America, Lu intends to arouse interest in reading, writing, and publishing science fiction in Taiwan. Du Jian of Hong Kong published *Shijia kehuan wentan daguan* (A General Introduction to World Science Fiction), in which he offers a brief survey of the development of the genre in Asia, Europe, and North America.

Also in 1980, Beijing's Popular Science Press published Ye Yonglie's *Lun kexue wenyi* (On Scientific Literature and Art), in which the author systematically expounds the general theories governing the creation of scientific literature and art. According to him, scientific literature and art refer to literary and artistic creations of all kinds with scientific content such as scientific fairy tales, scientific cross-talks, scientific poetry, scientific comics, and science fiction. He provides separate chapters to delineate the special features of each form of the genre with the approach combining history, theory, and reflections of his personal experiences in writing. Ye believes that all forms of scientific literature and art, though being literary and artistic creations, have the obligation to popularize scientific knowledge. In the chapter about science fiction, Ye states that science fiction consists of three indispensable elements: science, imagination, and fiction. Therefore, science fiction must base its story on experienced science and then make rational and reasonable extrapolations. Science fiction differs from scientific literature inasmuch as the former expresses ideas by means of images and the latter by logic.

Zuojia lun kexue wenyi (Writers on Scientific Literature and Art), edited by Huang Yi, includes twenty-nine articles by twenty authors on scientific literature and art, all stressing the importance of achieving an organic unity of scientific content and literary form. In this collection, nine articles are devoted to the studies of science fiction, representing the authors' different views on the nature and characteristics of science fiction. Tong Enzheng states that science fiction is not popular science writing and that he had no intention to propagandize laser technology in his "Death Ray on a Coral Island." He says that he wrote the story to expound scientists' principles as to whom they must serve. Representing the majority view on the issue, Rao Zhonghua avers that science fiction is part of popular science writing and that it is an unshakable obligation of science fiction to enrich readers with scientific knowledge.

In 1981 Huang Yi edited *Lun kexue huanxiang xiaoshuo* (On Science Fiction) for Beijing's Popular Science Press, including twenty-seven articles dealing with science fiction literary comment, theoretical studies, and writing experiences. In this book, thirteen chapters reveal controversial views in China regarding the fundamental character and functions of science fiction, six chapters offer general introduction to science fiction in other countries, and the rest comment on various individual authors, including Zheng Wenguang, Ye Yonglie, Xiao Jianheng, Jules Verne, H. G. Wells, Isaac Asimov, and A. Belyaev.

Rao Zhonghua compiled *Zhongguo kehuan xiaoshuo daquan* (A Complete Collection of Chinese Science Fiction Abstracts), a work that provides abstracts of more than 400 titles produced from 1905 to 1980 in chronological order. From these abstracts, readers can acquire a general idea of the subject matter, theme, and style of Chinese science fiction in the period, see how Chinese science fiction reflects the different historical times, and thus review the development of Chinese science fiction. This is a commendable reference book for those who are interested in the history of Chinese science fiction.

Zhao Shizhou edited *Kehuan xiaoshuo shijia* (Ten Science Fiction Writers), which includes criticism on ten Chinese science fiction authors: Zheng Wenguang, Tong Enzheng, Xiao Jianheng, Liu Xinshi, Ye Yonglie, Jin Tao, Chi Shuchang, Ye Zhishan, Zhao Shizhou, and Wang Guozhong. *Zhongwei kexue huanxiang xiaoshuo xishang cidian* (A Dictionary of Understanding Chinese and Foreign Science Fiction), edited by Ye Yonglie, is a 746-page volume that comments on more than 100 outstanding science fiction works published in China and elsewhere. Each entry includes a short excerpt from the original, a commentary, and a biographical note about the author. This reference book is very useful for studies of the genre.

The specific future of science fiction in China remains unclear, but that it will have a future is not in doubt.

NOTE

1. This essay is a revised version of the author's introduction to *Science Fiction from China: Eight Stories,* edited by Wu Dingbo and Patrick D. Murphy (Westport, Conn.: Greenwood Press, 1989).

BIBLIOGRAPHY

Aldiss, Brian. "Chengdu—A Personal View." *World SF Newsletter* 3 (1991): 2.

Ci hai (Encyclopedia of Chinese Words). Shanghai: Wordbook Press, 1979.

Du Jian. *Shijia kehuan wentan daguan* (A General Introduction to World Science Fiction). Hong Kong: Yuanjin Press, 1991.

Dunsing, Charlotte, and Ye Yonglie, eds. *Science Fiction from China.* Cologne, Germany: Goldmann, 1986.

Editorial Department of *Geology Gazette,* ed. *Kepu zuojia tan chuangzuo* (Popular Science Writers on Writing). Beijing: Geology Press, 1980.

Feng shen yanyi (The Canonization of the Gods). Circa 1800. Reprint. Beijing: People's Literature Press, 1955.

Gu Junzheng. *Heping de meng.* Includes "Heping de meng" (Dream of Peace), "Lundun qiyi" (The Strange Epidemic in London), and "Zai Beiji dixia" (Under the North Pole). Shanghai: Cultural Life Press, 1940.

Huang Fan. *Shangdi men* (Gods). Taipei, Taiwan: Hongfan Press, 1986.

Huang Hai. *Liulang xingkong* (Wandering in Starry Skies). Taipei, Taiwan: Juvenile Monthly Press, 1974.

———. *10101* (The Year of 10101). Taipei, Taiwan: Zhaoming, 1969.

———. *Tianwei yixiang ren* (A Stranger from Outer Space). Taipei, Taiwan: Zhaoming, 1980.

———. *Xinshiji zhelu* (Voyage to a New Era). Taipei, Taiwan: Zhaoming, 1972.

———. *Yinghe mihang ji* (Drifting Off Course in the Galaxy). Taipei, Taiwan: Zhaoming, 1979.

Huang Hai, Lu Yingzhong, and Zhang Zijian, eds. *Zhongguo dangdai kehuan xianji* (Selections of Contemporary Chinese Science Fiction). Taipei, Taiwan: Zhaoming, 1981.

Huang Yi, ed. *Lun kexue huanxiang xiaoshuo* (On Science Fiction). Beijing: Popular Science Press, 1981.

———. *Zuojia lun kexue wenyi* (Writers on Scientific Literature and Art). Nanjing: Jiangsu Science and Technology Press, 1980.

Jiang Yunsheng. "Spread SF Wings." *Renmin ribao* (People's Daily), Beijing, October 26, 1987.

Lao She [Shu Sheyu]. *Maocheng ji* (Cat Country). Shanghai: Modern Book Company, 1933. Translated by William A. Lyell. Columbus: Ohio State University Press, 1970. *City of Cats,* translated by James E. Dew. Ann Arbor: Center for Chinese Studies of the University of Michigan, 1964.

Li Qi. *Taohua yuan* (The Land of Peach Blossoms). Taipei, Taiwan: Lingxi Press, 1979.

Li Ruzhen. *Jinghua yuan* (Flowers in the Mirror). 1828. Rpt. Beijing: People's Literature Press, 1979.

Liu An. *Huai nan zi* (Works of Master Liu An). Circa second century B.C.E.

Lu Xun, trans. *From the Earth to the Moon* in *Lu Xun quanji* (Complete Works of Lu Xun). Vol. 11. Beijing: People's Press, 1973.

Lu Yingzhong. *Kehuan wenxue* (Science Fiction Literature). Taipei, Taiwan: Zhaoming, 1980.

Meng Weizai. *Fangwen shizong zhe* (Call on the Missing People). Tianjin: *Zhihuishu* (Tree of Knowledge); New Budding Press, 1981.

Ni Kuang. *Selections of Ni Kuang's Science Fiction.* Taipei, Taiwan: Hongfan Press, 1985.

Pu Songling. *Liao chai zhi yi (Strange Stories from a Chinese Studio).* 1679. Reprint. Beijing: People's Literature Press, 1962. Translated by Herbert A. Giles. New York: Boni and Liveright, 1925.

Qu Yuan. *Chu ci* (The Songs of the South). Translated by David Hawkes. London: Oxford, 1959.

Rao Zhonghua, comp. *Zhongguo kehuan xiaoshuo daquan* (A Complete Collection of Chinese Science Fiction Abstracts). Beijing: Ocean Press, 1982.

Shan hai jing (The Book of Mountains and Seas). Circa 500 B.C.E.

Shen Kuo. *Meng xi bi tan* (Sketches and Notes by Dream Creek). Circa eleventh century C.E.

Silverberg, Robert, ed. *Science Fiction Hall of Fame.* New York: Doubleday, 1970.

Tan Kai. "Why Has Cinderella Withdrawn from the Stage?" *Renmin ribao* (People's Daily), Beijing, June 10, 1987.

Tong Enzheng. "Shanhudao shang de siguang" (Death Ray on a Coral Island). *Renmin wenxue* (People's Literature) (August 1978). Beijing.

Verne, Jules. *Around the World in Eighty Days.* Translated by Sha Di. Beijing: Chinese Youth Press, 1958.

Wagner, Rudolf G. "Lobby Literature: The Archeology and Present Functions of Science Fiction in China." In *After Mao: Chinese Literature and Society, 1978–1981,* edited by Jeffrey Kinkley, 17–62. Cambridge, Mass.: Harvard University Press, 1985.

Wei Yahua. "Wenrou zhixiang de meng" (Conjugal Happiness in the Arms of Morpheus). *Beijing wenxue* (Beijing Literature) (January 1981), Beijing. Its sequel appears in *Yanhe* (Yanhe River) (May–July 1982). Jilin.

Wu Chengen. *Xi you ji* (Journey to the West). Beijing: People's Press, 1954. Translated by W.J.F. Jenner. Beijing: Foreign Language Press, 1982.

Wu Dingbo. "A Brief Survey of Chinese SF." *SF Gems* (April 1981). Japan.

Wu Dingbo, and Patrick D. Murphy, eds. *Science Fiction from China: Eight Stories.* Westport, Conn.: Greenwood Press, 1989.

Xiao Jianheng. "Buke de qiyu" (Pup Buke's Adventures). *Women ai kexue* (We Love Science) (July 1962). Beijing.

———. "Shaluomu jiaoshou de miwu" (Professor Solomon's Delusion). *Renmin wexue* (People's Literature) (December 1980). Beijing.

Xu Dishan. "Tieyu de sai" (Ironfish Gills). 1941. In *Selected Works of Xu Dishan.* Beijing: People's Literature Press, 1958.

Ye Lihua. *Shikong youxi* (The Game of Space and Time). Taipei, Taiwan: Hongfan Press, 1988.

Ye Yandu. *Haitian longzhan* (Dragon Wars in Ocean and Sky). Taipei, Taiwan: Hongfan Press, 1987.

Ye Yonglie. "Fushi" (Corrosion). *Renmin wenxue* (People's Literature) (November 1981). Beijing.

———. *Lun kexue wenyi* (On Scientific Literature and Art). Beijing: Popular Science Press, 1980.

Ye Yonglie, ed. *Zhongwei kexue huanxiang xiaoshuo xishang cidian* (A Dictionary of Understanding Chinese and Foreign Science Fiction). Jinan: Mintian Press, 1991.

Yu Zhi [Ye Zhishan]. "Shizong de gege" (The Missing Elder Brother). *Zhongxuesheng* (High School Student) (July–August 1957). Beijing.

Zhang Xiguo. *Longcheng hujiang* (Heroes in the Dragon City). Taipei, Taiwan: Hongfan Press, 1986.

———. *Wuyudie* (A Five-Jade Plate). Taipei, Taiwan: Hongfan Press, 1983.

———. *Xingyun zuqu* (Nebula Suite). Taipei, Taiwan: Hongfan Press, 1980.

———. *Yequ* (Nocturne). Taipei, Taiwan: Hongfan Press, 1985.

———. *Yiyumao* (A Feather). Taipei, Taiwan: Hongfan Press, 1991.

Zhang Xiguo, ed. *Boundless Love—1988 Best SF*. Taipei, Taiwan: Hongfan Press, 1991.

———. *1984 Best SF*. Taipei, Taiwan: Hongfan Press, 1985.

———. *1985 Best SF*. Taipei, Taiwan: Hongfan Press, 1986.

———. *1986 Best SF*. Taipei, Taiwan: Hongfan Press, 1987.

———. *1987 Best SF*. Taipei, Taiwan: Hongfan Press, 1988.

Zhang Zhan. *Lie zi* (The Book of Lie Zi). Circa 307–313. Translated by A. C. Graham. London: Murray, 1960.

Zhang Zhou. *Chao ye qian zai* (The Complete Records of the Court and Commoners). Circa seventh century C.E.

Zhao Shizhou, ed. *Kehuan xiaoshuo shijia* (Ten Science Fiction Writers). Taiyuan: Bei-yue Literature and Art Press, 1989.

Zhao Zifan. *Feidie zhengkong* (The Flying Saucer Conquers the Sky). Hong Kong: Asia Press, 1956.

———. *Taikong lixian ji* (Adventures in Space). Hong Kong: Asia Press, 1956.

———. *Yueliang shang kan Diqiu* (Watching Earth from the Moon). Hong Kong: Asia Press, 1956.

Zheng Wenguang. "Cong Diqiu dao Huoxing" (From Earth to Mars). Beijing: *Zhongguo shaonian bao* (Chinese Juvenile Daily), 1954.

———. *Feixiang Renmazuo* (Forward Sagittarius). Beijing: People's Literature Press, 1979.

15

Comic Art

JOHN A. LENT

HISTORY AND DEVELOPMENT

Dynastic Precursors

The history of Chinese comic art can be traced back thousands of years through grotesque drawings, serial story pictures, New Year's pictures, and wall paintings. Grotesque figures similar to some contemporary cartoons adorned burial paraphernalia as early as the Yangshao Culture (5000–3000 B.C.E.). One burial jar found in Shaanxi province during that period featured a cartoonlike image of a human face (Li, 1985, 20; qtd. in Liu-Lengyel 1993), and many stone statues and reliefs from the eleventh century B.C.E. represented humans in humorous or satirical ways.

Sarcasm and humor have been interpreted as part of other early stone carvings. One, found in Wuliang Ci, Shandong province, and dating from the Eastern Han Dynasty (147–157 C.E.), portrayed the tyrannical and licentious Jie, last king of the Xia Dynasty, holding a spear while sitting on the shoulders of two women. Liu-Lengyel (1993) claims that the drawing demonstrated, in a humorous manner, the king's negative attitude toward women.

In at least one case, an emperor, Xianzong, made a humorous drawing for political purposes. Entitled, "Keeping Good Terms with Everyone," the brush drawing appeared when Xianzong succeeded his tyrannical father, Yingzong, in 1465; with it, he intended to lighten the people's mood and let them know that a different style of rule was forthcoming. The print showed three men's faces on a common body, giving the impression that they were holding one another. The three portraits were composed in such a way as to form one smiling face (Mu 1991, 36).

Another precursor of comic art is the serial story picture, still common today in China. The tradition of telling a story with cartoonlike illustrations goes back to at least the Western Han Dynasty (206 B.C.E.–25 C.E.). A 1972 excavation found two picture stories on a coffin from that time (Zhu 1990). During the Eastern Han Dynasty, door guards, designed to ward off evil, used pictures of legendary heroes. Serial stories were prominently displayed on stone slabs and frescoes during the sixth and seventh century Wei and Sui dynasties. They were usually interpretations of Buddhist scriptures or biographical sketches of Sak-yamuni (Peng 1980, 2). Those that appeared during the Wei Dynasty were not fully developed as stories; that came about in the Sui Dynasty (Ah Ying 1982).

Other forerunners of the modern serial story pictures can be found during the Song (960–1279) and Yuan (1279–1368) dynasties, when fictional works flourished. Artists were asked to decorate storybooks with illustrations at the tops of the pages. According to one author, the Song Dynasty book paintings had cartoon characteristics (Shi 1989, 12). In the Yuan, Ming (1368–1644), and Qing (1644–1911) dynasties, popular romantic novels carried portraits of the main characters on the front and at the beginning of each chapter (Hwang 1978, 52).

New Year's pictures and wall paintings also have been lumped under comic art. But, it was much later, during the Qing Dynasty, when independent picture stories appeared as New Year's pictures, representing biographies, novels, and even the news. New Year's pictures were usually color prints. Before 1736, they were made up of a single panel or a story spread over several pages. After that, they were usually one page with sixteen, twenty-four, or thirty-two panels, relating stories of legendary heroes and episodes of operas; these were credited with later influencing picture storybooks. The serial wall paintings had similar themes; among the most prominent were the 112 paintings portraying the life of Confucius in the temple at Chu-fu (Hwang 1978, 52).

During the first half of the Qing Dynasty, examples of political satire and caricature were found in the works of painters such as Zhu Da (1626–1705) and Luo Liangfeng (1733–1799). Zhu Da's "Peacocks," made in 1690, showed local government officials as ugly peacocks standing on an unstable, egg-shaped rock as they waited for the emperor to pass by. In "Ghosts' Farce Pictures," Luo mocked ugly human behavior of the Qing Dynasty. Also during the Qing (and the latter Ming) Dynasty, the *nian hua,* the colored wood-block printing, used satire based on historical stories, folklore, current events, birds, and flowers. Popular during the New Year, the prints were put on walls as symbols of luck, or on doors to ward off evil.

The nineteenth century contributed a number of stimuli to the further development of Chinese comic art, contrary to some writers' claims. For example, A. L. Bader believed that China did not have a tradition of caricature before the twentieth century because

The Chinese racial genius has always been for the indirect, for suggestion, for compromising rather than for the outspoken from which caricature stems. Second, caricature demands freedom of expression. . . . Finally, caricature presupposes social and political consciousness in its audience. (Bader 1941, 229)

Cartoonist Fang Cheng said that cartoonists were virtually nonexistent in traditional China because (and here he quoted Lu Xun), "if the emperor was not in the mood to laugh, the slaves were forbidden to laugh" (Hua 1989, 9).

Others would disagree. Writing in 1877, James Parton told of a printer attracted to an American mission in China who brought back a "caricature," dating to the 1840s, showing an English foraging party. Parton believed that the Chinese had been caricaturing for decades:

Caricature, as we might suppose, is a universal practice among them; but, owing to their crude and primitive taste in such things, their efforts are seldom interesting to any but themselves. In Chinese collections, we see numberless grotesque exaggerations of the human form and face, some of which are not devoid of humor and artistic merit. (1877, 196)

Ample evidence of the use of cartoons in the first pictorial magazines and comic and other newspapers that appeared in the nineteenth century would also suggest that Bader and others were off the mark.

Between 1875 and 1911, at least seventy different newspapers and magazines appeared in China, a number of which carried "funnies," "burlesques," "current pictures," or "emblems," all forms of comic art. *Awakened World Pictorial Journal* in Beijing and *Man and Mirror Pictorial* in Tianjin used more caricatures than other periodicals (Lang et al. 1988, 924). Generally, Chinese newspapers and magazines became more appreciative of illustrations, using them in profusion to supplement articles and to focus on current events (Hung 1990, 42).

The first pictorial magazine was *Ying Huan Pictorial* (1877–1880), edited by a Britisher, but more important as an outlet for cartoonists was *Dianshi Studio Pictorial* (Dianshizhai huabao). Started in 1844, it became influential partly because of Wu Youru's drawings recording the decay and political conflicts of the Qing Dynasty. Because Wu's work was done in a realistic fashion, without exaggeration and satire, its categorization as comic art has been questioned. Other pictorials in the latter years of the Qing Dynasty were *Fairy Land Pictorial, Human Rights Pictorial, Wushen Yearly Pictorial, Truly Pictorial, Currents Pictorial, People's Pictorial, Guangdong Vernacular Pictorial Daily, Child's Monthly,* and *Primer Pictorial.*

Parton reported on an English language humor monthly, *Puck,* published in Shanghai in the 1870s. For the most part, the British ridiculed themselves in *Puck,* although occasionally they poked fun at Chinese ceremonies. Some Chinese patriots translated the British self-humor and printed it in anti-British flyers, thus making it appear that the "English barbarians" were criticizing themselves

(Parton 1877, 196). By 1909 the Chinese government had tired of the biting political satire and closed some of the periodicals.

Much like the first comic newspapers, serial pictures also had outside influences, one of which was the tendency to comment on contemporary problems, such as the Boxer movement and the devastating effects of opium on the families of smokers (Hwang 1978, 51). Some of the pictures were disseminated in a format modeled after later Western comic books (Hwang 1978, 53).

Cartoons appeared in flyer form during the patriotic movement of Yi He Tuan (the Boxers) in 1899. Drawn by self-taught cartoonists, the poster-sized cartoons, strategically placed on streets, denounced imperialism and foreign missionary activity. The cartoons contained familiar allusions to folklore and symbolic messages. Later, about the time of the revolts in China during the 1910s, cartoon leaflets drawn by amateurs were dispersed. Because they were done by amateurs and were not published in more permanent places, few remain. One that has survived, entitled, "Do Not Let Us Be Laughed at by the Japanese," implored the Chinese to boycott Japanese imports because of that country's occupation of parts of China.

Revolutionary Cartooning

Although some of the foregoing were press cartoons, the first one to be considered a real political newspaper cartoon appeared in *Russian Issues Alarming News*, December 15, 1903. It showed a map of China being torn apart by a group of animals, each representing a country: The Russian bear ended up with the northeast, the British dog hovered over the center, a French frog occupied a part of northern China, and other animals advanced to grab other parts.

Other political cartoons appeared. In the influential *People's Journal*, published in Japan by Sun Yat-sen's Chinese Alliance and smuggled back into China, numerous cartoons were published, especially in a 1907 issue entitled "Heaven Condemns." High-ranking Chinese officials were depicted in some as snakes or fish. About eighty important political cartoons were published in volume 20 of *Pictorials in the Year of "Wu-shen,"* a series of thirty-six books issued by Shanghai News Publishing House in 1909. The cartoons attacked corrupt and oppressive Qing officials and increased foreign aggression (Liu-Lengyel 1993).

The period around the 1911 revolution spawned a very lively cartoon scene exemplified in the works of He Jianshi (1877–1915), Zhang Yuguang (1885–1968), Ma Xingchi (1888–?), and Qian Binghe (1879–1944).

He Jianshi worked mainly in Guangzhou, although his cartoons also appeared in Shanghai newspapers. From 1905 to 1913, he and others published the *Journal of Current Pictorial,* in which their cartoons brought attention to the maltreatment of Chinese workmen in the United States. When a delegation of Americans, including the president's daughter, visited Guangzhou in 1905, the *Journal of Current Pictorial* cartoonists called upon palanquin carriers not to serve them. He painted a dozen large, anti-American cartoons and posted them in the streets. When one of the cartoons particularly offensive to the Americans was republished in a Hong Kong newspaper, its editor was expelled by British and Hong Kong officials (Jiang 1989).

The painter Zhang Yuguang worked as a cartoonist only from 1909 to 1911, yet his contributions were immeasurable. In one 1911 cartoon, Zhang showed the power-hungry Yuan Shikai, who had usurped the provisional presidency of China, on a rocking horse, implying that, despite his claims to be moving ahead with reforms, Yuan was actually standing in place. This may have been the first contemporary caricature. Zhang also pioneered in social cartooning, doing a number of drawings about the people's miserable living conditions.

As chief editor of Shanghai's *Fairy Land Pictorial,* founded in 1907, Ma Xingchi used the weekly newspaper supplement to point out the people's deplorable lives resulting from the officials' corruption. After 1912 Ma joined a group of cartoonists who contributed to *Truly Pictorial.* One of the techniques Ma employed was the separation of the radicals and components in the Chinese language, thus altering the meanings of the words.

Before and after the revolution, Qian Binghe published cartoons in *Human Rights Pictorial* in Shanghai, as well as the series, ''Old Ape's Hundred Manners,'' first appearing as individual cartoons and later collected in a book of more than 100 works. Using in the title the homonym of the Chinese words for ''ape'' and ''Yuan,'' the latter the family name of the president and self-appointed emperor, Qian made it obvious he did not plan to pull his punches.

A GOLDEN AGE

Influenced by both foreign and domestic factors, Chinese comic art blossomed from about the May 4, 1919, movement through the 1930s, in what must be called its golden age. A group of young cartoonists came onto the scene at a time when the situation bode well for cartooning, with the birth of a number of cartoon and humor periodicals and the development of newspaper supplements with children's pages.

The continuing internal revolutionary struggle provided much artistic fodder for such cartoonists as Dan Duyu (1896–1972), who published his *National Humiliation Pictures Collection,* which attacked the pro-Japanese attitude of the warlord government at about the time of the May 4th movement; Zhang Guangyu (1900–1964), who provided outlets for cartoonists in the fifteen magazines he set up over the years and who was responsible for getting China's leaders used to being caricatured without feeling they were losing face (Chen 1938, 312); Lu Zhiyang (1903–1990); Wang Dunqing (1910–1990); and Ding Song (1891–1972).

Cartoons were in demand during the early 1920s when the Chinese Communist Party was launched and trade unions sprang up to represent the growing working class. The unions took pains to illustrate their propaganda papers, especially with cartoons; many local unions brought out pictorials. The illustrated pages often were posted on walls or distributed as leaflets.

Simultaneously, cartoons were used as the main propaganda vehicle when the peasant associations were formed in the 1920s. Many provincial peasant associations published their own pictorials, abundantly illustrated with cartoons, or used comic art in posters or wall paintings. Early on, Mao Zedong acknowledged the great propaganda value of the peasant drawings, requiring lectures on "revolutionary drawings" as one of the important components of the Peasant Movement Institute's Sixth Session held in May 1926. Out of a curriculum of twenty-four hours, fourteen were given to cartoonist Huang Zhouhua to teach "revolutionary drawings" (Huang 1943, 26).

During the Northern Expedition, artists and cartoonists joined the army as it moved northward from Guangdong, using their skills to expose the decadence and inefficiency of the warlords and to strengthen the anti-imperialist spirit among local masses. Prominent among the army cartoonists was Huang Wennong (?–1934), whose works depicted the gang-up tendencies of the foreign imperialists and Chinese warlords, the devastation wrought by the warlords, and the difficult times experienced by the peasants. By mixing Western and Chinese drawing styles, Huang created his own individualistic approach which changed the way in which cartooning was done in China (Feng 1988, 2).

Mao Zedong used cartoons for propaganda purposes at other times as well. When the Central Revolutionary Base Area (CRBA) was established in Jiangxi province in 1929, and then, the China-Soviet Republic Temporary Central Government, Mao as president of the latter and head of the Red Army, emphasized artistic propaganda. Every army division had newspapers with cartoons, and wall cartoons were plastered everywhere in the CRBA. Cartoons in the CRBA were meant to praise the Communist leadership and Red Army victories, encourage the struggle against the ruling class and imperialist aggression, promote a new life in the CRBA, and propagate the Soviet Union revolution. Most of these works were rather crude and, except in a few instances, such as that of Huang Yuguang, their authors remain anonymous.

The *Shanghai Puck*, started in September 1918, was the first specialized magazine for cartoons. Although it lasted only four issues, succumbing in December 1918, the monthly attracted much public attention with its colorful drawings and well-written text in both Chinese and English. With few exceptions, all the cartoons in *Puck* were drawn by the editor, Shen Pochen (1889–1920), who targeted the Chinese warlords and German and Japanese imperialists.

In 1928 *Shanghai Cartoons* appeared as a weekly made up of color lithographs. Compared to *Shanghai Puck*, which was mainly political cartoons, *Shanghai Cartoons* delved into many genres—social, portrait, political, and series cartoons. Most of the portrait cartoons were done by Zhang Zhengyu; the important series cartoon (similar to comic strips in the United States) was Ye Qianyu's (1907–) "Mr. Wang."

Shanghai Sketch, begun in 1933, increasingly relied on "salacious humor" when political censorship became rampant in the following year (Chen 1938, 311). Other titles were *Modern Sketch, Cartoon Life, Modern Puck, Cartoons of the Times, Independent Cartoons, Time Cartoons,* and *Cartoons in Shanghai.* Some of the cartoon magazines had short lives; the smaller ones lasted only an issue or two before they ran out of money. The longest lived and most influential were *Time Cartoons* and *Cartoon Life.*

Time Cartoons was created as a reaction to the Japanese invasion of Manchuria in 1931, an act that stimulated cartoon activity because of its farcical nature. As one cartoon magazine editor wrote:

This was tragic farce in the grand manner. Adequate comment on it was possible only in the form of caricature. For it meant simply that a vast territory containing thirty million people was occupied because a rail and two sleepers had been damaged by a grenade. The young revolutionary students reacted to this in their demonstrations, artistically in their cartoons. (T. C. Wang qtd. in Chen 1938, 308)

Thus, *Time Cartoons* concentrated on resistance to Japan. Because of its stance, the magazine was fined and suspended in 1936. Consequently, it was forced to change its name (to *Cartoon Circle*) and chief editor. During its short life, *Time Cartoons* acted as the backbone of the cartooning community, publishing the works of about 100 cartoonists, many from remote areas, and teaching drawing skills to cartooning aspirants through correspondence from its chief editor, Lu Shaofei.

Cartoon Life, a monthly founded in 1934 in Shanghai, reflected the leftist ideological perspectives of its editors, Zhang Er (1910–), Huang Shiying, Wu Xilang, and Huang Ding. After one year of publication, *Cartoon Life* was closed by the government. Its replacement, *Cartoon and Life,* also had a short existence, suspended after three months because of governmental charges that it advocated class struggle, opposed the government, and promoted the October Revolution in the Soviet Union. The most active cartoonists for *Cartoon Life* and its clone were Zhang Er and Cai Ruohong (1910–), both members of the Leftist Artists Federation.

All of the main magazines were concentrated in Shanghai, which in the 1930s sported twenty titles. With circulations of as much as 40,000, the cartoon magazines were designed primarily for men because they indulged in some ''Elizabethan coarseness.'' One source reported, ''There is necessarily a certain amount of eroticism, influenced to a great extent by such journals as the American *Esquire,* but with an element of quite Chinese abandon'' (Chen 1938, 311).

Other outlets for cartoonists were provided by major journals, such as the *Eastern Miscellany* (Dongfang zazhi), *Analects* (Lun yu), and *Cosmos Wind* (Yuzhou feng), magazines which increased their solicitation of cartoons, and newspapers which added special cartoon sections. Thus, cartoons became a regular offering of nearly all publications (Hung 1990, 42).

The supplements that appeared in Chinese dailies by the 1930s occasionally included a children's page. North China dailies particularly sported the children's page, starting with Tientsin's *Social Welfare,* which had a Sunday children's page on July 2, 1929, followed by *Da Gong Bao* of the same city, which featured its "Kid's Weekly," beginning in 1930. Later that year, *Da Gong Bao* carried a half-page children's section daily. *Peiping Press* and *Peiping Social Welfare* also devoted a weekly page to children. All of these sections were successful, attracting women and children to their photographs, illustrations, poetry, essays, and, of course, cartoons (Cheng 1931, 103–4).

By the early 1930s, a group of young artists, some with strong political ideas, others a bit rebellious about traditional Chinese art, had already coalesced around the newly popularized genre of cartoons. In less than a generation preceding World War II, they had established the first cartoon associations, exhibitions, and training institutes, and had created comic strip characters who lived on for generations.

Four of them—Huang Wennong, Zhang Guangyu (1900–1964), Ding Song, and Wang Dunqing—founded the first cartoon society, Cartoon Association (Manhua hui), in 1927. The eleven-member group was an important rallying force for the profession, providing an esprit de corps and establishing a standard name (*manhua*) for their craft, even though other names (especially *katun*) were used well into the late 1930s. Headquartered in Shanghai, the association had as its purposes defining the social functions of cartoons and advocating them to society; exchanging artistic ideas and improving skills through seminars, exhibitions, and publications such as selected cartoon collections and the society's journal, *Shanghai Cartoons;* and organizing and training cartoonists.

Other cartoonist organizations were set up before World War II, including Cartoon Study Association (Manhua yanjiuhui) and Cartoon Service, the latter in Shanghai with Wang Wen-lung as head. Commenting about the Cartoon Service in 1931, one writer said:

In recent years, cartoons in newspapers have aroused a great deal of interest among painters and artists. A number of large papers of the port cities have used cartoons with good result. It is understood that the present organization is formed so as to make it easy for artists and newspapers to communicate with one another along the line of patronage and service. ("Cartoons" 1931, 101)

In the spring of 1937, the cartoonists organized a national association, China National Cartoonist Association, based in Shanghai with branches in Guangzhou, Xian, Wenzhou, and Hong Kong. The association's goals were to establish an annual national exhibition, a seasonal professional journal (*Cartoon's Friend*), regular training sessions, an annual cartoon award, a small research library, a loan scheme for cartoonists, and tours and lodging arrangements for visiting cartoonists.

The first national exhibition of cartoons was held in Shanghai in late 1936. Sponsored by *Time Cartoons* and *Cartoons in Shanghai,* it drew more attention than any preceding art show in the country. The critics, nevertheless, still had difficulties recognizing comic art, calling the exhibition "a small means of cutting up insects," or, in other words, inconsequential art (Chen 1938, 308). About 600 cartoons were shown first in Shanghai, and then in Nanjing, Suzhou, Hangzhou, and southern locations.

Another indication of the rise of cartooning as a profession was the establishment of training and correspondence schools, the two most famous of which were China First Art School (Zhongguo diyi huashe) and China Cartoon Correspondence School (Zhonghua manhua hanshou xuexiao), which, developed by Hu Kao, consisted of junior and senior classes. Usually, the courses were of six months' duration (Hung 1990, 43).

Pioneering in the cartoon field certainly did not provide much financial maneuverability; in the words of one cartoonist, they were offered "poverty and hard knocks" for their efforts (Chen 1938, 308). Jack Chen, who followed the destinies of what he called the original group of ten cartoonists (himself included), reported that one died without enough money for his own funeral, one joined the government, one "disappeared after publishing a particularly pointed anti-Kuomintang cartoon, six managed to hold together, to be joined by a seventh who has been in hiding for four years" (1938, 308). When the seven remaining cartoonists met at the home of their dead friend, only three had steady jobs, making about $50 gold a month, and another $50 for extra work. Chen said they were the best paid cartoonists in China.

Some characteristics of the early cartoonists that marked them as different were their political consciousness and their sense of realism. Describing them in 1938, Chen wrote:

They do not as a group belong to any particular political party, but represent in the main the interests of the young nationally conscious intelligentsia, and they are typical of China's revolutionary students. Not one of them is over forty. The vast majority of them are in their teens or late twenties. They are all former or parttime students, newspaper men, teachers, commercial artists, clerks. There are surprisingly few with a natural inclination for purely salacious humor; and ninety-nine per cent are animated by a sincere desire to save their country from colonial subjugation. This I stress, because the general level of political and national consciousness of Chinese artists is low. And it is a fact that there is not one avowedly reactionary cartoonist. *En masse* they are anti-imperialist, anti-feudalist. The sympathies are all with the underdog. (1938, 308)

Chen added that they showed "utter disregard" for the traditions of classical Chinese art and ridiculed the "old-fashioned 'bird and bamboo' painters and those would-be Westerners who 'spent their time with nudes and apples' " (308).

Few of them were true revolutionaries; instead, they were artists who wanted to express their feelings about the "grim reality of China" (311). In that sense, they *were* revolutionary because, as realists, they broke from the essence of Chinese art which was to strive for harmony with nature. According to Chen,

The young art of these militant young cartoonists marks a momentous, a revolutionary, change. They take Nature (or the Established Order of Things) by the forelock and give her a good walloping in order to make her behave. (311)

Among famous Chinese cartoonists with roots in the 1920s and 1930s were Feng Zikai (1898–1975), Ye Qianyu (1907–), Zhang Leping (1910–1992), and Hua Junwu.

Called the "founder and the unequalled master of the Chinese lyrical cartoon," Feng Zikai contributed much in the way of theory and technique to the new field through scores of books (at least twenty on art theory alone) and countless drawings. In fact, the term *manhua* (a direct translation of the Japanese *manga*) was first applied to his work by Zheng Zhenduo, when his "Zikai manhua" appeared in the impressive literary journal, *Wenxuezhoubao* (Literary Review) in 1925. The word has since entered the Chinese vocabulary as a synonym for cartoon. Previous to that, Feng had studied in Japan and taught high school.

Feng is credited with giving cartoons much needed respect because he contributed regularly to prestigious literary journals and influential dailies of the 1920s. His "Zikai manhua" was extremely popular because of its portrayal of "lovable, mischievous children" in an original style that combined the traditional Chinese brush technique with contemporary social settings, humor, and religious messages (Hung 1990, 46–47). He also introduced an important new genre into modern Chinese image literature with his literary comic strips based on the best modern Chinese literature.

Early on, Feng liked to combine poetry with his cartoons, which he wanted to be thought provoking and enlightening, a "highly reflective piece of art" (Hung 1990). Yet, he also insisted that the drawings be based on real experiences, focusing on what he saw in the streets and the happenings around him, and that they be plain, "humanly and morally constructive," and working-class affordable. As Christopher Harbsmeier explained, he was overlooked by Western connoisseurs because he "refused to work for the learned few" (1984, 10). As a result, he sought to be outside traditional Chinese art, which he found "elitist, esoteric, morally irrelevant and philosophically sterile" (Harbsmeier 1984, 9).

Influenced by the politicization of art in the 1930s, Feng moved from idyllic children's cartoons to social cartoons, although his work was never "ephemerally political" like that of his contemporaries. In fact, Feng's "social realism" was not really political, but rather artistic. His indignation at the social injustices and atrocities of the day can be compared to that of a powerless child (Harbsmeier 1984, 31).

By the time Ye Qianyu was twenty-one years old, he had a popular comic strip, "Mr. Wang" (Wangxiansheng), four to eight panels built around a "triangular-headed, middle-class philistine, proud possessor of all the typical Chinese vices" (Chen 1938, 312), a character similar to David Low's "Colonel Blimp." Dealing with the sensations of modern urban life—luxury, gluttony, deceit, pleasure seeking—the strip debuted in 1928 in *Shanghai Cartoons* (Shanghai manhua), switched to *Time Pictorial* in 1930 when *Shanghai Cartoons* merged with that periodical, and from 1934 to 1937, appeared in *Time Cartoons.*

Educated by "street-wise eclecticism," Ye went on to innovate as a painter of landscapes, actors, dancers, and the beauty of China's minority peoples. When he began as a cartoonist in 1927, he "holed up in a damp Shanghai shack, [from which] he cranked out one cartoon after another to meet editors' deadlines ("55 Years" 1982, 26). Ye described his work during that time: "Although I was motivated more by need than artistic fulfillment, I learned how to pick out that tell-tale trait that gives life to a character—and how to make my audience laugh or cry over it" ("55 Years" 1982, 26).

One of the longest lived comic strip characters in Asia was created during China's golden age. "Sanmao" (three hairs), the story of a vagabond waif, came from Zhang Leping's pen in 1935 and lasted into contemporary times. Originally, the strip featured Sanmao's attempts to eke out an existence on the streets of Shanghai, taking jobs as a shoeshine boy, restaurant worker, and even an unwilling pickpocket. By 1947 Sanmao was in the army, during which time the strip aimed at showing the backwardness and shortcomings of the military life with a view that the government had to take action. After 1949 Sanmao was shown as a bright, studious lad interested in scientific experiments (Peng 1980, 2) and as a precocious teacher, imploring his friends not to smoke, be selfish, or to show off ("Vagabond" 1982, 32).

Born into a lower-class family, Zhang was disturbed early in his life by the economic and social ills caused by the powerful. He vented his anger while working on the Shanghai daily, *Xiao chen kan,* where he developed "Sanmao." (In 1946, the strip began to appear in *Da gong bao.*) Without any formal art training, he had become a legend by the age of twenty-five, expressing the feelings of the abandoned street children in a style that often attacked social injustices.

Zhang's popularity helped lay the foundation for the recognition of cartoons as a serious art form. He, like other cartoonists of the era, showed disdain for artists who looked down upon cartooning as a low art meant for the masses. The very reason he chose the cartoon as his medium, he said, was "because, unlike many highbrow art forms, it can get directly at the heart of the masses" ("Vagabond" 1982, 32). One critic described Zhang's craftsmanship as "a style which, while remaining deceptively simple in conception and organization, permits the artist to incorporate into his work both obnoxious and inconspicuous facets of the experience of the man in the street—thus touching viewers with the relevance of art to life" ("Vagabond" 1982, 32).

Hua Junwu started drawing cartoons in 1934, when he was nineteen years old. Like some of his contemporaries, he was influenced by foreign cartoonists, such as the German E. O. Plauen and the Russian Sapajou, both appreciated in China at the time. While fighting against the Japanese, Hua realized that the peasants did not understand his cartoons, and accordingly, he changed his style and content to that of a folk artist (Hua 1984, 7–8).

Still another important cartoonist of this era was Wang Yao, creator of one of the most popular cartoon characters of the 1930s, "Mr. Willie Buffoon," noted for his big nose and equally big heart.

Apparently, cartooning as a profession was maturing by the 1930s, as many cartoonists, such as Huang Ding, Feng Zikai, Zhang Er, Huang Shiying, Wang Dunqing, Wang Zimei, Huang Miaozi (1913–), and Huang Mao (1917–), explored its history, conceptualized its theories, and discussed its basic components—characters, definitions, types, appreciation, and presentation (Bi and Huang 1986, 103).

Huang Mao said that cartoons had to concentrate on reality and politics, exaggeration and defamation, and satire and exposure, but they also should praise bright aspects of a subject or society. Feng Zikai, in the preface of his collection, wrote at the time that his works were neither decorative nor recreational, but recorded all unharmonious and unlovely behaviors of humans. A noncartoonist, the ideologist and revolutionary, Lu Xun (1881–1936), in his concern for all forms of art and culture, defined the requirements of cartoons and cartoonists and studied and introduced cartoons from other countries. He thought cartoons should attack society's sicknesses and reflect the views of the masses concerning trends, honestly show political reality, and base exaggeration upon honest observations (Jiang 1989, 187–88), while the cartoonist should have "progressive spirit and noble characters."

"CARTOON WARFARE"

As Japanese imperialism threatened throughout the 1930s, Chinese cartoonists spent even more time contemplating the role of the cartoon. Should it be a commercial product, an art form, an agent for social change, or a propaganda tool to resist aggression?

Most cartoonists chose the last role and for the next eight years, as individuals or in groups, they waged incessant cartoon warfare against the Japanese, moving about the country as they "etched cartoons on walls, published sketches in newspapers, and organized exhibitions to denounce the Japanese invasion and the imperialism of Western powers" ("Vagabond" 1982, 32).

Obviously, they were not sure for awhile. Bader, writing in 1941, said the Chinese tried to appease the Japanese until July 1937, forbidding artists from portraying a recognizable Japanese face or to use the words "Japan" or "Japanese" in their cartoons. Instead, the artists used symbols and subtle messages (Bader 1941, 233). After undeclared war broke out in the north and spread southward in late summer 1937, a new type of caricature appeared, more direct, Western, realistic, and powerful as an educative agent. "There is a violence, a grotesquely terrible quality about some of it, indicative of the strong feeling of both artists and audience" (Bader, 1941, 233).

Much credit for the change in style and emphasis must go to the National Salvation Cartoon Propaganda Corps. The corps adopted three major themes: Japanese brutality, imperialistic greed, and Chinese traitors (*han jian*). Discussing cartoon portrayals of Japanese brutality, Bader said:

Many of these can be called caricature only in the sense that Goya's realistic etchings of the Spanish civil war are so called. Some are entirely without the distortion that is the hallmark of caricature; others show a grotesque distortion of face and figure to express fear, hatred, pain and rage. All, however, are calculated to arouse hatred of the invader. (1941, 233–34)

Caricature attacking Japanese imperialism was more symbolic, according to Bader (234). The cartoonists drew Chinese who aided the Japanese as puppets, in one instance, showing a Chinese minister of communications playing on the floor with toy planes and boats.

The Japanese countered with their own propaganda cartoons, which tried to convince the Chinese that the Japanese conquest was beneficial to them (Bader 1941, 240). One cartoonist, Ding Cong, told how he and his colleagues took care of such propaganda: "We would sneak out at night, rip down posters put up by the Japanese troops, change them subtly so they poked fun at the Japanese, and then stick them up again" (WuDunn 1990, 2).

The most prominent anti-Japanese cartoonist was Feng Zikai, who, throughout the war, nurtured a belief that art and propaganda were irreconcilable. Hung Chang-Tai explained that intellectually, Feng, who abhorred war, was reluctant to paint propaganda cartoons, while emotionally, he realized they were useful and needed (Hung 1990, 67). Feng much preferred to draw what he called reflective (*ganxiang manhua*), rather than satirical (*fengci manhua*) or propaganda (*xuanchuan manhua*) cartoons. He felt that reflective cartoons touched a common chord between artist and reader and that they were the "most artistic" of all cartoons (Hung 1990, 65).

Feng's anti-Japanese cartoons materialized after his hometown was attacked in November 1937, and he and his family had to flee. The following March, Feng joined the All-China Resistance Association of Writers and Artists, becoming an editorial board member of the group's *Literature and Art of the War of Resistance* (Kangzhan wenyi). He produced cartoons and calligraphy for this journal, as well as for other periodicals (notably *Cosmos Wind*) and newspapers.

Hung described Feng's explicit cartoons concerning the war (1990, 55). On the surface, Feng Zikai's wartime cartoons resemble many of his contemporaries' works. He portrayed Japanese brutality, ridiculed traitors, depicted soldiers leaving for the front, painted the ruins caused by the war, and demonstrated the people's determination to defend their nation. He was set on recording the bestialities of aggression and the ensuing human suffering. In his wartime cartoons, the tragic parting of mother and child was a recurrent theme. Feng's wartime cartoons have been described as more than just pictorial documents of the time; they were statements condemning war as an "irremediable crime against humanity" (Hung 1990, 69).

Complementing individual efforts, such as those of Feng Zikai, were the various cartoonist associations' activities to deter the Japanese. Perhaps chief among these was the National Salvation Cartoon Propaganda Corps (Jiuwang manhua xuanchuandui), started in Shanghai in August 1937. The corps believed the country needed "cartoon warfare" (*manhua zhan*) to bring patriotic and anti-Japanese messages to the people (Hung 1990, 43). According to B. F. Chu, the group originally was made up of eleven cartoonists, most from the School of Fine Arts at Wuchang (1938, 72). Seven of them remained in Shanghai, and two each went to Guangzhou and Xian. Another source said that, after a month, the other seven left for Nanjing when Chinese troops withdrew from Shanghai. Later, they moved to Hankow and became part of the Political Department of the Military Affairs Commission (Hung 1990, 44).

After interviewing scores of Chinese cartoonists, many of whom were active during the war, Hongying Liu-Lengyel gave a slightly different version of the corps' development and structure. Her sources said that the Chinese Cartoonist Association organized the Shanghai Cartoonist Salvation Society (SCSS) in July 1937; after that city fell to the Japanese, the SCSS secretly organized the Cartoonist Propaganda Team (CPT), which shifted to Nanjing, and then to Wuhan, Changsa, Shangrao, and Chongqing. The CPT's main tasks were to make people aware of the meaning of the anti-Japanese war, to inspire spirit in the army, and to organize cartoonists everywhere to join the resistance.

Liu-Lengyel's sources said that the CPT had eight members when it left Shanghai in late August 1937; two others joined when the CPT arrived in Nanjing. Altogether, the CPT had eighteen members during its three years of operations: Ye Qianyu (team leader), Zhang Leping, Te Wei, Hu Kao, Liang Baibo, Xuan Wenjie, Zhang Ding, Lu Zhixiang, Tao Moji, Tao Jinji, Liao Bingxiong, Ye Gang, Mai Fei, Huang Mao, Zhang Xiya, Liao Weilin, Zhou Lingzhao, and Xi Yuqun.

Although small in number, the group was persistent in its propaganda pursuit. In its first year and a half, its members drew more than 1,000 scrolls and wartime cartoons, plastering them "on the walls along the streets, on posts, on banners carried by the numerous war service groups, in newspapers and magazines" (Chu 1938, 73). They also printed flyers that were air dropped over enemy lines to encourage safe surrenders.

While still in Shanghai, the corps published *Salvation Cartoons,* a journal that appeared every five days with contributions from thirty cartoonists spread throughout China. Very popular among cartoonists and the general public, *Salvation Cartoons* was published in other places such as Nanjing, Hankou, Guangzhou, and Hong Kong. By the time the CPT moved to Wuhan in October 1937, it was publishing a successor to *Salvation Cartoons,* called *Anti-War Cartoons.*

Cartoonists elsewhere were active in anti-Japanese campaigns. In Wuhan, the National Cartoonist Association organized the Wartime Executive Committee in early 1938, with tasks somewhat similar to those of the CPT. Wuhan also produced a few outlets for anti-Japanese cartoons, including *Xinhua Daily*—which carried daily political cartoons and whose art editor was the cartoonist Hu Kao—*In-Battle Pictorial, Fighting Pictorial,* and, of course, *Anti-War Cartoons.* After the Japanese occupation of Wuhan, the center of cartooning shifted to Guilin. There, the CPT held exhibitions and training sessions, while the National Woodcut Association and National Cartoonist Association published *Cartoon and Woodcut.*

Members of the Sichuan Cartoon Society made personal tours or staged street cartoon exhibitions in Chengdu and Kunmin, while in Xian the National Cartoonist Association branch held exhibitions and conducted training programs. Chongqing, which became an important city during the war, harbored about thirty cartoonists who had fled Shanghai and Wuhan. Hampered by publication censorship, these cartoonists resorted to using exhibitions as a means of getting across messages. The largest and most impressive of many was the Joint Cartoon Exhibition, a year-long affair launched in March 1945.

As cartoonists retreated southward with the advancement of the Japanese, cartooning became important in those areas. By 1938 the South China Branch of the National Cartoonist Association (NCA) had been founded in Guangzhou; its chief efforts were the publication of eight cartoon magazines and several collections. When Guangzhou was lost in 1939, the cartoonists moved to Hong Kong, where they established an NCA branch, staged an anti-Japanese exhibit, and set up training classes.

Through all the different areas, cartoonists seemed to agree that, during wartime, their work should wage ''cartoon warfare'' by building up hatred for the Japanese with cartoons that could be understood by the masses.

MAOIST CARTOONS

Mao Zedong recognized the importance of art to serve the millions in his speech at the 1942 Yanan Cultural Forum. Specifying the aims of propaganda art, he said, ''For the revolutionary artists, the only target to be aimed at is the aggressors, exploiters, oppressors, and the bad influences among our people, but never at our people themselves per se.'' Satire was needed too, Mao said, delineating the types of satire. The cartoonists understood that, in the 1940s, while conflicts with internal and external foes existed, the most important cartooning was that which dealt with enemies.

Between 1946 and 1949, a number of influential cartoonists returned to Shanghai, remaking it the cartoon capital of China. Because the Kuomintang did not permit the launching of newspapers other than those of old, the cartoonists started new magazines. These became the major outlets for a number of cartoonists, including many non-Communists, to ridicule the civil war, dictatorship, persecutions by the Kuomintang, inflation, and national traitors.

The cartoonists faced many hardships, such as lack of materials and the oppressive control of the government. In Kuomintang-occupied areas, the artists had to resort to exhibitions and underground publications for their works. In Shanghai, a Cartoon Worker-Student Group (CWSG) was secretly set up in 1946 to train young people in cartooning skills. Shen Tongheng, Ding Cong, Mi Gu (1918–1986), Hong Huang, and other famous cartoonists instructed from 40 to 100 teachers, art students, workers, and salespeople once a month. The group published a small journal of the students' works.

When the Kuomintang government closed all periodicals leaning toward the Communist Party in the summer of 1947, the CWSG participated in an underground Cartoon Monthly Exhibition that toured the country. The first exhibit, completely done by CWSG members, ridiculed United States aid to China and the National People's Congress of the ruling party. After six weeks of touring, the exhibit was disrupted by the government, which arrested three students and destroyed several of the cartoons.

The cartoonists were not deterred. After each of numerous bloody confrontations between the government and students and other strikers, amateur cartoonists blasted the Kuomintang or the civil war itself.

Leading art theoretician Wang Zhaowen, in a series of articles in 1950–1951, spelled out the official line on cartooning after the 1949 revolution. He wrote, in a 1950 *Guangming Ribao* article, that it was the sacred duty of cartoonists to use cartoons as vehicles of propaganda, and that this sacred duty included invoking hatred for the enemy in the Korean War and strengthening the determination for victory. "Cartoons must be directed towards mass thought," Wang said.

That same year, Wang advocated in the *People's Daily* that cartoons be varied in style and lively; he complained bitterly about the tendency toward standardization of all cartoonists' styles. He said that the twin tasks of the cartoonists were to sing the praise of the correct line and to attack the public enemy. In 1951 Wang wrote "We Need Children's Cartoons," an article that held up the work of Feng Zikai as a model. He also cautioned that the cartoonists should not imitate all of Feng's work because some of it was escapist, pessimistic, "old-fashioned humanism" (Harbsmeier 1984, 36–38).

Basically, after 1949, cartoonists were barred from ridiculing life in the new China and were coached to serve the political struggle and to jab at China's foreign enemies. Cartoons and cartoon magazines were not as plentiful as previously; some of the problems cartoonists lampooned had been obliterated by the Communists. One cartoon magazine wrote, "The crazy dictator and his shameless greedy running dogs have offered us innumerable subjects for cartoon drawing," but they were no longer around (Shi 1989, 14).

The cartoon pioneers adapted to the new environment. Zhang Leping became vice president of the Shanghai Artists Associations, and Ye Qianyu began lecturing at Peiping College of Art, where, in the 1950s, he gained national renown as a painter and propagandist for the Communist Party. Although Feng Zikai was trotted out as a model by Wang Zhaowen in 1951, he admitted to being ill equipped for indoctrination cartooning. In his public self-criticism, forced on many leading intellectuals, he said the sins of his past were his aestheticism, concern for wealth and fame, defense of the purity and independence of art, old-fashioned humanism, and an apolitical nature (Harbsmeier 1984, 36–37). His public responsibilities increased greatly during the next dozen years. In 1960 he was appointed head of the Institute of Chinese Painting in Shanghai, and two years later he was elected president of the Shanghai branch of the Chinese Artists' Association. He soon realized there was no place in China for his type of cartooning and writing, and between 1961 and 1965, he turned to translation work.

Feng, like other cartoonists, faced a bleak situation during the Cultural Revolution. Criticized from 1966 onward as a bourgeois intellectual, he was treated cruelly, and at the time of his death in 1975 he was still humiliated and embittered (Harbsmeier 1984, 40). Other cartoonists faced a similar fate. As part of the intelligentsia, they were called "stinky number nine" or antirevolutionaries, forbidden to do any cartoons, and banished to the remote countryside.

Zhang Leping was criticized as a "black cartoonist," his "Sanmao" as a "poisonous weed" advocating the bourgeois theory of human nature (Di 1991). Red Guards ransacked his apartment and ordered him to tear up early Sanmao cartoons. For his uncompromising views on art, Ye Qianyu was jailed for seven years; Ding Cong, labeled a rightist, had already served ten years by the time the Cultural Revolution started. Altogether, he was imprisoned for twenty-two consecutive years, during which time he did not draw a line (WuDunn 1990, 20). Hong Huang said he was not allowed to draw for eight years, two before and six during the Cultural Revolution. One cartoon he drew before the Cultural Revolution, which criticized young people sleeping on the job, resulted in an investigation of him (interview 1991).

The Cultural Revolution also had serious effects upon one of China's favorite ideological tools, *lien huan hua* (serial pictures). Having survived for centuries, *lien huan hua* had incorporated modern media by 1949, appearing as series of movie stills with captions, animated stills of marionette film, stage photographs on hand-drawn pictures adopted from famous stage plays and revolutionary Beijing operas, sketches based on *People's Daily* reports, and prints from woodcuts, paper cuts, traditional black-and-white sketches, and color sketches (Hwang 1978, 56).

Between 1949 and 1963, 12,700 different titles of *lien huan hua* were published, and more than 560 million copies were circulated. The numbers had increased quickly during those years, from 670 titles and 21 million copies in 1952, to 2,300 titles and more than 100 million copies in 1957 (Chiang 1959). The themes of these books changed from those concerning gods, ghosts, kings,

ministers, scholars, and beauties, to "praising the Party, Chairman Mao, socialism, heroes of the new era, workers, peasants,.and soldiers" (Ma Ke 1963).

During the Cultural Revolution, "revisionist, black" literary themes and subjects were further expunged, especially those considered anti-Mao, and the number of titles was shaved dramatically, to fewer than 150 in 1972 (Hwang 1978,
55–56). Nevertheless, *lien huan hua* remained popular in China despite the Cultural Revolution. In the early 1970s, as many as 7 million copies sold in Heilongjiang province alone, and the Beijing and Shanghai art institutes were
responsible for yearly outputs of 30 and 16 million copies, respectively (Moritz
1973, 9). As today, they were available at bookstores, libraries, schools, factory
cafeterias, department stores, military barracks, village markets, post offices, bus
terminals, and fruit stands. The usual press run was 1 million copies, although
some had as many as 10 million in first edition.

Their popularity has been attributed to their readability and their contents
(Nebiolo 1973). Picture storybooks have been based on children's stories, fairy
tales, stories of animals, adaptations of foreign books, and ancient legends (Peng
1980, 3). Exemplifying their emphasis on messages of loyalty, humble self-
sacrifice, and attendance to duty, Fredric A. Moritz cited *Twenty-Four Tales of
Filial Piety,* a picture storybook about a young boy who lowers his body onto
the ice to melt a hole to enable his starving father to fish (1973, 9).

Generally, John C. Hwang has categorized the subject matter of *lien huan
hua* as "serial pictures which mold the heroic image of the proletariat," "serial
pictures dealing with Chinese Communist revolutionary history and contemporary reconstruction campaigns," those based on traditional folklore (not very
popular since the Cultural Revolution), and those "dealing with the history of
the international Communist movements and struggles" (1978, 58–59).

Throughout most of their recent history, they have functioned to create images
of proletarian heroes; ensure the victory of the proletariat; protect communism;
extol Mao's virtues; praise young people who go to the countryside to work;
criticize feudalistic, bourgeois, and revisionist ideologies; raise class consciousness; and criticize "revisionist, black" literature (Sung 1974). *Lien huan hua*
have consistently reflected contemporary party policies, have incorporated an
extensive feedback mechanism, and have been the collective products of teams
of artists and writers working in a "Three-in-one union" of the "concrete leadership" of the party and the cooperation of professional and amateur artists
(Hwang 1978, 63).

The artists have worked under strict guidelines that stipulated the use of captions, not balloons (because captions allow for more narrative information, while
balloons are less aesthetic), the emphasis on many close-ups of hero/heroine,
and the centering of the main character in the pictures. Other rules have required
portraying enemies of the masses with sinister looks, drawing scenes and minor
characters to serve the main proletarian hero/heroine, and employing graphic
devices of contrast to reflect the relationship between the hero/heroine and the
enemy (Hwang 1978, 66–67).

A REBIRTH: 1976–1989

Comic art flowered again during the liberalization period after Mao's death. The topics and approaches broadened, although they still conformed to party campaigns; old-timers reappeared among cartoonists; and more outlets for comic art became available.

Mao's death and the fall of the Gang of Four fostered a comic art environment that was called the "most vivid" and "vicious" since 1949. One source wrote that some of the cartoons had become sensationalistic, "occasionally slipping into a sexual ribaldry that seemingly had little to do with the crimes or political issues then at hand" ("Sketching China's Scoundrels" 1983, 52). The peak of this freedom was reached during the "Beijing Spring" of 1979, when cartoonists such as Miao Yintang and Bi Keguan even hit out at the central contradictions of the Communist order.

After 1979, a chill set in that somewhat hindered cartooning. Cartoons were criticized for not being liberalized, for lacking innovativeness, and for using too many words in captions. The Twelfth Congress of the Chinese Communist Party, meeting in September 1982, strengthened some controls that affected cartoonists.

Most cartoonists hit, as they do today, topics already singled out for ridicule by party officials. Ian Findlay wrote that cartoonists, like other artists, stumbled along with the Chinese crises (1984, 108). Although their concerns broadened after 1976, most cartoonists drew their inspiration from the "officially sponsored political, social and economic campaigns, such as the fall of the Gang of Four, the Four Modernisations, and movement against 'spiritual pollution' and the negative influences of the West" (Findlay 1984, 108; see also "China Draws upon Humour" 1987, 53). They also concentrated on consumerism, adulteration of food and wine, logging, the ill-mannered, disrespectful young Chinese males who imitated Westerners (especially in works by Zuo Chuan and Tan Guquan), and materialism (especially in works by Xu Zhiqing and Tian Youkang).

Other social problems not satirized previously became fair game, the purposes of which were to show the people the errors of their ways and to give reasons for the lack of progress (Findlay 1984, 108). Singled out were the bureaucracy and intelligentsia. For example, Hua Junwu's "Fate of Efficiency" (1979) showed cadres moving at a snail's pace.

Although there were no written guidelines for cartoonists during most of this time, unspoken rules, such as not caricaturing contemporary leaders, existed that, if broken, led to trouble (Findlay 1984, 108). Later, even the regulation concerning caricatures of present-day leaders did not seem to apply. In August 1986, *Liberation Daily* ran caricatures of Deng Xiaoping, and avid bridge player, wielding a fistful of cards marked, "Chinese-style modernization," and Hu Yaobang, shown as a conductor of music over a caption that read, "Comrade Yaobang leads us in a new song" ("Look Who're Cartoon Characters" 1986, 6).

Throughout the 1980s then, cartoonists such as Zhang Qingguo, Wang Shuchen, and Hua Junwu continued to hit out at social and political issues, while others preferred more subtle approaches, playing on double meanings of words, subtle morals, and much symbolism. Their favorite subjects were bribery, favoritism, paternalism, and modernization.

A master at using subtlety in his work is Ding Cong, called a political cartoonist who never raises the topic of politics. Since his rehabilitation in 1979, Ding has been a prolific cartoonist, having turned out ten books of cartoons. Ironically, his works are rarely used in the official national newspapers despite the fact that he is one of the country's most popular cartoonists (WuDunn 1990, 2). Another source said that Ding's works were published regularly in *People's Daily* before 1989 (Liu-Lengyel 1993). His drawings have layers of meanings, avoid portraying current leaders explicitly, and draw on allusions to ancient history to illustrate contemporary points. WuDunn called his work "slippery," stating that "sometimes, the political zap is so veiled that a political explanation seems far-fetched, but Mr. Ding's background is rooted in politics and many of his cartoons have a bitter edge. To Mr. Ding, cartooning is wedded to politics" (1990, 2).

Ding said that, in China, "[A]ll cartoons are political. To be a cartoonist, if you want to satirize something, it's political. But because our social climate is not so good, there are not many political cartoons these days" (WuDunn 1990, 2). To accomplish his type of satire, Ding spends "days and days" thinking about what to draw and being extremely cautious in the process. "As soon as you look at a cartoon, one meaning jumps out at you immediately. But if you draw so that the real satire can be seen right away, ah, then you're finished" (WuDunn 1990, 2).

Ding's cautionary tendency is shared by many Chinese cartoonists who are taking a wait-and-see attitude, especially after the Tiananmen events, but also because of a long tradition of unsteadiness in the cartooning profession, much of it attributable to various governments' curtailment of freedom of expression.

REFERENCE WORKS

A rather large body of literature (most of which is in Chinese) exists concerning comic art in China. However, more general references are few. For example, no separate bibliography on Chinese cartoons is known, although a section of about 130 items in John A. Lent's forthcoming four-volume, worldwide comic art bibliography treats China. At least three dictionaries have appeared. Jiang Yihai compiled a dictionary of Chinese cartoon knowledge, which has been criticized for its many errors. Lang Shaojun, et al., and Yu Cheng, et al., brought out dictionaries on Chinese paintings and humor, respectively; both have implications for comic art.

Among theoretical books, imprints by Feng Zikai, some dating to the 1930s, set the standard concerning the purposes and styles of cartoons. Lent's forthcoming bibliography lists twenty-six Feng books on topics such as his selected essays, children's sketches, Yuanyuan Studio, painting and literature, methods, history of Western art, and art and national development. Feng's contemporary, Huang Mao, published another early theory book, *On Cartoon Art* (1943), which described the functions of cartoons during wartime. More recent studies in this realm were those done by Hong Shi, Li Jia, Miu Yintang, and Mo Ce. Fang Cheng has written books on amusement and humor, the art of laughing, and humor, satire, and cartoons.

History and biography were favorite topics of some writers. Christopher Harbsmeier wrote an excellent biography of Feng Zikai, discussing how changes in his life affected his cartoons. This is one of the few in-depth treatments of Chinese cartoonists in the English language. Hung Chang-Tai analyzed Feng's wartime cartoons, and Feng Yiyin, et al., compiled his biography. Mu Hui talked about the precursors of comic art in the Ming dynasty; Jack Chen, the militant cartoons of the 1930s; A. L. Bader and James Parton, early caricature; Yu Yueting, the *Dianshi Studio Pictorial;* Cheng Chi, Hwang; Fredric A. Moritz, serial pictures from earliest times to the Mao era; and Chiang Wei-pu and Peng Shan, the history of picture books. Other historical treatments of Chinese cartooning are found in Fu Chen and Wang Wang, Hong Kong Institute for Promotion of Chinese Culture, Bi Keguan and Huang Yuanlin, R. Croizier, and Wang Bomin.

Chinese comics have been discussed in works by Pierre Destenay, Antoine Roux, Jean Chesneaux, and Gerd Eversberg and in *Das Mädchen aus der Volkskommune, Bandes dessinées chinoises,* and *Chugoku no gekiga: Renkanga.*

Most plentiful are anthologies and collections of cartoons. Although many cartoonists are represented in this category, there are some whose works have not been collected, perhaps because they were lost or confiscated during different ideological movements (especially the Cultural Revolution), or because publishers were reluctant to publish them when more profitable books were in the offing.

RESEARCH COLLECTIONS

Public and Private Collections

China's museums and libraries are much less useful as reservoirs of primary research materials than the private collections of some cartoonists. Lack of funding to preserve cartoon materials on microfilm, or by other means, has played havoc with what does exist in museums and libraries. In some cases, works virtually ruined by the ravages of weather and insects can no longer be handled for fear of their disintegration.

The skimpy collections of original comic art in public depositories has resulted also from the ideological excesses of the Cultural Revolution when many materials were destroyed. Perhaps with that reckless period in mind, old-timer cartoonists have been reluctant to part with their private collections.

A few public institutions are helpful to comic art researchers; the difficulty, especially for foreigners, is gaining access to them in the cautious post-

Tiananmen period. The Beijing Library, which serves a capacity similar to the Library of Congress in the United States, collects a copy of everything that is published, including cartoons. In Shanghai, the Xujiahui Library contains back issues at least to the 1930s, of newspapers and periodicals, some of which include comic art; many of these resources are in a deteriorated state. The Tu Shen Wan Library, in the same city, has collections of New Year's pictures, as does the Chongqing Museum; and the Canton Fine Arts Academy has a collection of cartoons done immediately after Mao's death.

A wealth of Chinese cartoon art can be found in the homes of individual cartoonists. Most famous cartoonists (Ding Cong, He Wei, and so on) have their own collections; some of them collected the works of their predecessors and contemporaries, others their own work alone. Many cartoonists born before 1940 have works of their fellow cartoonists; among these is the excellent collection of Zhan Tong. Liao Bingxiong reportedly has collected sixty years' worth of his own work; Fang Cheng has preserved many of his works, as well as those of his deceased cartoonist wife, Chen Jinyan. The cartoons of Zhang Guangyu are in his widow's possession.

Knowledgeable Individuals

Many Chinese cartoon pioneers, whose works predate World War II, are important sources of information. However, because of their advanced ages and the lack of hard documentation for some of their statements, the credibility of their data is sometimes suspect.

Probably the most knowledgeable and one of the most credible individuals concerning the country's comic art is Wang Dazhuang, a cartoonist who is also chief editor of Heilongjiang Television in Harbin. Since 1986 Wang has interviewed numerous Chinese cartoonists on film, including some since deceased, for a television series, "Overview of Chinese Cartooning," made up of thirty fifteen-minute segments. Thus far, twenty-six shows have been taped, and Wang will continue the series to sixty segments.

Hongying Liu-Lengyel has voluminous data and materials. Nearly every year, she and her professor husband, Alfonz Lengyel, return to her homeland to conduct research. In the summers of 1991 and 1992, Liu-Lengyel interviewed eighty-three cartoonists. Liu-Lengyel and John A. Lent are preparing a book-length manuscript of Chinese comic art, based in part on these interviews and others that they conducted together in 1993.

Organizations and Cartoon Magazines

The many associations devoted to art and cartooning are excellent sources of information about the field and its practitioners. Some of their activities aim to professionalize cartooning, including the collection, preservation, and publishing of cartoonists' works. For example, the National Cartoon Art Commission advises the Sichuan Fine Arts Publishing House on which cartoon collections to publish. Started at the advent of the 1990s, the publishing house has already published the cartoon collections of Fang Cheng and others. Among other associations are the National Chinese Artists Association and its local branches; the Chinese Cartoonist Federation; the Chinese National Press Cartoon Research Association; provincial or city cartoon societies; and others made up of peasants (such as the twenty-five-member Hebei Qiuxian Peasant Cartoonist Group), military (such as the defunct Military Cartoonist Group of Harbin), workers (Worker Cartoonist Group in each city and province), and college and high school students.

Three magazines devoted to cartooning survive in China. *China Cartoons* (Zhongguo manhua), a monthly, is the most important, being the official publication of the National Cartoon Art Commission. *Cartoon World* (Manhua shijie), published in Shanghai since the 1980s, is also a monthly; its importance has reportedly dwindled with the deaths of the older members of its editorial board. *Cartoon Monthly* (Manhua yuekan), which appears less frequently than monthly, contains cartoons, announcements, and a column by Fang Cheng on the history and theory of cartooning.

Other cartoon magazines had appeared, some ever so briefly, after the launching of *Satire and Humour* as a monthly (changed to fortnightly one year later) supplement of *People's Daily* in January 1979. The editor made his intention quite clear in the first number of *Satire and Humour*, writing that cartoons are for revolution, "to be used for enhancement of unity, self-education, and exposure of as well as dealing of blows at enemies" (Chen, "Cartoons" 1980, 3). By the late 1980s, *Satire and Humour* had become one of China's most sought-after periodicals, attaining a circulation of 700,000. Other cartoon periodicals that came in its wake were the magazines *Children's Cartoons, Selected Cartoons, Laugh, Humour Master, The World of Cartoons,* and *Cartoon Monthly,* about ten cartoon newspapers (some with names such as *Thorny Roses, Little Hot Pepper,* and *Gag Cartoon Paper*), and at least twenty cartoon columns in various newspapers and magazines.

NOTE

The author wishes to thank sincerely Hongying Liu-Lengyel for sharing information she gathered in China. This chapter was strengthened considerably because of her generous help.

BIBLIOGRAPHY

Ah Ying. *Essays on Art.* Beijing: People's Art Publishing House, 1982.
Bader, A. L. "China's New Weapon—Caricature." *American Scholar* (April 1941): 228–40.
Bandes dessinées chinoises. Paris: Centre Georges Pompidou, 1982.

Bi Keguan. *Bi Keguan manhua xuan* (Selected Cartoons of Bi Keguan). Chengdu: Sichuan Arts Publishing House, 1985.

Bi Keguan and Huang Yuanlin. *Zhongguo manhua shihua* (Chinese Cartoons). Beijing: Cultural Publishing House, 1986.

Cartoon Arts Commission, ed. *Selected Works of Chinese Cartoonists.* Chengdu: Fine Arts Publishing House, 1988.

"Cartoons Come to Stay." *The New China* (February 1931): 101.

Chang Tiejun. *Chang Tiejun manhua xuan* (Selected Cartoons of Chang Tiejun). Beijing: Chinese Workers' Publishing House, 1989.

Chen, Jack. "China's Militant Cartoons." *Asia* (May 1938): 308–12.

Chen, L. "Cartoons Ain't Just for Fun." *Free China Weekly,* August 31, 1980, 3.

———. "How Cartoons Have Been Used." *Free China Weekly,* May 18, 1980, 3.

———. "Stories behind Some Cartoons." *Free China Weekly,* May 25, 1980, 3.

Cheng Chi. "New Serial Pictures." *Chinese Literature* 2 (1974): 111–17.

Cheng Hsi Chang. "The Children's Page in Chinese Newspapers." *The New China* (February 1931): 103–4.

Chesneaux, Jean, comp. *The People's Comic Book: Red Women's Detachment, Hot on the Trail, and Other Chinese Comics.* New York: Anchor Press, 1973.

Chiang Wei-pu. "Chinese Picture Story Books." *Chinese Literature* (March 1959): 144–47.

"China Draws upon Humour." *Asiaweek,* October 30, 1987, 53.

"Chinese Cartoons of the Day." *Asia* (August 1936): 507.

Chu, B. F. "Chinese Cartoonist in Wartime." *Far Eastern Mirror,* April 21, 1938, 72–73.

Chūgoku no gekiga: Renkanga (Chinese Drama Comics: Renkanga). Tokyo: Tabata Shoten, 1974.

Croizier, R. "Crimes of the Gang of Four: A Chinese Artist's Version." *Pacific Affairs* (Summer 1981): 311–22.

Das Mädchen aus der Volkskommune. Hamburg: Rowohlt, 1972.

Destenay, Pierre. "Les bandes dessinées." *La Nouvelle Chine* (Paris) 4 (1971): 38–43.

Di Jiexian. "Father of Sanmao—Zhang Leping." *World Time* (Taipei), July 24, 1991.

Ding Cong, ed. *Wit and Humour from Ancient China: 100 Cartoons by Ding Cong.* Beijing: New World Press, 1986.

Duan Jifu. *Lao Ma zhengzhuan* (Series of Lao Ma). Tianjin: Yangliuqing Pictorial House, 1990.

Eversberg, Gerd. "Chinesische Comics." *Science Fiction Times* (Bremerhaven) 14, 4 (1972): 21–22.

Fang Cheng. *Dangdai Zhongguo manhua jing xuan* (Selected Contemporary Chinese Cartoons). Hong Kong: Nan Yu Publishing House, 1991.

———. *Fang Cheng lianhuan manhua yuanji* (Collection of Comic Strips of Fang Cheng). Changchun: Jilin Arts Publishing House, 1985.

———. *Fang Cheng manhua xuan* (Selected Cartoons of Fang Cheng). Tianjin: Tianjin People's Arts Publishing House, 1981.

———. *Fang Cheng manhua xuan* (Selected Cartoons of Fang Cheng). Shanghai: Shanghai People's Arts Publishing House, 1982.

———. *Huaji yu youmo* (Amusement and Humor). Beijing: China Overseas Publishing Co., 1989.

———. *Xiao de yishu* (The Art of Laughing). Shenyang: Spring City Cultural Publishing House, 1984.

————. *Youmo, fengci, manhua* (Humor, Satire, and Cartoon). Beijing: Sanlian Bookstore, 1984.

Feng Yiyin, et al. *Feng Zikai zhuan* (Biography of Feng Zikai). Hangzhou: Zhejiang People's Publishing House, 1983.

Feng Zikai. *Feng Zikai ertong manhua xuanji* (Collection of Feng Zikai's Children's Cartoons). Chengdu: Sichuan Children's Publishing House, 1988.

"55 Years of Innovation." *Asiaweek,* December 24–31, 1982, 26–27.

Findlay, Ian. "Drawing the Party Line: From Fallen Leaders to Consumers." *Far Eastern Economic Review,* November 15, 1984, 108.

Fu Chen and Wang Wang. *Xiao shi manhua* (Historical Laughing Stories and Cartoons). Shanghai: Shanghai Ancient Book Publishing House, 1991.

Fuyu manhua (Fuyu Cartoons). Harbin: Liberation Army Arts and Culture Publishing House, 1991.

Government Information Service. *Mian xiang weilai* (From Past to the Future: Cartoon Collection). Taipei: Government Information Service, 1989.

————. *Zhonghua ernu de nuhou* (Angry Roar of the Chinese: Cartoon Collection). Taipei: Government Information Service, 1989.

Han Shangyi. Interview with Hongying Liu-Lengyal. Shanghai, July 12, 1991.

Harbsmeier, Christopher. *The Cartoonist Feng Zikai.* Oslo: Universitetsforlaget, 1984.

Hebei Qiuxian "Frog" Cartoonist Group. *Heibei Qiuxian nongmin manhua xuan* (Selected Cartoons of the Peasants in Qiu County). Shijiazhuang: Hebei Arts Publishing House, 1989.

Hong Huang. Interview with Hongying Liu-Lengyel. Shanghai, July 12, 1991.

Hong Kong Institute for the Promotion of Chinese Culture. *Chinese Satirical Drawings Since 1900.* Hong Kong: Hong Kong Institute for the Promotion of Chinese Culture, 1987.

Hong Shi, ed. *Manhua jialun* (On Cartoons). Harbin: North Publishing House, 1991.

————. *Zhongguo manhua yishu lun* (On Chinese Cartoon Art). Changchun: Changchun Publishing House, 1991.

Hua Junwu. *Cartoons from Contemporary China.* Beijing: New World Press, 1989.

————. *Chinese Satire and Humour: Selected Cartoons of Hua Junwu (1955–1982).* Beijing: New World Press, 1984.

Huang Mao. *On Cartoon Art.* Shangai: Life Bookstore, 1943.

Huang Yongyu. *Liqiu yansu renzhen sikao de zhaji* (Collection Which Tried to Have Serious Thinking). Beijing: Sanlin Bookstore, 1985.

Hung Chang-tai. "War and Peace in Feng Zikai's Wartime Cartoons." *Modern China* (January 1990): 39–83.

Hwang, John C. "Lien Huan Hua: Revolutionary Serial Pictures." In *Popular Media in China,* edited by Godwin Chu, 51–72. Honolulu: East West Center, 1978.

Jiang Yihai, ed. *Manhua zhishi cidian* (Dictionary of Cartoon Knowledge). Nanjing: Nanjing University Press, 1989.

Lan Jian'an and Shi Jicai, eds. *Cartoons from the Contemporary China.* Beijing: New World Press, 1989.

Lang Shaojun et al., eds. *Zhongguo shuhua jianshang cidian* (Dictionary of Chinese Paintings and Calligraphy Appreciation). Beijing: China Youth Publishing House, 1988.

Lent, John A. *Comic Art in Africa, Asia, Australia, and Latin America: An International Bibliography.* Westport, Conn.: Greenwood Press, forthcoming.

Li Jia. *Manhua qutan* (On Cartoons). Heifei: Anhui Fine Arts Publishing House, 1985.

Li Mu and Yi Xie, eds. *Mei ri yi xiao* (One Laugh a Day). Guangzhou: Guangzhou Traveling Publishing House, 1991.

Li Qing. *Li Qing manhua* (Cartoons of Li Qing). Yantai: Shandong Arts Publishing House, 1989.

Liu-Lengyel, Hongying. "Chinese Cartoons: History and Present Status." Ph.D. diss., Temple University, 1993.

Long Shengming and Liu Yongguo, eds. *Zhongguo dangdai youmo huajia zuopinxuan* (Selected Works of Contemporary Chinese Humorous Drawings). Nanning: Guangxi Arts Publishing House, 1992.

"Look Who're Cartoon Characters." *Mayala* (Manila), August 19, 1986, 6.

Ma Ke. "Cheers to the New Achievement of the Serial Picture." *People's Daily,* December 29, 1963.

Mi Gu. *Mi Gu manhua xuan* (Selected Cartoons of Mi Gu). Chengdu: Sichuan People's Publishing House, 1982.

Miu Yintang. *Manhua yishu ABC* (The Art of Cartooning). Beijing: Chinese Series Pictures Publishing House, 1990.

————. *Miu Yintang manhua xuan* (Selected Cartoons of Miu Yintang). Beijing: Knowledge Publishing House, 1990.

Mo Ce, ed. *Manhuajia tan manhua* (Cartoonist on Cartoons). Beijing: Beijing Arts and Handicrafts Publishing House, 1989.

Moritz, Fredric A. "Chinese Comics Teach Mao's Lessons." *Christian Science Monitor,* August 15, 1973, 9.

Mu Hui. "Cartoons in Ming Dynasty." *Outlook Weekly* 22 (1991): 36.

Nebiolo, Gino. *The People's Comic Book.* Translated by Endymion Wilkinson. Garden City, N.Y.: Anchor Press, 1973.

Pan Shunqi. *Pan Shunqi youmo hua* (Humorous Drawings of Pan Shunqi). Shanghai: People's Arts Publishing House, 1991.

Parton, James. *Caricature and Comic Art in All Times and Many Lands.* New York: Harper Brothers, 1877.

Peng Shan. "Picture Story Books of China." *Asian Culture* (January 1980): 2–3.

People's Arts Publishing House, ed. *Chen Jinyan meishu zuopin xuanji* (Selected Artistic Works of Chen Jinyan). Beijing: People's Arts Publishing House, 1981.

Roux, Antoine. "Les bades rouges du President Mao." *Communication et Languages* (Paris) 12 (1971): 101–17.

Satire and Humour Editorial Group, ed. *Fengci yu youmo* (Satire and Humor). Beijing: People's Arts Publishing House, 1989.

Shi Jicai. "Introduction." In *Cartoons from Contemporary China,* edited by Hua Junwu, 12–15. Beijing: New World Press, 1989.

"Sketching China's Scoundrels." *Asiaweek,* September 2, 1983, 52.

Sun Yizeng. *Sun Yizeng manhua xuan* (Selected Cartoons of Sun Yizeng). Beijing: Knowledge Publishing House, 1991.

Sung Yin. "A Talk on Moulding the Characters of Serial Pictures." *People's Daily,* June 6, 1974.

"Vagabond Waif of Shanghai." *Asiaweek,* August 13, 1982, 32–33.

Wang Bomin. *Zhonggou huihua shi* (History of Chinese Paintings). Shanghai: Shanghai People's Arts Publishing House, 1982.

Wang Fuyang et al., eds. *Shixiang baitu* (One Hundred Cartoons on Social Phenomena). Beijing: People's Daily Publishing House, 1991.

Wang Schuchen. *Wang Schuchen manhua xuan* (Selected Cartoons of Wang Schuchen). Chengdu: Sichuan Arts Publishing House, 1991.

Worker's Daily Agency, ed. *Dierjie Gongren Ribao manhua dasai zuopin xuan* (Selected Works of the Second Worker's Daily Cartoon Competition). Beijing: Worker's Daily Agency, 1987.

WuDunn, Sheryl. ''Chinese Cartoonist Is the Master of the Fine Line.'' *New York Times,* December 31, 1990, 2.

Xu Changming. *Xu Changming manhua xuan* (Selected Cartoons of Xu Changming). Shanghai: Translation Company, 1991.

Xu Jingxiang, ed. *200 Cartoons from China.* Beijing: China Today Press, 1990.

———. *Zhongguo youmohua xuan* (Selected Chinese Humorous Drawings). Shanghai: Fudan University Press, 1989.

Yang Changfei, ed. *Shijie yinyue youmo* (World Cartoons of Music). Beijing: Chinese Youth Publishing House, 1991.

Ye Chunyang. *Ye Chunyang manhua xuan* (Selected Cartoons of Ye Chunyang). Beijing: Chinese Workers' Publishing House, 1990.

Ye Qianyu. *Ye Qianyu manhua xuan 1928–1959* (Selected Cartoons of Ye Qianyu 1928–1959). Chengdu: Sichuan Arts Publishing House, 1986.

Yu Cheng et al., eds. *Shiyong youmo cidian* (Practical Dictionary of Humor). Beijing: China Metropolitan Economy and Society Publishing, 1990.

Yu Henxi and Xu Jin, eds. *Disanjie Gongren Ribao manhua dasai zuopin xuan* (Selected Works of the Third Worker's Daily Cartoon Competition). Beijing: Popular Science Publishing House, 1990.

Yu Yueting. ''Woguo huabo de shizu—Dianshizhai Huabao Chutan'' (The Pioneer of Chinese Pictorials: A Preliminary Study of Dianshi Studio Pictorial). *Xinwen Yanjiu Ziliao* (Beijing) 10 (1981): 149–81.

Zhan Tong. *Zhan Tong ertong manhua xuan* (Selected Children's Cartoons of Zhan Tong). Chengdu: Sichuan Children's Publishing House, 1985.

Zhang Bin and Sun Maoju, eds. *Junxiao manhua xuan* (Selected Cartoons from the Military School). Beijing: Jiefangjun Arts Publishing House, 1992.

Zhang Ding. *Zhang Ding manhua* (Cartoons of Zhang Ding, 1936–1976). Shenyang: Liaoning Arts Publishing House, 1985.

Zhang Leping. *San Mao can jun ji* (San Mao Joins the Army). Shanghai: Tongji University Press, 1990.

Zheng Xinyao. *Zheng Xinyao manhua xuan* (Selected Cartoons of Zheng Xinyao). Shanghai: Shanghai Cartoonist Studies, 1988.

Zhu Genhua and Shen Tongheng, eds. *Manhua xuankan* (Selected Cartoons). Beijing: People's Arts Publishing House, 1982–1987.

Zhu Guorong. *China Art: The Ultimate.* Shanghai: Knowledge Publishing House, 1990.

16

Chinese Calligraphy

QINGXIANG WANG

Chinese calligraphy is the key to understanding Chinese civilization. To the Chinese, calligraphy is not just a graphic art, but a genuine art. It is a discipline of learning that embodies the philosophy for various art forms, a fundamental training for all forms of genuine art. Its criteria for excellence are regarded as the theoretical foundation of art criticism in general. More utilitarian purposes, such as decoration, advertising, exercise for mental health and physical relaxation, however, extend the use of Chinese calligraphy beyond the bounds of art to become an essential element of Chinese culture and Chinese life.

Calligraphy is broadly and diversely applied in Chinese society for various purposes. It is, first of all, a scholastic accomplishment. Scholars who are outstanding in calligraphy are more respected. There are historical examples that calligraphers were appointed to important governmental positions to award their calligraphic achievement. Liu Gongquan, Tang Dynasty calligrapher, for example, was appointed to the position of *Taizi Shaoshi,* tutor of the young prince, and he served three emperors of the Tang Dynasty as the royal calligrapher.

Chinese calligraphy is an art of lines, the structuring of lines, and the harmonious and rhythmical motion of lines. It presents a form of beauty that does not rely on realistically copying nature, but, instead, depends on abstraction. Therefore, Chinese calligraphy, as art, can be applied to various situations. In China, calligraphy, in its simplest form—black and white—is seen everywhere: in palaces, museums, and meeting halls, on mountain rocks, and in private studies. It is an art form that reveals its owner's taste, beliefs, and philosophy.

It has been a tradition for centuries to use calligraphy as a means of advertising. In ancient times, calligraphers usually disapproved of mixing their art with commerce, but in modern China, particularly today, calligraphy is more and more used to enhance the status and reputation of commercial institutions and their products. Not only major stores, but also teahouses and fruit stands by the roadside, invite calligraphers to write their signboards. Wang Xizhi (307–365), saint of Chinese calligraphy, once saw an old lady who was peddling fans by the roadside but could not sell any because her fans were too plain. Wang offered to write on her fans in exchange for the geese she had brought with her. As soon as Wang had finished the writing, her fans sold for good prices. This is perhaps the earliest recorded case of using calligraphy as advertisement.

Since the beginning, Chinese calligraphy has been used as an instrument for ideological control and political struggle. During the Great Cultural Revolution, calligraphic criticism unexceptionably became part of the critical movement which was manipulated to serve the current politics. Before the death of Mao Zedong, for example, great Tang Dynasty calligraphers Zhang Xu, Yan Zhenqing, and Sun Guoting were all overshadowed by the superfluous praising comments on their contemporary monk calligrapher Huai Su, who was Mao Zedong's native fellow and calligraphic model. After Mao's death, calligraphic critics turned to the eulogy upon Yan Zhenqing, another Tang Dynasty calligrapher who enjoys a greater fame than Huai Su, because Hua Guofeng, Mao Zedong's successor, is an imitator of Yan Zhenqing's style.

The application of calligraphy is not confined to those purposes mentioned. It is also a way of mental cultivation and health preservation. Some exercise calligraphy to restrain a hot temper and improve patience; others use calligraphy to relax and maintain mental stillness. When people talk about therapeutic exercises, calligraphy is often mentioned side by side with *taijiquan.*

To understand Chinese calligraphy, it is necessary to appreciate the factors that molded it as a unique art form of various styles and tremendous use. Such factors are numerous, but the following have been playing the decisive roles in its evolution: the block-shaped Chinese characters, the unique tools for presentation, the highly cultivated calligraphic criticism, and the extensive application.

CHINESE CHARACTERS AND THE MAJOR STYLES OF CHINESE CALLIGRAPHY

It is the block-shaped Chinese characters that gave rise to and decided the direction of the development of Chinese calligraphy. According to *The Book of Changes,* Pao Xi, the first ancestor of the Chinese, invented characters by observing the phenomena of the sky and the earth and by following the patterns found on the bodies of birds and animals. Judging by the legend that he tried to reproduce the natural phenomena and patterns he observed, the characters Pao Xi invented must be descriptive and figurative in nature. Although the legend has not yet been proved by archaeological discoveries, the block-shaped characters have been the basis for the five major styles of Chinese calligraphy: the seal style (*Zhuanshu*), the official style (*Lishu*), the regular style (*Kaishu*), the running style (*Xingshu*), and the hasty style (*Caoshu*).

Seal Style

The Seal Style comprises three phases in its development: the tortoiseshell and bone style (*Jiaguwen*) period, the bronze style (*Jinwen*) period, and the minor seal style (*Xiaozhuan*) period. The three styles are named generally the Seal Style because they have been found widely used for seal-carving since the Han Dynasty.

The tradition of the block-shaped character began with the tortoiseshell and bone style (Figure 1), the earliest written form of Chinese characters regarded as full-grown calligraphy. Each character of the style is an independent block that contains a certain number of strokes. Due to the block shape of the characters, calligraphers of the tortoiseshell and bone style enjoyed tremendous freedom of compositional arrangement. They could arrange the characters to suit the shape of the tortoiseshell or the bone. Such has been a heritage of thousands of years, and it is still benefiting calligraphers today. A piece of Chinese calligraphy can be presented either from left to right or from right to left when written horizontally. It can also be written from top to bottom when written vertically. Specific designs are used to suit specific purposes and to add unusual beauty to the work. The compositional flexibility inspires calligraphers' imagination and encourages them to innovate.

Characters of the tortoiseshell and bone style are not regular square blocks of the same size like the characters used today, but, on the contrary, they are of different sizes and different shapes which are decided by the characteristics and number of the predominant strokes in the individual characters. For example, a character can be vertically longer if the predominant stroke in the character is vertically long. If the predominant stroke is horizontally long, the character will then be horizontally broader. If the predominant stroke is a circle embodying the other strokes of the character, the character will be of a round shape, and so on. Furthermore, there is no fixed standard of how long or how broad a character should be. The shape of a character is rather a matter of the calligrapher's personal understanding and creative intention. This tradition initiated by the tortoiseshell and bone style has been fully developed in later styles, such as the running style and the hasty style, although it disappeared in the official style and the regular style, which leveled the difference between characters in size and shape.

Another stylistic character of the tortoiseshell and bone style is its emphasis on stroke variation. The best of tortoiseshell and bone style calligraphy manifests the efforts made by its calligraphers to create personal styles by adding original characteristics to strokes. The 5,000 pieces of tortoiseshell and animal bones with characters of the style form an enormous exhibition of stroke variation. Some are characteristic of thin and delicate strokes; others are characteristic of thick and bold strokes. Some have strokes round and smooth at the curves, while some have strokes square and sharp. Calligraphers of the tortoiseshell and bone style had reached considerable sophistication in creating personal style by presenting the strokes originally.

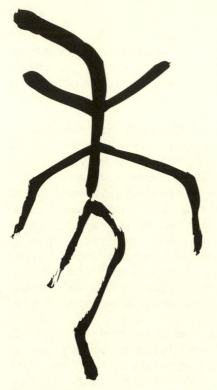

Figure 1
The Tortoiseshell and Bone Style

The bronze style (Figure 2), which was popular during the 800 years of the Zhou Dynasty, inherited and further developed the three elements of the tortoiseshell and bone style: stroke variation, character structure, and composition. Early bronze style resembles the tortoiseshell and bone style in several respects, such as irregular character size, sharp and square turns of the stroke, and the beauty of simplicity. Later, however, the bronze style became more and more characteristic of round and smooth turns of the stroke, regular character size, and greater and greater labor on the balance of composition. Consequently, the strokes became more steady, the character size more regular, and the space of the whole piece of calligraphic work more evenly divided among the characters. The bronze style marked, therefore, the period of history during which Chinese calligraphy was transforming from its primitive forms to maturity.

The Qin Dynasty (221–206 B.C.E.), which lasted for only fifteen years, was important in the history of Chinese calligraphy. During its short span, the first emperor of Qin unified the Chinese characters, and General Meng Tian, as legend goes, invented the writing brush that has been a unique writing vehicle

Figure 2
The Bronze Style

ever since. Calligraphy was no longer carved on tortoiseshell and animal bones, but, instead, written on bamboo and wooden slips or on silk. Chinese calligraphy for the first time became deliberate efforts of artistic innovation and ended its history of anonymity. There appeared the first group of calligraphers whose names were recorded in history. Among them, Li Si, Zhao Gao, and Shi Zhou were the most outstanding.

The predominant style of the Qin Dynasty is known as the minor seal style (Figure 3), which was created by Prime Minister Li Si. Compared with the bronze style, the minor seal style demonstrates tremendous progress. Its strokes are even, smooth, symmetrical, and controlled. The structure and size of the character are no longer irregular but uniform. The exaggerated long strokes and curves make the style extremely refined and decorative.

Nevertheless, the long, smooth, symmetrical strokes of the minor seal style were difficult to present. They were particularly burdensome for the administrators and officials who had to handle the administrative and legal documents that accumulated day by day. It became necessary, therefore, to simplify the minor seal style. As a result, the official style replaced the minor seal style during the Han Dynasty (206 B.C.E.–220 C.E.).

Figure 3
The Minor Seal Style

Official Style

In the official style (Figure 4), the long, curved strokes of the minor seal style were straightened. Dots were introduced to replace some of the shorter strokes. Chinese characters underwent a major change of shape. To compensate for the simplification, calligraphers of the official style paid more attention to the internal variation of the stroke. The beginning of the prominent horizontal stroke, for example, is made into a "silkworm head," while the end of the same stroke resembles "the swallow tail." The complication of stroke technique successfully maintained and developed the artistic beauty of Chinese calligraphy.

The transformation from the seal style to the official style is a revolution in the history of Chinese calligraphy. Before the official style, the various styles were all basically pictographic, which is not only difficult for presentation, but also makes it impossible to fix the shape and number of strokes of a character. One stroke might be written in different ways by different calligraphers, and the same character might have different shapes. The official style, which eventually abandoned the pictographic characteristics of Chinese characters, is the beginning of a new phase of abstraction. It fixed the square shape of Chinese char-

Figure 4
The Official Style

acters and is usually regarded as the basis for the regular style, the running style, and the hasty style.

As a matter of fact, during the Han Dynasty when the official style dominated, there were already signs of the regular, the running, and the hasty styles. During the later Han Dynasty, these four styles actually developed simultaneously. It is not until the Wei (220–265) and Jin (265–420) dynasties, however, that the regular, the running, and the hasty styles matured and flourished. Therefore, the transformation of the major styles of Chinese calligraphy was completed during the 200 years of the Wei and Jin dynasties.

Regular Style

The regular style (Figure 5) is an evolutionary modification rather than a revolutionary development of the official style. Its contribution to Chinese calligraphy is that it modified almost every stroke of the official style to make the writing easier and faster, while it preserved the basic shape of the Chinese characters set by the official style. Although the appearance of the regular style is not a matter of "invention," Zhong You of the Wei Dynasty and Wang Xizhi of the Jin Dynasty, who completed the transition from the official style to the regular style, are regarded as the most important figures in the history of Chinese calligraphy. Wang is even called the saint of Chinese calligraphy, both in China and in Japan.

Figure 5
The Regular Style

Distinguished calligraphers of the regular style all attempted to generalize the characteristics of the style. The classification by Wang Xizhi is, however, considered the best. In his book, *The Eight Components of the Character "Yong,"* Wang uses the eight strokes of the character "yong" (eternal) to illustrate the characteristics of all the strokes of the regular style, and he gives a different name to each of the eight strokes (Figure 6):

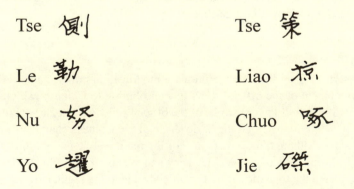

Each of the eight strokes stands for a class of strokes which share common characteristics. According to Wang Xizhi, the calligrapher would become good

Figure 6
The Eight Strokes of the Character "Yong"

at all sorts of strokes by mastering the techniques of these eight strokes through arduous practice. Although the summary does not comprehensively include all the necessary strokes of the regular style, it is still a clever way to use one character to illustrate the essential characteristics of the style.

The regular style reached the peak of its achievements during the Tang Dynasty. To name a few, Yu Shinan, Ouyang Xun, Chu Suiliang, Yan Zhenqing, and Liu Gongquan were the most outstanding masters of the regular style. Stone rubbings of their calligraphy have been treasured by artists and used as models for learners for centuries. Economical copies of the rubbings can be found almost in every pupil's schoolbag.

Running Style

The running style (Figure 7) was a parallel development with the official and the regular styles. Signs of the style appeared as early as on the bamboo slips of the Han Dynasty. It is by nature a sort of free hand of both the official and

Figure 7
The Running Style

the regular styles. The calligrapher who is good at the official style or the regular style can be good at the running style without any special training. As a matter of fact, the calligrapher's personal characteristics in the official and regular styles are usually reflected in his running style.

It is, however, no easy matter to become a real master of the running style because there is no regularity for the calligrapher to follow. Some critics even believe that the running style is the most difficult to handle, although it appears to be easy. The only secret to becoming a master of the style is perhaps to become first of all a real master of the official and the regular styles.

The strokes of the running style do not need to be as neat and accurate as those of the regular style. There can be some free connection between the strokes in a sequence. The rigid angles and sharp points of the official and the regular styles can be softened. In the ease and casualness lie the charm and vitality of the style. Nevertheless, to maintain the beauty of simplicity, one of the major principles of Chinese calligraphy, none of those characteristics should be overdone.

Figure 8
The Hasty Style

Of the large number of masters of the running style since the Wei and Jin dynasties, Wang Xizhi is universally considered the greatest, and his "Preface to the Orchid Pavilion Poetry" ("Lantingxu") is the greatest masterpiece of the running style in history. Unfortunately the original work was lost. What we have today are copies by famous calligraphers of the Tang Dynasty.

Compared with the other styles, the running style enjoys the first position of popularity for daily use. Because it is convenient to write and easy to identify, it is widely used for correspondence, note taking, diary writing, manuscripts, and so on, leaving the other styles for more artistic and serious purposes.

Hasty Style

The hasty style (Figure 8) is another parallel development since the Han Dynasty with the official and the regular styles. Judging by the name, the style may be supposed to be a careless way of calligraphy. It has its own formality and regularities, however, which calligraphers should follow closely. Violations of the rules will not only reduce the beauty of the style but also cause difficulty in understanding.

The greatest characteristic of the hasty style is perhaps the use of cursive, connected, and sometimes intertwined strokes. During the early periods of the style, only strokes within a character could be cursive and connected. Individual characters of one piece of calligraphy were kept distinctively separate. Since the Tang Dynasty, some calligraphers of the hasty style started to promote a unique style initiated by Wang Xianzhi, who was famous for running one stroke of a character into the following character, so that characters in his calligraphy were all connected. Zhang Xu and Huai Su of the Tang Dynasty were celebrated masters of the style. Due to the prominent characteristic of intertwining strokes, their calligraphy of the hasty style is called by critics "calligraphy of one stroke." If such a technique is abused, however, the work will be considered vulgar and immature.

The hasty style is the most romantic form of Chinese calligraphy. The execution of strokes, the linking between them and between characters, and the overall compositional design do not allow the calligrapher to take time to consider once he or she has started the writing. Decisions are instantaneous and spontaneous. Therefore, the charm of the hasty style is natural overflow of the artist's accomplishments, personality, and passion at the moment when the work is done. That is why it is always exciting to watch a master calligrapher working the brush in the hasty style.

TOOLS AND TECHNIQUE

Chinese calligraphy emphasizes the importance of tools and takes them as part of the art. The four fundamental tools—the brush, the paper, the ink, and the inkstone—are called "the four treasures in a study." Good quality of the tools is the material guarantee for good work, while beautiful design creates artistic atmosphere.

Brush

Chinese calligraphy pays special attention to the handling of the brush, the paper, and the ink. First of all, the calligrapher must learn the choice of the right quality and size of brush. The Chinese brush is made of animal hair, tied together and fixed into the hollow at one end of a piece of bamboo. To make brushes of different sizes and different qualities, the hair of various animals is used: Sheep, weasel, badger, wolf, and rabbit are the most popular.

Brushes can be classified into three different categories according to the quality of the hair they are made of: soft, resilient, and stiff. Those made of sheep hair, for example, are soft, while those made of wolf hair are stiff. Weasel hair is preferred for resilient brushes. Sometimes, two or several kinds of hair are combined to produce a mixed quality in the brush. There is no definite rule about what kind of brush should be used for a certain style of calligraphy, although the right choice usually does fit a certain style better and make the work easier. It is true that calligraphers often prefer a certain kind of brush to produce the effect they desire. The size of the brush varies from one-third of an inch, or even smaller, to several inches. Specially made brushes can be as big as several feet long. It is common sense that the larger the character is the bigger the brush that should be used and vice versa. However, learners are always advised that it is much better to use a comparably bigger brush to write characters of comparably smaller size because the bigger brush holds more ink and has greater flexibility and potentiality when it is used to write smaller characters.

The handling of the brush is important but, as Su Dongpo, great poet and calligrapher of the Song Dynasty, once said, there is no definite way to hold the brush. True masters sometimes use unusual ways to handle their brush. Yet, some principles might be helpful to beginners: (1) Keep the wrist of the hand that holds the brush off the table to give the wrist freedom to maneuver; (2) if the size of the characters the calligrapher is to write is not very small, stand to gain better balance and concentration of the whole body; (3) the fingers of the hand that holds the brush should be firm, while the palm should be an empty hollow; (4) the brush should always be kept upright.

The tip of the brush is the center of concentration and gravity. When held in the right position and method, the brush generates great power. Whichever way it is held, the brush should be firm and flexible, so that the strokes made can be steady and graceful.

Paper

Although Chinese calligraphy can be written on all kinds of materials—paper, fabrics, boards, and so on—masters of calligraphy favor, in particular, Xuan paper, a paper made of the bark of a special tree and named after the town in Anhui province where it is made. Xuan is classified into dozens of different types according to their different textures and levels of ink absorption.

After many years of trying, the calligrapher will eventually learn the qualities of various types of Xuan paper and decide the most ideal types for particular purposes. The use of paper, however, is a technique that requires the proper use of brush and ink. Before the brush touches the paper, the texture and level of absorption of the paper should be carefully judged. Then the type of brush and the speed of brush motion can be decided. Ink should also be prepared according to the quality of the paper.

Ink

Before the recent invention of water-based liquid ink, an ink stick was one of the essentials for Chinese calligraphy. Calligraphers not only cherish the good quality but also treasure the brands, decoration, and packaging of their ink sticks. The aged ink sticks of famous brands have become antiques.

The major ingredient of Chinese ink is smoke, of which there are two kinds: pine smoke and oil smoke. Ink made of oil smoke has a beautiful gloss after it dries; therefore, it is particularly good for calligraphy. The grinding of ink stick on an inkstone demands steady pressure, time, and patience. The calligrapher usually takes advantage of the time for ink preparation to work out the style, size, composition, and other details of the execution. Today, ink sticks are increasingly being replaced by liquid ink, which is ready for use and mixes as well as the ink sticks.

Inkstone

The inkstone is another treasure of the study which has the value of both practical use and artistic appreciation. The best inkstones are made of rocks of special quality from Guangdong province, called Duan stone; from Anhui province, called She stone; or from Shandong province, called Lu stone. The middle of the stone is a hollow where ink is ground from the stick and mixed with water, while one end of the stone is a deeper hollow where more water is kept ready for use. Exquisite inkstones have gracefully designed patterns carved out around the edge: flowers, birds, insects, animals, clouds and dragons, or landscapes. Such beautifully crafted stones are usually set in mahogany or sandalwood cases, the covers of which are usually engraved with calligraphy.

Before the age of the inkstone, bricks and tiles were used to grind ink. The best of them were made during the Han Dynasty. Those rare ones left to us are cherished as precious antiques.

CHINESE CALLIGRAPHY AND ITS CRITICISM

The achievements of Chinese calligraphy owe much to its criticism, which has long established itself as an independent genre of aesthetics. It contributes not only to the development of Chinese calligraphy but also to the flourishing of Chinese culture in general.

The critical approaches of Chinese calligraphy have been tremendously influenced by classic Chinese philosophies, such as Taoism, Zhuangism, and Confucianism. The basic Taoist precepts have been applied to elucidate the basic principles and abstract beauty of Chinese calligraphy, while the Confucian approach is more concerned with the social and ethical values. The philosophy of Zhuang Zhou has been quoted, on the one hand, to emphasize perfection through practice, while, on the other, to advocate spontaneity and free expression. The combination of such approaches has been a traditional vehicle for the interpretation and appreciation of Chinese calligraphy until recently.

The most important precept of Taoism is *qi,* the harmony of yin and yang, the original force, the source of life, which makes the universe rotate. Critics do not view a piece of calligraphic work as something lifeless but as creation with life. The origin of this life is *qi*. Chinese calligraphy emphasizes the existence and use of *qi*. Without *qi*, a stroke, a character, or the whole piece of calligraphy is dull and lifeless. A masterpiece is said to be lively and vigorous for having *qi* throughout. To have the whole piece of calligraphy permeated with *qi*, the calligrapher should be ready with *qi* before the writing is started, keep it working while the work is being executed, and never stop it until the writing is completed.

Xie Ho, famous artist and critic of the Southern Qi Dynasty (479–502), developed the concept *qi* into *qiyun*, meaning "the rhythmical motion of vitality." He emphasized the lively motion of *qi* and made it the first of his Six Methods. Xie Ho's theory of *qiyun* has a far-reaching influence on the practice and criticism of Chinese calligraphy, although it was originally meant for the art of painting. Since Xie, the rank of a piece of calligraphic work is first judged by whether it is lively in *qiyun*. Those displaying superior *qiyun* are said to have *shenyun*, meaning the divine state of charm.

To create *qiyun*, the calligrapher has to transfer his or her mind into the state of *xukong*, meaning void and stillness, another Taoist precept. According to Taoism, to enter the state of *xukong*, the individuals should rid themselves of worldly concerns and pursuits, to withdraw from worldly affairs. There were stories about calligraphers who shut themselves up for days to empty their minds for the state of *xukong* and about those who faced the blank paper on the wall until they visualized each of the characters and the whole piece of calligraphy they were going to execute. Those stories have become legends. The original Taoist preachings of *xukong* are almost impossible for today's artists to practice. The concepts have, however, been modulated into a means for concentration.

Another precept that has a profound influence on Chinese calligraphy is Taoist dualism, of which the union of yin and yang is the core. According to Taoism, the essence of the universe is the unity of yin and yang, which oppose each other and are harmonized by the force of *qi*. The unity of yin and yang, which exists everywhere, in the stroke, the character, and the whole piece of calligraphy, generates various concepts based on the Taoist understanding that opposites oppose and complement each other at the same time, to name a few of the most important: *xu* and *shi* (emptiness and substantiality), *shu* and *mi* (density and sparsity), *sheng* and *shu* (unskillfulness and skillfulness), and *yi* and *bi* (intention and brushwork).

The concept of *xu* and *shi* is a matter of space consciousness. To the Chinese calligraphy, the space between characters that are written in black ink is as important as the space occupied by the characters themselves. It is what calligraphers mean in the saying: White should be regarded as black.

The concept of *shu* and *mi* concerns the arrangement of the strokes in the character. It is said that Zhang Xu, great calligrapher of the Tang Dynasty, suddenly realized the secret of stroke arrangement when he saw farmers who carried with poles heavy loads on their shoulders vying with each other for the path without knocking each other off the road. Deng Shiru, a great calligrapher of the seal style of the Qing Dynasty, once commented on stroke arrangement, saying that wind cannot pass where the strokes are dense; horses are able to walk where the strokes are sparse.

The concept of *sheng* and *shu* is one of the hardest to grasp. A green hand, who is unskilled with the techniques, is confined in the realm of *sheng,* and needs to transcend the state of unskillfulness by mastering the techniques to enter the realm of *shu.* Familiarity with the rules leads to sophistication, however, which blocks the way to originality. True masters struggle to return to the state of simplicity after the mastery of techniques. As Zheng Xie, famous painter and calligrapher of the Qing Dynasty, put it, dealing with the relation between *sheng* and *shu,* "You are really skilled when you feel you are again unskilled." Qi Baishi, modern master of calligraphy, painting, and seal engraving, went to the extreme on the same topic, "Only those who have never learned to paint paint well." Obviously, both Zheng Xie and Qi Baishi favored regained simplicity, a realm higher than normal skillfulness, over sophistication.

The state of *sheng* is sometimes gained by accidents that bring about unexpected effects valued by calligraphers as divine touches. Gao Fenghan, one of the so-called eight Yangzhou grotesque artists of the Qing Dynasty, has been especially admired for his calligraphy and paintings done with his left hand after his right hand became paralyzed at the age of fifty. In the artist's own words, "with the left hand [while he was not left-handed], beaten tracks can be avoided."

Although the relation between *yi* and *bi* affects the whole procedure of writing, two phases claim calligraphers' attention in particular: the precreation drafting of brushwork and the brush activity directed by *yi.* During the pre-creation phase, *yi* is set while *qi* is gathered. This is what calligraphers call *yi* (intention) first and *bi* (brushwork) second. The strokes written with the Chinese brush in black ink on white paper cannot be corrected once they are done; therefore, direction of *bi* (the brush) by *yi* (the intention) demands extreme delicacy. When unexpected results occur, particularly in the running and the hasty styles, the relation between *bi* and *yi* is of vital importance. Sometimes, for example, the stroke is disconnected in the middle because the brush runs out of ink. So far as *yi* is not discontinued, the stroke thus made is even of greater calligraphic beauty.

Zhuang Zhou influenced later critics through his philosophical fables. He advised artists to make painstaking efforts to perfect their art after the model, Master Cook Pao Ding, who, as Zhuang Zhou tells us, spent three years to learn to view the ox as parts instead of a whole ox and to move his knife at great ease in between the joints. According to Zhuang Zhou, the sublime state of artistic creation, however, is a sort of supernatural situation, which is gained only when the artist's self is absolutely forgotten, which happens in his fable

"Zhuang Zhou Dreams of the Butterfly," wherein he cannot tell whether he has turned into the butterfly or vice versa.

Confucianism emphasizes unity, harmony, duty, and morality. Its influence on Chinese calligraphy is mainly in regard to the strict training in rules and using calligraphy as a means of self-cultivation. Liu Gongquan (778–685), for example, believed that "the use of the brush depends on the use of the mind. If you are righteous in the mind, your brush will be naturally upright." Unfortunately, Confucian preaching does not encourage originality as does Taoism.

Alongside of the philosophical elucidation of the criteria of Chinese calligraphy are the critics' arduous efforts to present the beauty of Chinese calligraphy through association and particularization.

After the pictographic period, Chinese characters became mere linguistic symbols. When we read, we are not viewing pictures, nor trying to work out what picture a character or stroke stands for, but, instead, we are perceiving the linguistic meanings of characters. The appreciation of calligraphy, however, is contrary to such linguistic experience. We rather forget the meanings of characters but concentrate on the beauty the work represents. That is why the collector, who does not know a single word of the Chinese language, is still intoxicated with the great beauty in the calligraphy he hangs upside down.

The abstract beauty of Chinese calligraphy, like that of other abstract arts, arouses different reactions from different viewers. Chinese calligraphic criticism has been interpretative and descriptive. Critics of the Tang and Song dynasties were particularly characteristic of this approach. In their works, the beauty of calligraphy is always associated to actual phenomena in nature. Therefore, Zhong You's calligraphy looks like, as Emperor Wu Di of the Liang Dynasty told us, "a flock of geese playing on the sea, and a flock of cranes hovering in the sky." Wang Xizhi's calligraphy is said to be a "gentle breeze caressing the sleeves or the bright moon reflected in the wine glass." Comments on his calligraphy by Tang Dynasty critics have stronger mythical color. *Tangren shupen* (Critical Remarks on Calligraphy by Tang Dynasty Critics) compares Wang Hsi-Chi's calligraphy to

a hero drawing his sword to stop the flood in the middle. The dot he places on top of the character is like the rock rolling down from a high peak; his horizontal stroke resembles the dark cloud which runs a thousand miles long; his *Na* stroke has the power of thunders; his vertical stroke looks like a dry vine of ten thousand years; his declining stroke seems a tiger lying in the yard of the Phoenix Palace.

In trying to relate calligraphy as an object of appreciation to images and phenomena in imagination, such critical approaches focus upon subjective response. Although they lack the profundity of analysis and often lead to simplistic interpretations of the unique beauty of Chinese calligraphy, they do, however, inspire imagination and encourage us as readers to dig out on our own the beauty hiding under the abstract surface.

RECENT DEVELOPMENTS

In the last fifty years, Chinese calligraphy has experienced the most unusual situation. It survived politically motivated attacks on the Chinese characters, the proposed Romanization of the Chinese writing system, and the Cultural Revolution, the most devastating political movement in Chinese history. Since the beginning of the economic reforms, the art of Chinese calligraphy has entered a new era of growth.

Despite the fact that the Chinese people created one of the most splendid civilizations of the world with the square characters they have been using for 5,000 years, ultraleftist forces have continuously attacked the Chinese writing system, blaming the "square characters" for China's poverty and backwardness since the last century. Communist leaders, such as Chen Duxiu, Mao Zedong, and Zhou Enlai, all insisted that Chinese characters be abandoned because they could not communicate revolutionary ideas. They believed that Romanization was the only way out for the Chinese language. Although Chinese calligraphy as a unique art form will survive any type of reform, politically motivated intentions to reform the square characters seriously harmed the nation's enthusiasm and impeded calligraphers' artistic progress. For half a century, there has been nobody whose calligraphy can be considered great and compare favorably with those in history.

During the Cultural Revolution, calligraphy was practiced only for revolutionary purposes—to copy Mao's poems and quotations, and to write *dazibao* (big-character posters). Ironically, the Chinese nation perhaps had never written so many big characters within ten years, since it was often a required task for each person to complete a certain number of big-character posters within a certain period of time. It does not mean, however, that calligraphy as an art was encouraged. On the contrary, stone rubbings and authentic works of master calligraphers were burnt as *sijiu* (four olds—old ideas, old culture, old customs, and old habits). Calligraphers who practiced less popular styles, such as *zhuanshu* and *caoshu*, were criticized as "intentionally not to let the masses understand."

A revival of calligraphic interest began in the 1980s as a result of economic reforms. The hubbub for Romanization of Chinese characters has withered away, and successful research work in linguistics has proven the advantages of Chinese characters over other writing systems in the age of the computer. Famous stone rubbings and works of master calligraphers have been reprinted despite their contents. There appeared for the first time in history a number of journals that specialize in calligraphy, such as *Shufa* (Calligraphy), *Zhongguo Shufa* (Chinese Calligraphy), and *Shufa Bao* (Calligraphy Monthly). Calligraphers were allowed to form their own associations, local and national. There have been more and more exchanges between calligraphers on the mainland and those from Hong Kong, Taiwan, Japan, and other parts of the world. Such developments will probably lead to another upsurge of Chinese calligraphy.

BIBLIOGRAPHY

Billeter, Jean François. *The Chinese Art of Writing*. New York: Skira/Rizzoli, 1990.

Chang, Leon Long-yien. *Four Thousand Years of Chinese Calligraphy*. Chicago: University of Chicago Press, 1990.

Chiang, Yee. *Chinese Calligraphy: An Introduction to Its Aesthetics and Technique*. Cambridge, Mass.: Harvard University Press, 1973.

Fu, Shen C. Y. *Traces of the Brush: Studies in Chinese Calligraphy*. New Haven, Conn.: Yale University Art Gallery, 1977.

Kraus, Richard Curt. *Brushes with Power: Modern Politics and the Chinese Art of Calligraphy*. Berkeley: University of California Press, 1991.

Kwo Da-Wei. *Chinese Brushwork in Calligraphy and Painting: Its History, Aesthetics, and Techniques*. Dover, England: Allanheld and Schram, 1981.

Lai, T. C. *Chinese Calligraphy: An Introduction*. Seattle: University of Washington Press, 1973.

————. *Chinese Calligraphy: Its Mystic Beauty*. Hong Kong: Swinden, 1973.

Legeza, Ireneus Laszlo. *Tao Magic: The Secret Language of Diagrams and Calligraphy*. London: Thames and Hudson, 1975.

Mi Fu. *Shushi* (History of Calligraphy). N.d.

Sanxitang fatie (Stone Rubbings of the House of Three Treasures). Beijing: China Books, 1986.

Tangren shuping (Critical Remarks on Calligraphy by Tang Dynasty Critics). N.d.

Willetts, Williams Y. *Chinese Calligraphy: Its History and Aesthetic Motivation*. Hong Kong: Oxford University Press, 1981.

Zhang Huaiguan. *Shuduan* (Conclusive Remarks on Calligraphy).

Zhong Mingshan. *Zhongguoshufa jianshi* (A Brief History of Chinese Calligraphy). Shijiazhuang: Hebei Fine Arts, 1983.

17

Popular Rural Architecture

RONALD G. KNAPP

Chinese rural dwellings are more than simply vessels for daily life or havens against the changing forces of nature. Common dwellings, which on the surface appear to be nondescript and mute structures, indeed are able to reveal and communicate important aspects of Chinese popular culture. Throughout much of Chinese history, building sites were chosen and structures built based upon an organic view of the cosmos. House construction traditionally has not been seen simply as a progression of technical tasks, but as a means to increase worldly benefits and avoid misfortune. Ordinary houses, just as with other elements of Chinese popular and even elite culture, are texts, tangible manifestations of people's behaviors, beliefs, and aspirations.

It should not come as a surprise that China—a nation with a lengthy history of unparalleled continuity, a territory of nearly 10 million square kilometers, strikingly complex physical environments, and a population of more than 1.16 billion—encompasses richly diverse folk architectural traditions. Even without speaking of the vernacular traditions characteristic of the fifty-five minority nationalities within the country, there is indeed an extraordinary degree of heterogeneity even among the majority nationality, the Han Chinese. Thus, as with other aspects of popular culture, it makes little sense to speak of Chinese patterns as if they were essentially homogeneous. One must not only acknowledge regional and subethnic variations, but also examine the ongoing tensions between cultural integration and differentiation. Chinese monumental architecture has long been a concern of Chinese and Western scholars. Even though many have made important contributions to our understanding of the principles and symbolism of imperial palaces, walled cities, temples, imperial tombs, and gentry mansions, the study of Chinese architecture in the West is relatively undeveloped (Chang 1970; Liang 1981, 1984; Liu 1980b; Steinhardt 1984, 1990a, 1990b;

Thorp 1983, 1986; Yang 1980; Zhang 1985, 1986). Recognition of the significance of Chinese folk architecture, as with other forms of popular material
culture, has come even more slowly. This is in spite of the great potential that
vernacular structures have for telling us things that texts and monuments cannot
about common people in the past and in the present.

Geographers in the United States have a well-documented tradition of looking
at vernacular architecture and other forms of material culture as keys to understanding cultural history. In studying American landscapes, geographers have
described buildings as cultural artifacts by documenting local house types and
materials, as elements in culturogeographic regionalization, as well as evidence
in tracing the diffusion of landscape features across the country (Jackson 1970,
1984; Kniffen 1965, 1990; Meinig 1979, 1986; Noble 1984; Sauer 1941, and
Zelinsky 1992, among many others). Among useful resources for geographers
are publications by architects and architectural historians, such as those by Amos
Rapoport (1969), Dell Upton and John Michael Vlach (1986), and Paul Oliver
(1987, forthcoming 1994). Much of the work done by geographers admittedly
has been descriptive and historical with only rare excursions into and relationships with theory.

Aside from generally brief descriptions of Chinese villages and houses in the
writings of Western visitors and residents during the nineteenth and twentieth
centuries, few attempts were made in the past to survey Chinese dwellings. Some
useful information may be gleaned from brief articles written by Helena von
Poseck (1905), Gregorio Arnaiz (1910), Myron L. Fuller and Frederick G. Clapp
(1924), George B. Cressey (1932), and Kay Baker-Carr (1951), but all of these
are essentially mere glimpses of fragments of China's rich vernacular traditions,
simple records of conditions as encountered. None of these authors published a
second article on the topic of rural architecture in China. Noteworthy, however,
were the efforts made by John Dudgeon (1884) and Herbert Day Lamson (1935).

The first academic article concerning "the houses of the Chinese" was Joseph
Spencer's in 1947. Although his survey was admittedly "preliminary observations," its text, footnotes, and photographs clearly suggested important research
themes concerning regional differences in roofs, walls, and minor architectural
features of rural dwellings. Spencer faulted even those few observers of Chinese
rural architecture who unsatisfactorily "generalized into a relatively uniform
'Chinese' pattern, a single simplified style somewhat at variance with the facts."
The fact that no foreign geographer was able to build upon Spencer's work in
China was, of course, the direct result of the changed political environment in
China and the country's isolation from the world community for nearly a quarter
of a century after 1949.

THE 1950s–1970s

Substantial fieldwork was carried out by Chinese architects and others in the
1950s and 1960s to survey, document, and assess not only vernacular dwellings
but also the magnificent dwellings of gentry and merchants, many of which had

historic significance. The sporadic mention in Western architectural publications of conference reports, writings, and drawings by Chinese researchers aroused some hope that the recording of Chinese rural popular architecture was under way.

Chinese language architectural journals in the 1950s and 1960s included a small number of articles concerning *minjian jianzhu* (folk architecture), but unfortunately most of the work done during this period—drawings, photographs, and texts—was not published at the time. Much rested unanalyzed and unappreciated for a quarter century before changes in the political environment in the 1980s led to their long awaited publication. These belatedly issued studies will be discussed below. Undoubtedly and sadly, some documentation must have been destroyed or lost.

An exception to the above was the publication in 1957 of several important books. Primary among these was the architect Liu Dunzhen's *Zhongguo zhuzhai gaishuo* (Introduction to Chinese Dwellings), which suggested the richness of Chinese vernacular architecture. The book was expanded from a lengthy article of Liu's published in the *Jianshu xuebao* (Architectural Journal) in 1956. In the preface to the book, Liu informs readers that his travels in southwestern China during the anti-Japanese war (1937–1945) opened his eyes to vernacular architecture, but that it was not until the formation of a Chinese Architectural Research Unit by the Nanjing College of Engineering and the former East China Architectural Design Company in 1953 that it was possible to carry out systematic surveys. Liu unapologetically admitted that his book was preliminary and that the story of vernacular architecture in China could not be adequately told until a comprehensive survey was completed countrywide. His book was an appeal for such an effort.

Liu presented a brief historical summary of the development of the Chinese house from neolithic times through the Qing Dynasty (1644–1911). While the book focused on existing dwellings that reach back to the Ming Dynasty (1368–1644), his approach was less historical than morphological. He categorized rural dwellings into nine types according to house shape and made tentative excursions into ways of improving contemporary rural dwellings. The book is illustrated with useful drawings and photographs.

Politics within China and international events, as well as the limited circulation of the book at the time, limited the impact of this important publication in China and abroad. In the West, note was made of the book in 1958 by R.T.F. Skinner in the *Journal of the Royal Institute of British Architects,* noting that ''it is perhaps difficult for us in Europe, where at least all the main types of domestic architecture have been studied and presented in innumerable excellent publications, to realize how important it is that this research work has been started in China.'' Nonetheless, by 1958, vernacular architectural study in China had already entered a stage of dormancy, striking, and melancholy inactivity, rather than the period of vigorous and healthy development hoped for by Liu and others just a short time before.

An abridged typescript translation of Liu's book was done by Liao Hung-ying, but it and even the Chinese edition of *Zhongguo zhuzhai gaishuo* were not widely available in libraries in the West. Andrew Boyd's *Chinese Architecture and Town Planning,* published in 1962, depended upon books by Liu and other Chinese architects for its descriptions, drawings, and photographs of Chinese dwellings but unfortunately did not clearly acknowledge their Chinese origins. Because of careless attribution to Liu's work in Boyd's book, many of Liu's photographs and drawings subsequently were credited to Boyd rather than to Liu, such as can be seen in the interesting and useful article on Chinese regional house types published in Hong Kong in 1972 by Linda F. Sullivan. Boyd's generously illustrated volume subsequently became a standard reference work on the subject of Chinese architecture.

In 1957 two other important vernacular architecture books were published in China: *Zhongguo jianzhu leixing ji jiegou* (Chinese Architectural Types and Structural Forms), by Liu Zhiping, and *Huizhou Mingdai zhuzhai* (Ming Dynasty Houses in Huizhou), by Zhang Zhongyi et al. Liu's book ranged widely across Chinese architectural forms from palaces to common house types, from bridges to gardens. The book is flush with original drawings and observations. Zhang's book, which emphasized the merchant mansions of southern Anhui province, still stands today as the best source on these magnificent dwellings. Illustrations as well as translated texts from both of these books found their way also into English language treatments of Chinese architecture without proper attribution.

THE 1980s

Chinese Language Materials

The languished state of China's architectural studies slowly was invigorated by the political events of the late 1970s, leading in the 1980s to an avalanche of publications of interest to researchers of vernacular architecture. China's emergence from international isolation began with admission to the United Nations in 1971 and continued with increasing contact with nations from which it had been separated in the decades since 1949. The death of Chairman Mao and the formal conclusion of the Great Proletarian Cultural Revolution in 1976 set in train the circumstances that came to invigorate Chinese academic life for much of the following decade and a half. The number of Chinese language and Western language publications concerning popular architecture during this decade far exceeds that of earlier times. There has been not only a substantial increase in the number of descriptive regional studies concerning Chinese vernacular architecture but also an overall maturation of approaches. This section will first present Chinese language publications before examining Western language publications during the decade.

The publication of *Zhejiang minju* (Folk Houses of Zhejiang) in 1984 marked a turning point in the study of China's popular architecture, providing at once a link with Liu Dunzhen's earlier work in the 1950s and a promise of additional regional studies of China in the 1980s. Fieldwork had begun for this book in 1961, and a draft manuscript had been completed by 1963. Prior to its 1984 publication, supplementary fieldwork, several new chapters, and overall reorganization were carried out to improve the manuscript. Participants in the project for more than twenty years included China's most prominent architectural historians. As appropriate for the political climate of the early 1980s, the book's authorship was officially collective, a joint project of the Center for Chinese Architectural Technology Development Center's Research Unit for Architectural History. Focusing on a single province, *Zhejiang minju* examines the building materials, as well as the climatic, topographic, social, and historical contexts in which one of the country's most important vernacular traditions emerged. The book's drawings, photographs, and text clearly have enriched the earlier countrywide observations of Liu Dunzhen.

The appearance of Zhang Yuhuan's *Jilin minju* (Folk Dwellings of Jilin) in 1985 revealed that fieldwork had been completed in 1956–1957 and a manuscript completed in 1958. The preface noted somewhat elliptically and with an implied sense of sadness that publication had been delayed "for various reasons." The manuscript for this book was added to as a result of current field research, but unfortunately it also does not differentiate between information and illustrations pertinent to the late 1950s or early 1980s. While emphasizing the majority Han's vernacular architecture forms, Zhang presents useful information about the folk dwellings of the Manchu, Korean, and Mongol ethnic minorities in Jilin province.

With the publication of *Yunnan minju* (Folk dwellings of Yunnan) by Yunnan sheng sheji yuan (Yunnan Provincial Design Institute) in 1986, it appeared as if there was an annual schedule planned for this building series by the China Building Industry Press. As with its two recent precursors, this volume had its origins decades earlier and had benefited from recent revision. More explicitly perhaps than the others, the book's purpose was to go beyond mere documentation and analysis of building traditions to "make the past serve the present" (*gu wei jin yong*). This notion of a need for practical relevance rather than mere scholarship has come to characterize much academic work in China. Since Yunnan province is one of China's most ethnically diverse areas, with twenty-four of the country's fifty-five minority nationalities, it is not surprising that this book focuses on nine of the most important minority nationalities. Peculiarly, little mention is made of Han house forms in the province, although the book offers a rich resource for making comparisons across cultural boundaries.

Fujian minju (Folk Dwellings of Fujian), published in 1987, was jointly authored by Gao Zhenming, Wang Naixiang, and Chen Yu, each of whom took responsibility for different sections. The book's preface does not indicate that the research had been completed decades before and thus the work appears to document more recent and existing vernacular traditions than the earlier books. More than fifty locations throughout the province were studied. While the volume surveys overall settlement ensembles, housing plans, the organization of domestic space, building structure and construction materials, as well as architectural details, the bulk of the book highlights nearly ninety specific dwellings with drawings and photographs.

Although 1988 passed without a volume in the series, 1989 brought an important volume by Hou Jiyao, Ren Zhiyuan, Zhou Peinan, and Li Zhuanzi, *Yaodong minju* (Subterranean Folk Dwellings), which is superior in design, clarity, and presentation to earlier volumes in the series. Ranging across six provinces in the loessial plateau region of north and northwestern China, this book focuses on the earth-sheltered habitats of some 40 million Chinese. The collaborative nature of this work was stimulated by the 1985 international conference on earth-sheltered housing held in Beijing. A particular strength of this volume is the effort made to work within a comparative approach and toward improving techniques of subterranean construction as well as bettering the overall residential environment in "cave" dwellings.

Lu Yuanding and Wei Yanjun's *Guangdong minju* (Folk Dwellings of Guangdong), published in 1990, further advanced the regional treatment of folk architectural forms in China. While following a chapter sequence and earlier genesis reminiscent of the 1984 Zhejiang volume, the book broke new ground with its emphasis on historical context, cultural factors important in site selection and directional orientation of dwellings, measurements and proportions, and a glossary that indicates the localized use of building terminology. The authors acknowledge that the volume was enriched through thesis research completed by their students. While one might assume that the market for this series was expanding, it is curious to note that the print run for both *Yaodong minju* and *Guangdong minju* was less than half of the *Zhejiang* volume and a third of the others.

Two volumes broke the convention of a provincewide survey. *Guibei minjian jianzhu* (Folk Architecture of Northern Guangxi) edited by Li Changjie in 1990, focuses on a corner of the Guangxi Zhuang Autonomous Region in southern China. This book includes extraordinarily detailed drawings of Han, Zhuang, Tong, and Yao dwellings, as well as village settlements, drum towers, covered bridges, opera stages, gatehouses, wayside pavilions, and even country toilets and shrines to earth gods. *Suzhou minju* (Folk Dwellings of Suzhou), edited by Xu Minsu and others in 1991, focuses on common and high-style dwellings in one of China's most historic and picturesque small cities.

In addition to these eight valuable Chinese language books, journal articles, sketch books, pamphlets, popular and news articles, as well as several somewhat idiosyncratic books have appeared over the past decade to further enrich our knowledge of China's rich and diverse vernacular building traditions. Although space does not permit mention of them all, note should be made of the work of, among many others, Cheng Jiyue and Hu Chengen (1980), Huang Hanmin (1982, 1984), Huang Shuangwu (1984), Huang Weijuan (1987), Jing Qimin (1985), Liu Baozhong (1981), Niu Weina (1988), Shan Deqi (1984, 1987), Shen Dongqi (1985, 1991), Tang Baoheng (1987), Tongji Daxue (1986a, 1986b),

Wang Shaozhou (1980), Wang Shuangwu (1984), and Yang Hongxun (1980). The two-volume conference set *Zhongguo chuantong minju yu wenhua* (China's Traditional Folk Dwellings and Culture), edited by Lu Yuanding in 1991 and 1992, expressly attempts to relate building form to the cultural context of people's lives. Although each of the fifty-seven included papers is relatively brief, collectively they reveal the breadth of interest in this topic throughout China as the 1980s ended. Included in the second volume is a comprehensive list of Chinese publications on vernacular architecture from 1949 to 1991. Recent sophisticated excursions by Chinese architects into traditional symbolization, by Xu Yinong (1990); phenomenology, by Miao Po (1989); and architectonics, by Lu Yuanding (1990), as they related to monumental architecture, suggest insights into vernacular forms as well. The appearance of *Zhongguo minju* (China's Folk Architecture), an expensive and lavishly illustrated survey by Chen Congzhou, Pan Hongxuan, and Lu Bingjie (1993), is a successful effort of mainland authors to bring the fruits of their important work to the world. An English translation is promised for 1994.

It is important to realize that these useful books and articles on Chinese vernacular architecture appeared at a time in which a rural housing building boom was also taking place in China. New rural economic policies spurred unprecedented housing construction throughout the country. In the six years between 1979 and 1985, more construction took place than in the previous thirty. While the pace of construction has slowed in recent years, it is an inescapable fact that there was as well widespread destruction of traditional rural housing as new construction took place. Although architects and others continue to make valiant efforts to document structures slated for destruction and have been victorious in saving many valuable buildings, undoubtedly many fine examples of popular architecture continue literally to be expunged from both rural and urban landscapes. Dissatisfaction with many current designs and the inadequacies of new models inevitably have caused many in China to reexamine traditional housing forms and patterns in a search for ways to improve new habitats.

Western Language Materials

Accompanying Chinese efforts at documenting and understanding their own vernacular architectural forms has been a growing interest in the same topics by American, European, and Japanese researchers. In 1980 Liu Dunzhen's path-breaking 1957 *Zhongguo zhuzhai gaishuo* (Introduction to Chinese Dwellings) was translated into French as *La Maison Chinoise* with some rearranging and additions to make the volume more useful.

Drawing on extensive fieldwork in China and published Chinese sources, *China's Traditional Rural Architecture: A Cultural Geography of the Common House* was published by Ronald G. Knapp in 1986. The volume was the first in English to survey the evolution, variety, construction techniques, social context, and contemporary transformations of Chinese dwellings. Its nearly 200 photographs and drawings draw attention to the richness of Chinese vernacular traditions, but the book is not a definitive treatment of the topic. Unlike similar surveys in China for Chinese audiences, this volume explores the ways in which Chinese dwellings communicate folk beliefs and employ *fengshui* (geomancy), almanacs, and charms in house construction. The volume is now being extensively rewritten to take into account new research in China over the past decade. Brief treatments of Chinese houses (1990) and Chinese bridges (1993) were written by Knapp for the Oxford University Press Images of Asia Series.

Going beyond a countrywide survey to focus on the local vernacular traditions found in Zhejiang province is Knapp's *China's Vernacular Architecture: House Form and Culture* (1989). While covering topics similar to those of his 1986 book, this volume details one of China's most striking vernacular architectural traditions. Emphasis in the book is placed on settlement sites and sensitivity to the natural environment, as well as the use of space, construction principles and techniques, exterior and interior ornamentation, and folk traditions associated with the building of and living within rural dwellings. Each chapter of the book examines the ways in which these elements are changing, the ways in which rural housing resonates the tensions between continuity and innovation as rapid economic changes subject rural China to a stressful transformation unparalleled in Chinese history.

Prior to the publication of Gideon Golany's three books on the earth-sheltered dwellings of northern China that are home to some 40 million Chinese (1989, 1990, 1992), only general information concerning this unique type of vernacular housing was available in the West. Golany's comprehensive research not only documents, with drawings and photographs, the design elements and related thermal performance of below-ground dwellings in China, but also explores ways to improve traditional rural patterns and suggests lessons that can be learned even for modern urban construction.

Often seen as the prototypical Chinese dwelling, the Beijing *siheyuan* or courtyard house has been described well by Werner Blaser (1979) and Chin Pai (1987, 1989). Although this important house type varies in scale and proportion from place to place in China, the regularity of rectangular shape, symmetrical layout, axiality, and hierarchical layout together underscore the fact that clear sociocultural forces undergird its development and importance as an archetype in Chinese popular architecture.

A college-level course titled ''Vernacular Chinese Architecture'' was initiated at the University of Hong Kong by David P. Y. Lung in 1985, perhaps the only course offered in English on this subject. Field research by Lung and his students in Hong Kong and in China led to two important exhibitions on vernacular architecture in 1985 and 1991. Especially important was the 1991 exhibition ''Chinese Traditional Vernacular Architecture,'' which was an extraordinary multimedia presentation of Chinese vernacular patterns. The bilingual catalog by Lung (1991) provides a fine survey of a broad range of relevant topics.

Many of the Chinese and Western language treatments of Chinese housing

explore traditional construction materials and technologies. None, however, examines within this topic the specific tools used by carpenters and masons or the
methods of brick and tile manufacture as thoroughly as Rudolf Hommel's *China
at Work* (1937). This is a subject worthy of further attention.

Klaas Ruitenbeek has documented well the interplay of ritual and craft used
by carpenters in Chinese house construction (1986, 1993). Basing his research
on the fifteenth-century carpenter's manual *Lu Ban jing,* his research goes beyond that of the folklorist Wolfram Eberhard (1970) in documenting the ways
in which house construction was more than a series of technical operations. In
addition to assessing and translating important Chinese materials, his work is
enriched by contemporary fieldwork.

While there are several accessible studies of general geomantic theory
(Feuchtwang 1974; Bennett 1978), Richard J. Smith's (1991) comprehensive
and informed survey of divination in traditional Chinese society should lead
some researchers to examine further the role of *fengshui* in site selection for
dwellings. The unpublished dissertation by Sang Hae Lee is a useful treatment
of the topic, especially the application of *fengshui* theories to house construction
(1986). Sophie Clément, Pierre Clément, and Shin Yong-hak (1987) explore the
spread of these geomantic ideas elsewhere in East Asia.

Just as with Chinese monumental architecture, vernacular architecture expresses the conjoined relationships between secular and spiritual realms. Rolf
Stein's compelling discussion of "the religious role of the dwelling place in
China," published originally in French in 1957, was made available in English
in 1990. He emphasizes the ways in which Chinese cosmological speculations
were given material form in their dwellings, an important element in understanding Chinese architecture.

It is clear that the ornamentation around and about Chinese dwellings includes a rich symbolic vocabulary that expresses broad features of shared cosmology as well as folk beliefs in concrete forms. Common dwellings in China
utilize decorative features that echo and imitate the fancied norms of the elite in
order to summon prosperity and keep misfortune at bay. Daniel Sheets Dye's *A
Grammar of Chinese Lattice* (1937) and Clarence Burton Day's *Chinese Peasant Cults: Being a Study of Chinese Paper Gods* (1940) are important comprehensive twentieth-century, illustrated source materials for this topic. Valuable
information and insights that help inform our understanding are found as well
in *Researches into Chinese Superstitions* by Henry Dore (1917), *The Religious
System of China* by J.J.M. deGroot (1897), and *The Five Happinesses: Symbolism in Chinese Popular Art* by Edouard Chavannes (1901).

The variety and meaning of New Year couplets has been studied by Jiann
Hsieh and Ying-hsiung Chou (1981). Wang Shucun (1985) provides a compre-
hensive illustrated treatment of the history and meaning of New Year pictures,
emphasizing the five distinct production traditions. Eberhard's *Dictionary of
Chinese Symbols: Hidden Symbols in Chinese Life and Thought* (1983) and
C.A.S. Williams's *Outlines of Chinese Symbolism and Art Motifs* (1932) are

remarkably handy reference tools for examining this complex topic. An imaginative and extremely useful excursion into the manner in which human activities, including shelter, were given form in the Chinese written language has been written by Cecilia Lindqvist (1991).

Although a great deal of substantial research has been completed concerning high-style Chinese furniture by Wang Shixiang (1986), much less work has been done concerning the furnishing of common dwellings. Ellen Johnston Laing's interesting article (1989) concerning the "correct" arrangement of furniture and selection of decorative paintings points clearly to the persistence of traditional attitudes concerning what is proper in contemporary Chinese households. Deborah Davis (1989) shows how urban apartment dwellers use interior space in ways that clearly distinguish private and public domains. Laing (1988–1989) also has imaginatively used Jin Dynasty (1115–1234) paintings, tomb murals, and decorated ceramics to assess the increasing ornateness of household decoration and furnishings during a historical period.

While most of the research described above focuses on individual dwellings, it is increasingly clear that understanding may be augmented if one changes the scale of inquiry and examines settlement ensembles; that is, villages. One recent edited collection, by Knapp (1992), draws upon the perspectives of anthropologists, architects, geographers, historians, a sociologist, and a veterinary ecologist in examining the various settings of habitation, work, and leisure of China's rural population. The book includes general discussions of the regional differences in size and morphology of village settlements, traditional principles used in siting villages, and the impact of politics on contemporary village form. Eighteen village case studies, generously illustrated with photographs, drawings, and maps, form the core of *Chinese Landscapes: The Village as Place*.

TAIWAN AND HONG KONG

One might assume that, without the political factors that had slowed the development of vernacular architectural studies on the China mainland, research in Taiwan and Hong Kong would have taken off early and developed quickly. Such was not quite the case, however. A small number of very useful publications came early, but there are many gaps yet to be filled.

Reed Dillingham and Chang-lin Dillingham's *A Survey of Traditional Architecture of Taiwan* (1971), with its excellent measured drawings and photographs, documented well traditional farmhouses and other structures at a time when many of these were being destroyed or renovated as Taiwan modernized. Many useful observations concerning the historical, social, and structural aspects of these dwellings were discussed in a "Notes" section. The book acknowledges the research of Chinese scholars on these topics, especially that of Lin Hengtao (1975) and Shao Mei (1968), but it does not call attention to numerous articles in Japanese completed during the Japanese occupation of Taiwan between 1895 and 1945.

A number of general articles on vernacular architecture in Taiwan appeared in English in the magazine *Echo* in the 1970s. Calling attention to the importance of material culture in understanding China, they together suggested what work was yet to be done (Lin 1975 and Lee 1977 are but two examples). Chinese language publications on the island also increasingly carried articles on local architecture. Han Pao-teh and others played important roles in the preservation of historic structures, such as the important Lin family villa in Banqiao (1973, 1983).

As anthropologists and others carried out fieldwork on Taiwan, their books and articles increasingly called attention to domestic space. Wang Sung-hsing's "Taiwanese Architecture and the Supernatural" (1974) helped move researchers away from focusing on mere form to consideration of meaning. Emily M. Ahern (1979) looked at continuity and change in some of these patterns. General articles by Knapp (1981, 1982) suggested looking at Taiwan's house forms only as an initial step in seeking an understanding of China's overall social geography, warning of the difficulty of generalizing about Chinese vernacular patterns before the completion of extensive fieldwork on the mainland. The development of housing on the Taiwan frontier was examined in Knapp (1986).

Liu Dunzhen's work entered academic discourse in Taiwan through the thesis written by Chang Wen-jui (1976). Kwan Hwa-san (1980) extended the discussion with an examination of the components of "space conceptualization" in traditional folk architecture. The impact of changing forms of the family on housing in Taiwan was examined by John K. C. Liu (1980) in a way that has not yet been applied elsewhere in China. The work of Hsu Min-fu (1990) combined theory and fieldwork in a way that promises further advances in the development of a comprehensive understanding of folk architecture in Taiwan using local historical materials. Kao Ts'an-jung's study of the structural, ornamental, and symbolic meanings of the roofs of Taiwan dwellings (1989) focused on a detail that heretofore had only been generally studied.

No individual has carried out more research and has had a greater impact on understanding Taiwan's architecture than Lee Chien-lang. His detailed bilingual Chinese-English study (1978) of rural architecture on the island of Jinmen, just off the coast of the mainland city of Xiamen, clearly suggested the island's intermediate role as a link between mainland patterns and those found in Taiwan. Lee placed vernacular housing patterns within the context of overall architectural developments on Taiwan from 1600 to 1945 in a comprehensive architectural history (1980). Numerous survey reports and booklets by Lee over the past decade have not only documented a broad range of vernacular patterns in Taiwan, they have also served to stimulate concern for the historical preservation of important elements of Chinese material culture on Taiwan for future generations. Lee's important role in nurturing popular appreciation of Taiwan's architectural heritage was underscored by the publication of a richly illustrated children's book by Liu Siyuan (1989).

Documentation of Hong Kong's vernacular traditions has come slowly. While the Hong Kong government publication *Rural Architecture in Hong Kong* (1979) appeared likely to stimulate research within the colony, little appeared in the 1980s. This is partly explained by the fact that field opportunities in adjacent areas of the mainland drew the interests of Hong Kong researchers. The 1991 volume by David Lung, discussed above, also clearly represented the Hong Kong building heritage of rural dwellings, study halls, ancestral halls, markets, and temples.

CONCLUSIONS

Over the millennia, rural architecture—whether one calls it vernacular, folk, or popular—changed slowly in China's villages. Each generation bequeathed cultural landscapes not too different from the ones they themselves inherited. Aside from a penchant for cultural conservatism, it is also likely that the slow pace of technological change contributed significantly to the maintenance of old housing patterns. Many of these patterns were carried well into the twentieth century and are only now undergoing accelerated change. One might assume that the combined effect of population pressures on limited resources and the onslaught of modernization would have led inevitably to the subversion of traditional patterns of popular architecture. It is nonetheless paradoxical that such has not been the case because of the apparent extraordinary resilience of traditional patterns of thought and behavior in China.

Much folk architecture in China today is hybrid, a mélange of traditional patterns necessarily intermixed with contemporary elements derived from, among others, the series of political campaigns that have buffeted Chinese culture in the forty years since the founding of the People's Republic of China. Many fine large residences, temples, and lineage halls, indeed, were razed, abandoned, or turned to alternative uses, especially between 1949 and 1979. In China's villages, common dwellings were divided and subdivided in order to provide housing for a population that doubled between 1949 and 1990.

As in other areas of the world, the Chinese appreciation of their rural built heritage has come about only slowly—a striking contrast with the well-known Chinese reverence for their imperial architectural patrimony. There is nonetheless an enthusiasm in some quarters in China for historic preservation, an increasing effort to reclaim and restore the magnificence of past vernacular architectural forms before forces destroy them. Many unnoticed and unheralded traditional dwellings and village landscapes, however, face modification and destruction because their residents regard them as too ordinary, outdated, and dysfunctional to preserve.

It is important that efforts be made to evaluate dwellings and other rural buildings before they are razed to ensure that those of historical significance or even typicality be preserved. Many such structures certainly have deteriorated over the years or were vandalized to the degree that they are no longer safe to use. Nonetheless, whenever it is impossible to save structures, at the least they should be photographed and documented with drawings. Recently, architects and others have been able to stave off destruction of some villages by proclaiming them "living fossils" (*huo huashi*). It is indeed a peculiarity that at Shenzhen in Guangdong province and Wuxi in Jiangsu province, as well as at several other sites in China, efforts are being made to create "folklore parks," recreations of traditional villages with farmhouses and other buildings that recall vernacular patterns in the past for people living in modernizing China today.

Field researchers must continue to carry out basic documentation of rural architecture before it will be possible to speak confidently of origins, culture regions, patterns of diffusion, adaptations, and shared or unique symbolic motifs. In addition to emphasizing the plans of individual dwellings with measured drawings and architectural details, more attention must be paid to the historical contexts and time periods of common old buildings. There is a need to use literary and artistic sources for insights into the nature of individual as well as groups of structures. Popular architecture needs to be examined at different scales of inquiry, including individual buildings, ensembles of structures in villages and towns, and regions. Increasingly it will be necessary to collect information in a form that invites comparison. Glossaries of building and ornamental terms that speak to regional differences are a priority. Folk architecture and other topics regarding Chinese material culture remain part of a wide-open field of inquiry.

BIBLIOGRAPHY

Ahern, Emily M. "Domestic Architecture in Taiwan: Continuity and Change." In *Value Change in Chinese Society,* edited by R. W. Wilson, A. A. Wilson, and S. L. Greenblatt, 155–70. New York: Praeger, 1979.

Arnaiz, Gregorio. "Construccion de los edificios en las prefecturas de Coan-ciu y Cianciu, Fu-kien sur, China." *Anthropos* 5 (1910): 907–33.

Baker-Carr, Kay. "The Chinese House." *Journal of the Royal Anthropological Institute of Canada* 5 (1951): 234–35.

Bennett, Steven. "Patterns of Sky and Earth: The Chinese Science of Applied Cosmology." *Chinese Society* 3 (1978): 1–26.

Blaser, Werner. *Courtyard House in China: Tradition and Present.* Basel: Birkhauser, 1979.

Boyd, Andrew. *Chinese Architecture and Town Planning.* Chicago: University of Chicago Press, 1962.

Cen Shuhuan. "Guangdong zhongbu yanhai diqu de minjian jianzhu" (Folk Architecture in the Coastal Areas of Guangdong Province). *Jianzhu xuebao* (Architectural Journal) 2 (1956): 36–46.

Chang, Sen-dou. "Some Observations on the Morphology of Chinese Walled Cities." *Annals, Association of American Geographers* 60 (1970): 63–91.

Chang Wen-jui (Zhang Wenrui). "Zhongguo minju de fazhan he shigong fangfa" (The Development and Construction Methods of Chinese Folk Housing). Master's thesis, Chinese Culture University, Taipei, 1976.

Chavannes, Edouard. *The Five Happinesses: Symbolism in Chinese Popular Art.* Translated by Elaine S. Atwood. New York: Weatherhill, 1973. Text originally published as "De l'expression des voeux dans l'art populaire chinois." *Journal Asiatique* 9, 18 (September–October 1901).

Chen Congzhou, Pan Hongxuan, and Lu Bingjie. *Zhongguo minju* (China's Folk Architecture). Hong Kong: Joint Publishing Company 1993.

Cheng Jiyue and Hu Chengen. "Shexian Mingdai juzhu jianzhu 'lao wujiao (ge)' diaocha jianbao" (Brief Report on the Ming Dynasty Houses "Lau Wu Guo" in Shexian). *Jianzhu lishi yu lilun* (Corpus of Architectural History and Theory) 1 (1980): 104–11.

Clément, Sophie, Pierre Clément, and Shin Yong-hak. *Architecture du paysage en Extrême-Orient.* Paris: Ecole nationale supérieure des Beaux-Arts, 1987.

Cressey, George B. "Chinese Homes and Homesites." *Home Geographic Monthly* 2 (1932): 31–36.

Davis, Deborah. "My Mother's House." In *Unofficial China: Popular Culture and Thought in the People's Republic,* edited by Perry Link, Richard Madsen, and Paul G. Pickowicz, 88–100. Boulder, Colo.: Westview Press, 1989.

Day, Clarence Burton. *Chinese Peasant Cults: Being a Study of Chinese Paper Gods.* Shanghai: Kelly and Walsh, 1940.

Dillingham, Reed, and Chang-lin Dillingham. *A Survey of Traditional Architecture of Taiwan.* Taizhong: Donghai University, 1971.

Dore, Henry. *Researches into Chinese Superstitions.* Translated by M. Kennelly. Shanghai: T'usewei Printing Press, 1917.

Dudgeon, John. "Diet, Dress, and Dwellings of the Chinese in Relation to Health." In *International Health Exhibition, London, 1884: The Health Exhibition Literature,* 379–467. London: William Clowes and Sons, 1884.

Dye, Daniel Sheets. *A Grammar of Chinese Lattice.* Cambridge, Mass.: Harvard University Press, 1937.

Eberhard, Wolfram. "Chinese Building Magic." In *Studies in Chinese Folklore and Related Essays,* 49–65. Bloomington: Indiana University Folklore Institute, 1970.

———. *Dictionary of Chinese Symbols: Hidden Symbols in Chinese Life and Thought.* London: Routledge and Kegan Paul, 1983.

Feuchtwang, Stephen. *An Anthropological Analysis of Chinese Geomancy.* Vientiane, Laos: Vithagna, 1974.

Fong, Mary H. "The Iconography of the Popular Gods of Happiness, Emolument, and Longevity (Fu Lu Shou)." *Artibus Asiae* 44(2/3) (1983): 159–99.

Fuller, Myron L., and Frederick G. Clapp. "Loess and Rock Dwellings of Shensi, China." *Geographical Review* 14 (1924): 215–26.

Gao Zhenming, Wang Naixiang, and Chen Yu. *Fujian minju* (Folk Dwellings of Fujian). Beijing: China Building Industry Press, 1987.

Golany, Gideon. *Chinese Earth-sheltered Dwellings: Indigenous Lessons for Modern Urban Design.* Honolulu: University of Hawaii Press, 1992.

———. *Design and Thermal Performance: Below-Ground Dwellings in China.* Newark: University of Delaware Press, 1990.

———. *Underground Space Design in China: Vernacular and Modern Practice.* Newark: University of Delaware Press, 1989.

Groot, J.J.M. de. *The Religious System of China.* 6 vols. 1892–1910. Reprint. Taipei: Ch'eng-wen Publishing, 1972.

Guowuyuan bangongting diaocha, yanjiushi (Investigation and Research Office, State

Council). *Nongfang jianshe yanjiu ziliao* (Research Materials for the Construction of Rural Houses). Beijing: China Building Industry Press, 1984.

Han Pao-teh (Han Baode). *Guji de weihu* (The Preservation of Historic Sites). Taipei: Cultural Buildings Administrative Council, 1983.

Han Pao-teh and Hung Wen-hsiung (Hong Wenxiong). *Banqiao Lin zhai: Diaocha yanjiu ji xiufu jihua* (Banqiao Lin Family Compound: The Survey, Study, and Restoration). Taizhong: Donghai University, 1973.

Hayes, James. "Specialists and Written Materials in the Village World." In *Popular Culture in Late Imperial China,* edited by David Johnson, Andrew J. Nathan, and Evelyn S. Rawski, 75–111. Berkeley: University of California Press, 1985.

Hommel, Rudolf P. *China at Work.* New York: John Day, 1937.

Hong Kong Government. *Rural Architecture in Hong Kong.* Hong Kong: Government Information Services, Hong Kong Government Printer, 1979.

Hou Jiyao, Ren Zhiyuan, Zhou Peinan, and Li Zhuanzi. *Yaodong minju* (Subterranean Folk Dwellings). Beijing: China Architecture and Building Press, 1989.

Hsieh, Jiann, and Ying-hsiung Chou. "Public Aspirations in the New Year Couplets: A Comparative Study between the People's Republic and Taiwan." *Asian Folklore Studies* 40.2 (1981): 125–49.

Hsu Min-fu (Xu Mingfu). *Taiwan chuantong minzhai ji qi difangxing shiliao zhi yanjiu* (Traditional Dwellings in Taiwan and Local Research Materials). Taipei: Hushi Book Company, 1990.

Huang Hanmin. "Fujian minju de chuantong tese yu difang fengge, shang" (The Traditional Character and Local Styles of Folk Dwellings in Fujian, Part 1). *Jianzhushi* (The Architect) 19 (1982): 178–203.

———. "Fujian minju de chuantong tese yu difang fengge, xia" (The Traditional Character and Local Styles of Folk Dwellings in Fujian, Part 2). *Jianzhushi* (The Architect) 21 (1984): 182–94, 134.

Huang Shuangwu. "Ming-Qing jianzhu chun Hongcun cunluo minju" (Ming and Qing Period Village Houses in Hongcun). *Jianzhu xuebao* (Architectural Journal) 10 (1984): 74–77.

Huang Weijuan. "Qu xing, qu yi, qu fa: Chuantong de qidi, chuanzuo de tansuo" (Modeling Form, Shaping Meaning, and Following the Laws of Nature: Traditional Enlightenment and the Exploration of Creativity). *Jianzhu xuebao* (Architectural Journal) 22 (1987): 7–13.

Inn, Henry. *Chinese House and Gardens.* New York: Bonanza, 1950.

Jackson, John Brinckerhoff. *Discovering the Vernacular Landscape.* New Haven, Conn.: Yale University Press, 1984.

———. *Landscapes: Selected Writings of J. B. Jackson.* Edited by Ervin H. Zube. Amherst: University of Massachusetts Press, 1970.

Jing Qimin, ed. *Zhongguo chuantong minju baiti* (One Hundred Topics on Chinese Traditional Dwellings). Tianjin: Tianjin Science and Technology Press, 1985.

Johnson, David, Andrew J. Nathan, and Evelyn S. Rawski, eds. *Popular Culture in Late Imperial China.* Berkeley: University of California Press, 1985.

Kao Ts'an-jung (Gao Canrong). *Yenwei Mabei Wazhen: Taiwan gucuo wuding de xingtai* (Swallows' Tails, Horses' Backs, Tiles—The Form of Roofs in Old Villages in Taiwan). Taipei: Nantian Press, 1989.

Knapp, Ronald G. *China's Traditional Rural Architecture: A Cultural Geography of the Common House.* Honolulu: University of Hawaii Press, 1986.

———. *China's Vernacular Architecture: House Form and Culture.* Honolulu: University of Hawaii Press, 1989.

————. *Chinese Bridges.* New York: Oxford University Press, 1993.

————. *The Chinese House: Craft, Symbol, and the Folk Tradition.* New York: Oxford University Press, 1990.

————. "Chinese Rural Dwellings in Taiwan." *Journal of Cultural Geography* 3, 1 (1982): 1–18.

————. "Taiwan's Vernacular Architecture." *Orientations* 12 (1981): 38–47.

Knapp, Ronald G., ed. *Chinese Landscapes: The Village as Place.* Honolulu: University of Hawaii Press, 1992.

Kniffen, Fred B. *Cultural Diffusion and Landscapes: Selections by Fred B. Kniffen.* Baton Rouge, La.: Geosciences Publications, 1990.

————. "Folk Housing: Key to Diffusion." *Annals, Association of American Geographers* 55 (1965): 549–77.

Kwan Hwa-san (Guan Huashan). "Taiwan chuantong minzhai biaoxian de kongjian guannian" (Traditional Houses and Folk Space Concepts in Taiwan). *Zhongyang yanjiuyuan, minzuxue yanjiusuo jikan* (Bulletin of the Institute of Ethnology, Academia Sinica) 49 (1980): 175–215.

Laing, Ellen Johnston. "Chin 'Tartar' Dynasty (1115–1234) Material Culture." *Artibua Asiae* 49 (1988–1989): 73–121.

————. "The Persistence of Propriety in the 1980s." In *Unofficial China: Popular Culture and Thought in the People's Republic,* edited by Perry Link, Richard Madsen, and Paul G. Pickowicz, 156–71. Boulder, Colo.: Westview Press, 1989.

Lamson, Herbert Day. *Social Pathology in China.* Shanghai: The Commercial Press, 1935.

Lee Chien-lang. "The An Tai Lin Family House." *Echo* 6 (1977): 18–25, 55.

———— (Li Qianlang). *Jinmen minju jianzhu* (Architecture of Folk Dwellings in Kinmen). Taipei: Xiongshi Book Company, 1978.

————. *Taiwan jianzhu shi* (History of the Architecture of Taiwan). Taipei: Beiwu Press, 1980.

————. *Yangmingshan Guojia Gongyuan chuantong juluo ji jianzhu diaocha yanjiu* (Research Survey on Traditional Villages and Architecture in the Yangmingshan National Park). Taipei: Ancient Architecture Research Center, 1988.

Lee, Sang Hae. "Feng-shui: Its Content and Meaning." Ph.D. diss., Cornell University, 1986.

Li Changjie, chief ed. *Guibei minjian jianzhu* (Folk Architecture of Northern Guangxi). Beijing: China Architecture and Building Press, 1990.

Liang Sicheng. *A Pictorial History of Chinese Architecture: A Study of the Development of Its Structural System and the Evolution of Its Types.* Edited by Wilma Fairbank. Cambridge, Mass.: Massachusetts Institute of Technology Press, 1984.

————. *Zhongguo jianzhushi* (A History of Chinese Architecture). Taipei: Historic Books Publishing Company (reprint of 1955 *Shangwu yinshuguan banshe*), 1981.

Lin Heng-tao. "Taiwan's Traditional Chinese Houses." *Echo* 5 (1975): 23–27, 54, 56.

Lindqvist, Cecilia. *China: Empire of Living Symbols.* Translated from the Swedish by Joan Tate. Reading, Pa.: Addison-Wesley Publishing House, 1991.

Link, Perry, Richard Madsen, and Paul G. Pickowicz, eds. *Unofficial China: Popular Culture and Thought in the People's Republic.* Boulder, Colo.: Westview Press, 1989.

Liu Baozhong. *Gu jianzhu zhinan* (Guidebook to China's Ancient Buildings). Beijing: China Architecture and Building Press, 1981.

Liu Dunzhen. *La Maison Chinoise* (The Chinese House). Translated and adapted by

Georges Métailie, Marie-Hélène Métailie, Sophie Clément-Charpentier, and Pierre Clément. Paris: Bibliotheque Berger-Levrault, 1980a.

———. *Zhongguo zhuzhai gaishuo* (Introduction to Chinese Dwellings). Beijing: Architectural Engineering Press, 1957.

Liu Dunzhen, chief ed. *Zhongguo gudai jianzhu shi* (A History of Traditional Chinese Architecture). Beijing: China Building Industry Press, 1980b.

Liu, John K. C. "Housing Transformations: A Study of Family Life and Built Form in Taiwan." Ph.D. diss., University of California, Berkeley, 1980.

Liu Siyuan. *Taiwan minzhai* (Folk Residences in Taiwan). Taipei: Yezhulin, 1989.

Liu Zhiping. *Zhongguo jianzhu leixing ji jiegou* (Chinese Architectural Types and Structural Forms). Beijing: Architectural Engineering Press, 1957.

Lu Yuanding. "Nangfang diqu chuantong jianzhu de tongfeng yu fangre" (The Ventilation and Heat Insulation of Traditional Architecture in South China). *Jianzhu xuebao* (Architectural Journal) 4 (1978): 36–41.

———. "Zhongguo chuantong jianzhu goutu de tezheng, bili yu wending" (Compositional Characteristics of Traditional Chinese Architecture—Scale and Stability). *Jianzhushi* (The Architect) 39 (1990): 97–113.

Lu Yuanding, chief ed. *Zhongguo chuantong minju yu wenhua* (China's Traditional Folk Dwellings and Culture). Beijing: China Architecture and Building Press, vol. 1, 1991; vol. 2, 1992.

Lu Yuanding and Wei Yanjun. *Guangdong minju* (Folk Dwellings of Guangdong). Beijing: China Architecture and Building Press, 1990.

Lung, David P. Y. *China's Traditional Vernacular Architecture* (Zhongguo chuantong minju jianzhu), bilingual ed. Hong Kong: Regional Council, Museums Section, 1991.

———. "Fung Shui: An Intrinsic Way to Environmental Design with Illustrations of Kat Hing Wai." *Asian Architect and Builder* (October 1979): 16–23.

McColl, Robert. "By Their Dwellings Shall We Know Them: Home and Setting among China's Inner Asian Ethnic Groups." *Focus* 39 (1989): 1–6.

Meinig, Donald W., ed. *The Interpretation of Ordinary Landscapes*. New York: Oxford University Press, 1979.

———. *The Shaping of America: A Geographical Perspective on 500 Years of History*. New Haven, Conn.: Yale University Press, 1986.

Miao Po. "Chuangtong de benzhi—Zhongguo chuangtong jianzhu de shisan ge tedian" (The Essence of Tradition—Thirteen Special Characteristics of Traditional Chinese Architecture). *Jianzhushi* (The Architect) 36 (1989): 56–69, 80.

Niu Weina. "Nongcun zhuzhai sheji de huigu yu zhanwang" (Review and Prospect concerning Rural Housing Design). In *Nongcun jizhen yu zhuzhai* (Rural Towns and Housing), 25–47. Beijing: Center for Chinese Architectural Technology and Development, Research Unit for Planning and Design, 1988.

Noble, Allen G. *Wood, Brick, and Stone: The North American Settlement Landscape*. Amherst: University of Massachusetts Press, 1984.

Oliver, Paul. *Dwellings: The House across the World*. Oxford, England: Phaidon Press, 1987.

Oliver, Paul, ed. *Encyclopedia of Vernacular Architecture of the World*. Oxford, England: Blackwell Publishers, forthcoming 1994.

Pai, Chin. "City Transformation: A Study of City Form and City Life in China." Ph.D. diss., University of Michigan, 1987.

———. "Traditional Chinese House Form: The Courtyard House Compound of Peking." *Asian Culture* 17 (1989): 39–56.

Penn, Colin. "Chinese Vernacular Architecture." *Journal of the Royal Institute of British Architects* 72 (1965): 502–7.

Rapoport, Amos. *House Form and Culture.* Englewood Cliffs, N.J.: Prentice-Hall, 1969.

Ruitenbeek, Klaas. *Carpentry and Building in Late Imperial China: A Study of the Fifteenth Century Carpenter's Manual Lu Ban Jing.* Leiden, Netherlands: E. J. Brill, 1993.

———. "Craft and Ritual in Traditional Chinese Carpentry." *Chinese Science* 7 (1986): 1–23.

Rural Architecture in Hong Kong. Hong Kong: Government Information Services, 1979.

Sauer, Carl O. "Foreword to Historical Geography." *Annals, Association of American Geographers* 31 (1941): 1–24.

Shan Deqi. "Cunxi, tianjing, matouqiang—Huizhou minju biji" (Village Streams, Skywells, Gable Walls—Notes on the Vernacular Architecture of Huizhou). *Jianzhu shi luwenji* (Treatise on the History of Architecture) 6 (1984): 120–34.

———. "Yixian Hongcun guihua tanyuan" (Planning of Hongcun in Yixian). *Jianzhu shi luwenji* (Treatise on the History of Architecture) 8 (1987): 87–95.

Shao Mei. *Taiwan minju jianzhu zhi chuantong fengge* (Traditional Styles of Taiwan's Folk Architecture). Taizhong: Donghai University, 1968.

Shen Dongqi. *Nongcun zhuzhai jianzhu sheji* (The Design and Construction of Rural Settlements). Beijing: China Architecture and Building Press, 1991.

———. "Quan sheng jizhen wenhua zhongxin he nongcun zhuzhai sheji fangan jingsai shuping ji huojiang fangan xuandeng" (Commentary on the Award-winning Plans for the Provincewide Town Cultural Center and Rural Housing Competition). *Zhejiang jianzhe* (Zhejiang Architecture) 6, 4 (1985): 34–37.

Siu, Helen F. "Recycling Rituals: Politics and Popular Culture in Contemporary Rural China." In *Unofficial China: Popular Culture and Thought in the People's Republic,* edited by Perry Link, Richard Madsen, and Paul G. Pickowicz, 121–37. Boulder, Colo.: Westview Press, 1989.

Skinner, R.T.F. "Chinese Domestic Architecture." *Journal of the Royal Institute of British Architects* 65 (1958): 430–31.

Smith, Richard J. *Fortune-tellers and Philosophers: Divination in Traditional Chinese Society.* Boulder, Colo.: Westview Press, 1991.

Spencer, Joseph. "The Houses of the Chinese." *Geographical Review* 37 (1947): 254–73.

Stein, Rolf. *The World in Miniature.* Stanford, Calif.: Stanford University Press, 1990.

Steinhardt, Nancy Shatzman, ed. *Chinese Imperial City Planning.* Honolulu: University of Hawaii Press, 1990a.

———. *Chinese Traditional Architecture.* New York: China Institute in America, 1984.

———. "East Asia: Architectural History across War Zones and Political Boundaries." In *The Architectural Historian in America,* edited by Elizabeth Blair MacDougall. Washington, D.C.: National Gallery of Art, 1990b.

Sullivan, Linda F. "Traditional Chinese Regional Architecture: Chinese Houses." *Journal of the Royal Asiatic Society of Great Britain and Ireland, Hong Kong Branch* 12 (1972): 131–49.

Tang Baoheng. "Zhejiang diyu de chuantong he jianzhu xingshi" (The Traditions of the Zhejiang Region and Architectural Forms). *Jianzhu xuebao* (Architectural Journal) 221, 1 (1987): 40–45.

Thorp, Robert L. "Architectural Principles in Early Imperial China: Structural Problems and Their Solution." *Art Bulletin* 68 (1986): 360–75.

————. "Origins of Chinese Architectural Style: The Earliest Plans and Building Types." *Archives of Asian Art* 36 (1983): 22–39.

Tongji Daxue Jianzhu Chengshi Guihua Xueyuan (College of Architecture and Planning, Tongji University). *Zhouzhuang shuixiang jiexiang minju diaocha* (A Survey of Zhouzhuang: Its Streets and Dwellings). Unpublished report, 1986a.

Tongji Daxue Jianzhu Chengshi Guihua Xueyuan (College of Architecture and Planning, Tongji University) and Jiangsu Sheng Kunshan Xian Chengshi Jianshe Ju (Bureau of Urban Construction, Kunshan County, Jiangsu Province), eds. *Shuixiang gu zhen Zhouzhuang zongti ji baohu guihua* (A Master Plan and Preservation Study for the Watertown Zhouzhuang). Unpublished report, 1986b.

Upton, Dell, and John Michael Vlach, eds. *Common Places: Readings in American Vernacular Architecture.* Athens: University of Georgia Press, 1986.

von Poseck, Helena. "How John Chinaman Builds His House." *East of Asia Magazine* 4 (1905): 348–55.

Wang Shaozhou. "Beijing siheyuan zhuzhai de zucheng yu gouzao" (The Composition and Structure of the Courtyard Dwellings of Beijing). *Keji shi wenji* (Collection on the History of Science and Technology) 5 (1980): 92–101.

Wang Shixiang. *Classic Chinese Furniture.* Hong Kong: Joint Publications, 1986.

Wang Shuangwu. "Ming-Qing jianzhu qun Hongcun cunluo minju" (Hongcun Village Residences: A Ming-Qing Architectural Ensemble). *Jianzhu xuwbao* (Architectural Journal) 10 (1984): 74–77.

Wang Shucun. *Ancience Chinese Woodblock Prints.* Beijing: Foreign Languages Press, 1985.

Wang Sung-hsing. "Taiwanese Architecture and the Supernatural." In *Religion and Ritual in Chinese Society,* edited by Arthur P. Wolf, 183–92. Stanford, Calif.: Stanford University Press, 1974.

Williams, C.A.S. *Outlines of Chinese Symbolism and Art Motifs.* Shanghai: Kelly and Walsh, 1932.

Xu Minsu et al., eds. *Suzhou minju* (Folk Dwellings of Suzhou). Beijing: China Architecture and Building Press, 1991.

Xu Yinong. "Zhongguo chuantong fuhe kongjian guannian" (Composite Space Concepts in Traditional Chinese Architecture). *Jianzhushi* (The Architect) 12 (1989): 68–87; 6 (1990): 67–82; 12 (1990): 71–96, 37.

Xue Qiuli. "Zhongguo chuantong yingzao yishi de xiangzhengxing" (The Symbolism of China's Traditional Building Ideas). *Jianzhushi* (The Architect) 38 (1990): 1–13.

Yang Hongxun. "Zhongguo zaoqi jianzhu de fazhan" (The Development of Early Architecture in China). *Jianzhu lishi yu lilun* (Corpus of Architectural History and Theory) 1 (1980): 112–35.

Yunnan sheng sheji yuan (Yunnan Provincial Design Institute). *Yunnan minju* (Folk Dwellings of Yunnan). Beijing: China Building Industry Press, 1986.

Zelinsky, Wilbur. *The Cultural Geography of the United States.* New York: Prentice Hall, 1992.

Zhang Yuhuan. *History and Development of Ancient Chinese Architecture.* Beijing: Beijing Science Press, 1986.

————. *Jilin minju* (Folk Dwellings of Jilin). Beijing: China Building Industry Press, 1985a.

Zhang Yuhuan, chief ed. *Zhongguo gudai jianzhu shi* (History and Development of Ancient Chinese Architecture). Beijing: Science Press, 1985b.

Zhang Zhongyi et al. *Huizhou Mingdai zhuzhai* (Ming Dynasty Houses in Huizhou). Beijing: Architectural Engineering Press, 1957.

Zhongguo jianzhu jishu fazhan zhongxin, jianzhu lishi yanjiusuo (Center for Chinese Architectural Technology and Development, Research Unit for Architectural History). *Zhejiang minju* (Folk Dwellings of Zhejiang). Beijing: China Building Industry Press, 1984.

18

Transportation in the People's Republic of China

JOHN MARNEY

Two essential elements affect transportation: demographics and topography. In China, the billion and more population is distributed unevenly over a widely disparate terrain, where densities of fewer than a dozen people per square kilometer, in the highlands of Tibet and the deserts of Xinjiang and Mongolia, contrast with the overcrowding of a thousand souls into a similar space in the eastern seaboard cities of Shanghai and Tianjin. Other populous and industrial urban centers like Xian, Lanzhou, and Chengdu lie a thousand miles inland behind barriers of mountainous peaks and grotesque moonscapes of yellow dust ravines, and within the great watersheds of the Yangtze, Wei, and Yellow rivers.

Political economics contribute problems. The People's Republic has been impoverished by four decades of radically conflicting social experimentation. Until his death in 1976, Mao Zedong kept localities throughout China self-reliant and independent of each other, the better to resist and survive an invading force. This regionalism and its effect on marketing and transportation is specifically addressed in Wu Yuan-li's *The Spatial Economy of Communist China: A Study on Industrial Location and Transportation*. With the reform movement in 1978 came lateralism, which encouraged traditionally aloof communities to interact and trade with each other. Wu Yuan-li's concerns are brought up to the end of the 1980s in Daniel Little's *Understanding Peasant China: Case Studies in the Philosophy of Social Science*.

The larger expression of lateralism, "opening up to the world," has revealed to the Chinese the inadequacies of their economic infrastructure, especially communications and transportation, whether it be expediting oil supplies from distant Xinjiang oil fields, or hastening foreign tourists on their way. Priority in public spending is now given to improving facilities, such as double-tracking and electrifying rail lines, developing airports, and improving highways.

Historically, earthbound agricultural Chinese society had little need for extensive transportation systems. What worked locally was adequate, and in the vast Chinese hinterland that is still generally true today. Farmers trudge their produce slung on the all-purpose bamboo shoulder pole the several miles to market along dusty, unpaved country tracks, or balance a wheelbarrow, with family members sitting atop the load. Grossly overburdened mule trains reach into big-city streets. High-booted horsemen gallop the grimy grasslands of Mongolia and western regions; black-caped Tibetan nomads trailing a yak-sled piled with yurtpoles and cakes of dried tea trek the windy plateaus of Kokonor. Mule-carts amble among the vine-covered alleys of Turfan; oxcarts creak along the rutted paths of the Guangzhou countryside. Camel caravans string past Dunhuang sand dunes; motorized pedicabs splutter their breezy way above the sunny beaches of Hainan. Snorting tractors of indeterminate vintage and model ubiquitously snarl urban traffic.

Poor areas are desperate. In the backlands of southwest Guizhou province, witness a woman dragging a bamboo A-frame to which is swaddled an invalid relative, stumping along to a township hospital twenty miles down the road. Conversely, at scenic resorts like Mount Emei, brute human labor commercially renders skylift facilities: For a pittance, tourists may trust themselves to be piggybacked up the precipitous flights of rockhewn steps. In such mountainous areas where neither wheel nor hoof can go, goods are portered with backframe and headstrap. Ronald Hsia raises this stoic, day-to-day drudgery of local transportation to an intellectual level in his study, *The Role of Labor-Intensive Investment Projects in China's Capital Formation.*

With probably the sole exception of hilly Chongqing, the bicycle is in China what the automobile is in the United States. Relative cost is about the same: six months' pay for a coveted top-of-the-line Phoenix or Flying Pigeon model (these in short supply and reserved for privileged purchasers). The bicycle serves the overcrowded community well. It creates no chemical or undue noise pollution and almost never wears out, becomes outmoded, or ends up in the scrapyard. Parking is convenient and cheap (at less than half a U.S. penny) in a controlled lot—a roped-off area on the sidewalk licensed to a senior citizen. Numbered wooden or metal tokens permit redemption. The row of bicycle stands is a feature of urban Chinese scenery.

Speeds are moderate and most accidents end up in a bruised kneecap or torn trousers. The vehicle requires no great amount of resources or hi-tech industry to produce or run, and repair businesses, tooled only with a wrench and a tire pump, operate handily at roadside street corners. Such considerations are important since China has not developed the personal legal and insurance mechanisms that protect the individual in the West.

In China, each machine must be registered with the police. An identity number is stamped into the frame, and a license plate is displayed. Bicycles come with a fitted lock, but theft is very common. However, chances of getaway are extremely limited in every respect, and thanks to registration, recovery is equally common. More pesky is the theft of small parts and fittings, like a leather saddle or the resonator element of the bell.

The bicycle itself, made in China, is a dour object. Models are uniform, heavy and lumpish, and strictly utilitarian, with standard fittings like upright handlebars and rod brakes. Color may vary, although black by far predominates. There are no ingenious entrepreneurs marketing offshoot merchandise like special toeclips or fancy helmets, or expensive faddish outfits. Needless to say, the appearance of an imported ten-speed, the property of a resident foreigner, draws a circle of mightily impressed gawkers. Nor are there vivid television ads and "biker" magazines to suggest that bicycling is anything more than pedaling sedately along a flat road to a daily job.

The Western image is of a sea of faceless cyclists, tinkling like the singing sands of Dunhuang. But regulations single out each individual. Passengers are forbidden and fines, say for taking a shortcut across an intersection, are usually fifty cents, exacted on the spot (equivalent to about U.S. $10). Tearaway "hero vehiclists" are but an odd nuisance.

Since the private car is still a rarity in China, the immediate alternative to the bicycle is the public bus. Vehicles are more or less modern and well maintained according to the local economy. In bigger cities, articulated electric or motor buses, decently washed and swept, offer regular, pennies-cheap, and convenient service along efficiently planned routes. In smaller country towns, ramshackle rattletraps bump their muddy way between stops. Long-distance buses, covering routes from a few hours to a week long, operate where rail lines do not extend, or as a more frequent and cheaper, if less comfortable, alternative to the train.

Buses are not for the claustrophobic. Here, Chinese civility and orderly precedence give way to the mob. The crush of passengers inside and out, with all their fantastic impedimenta, contend in opposing tides against the compressed-air folding doors. The crowding results in other social disorders. Pickpocketing is rife and frequently accomplished by slitting the victim's purse or pocket with a razor blade pasted between two rail tickets. Clothing may be slit without concomitant theft out of frustration and spite. Cigarette burns are an irritating hazard, but they seem to be accepted philosophically. Sexual impudences go undetected and modestly unreported. Entertainingly colorful arguments break out between passengers, or commonly between passenger and ticket collector over change or nonpayment of fare. Courtesy is not expected. Only the "little emperor" (a healthy male child born into the "one child per family" system) may demand that passengers yield their seat to him.

Fare collection systems vary with the sophistication of the management. Season tickets, ticket packs, and transfers may be available. Some long-distance routes designate seating. On more orderly routes, passengers pay the driver as they board. Most commonly, to provide employment, one or two girls are assigned to each bus to roam among the passengers or sit behind a tiny cash desk by the exits, punch flimsy tickets, and call the stops.

Privately operated minivan buses supplement city, local, and long-distance public systems. At about double the cost of a public bus ticket, and with limited seating, they are a reasonable means of transportation for the more affluent citizen.

For more pressing or official occasions, the Chinese may resort to the extra expense of a taxi. Taxi ranks are run by both state-controlled and private companies licensed by the state. The passenger pays cash, and the driver issues tickets of various denomination for reimbursement by the passenger's work unit if the journey was a business expense. Fares vary according to the size of the cab, and may be doubled to cover the taxi's return to base. After ten kilometers, the Beijing cabby switches the meter to increase the fare by 50 percent. Originally this was to cover the extra cost of journeys outside the city limits, but drivers now increase the fare even within the city. At night, the meter is switched off altogether. In smaller towns, unmetered gouging has compelled local authorities to crack down on the profiteering, and a hot line was set up in Beijing to handle complaints. By law, taxis (and other cars) may carry only four passengers.

The Chinese are credited with the invention of the wheelbarrow, the double-shaft cart, the stirrup, the breast harness, and the horse collar (although the horse was not indigenous to China proper). Specifically addressing the technological development of transportation is Joseph Needham, *Science and Civilization in China*. In systematic detail, and with illustrations from original texts, Needham researches chariots in ancient China, wagons and handcarts, the wheelbarrow and sailing carriage, the hodometer, and the south-pointing carriage. In a following section, he discusses harnesses and their history. A vast bibliography enhances the seminal utility of his text. Suzanne Ogden, *Global Studies, China*, provides several columns on the Chinese invention of the stirrup, dated at the third century C.E., and the wheelbarrow she attributes to the first-century B.C.E., semi-legendary Guo Yu. Jacques Gernet's general survey, *A History of Chinese Civilization*, discusses the fourth-century B.C.E. technical development in China of the double-shafted cart, wheel "dishing," the breast harness which replaced the strangling neck yoke, and the horse collar, which appeared there between the fifth and ninth centuries.

More recently, if there is anything that can be done with bicycle wheels, the Chinese have done it. There are bicycle trailers, bicycle sidecars, and trucked tricycles. Tiny two-stroke engines add a useful fraction of a horsepower. Motorcycles range from quarter-horsepower, Chinese-Japanese joint venture mopeds to the heavy, showpiece all-Nippon Yamaha.

Perhaps the most dangerously unstable vehicle the Chinese ever contrived is the motorized three-wheeler. The rear axle of a motorcycle is extended to accommodate two wheels, a small truckbed is added behind the driver's saddle, two boards are fitted along the insides to seat six or eight people, and the contraption is covered with a bamboo or metal hooped canvas canopy. A clear plastic-sheet cabin encloses the driver's seat. Private entrepreneurs operate them as short-range buses, taxis, and pickups, and to make the extra dollar or so, at times and places and under conditions eschewed by their competition. Their economical utility and maneuverability are undeniable, but they are much attenuated by safety risks.

For the mass of Chinese citizenry, air travel is not an option. Cost is prohibitive, and, in any case, available seating is reserved for those on official business and foreign tourists. A letter of introduction and an explanation of the business sealed by the traveler's work unit is usually required for individual purchase of a ticket. In most cases, the unit itself acquires and issues the vouchers. To prevent long-term booking, whereby seats on popular routes might be sold out months in advance, ticketing agencies require the traveler to make advance application for a specific departure, and, depending on the agency, within one to four days of the flight pay for the ticket on a first-come first-served basis.

Until recently, all civilian domestic and international air travel in China came under the purview of the State Council Civil Aviation General Administration of China (CAAC, i.e., China Airlines). Large regional administrations under CAAC in turn controlled local air stations. However, under the new reforms, to encourage CAAC to improve its notoriously unreliable services, private domestic airlines, for example, Dragon Air, have been licensed to operate along certain popular routes in competition with the state's line.

The development and expansion of airport facilities are a state priority. Airports at major coastal cities approach international standards, but there still exist public landing fields that do not have tarmac runways, and the shorthop 1950s Soviet Illyushins or Antonovs trundle their terrified passengers in their canvas bucket seats across grassy meadows. Navigational and all-weather operation gear, plus maintenance and repair facilities, are mercifully scheduled for modernization. But pilots often refuse to fly in adverse conditions, adding perhaps days to delays in scheduled flights. The government does not announce accident statistics, but the record is not good, and the occasional planeload of foreign tourists that goes down excites international concern.

Paul Theroux's anecdotal *Riding the Iron Rooster* describes his rare flight aboard an "old Russian jet, its metal covering wrinkled and cracked like cigarette pack tinfoil," with "stewardesses in old mailman's uniforms" there as much to keep order as to issue the hard candy, tepid green tea, and cheap souvenir gift (a paper fan, a brocade purse, or plastic wallet). Alcohol is not served inflight, but the passenger cabin soon fills with cigarette smoke, and even the girls' combined forces are insufficient to control the pandemonium that breaks out upon touchdown, with passengers scrambling to retrieve their carryons and throng the sealed exits.

The Chinese prehistory of aeronautical engineering, including the kite, the helicopter top, the parachute, and balloon, is discussed in Needham's *Science and Civilization in China*. Nowadays, China has its own fledgling aircraft industry, producing the small Yun class planes. However, the majority of its main domestic line and international fleet are U.S. or British Boeings, Lockheed Tristars, and Viscounts. Airfreight services, integral in Western economies, are only in their infancy in China. Cargoes are usually emergency items or hi-tech machinery needed on-site in remote areas.

Throughout history, waterways have provided the means of long-distance transportation in China. Scholar-officials en route to and from provincial postings across the face of the country over the centuries have left an enduring literature of poetic and artistic impressions of their voyages. The myriad rivers and streams became the veins and arteries of commerce. T. R. Tregear, *A Geography of China,* cites original materials to describe the historical development of China's water communications and domestic and international trade routes from earliest times. General histories of China invariably mention the early seventh-century Grand Canal, on the scale of the construction of the Great Wall and of far greater utility, and how the canal served for ten centuries thereafter in the transportation of tax grain and products from the empire south of the Yangtze River to the capital domains in the north.

Today, China has more than 100,000 miles of navigable, though seasonal, inland waterways. Winter icing of the Amur River in the extreme north, for example, and catastrophic silting of the Yellow River and its tributaries attenuate the commercial value of these great systems. The Grand Canal, once China's major north-south waterway, like the Great Wall, is largely derelict. To date only southern stretches, as much tourist attraction as channel for freight, have been repaired.

The West River system drains southeast China and flows into the Pearl River and the China Sea at Guangzhou (Canton). The great bulk of Hong Kong–China commerce plies the Pearl and from the blanketing white morning river mist emerges a cacophony from the motley craft that tie up at its quaysides.

As ever, the Yangtze River remains the principal artery of China's commercial waterways. Its 1,500-mile navigable length extends from Shanghai on the central eastern seaboard upriver westward via the major ports of Nanjing, and Wuhan, through the spectacular Gezhouba hydroelectric dams at Ichang and the Scylla and Charybdis of the towering Three Gorges to Chongqing, and thence to Chengdu and beyond. A thousand smaller ports thrive on its banks. Tourists may take the scenic three-day steamer trip from Chongqing to Wuhan; the return voyage upstream takes five days, such being the force of the current. In the eerie yellow light of these upper reaches, gangs of haulers still bend and strain on steep levees and footpaths worn smooth by centuries of calloused feet. Yoked to webs of massive ropes, they heave flat-bottomed, sluggish barges a pace at a time against the roiling tide.

One of the most eloquent and touching Yangtze travelogs, John Hersey's novel, *A Single Pebble,* dispatches a youthful American engineer to survey the Gorges for a hydroelectric dam project. Berthed on a Chinese fishing junk, the lad observes the hard life and camaraderie of the crew, and their river lore and superstitions. Similarly realistic, quasi-autobiographical description, however much presented as fiction, is U.S. Navy engineer Richard McKenna's *The Sand Pebbles,* which remembers life on the middle reaches of the Yangtze and its tributaries at the time of Chiang Kai-shek's accession to power as leader of the Nationalist Party in 1925.

In the hilly, riverine terrain and lake district south of the Yangtze, waterways serve as roads. Indeed, the capital of fifteenth-century Ming China, Hangzhou, is known as the "Venice of the East." Waterborne vendors sell daily provisions door to door to canalside Suzhou housewives; along limpid Guangxi streams, graceful youngsters pole their slender bamboo rafts.

Chinese shipbuilding and designs are unique and effective. Needham describes early Chinese experiments with the paddleboat. General histories of China, for example, Dun J. Li's *The Ageless Chinese,* recount the great Ming armadas which, a century earlier than Columbus, from 1405 to 1431 made half-a-dozen voyages reaching as far as the east coast of Africa. One such fleet consisted of sixty-two ocean-going vessels manned by 27,800 souls dispatched, says Li, "to glorify Chinese arms in the remote regions and show off the wealth and power of the Central Kingdom." Li notes that the material and commercial motives that prompted European expansion in later times was notably absent. Curiously, these initiatives failed to develop, and by the nineteenth century, when illegal traffic in opium was the major enterprise, China's seas had become dominated by Western sea power.

The bulk of China's modern maritime fleet, some 10,000 tons, is built to serve the nation's transportation needs along its 3,500-mile coastline. Larger deep-sea vessels are constructed domestically for international trade, but China also purchases tanker and specialized shipping from overseas. Much of the merchant fleet sails under flags of convenience, particularly Hong Kong registration. For more than a decade, priority has been given to shipbuilding and also to enlarging and deepening major ports, and to developing and modernizing quayside loading and other port facilities. International joint ventures for such projects are encouraged.

Ferryboats are an everyday aspect of transportation on inland rivers as well as on coastal waters. The relatively small number of highways and bridges and the lack of convenient access to those that do exist necessitate local ferry services. These can range from small steamers and paddlewheelers to rope-pulled rafts and, in at least one remote area of the Yellow River, a cowhide into which the passenger crawls. Therein he is sealed, with half-an-hour's air supply, and paddled across the river by the ferryman who is seated or lying on top.

Coastal liners, for example, steamships that cross Beihai from Dalian on the Liaoning Peninsula to Yantai on the Shandong Peninsula, and the South China Sea from Haikou on Hainan Island to Hong Kong or Guangdong, save days of overland travel around the coast, but conditions on board are unkempt. Classes from second to fifth determine the deck and location, and the number of inmates to a cabin. Second class, open to a seadeck, has six or eight berths, three to a tier. Steerage passengers crowd the alleys, gravitating to areas around the smokestack to warm themselves on the deckplates.

The absence of an interstate network of highspeed superhighways in China precludes rapid road transportation and distribution. Rather, as noted above, trucking tends to be local, whether it be the unbroken columns of coal-haulers inbound from the Shanxi mines to the railhead at Datong, or a load of raw cotton for the dusty looms of Xianyang. Only in the far west, beyond China proper, has trucking developed into a large-scale organized enterprise. Truck depots, perhaps dispatching several hundred long-distance vehicles, have been established at the opposite ends of the military road, constructed by the People's Liberation Army. Lhasa, capital of Tibet, connects with Golomud, the railhead in central Qinghai province, Dunhuang, further northwest in Gansu province, and on to Urumuchi in far northwest Xinjiang province. Obsolete, no-frills Liberation four-tonners, produced at the No. 1 Changchun Vehicle Plant in the industrial northeast; newer East Wind lorries; and imported, air-conditioned Mitsubishi trucks make their dash along the bumpy surface across the perilous and circuitous northern slopes of the Himalayas to the high point at Tanggula Pass (whose appellative peak rises to more than 20,000 feet), and upon elevated two-way lanes traversing the deserts and marshes of Qinghai.

Public buses too make the six-day journey from Golomud to Lhasa, but thumbing a ride on a truck is faster by half, if twice the price. Hitchhiking is not an institution in China, but in these remote localities, it is possible to win the services of the two codrivers, who are usually of central Asian Kazak or Uighur minority nationality. By law, trucks may carry only three persons in the cab, so any companion wayfarer must jump off before arrival at Chinese police and military checkpoints, which abound in Tibet to inspect papers and check for illicit weapons, and rejoin his group down the road.

The People's Liberation Army, of course, controls the largest fleet of serviceable long-distance, heavy trucks. These vehicles are not subject to the stop-and-search authority of the civilian police, or to provincial customs duty. It is profitable and expedient, therefore, for private entrepreneurs to suborn army drivers into transporting civilian goods free but for the price of the bribe. Conversely, army drivers may be assigned civilian service, and are known to help out, gratis, in quite private emergencies.

Work unit transportation is the nearest thing the ordinary Chinese comes to in private travel. Units are authorized to operate motorpools, and in more affluent enterprises, the pool may boast several limousines for its senior officials, school and personnel buses, and a repair shop. The buses, restricted to unit residents (and friends and relatives of the driver), run on a regular schedule and to set pickup points. The limousines are predominantly ponderous Shanghai models, Chinese manufactured with minimal fittings in the 1950s Russian style. The behemoth Red Flag is for senior statesmen. But any private car is a matter of great privilege and status, and most workers never see the inside of one during their entire lifetimes.

Control of motor facilities confers real power. Subunits are not permitted their own transportation, but even quite lowly officials who, for one reason or another, command transportation authorizations or access to gas allocations, normally very scarce, can wield considerable clout. The use of public resources for personal favors—and a wealth of often bizarre anecdotes supports the contention—is of course corrupt. But such pervasive petty corruption has become a necessary means of circumventing the stultifying hand of Communist bureaucracy.

Certification for a driving license in China requires Chinese drivers to complete a two-year course at polytechnic level, during which they learn driver's regulations, skills, and vehicle repair. Nevertheless, road accidents are endemic. Prison sentences for vehicular homicide are swift and certain. But penalties seem not to diminish the numbers of tractors, with their monstrously overloaded trailers, lying belly-up in ditches, and the mangled remains of trucks and motorcycles caught in head-on collisions across the ill-defined centerline, at frequent intervals along country roads.

Road conditions do not favor the motorized driver. Intersection traffic lights disappear amid the boughs of trees planted beneath them. At night, the lights of urban traffic must be extinguished to avoid dazzling on-coming drivers and to pick out the chaos of straggling chickens and children, pigs and pedestrians who innocently roam the pavement. Except in designated central streets and hospital precincts, as a courtesy, drivers sound their horns continuously.

The subject of Chinese railways has perennially attracted the interest of moviemakers and writers, notably Patrick Bruce Whitehouse, in *China by Rail,* and most recently, train-veteran Paul Theroux, whose *Riding the Iron Rooster* may have said the last word. In China, rail is the cheapest and most efficient means of transportation. It is estimated that more than two-thirds of the nation's freight is shipped by rail, and that trains carry more than 3 million passengers a day.

The history of railways in China and their political and economic significance are discussed in Leung Chi-keung's *China, Railway Patterns and National Goals* and in Ernest P. Liang's *China, Railways and Agricultural Development, 1875–1935.* Prior to the Communist victory in 1949, China's railways were in what the *Encyclopedia of China Today* describes as a state of shambles. An ''incoherent array'' of more than 100 track gauges and rail sizes, the heritage of a century of foreign concessions, littered the northeast and more accessible coastal areas. At Sino-Soviet border crossings, passengers must still disembark and wait nine or ten hours while the coaches are jacked up and the appropriate wheel assemblies are refitted (Kaplan and Sobin, eds.).

Chao Yung-hsin describes the condition of China's railways shortly after the Communist takeover in his *Railways in Communist China.* In China today, with the exception of Lhasa in Tibet and Kashgar in southwestern Xinjiang, standardized heavy-duty rail networks reach to virtually every city and town. Under the Ministry of Railways (now a commission), new lines are being extended, for example, from Urumuchi across the Soviet border to Alma Ata. Established lines are being double-tracked and electrified. The picturesque old iron steam engines, whose manufacture at Datong is still a tourist attraction, are being phased out in favor of more efficient diesel-electric locomotives. Train-buff Robert Adley contributes a description of Chinese railways and the locomotives that ran on them in his *To China for Steam.*

Railway engineering used to be the province of the Western professional, for example, William Barclay Parsons (1859–1932), who wrote *An American Engineer in China*. However, the engineering achievement of China's modern rail network lives up to the country's historical propensity for completing grand public works. The scenic Bao-Cheng line, from the railhead at Baoji crossing the Qinling Mountains south to Chengdu, might be considered a modern wonder of the world. Two hundred miles of the 600-mile main line continuing south to Kunming comprise tunnels and bridges across range upon range of eastern Himalayan foothills. Such lines, communicating with border regions, are considered strategic and are maintained in part by military personnel, many thousands of whose lives were sacrificed in their construction.

Heroics aside, rail accidents on the single track or mountainous routes are frequent. Derailments take a steep toll of lives and property and cause delays of thousands of hours annually to traffic already bottlenecked by other obstacles. The system itself is overburdened, and corrupt rail officials make a tidy side income from reassigning freight space to favored enterprises. Conversely, according to complaints in the official press, freight handlers, frustrated by their lack of access to desirable products because of cash or status constraints, occasionally conspire to sabotage consignments.

Much has already been written about the passenger service. It too is overcrowded and cannot keep up with the demand, and as with the airlines, the ticketing system is designed to allow equitable access. Tickets are valid for a specified date and only to the terminus of a particular route. Through tickets beyond that terminus to other destinations are not available, and stopovers en route are not permitted. Return tickets may be ordered and paid for in advance, but in all other respects, the actual issuing of the ticket follows the same time-consuming and fatiguing procedure as in the purchase of the outbound ticket.

Ticket scalpers in the station yard run a thriving business, although the rail police now and then mount campaigns to suppress the profiteering. The desperate traveler may also buy a platform ticket, pile on the train with the crush of peasantry, and pray that the conductor will permit him to upgrade.

To allow downline passengers a chance at rail service, ticket quotas are apportioned to provincial stations according to their size and importance. Thus, the number of Beijing through passengers on the Beijing-Chengdu line, for example, will be restricted to reserve berths for passengers at Zhengzhou, Xian, and Baoji. Lack of nationally linked computerized vending and accounting, however, attenuates the efficiency of the device.

Chinese train stations have none of the purposeful bustle and excitement of their Western counterparts. They are crowded, and a sporadic surge occurs whenever a platform is opened, but it is the movement of panic and desperation. At such moments, crowd control can be craven or gallant. Otherwise, the bleak halls convey an air of helplessness and frustration. Sleeping bodies occupy the rows of wooden benches. Sweepers come by at intervals to clean away the mounds of discarded melon and fruit peel, cigarette butts, and the detritus of a rural population. Foyers and lobbies are blocked by peasantry squatting on the dirty ground with their burlap bundles and shoulder poles, blankly resigned to an interminable wait.

The three classes of passenger seating accommodation are also well documented, for example, in Theroux. First-class "soft sleeper" was for a while open to the general public, but the privilege was rescinded, and the four-bunk cabins remain the preserve of government officials and foreigners. Theroux devotes much of his space to describing the conditions in these accommodations, his fellow passengers, the quality of the food, and the service.

At half the cost of first class and available to the public, "hard sleepers" are the most desirable accommodations and consequently the most difficult to obtain. A coach is partitioned into open compartments housing six berths in tiers of three. Logically, the middle bunk is slightly more costly: The bottom bunk becomes a seat for all and sundry; the top bunk is difficult of access by a ladder and close in all weathers. Theroux describes the crowded compartments as "a great sluttish pleasure for everyone—a big middle-aged pajama party, full of reminiscences, chatter, smoking and slurping tea, playing cards, and shuffling around in slippers."

"Hard seats" are for the peasant masses, and unfortunate travelers who cannot obtain a sleeper accommodation. The large, high-backed, green vinyl benches seat six or, at the ends of the cavernous coach, four. Seats are numbered, but disputes over possession can be violent and have to be settled by the guards. Tables fold beneath the windows, and continuous overhead racks accommodate some of the voluminous baggage. The aisles are blocked by seatless passengers, who must stand the duration of their three- or four-day journey. Constant flows of people shove to and fro, obstructing ticket inspectors; floor sweepers; guards; vendors of cigarettes, candy, and bottled soft drinks; and attendants with their large kettles of hot water and box lunches of rice and meat for sale. Hard-seat passengers have access to the dining cars, but like everyone else aboard, they are more likely to stock up on provisions at wayside stations, whose platform vendors supply fresh local produce.

Perhaps less worldly, these peasant people are more cautious in their social relations, more conservative or shy, and less ready to tell their business. But in the adversity of hard-seat travel, the Chinese traits of patience, kindness, and sharing shine through.

As with other activities in China, transportation is less system than people. Bureaucratic administration may be uncivil and obstructive, but it is people who overcome the myriad obstacles in this overcrowded society. "People" also translates into "back door," the essential network of personal associations and connections by which cramping official regulations are circumvented, and scarce commodities like tickets and vouchers, gasoline, and spare parts are obtained. The Chinese leadership has been properly responsive to the need for improving and developing national transportation systems. But as a country in which 80 percent of the population lives in rural conditions, China will long remain a land of the bicycle and shoulder pole.

APPENDIX: RECENT STATISTICS

Railways

State-funded railways to 1989	53,186 km
Local-funded railways	4,424.4 km
National cargo volume, 1991	1.47 billion tons
Local cargo volume	200 million tons
	9 billion tons/km
Local railway funding, 1986–1991	RMB Y1.72 billion
	(U.S. $400 million)
Local passenger volume, 1986–1991	31.67 million
Local turnover volume, 1986–1991	1.5 billion passengers/km
Local railways profit	RMB Y100 million (U.S. $25 million)
Taxes to state	RMB Y40 million (U.S. $10 million)

Plans are to extend locally funded and locally administered railways another 6,000 km during the 1990s, bringing the total length of China's local railways to over 10,000 km by the end of the century. (Xinhua News Agency, June 9, 1991.)

Roadways   1.04 million km

Traffic Accidents

Total motor vehicles in PRC (2% of world total)	13 million
Total bicycles (average 1 per 3 persons)	400 million
Traffic control police	130,000
1990 total accidents	250,297
Deaths	49,271
Injuries	155,072
Damages	RMB Y363 million (U.S. $91 million)

Cause of Accidents

Motorized vehicles	48%
Bicycles	36%
Pedestrians	14%
Other	2%

Further analysis shows that driving on the wrong side of the road, carelessness, and driving through red lights are by far the major causes of accidents. Delays in medical treatment and lack of medical facilities are cited as exacerbating traffic accident–related fatalities and serious injuries. (*China Daily,* October 1, 1991.)

Airways

Civil airports	98
CAAC air routes	
Domestic	393
International (connecting with 37 cities in 27 countries)	44
CAAC fleet	206 planes
Passengers (1990)	16.6 million
Cargo	370,000 tons
Air-control facilities expenditures	
1986–1991	RMB Y350 million (U.S. $10 million)

BIBLIOGRAPHY

The importance of transportation in society ensures that even the most general surveys of China include more or less detail, with general agreement, on the subject. For example, see John K. Fairbank and Edwin O. Reischauer, *China, Tradition and Transformation* (Boston: Houghton-Mifflin, 1978); Charles O. Hucker, *China's Imperial Past* (Stanford, Calif.: Stanford University Press, 1975); and John T. Meskill, *An Introduction to Chinese Civilization* (London: D. C. Heath, 1973). Conditions and means of travel by air, rail, and road are described in widely available guidebooks and timetables; routes are indicated in atlases and maps.

Adley, Robert. *To China for Steam.* Poole, Dorset, England: Blandford Press, 1983.

Chao Yung-hsin. *Railways in Communist China.* Kowloon, Hong Kong: Union Research Institute, 1956.

Gernet, Jacques. *A History of Chinese Civilization.* Translated by J. R. Foster. Cambridge, England: Cambridge University Press, 1982.

Hersey, John. *A Single Pebble.* New York: Alfred A. Knopf, 1956.

Hsia, Ronald. *The Role of Labor-Intensive Investment Projects in China's Capital Formation.* Cambridge, Mass.: Massachusetts Institute of Technology, 1954.

Kaplan, Frederick M., and Julian M. Sobin, eds. *Encyclopedia of China Today.* 3d rev. ed. New York: Harper and Row, 1981.

Leung Chi-keung. *China, Railway Patterns and National Goals.* Chicago: University of Chicago, Department of Geography, 1980.

Li, Dun J. *The Ageless Chinese.* New York: Scribner, 1965.

Liang, Ernest P. *China, Railways and Agricultural Development, 1875–1935.* Chicago: University of Chicago, Department of Geography, 1982.

Little, Daniel. *Understanding Peasant China: Case Studies in the Philosophy of Social Science.* New Haven, Conn.: Yale University Press, 1989.

McKenna, Richard. *The Sand Pebbles.* New York: Harper and Row, 1962.

Needham, Joseph. *Science and Civilization in China.* Vol. 4, Pt. II, *Mechanical Engineering.* Cambridge, England: Cambridge University Press, 1962.

Ogden, Suzanne. *Global Studies, China.* 4th ed. Guilford, Conn.: Dushkin, 1991.

Parsons, William Barclay. *An American Engineer in China.* New York: McClure, Philips and Co., 1900.

Theroux, Paul. *Riding the Iron Rooster.* Cape Cod, Mass.: Scriveners, 1988.

Tregear, T. R. *A Geography of China.* London: University of London Press, 1965.

Whitehouse, Patrick Bruce. *China by Rail.* New York: Vendome Press, 1988.

Wu Yuan-li. *The Spatial Economy of Communist China: A Study on Industrial Location and Transportation.* New York: Praeger, 1967.

Selected Bibliography

BIBLIOGRAPHIES, DICTIONARIES, ENCYCLOPEDIAS, INDEXES

Andrews, Theodora. *A Bibliography on Herbs, Herbal Medicine, "Natural" Foods, and Unconventional Medical Treatment.* Littleton, Colo.: Libraries Unlimited, 1982.

Bailey, Liberty Hyde. *Manual of Cultivated Plants.* New York: Macmillan, 1949.

———. *The Standard Cyclopedia of Horticulture.* 3 vols. New York: Macmillan, 1942.

Beijing Municipal Bureau of Postal Service. *Quanguo baokan neirong huibian* (A Nationwide Compilation of Newspaper Contents). Beijing: The Bureau's publications, 1985– .

Berton, Peter, and Eugene Wu. *Contemporary China: A Research Guide.* Stanford, Calif.: Joint Committee on Contemporary China of the American Council of Learned Societies and the Social Science Research Council, Hoover Institute on War, Revolution, and Peace, 1967.

Center for Book and Newspaper Materials. *Quanguo baokan suoyin* (An Index to the Country's Newspapers and Periodicals). Beijing: People's University Press, 1980– .

Chan, Ming K. *Historiography of the Chinese Labor Movement, 1895–1945: A Bibliography of Chinese Source Materials at the Hoover Institute.* Stanford, Calif.: Hoover Institute Press, 1981.

Chang, Lucie, Charlotte Furth, and Hon-Ming Yip, eds. *Women in China: A Bibliography of Available English-Language Materials.* Berkeley: University of California, Institute of East Asian Studies, 1984.

Chang, T. C., et al., eds. *Zhongguo dalu dixia wenxue mulu* (Catalog of Chinese Underground Literatures). Taipei: Institute of Current China Studies, 1981.

Chen, C. R. *Zhong chao yao bai ke quan shu* (Encyclopedia of Chinese Drugs). 2 vols. Hong Kong: Shanghai Publishing Co., 1962.

Chinese Academy of Social Sciences. *Zhongguo jingjishi tiyao* (A Bibliography of China's Economic History). Jinan: Social Sciences Press, 1988.

Ci hai (Encyclopedia of Chinese Words). Shanghai: Wordbook Press, 1979.

Communist China: A Bibliographic Survey. Washington, D.C.: U.S. Government Printing Office, 1971.

Dale, Ralph A. *The Complete Guide to Acupuncture: The Five-Volume Reference Library.* North Miami Beach, Fla.: Dialectic Publications, 1990.

Dictionary of Traditional Chinese Medicine. San Francisco: China Books and Periodicals, 1984.

Eberhard, Wolfram. *A Dictionary of Chinese Symbols: Hidden Symbols in Chinese Life and Thought.* London: Routledge and Kegan Paul, 1983.

Editorial Board. *Encyclopedia of New China.* Beijing: Beijing Foreign Language Press, 1987.

English-Chinese Medical Dictionary. New York: French and European Publications, 1980.

Hook, Brian, ed. *The Cambridge Encyclopedia of China.* New York: Cambridge University Press, 1991.

Hu Fuming, ed., with James Townsend. *Zhengzhixue cidian* (A Dictionary of Political Science). Zhejiang: Zhejiang Educational Publishing House, 1989.

Hu Wenbin, ed. *Zhongguo xiandai wuxia xiaoshuo jianshang cidian* (A Dictionary of Modern Chinese Gallant Fiction Appreciation). Shijiazhuang: Huashan Literature and Art Press, 1991.

Hu Wenbin, Wang Hailin, and Luo Liqun, eds. *Zhongguo wuxia xiaoshuo cidian* (A Dictionary of Chinese Gallant Fiction). Shijiazhuang: Huashan Literature and Art Press, 1991.

Hunyin yu jiating cidian (The Dictionary of Marriage and Family). Beijing: International Broadcast Press, 1989.

Jiang Yihai, ed. *Manhua zhishi cidian* (Dictionary of Cartoon Knowledge). Nanjing: Nanjing University Press, 1989.

Kan, Lai-bing. *Parasitic Infections of Man and Animals: A Bibliography of Articles in Chinese Medical Periodicals, 1949–1964.* Ann Arbor, Mich.: Books on Demand, 1966. Reprint. 1991.

Kaplan, Frederick M., and Julian M. Sobin, eds. *Encyclopedia of China Today.* 3d rev. ed. New York: Harper and Row, 1981.

Lang Shaojun et al., eds. *Zhongguo shuhua jianshang cidian* (Dictionary of Chinese Paintings and Calligraphy Appreciation). Beijing: China Youth Publishing House, 1988.

Lent, John A. *Comic Art in Africa, Asia, Australia, and Latin America: An International Bibliography.* Westport, Conn.: Greenwood Press, forthcoming.

Leung, Albert Y. *Encyclopedia of Common Natural Ingredients Used in Food, Drugs and Cosmetics.* New York: Wiley-Interscience, 1980.

Lin Dehai. *Zhongguo xinwen shumu daquan* (An Annotated Bibliography of Chinese Press Publications 1903–1987). Beijing: Xinhua Press, 1989.

Lu, K. S. *Encyclopedia of Chinese Drugs and Their Chemical Constituents.* Hong Kong: Shanghai Press, 1955. (In Chinese)

Nelson, Randy, and Katherine C. Whitaker. *The Martial Arts: An Annotated Bibliography.* New York: Garland, 1988.

Newman, Jacqueline. *Chinese Cookbooks: An Annotated English Language Compendium/Bibliography.* New York: Garland Publishing Co., 1987.

Ning Zhongyi and Lin Guohi, eds. *Zhongguo wuxia xiaoshuo jianshang cidian* (A Dictionary of Chinese Gallant Fiction Appreciation). Beijing: International Culture Press, 1992.

Lindqvist, Cecilia. *China: Empire of Living Symbols.* Translated from the Swedish by Joan Tate. Reading, Pa.: Addison-Wesley Publishing House, 1991.

Link, Perry, Richard Madsen, and Paul G. Pickowicz, eds. *Unofficial China: Popular Culture and Thought in the People's Republic.* Boulder, Colo.: Westview Press, 1989.

Little, Daniel. *Understanding Peasant China: Case Studies in the Philosophy of Social Science.* New Haven, Conn.: Yale University Press, 1989.

Liu, Da. *The Tao of Health and Longevity.* New York: Schocken, 1978.

McKenna, Richard. *The Sand Pebbles.* New York: Harper and Row, 1962.

Medley, Margaret. *The Chinese Potter, A Practical History of Chinese Ceramics.* Oxford, England: Phaidon, 1976.

Meskill, John T. *An Introduction to Chinese Civilization.* London: D. C. Heath, 1973.

Moore, Charles A. *The Chinese Mind: Essentials of Chinese Philosophy and Culture.* Honolulu: University of Hawaii Press, 1967.

Needham, Joseph, et al. *Science and Civilisation in China.* 14 vols. to date. Cambridge, England: Cambridge University Press, 1954– .

Ogden, Suzanne. *Global Studies, China.* 4th ed. Guilford, Conn.: Dushkin, 1991.

Osgood, Cornelius. *The Chinese.* Tucson: University of Arizona Press, 1975.

Ropp, Paul S., ed. *Heritage of China: Contemporary Perspectives on Chinese Civilization.* Berkeley: University of California Press, 1990.

Rowe, William. *Hankow: Conflict and Community in a Chinese City, 1976–1985.* Stanford, Calif.: Stanford University Press, 1989.

Sima Qian. *Shiji* (The Historical Records, annotated). Changsha: Yuelu Press, 1988.

Skinner, G. William. "Marketing and Social Structure in Rural China." *Journal of Asian Studies* 24 (1964–65): 3–43, 195–228, 363–400.

Smith, Richard J. *Fortune-tellers and Philosophers: Divination in Traditional Chinese Society.* Boulder, Colo.: Westview Press, 1991.

Tregear, T. R. *A Geography of China.* London: University of London Press, 1965.

Van Gulik, R. H. *Sexual Life in Ancient China: A Preliminary Survey of Chinese Sex and Society from ca. 1500 B.C. till 1644 A.D.* Leiden, Netherlands: E. J. Brill, 1961.

Wang Bomin. *Zhongguo huihua shi* (History of Chinese Paintings). Shanghai: Shanghai People's Arts Publishing House, 1982.

Wang Shixiang. *Classic Chinese Furniture.* Hong Kong: Joint Publications, 1986.

Wang Shucun. *Ancient Chinese Woodblock Prints.* Beijing: Foreign Languages Press, 1985.

Watson, James L., and Evelyn S. Rawski, eds. *Death Ritual in Late Imperial and Modern China.* Stanford, Calif.: Stanford University Press, 1988.

Williams, C.A.S. *Outlines of Chinese Symbolism and Art Motifs.* 2d ed. Shanghai: Kelley and Walsh, 1932.

Wilson, R. W., A. A. Wilson, and S. L. Greenblatt, eds. *Value Change in Chinese Society.* New York: Praeger, 1979.

Wu Kuocheng. *The Chinese Heritage.* New York: Crown, 1982.

Yin Falu and Wu Shuan, eds. *Zhongguo wenhua shi* (The History of Chinese Culture). Beijing: Beijing University Press, 1990.

Yu Longyu, ed. *Zhongxi wenhua yitong lun* (On the Differences of Culture in China and in the West). Beijing: Sanlian Bookstore, 1989.

Zhu Guorong. *China Art: The Ultimate.* Shanghai: Knowledge Publishing House, 1990.

ARCHITECTURE

Blaser, Werner. *Courtyard House in China: Tradition and Present.* Basel: Birkhauser, 1979.

Boyd, Andrew. *Chinese Architecture and Town Planning.* Chicago: University of Chicago Press, 1962.

Chang, Sen-dou. "Some Observations on the Morphology of Chinese Walled Cities." *Annals, Association of American Geographers* 60 (1970): 63–91.

Chen Congzhou, Pan Hongxuan, and Lu Bingjie. *Zhongguo minju* (China's Folk Architecture). Hong Kong: Joint Publishing Company, 1993.

Clément, Sophie, Pierre Clément, and Shin Yong-hak. *Architecture du paysage en Extrème-Orient.* Paris: Ecole nationale supérieure des Beaux-Arts, 1987.

Dillingham, Reed, and Chang-lin Dillingham. *A Survey of Traditional Architecture of Taiwan.* Taizhong: Donghai University, 1971.

Dye, Daniel Sheets. *A Grammar of Chinese Lattice.* Cambridge, Mass.: Harvard University Press, 1937.

Gao Zhenming, Wang Naixiang, and Chen Yu. *Fujian minju.* (Folk Dwellings of Fujian). Beijing: China Building Industry Press, 1987.

Golany, Gideon. *Chinese Earth-sheltered Dwellings: Indigenous Lessons for Modern Urban Design.* Honolulu: University of Hawaii Press, 1992.

———. *Design and Thermal Performance: Below-Ground Dwellings in China.* Newark: University of Delaware Press, 1990.

———. *Underground Space Design in China: Vernacular and Modern Practice.* Newark: University of Delaware Press, 1989.

Guowuyuan bangongting diaocha, yanjiushi (Investigation and Research Office, State Council). *Nongfang jianshe yanjiu ziliao.* (Research Materials for the Construction of Rural Houses). Beijing: China Building Industry Press, 1984.

Han Pao-teh (Han Baode). *Guji de weihu.* (The Preservation of Historic Sites). Taipei: Cultural Buildings Administrative Council, 1983.

Han Pao-teh and Hung Wen-hsiung (Hong Wenxiong). *Banqiao Lin zhai: Diaocha yanjiu ji xiufu jihua* (Banqiao Lin Family Compound: The Survey, Study, and Restoration). Taizhong: Donghai University, 1973.

Hong Kong Government. *Rural Architecture in Hong Kong.* Hong Kong: Government Information Services, Hong Kong Government Printer, 1979.

Hou Jiyao, Ren Zhiyuan, Zhou Peinan, and Li Zhuanzi. *Yaodong minju* (Subterranean Folk Dwellings). Beijing: China Architecture and Building Press, 1989.

Hsu Min-fu (Xu Mingfu). *Taiwan chuantong minzhai ji qi difangxing shiliao zhi yanjiu* (Traditional Dwellings in Taiwan and Local Research Materials). Taipei: Hushi Book Company, 1990.

Inn, Henry. *Chinese House and Gardens.* New York: Bonanza, 1950.

Jing Qimin, ed. *Zhongguo chuantong minju baiti* (One Hundred Topics on Chinese Traditional Dwellings). Tianjin: Tianjin Science and Technology Press, 1985.

Kao Ts'an-jung (Gao Canrong). *Yenwei Mabei Wazhen: Taiwan gucuo wuding de xingtai* (Swallows' Tails, Horses' Backs, Tiles—The Form of Roofs in Old Villages in Taiwan). Taipei: Nantian Press, 1989.

Knapp, Ronald G. *China's Traditional Rural Architecture: A Cultural Geography of the Common House.* Honolulu: University of Hawaii Press, 1986.

―――. *China's Vernacular Architecture: House Form and Culture*. Honolulu: University of Hawaii Press, 1989.

―――. *Chinese Bridges*. New York: Oxford University Press, 1993.

―――. *The Chinese House: Craft, Symbol, and the Folk Tradition*. New York: Oxford University Press, 1990.

―――. "Chinese Rural Dwellings in Taiwan." *Journal of Cultural Geography* 3, 1 (1982): 1–18.

―――. "Taiwan's Vernacular Architecture." *Orientations* 12 (1981): 38–47.

Knapp, Ronald G. ed. *Chinese Landscapes: The Village as Place*. Honolulu: University of Hawaii Press, 1992.

Kwan Hwa-san (Guan Huashan). "Taiwan chuantong minzhai biaoxian de kongjian guannian" (Traditional Houses and Folk Space Concepts in Taiwan). *Zhongyang yanjiuyuan, minzuxue yanjiusuo jikan* (Bulletin of the Institute of Ethnology, Academia Sinica) 49 (1980): 175–215.

Li Changjie, chief ed. *Guibei minjian jianzhu* (Folk Architecture of Northern Guangxi). Beijing: China Architecture and Building Press, 1990.

Li Qianlang. *Jinmen minju jianzhu* (Architecture of Folk Dwellings in Kinmen). Taipei: Xiongshi Book Company, 1978.

―――. *Taiwan jianzhu shi* (History of the Architecture of Taiwan). Taipei: Beiwu Press, 1980.

―――. *Yangmingshan Guojia Gongyuan chuantong juluo ji jianzhu diaocha yanjiu* (Research Survey on Traditional Villages and Architecture in the Yangmingshan National Park). Taipei: Ancient Architecture Research Center, 1988.

Liang Sicheng. *A Pictorial History of Chinese Architecture: A Study of the Development of Its Structural System and the Evolution of Its Types*. Edited by Wilma Fairbank. Cambridge, Mass.: Massachusetts Institute of Technology Press, 1984.

―――. *Zhongguo jianzhushi* (A History of Chinese Architecture). Taipei: Historic Books Publishing Company (reprint of 1955 *Shangwu yinshuguan banshe*), 1981.

Liu Baozhong. *Gu jianzhu zhinan* (Guidebook to China's Ancient Buildings). Beijing: China Architecture and Building Press, 1981.

Liu Dunzhen. *La Maison Chinoise* (The Chinese House). Translated and adapted by Georges Métailie, Marie-Hélène Métailie, Sophie Clément-Charpentier, and Pierre Clément. Paris: Bibliotheque Berger-Levrault, 1980.

―――. *Zhongguo zhuzhai gaishuo* (Introduction to Chinese Dwellings). Beijing: Architectural Engineering Press, 1957.

Liu Dunzhen, chief ed. *Zhongguo gudai jianzhu shi* (A History of Traditional Chinese Architecture). Beijing: China Building Industry Press, 1980.

Liu Siyuan. *Taiwan minzhai* (Folk Residences in Taiwan). Taipei: Yezhulin, 1989.

Liu Zhiping. *Zhongguo jianzhu leixing ji jiegou* (Chinese Architectural Types and Structural Forms). Beijing: Architectural Engineering Press, 1957.

Lu Yuanding. "Zhongguo chuantong jianzhu goutu de tezheng, bili yu wending" (Compositional Characteristics of Traditional Chinese Architecture—Scale and Stability). *Jianzhushi* (The Architect) 39 (1990): 97–113.

Lu Yuanding, chief ed. *Zhongguo chuantong minju yu wenhua* (China's Traditional Folk Dwellings and Culture). Beijing: China Architecture and Building Press, vol. 1, 1991; vol. 2, 1992.

Lu Yuanding and Wei Yanjun. *Guangdong minju* (Folk Dwellings of Guangdong). Beijing: China Architecture and Building Press, 1990.

Lung, David P. Y. *China's Traditional Vernacular Architecture* (Zhongguo chuantong minju jianzhu), bilingual ed. Hong Kong: Regional Council, Museums Section, 1991.

Niu Weina. "Nongcun zhuzhai sheji de huigu yu zhanwang" (Review and Prospect concerning Rural Housing Design). In *Nongcun jizhen yu zhuzhai* (Rural Towns and Housing), 25–47. Beijing: Center for Chinese Architectural Technology and Development, Research Unit for Planning and Design, 1988.

Oliver, Paul. *Dwellings: The House across the World.* Oxford, England: Phaidon Press, 1987.

Pai, Chin. "Traditional Chinese House Form: The Courtyard House Compound of Peking." *Asian Culture* 17 (1989): 39–56.

Ruitenbeek, Klaas. *Carpentry and Building in Late Imperial China: A Study of the Fifteenth Century Carpenter's Manual Lu Ban Jing.* Leiden, Netherlands: E. J. Brill, 1993.

Rural Architecture in Hong Kong. Hong Kong: Government Information Services, 1979.

Shan Deqi. "Cunxi, tianjing, matouqiang—Huizhou minju biji" (Village Streams, Skywells, Gable Walls—Notes on the Vernacular Architecture of Huizhou). *Jianzhu shi luwenji* (Treatise on the History of Architecture) 6 (1984): 120–34.

———. "Yixian Hongcun guihua tanyuan" (Planning of Hongcun in Yixian). *Jianzhu shi luwenji* (Treatise on the History of Architecture) 8 (1987): 87–95.

Shao Mei. *Taiwan minju jianzhu zhi chuantong fengge* (Traditional Styles of Taiwan's Folk Architecture). Taizhong: Donghai University, 1968.

Shen Dongqi. *Nongcun zhuzhai jianzhu sheji* (The Design and Construction of Rural Settlements). Beijing: China Architecture and Building Press, 1991.

Steinhardt, Nancy Shatzman, ed. *Chinese Imperial City Planning.* Honolulu: University of Hawaii Press, 1990.

———. *Chinese Traditional Architecture.* New York: China Institute in America, 1984.

Wang Shaozhou. "Beijing siheyuan zhuzhai de zucheng yu gouzao" (The Composition and Structure of the Courtyard Dwellings of Beijing). *Keji shi wenji* (Collection on the History of Science and Technology) 5 (1980): 92–101.

Xu Minsu et al., eds. *Suzhou minju* (Folk Dwellings of Suzhou). Beijing: China Architecture and Building Press, 1991.

Xu Yinong. "Zhongguo chuantong fuhe kongjian guannian" (Composite Space Concepts in Traditional Chinese Architecture). *Jianzhushi* (The Architect) 12 (1989): 68–87; 6 (1990): 67–82; 12 (1990): 71–96, 37.

Yunnan sheng sheji yuan (Yunnan Provincial Design Institute). *Yunnan minju.* (Folk Dwellings of Yunnan). Beijing: China Building Industry Press, 1986.

Zhang Yuhuan. *History and Development of Ancient Chinese Architecture.* Beijing: Beijing Science Press, 1986.

———. *Jilin minju* (Folk Dwellings of Jilin). Beijing: China Building Industry Press, 1985.

Zhang Yuhuan, chief ed. *Zhongguo gudai jianzhu shi* (History and Development of Ancient Chinese Architecture). Beijing: Science Press, 1985.

Zhang Zhongyi et al. *Huizhou Mingdai zhuzhai* (Ming Dynasty Houses in Huizhou). Beijing: Architectural Engineering Press, 1957.

Zhongguo jianzhu jishu fazhan zhongxin, jianzhu lishi yanjiusuo (Center for Chinese Architectural Technology and Development, Research Unit for Architectural History). *Zhejiang minju* (Folk Dwellings of Zhejiang). Beijing: China Building Industry Press, 1984.

CALLIGRAPHY

Billeter, Jean François. *The Chinese Art of Writing.* New York: Skira/Rizzoli, 1990.

Chang, Leon Long-yien. *Four Thousand Years of Chinese Calligraphy.* Chicago: University of Chicago Press, 1990.

Chiang, Yee. *Chinese Calligraphy: An Introduction to Its Aesthetics and Technique.* Cambridge, Mass.: Harvard University Press, 1973.

Fu, Shen C. Y. *Traces of the Brush: Studies in Chinese Calligraphy.* New Haven, Conn.: Yale University Art Gallery, 1977.

Kraus, Richard Curt. *Brushes with Power: Modern Politics and the Chinese Art of Calligraphy.* Berkeley: University of California Press, 1991.

Kwo Da-Wei. *Chinese Brushwork in Calligraphy and Painting: Its History, Aesthetics, and Techniques.* Dover, England: Allanheld and Schram, 1981.

Lai, T. C. *Chinese Calligraphy: An Introduction.* Seattle: University of Washington Press, 1973.

———. *Chinese Calligraphy: Its Mystic Beauty.* Hong Kong: Swinden, 1973.

Legeza, Ireneus Laszlo. *Tao Magic: The Secret Language of Diagrams and Calligraphy.* London: Thames and Hudson, 1975.

Sanxitang fatie (Stone Rubbings of the House of Three Treasures). Beijing: China Books, 1986.

Willetts, Williams Y. *Chinese Calligraphy: Its History and Aesthetic Motivation.* Hong Kong: Oxford University Press, 1981.

Zhong Mingshan. *Zhongguoshufa jianshi* (A Brief History of Chinese Calligraphy). Shijiazhuang: Hebei Fine Arts, 1983.

COMIC ART

Ah Ying. *Essays on Art.* Beijing: People's Art Publishing House, 1982.

Bader, A. L. ''China's New Weapon—Caricature.'' *American Scholar* (April 1941): 228–40.

Bandes dessinées chinoises. Paris: Centre Georges Pompidou, 1982.

Bi Keguan. *Bi Keguan manhua xuan* (Selected Cartoons of Bi Keguan). Chengdu: Sichuan Arts Publishing House, 1985.

Bi Keguan and Huang Yuanlin. *Zhongguo manhua shihua* (Chinese Cartoons). Beijing: Cultural Publishing House, 1986.

Cartoon Arts Commission, ed. *Selected Works of Chinese Cartoonists.* Chengdu: Fine Arts Publishing House, 1988.

Chang Tiejun. *Chang Tiejun manhua xuan* (Selected Cartoons of Chang Tiejun). Beijing: Chinese Workers' Publishing House, 1989.

Chen, Jack. ''China's Militant Cartoons.'' *Asia* (May 1938): 308–12.

Cheng Chi. ''New Serial Pictures.'' *Chinese Literature* 2 (1974): 111–17.

Chesneaux, Jean, comp. *The People's Comic Book: Red Women's Detachment, Hot on the Trail, and Other Chinese Comics.* New York: Anchor Press, 1973.

Chiang Wei-pu. ''Chinese Picture Story Books.'' *Chinese Literature* (March 1959): 144–47.

Chūgoku no gekiga: Renkanga (Chinese Drama Comics: Renkanga). Tokyo: Tabata Shoten, 1974.

Croizier, R. "Crimes of the Gang of Four: A Chinese Artist's Version." *Pacific Affairs* (Summer 1981): 311–22.

Das Mädchen aus der Volkskommune. Hamburg: Rowohlt, 1972.

Ding Cong, ed. *Wit and Humour from Ancient China: 100 Cartoons by Ding Cong.* Beijing: New World Press, 1986.

Duan Jifu. *Lao Ma zhengzhuan* (Series of Lao Ma). Tianjin: Yangliuqing Pictorial House, 1990.

Fang Cheng. *Dangdai Zhongguo manhua jing xuan* (Selected Contemporary Chinese Cartoons). Hong Kong: Nan Yu Publishing House, 1991.

———. *Fang Cheng lianhuan manhua yuanji* (Collection of Comic Strips of Fang Cheng). Changchun: Jilin Arts Publishing House, 1985.

———. *Fang Cheng manhua xuan* (Selected Cartoons of Fang Cheng). Tianjin: Tianjin People's Arts Publishing House, 1981.

———. *Fang Cheng manhua xuan* (Selected Cartoons of Fang Cheng). Shanghai: Shanghai People's Arts Publishing House, 1982.

———. *Huaji yu youmo* (Amusement and Humor). Beijing: China Overseas Publishing Co., 1989.

———. *Xiao de Yishu* (The Art of Laughing). Shenyang: Spring City Cultural Publishing House, 1984.

———. *Youmo, Fengci, Manhua* (Humor, Satire, and Cartoon). Beijing: Sanlian Bookstore, 1984.

Feng Yiyin, et al. *Feng Zikai zhuan* (Biography of Feng Zikai). Hangzhou: Zhejiang People's Publishing House, 1983.

Feng Zikai. *Feng Zikai ertong manhua xuanji* (Collection of Feng Zikai's Children's Cartoons). Chengdu: Sichuan Children's Publishing House, 1988.

Fu Chen and Wang Wang. *Xiao shi manhua* (Historical Laughing Stories and Cartoons). Shanghai: Shanghai Ancient Book Publishing House, 1991.

Fuyu manhua (Fuyu Cartoons). Harbin: Liberation Army Arts and Culture Publishing House, 1991.

Government Information Service. *Mian xiang weilai* (From Past to the Future: Cartoon Collection). Taipei: Government Information Service, 1989.

———. *Zhonghua ernu de nuhou* (Angry Roar of the Chinese: Cartoon Collection). Taipei: Government Information Service, 1989.

Harbsmeier, Christoph. *The Cartoonist Feng Zikai.* Oslo: Universitetsforlaget, 1984.

Hebei Qiuxian "Frog" Cartoonist Group. *Hebei Qiuxian nongmin manhua xuan* (Selected Cartoons of the Peasants in Qiu County). Shijiazhuang: Hebei Arts Publishing House, 1989.

Hong Kong Institute for the Promotion of Chinese Culture. *Chinese Satirical Drawings Since 1900.* Hong Kong: Hong Kong Institute for the Promotion of Chinese Culture, 1987.

Hong Shi, ed. *Manhua jialun* (On Cartoons). Harbin: North Publishing House, 1991.

———. *Zhongguo manhua yishu lun* (On Chinese Cartoon Art). Changchun: Changchun Publishing House, 1991.

Hua Junwu. *Cartoons from Contemporary China.* Beijing: New World Press, 1989.

———. *Chinese Satire and Humour: Selected Cartoons of Hua Junwu (1955–1982).* Beijing: New World Press, 1984.

Huang Mao. *On Cartoon Art.* Shanghai: Life Bookstore, 1943.

Huang Yongyu. *Liqiu yansu renzhen sikao de zhaji* (Collection Which Tried to Have Serious Thinking). Beijing: Sanlin Bookstore, 1985.

Hung Chang-tai. "War and Peace in Feng Zikai's Wartime Cartoons." *Modern China* (January 1990): 39–83.

Lan Jian'an and Shi Jicai, eds. *Cartoons from Contemporary China.* Beijing: New World Press, 1989.

Li Jia. *Manhua qutan* (On Cartoons). Heifei: Anhui Fine Arts Publishing House, 1985.

Li Mu and Yi Xie, eds. *Mei ri yi xiao* (One Laugh a Day). Guangzhou: Guangzhou Traveling Publishing House, 1991.

Li Qing. *Li Qing manhua* (Cartoons of Li Qing). Yantai: Shandong Arts Publishing House, 1989.

Long Shengming and Liu Yongguo, eds. *Zhongguo dangdai youmo huajia zuopinxuan* (Selected Works of Contemporary Chinese Humorous Drawings). Nanning: Guangxi Arts Publishing House, 1992.

Mi Gu. *Mi Gu manhua xuan* (Selected Cartoons of Mi Gu). Chengdu: Sichuan People's Publishing House, 1982.

Miu Yintang. *Manhua yishu ABC* (The Art of Cartooning). Beijing: Chinese Series Pictures Publishing House, 1990.

———. *Miu Yintang manhua xuan* (Selected Cartoons of Miu Yintang). Beijing: Knowledge Publishing House, 1990.

Mo Ce, ed. *Manhuajia tan manhua* (Cartoonist on Cartoons). Beijing: Beijing Arts and Handicrafts Publishing House, 1989.

Nebiolo, Gino. *The People's Comic Book.* Translated by Endymion Wilkinson. Garden City, N.Y.: Anchor Press, 1973.

Pan Shunqi. *Pan Shunqi youmo hua* (Humorous Drawings of Pan Shunqi). Shanghai: People's Arts Publishing House, 1991.

People's Arts Publishing House, ed. *Chen Jinyan meishu zuopin xuanji* (Selected Artistic Works of Chen Jinyan). Beijing: People's Arts Publishing House, 1981.

Satire and Humour Editorial Group, ed. *Fengci yu youmo* (Satire and Humor). Beijing: People's Arts Publishing House, 1989.

Sun Yizeng. *Sun Yizeng manhua xuan* (Selected Cartoons of Sun Yizeng). Beijing: Knowledge Publishing House, 1991.

Wang Fuyang et al., eds. *Shixiang baitu* (One Hundred Cartoons on Social Phenomena). Beijing: People's Daily Publishing House, 1991.

Wang Schuchen. *Wang Schuchen manhua xuan* (Selected Cartoons of Wang Schuchen). Chengdu: Sichuan Arts Publishing House, 1991.

Worker's Daily Agency, ed. *Dierjie Gongren Ribao manhua dasai zuopin xuan* (Selected Works of the Second Worker's Daily Cartoon Competition). Beijing: Worker's Daily Agency, 1987.

Xu Changming. *Xu Changming manhua xuan* (Selected Cartoons of Xu Changming). Shanghai: Translation Company, 1991.

Xu Jingxiang, ed. *200 Cartoons from China.* Beijing: China Today Press, 1990.

———. *Zhongguo youmohua xuan* (Selected Chinese Humorous Drawings). Shanghai: Fudan University Press, 1989.

Yang Changfei, ed. *Shijie yinyue youmo* (World Cartoons of Music). Beijing: Chinese Youth Publishing House, 1991.

Ye Chunyang. *Ye Chunyang manhua xuan* (Selected Cartoons of Ye Chunyang). Beijing: Chinese Workers' Publishing House, 1990.

Ye Qianyu. *Ye Qianyu manhua xuan 1928–1959* (Selected Cartoons of Ye Qianyu 1928–1959). Chengdu: Sichuan Arts Publishing House, 1986.

Yu Henxi and Xu Jin, eds. *Disanjie Gongren Ribao manhua dasai zuopin xuan* (Selected

Works of the Third Worker's Daily Cartoon Competition). Beijing: Popular Science Publishing House, 1990.

Yu Yueting. "Woguo Huabo de shizu—Dianshizhai Huabao Chutan" (The Pioneer of Chinese Pictorials: A Preliminary Study of Dianshi Studio Pictorial). *Xinwen Yanjiu Ziliao* (Beijing) 10 (1981): 149–81.

Zhan Tong. *Zhan Tong ertong manhua xuan* (Selected Children's Cartoons of Zhan Tong). Chengdu: Sichuan Children's Publishing House, 1985.

Zhang Bin and Sun Maoju, eds. *Junxiao manhua xuan* (Selected Cartoons from the Military School). Beijing: Jiefangjun Arts Publishing House, 1992.

Zhang Ding. *Zhang Ding manhua* (Cartoons of Zhang Ding, 1936–1976). Shenyang: Liaoning Arts Publishing House, 1985.

Zhang Leping. *San Mao can jun ji* (San Mao Joins the Army). Shanghai: Tongji University Press, 1990.

Zheng Xinyao. *Zheng Xinyao manhua xuan* (Selected Cartoons of Zheng Xinyao). Shanghai: Shanghai Cartoonist Studies, 1988.

Zhu Genhua and Shen Tongheng, eds. *Manhua xuankan* (Selected Cartoons). Beijing: People's Arts Publishing House, 1982–1987.

DRAMA

Allen, B. S. *Chinese Theater Handbook.* Tianjin: Oriental Press, n.d.

Beijing Art Research Institute and Shanghai Art Research Institute, comp. *Zhongguo jingju shi* (A History of China's Beijing Drama). Beijing: China Drama Press, 1990.

Hong Shen. *Xi de nianci yu shi de langsong* (Recitations of Drama and Poetry). Beijing: China Drama Press, 1962.

Jiang Xingyu. *Mingkanben Xixiang ji yanjiu* (On the Editions of *The West Chamber* in the Ming Dynasty). Beijing: China Drama Press, 1982.

———. *Xixiang ji kaozheng* (Textual Studies on *The West Chamber*). Shanghai: Ancient Books Press, 1988.

Johnston, R. F. *The Chinese Drama.* Hong Kong: Kelly and Walsh, 1921.

Mei Lanfang. *Wutai shenghuo sishi nian* (My Forty Years of Stage Life). 2 vols. Shanghai: Pingming Press, 1952 and 1954.

Ren Erbei. *Tang xi rong* (Drama under the Tang Dynasty). Beijing: Writers Press, 1958. Reprint. 1984. Shanghai: Shanghai Ancient Books Press.

Scott, A. C. *An Introduction to the Chinese Theatre.* New York: Theatre Arts Books, 1960.

Snow, Lois Wheeter. *China on Stage: An American Actress in the People's Republic.* New York: Random House, 1972.

Stanton, William. *The Chinese Drama.* Hong Kong: Kelly and Walsh, 1899.

Wang Guowei. *Song Yuan xiqu kao* (A History of Traditional Drama under the Song and Yuan Dynasties). Shanghai: Commercial Press, 1915.

———. *Wang Guowei xiqu lunwen ji* (Wang Guowei's Treatises on Traditional Drama). 1957. Reprint. Beijing: China Drama Press, 1986.

Yu Zengfei. *Zengfei qupu* (Yu Zengfei Drama Music). Shanghai: Shanghai Literature and Art Press, 1983.

Zhongguo xiqu yishu guoji xueshu taolunhui wenji (Papers from the 1987 International Symposium on Traditional Chinese Drama). Beijing: Culture and Art Press, 1988.

Zucker, A. E. *The Chinese Theater.* London: Jarrolds, 1925.

FILM

Berry, Chris, ed. *Perspectives on Chinese Cinema.* 2d exp. ed. London: BFI, 1991.

Cai Chusheng, et al. *Lun dianying juben changzuode tezheng* (On the Special Characteristics of Film-Script Writing). Beijing: China Film Press, 1959.

Chen Huangmei, ed. *Dangdai zhongguo dianying* (Contemporary Chinese Film). Beijing: China Social Science Press, 1989.

Chen Kaiyan, ed. *Hua shuo Huang Tudi* (Talking about Huang Tudi). Beijing: China Film Press, 1986.

Chen, Li. *Film: Chinese Film and Film Audience.* London: Massachusetts Institute of Technology Press, 1972.

Cheng Jihua, ed. *Zhongguo dianying fazhan shi* (The History of the Development of Chinese Film). 1963. Reprint. Beijing: China Film Press, 1980.

China Film Association, ed. *Zhongguo dianying jia liezhuan* (Biographies of the Chinese Film Artists). Beijing: China Film Press, 1991.

———. *Zhongguo dianying jinjijiang wenji* (A Collection of the Golden Rooster Prize Essays). Beijing: China Film Press, 1983.

Clark, Paul. *Chinese Cinema: Culture and Politics Since 1949.* Cambridge, England: Cambridge University Press, 1988.

Leyda, Jay. *Dianying: An Account of Films and the Film Audience in China.* Cambridge, Mass.: Massachusetts Institute of Technology Press, 1972.

Li Shuangshang: Cong juben dao dianying (Li Shuangshang: From Short Story to Film). Beijing: China Film Press, 1963.

MacKerras, Colin. *The Performing Arts in Contemporary China.* London: Routledge and Kegan Paul, 1981.

Mei Duo. *Mei Duo dianying pinglun ji* (Mei Duo's Critical Essays on Films). Chengdu: Sichuan Literature and Art Press, 1985.

Ouyang Yuqian. *Xie dianying juben de jige wenti* (Some Problems of Film Script Writing). Beijing: China Film Press, 1959.

Rayns, Tony, and Scott Meek. *Electric Shadows: 45 Years of Chinese Cinema.* London: BFI, 1980.

Semsel, George Stephen, ed. *Chinese Film: The State of the Art in the People's Republic of China.* New York: Praeger, 1987.

Shi Doshang. *Dianying yishu zai biaoxian xingshi shang de jige tedian* (Some Characteristics in the Representational Form of Film Art). Beijing: Yishu Press, 1954.

Wusi yilai dianying juben xuanji (Selected Film Scripts Since the May Fourth Era). Beijing: China Film Press, 1962.

Yang Sheng et al., eds. *Zhongguo dianying yanyuan beiren zhuan* (Biographies of a Hundred Chinese Film Stars). Wuhan: Changjiang Literature and Art Press, 1984.

Yang Wenming and Xie Xizhang, eds. *Zhongguo dianying mingxing lu* (Chinese Film Stars). Beijing: Xuewan Press, 1990.

Zhongguo dianying nianjian (China Film Yearbook). Beijing: China Film Press, 1981–1985.

FOOD AND TEA

Anderson, E. N. *The Food of China.* New Haven, Conn.: Yale University Press, 1988.

Blofeld, John. *The Chinese Art of Tea.* Boston: Shambhala, 1985.

Chang Kwang-chih, ed. *Food in Chinese Culture.* New Haven, Conn.: Yale University Press, 1977.

Chen Chuan. *Chaye tongshi* (History of Tea). Beijing: Agriculture Press, 1974.

Chow, Kit, and Ione Kramer. *All the Tea in China.* San Francisco: China Books, 1990.

Croll, Elisabeth. *The Family Rice Bowl.* London: United Nations Research Institute for Social Development and Zed Press, 1983.

Dorje, Rinching. *Food in Tibetan Life.* London: Prospect Books, 1985.

Etherington, Dan M., and Keith Forster. "The Complex Case of the Chinese Tea Industry." Palo Alto, Calif.: Food Research Institute Studies, Food Research Institute of Stanford University, vol. 21, no. 3, 1989.

Flaws, Bob, and Honora Wolfe. *Prince Wen Hui's Cook: Chinese Dietary Therapy.* Brookline, Mass.: Paradigm Publications, 1983.

Gong Dan. *Food and Drink in China.* Beijing: New World Press, 1986.

Gu Jingzhou, ed. *Yixing zisha taoci* (Yixing Purple Clay Pottery). Hong Kong: Joint Publishers, 1993.

Gwinner, Thomas. *Essen und Trinken: Die klassische Kochbuchliteratur Chinas.* Heidelberger Schriften zur Ostasienkunde, Band 11. Heidelberg: Haag & Herchen, 1988.

Hong Kong Urban Council. *The Art of the Yixing Potter. The K. S. Lo Collection, Flagstaff House Museum of Tea Ware.* Hong Kong: 1990. (Bilingual English/Chinese)

———. *Innovations in Contemporary Yixing Pottery.* Hong Kong: 1988. (Bilingual English/Chinese)

Huang, H. T. "Han Gastronomy—Chinese Cuisine *in statu nascendi.*" *Interdisciplinary Science Reviews* 15 (1990): 139–52.

Ishige, Naomichi, ed. *Ronshu: Higashi Ajia no Shokuji Bunka* (Collected Essays on East Asian Food Culture). Tokyo: Heibonsha, 1985.

Jia Sixie. *Qimin yaoshu (heshi bufen)* (Necessary Knowledge for the Ordinary People: Drinking and Eating Section). Beijing: Commercial Press, 1984.

Kong Xianlo, ed. *Cha yu wenhua* (Tea and Culture). Shenyang: Chunfeng Culture Press, 1990.

Lao She. *Teahouse.* Translated by Yang Xianyi and Gladys Yang. Beijing: Foreign Languages Press, 1978.

Lin Yutang. "On Tea and Friendship." In *The Importance of Living.* 1937. New York: John Day, 1966.

Lo, K. S. *The Stonewares of Yixing from the Ming Period to the Present Day.* Hong Kong: Sotheby's and Hong Kong University Press, 1987.

Lu, Henry C. *Chinese System of Food Cures.* New York: Sterling, 1986.

Lu Yu. *The Classic of Tea.* Translated with introduction by Francis Ross Carpenter. Boston: Little, Brown, 1974.

Maitland, Derek. *5000 Years of Tea, a Pictorial Companion.* Hong Kong: CFW Publications, 1983.

Mallory, Walter. *China, Land of Famine.* New York: American Geographic Society, 1926.

Read, Bernard E. *Famine Foods Listed in the Chiu Huang Pen Ts'ao.* Shanghai: Henry Lester Institute of Medical Research, 1946. Reprint. Pasadena, Calif.: Oriental Book Store, 1977.

Rozin, Elisabeth. *Ethnic Cuisine: The Flavor Principle Cookbook.* New York: Greene, 1983.

Ruddle, Kenneth, and Gongfu Zhong. *Integrated Agriculture-aquaculture in South China: The Dike-pond Systems of the Zhujiang Delta*. Cambridge, England: Cambridge University Press, 1988.

Sabban, Françoise. "Cuisine à la cour de l'empereur de Chine: Les aspects culinaires du Yinshan Zhengyao de Hu Sihui." *Médiévales* 5 (1983): 32–56.

———. "De la Main à la pâté." *L'Homme* 113 (1990): 102–37.

———. "Un savoir-faire oublié: Le travail du lait en Chine ancienne." *Zinbun: Memoirs of the Research Institute for Humanistic Studies, Kyoto University* 21 (1986): 31–65.

———. "Sucre candi et confiseries de Quinsai: L'essor du sucre de canne dans la chine des Song (Xe–XIIIe siècle)." *Journal d'Agriculture Traditionelle et de Botanique Appliquée* 35 (1988): 195–214.

———. "Le système des cuissons dans la tradition culinaire chinoise." *Annales: Economies, Sociétés, Civilisations* (1983): 341–68.

Shih Sheng-han. *A Preliminary Survey of the Book Ch'i Min Yao Shu*. Beijing: Science Press, 1974.

Simoons, Frederick. *Food in China*. New York: CRC Press, 1990.

Sung Ying-hsing. *T'ien-kung K'ai-wu*. Tr. E.-tu Zen Sun and Shiou-chuan Sun. University Park: Pennsylvania State University Press, 1966.

Tea Research Institute of the Chinese Academy of Agricultural Sciences. *Cha—pinzhi—renlei Jiankang Guoji Xueshu Taolun Hui, Taolun Wenzhang Gaoyao* (Tea, Quality and Human Health, International Scholarly Symposium, Papers Presented, November 4–9, 1987). Hangzhou, 1988.

Ukers, William. *All about Tea*. Whitestone, N.Y.: Tea and Coffee Trade Journal Co., 1935.

———. *The Romance of Tea*. New York: Alfred A. Knopf, 1936.

Wang Yuefen, chief ed. *China—Homeland of Tea*. Beijing: China National Native Produce and Animal By-Products Import and Export Corp., and Hong Kong: Educational and Cultural Press, 1989.

Wittwer, Sylvan, Yu Youtai, Sun Han, and Wang Lianzheng. *Feeding a Billion*. East Lansing: Michigan State University Press, 1987.

Yang, Billy Wen-Chi. *History of Chinese Food Culture and Food Industries*. Beijing: Agricultural History Press, 1984. (In Chinese; bilingual title)

Zee, A. *Swallowing Clouds*. New York: Simon and Schuster, 1990.

Zhuang Wanfang, Tang Qingzhong, Tang Li-xing, Chen Wen Huai, and Wang Jiabin. *Zhongguo mingcha* (Famous Chinese Teas). Hangzhou: Zhejiang People's Publishing House, 1979.

Zhuang Wansu, ed. *Zhongguo cha shi jielun* (Some Conclusions on Chinese Tea History). Beijing: Science Press, 1988.

LIFESTYLES

Andors, Phyllis. *The Unfinished Liberation of Chinese Women: 1949–1980*. Bloomington: Indiana University Press, 1983.

Andors, Stephen, ed. *Workers and Workplaces in Revolutionary China*. White Plains, N.Y.: M. E. Sharpe, 1977.

Baker, Hugh D. R. *Chinese Family and Kinship.* New York: Columbia University Press, 1979.

Bense, chuantong, shiming: Gongren jieji changshi duben (Character, Tradition, and Historical Mission: A Working Class Reader). Beijing: Workers' Publishing House, 1983.

Broyelle, Claudie. *Women's Liberation in China* (translated from *La Motie du ciel* and prefaced in English by Han Su-yin). New York: Hunter's Press, 1977.

Burns, John P. *Political Participation in Rural China.* Berkeley: University of California Press, 1988.

Buxbaum, David C., ed. *Chinese Family Law and Social Change.* Seattle: University of Washington Press, 1978.

Can Shijie, You Zhonglun, and Tang Xiaoqing. *Zenyang ban hunshi* (How to Get Married). Chengdu: Sichuan People's Publishing House, 1984.

Central People's Broadcasting Station Lecture Series. *Laodong wenti jianghua* (Answers to Labor Questions). Beijing: Guang Fan Publishing House, 1983.

———. *Zhengque chuli hunyin yu jiating wenti* (On the Correct Handling of Marital and Family Problems). Guilin: Guizhou People's Publishing House, 1979.

Chan, Anita. *Children of Mao: Personality Development and Political Action in the Red Guard Generation.* Seattle: University of Washington Press, 1985.

Chao, Paul. *Chinese Kinship.* London: Kegan, Paul, International, 1983.

Chen, Jack. *A Year in Upper Felicity: Life in a Chinese Village during the Cultural Revolution.* New York: Macmillan, 1973.

Chen Liaohsiang. *Zhonggong jianyu sanshisan nian* (33 Years of Imprisonment by the Chinese Communists). Taipei: National Security Bureau, Political Work Section, 1982.

Chen Peng. *Zhongguo hunyin shi* (A History of Marriage in China). Beijing: Zhong Hua Publishing House, 1990.

Chin, Ann-Ping. *Children of China: Voices from Recent Years.* New York: Knopf, 1988.

China Institute of Marriage and the Family. *Hunyin jiating wenji* (Essays on Marriage and the Family). Tianjin: Legal Publishing House, 1984.

Ch'ou Pai-Yun. *Dalu nannu* (Men and Women on the Mainland). Taipei: Huan-Ning Press, 1968.

Chu Jianquan, Tian Ming, and Yang Hao, eds. *Guoying qiye laodong zhidu gaige daxiang* (Answers to Questions on Reform of the State Enterprise Work System). Beijing: Worker's Publishing House, 1986.

Chuan Weitian. *Zhongguo shaoshu minzu zibenzhuyi fazhan* (Developing Capitalism among China's Minorities). Kaifeng: Henan People's Publishing House, 1982.

Coale, Ansley J., Shaomin Li, and Jing-Qing Han. *Distribution of Interbirth Intervals in Rural China, 1940s–1970s.* Honolulu: East-West Center Press, Papers of the East-West Population Institute, no. 109, August 1988.

Croll, Elisabeth. *Chinese Women Since Mao.* London: Zed Books, 1983.

———. *The Politics of Marriage in Contemporary China.* New York: Cambridge University Press, 1981.

Croll, Elisabeth, ed. *The Women's Movement in China: A Selection of Readings, 1949–1973.* London: Anglo-Chinese Educational Institute, Modern China Series no. 6, 1974.

Croll, Elisabeth, Delia Davin, and Penny Kane, eds. *China's One-Child Family Policy.* New York: St. Martin's Press, 1985.

Crook, Isabel, and David Crook. *Revolution in a Chinese Village: Ten Mile Inn.* London: Routledge and Kegan Paul, 1959.

————. *Ten Mile Inn: Mass Movement in a Chinese Village.* New York: Pantheon, 1979.

Curtin, Katie. *Women in China.* New York: Pathfinder Press, 1975.

Davin, Delia. *Woman-Work: Women and the Party in Revolutionary China.* New York: Oxford University Press, 1979.

Davis, Deborah, and Steven Harrell, eds. *Chinese Families in the Post-Mao Era.* Berkeley: University of California Press, 1993.

Deng Weizhi. *Jiating de mingtian* (The Family Tomorrow). Guiyang: Guizhou People's Publishing House, 1986.

————. *Jiating wenti zhongzhong* (Types of Family Problems). Tianjin: Tianjin People's Publishing House, 1983.

Deng Weizhi, with Zhang Daiyu. *Zhongguo jiating de yanbian* (The Changing Chinese Family). Shanghai: Shanghai People's Publishing House, 1987.

Domenach, Jean-Luc, and Hua Changming. *Marriage en Chine* (Marriage in China). Paris: Presses de la Fondation Nationale des Sciences Politiques, 1987.

Dunn, Robert, trans. and ed. *Chinese Approaches to Family Planning.* White Plains, N.Y.: M. E. Sharpe, 1979.

Ebrey, Patricia Buckley, and James L. Watson. *Kinship Organization in Late Imperial China, 1000–1940.* Berkeley: University of California Press, 1986.

Etheridge, James M. *China's Unfinished Revolution.* San Francisco: China Books and Periodicals, 1990.

Falkenheim, Victor C., ed. *Citizens and Groups in Contemporary China.* Ann Arbor: Center for Chinese Studies, University of Michigan, Michigan Monographs in Chinese Studies no. 56, 1987.

Feng Jicai, ed. *Voices from the Whirlwind: An Oral History of the Cultural Revolution.* New York: Pantheon, 1991.

Freedman, Maurice. *Lineage and Society in Fukien and Kwangtung.* London: London School of Economics Monographs of Sociological Anthropology no. 33, University of London Athlone Press, 1971.

————. *Lineage Organization in Southeast China.* London: London School of Economics Monographs of Sociological Anthropology no. 18, University of London Athlone Press, 1966.

Freedman, Maurice, ed. *Family and Kinship in Chinese Society.* Palo Alto, Calif.: Stanford University Press, 1958.

Goldstein, Avery. *From Bandwagon to Balance-of-Power Politics.* Palo Alto, Calif.: Stanford University Press, 1991.

Gongmin shouce (Citizen's Handbook). Beijing: Huayi Publishing House, 1988.

Goodman, David S. E. *Beijing Street Voices.* Boston: Marian Boyars, 1981.

Goodman, David S. G., ed. *Groups and Politics in the People's Republic of China.* Armonk, N.Y.: M. E. Sharpe, 1984.

Gravereau, Jacques. *La Chine apres l'utopie* (China after Utopia). Paris: Berger-Levrault, 1983.

Guisso, Richard W., and Stanley Johannesen, eds. *Women in China: Current Directions in Historical Scholarship.* Youngstown, Ohio: Philo Press, 1981.

Hinsch, Bret. *Passions of the Cut Sleeve.* Berkeley: University of California Press, 1990.

Hinton, William. *Fanshen.* New York: Vintage, 1966.

————. *Shenfan.* New York: Random House, 1983.

Honig, Emily, and Gail Hershatt. *Personal Voices: Chinese Women in the 1980s.* Palo Alto, Calif.: Stanford University Press, 1988.

Hua Changming. *La Condition feminine et les Communistes Chinoises en action: Yan'an, 1935–46* (The Feminine Condition and the Chinese Communists in Action: Yan-'an, 1935–46). Paris: Editions de l'Ecole des Hautes Etudes en Sciences Sociales, 1981.

Jacob, Alain. *Un Balcon à Pekin* (A Balcony in Beijing). Paris: Edition Grasset et Fasquelle, 1982.

Jia Wenqing. *Lao gai chun qiu* (A Spring and Autumn Annals of My Labor Reform). Beijing: Masses Publishing House, 1985.

Johnson, Kay Ann. *Women, the Family and Peasant Revolution in China.* Chicago: University of Chicago Press, 1983.

Kessen, William, ed. *Childhood in China.* New Haven, Conn.: Yale University Press, 1975.

Lao Feng. *Jiating yu shaonian fanzui* (Families and Juvenile Delinquency). Beijing: China People's Security University Press, 1987.

Leary, Marvin, Jr. *The Family Revolution in Modern China.* New York: Octagon Books, 1971.

Leijonhufvud, Goran. *Going against the Tide: On Dissent and Big Character Posters in China.* n.p.: Curson Press, Scandinavian Institute of Asian Studies Monograph Series no. 58, 1990.

Lemieux, Claude. *La Chine: Une histoire de famille* (China: A History of the Family). Montreal: Editions Saint Martins, 1984.

Li Saochen and Jiang Yuanming. *Fuqi zhijian* (Between Husbands and Wives). Jiangsu: Jiangsu People's Publishing House, 1983.

Li Songnong, ed. *Jiating daode jiahua* (Moral Family Life). Beijing: China Gong-guang Press, 1983.

Lin, Alice Murong P. *Grandmother Had No Name.* San Francisco: China Books and Periodicals, 1988.

Lin Yueh-Hua. *The Golden Wing.* London: Kegan, Paul, Trachy, Trubner and Co., 1947.

Link, Perry, ed. *Mandarin Ducks and Butterflies.* Berkeley: University of California Press, 1981.

———. *Roses and Thorns.* Berkeley: University of California Press, 1984.

Liu, Alan P. L. *Political Culture and Group Conflict in Communist China.* San Francisco: Cho Books, 1971.

Liu Bin-Yan. *A Higher Kind of Loyalty.* New York: Pantheon, 1990.

Liu Hulin. *Hunyin jiating daode* (Morality in Marriage and Family). Beijing: Beijing Press, 1986.

Liu Jia-Lin and Mafeng Huadeng, eds. *Zhongguo laodong zhidu gaige* (Reforms in China's Work System). Jing'an: Economic Press, 1988.

Lun jingji xiaoguo (On Economic Efficiency). Beijing: Chinese Academy of Social Sciences Press, 1981.

Maxwell, Neville, and Bruce McFarlane, eds. *China's Changed Road to Development.* New York: Pergamon Press, 1984.

Meyer, Charles. *Histoire de la femme chinoise: 4000 ans de pouvoir* (A History of Chinese Women: 4,000 Years of Power). Paris: Editions Jean-Claude Lattier, 1986.

Michael, Franz. *China and the Crisis of Marxism-Leninism.* Boulder, Colo.: Westview Press, 1990.

Morrison, Charles E., and Robert F. Dernberger, eds. *Asia Pacific Report: Focus—China in the Reform Era*. Honolulu: East-West Center Press, 1989.

Mosher, Steven. *Broken Earth: The Rural Chinese*. New York: Free Press, 1983.

Myrdal, Jan. *Report from a Chinese Village*. New York: Vintage, 1965.

———. *Return to a Chinese Village*. New York: Pantheon, 1984.

Nathan, Andrew J. *Chinese Democracy*. New York: Knopf, 1985.

Pasternak, Burton. *Marriage and Fertility in Tianjin, China: Fifty Years of Transition*. Honolulu: East-West Center Press, Papers of the East-West Population Institute, no. 99, July 1986.

Pruitt, Ida, ed. *A Daughter of Han: The Autobiography of a Chinese Working Woman*. Palo Alto, Calif.: Stanford University Press, 1967.

Pye, Lucian W. *The Dynamic of Factions and Consensus in Chinese Politics*. Project AIR FORCE Report, USAF, July 1980.

———. *The Mandarin and the Cadre: China's Political Cultures*. Ann Arbor: Center for Chinese Studies, University of Michigan, Michigan Monographs in Chinese Studies no. 59, 1988.

Qiu Qianshou, Yang Shubiao, and Wang Tianwen. *Minzhu geming de minzhu yundong* (The Democratic Movement of the Democratic Revolution). Changsha: Hunan People's Publishing House, 1986.

Selden, Mark. *The Yenan Way in Revolutionary China*. Cambridge, Mass. Harvard University Press, 1971.

Seymour, James D. *The Fifth Modernization: China's Human Rights Movement, 1978–79*. New York: Human Rights Publishing Group, 1980.

Sha Qianli. *Qi ren zhi yu* (The Story of Seven Prisoners). Beijing: San Lian Publishing Company, 1984.

Shao Qing-wen. *Pochu jiazu guannian* (Pushing Out the Concepts of Ancestry). Guangzhou: Guangdong People's Publishing House, 1975.

Sheridan, Mary, and Janet W. Salaff, eds. *Lives: Chinese Working Women*. Bloomington: Indiana University Press, 1984.

Shinian dongluan (Ten Years of Chaos). Beijing: Masses Publishing House, 1986.

Shi Tianyang, Ma Suwen, Li Yanshu, and Ying Xianyu. *Xinhun bidu* (Required Reading for Newlyweds). Nanjing: Nanjing People's Publishing House, 1985.

Sidel, Ruth. *Women and Child Care in China*. New York: Hill and Wang, 1972.

Siu, Bobby. *Fifty Years of Struggle: The Development of the Women's Movement in China, 1900–1949*. Hong Kong: Revomen Publications, 1975.

———. *Women of China: Imperialism and Women's Resistance, 1900–1949*. London: Zed Press, 1982.

Spence, Jonathan. *The Death of Woman Wang*. New York: Penguin, 1978.

Stacey, Judith. *Patriarchy and Socialist Revolution in China*. Berkeley: University of California Press, 1983.

Tang Tao. *Hunyin xinlixue* (The Psychology of Marriage). Shanghai: Shanghai People's Publishing House, 1986.

Tang Yuliang. *Zhongguo minzhu shiqi de gongren yundong shilu* (A History of Workers' Movements in the Chinese Democratic Revolutions). Beijing: Worker's Publishing House, 1985.

Thurston, Anne F. *Enemies of the People*. New York: Knopf, 1987.

Townsend, James R. *Political Participation in Communist China*. Berkeley: University of California Press, 1968.

Wagner, Augusta. *Labor Legislation in China*. New York: Garland Publishing, 1980.

Walder, Andrew G. *Communist Neo-Traditionalism: Work and Authority in Chinese In-dustry*. Berkeley: University of California Press, 1986.

Wang Guichen. *Smashing the Communal Plot: Formulation and Development of the Rural Responsibility System*. Beijing: New World Press, 1985.

Watson, James L. *Emigration and the Chinese Lineage: The Mans in Hong Kong and London*. Berkeley: University of California Press, 1975.

Watson, James L., ed. *Class and Social Stratification in Post-Revolutionary China*. Cam-bridge, England: Cambridge University Press, 1984.

Weiner, Rebecca, Margaret Murphy, and Albert Li. *Living in China*. San Francisco: China Books and Periodicals, 1991.

Whyte, Martin King. *Urban Life in Contemporary China*. Chicago: University of Chi-cago Press, 1984.

Widor, Claude, ed. *Documents on the Democratic Movement, 1978–1980*. Paris: Editions de L'Ecole des Hautes Etudes en Sciences Sociales, 1984.

Wolfe, Margery. *The House of Lim*. New York: Meredith Corp., 1960.

Wolfe, Margery, and Roxanne Witke, eds. *Women in Chinese Society*. Palo Alto, Calif.: Stanford University Press, 1975.

"Women of China," ed. *When They Were Young*. Beijing: China Spotlight Series, New World Press, 1983.

Wong, George C., trans. and ed. *Economic Reform in the PRC: In Which China's Econ-omists Make Known What Went Wrong, Why, and What Should Be Done about It*. Boulder, Colo.: Westview Press, 1982.

Wortel, Larry M. *Class in China: Stratification in a Classless Society*. New York: Green-wood Press, 1987.

Xiao Fengxi, ed. *Wo guo ziran ziyuan* (Our Nation's Natural Resources). Baoding: Hebei People's Publishing House, 1957.

Xiao Mingxiong (pen name, Takeshi Koake). *Zhongguo tongxingai shilu* (A History of Homosexuality in China). Hong Kong: Fenhong Sanjian Press, 1984.

Xiu Dingben. *Jiating wenti ershi jiang* (Twenty Answers to Familial Questions). Xi'an: Shaanxi People's Publishing House, 1983.

Yinchuan Family Planning Committee. *Jiating jihua* (Family Planning). Yinchuan: Ni-ngxia People's Publishing House, 1982.

Yingzi sashuang de Guangxi funu (Heroic and Sacrificial Women of Guangxi Province). Guangxi People's Publishing House, 1975.

Youth Marxist-Leninist Studies Committee. *Lishi shi nulimen chuangzao de* (History Is Written by the Slaves). Shenyang: Liaoning People's Publishing House, 1976.

Zeng Zhi. *Changzheng nu zhanshi* (Women Fighters of the Long March). Beijing: China Women's and Children's Publishing Company, 1987.

Zhang Qingfu and Wang Deyang. *Woguo gongmin jiben quanli he ziren* (Basic Rights and Responsibilities of the Citizens of Our Nation). Beijing: Masses Publishing Company, 1987.

Zhang Xin-xin and Sang Ye. *Chinese Lives*. Translated and edited by W.J.F. Jenner and Delia Davin. New York: Pantheon, 1987.

———. *Chinese Stories*. Beijing: Panda Books, 1989.

Zhongguo chengshi jiating (Chinese Urban Families). Jinan: Shandong People's Pub-lishing House, 1985.

Zhongguo funu da fanshen (The Great Transformation of Women in China). Beijing: New Democracy Press, 1975.

Zhongguo gongmin xuzhi (What Every Chinese Citizen Needs to Know). Jiangsu: Jiangsu People's Publishing House, 1987.

Zhongguo jingji jinzhan (Chinese Economic Growth). Beijing: People's Publishing House, 1982.

LITERATURE: GALLANT FICTION AND SCIENCE FICTION

Cao Zhengwen. *Jin Yong bixia de yibailingba jiang* (One Hundred and Eight Heroes in Jin Yong's Novels). Hangzhou: Zhejiang Literature and Art Press, 1991.

————. *Wuxia shijie de guaicai—Gu Long xiaoshuo tan* (A Rare Genius in the World of Gallant Fiction—Gu Long's Artistry). Shanghai: Xuelin Press, 1990.

————. *Zhongguo xia wenhua shi* (A History of Chinese Gallant Culture). Shanghai: Shanghai Literature and Art Press, 1993.

Chen Mo. *Jin Yong xiaoshuo shangxi* (Appreciating Jin Yong's Fiction). Nanchang: Baihuazhou Literature and Art Press, 1990.

Du Jian. *Shijia kehuan wentan daguan* (A General Introduction to World Science Fiction). Hong Kong: Yuanjin Press, 1991.

Dunsing, Charlotte, and Ye Yonglie, eds. *Science Fiction from China*. Cologne, Germany: Goldmann, 1986.

Editorial Department of *Geology Gazette,* ed. *Kepu zuojia tan chuangzuo* (Popular Science Writers on Writing). Beijing: Geology Press, 1980.

Feng shen yanyi (The Canonization of the Gods). Circa 1800. Reprint. Beijing: People's Literature Press, 1955.

Giles, Herbert A. *A History of Chinese Literature*. New York: D. Appleton and Company, 1915.

Gu Junzheng. *Heping de meng*. Includes "Heping de meng" (Dream of Peace), "Lundun qiyi" (The Strange Epidemic in London), and "Zai Beiji dixia" (Under the North Pole). Shanghai: Cultural Life Press, 1940.

Gu Long [Xiong Yaohua]. *Duoqing jianke wuqing jian* (The Affectionate Gallant and the Affectionless Sword). Taiwan: Wansheng Press, 1969.

————. *Juedai shuangjiao* (Two Peerless Heroes). Taiwan: Wansheng Press, 1967.

————. *Lu Xiaofeng*. Taiwan: Wansheng Press, 1972.

————. *Xiadao Chu Liuxiang* (Gallant Outlaw Chu Liuxiang). Taiwan: Wansheng Press, 1970.

Han Fei. *Hanfeizi* (The Prose of Master Han Fei, annotated). Nanjing: Jiangsu People's Press, 1982.

Huang Fan. *Shangdi men* (Gods). Taipei, Taiwan: Hongfan Press, 1986.

Huang Hai. *Liulang xingkong* (Wandering in Starry Skies). Taipei, Taiwan: Juvenile Monthly Press, 1974.

————. *10101* (The Year of 10101). Taipei, Taiwan: Zhaoming, 1969.

————. *Tianwei yixiang ren* (A Stranger from Outer Space). Taipei, Taiwan: Zhaoming, 1980.

————. *Xinshiji zhelu* (Voyage to a New Era). Taipei, Taiwan: Zhaoming, 1972.

————. *Yinghe mihang ji* (Drifting Off Course in the Galaxy). Taipei, Taiwan: Zhaoming, 1979.

Huang Hai, Lu Yingzhong, and Zhang Zijian, eds. *Zhongguo dangdai kehuan xianji*

(Selections of Contemporary Chinese Science Fiction). Taipei, Taiwan: Zhao-ming, 1981.

Huang Yi, ed. *Lun kexue huanxiang xiaoshuo* (On Science Fiction). Beijing: Popular Science Press, 1981.

———. *Zuojia lun kexue wenyi* (Writers on Scientific Literature and Art). Nanjing: Jiangsu Science and Technology Press, 1980.

Jin Yong [Zha Liangyong]. *Ruding ji* (On Ruding Mountain). Hong Kong: Minghe Press, 1969.

———. *Shujian enchou lu* (A Scholarly Gallant's Revenge). Hong Kong: Minghe Press, 1955.

———. *Tianlong Babu* (Eight Books of the Heavenly Dragon). Hong Kong: Minghe Press, 1965.

———. *Xiaoao jianghu* (The Peerless Gallant Errant). Hong Kong: Minghe Press, 1967.

———. *Yitian tulong ji* (The Sword and the Knife). Hong Kong: Minghe Press, 1964.

Lai, T. C. *Duilian: Chinese Couplets.* Hong Kong: Kelly and Walsh, 1969.

Lao She [Shu Sheyu]. *Maocheng ji* (Cat Country). Shanghai: Modern Book Company, 1933. Translated by William A. Lyell. Columbus: Ohio State University Press, 1970. *City of Cats,* translated by James E. Dew. Ann Arbor: Center for Chinese Studies of the University of Michigan, 1964.

Li Qi. *Taohua yuan* (The Land of Peach Blossoms). Taipei, Taiwan: Lingxi Press, 1979.

Li Ruzhen. *Jinghua yuan* (Flowers in the Mirror). 1828. Rpt. Beijing: People's Literature Press, 1979.

Liang Yusheng [Zheng Wentong]. *Longhu dou jinghua* (Contesting of Dragons and Ti-gers in the Capital). Hong Kong: Tiandi Press, 1954.

Liu An. *Huai nan zi.* (Works of Master Liu An). Circa second century B.C.E.

Liu, James J. *The Chinese Knight-Errant.* Routledge and Kegan Paul, 1967.

Lu Xun, trans. *From the Earth to the Moon* in *Lu Xun quanji* (Complete Works of Lu Xun). Vol. 11. Beijing: People's Press, 1973.

Lu Yingzhong. *Kehuan wenxue* (Science Fiction Literature). Taipei, Taiwan: Zhaoming, 1980.

Luo Liqun. *Zhongguo wuxia xiaoshuo shi* (A History of Chinese Gallant Fiction). Shen-yang: Liaoning People's Press, 1990.

Meng Weizai. *Fangwen shizong zhe* (Call on the Missing People). Tianjin: *Zhihuishu* (Tree of Knowledge); New Budding Press, 1981.

Ni Kuang. *Erkan Jin Yong xiaoshuo* (My Second Reading of Jin Yong's Fiction). Taipei: Yuanliu Press, 1987.

———. *Sankan Jin Yong xiaoshuo* (My Third Reading of Jin Yong's Fiction). Taipei: Yuanliu Press, 1987.

———. *Selections of Ni Kuang's Science Fiction.* Taipei, Taiwan: Hongfan Press, 1985.

———. *Wokan Jin Yong xiaoshuo* (My Reading of Jin Yong's Fiction). Taipei: Yuanliu Press, 1987.

Pu Songling. *Liao chai zhi yi (Strange Stories from a Chinese Studio).* 1679. Reprint. Beijing: People's Literature Press, 1962. Translated by Herbert A. Giles. New York: Boni and Liveright, 1925.

Qu Yuan. *Chu ci* (The Songs of the South). Translated by David Hawkes. London: Oxford, 1959.

San Mao, et al. *Zhuzi baijia kan Jin Yong* (Hundred Schools' Views on Jin Yong). Taiwan: Yuanjin Press, 1988.

Shan hai jing (The Book of Mountains and Seas). Circa 500 B.C.E.

Shen Kuo. *Meng xi bi tan* (Sketches and Notes by Dream Creek). Circa eleventh century C.E.

Tong Enzheng. "Shanhudao shang de siguang" (Death Ray on a Coral Island). *Renmin wenxue* (People's Literature) (August 1978). Beijing.

Wagner, Rudolf G. "Lobby Literature: The Archeology and Present Functions of Science Fiction in China." In *After Mao: Chinese Literature and Society, 1978–1981* edited by Jeffrey Kinkley, 17–62. Cambridge, Mass.: Harvard University Press, 1985.

Wang Hailin. *Zhongguo wuxia xiaoshuo shilue* (A Brief History of Chinese Gallant Fiction). Taiyuan: Beiyue Literature and Art Press, 1988.

Wei Yahua. "Wenrou zhixiang de meng" (Conjugal Happiness in the Arms of Morpheus) *Beijing wenxue* (Beijing Literature) (January 1981), Beijing. Its sequel appears in *Yanhe* (Yanhe River) (May–July 1982), Jilin.

Weng Reian. *Baiyi Fang Zhenmei* (The Commoner Fang Zhenmei). Hong Kong: Dunhuang Press, 1983.

———. *Daxia Xiao Qiushui* (The Great Hero Xiao Qiushui). Hong Kong: Dunhuang Press, 1980.

———. *Jianghu xianhua* (An Errant's Chitchat). Taipei: Wansheng Press, 1988.

———. *Shenxiang Li Buyi* (The Fortune Teller Li Buyi). Hong Kong: Dunhuang Press, 1982.

———. *Sida minbu* (The Four Famous Detectives). 4 vols. Hong Kong: Dunhuang Press, 1988.

———. *Xi Xueshanfeihu yu Yuanyangdao* (The Flying Fox in Snow Mountain and The Twin Swords). Taipei: Yuanjin Press, 1987.

Wu Chengen. *Xi you ji* (Journey to the West). Beijing: People's Press, 1954. Translated by W.J.F. Jenner. Beijing: Foreign Language Press, 1982.

Wu Dingbo and Patrick D. Murphy, eds. *Science Fiction from China: Eight Stories.* Westport, Conn.: Greenwood Press, 1989.

Xiao Jianheng. "Buke de qiyu" (Pup Buke's Adventures). *Women ai kexue* (We Love Science) (July 1962). Beijing.

———. "Shaluomu jiaoshou de miwu" (Professor Solomon's Delusion). *Renmin wexue* (People's Literature) (December 1980). Beijing.

Xu Dishan. "Tieyu de sai" (Ironfish Gills). 1941. In *Selected Works of Xu Dishan.* Beijing: People's Literature Press, 1958.

Ye Lihua. *Shikong youxi* (The Game of Space and Time). Taipei, Taiwan: Hongfan Press, 1988.

Ye Yandu. *Haitian longzhan* (Dragon Wars in Ocean and Sky). Taipei, Taiwan: Hongfan Press, 1987.

Ye Yonglie. "Fushi" (Corrosion). *Renmin wenxue* (People's Literature) (November 1981). Beijing.

———. *Lun kexue wenyi* (On Scientific Literature and Art). Beijing: Popular Science Press, 1980.

Yu Zhi [Ye Zhishan]. "Shizong de gege" (The Missing Elder Brother). *Zhongxuesheng* (High School Student) (July–August 1957). Beijing.

Zhang Xiguo. *Longcheng hujiang* (Heroes in the Dragon City). Taipei, Taiwan: Hongfan Press, 1986.

———. *Wuyudie* (A Five-Jade Plate). Taipei, Taiwan: Hongfan Press, 1983.

———. *Xingyun zuqu* (Nebula Suite). Taipei, Taiwan: Hongfan Press, 1980.

———. *Yequ* (Nocturne). Taipei, Taiwan: Hongfan Press, 1985.

———. *Yiyumao* (A Feather). Taipei, Taiwan: Hongfan Press, 1991.

Zhang, Xiguo, ed. *Boundless Love—1988 Best SF*. Taipei, Taiwan: Hongfan Press, 1991.

———. *1984 Best SF*. Taipei, Taiwan: Hongfan Press, 1985.

———. *1985 Best SF*. Taipei, Taiwan: Hongfan Press, 1986.

———. *1986 Best SF*. Taipei, Taiwan: Hongfan Press, 1987.

———. *1987 Best SF*. Taipei, Taiwan: Hongfan Press, 1988.

Zhang Zhan. *Lie zi* (The Book of Lie Zi). Circa 307–313. Translated by A. C. Graham. London: Murray, 1960.

Zhao Shizhou, ed. *Kehuan xiaoshuo shijia* (Ten Science Fiction Writers). Taiyuan: Beiyue Literature and Art Press, 1989.

Zhao Zifan. *Feidie zhengkong* (The Flying Saucer Conquers the Sky). Hong Kong: Asia Press, 1956.

———. *Taikong lixian ji* (Adventures in Space). Hong Kong: Asia Press, 1956.

———. *Yueliang shang kan Diqiu* (Watching Earth from the Moon). Hong Kong: Asia Press, 1956.

Zheng Wenguang. "Cong Diqiu dao Huoxing" (From Earth to Mars). Beijing: *Zhongguo shaonian bao* (Chinese Juvenile Daily), 1954.

———. *Feixiang Renmazuo* (Forward Sagittarius). Beijing: People's Literature Press, 1979.

MASS MEDIA

Beijing Municipal Bureau of News Publications. *Xinwen chuban zhengce guizhang xianbian* (A Selective Compilation of Rules and Regulations for News Publications). Beijing: The Beijing Municipal Bureau of News Publications, 1989.

Bureau of Policy Research in the Ministry of Radio, Film, and Television. *Guangbo dianshi gongzuo wenjian xianbian 1978–1980* (A Selection of Radio and Television Documents 1978–1980). Beijing: Chinese Radio and Television Press, 1988.

———. *Guangbo dianshi fagui guizhang huibian* (A Compilation of Rules and Regulations for Radio, Film, and Television). Beijing: Chinese Radio and Television Press, 1988.

Bureau of Propaganda in the Ministry of Radio, Film, and Television. *Guangbo jiemu gaige chutan* (Broadcasting Program Reform Exploration). Beijing: Chinese Radio and Television Press, 1987.

———. *Xinshiqi yu xinwen guangbo* (New Era and News Broadcasting). Beijing: Chinese Radio and Television Press, 1987.

CCTV's Group for History. *Zhongguo Zhongyang Dianshitai Sanshinian* (Thirty Years of China's Central Television Station). Beijing: Chinese Radio and Television Press, 1988.

CCTV's Group for Mass Correspondence. *Zhongyang Dianshitai guanzhong laixin xianbian* (A Selective Compilation of the CCTV's Letters from Viewers). Beijing: Chinese Radio and Television Press, 1989.

Center for Chinese Studies. *Current Chinese Communist Newspaper Terms and Sayings*. Berkeley: University of California, 1971.

Chang, Won Ho. *Mass Media in China: The History and the Future*. Ames: Iowa State University Press, 1989.

Chinese International Radio Station. *Zhongguo zhisheng youyi zhiqiao* (Voice of China and Bridge of Friendship). Beijing: Chinese International Broadcasting Press, 1987.

CPBS's Group for History. *Zhongyang renmin Guangbo Diantai Jianshi* (A Concise History of the Central People's Broadcasting Station). Beijing: Chinese Radio and Television Press, 1987.

Editorial board. *Beijing duzhe tingzhong guanzhong diaocha* (Beijing Survey on Readers, Listeners, and Viewers). Beijing: Workers' Press, 1985.

Editorial board. *Dangdai Zhongguo guangbo dianshi* (Contemporary Radio and Television in China). Vols. 1–2. Beijing: Chinese Social Sciences Press, 1987.

Editorial board. *Diwujie quanguo youxiu guangbo jiemu gaoxian* (A Selection of the Fifth Nationwide Winning Programs). Beijing: Chinese Radio and Television Press, 1987.

———. *Jiefangqu guangbo ziliao xianbian 1940–1949* (A Compilation of Historical Materials on Broadcasting on the Liberated Areas 1940–1949). Beijing: Chinese Radio and Television Press, 1985.

Editorial board. *Zhongguo guangbo dianshi nianjian* (China's Radio and Television Yearbook). Beijing: Beijing Broadcasting College Press, 1986– .

———. *Zhongguo guangbo dianshi shiliao xianbian* (A Selected Collection of Chinese Radio and Television History). Vols. 1–5. Beijing: Beijing Broadcasting College Press, 1987–1988.

Editorial board. *Zhongguo nujizhe* (China's Female Correspondents). Vols. 1–2. Beijing: Xinhua Press, 1989.

Editorial board. *Zhongguo renmin Guangbo huiyilu* (A Reminiscence of the Chinese People's Radio). Beijing: Chinese Broadcasting Press, 1983.

Editorial board. *Zhongguo xiandai baokanshi congshu* (A Book Series of China's Modern Newspaper History). Beijing: Xinhua Press, 1983– .

Fang Hanqi. *Zhongguo jindai baokanshi* (A History of China's Modern Newspapers). Taiyuan: Shanxi People's Publishing House, 1981.

Fang Jigen and Wenying Hu. *Haiwai Huawen Baokan de Lishi yu Xianzhuang* (Historical and Current Situations of the Overseas Chinese Newspapers). Beijing: Xinhua Press, 1989.

Howkins, John. *Mass Communication in China*. New York: Longman, 1982.

Huang He and Zhihua Zhang. *Zhongguo renmin Jiefangjun baokanshi* (A History of the Chinese People's Liberation Army's Newspapers). Beijing: PLA Press, 1986.

Huang Zhuomin. *Zhongguo gudai baozhi tanyuan* (An Exploration into China's Ancient Newspapers). Beijing: People's Daily Press, 1983.

Lai Kuang-lin. *Qishinian zhongguo baoyeshi* (Seventy Years of China's Newspapers). Taipei: Central Daily Press, 1981.

Li Zhengjie et al. *Zhongguo baokan xinciyu* (New Words in the Chinese Newspapers). Beijing: Chinese Language Learning Press, 1987.

Liu, Alan P. L. *Communications and National Integration in Communist China*. Berkeley: University of California Press, 1971.

Liu Sheng-chi. *Zhongguo dalu dixia kanwu yanjiu 1978–1982* (A Study of Underground Periodicals in Mainland China 1978–1982). Taipei: Commercial Publishing House, 1985.

Lu Yunfan. *Zhongguo shida mingjizhe* (China's Contemporary Top Ten Correspondents). Hefei: Anhui People's Press, 1985.

Markham, James W. *Voices of the Red Giants.* Ames: Iowa State University Press, 1967.

Press Institute in the Chinese Academy of Social Sciences. *Xinwenxue yanjiu shinian 1978–1988* (Ten Years of Press Study 1978–1988). Beijing: People's Publishing House, 1989.

Press Institute in the Chinese Academy of Social Sciences, ed. *Xinwenjie renwu* (Who's Who in the Press). Vol. 1– . Beijing: Xinhua Press, 1983– .

Press Institute in the Chinese Academy of Social Sciences and the Association of the Chinese Press Societies, eds. *Zhongguo xinwen nianjian* (The Chinese Press Almanac). Beijing: Chinese Social Science Press, 1982– .

Radio and Television Group, ed. *Quanguo guangbo xinwen youxiu zuopin xianping* (A Selective Commentary of All-China's Excellent Broadcasting Works). Beijing: People's University Press, 1989.

Shanghai Library. *Zhongguo jindai qikan pianmu huilu 1857–1918.* (A Compilation of China's Modern Newspapers and Periodicals 1857–1918). Shanghai: Shanghai People's Publishing House, 1979.

Shi Tianchuan. *Guangbo dianshi gailun* (An Introduction to Radio and Television). Shanghai: Fudan University Press, 1987.

Wang, Ting. *A Compilation of Press Articles on Peking's News Policy during the Cultural Revolution.* Hong Kong: Chinese University of Hong Kong, 1973.

Wang Xueqi. *Disi Zhanxian: Guomindang Zhongyang Guangbo Diantai Duoshi* (The Fourth Front: The KMT Central Broadcasting Station). Beijing: Chinese Culture and History Press, 1988.

Wen Shih-kuang. *Zhongguo guangbo dianshi fazhanshi* (A Development History of China's Radio and Television). Taipei: Three People's Principles Publishing House, 1983.

Womack, Brantly, ed. *Media and the Chinese Public: A Survey of the Beijing Media Audience.* Armonk, N.Y.: M. E. Sharpe, 1986.

Xu Huanlong. *Zhongguo xiandai xinwenshi jianbian* (A Concise History of the Chinese Press). Zhengzhou: Henan People's Publishing House, 1989.

Yang Guanghui et al. *Zhongguo jindai baokan fazhan gaikuang* (A General Survey of China's Modern Newspaper Development). Beijing: Xinhua Press, 1986.

Yu Wenhai, et al. *Zhongguo baokan tougao zhinan* (A Manuscript Submission Guide for the Chinese Newspapers). Beijing: Xinhua Press, 1988.

Zeng Xubai. *Zhongguo xinwenshi* (A History of the Chinese Press). Vols. 1–2. Taipei: University of Politics Press, 1966.

Zhao Xin, ed. *Zhongguo xinwenxue daxi—Dianshipian 1976–1982* (China's New Literature—Television 1976–1982). Beijing: China's Literature Association Press, 1990.

Zhao Yuming. *Zhongguo xiandai guangbo jianshi* (A Concise History of China's Modern Radio Broadcasting). Beijing: Chinese Radio and Television Press, 1987.

Zhuang Chunyu. *Zhongguo Dianshi Gaishu* (An Introduction to Chinese Television). Beijing: Chinese Radio and Television Press, 1985.

Zuo Moye. *Dangdai Zhongguo de guangbo dianshi* (Contemporary Radio and Television in China). Beijing: Chinese Social Science Press, 1987.

MEDICINE

A Barefoot Doctor's Manual (Contemporary Chinese Paramedical Manual). Philadelphia: Running Press, 1977.

Academy of Traditional Chinese Medicine, Peking Staff. *An Outline of Chinese Acupuncture.* Monterey Park, Calif.: Chan's Corporation, n.d.

Beijing Institute of Traditional Chinese Medicine Staff. *Fundamentals of Chinese Medicine.* Translated by Nigel Wiseman and Andrew W. Ellis; edited by Paul Zmiewski. Brookline, Mass.: Paradigm Publications, 1987.

Bensky, Dan, Andrew Gamble, Lilian L. Bensky, and Ted Kaptchuk, comp. and trans. *Chinese Herbal Medicine: Materia Medica.* Seattle: Eastland Press, 1986.

Bensky, Dan, and Randall Barolet. *Chinese Herbal Medicine: Formulas and Strategies* (translation from Chinese). Seattle: Eastland Press, 1990.

Berk, William, ed. *Chinese Healing Arts: Internal* Kung Fu. Translated by John Dudgeon. 1979. Reprint. Burbank, Calif.: Unique Publications, 1986.

Bowers, John Z., J. William Hess, and Nathan Sivin, eds. *Science and Medicine in Twentieth-Century China.* Ann Arbor: University of Michigan, Center for Chinese Studies, 1989.

Braun, R. *List of Medicines Exported from Hangkow and Other Yangtze Ports.* Shanghai: Inspector General of Customs, 1909.

Buchman, D. D. *Herbal Medicine.* New York: Outlet Book Company, 1988.

Buchman, Dian D. *Herbal Medicine: The Natural Way to Get Well and Stay Well.* New York: McKay, David, Company, 1979.

Chang, H. M., and P. P. But, eds. *Pharmacology and Applications of Chinese Materia Medica.* Vol. 1. River Edge, N.J.: World Scientific Publishing Company, 1988.

Chang, Po-tuan. *Understanding Reality: A Taoist Alchemical Classic.* Translated by Thomas Cleary. Honolulu: University of Hawaii Press, 1987. ´

Cheung, S. C., and N. H. Li, eds. *Xiang Gang de Zhong yi chao yao* (Chinese Medicinal Herbs of Hong Kong). Vol. 1. Hong Kong: Commercial Press, 1978. (In Chinese and English)

Chinese Herbs Made Easy. Provo, Utah: Woodland Health Books, n.d.

Chinese Tonic Herbs. New York: Gordon Press Publishers, 1992.

Claus, Edward P. *Phamacognosy.* 4th ed. Philadelphia: Lea and Fibiger, 1961.

Croizier, Ralph C. *Traditional Medicine in Modern China.* Cambridge, Mass.: Harvard University Press, 1968.

Current Topics in Chinese Science, Section G: Medical Science. Vol. 2. New York: Gordon and Breach Science Publishers, 1984.

Current Topics in Chinese Science, Section G: Medical Science. Vol. 3. New York: Gordon and Breach Science Publishers, 1984.

Eisen, Andrew W. *Fundamentals of Chinese Acupuncture.* Edited by Richard Feit. Rev. ed. Brookline, Mass.: Paradigm Publications, 1991.

Eisenberg, David, and Thomas Lee Wright. *Encounters with Qi: Exploring Chinese Medicine.* New York: W. W. Norton, 1985.

Finnegan, John. *Regeneration of Health: Nourishing Body Systems with Chinese Herbal Formulas.* 5th ed. Mill Valley, Calif.: Elysian Arts, 1991.

J. E. Fogarty International Center for Advanced Study in the Health Sciences. *A Barefoot Doctor's Manual.* Washington, D.C.: National Institutes of Health, 1974. (U.S.

Department of Health, Education, and Welfare Publication no. NIH 75-695; translation of Chinese text)

Foster, Steven, and Yve Chongxi. *Herbal Emissaries: Bringing Chinese Herbs to the West.* Rochester, Vt.: Inner Traditions International, 1992.

Fulder, Stephen. *Tao of Medicine.* Rochester, Vt.: Inner Traditions International, 1991.

Grieve, Maude. *A Modern Herbal.* 2 vols. New York: Dover, 1971.

Griffin, LaDean. *The Return to Herbal Medicine.* Salt Lake City, Utah: Hawkes Publishing, 1979.

Gumbel, Dietrich. *Principles of Holistic Skin Therapy with Herbal Essences.* Translated by Ritva Abao. Portland, Oreg.: Medicina Biologica, 1986.

Hallowell, Michael. *Herbal Healing: A Practical Introduction to Medicinal Herbs.* Garden City Park, N.Y.: Avery Publishing Group, 1989.

Hammer, Leon. *Dragon Rises, Red Bird Flies: Psychology and Chinese Medicine.* Barrytown, N.Y.: Station Hill Press, 1980.

Herbal Pharmacology in the People's Republic of China: A Trip Report of the American Herbal Pharmacology Delegation. Washington, D.C.: National Academy of Sciences, 1975.

————. *Immediate Hints to Health Problems.* Edited by Betty Elkan. New York: Juvenescent Research Corporation, 1991.

Ho, Betty Yu-Lin. *How to Stay Healthy a Lifetime without Medicines.* New York: Juvenescent Research Corporation, 1979.

Holmes, Peter. *The Energetics of Western Herbs: Integrating Western & Oriental Herbal Medicine Traditions.* Vol. I. Boulder, Colo.: Artemis Press, 1989.

Hsu, Hong-yen, Yuh-pan Chen, and Shuenn-jyi Shen. *Oriental Materia Medica.* Long Beach, Calif.: Orient Heal Arts, 1986.

Hsu Ta-chun. *Forgotten Traditions in Ancient Chinese Medicine.* Brookline, Mass.: Paradigm Publications, 1989.

Huang, Bing-shan. *AIDS and Its Treatment: According to Traditional Chinese Medicine.* Translated by Di Fu and Bob Flaws. Boulder, Colo.: Blue Poppy Enterprises Press, 1991.

Huang ti nei ching su wen—The Yellow Emperor's Classic of Internal Medicine. New ed. Translated by Ilza Veith. Berkeley: University of California Press, 1972.

Huard, Pierre, and Ming Wong. *Chinese Medicine.* New York: McGraw-Hill, 1968.

Hume, Edward H. *Chinese Way in Medicine.* 1940. Reprint. Westport, Conn.: Hyperion Press, 1975.

Hyatt, Richard. *Healing with Chinese Herbs.* New York: Schocken Books, 1978.

Jain, K. K. *The Amazing Story of Health Care in New China.* Emmaus, Pa.: Rodale Press, 1973.

Johnson, Obed S. *A Study of Chinese Alchemy.* 1928. Reprint. Salem, N.H.: Ayer Company Publishers, 1974.

Kaptchuk, Ted J. *The Web That Has No Weaver: Understanding Chinese Medicine.* Chicago: Congdon and Weed, 1985.

Keys, John. *Chinese Herbs: Their Botany, Chemistry and Pharmacodynamics.* Boston: Charles E. Tuttle, 1991.

Kleinman, Arthur, Peter Kunstadter, E. Russell Alexander, and James L. Gale, eds. *Medicine in Chinese Cultures: Comparative Studies of Health Care in Chinese and Other Societies.* Washington, D.C., National Institutes of Health, 1974.

Koo, A., H. W. Yeung, and W. W. Tso, eds. *Advances in Chinese Medicinal Materials Research: Proceedings of the International Symposium.* River Edge, N.J.: World Scientific Publishing Company, 1985.

Lampton, David M. *The Politics of Medicine in China: The Policy Process, 1949–1977.* Boulder, Colo.: Westview Press, 1977.

Larre, Claude, Jean Schatz, and Elisabeth Rochat de la Valle. *Survey of Traditional Chinese Medicine.* Columbia, Md.: Traditional Acupuncture Institute, 1986.

Leslie, Charles, ed. *Asian Medical Systems: A Comparative Study.* Berkeley: University of California Press, 1977.

Leung, Albert Y. *Chinese Herbal Medicine.* New York: Universe Books, 1984.

Li, Shi-Zhen. *Ben cao gang mu.* (Chinese Medicinal Herbs). Translated by F. Porter Smith and G. A. Stuart. New ed. San Francisco: Georgetown Press, 1973.

Liang, Jian-Hui. *A Handbook of Traditional Chinese Dermatology.* Edited by Bob Flaws; translated by Zhang Ting-Liang. Boulder, Colo.: Blue Poppy Enterprises Press, 1987.

Liu, F., and Yan Mau Liu. *Chinese Medical Terminology.* Hong Kong: Commercial Press, 1980.

———. *English-Chinese Medical Terminology.* New York: French and European Publications, 1980. (In English and Chinese)

Liu, Yanchi. *The Essential Book of Traditional Chinese Medicine.* Translated by Fang Tingyu and Chen Laidi. New York: Columbia University Press, 1988.

Lu, Henry C. *Legendary Chinese Healing Herbs.* New York: Sterling Publishing Company, 1991.

Lu, S. *Chinese Drugs in the West.* Hong Kong: Deli Book Co., 1978.

Lucas, Anelissa. *Chinese Medical Modernization: Comparative Policy Continuities, 1930's–1980's.* Westport, Conn.: Greenwood Press, 1982.

Lucas, Richard M. *Secrets of the Chinese Herbalists.* Rev. ed. New York: Prentice Hall, 1987.

Lust, John B. *The Herb Book.* Simi Valley, Calif.: Benedict Lust, 1974.

Mann, Felix. *Acupuncture: The Chinese Art of Healing.* 3d ed. London: William Heinemann Medical Books, 1978.

Maoshing Ni. *Chinese Herbology Made Easy.* Santa Monica, Calif.: Shrine of the Eternal Breath of Tao, 1986.

March, Kathryn G., and Andrew L. March. *The Wild Plant Companion: A Fresh Understanding of Herbal Food and Medicine.* Lakewood, Colo.: Meridian Hill Publications, 1986.

Miller, S. M., and J. A. Jewell. *Health Care and Traditional Medicine in China, 1800–1982.* London: Routledge and Kegan Paul, 1983.

Moody, Ramona A., and Lee C. Overholser, eds. *Signs of Health: Traditional Chinese Medicine for Modern Living.* San Diego, Calif.: Empire Publishing, 1991.

Morse, William R. *Chinese Medicine.* New York: Paul B. Hoeber, 1934.

Nan-Ching: The Classic of Difficult Issues. Translated by Paul U. Unschuld. Berkeley: University of California Press, 1986.

Naeser, Margaret A. *Outline Guide to Chinese Herbal Patent Medicines in Pill Form.* 2d ed. Boston: Boston Chinese Medicine, 1990.

Palos, Stephan. *The Chinese Art of Healing.* New York: Herder and Herder, 1971.

Pillsbury, Barbara. " 'Doing the Month': Confinement and Convalescence of Chinese Women after Childbirth." *Social Science and Medicine* 12 (1978): 11–22.

Porkert, Manfred, and Christian Ullmann. *Chinese Medicine.* New York: Henry Holt and Company, 1990.

Read, Bernard E. *Chinese Materia Medica: Animal Drugs.* Hong Kong: Commercial Press, 1931. Reprint. Pasadena, Calif.: Oriental Book Store, 1982.

————. *Chinese Materia Medica: Insect Drugs, Dragon and Snake Drugs, Fish Drugs.* Hong Kong: Commercial Press, 1934. Reprint. Chinese Materia Medica Series no. 2. Pasadena, Calif.: Oriental Book Store, 1984.

————. *Chinese Materia Medica: Turtle and Shellfish Drugs, Avian Drugs, a Compendium of Minerals and Stones.* Hong Kong: Commercial Press, 1932. Reprint. Chinese Material Medica no. 3. Pasadena, Calif.: Oriental Book Store, 1982.

————. *Chinese Medicinal Plants from the Pen T'sao Kang Mu.* Pasadena, Calif.: Oriental Book Store, 1977.

Reid, Daniel P. *Chinese Herbal Medicine.* Boston: Shambhala, 1987.

Risse, Guenter B., ed. *Modern China and Traditional Chinese Medicine.* Springfield, Ill.: Charles C. Thomas Publisher, 1973.

Rosenthal, Marilynn M. *Health Care in the People's Republic of China.* Boulder, Colo.: Westview Press, 1987.

Ross, Jeremy. *Zang Fu: The Organ Systems of Traditional Chinese Medicine.* 2d ed. New York: Churchill Livingstone, 1985.

Said, Hakim Mohammed. *Medicine in China.* Karachi, Pakistan: Hamdard Foundation, 1981.

Shen, John H. *Chinese Medicine.* New York: Educational Solutions Incorporated, 1980.

Shen Nong ben cao (The Shennong Herbal). Taipei: Five Continent, 1977.

Sidel, Victor W., and Ruth Sidel. *The Health of China.* Boston: Beacon Press, 1982.

————. *Serve the People: Observations on Medicine in the People's Republic of China.* Boston: Beacon Press, 1973.

Sivin, Nathan. *Traditional Medicine in Contemporary China.* Science, Medicine, and Technology in East Asia Series no. 2. Translated from Chinese. Ann Arbor: University of Michigan, Center for Chinese Studies, 1987.

Stuart, G. A. *Chinese Materia Medica: Vegetable Kingdom.* Shanghai: American Presbyterian Press, 1911. Reprint. Taipei: Southern Materials Press, 1976.

Teeguarden, Ron. *Chinese Tonic Herbs.* Briarcliff Manor, N.Y.: Japan Publications (U.S.A.), 1987.

Temple, Robert. *The Genius of China: 3,000 Years of Science, Discovery, and Contemporary Perspectives on Chinese Civilization.* New York: Simon and Schuster, 1986.

Tierra, Leslie. *The Herbs of Life: Health and Healing Using Western and Chinese Techniques.* Freedom, Calif.: Crossing Press, 1992.

Tsuei, Wei. *Roots of Chinese Culture and Medicine.* Academy of Chinese Culture and Health Sciences Series no. 1. Oakland, Calif.: Chinese Culture Books Company, 1990.

Tsung, Pi-Kwang, and Hong-yen Hsu. *Allergies and Chinese Herbal Medicine.* Educational Series on Chinese Medicine no. 3. Long Beach, Calif.: Oriental Healing Arts Institute, 1987.

————. *Arthritis and Chinese Herbal Medicine.* Long Beach, Calif.: Oriental Healing Arts Institute, 1987.

————. *Immunology and Chinese Herbal Medicine.* Educational Series on Chinese Medicine no. 1. Long Beach, Calif.: Oriental Healing Arts Institute, 1986.

Unschuld, Paul U. *Medical Ethics in Imperial China: A Study in Historical Anthropology.* Berkeley: University of California Press, 1979.

————. *Medicine in China: A History of Ideas.* Berkeley: University of California Press, 1985.

————. *Medicine in China: A History of Pharmaceutics.* Berkeley: University of California Press, 1985.

Unschuld, Paul U., ed. *Approaches to Traditional Chinese Medical Literature: Proceedings of an International Symposium on Translation Methodologies and Terminologies.* Norwell, Mass.: Kluwer Academic Publishers, 1989.

————. *Introductory Readings in Classical Chinese Medicine.* Norwell, Mass.: Kluwer Academic Publishers, 1988.

Willmott, Jonathan C. *Western Astrology and Chinese Medicine.* Rochester, Vt.: Inner Traditions International Limited, 1985.

Wiseman, Nigel A., and Ken Boss. *Complete Chinese Materia Medica.* Brookline, Mass.: Paradigm Publications, 1991.

Wolfe, Honora L. *Second Spring: A Guide to Healthy Menopause through Traditional Chinese Medicine.* Edited by Bob Flaws. Boulder, Colo.: Blue Poppy Enterprises Press, 1990.

Wong, K. C., and Lien-Teh Wu. *History of Chinese Herbal Medicine.* 2 vols. Shanghai: National Quarantine Service, 1936. Reprint. New York: Gordon Press Publishers, 1976.

Wu, Shan M. *The Mending of the Sky and Other Chinese Myths.* Translated by Xiao M. Li. Durham, N.H.: Oyster River Press, 1989.

Zhang Zhong-Jing. *Shanghan lun* (Treatise on Febrile and Miscellaneous Diseases). Shanghai: Commercial Press, 1983.

Zhong chao yao he chao yao shi pu (Chinese Herbs and Herbal Recipes). Hong Kong: Commercial Press, 1970.

QIGONG

China Sports Magazine. The Wonders of Qigong: A Chinese Exercise for Fitness, Health and Longevity. Los Angeles: Wayfarer Publications, 1985.

Dong, Paul, and Aristide Esser. *Chi Gong: The Ancient Way to Health.* New York: Paragon Press, 1990.

Takahashi, Masaru, and Stephen Brown. *Qigong for Health: Chinese Traditional Exercises for Cure and Prevention.* New York: Japan Publications, 1986.

Zhang Mingwu and Sun Xingyuan. *Chinese Qigong Therapy.* Translated by Yang Entang. Jinan: Shangdong Science and Technology Press, 1985.

RELIGION

Ahern, Emily. *The Cult of the Dead in a Chinese Village.* Stanford, Calif.: Stanford University Press, 1973.

Allan, Sarah. *The Shape of the Turtle: Myth, Art and Cosmos in Early China.* Albany: State University of New York Press, 1991.

Baity, Philip Chesley. *Religion in a Chinese Town.* Taipei: Orient Cultural Service, 1975.

Baker, Dwight Condo. *T'ai Shan.* Shanghai: Commercial Press, 1925.

Bell, Catherine. "Religion and Chinese Culture: Toward an Assessment of 'Popular Religion.'" *History of Religions* 29 (1989): 35–57.

Bilsky, Lester James. *The State Religion of Ancient China.* 2 vols. Taipei: Orient Cultural Service, 1975.

Biot, Edouard, trans. *Le Tchou-Li ou Rites des Tchou.* 2 vols. 1851. Reprint. Taipei: Ch'eng-wen Publishing, 1969.

Bodde, Derk. *Festivals in Classical China, New Year and Other Annual Observances during the Han Dynasty, 206 B.C.–A.D. 220.* Princeton, N.J.: Princeton University Press, 1975.

Brown, G. Thompson. *Christianity in the People's Republic of China.* Rev. ed. Atlanta: John Knox Press, 1986.

Burkhardt, Valentine R. *Chinese Creeds and Customs.* 3 vols. Hong Kong: South China Morning Post, 1952–1958.

Ch'en, Kenneth K. S. *Buddhism in China, An Historical Survey.* Princeton, N.J.: Princeton University Press, 1964.

Day, Clarence Burton. *Chinese Peasant Cults: Being a Study of Chinese Paper Gods.* 2d ed. Taipei: Ch'eng-wen Publishing, 1969.

DeWoskin, Kenneth J., trans. *Doctors, Diviners and Magicians of Ancient China: Biographies of Fang-shih.* New York: Columbia University Press, 1983.

Doré, Henri. *Researches into Chinese Superstitions.* Translated by M. Kennedy et al. 13 vols. 1914–1938. Reprint. Taipei: Ch'eng-wen Publishing, 1966–1967.

Dudbridge, Glen. *The Legend of Miao-shan.* London: Ithaca Press, 1978.

Dun Lichen. *Yenjing suishi ji* (Annual Customs and Festivals in Beijing). Translated by Derk Bodde. Hong Kong: Henri Vetch, 1936.

Eberhard, Wolfram. *Chinese Festivals.* Taipei: Orient Cultural Service, 1972.

Ebrey, Patricia Buckley. *Chu Hsi's Family Rituals.* Princeton, N.J.: Princeton University Press, 1991.

Elliot, Alan J. A. *Chinese Spirit Medium Cults in Singapore.* London: Royal Anthropological Institute, 1955.

Girardot, Norman. *Myth and Meaning in Early Taoism: The Theme of Chaos (hun-tun).* Berkeley: University of California Press, 1983.

Graham, David Crockett. *Folk Religion in Southwest China.* Washington, D.C.: Smithsonian Press, 1961.

Groot, J.J.M. de. *The Religious System of China.* 6 vols. 1892–1910. Reprint. Taipei: Ch'eng-wen Publishing, 1972.

Hansen, Valerie. *Changing Gods in Medieval China, 1127–1276.* Princeton, N.J.: Princeton University Press, 1990.

Jordan, David K. *Gods, Ghosts and Ancestors: Folk Religion in a Taiwanese Village.* Berkeley: University of California Press, 1972.

Jordan, David K., and Daniel L. Overmeyer. *The Flying Phoenix: Aspects of Chinese Sectarianism in Taiwan.* Princeton, N.J.: Princeton University Press, 1986.

Kaltenmark, Max. *Lao Tzu and Taoism.* Translated by Roger Greaves. Stanford, Calif.: Stanford University Press, 1969.

Karlgren, Bernhard, trans. *The Book of Odes.* Stockholm: The Museum of Far Eastern Antiquities, 1950.

Latourette, Kenneth Scott. *A History of Christian Missions in China.* 1929. Reprint. Taipei: Ch'eng-wen Publishing, 1966.

Legge, James, trans. "The Li Ki." In *The Sacred Books of the East,* edited by F. Max Müller. Vols. 27 and 28. Oxford, England: The Clarendon Press, 1885.

Loewe, Michael. *Ways to Paradise: The Chinese Quest for Immortality.* London: George Allen and Unwin, 1979.

Overmeyer, Daniel L. *Folk Buddhist Religion, Dissenting Sects in Late Traditional China.* Cambridge, Mass.: Harvard University Press, 1976.

Palmer, Martin, ed. *T'ung Shu, The Ancient Chinese Almanac.* Boston: Shambhala, 1986.

Paper, Jordan. "Further Notes Regarding Religion in China—1992." *Journal of Chinese Religion* 20(1992): 215–220.

———. "The Normative East Asian Understanding of Christian Scriptures." *Studies in Religion* 18 (1989): 451–65.

———. "The Persistence of Female Spirits in Patriarchal China." *Journal of Feminist Studies in Religion* 6 (1990): 25–40.

———. "The Ritual Core of Chinese Religion." *Religious Studies and Theology* 7, 2–3 (1987): 19–35.

Pas, Julian, ed. *The Turning of the Tide: Chinese Religion Today.* Hong Kong: Royal Asiatic Society, Hong Kong Branch, 1989.

Saso, Michael. *Blue Dragon White Tiger: Taoist Rites of Passage.* Washington, D.C.: The Taoist Center, 1990.

———. *Taoism and the Rite of Cosmic Renewal.* N.p.: Washington State University Press, 1972.

———. *The Teachings of the Taoist Master Chuang.* New Haven, Conn.: Yale University Press, 1978.

Seidel, Anna K. *La divinisation de Lau Tseu dans le Taoisme des Han.* Paris: Ecole Française d'Extrême-Orient, 1969.

Seiwert, Hubert. *Volksreligion und nationale Tradition in Taiwan: Studies zur regionalen Religionsgeschichte einer chinesischen Provinz.* Stuttgart, Germany: Franz Steiner Verlag, 1985.

Shapiro, Sidney, ed. and trans. *Jews of Old China.* New York: Hippocrene Books, 1984.

Shen Fu. *Six Records of a Floating Life.* Translated by Leonard Pratt and Chiang Su-hui. Harmondsworth, England: Penguin Books, 1983.

Shinohara, Koichi, and Gregory Schopen, eds. *From Benares to Beijing: Essays on Buddhism and Chinese Religion in Honour of Prof. Jan Yün-hua.* Oakville, Ontario: Mosaic, 1991.

Steel, John, trans. *The I-Li or Book of Etiquette and Ceremonial.* 2 vols. Taipei: Ch'eng-wen Publishing, 1966.

Thompson, Lawrence. *Chinese Religion: An Introduction.* 4th ed. Belmont, Calif.: Wadsworth Publishing, 1989.

Waley, Arthur, trans. *The Book of Songs.* New York: Grove Press, 1960.

Watson, James L., and Evelyn S. Rawski, eds. *Death Ritual in Late Imperial and Modern China.* Berkeley: University of California Press, 1988.

Wechsler, Howard J. *Offerings of Jade and Silk: Ritual and Symbol in the Legitimation of the T'ang Dynasty.* New Haven, Conn.: Yale University Press, 1985.

Welch, Holmes. *The Parting of the Way: Lao Tzu and the Taoist Movement.* London: Methuen, 1958.

———. *The Practice of Chinese Buddhism, 1900–1950.* Cambridge, Mass.: Harvard University Press, 1967.

Welch, Holmes, and Anna Seidel. *Facets of Taoism: Essays in Chinese Religion.* New Haven, Conn.: Yale University Press, 1979.

Werner, E.T.C. *Myths and Legends of China.* New York: Brentano's, 1922.

Wolf, Arthur P., ed. *Religion and Ritual in Chinese Society.* Stanford, Calif.: Stanford University Press, 1974.

Yang, C. K. *Religion in Chinese Society.* Berkeley: University of California Press, 1961.

Zhen Zhiming. *Zhongguo shanshu yu congjiao* (Chinese 'Good Books' and Religion). Taipei: Hsüeh Sheng Shu Chü, 1988.

Zong Li and Liu Chun. *Zhongguo minjian zhushen* (Chinese Folk Deities). Shijiazhuang: Hebei renming chupanshe, 1986.

Zürcher, E. *The Buddhist Conquest of China: The Spread and Adaptation of Buddhism in Early Medieval China.* 2 vols. Leiden, Netherlands: E. J. Brill, 1959.

SPORTS

Beijing Review, ed. *XI Asian Games, Beijing, 1990.* Beijing: New Star Publishers, 1990.

Brownell, Susan E. "The Changing Relationship between Sport and the State in the People's Republic of China." In *Sport . . . the Third Millennium,* 295–302. Proceedings of the International Symposium, May 21–25, 1990. Quebec City, Canada: Les Presses de l'Université Laval, 1991.

————. "Sports in Britain and China, 1850–1920: An Explanatory Overview." *International Journal of the History of Sport* 8, 2 (1991): 114–20.

Cao Xiangjun. *Tiyu gailun* (A General Theory of Physical Culture). Beijing: Beijing Institute of Physical Education Press, 1985.

China Sports and New World Press. *Traditional Chinese Fitness Exercises.* China Spotlight Series. Beijing: New World Press, 1984.

Diem, Carl. *Asiatische Reiterspiele: Ein Beitrag zur Kulturgeschichte der Völker.* Berlin: Deutscher Archiv-Verlag, 1941.

Espy, Richard. *The Politics of the Olympic Games.* Berkeley: University of California Press, 1979.

Guojia tiwei zhengce yanjiushi (State Sports Commission Policy Research Division). *Tiyu yundong wenjian xuanbian 1949–1981* (Selected Sport and Physical Culture Documents 1949–1981). Beijing: Renmin tiyu chubanshe, 1982.

Hoberman, John M. *Sport and Political Ideology.* Austin: University of Texas Press, 1984.

————. "Sport and Social Change: The Transformation of Maoist Sport." *Sociology of Sport Journal* 4 (1987): 156–79.

Knuttgen, Howard G., Ma Qiwei, and Wu Zhongyuan, eds. *Sport in China.* Champaign, Ill.: Human Kinetics Books, 1990.

Kolatch, Jonathan. *Sports, Politics, and Ideology in China.* Middle Village, N.Y.: Jonathan David Publishers, 1972.

Kong Xiang'an, Niu Xinghua, and Qiu Bo. "A Summary of Sport Sociology Research in the PRC." Translated by Susan E. Brownell. *International Review for the Sociology of Sport* 25, 2 (1990): 93–108.

Lewis, Mark Edward. *Sanctioned Violence in Early China.* Albany: State University of New York Press, 1990.

Liu, James J. Y. *The Chinese Knight-Errant.* Chicago: University of Chicago Press, 1967.

Lowe, Benjamin, David B. Kanin, and Andrew Strenk, eds. *Sports and International Relations,* Champaign, Ill.: Stipes Publishing, 1978.

Nelson, Randy, ed. *Martial Arts Reader: An Anthology of Historical and Philosophical Writings.* Woodstock, N.Y.: Overlook Press, 1989.

People's Sports Editorial Group. *Minzu tiyu jijin* (Outstanding Examples of Minority Physical Culture). Beijing: Renmin tiyu chubanshe, 1985.

People's Sports Publishing House. *Sports in Ancient China.* Hong Kong: Tai Dao, 1986.

Potter, Sulamith Heins, and Jack M. Potter. *China's Peasants: The Anthropology of a Revolution.* Cambridge, England: Cambridge University Press, 1990.

Riordan, James. *Sport, Politics and Communism.* Manchester, England: Manchester University Press, 1991.

Riordan, James, ed. *Sport under Communism: The U.S.S.R., Czechoslovakia, The G.D.R., China, Cuba.* Montreal: McGill-Queen's University Press, 1978.

Rizak, Gene. "Sport in the People's Republic of China." In *Sport in Asia and Africa: A Comparative Handbook,* edited by Eric A. Wagner, 101–20. Westport, Conn.: Greenwood Press, 1989.

Rong Gaotang et al. *Dangdai zhongguo tiyu* (Contemporary Chinese Sports). Beijing: Chinese Academy of Social Sciences Press, 1984.

Shih Chi-wen. *Sports Go Forward in China.* Peking: Foreign Languages Press, 1963.

Sports and Games in Ancient China. Beijing: New World Press, 1986.

Sports and Public Health. Beijing: Foreign Language Press, 1983.

Tang, Hao. *Shenzhou wuyi* (Chinese Martial Arts). Changchun: Jilin Culture and History Press, 1986.

Xu Yongchang, ed. *Zhongguo gudai tiyu* (Ancient Chinese Physical Culture). Beijing: Beijing Normal University Press, 1983.

Yang, Jwing-Ming. *The Root of Chinese Chi Kung.* Jamaica Plain, Mass.: Yang's Martial Arts Association, 1989.

Zhao Yu. "Qiangguo meng" (Superpower Dream). *Dangdai* (Contemporary Times), February 1988, 163–98.

Zhuang Kongshao, producer and director. *The Dragon-Boat Festival* (videocassette). Seattle: University of Washington Press, 1992.

TAIJIQUAN AND WUSHU

Cheng Man-Ch'ing. *Cheng Man-Ch'ing's Advanced T'ai-chi Form Instructions.* Translated and edited by Douglas Wile. Brooklyn, N.Y.: Sweet Ch'i Press, 1985.

————. *T'ai Chi Ch'uan: A Simplified Method of Calisthenics for Health and Self-defense.* Translated by Beauson Tseng. Berkeley, Calif.: North Atlantic Books, 1981.

Cheng Man-Ch'ing and Robert Smith. *T'ai-chi: The "Supreme Ultimate" Exercise for Health, Sport, and Self-defense.* Rutland, Vt.: Charles E. Tuttle, 1986.

Crompton, Paul. *The T'ai Chi Workbook.* Boston: Shambhala Publications, 1986.

Delza, Sophia. *T'ai-Chi Ch'uan: Body and Mind in Harmony, the Integration of Meaning and Method.* 1961. Rev. Albany: State University of New York Press, 1985.

Horwitz, Tem, Susan Kimmelman, and H. H. Lui. *Tai Chi Ch'uan: The Technique of Power.* Chicago: Chicago Review Press, 1976.

Huang Wen-shan. *Fundamentals of T'ai Chi Ch'uan.* 1973. 5th rev. ed. Seattle, Wash.: South Sky Book Company, 1984.

Jou, Tsung Hwa. *The Tao of Tai-chi Chuan: Way to Rejuvenation.* Edited by Shoshana Shapiro. 1981. 3d rev. ed. Rutland, Vt.: Charles E. Tuttle, 1983.

Lee, Douglas. *Tai Chi Chuan: The Philosophy of Yin and Yang and Its Application.* Burbank, Calif.: Ohara Publications, 1976.

Li Cheng, ed. *Wushu daquan* (Compendium of Wushu). Beijing: Beijing Physical Culture Institute Press, 1990.

Liang, T. T. *T'ai Chi Ch'uan for Health and Self-defense: Philosophy and Practice.* Edited by Paul Gallagher. 1974. Rev. New York: Vintage Books, 1977.

Liu, Da. *T'ai Chi Ch'uan and Meditation.* New York: Schocken, 1986.

Lo, Benjamin Peng Jeng, ed. *The Essence of T'ai Chi Ch'uan: The Literary Tradition.* Richmond, Calif.: North Atlantic Books, 1979.

Matsuda Takachi. *Zhongguo wushu shilue* (A Brief History of the Chinese Wushu). Translated by Lu Yan and Yan Hai. Chengdu: Sichuan Science and Technology Press, 1984.

Sohn, Robert C. *Tao and T'ai Chi Kung.* Rochester, Vt.: Destiny Books, 1989.

Soo, Chee. *The Chinese Art of K'ai Men.* New York: Gordon and Cremonesi Publishers, 1977.

Wang, Paisheng, and Zeng Weiqi. *Wu Style Tradition: A Detailed Course for Health and Self-defence and Teachings of Three Famous Masters in Beijing.* Beijing: Zhaohua Publishing House, 1983.

Wang Peikun and Shing Yen-Ling. *T'ai Chi Ch'uan: The Basic Exercises.* Translated by Sue-Shion Mei. Vol. 1, Chinese Martial Arts Series. Tokyo: Minato Research and Publishing, 1990.

Weng, Chi-Hsiu Daniel. *Ch'ang Style T'ai-Chi-Ch'uan.* Taipei: n.p., 1987. Available through Dr. Daniel Weng, P.O. Box 1221, Cupertino, Calif., 95015.

Wile, Douglas. *T'ai-chi Touchstones: Yang Family Secret Transmissions.* Translated by Douglas Wile. Brooklyn, N.Y.: Sweet Ch'i Press, 1983.

Xi Yuntai. *Zhongguo wushu shi* (A History of the Chinese *Wushu*). Beijing: People's Physical Culture Press, 1985.

Xu Cai, ed. *Wushu kexue tanmi* (Exploring Science in *Wushu*). Beijing: People's Physical Culture Press, 1990.

Yu Shenquan, ed. *Yang Style Taijiquan.* Beijing: Morning Glory Press, 1988.

TRANSPORTATION

Adley, Robert. *To China for Steam.* Poole, Dorset, England: Blandford Press, 1983.

Chao Yung-hsin. *Railways in Communist China.* Kowloon, Hong Kong: Union Research Institute, 1956.

Leung Chi-keung. *China, Railway Patterns and National Goals.* Chicago: University of Chicago, Department of Geography, 1980.

Liang, Ernest P. *China, Railways and Agricultural Development, 1875–1935.* Chicago: University of Chicago, Department of Geography, 1982.

Parsons, William Barclay. *An American Engineer in China.* New York: McClure, Philips and Co., 1900.

Theroux, Paul. *Riding the Iron Rooster.* Cape Cod, Mass.: Scriveners, 1988.

Whitehouse, Patrick Bruce. *China by Rail.* New York: Vendome Press, 1988.

Wu Yuan-li. *The Spatial Economy of Communist China: A Study on Industrial Location and Transportation.* New York: Praeger, 1967.

Index

Contributors

E. N. ANDERSON is Professor of Anthropology, University of California, Riverside. He has conducted field research in Hong Kong, Malaysia, and elsewhere throughout the Pacific Rim. His major work is *The Food of China*. Among earlier works are *The Floating Worlds of Castle Peak Bay, Essays on South China's Boat People*, and, with Marja L. Anderson, *Mountains and Waters: The Cultural Ecology of South Coastal China*.

SUSAN E. BROWNELL, a former nationally-ranked U.S. track and field athlete, won a gold medal for Beijing City in the 1986 National College Games. In 1988 she took a Senior Advanced Studies Degree at the Beijing Institute of Physical Education. She earned a Ph.D. in Cultural Anthropology from the University of California, Santa Barbara, in 1990. She has taught at Middlebury, University of Washington, and Yale, and is currently completing *Training the Body for China: Sports in the Moral Order of the People's Republic*.

CAO ZHENGWEN, correspondent for *Xinmin Evening Paper*, is a member of the Chinese Writers' Association and a member of the Council of the Popular Literature Society. To date he has published 25 works of fiction. He is best known for his novel *The Dilemma of Men in Their Forties* and his criticism *One Hundred and Eight Heroes in Jin Yong's Novels*.

J. A. ENGLISH-LUECK earned a Ph.D. in Cultural Anthropology from the University of California, Santa Barbara, and has done research in Suriname, the United States, and the People's Republic of China in ethnomedicine and psychological anthropology. Assistant Professor at San Jose State University, she is currently doing comparative research on California's Silicon Valley and Hong Kong.

JIANG XINGYU is a research fellow at the Shanghai Art Research Institute, a guest professor at the East Normal University, and a member of the Chinese Writers' Association. He specializes in traditional Chinese drama and has published widely on the subject.

RONALD G. KNAPP, Professor of Geography at the State University of New York, College at New Paltz, has authored or edited seven books on China's cultural geography, including *Chinese Bridges, Chinese Landscapes: The Village as Place, The Chinese House, China's Vernacular Architecture: House Form and Culture,* and *China's Traditional Rural Architecture.*

IONE KRAMER, a journalist by profession, spent over twenty years in Beijing as an editor of *China Today* (then *China Reconstructs*). There she also edited the English edition of a popular history of the Chinese dynasties, *Legends and Tales from Chinese History.* With Kit Chow she has authored *All the Tea in China.* She is currently working on a companion book about silk.

HSIAO-HUNG LEE is Reference Librarian at the University of Central Arkansas, where he also teaches English. He has published several Chinese translations of short stories by Nathaniel Hawthorne and Richard Wright and is currently researching the history of Chinese libraries.

JOHN A. LENT has authored or edited forty-six books and monographs and has written hundreds of articles. A Fulbright scholar to the Philippines in 1964–65, and the first coordinator of the pioneering mass communications program in Malaysia in 1972–74, Dr. Lent has returned to Asia on thirteen other occasions to conduct research. He has been managing editor of *Witty World International Cartoon Magazine* since its 1987 founding, is founding chair of a comic art working group within the International Association for Mass Communication Research since 1984, and has served as editor or editorial board member of *Comics Journal, Big O Magazine,* and other periodicals.

JOHN MARNEY was born in London and spent the first decades of his career as a professional violinist. On tour in the Far East, he became attracted to Oriental Studies and studied at London and Oxford universities and at the University of Wisconsin, where he earned his Ph.D. in classical Chinese literature. After living and working for many years in the Far East, he is now Professor of Chinese at Oakland University, Michigan.

PATRICK D. MURPHY, Director of the Graduate Program in Literature and Criticism in the English Department at Indiana University of Pennsylvania, coedited with Wu Dingbo *Science Fiction From China.* He has also authored *Understanding Gary Snyder* and has edited and co-edited a variety of other books, such as *Staging the Impossible, Essentials of the Theory of Fiction,* and *Critical Essays on American Modernism.* He recently founded *ISLE: Interdisciplinary Studies in Literature and Environment.*

JORDAN PAPER, a Professor of Comparative Religion at York University in Toronto, has written on various aspects of Chinese religion. His research topics include ritual practices, ecstatic experience, female spirituality, and religion and art. His book, *Chinese Religion: New Approaches,* is forthcoming from SUNY press.

QINGXIANG WANG taught for many years in northern China before undertaking graduate study in the United States, where he earned his Ph.D. in English from Indiana University of Pennsylvania. A noted calligrapher, he has taught courses in calligraphy as well as English. Currently he is an independent scholar.

TAN XIUJUN is an English teacher at the Shanghai Sports Technology Institute.

REBECCA HELEN WEINER has been a freelance China specialist since graduating from Yale University. As an interpreter and escort, she has worked for the U.S. Department of State, the National Committee on U.S.–China Relations, Academic Travel Abroad, and various private corporations. Ms. Weiner has published extensively on China, serving as principal researcher for the 1990 edition of *The China Guidebook* and as co-author of *Living in China.*

WU DINGBO, who earned his Ph.D. in English from Indiana University of Pennsylvania, has been teaching at Shanghai International Studies University since 1964. He has written about American literature, Chinese culture, and science fiction. In addition to *Science Fiction from China, Star Ducks,* and *Selections of American Science Fiction,* which he edited, more than forty of his articles and translations in Chinese and English have been published in China and elsewhere. He is a member of World SF.

XU XINYI is currently a Ph.D. candidate in Sociology at the University of Hawaii. He has researched and written on policy analysis, social control, and East Asia.

ZHANG WEI, correspondent for *Sports Herald* in China, has published *Future World Champions, A Marvellous Prince, Champions Who Have Won Honor for the Nation* and articles in various journals and newspapers.